History of Manufactures in the United States

Volume III
1893-1928

BY

VICTOR S. CLARK

With an Introductory Note by
HENRY W. FARNAM

1929 EDITION

PUBLISHED FOR THE

CARNEGIE INSTITUTION OF WASHINGTON

BY THE

McGRAW-HILL BOOK COMPANY, INC.
NEW YORK: 370 SEVENTH AVENUE
LONDON: 6 & 8 BOUVERIE ST., E. C.4
1929

Copyright, 1929, by the
CARNEGIE INSTITUTION OF WASHINGTON

Printed in the United States of America

CONTENTS

THE INDUSTRIAL STATE

CHAPTER I

                                              PAGE

General Characteristics of the Period from 1893 to 1914 1

    Foreign Trade, 1. Hydro-electric Power, 2. Big Industry, 5. The Crisis of 1893, 8. The Revival of the Later Nineties, 10. The Recession of 1907, 11. Labor Questions, 12.

CHAPTER II

Manufacture of Pig Iron 15

    Domestic Ores, 15. Ore Imports, 16. Lake Superior Ores, 17. Organization of Ore Trade, 19. Iron Smelting in the North, 22. Iron Smelting in the South, 24. Furnace Statistics, 28. Pig-Iron Output, 31.

CHAPTER III

Steel Making in the Eastern States 34

    Steel Works Geography, 34. Organization of the Steel Industry, 35. Influences Determining Plant Location, 36. Lackawanna Steel Company, 36. The Tidewater Steel Makers, 37. Pennsylvania Steel Company, 38. Bethlehem Steel Corporation, 39. Cambria Steel Company, 41. Republic Iron and Steel Company, 36. National Steel Company, 43. Carnegie Steel Company, 44.

CHAPTER IV

Newer Steel Centers and the Great Consolidation 45

    Federal Steel Company, 45. Tennessee Coal, Iron and Railroad Company, 47. Colorado Fuel and Iron Company, 52. United States Steel Corporation, 54.

CHAPTER V

Statistical and Technical Features of the Iron and Steel Industry 65

    Steel Output, 65. The Open-Hearth Processes, 67. Crucible Steel, 71. Charcoal Iron, 71. Furnace Fuels, 72. Blast Furnace Practice and Outputs, 73. Ore Treatment, 75. Electric Driving and Smelting, 75. Basic Steel, 77. Variants of the Bessemer Process, 77. Steel Furnace Capacity and Practice, 79. Alloys and Special Steels, 80. Wrought Iron, 82.

CHAPTER VI

Miscellaneous Features of the Iron and Steel Industry 84

    Rolling mills, 84. Foundries, 85. Forging, 85. Labor Conditions, 86. Pools and Consolidations, 87. General Organization, 89. Production Costs, 91.

CHAPTER VII

Commercial Features of the Iron and Steel Industries 94

    Low Prices, 94. Price Recovery of 1899, 98. Some Causes of Price Instability in America, 99. The New Century's Prosperous Beginning, 101. Depression of 1907, 104. Pre-war Dulness, 105. Marketing Methods, 105. Our Foreign Iron Trade, 108. International Comparisons, 115.

Contents

Chapter VIII

Iron and Steel Shapes.. 118
    Rails, 118. Structural Shapes, 119. Wire and Wire Products, 122. Nails, 125. Pipes and Tubes, 127. Tin Plate, 129.

Chapter IX

Engineering Industries... 136
    Locomotives and Rolling Stock, 136. Shipbuilding, 141. Agricultural Machinery, 146. Ordnance and Armor, 147. Hardware, 148. Tools and Cutlery, 148. Stoves and Furnaces, 150. Prime Movers, 150. Machine Tools, 153. Bicycles, 155.

Chapter X

The Automobile and the Dynamo....................................... 157
    Pioneer Motor Cars, 157. Early Promoting, 158. First Manufacturing Companies, 160. Motor Shows, 160. Status of the Industry in 1910, 162. Culmination of Pre-war Development, 163. Electrical Industries, 165. Electric Generators, 166. Industrial Consumption, 167. Company Organization, 168.

Chapter XI

Cotton Manufacture.. 171
    Cotton Consumption, 171. Spindle Statistics and Geography, 172. North and South, 173. Technical Progress, 177. Organization, 180. Trade Conditions, 184. Exports of Cotton Goods, 187. Labor, 188.

Chapter XII

Wool Manufacture... 191
    Wool Production, 191. Wool Substitutes, 194. Geography of the Wool Manufacture, 196. Fabrics, 197. Technical Aspects, 197. Trade Conditions, 199. Foreign Competition, 202. Labor, 213. Exports, 204. Organization, 205. Carpets, 207.

Chapter XIII

Silk Manufacture.. 210
    Rapid Growth, 210. Geography, 210. Specialization of Process, 211. Technical Progress, 212. Fabrics, 213. Organization, 215.

Chapter XIV

Minor Textiles and Allied Industries................................... 218
    Flax Manufactures, 218. Hemp and Other Fibers, 219. Knit Goods, 221. Dyeing and Finishing, 221. Hats, 222. Clothing, 222.

Chapter XV

Leather and the Rubber Manufacture.................................. 225
    Tanning Technology, 225. Geography and Organization, 226. Leather Varieties, 228. Leather Exports and Hide Imports, 229. Boot and Shoe Making, 230. Boot and Shoe Exports, 231. Geography of Boot and Shoe Making, 232. Shoe Machinery Business, 233. Glove Making, 234. Organization of the Rubber Manufacture, 235. Rubber Tire Manufacture, 236.

Chapter XVI

Manufactures of Wood... 238
    Lumber Industry, 238. Technical Development, 239. Organization, 241. Miscellaneous Timber Manufactures, 242. Naval Stores, 243. Furniture, 244. Paper Making, 245.

Contents

Chapter XVII

Cement, Clay, and Glass.. 253

The Cement Age, 253. Clay Manufactures, 256. Glass Making, 259.

Chapter XVIII

Manufacture of Food, Drink, and Tobacco............................. 263

Food Manufacture in General, 263. Meat Packing, 263. Flour Milling, 266. Cereals, Bakery Goods and Miscellaneous Grain Products, 268. Canning, 269. Cane Sugar, 272. Beet Sugar, 272. Sugar Refining, 274. Alcoholic Liquors 275. Tobacco, 278.

Chapter XIX

Industrial Fuels and Miscellaneous Manufactures..................... 281

Industrial Fuels, 281. Mineral and Vegetable Oils, 283. Chemical Industries, 284. Fertilizers, 293. Miscellaneous Industries of the Chemical Group, 291. Cultural Manufactures, 293.

Chapter XX

The World War Episode... 298

Some Historical Parallels, 298. The Government and Business, 300. Iron and Steel, 306. Non-ferrous Metals, 310. Engineering Industries, 312. Chemical Industries, 315. Textiles, 318.

Chapter XXI

Post-Bellum Development... 324

Industry Becomes Socialized, 324. Tariff Laws, 328. Industrial Organization, 330. Merchandizing and Consumer's Credits, 332. Iron and Steel, 333. Engineering Industries, 336. Textiles, 339. Chemical Industries, 346. Miscellaneous Manufactures, 348.

Chapter XXII

Conclusion... 351

Fifty-five Years' Growth, 351. Geography of Manufactures, 351. Industrial Concentration, 353. Market Policy, 355. Service Supply, 356. Manufacturing and Society, 357. Last Developments, 358.

Appendices

I. Colonial Currency and Exchange.................................	359
II. Colonial Price of Lumber per M feet............................	363
III. Colonial Price of Tar per Barrel..............................	365
IV. Colonial Price of Shipbuilding per Ton........................	367
V. Colonial Price of Iron per Ton.................................	368
VI. Colonial Price of Flour per Hundredweight.....................	370
VII. George Washington's Weaving Accounts.........................	376
VIII. Statistics Relating to the Tariff...........................	380
IX. Price Changes of Raw Materials and Manufactures...............	387
X. A British Opinion of American Industrial Organization and Labor in 1854...	394
XI. Extracts from Governor Williams' Correspondence relating to an Early Cotton Factory in South Carolina........................	395

Contents

	PAGE
XII. Table Showing Relation of Population and Railway Mileage to Value of Manufactures Produced in Shops and Factories and in Households, 1840, 1850, 1860..	398
XIII. New Orleans Receipts of Inland Manufactures by River, 1822–1829.	399
Bibliography..	400

    Colonial Period, 400. The Early Republic, 401. The Civil War and After, 405. List of Authorities, 407.

| Index.. | 443 |

PLATES

	FACING PAGE
1. Fig. 1.—First Direct Connected Dynamo (1881)................................	166
Fig. 2.—Modern Connected Turbine Generator..................................	166
2. Fig. 1.—Cotton Weaving in the Thirties...	178
Fig. 2.—Modern Cotton Weaving Room..	178
3. Fig. 1.—Hoe 10-Cylinder Newspaper Press of the Seventies........................	294
Fig. 2.—Modern Hoe Perfecting Newspaper Press...............................	294

CHAPTER I

GENERAL CHARACTERISTICS OF THE PERIOD FROM 1893 TO 1914

Foreign Trade, 1. Hydro-electric Power, 2. Big Industry, 5. The Crisis of 1893, 8. The Revival of the Later Nineties, 10. The Recession of 1907, 11. Labor Questions, 12.

FOREIGN TRADE

When the effects of the panic of 1893 finally passed away and the country swung into a new current of prosperity and expansion, manufacturing was on the eve of attaining a position in our national economy that it had never before occupied. Significant indications of this change appeared in the character of our foreign trade. In 1890 our exports of manufactures reached a total of $151,000,000; five years later they had risen to nearly $184,000,000, an increase ascribed at the time to the willingness of American producers to unload surplus goods abroad at a sacrifice in order to relieve the domestic market.[1] It began to be noticed as a curious feature of our foreign commerce that we imported growing quantities of raw materials that were extensively produced within the country, and that even formed an important item of our export trade. For instance, though the United States produced half of the world's copper and shipped abroad far more than any other country, it was one of the largest importers of that commodity. Over $30,000,000 worth of pig copper and copper ore entered the country annually before 1906, although we exported $90,000,000 worth of that metal. The explanation was that the United States, for the very reason that it was a large copper producer, possessed the best refining and manufacturing plants. We thus attracted to our own manufacturing establishments large quantities of ore from Canada and Mexico, and of pig metal even from Europe. While the United States produced three-quarters of the world's cotton, it annually imported $12,000,000 worth of cotton and cotton waste, that brought into the country being of a different quality from the cotton produced in America. Incidentally, although we were one of the world's largest manufacturers of cotton goods, we purchased abroad manufactures of cotton to the value of nearly $70,000,000, or double the value of the cotton manufactures that we exported.[2]

It was noted further as a remarkable fact that, during the month of May 1904, the value of our exports of manufactures exceeded by a million dollars the value of the agricultural products we shipped abroad. Averaged by the year, however, our exports of agricultural products were still double our

[1] American Iron and Steel Association, *Bulletin*, xxx, 163, July 20, 1896; xl, 245, Nov. 1, 1896.
[2] American Iron and Steel Association, *Bulletin*, xli, 25, Mar. 9, 1907.

exports of manufactures. During the fiscal year ending with June 30, 1912, the value of our exports of manufactures for the first time passed the billion-dollar line, reaching a total of $1,022,000,000, of which two-thirds were goods ready for immediate consumption. In 1893 manufactures had formed less than one-fifth of our total exports. Ten years later the proportion had risen to one-third. In 1912 it had become 47 per cent, and it was soon to exceed the value of all our other shipments abroad.[3]

HYDRO-ELECTRIC POWER

Another outstanding feature of this period was the growing use of hydro-electric power. The first great development of this kind in the United States was at Niagara Falls, where after nearly five years' work and the expenditure of vast sums of money, a power plant, capable of developing more than 100,000 horse-power in 5,000 horse-power turbine and dynamo units, went into operation in 1894 and 1895. The first manufacturing establishments to benefit by this development was a paper mill, said to be the largest of its kind in the world. Long-distance transmission was still in its infancy even at this recent date, and it remained to be demonstrated whether this power could be profitably delivered at the neighboring city of Buffalo. In 1895 the Niagara Falls Company was supplying power to the Pittsburgh Reduction Company, manufacturing aluminum, about half a mile from the power house, and to the Carborundum Company, one-third of a mile distant. The following year the Power Company contracted with the Buffalo Traction lines to deliver 10,000 horse-power, with a proviso that this be increased to 40,000 horse-power at the rate of $36 per horse-power per year. In 1900 the Company, now a demonstrated success, increased its capital by an issue of debentures for the purpose of doubling its plant.[4]

By the latter date other large developments were already in progress. Among the most important of these was that begun by several companies, ultimately combined under the name of the Consolidated Lake Superior Company, at the Falls of the St. Mary's River between Michigan and Canada. This ambitious project, which was destined to experience many vicissitudes and to pass for a period into the hands of a receiver, differed from the Niagara Falls Power Company in combining the development and delivery of power with the manufacturing processes that utilized that power, thus becoming its own consumer. It was estimated that 200,000 horse-power could be developed at this point, and in the surrounding territory pulpwood, iron and nickel ores and other raw materials were abundant. For a time all went well. Mills for producing both mechanical and sulphide pulp were erected and soon were serving a large market extending

---

[3] American Iron and Steel Association, *Bulletin*, XXXVIII, 101, July 10, 1904; XLVI, 80, Sept. 1, 1912.

[4] *Commercial and Financial Chronicle*, LVI, 819, May 20, 1893; LVII, 723, Oct. 28, 1893; LVIII, 178, Jan. 27, 1894; LVIII, 815, May 12, 1894; LXI, 69, July 13, 1895; LXIII, 1114, Dec. 19, 1896; LXX, 689, Apr. 7, 1900; American Iron and Steel Association, *Bulletin*, XXIX, 197, Sept. 1, 1895.

from Japan to France and Germany. This was perhaps the first experiment with the long-distance shipment of dried pulp—a process developed at this mill—in the history of the paper trade. Large sums were expended in various metallurgical enterprises—the manufacture of nickel steel in electric furnaces, refining copper ore by an electrolytic process, and the production of certain chemicals, especially sulphide, for the use of the pulp mill. The Company leased 40,000 horse-power to the Union Carbide Company and the United Electrical Company at rates said to be one-third those charged at Niagara.[5]

From an engineering point of view this development differed notably from that at Niagara, in that the generating units instead of being very large, 5,000 horse-power as at the former point—were comparatively small, 316 turbine wheels being used to develop the 60,000 estimated horse-power produced on the American side of the River.[6]

Meanwhile the use of electric power was rapidly introduced in textile mills. The first establishment to utilize this source of energy is said to have been the Ponemah Mills at Taftville, Connecticut, which used electricity from a water power 4 miles away as early as January 1894. Two years later the Boston Duck Company, at Pondville, Massachusetts, installed electricity, being the second mill in the country to do this. The third and fourth mills to follow this example were at Columbia, South Carolina, and in its immediate vicinity. Thereafter the utilization of this power extended rapidly, particularly in the South. In 1905, the New England Cotton Manufacturers' Association reported that some 175 textile mills used electricity, to the amount of 140,000 horse-power, for driving machinery. Of the new mills a large number bought their power from outside corporations, indicating that the tendency to specialize in power production had already begun.[7]

During the decade ending with 1914 hydro-electric development proceeded apace in the South, encouraged by the large market for electric power afforded by cotton mills and by the numerous public service corporations that were organized about this time in that section. By 1914 the quantity available for use in the Southern Appalachians considerably exceeded half a million horse-power. A striking feature of recent progress in that region was the extent to which the greater systems had dovetailed so that power could be exchanged by means of meters and switching apparatus between different companies. One net-work of transmission lines covered a territory 550 miles in length and from 100 to 250 miles broad. Half a dozen systems operated within this region. Their relations were such that when the end of one line was near a power station belonging to another company, it pur-

[5] *Commercial and Financial Chronicle*, LXVIII, 1075, June 3, 1899; LXXI, 912, Nov. 3, 1900, American Iron and Steel Association, *Bulletin*, XXXIV, 154–155, Sept. 15, 1900.
[6] American Iron and Steel Association, *Bulletin*, XXXVI, 124, Aug. 25, 1902; XXXVII, 133 Sept. 10, 1903; XXXVIII, 85, June 10, 1904.
[7] Southern Cotton Spinners' Association, *Proceedings, 1900*, pp. 88–94; New England Cotton Manufacturers' Association, *Transactions, April 1905*, 262.

chased power regularly from that neighbor. In times of drought or when plants were temporarily shut down for repairs, power was also passed on from one company to another. In addition, there were isolated developments of the first magnitude in this region, such as the plant of the Aluminum Company of America in East Tennessee, and of the Alabama Power Company in the latter state. Although but eight years had passed since the first important enterprise in the southern Appalachian territory—the Southern Power Company—began the erection of its plant, this development alone gridironed the Piedmont Section of North and South Carolina with 1,600 miles of transmission line. It supplied 98,000 horsepower generated by water and 30,000 horse-power generated by steam. Numerous smaller companies serving more limited and isolated districts had sprung up in other parts of the South.[8]

Naturally this development was not limited to any section of the country, though it was most marked where water heads and manufacturing industries already existed within reasonable proximity of each other. A single plant developing 300,000 horse-power was installed on the Mississippi at Keokuk, Iowa; while still farther West, at Great Falls, Montana, and other points in the Rocky Mountain and Pacific Coast states, electric power was revolutionizing industrial conditions in regions of high-priced coal. Although progress was not equally rapid in New England during the period we are now discussing, partly because the more eligible sites had long since been occupied by great manufacturing establishments, a disposition was shown to improve existing plants. In 1900 the Holyoke Water Power Company completed a new dam across the Connecticut River, adding largely to the power available at that point.[9]

Each advance in the application of power liberated manufacturing from some of its former geographical and physical limitations. Water heads, that had remained unutilized because the topographical peculiarities of their sites made the construction of mills in their immediate vicinity too expensive to be profitable, were now available as sources of power for distant and more conveniently located establishments. Early mills driven by undershot or by breast wheels were of necessity placed close to the face of the dam that supplied their power. The overshot wheel of later date made it possible to place the mill somewhat farther from the dam, but oftentimes in a deep valley where the space between the canal and the river below was necessarily narrow. This led to the construction of a building of several stories to make up for the limited area of the site it occupied. The turbine waterwheel made it possible to remove the mill still farther from the dam and correspondingly increased the choice of mill locations. The introduction of steam power liberated the mill entirely from the river and made possible even greater freedom of design. With the introduction of elec-

[8] Manufacturers' Record, LXV (1), 62, Feb. 5, 1914; LXV (2), 41–42, May 28, 1914.
[9] *Commercial and Financial Chronicle*, LXX, 233, Feb. 3, 1900; cf. New England Cotton Manufacturers' Association, *Transactions, April 1895*, 125.

tricity, the source of power and the method of its transmission almost ceased to be a factor in mill construction. Simultaneously, in order to meet the competition of electricity and also to serve more efficiently in its generation, the steam engine was rapidly improved. This development, as we have seen, was in the direction of higher boiler pressures and superheating, the use of compound engines and the introduction of steam turbines.[10]

BIG INDUSTRY

About the turn of the century the movement toward consolidating industries that had been in progress for ten years or more reached a climax. The Trust in the original sense of the word was already an outlived institution. In 1889 the New York Court of Appeals, in the famous Sugar Trust decision, declared that the practice that had grown up of assigning the stock of several corporations engaged in the same line of business to a board of trustees in return for certificates issued by the latter, and the practice of authorizing such trustees virtually to control the policies, prices and methods of operation of the constituent companies, was illegal.[11]

Trusts of the character mentioned were primarily devices for controlling competition. In the latter respect they were a step forward in the line of evolution indicated by pools and associations of independent companies operating under short-term agreements, in accordance with which business was allotted in an agreed ratio to the members and prices were regulated. Indeed, associations of the latter character were sometimes known as trusts. In 1894 the cottonseed-oil mills of Texas associated themselves in a loose organization called a trust, or "Crushers' Association," that fixed the price paid for seed. They thereby invited prosecution by the Attorney General under the state's anti-trust laws.[12] Pools continued to be formed in the iron and steel trades throughout the nineties. In 1896 the steel billet pool fixed prices, and during this season pools and combines were for a time in control of the iron and steel market.[13] This understanding was broken up as a result of an arrangement between the Rockefeller and Carnegie interests, by which the former's large ore holdings in the Lake Superior districts and his transportation lines became the property of the Pittsburgh steel king. This development, which properly belongs to the history of the Carnegie Steel Company, gave that firm absolute control of the market. Commenting upon this situation a contemporary authority said:

"We have had pools and combinations without number in the iron market, but never before a position like this by which a single company can absolutely dominate the trade, and make any combination which can be formed simply the register of its own wishes."[14]

[10] National Association of Wool Manufacturers, *Bulletin*, XXIX, 26–28, Mar. 1899; New England Cotton Manufacturers' Association, *Transactions*, April 24, 1895, 112–114, 125.
[11] *Commercial and Financial Chronicle*, L, 888–889, June 28, 1890.
[12] *Manufacturers' Record*, XXVI, 83, Sept. 8, 1894; XXVII, 275, May 31, 1895.
[13] *Mineral Industry*, IV, 1895, p. 402; V, 1896, p. 339, 402.
[14] *Mineral Industry*, V, 1896, 340.

Agitation against the trusts did not cease with the 1889 decision, and in 1897 a special committee of the New York Legislature appointed for that purpose presented an elaborate report dealing with this question. By this time, however, the trust proper was rapidly making place for the gigantic corporation, improperly called by the same name. These vast companies were integrations of smaller firms and corporations, not to be confounded with mere trading combinations like the steel-rail pool, the Western Nail Association, and similar associations. The new organization represented a concentration of productive power as well as a concentration of selling control. It therefore served a broader economic purpose, and one in some respects beneficial for the general public as well as for the investor.[15]

The movement toward combination that now dominated so many fields of industry was due to a variety of causes. Mere imitation played a part. A policy that had behind it the prestige and authority of the country's greatest financiers and captains of industry was accepted more or less uncritically by minor industrial managers and promoters. These often made mistakes in their calculations, and the path of industrial progress during this period is paved with the wrecks of many unfortunate undertakings of this sort.

Another condition that favored the formation of gigantic corporations was the abundance of capital and the curtailment of traditional fields of investment, especially in the railways. While our railway system was by no means complete as yet, and millions were soon to be invested in rebuilding and improving existing lines, this field of enterprise could no longer absorb the same proportion as hitherto of the nation's surplus capital. Funds accumulated, sought new outlets for profitable employment and almost solicited the attention of the promoter.[16]

An estimate made at the end of 1898 placed the authorized capital of the great corporations organized within twelve months at more than $900,000,000. It was characteristic of the financing of this period that 95 per cent of this capital represented stocks, and only 5 per cent represented bonds. Many of these new companies were combinations of special branches of iron and steel manufacturing that had hitherto been controlled by pools. For instance, in 1898, the American Steel and Wire Company, The American Sheet Metal Company, and the National Tube Company were incorporated, with an aggregate capitalization of nearly $200,000,000.[17]

This movement was not as noticeable in textile manufacturing although, as we shall see, the American Thread Company was formed in 1898 to effect a combination of thirteen mills, some of which were to be closed and others to be devoted exclusively to the manufacture of a single specialty. This combination embraced practically every thread maker in New Eng-

---

[15] *Cf.* American Iron and Steel Association, *Bulletin*, xxi, 74, Apr. 1, 1897; xxxiii, 59, Apr. 10, 1899.

[16] *Commercial and Financial Chronicle*, LXVIII, 5, Jan. 7, 1899.

[17] *South and Western Textile Excelsior*, vi, 11, Dec. 10, 1898; U. S. Industrial Commission, *Reports*, xiii, 343, 347.

land.[18] Meanwhile a normal tendency existed for successful manufacturing firms to grow and for successful manufacturers to extend their investments in the branch of industry with which they were most familiar. In 1899 the Knights of Rhode Island, who were popularly reputed to be the largest cotton manufacturing firm in the world, operated 15 mills with 11,000 looms and 425,000 spindles.[19]

The constantly accelerated expansion of capital that accompanied this movement toward industrial combination was illustrated when the figures for 1899 were published. These showed that during the year bonds and shares with a par value of nearly $3,594,000,000, issued by new industrial combinations in the field of manufacturing alone, had been absorbed by American investors. Of this huge total, however, less than 10 per cent consisted of bonds and only about one-fourth of preferred stock. The great bulk of this nominal capital was represented by common stock, which in many cases stood for little else than theoretical good will and promoters' profits.[20]

According to the Twelfth Census of Manufactures, 185 large corporations controlling 2,040 plants, employed about 8 per cent of the workers and produced about 14 per cent of the goods made in their respective lines in the United States. This did not suggest that our industries as a whole were at this time likely to fall immediately in the hands of great industrial combinations. The percentage of output produced by these nominal trusts varied in different branches of manufacturing. It was less than 4.5 per cent in textiles and 8 per cent in leather; but it rose to 22 per cent in case of liquors, 24 per cent in miscellaneous metals, 28.5 per cent in iron and steel, and 33.5 per cent in chemicals. It should be observed that in the last instance this concentration was due partly to the existence of patent monopolies.[21]

By 1903 the period of active combination and consolidation seemed to be over, especially in the mineral industries. The industrial leaders of the country were eagerly explaining to the public the economies of large corporations, their ability to produce cheaper and better goods at lower prices, and at the same time to pay high wages to their employes and higher returns to their investors, than small and presumable less ably managed plants. Charles Schwab addressing the Bankers Club in Chicago, in 1902, declared that the trust as such was—

"A dead business proposition built on a trinity that would wreck anything— restriction of trade, increase of prices, and throttling of competition."

He asserted that consolidations instead of restricting trade expanded it, created new avenues of consumption and reduced prices. At the same

---

[18] *Commercial and Financial Chronicle*, LXVIII, 6, Jan. 7, 1899; *Mineral Industry*, v, 1896, 354–355.
[19] *South and Western Textile Excelsior*, VI, 15, Jan. 7, 1899.
[20] *Commercial and Financial Chronicle*, LXX, 560–563, Mar. 24, 1900.
[21] Twelfth Census, *Reports*, VII, lxxv–xci; American Iron and Steel Association, *Bulletin*, XXXVI, 173, Nov. 25, 1902.

time, however, Congress was legislating for the control of such combinations, and during the session of 1902–1903 appropriated half a million dollars for the enforcement of the Sherman Anti-trust Law, transferred preferential jurisdiction over suits of this nature to the Federal Courts, amended the Interstate Commerce Law to extend the penalties for violation to shippers as well as to carriers, and established a Bureau of Corporations to investigate the operations of great firms engaged in interstate or foreign commerce.[22]

Meanwhile, the financing of these vast corporations tended to concentrate ultimate control over them in a comparatively small group of financial institutions in New York City. To be sure underwriting new industrial enterprises was not always a profitable undertaking. The underwriters were usually paid by a bonus in common stock. In numerous instances the market value of this promotion stock did not cover the depreciation in the company's securities held by the underwriters during the period of promotion, and the latter consequently suffered a net loss through the operation. In 1900 the *Commercial and Financial Chronicle* published a list of 15 large corporations with capital ranging from $2,000,000 to $50,000,000, that had paid their underwriters profits ranging from 1.25 to 20 per cent upon the total capitalization of the companies. Sixteen other companies, however, with a capitalization ranging from $8,000,000 to $200,000,000 had, according to this statement, proved losing ventures to the underwriters, whose losses ranged from less than 2 per cent to a maximum of over 74 per cent.[23]

THE CRISIS OF 1893

The crisis of 1893 was accompanied by one of the severest and most protracted financial strains to which the country was ever subjected. Manufacturers felt its effect in an abrupt cessation of demand for their products and a correspondingly sudden and extreme decline in prices. R. G. Dun and Company reported, in March 1894, that the volume of domestic trade as measured by bank clearings was nearly one-third less than a year before. Although business had begun to expand it was not more profitable, because prices did not respond to increased sales; rather they continued to fall and were nearly 13 per cent lower than the previous year.[24] Some relief was felt in the course of the following summer from the enactment of a new tariff, not so much because of its provisions, as because the business uncertainty that prevailed during its discussion in Congress was removed as a disturbing factor in the calculations of manufacturers and merchants. The volume of business was reported to have increased by autumn one-fifth over that of a year before, yet the season was one of unexampled depression, instead of general recuperation as had been antici-

---

[22] *Mineral Industry*, XII, 1903, 188; American Iron and Steel Association, *Bulletin*, XXXIV, 107, June 15, 1900; XXXVI, 2, Jan. 10, 1902; XXXVII, 35, Mar. 10, 1903.
[23] *Commercial and Financial Chronicle*, LXXI, 545, Sept. 15, 1900.
[24] Quoted in American Iron and Steel Association, *Bulletin*, XXXVIII, 69, Mar. 31, 1894.

pated. Strikes, floods and drought coöperated to check the normal processes of recovery.[25]

By the following spring, however, conditions were decidedly better, especially at Pittsburgh and in the iron-working districts of the West. Marked advances occurred in the price of iron, leather and cotton goods, due to heavy orders from consumers, which exceeded for a time the capacity of works in operation. Excellent crops contributed to a betterment of business conditions, especially in the West. There were no labor troubles of any magnitude. An arrangement between the Treasury and a syndicate of Wall Street bankers checked the heavy exports of gold that had excited deep concern for the financial stability of the country.[26]

This period was characterized by constant money stringency, due partly to the fact that the agitation for cheap money in America had weakened confidence in our financial soundness abroad. Foreign investments in America had received a sudden check on account of the shock of the Baring failure in London and the general contraction of enterprise that followed the overexpansion of the years immediately preceding; but the curtailment in the flow of investment capital from Europe to the United States was greater than it would have been had foreign investors had faith in our currency policy. American securities owned abroad were thrown upon the American market more rapidly than our investors at home could buy them back. Our surplus exports were not sufficient to meet the demands thus created, and we were compelled to ship specie abroad to make up the deficit.

As long as agitation for cheap money continued the money stringency persisted, and even occasional revivals in certain lines of manufacturing, due to recurrent demands that could not be postponed in a large national market like our own, proved temporary. In the summer of 1896 the textile industry, particularly at Fall River and in Philadelphia and vicinity, passed through a period of depression such as had seldom been experienced.[27] The market for watches fell off to such an extent that the large factories at Waltham, and even the Waterbury Company which catered to the cheapest trade, were forced to shut down for considerable periods. This depression was partly due to the normal let-down of business prior to a Presidential election, particularly an election in which an important economic issue like that of the future coinage of silver was before the country. Prices, especially of grain, cotton and wool, fluctuated widely and erratically, falling toward the middle of the year and recovering part of their losses toward the end of the season. There were more commercial failures in 1896 than in any previous year except 1893, total liabilities increasing 29 per cent over those of 1895.[28]

[25] American Iron and Steel Association, *Bulletin*, XXXVIII, 196, Sept. 5, 1894; *Commercia and Financial Chronicle*, LX, 9, Jan. 5, 1895.
[26] American Iron and Steel Association, *Bulletin*, XXIX, 92, Apr. 20, 1895; XXIX, 233, Oct. 20, 1895; *Commercial and Financial Chronicle*, LXII, 5–6, Jan. 4, 1896.
[27] American Iron and Steel Association, *Bulletin*, XXX, 181, Aug. 10, 1896.
[28] American Iron and Steel Association, *Bulletin*, XXX, 181, Aug. 10, 1896; XXX, 189, Aug. 20, 1896; XXX, 197, Sept. 1, 1896; XXXI, 11, Jan. 10, 1897; *Commercial and Financial Chronicle*, LXIV, 6–8, Jan. 2, 1897.

THE REVIVAL OF THE LATER NINETIES

Following the Presidential election of 1896, however, a progressive betterment of the industrial situation occurred. The enactment of the Dingley Tariff removed one uncertainty from the manufacturer's horizon, and the popular verdict in favor of sound money strengthened business confidence. An abundant harvest in the autumn of 1897, accompanied by a good demand for American agricultural staples abroad, converted this confidence into optimism.[29]

During the era of low prices and keen competition for markets that followed the panic of 1893, when American exports of manufactures increased rapidly, the specter of American competition rose for the first time in the minds of European statesmen and industrialists, who became conscious of a new rival in a field of production which they hitherto had supposed to be their preculiar province. The Premier of Austria Hungary delivered a speech on foreign affairs in November 1897, which attracted wide attention because of its urgent advocacy of closer cooperation, both political and economic, among the nations of Europe. In the light of later events it has now acquired new interest. Count Goluchowski declared that the competion of transatlantic countries, present and prospective, would gravely compromise the vital interests of the peoples of Europe unless they took common action to avert this peril. Just as the sixteenth and seventeenth centuries had been absorbed by religious wars, the eighteenth century by political revolution, and the nineteenth century by the development of nationalities, the twentieth century would be a period of struggle for economic world supremacy. In this struggle America was likely to be arrayed against Europe.[30]

By the autumn of 1897 it was becoming clear, even to conservative and skeptical observers, that an era of real recovery from the past four years of depression and languid convalescence was in sight. Good crops and high prices enabled farmers to reduce their mortgages and increase their purchases. The tonnage and revenues of the western railroads were growing. Although the country was exporting heavily, and there was a large trade balance in our favor, so that the debt of foreign countries to the United States upon the year's business exceeded $300,000,000, our net gold imports were less than 10 per cent of this amount. In other words, American investors were buying back their securities owned abroad. Iron and steel outputs reached new records. The only industry that lagged behind was cotton manufacturing, where print cloths fell to the lowest point on record. In fact, New England's three chief industries, wool, cotton and leather, experienced abnormal dullness up to the end of the season.[31]

[29] American Iron and Steel Association, *Bulletin*, XXXI, 189, Aug. 20, 1897; *Commercial and Financial Chronicle*, LXV, 2, July 3, 1897.
[30] *Commercial and Financial Chronicle*, LXV, 1147, Dec. 18, 1897.
[31] American Iron and Steel Association, *Bulletin*, XXXI, 196, Sept. 1, 1897; XXXII, 178, Nov. 20, 1898; *Commercial and Financial Chronicle*, LXVI, 4–6, Jan. 1, 1898.

During 1898 the tide of prosperity continued to rise. Good crops, unprecedented exports of merchandise, further victories for the champions of sound money and the successful war against Spain cooperated to fortify confidence and to stimulate business activity. This favorable situation continued throughout the year, the closing month being the most auspicious of the season. Our balance of trade was again extremely favorable, thanks to good crops, active foreign demand and growing exports of manufactured products, especially iron and steel. Reversing recent conditions, the country was entering upon an era of easy money, and in fact of superabundant capital, reflected as we have previously seen, in the financing of great trusts and giant corporations that characterized the following four or five years. Between 1896 and 1899 per capita circulation rose from approximately $21.50 to $25.50.[32]

Naturally the period of prosperity that followed was interrupted by occasional intervals of recession. In 1899, while trade and industry continued to expand, there was a brief period of money stringency and alarm in the financial market, due partly to the over-rapid absorption of floating capital by great industrial undertakings. Fear that many of the new trusts were overcapitalized and that their securities were likely to decline when the limit to their earning powers was definitely ascertained, was largely responsible for this salutary timidity.[33] This check to the prevailing spirit of confidence was but temporary, however, and the turn of the century found the country enjoying a period of extraordinary business activity, which began in 1899 and was not materially interrupted even by a severe and widespread drought in 1901. It was reported in 1903 that "the general prosperity of the country is probably at as high a stage as at any period during the present golden era." Steel works were overwhelmed with business.[34]

THE RECESSION OF 1907

Not until 1907 did a decided set-back interrupt this period of expansion and rising prices. The previous twelve months had been the most prosperous in the history of our great industries. Steel and affiliated companies had established new high records of productions and earnings. In the spring of 1907, however, a decline set in, marked by an abrupt fall in the price of railroad stocks, followed by a sympathetic settling of prices in other lines of business. The unfilled tonnage on the books of the United States Steel Corporation was one-fourth less on the first of July than on the same date a year before. Money was dearer all over the world than it had been for some seasons. Industries were practicing ultra-conservatism, curtailing improvements and avoiding expenditures that were not absolutely necessary. Over-expansion had absorbed capital too rapidly. In the

---

[32] *Commercial and Financial Chronicle*, LXVIII, 5–6, Jan. 7, 1899; American Iron and Steel Association, *Bulletin*, XXXIII, 92, June 1, 1899.
[33] *Commercial and Financial Chronicle*, LXX, 4, Jan. 6, 1900.
[34] American Iron and Steel Association, *Bulletin*, XXXV, 116, Aug. 10, 1901; XXXVII, 117, Aug. 10, 1903.

United States, securities to the value of $1,300,000,000 were marketed between the first of January and the first of August, while the gross earnings of railways, which were less affected at first than were manufacturing industries by the recession, continued to rise, though net profits did not increase. This temporary crisis, however, was not as prolonged and did not have as far-reaching results as the great panics of 1873 and 1893.[35]

After the recovery from this brief set-back, business continued fairly active, although the height of the boom had passed, until shortly before the outbreak of the World War, when, notwithstanding the absence of any acute derangement of the country's financial and industrial machinery, signs of a period of declining prosperity were everywhere visible. During these twenty years the general price level rose steadily from the extraordinarily low point that it occupied after the panic of 1893, when mercantile calculations showed that the purchasing power of money in certain lines—for instance, dry goods—was practically five times as great as a few years before. This recovery of prices was slow and laborious, but was not interrupted by more than partial and temporary reactions.[36]

LABOR QUESTIONS

Labor questions occupied a larger place in the history of manufacturing than during any equal period preceding. The rapid expansion of our great industries, and the development of manufacturing in regions that had hitherto been mainly devoted to other pursuits, raised new problems of labor supply and caused a constant change in the character of the working force. Labor legislation and social welfare experiments acquired a new importance. Technical education received more attention than formerly. There had been several excellent engineering schools in the country since the period of the Civil War or immediately thereafter. The first textile school in the United States was founded at Philadelphia in 1883, and was followed by the Lowell Textile School, which was opened in 1897. Similar schools were established at New Bedford in 1899, at Fall River five years later, and also at several points in the South.[37] The sources of labor supply in the North and South exhibited a striking contrast. In the North the immigrant, and particularly the unskilled immigrant, was supplanting the native skilled worker in many occupations that the former had hitherto controlled. In the South, where new industries were springing up and old ones were expanding rapidly, native labor, both white and black, continued to be mainly employed. And this employment, which was in distinct fields, resulted in the increasing use of male negro labor and white female and child labor, while negro women and children and white men were in relatively less demand.

[35] American Iron and Steel Association, *Bulletin*, XLI, 85, July 10, 1907; XLI, 36, Apr. 1, 1907; XLI, 100, Aug. 15, 1907; XLII, 20, Feb. 1, 1898.
[36] *Commercial and Financial Chronicle*, LIX, 668–669, Oct. 20, 1894.
[37] Eleventh Census, *Report on Manufactures*, III, 67–68; National Association of Wool Manufacturers, *Bulletin*, XXVII, 102–103, Mar. 1897; National Association of Cotton Manufacturers, *Transactions*, 1906, p. 106.

Negroes were mainly employed as miners, furnace laborers and unskilled and semi-skilled hands in iron and steel works and about lumber mills. In 1890 negroes had taken the place of strikers in the Alabama coal field. In 1908 the Amalgamated Association of Iron and Steel Workers at Youngstown, Ohio, was compelled to wipe out the color line and to give negro mill hands consideration and protection, an action said to have been brought about as a matter of self presevation, since the mills of the West were filled with negro help.[38] Attempts to use negroes in cotton mills, though tried in several places, seem nowhere to have succeeded. To be sure, a number of hopeful experiments were made and there was much optimistic discussion of this possibility. A manufacturing company was organized by negroes here and there. For instance, a factory was projected and perhaps put into operation at Concord, North Carolina, of which the officers and all the directors but one were negroes, to be operated entirely with colored labor. A similar mill was projected at Columbia, but proved a failure. Knitting mills were established at Charleston, South Carolina, to employ colored girls, who were paid only 20 cents a day. Although white labor cost several times this amount, the Charleston experiment was a failure and the company became bankrupt. Yet as recently as 1906 a knitting mill was in operation at Henderson that employed negroes exclusively and was reported to be successful.[39]

But the main reliance of Southern cotton spinners was upon the native whites, who migrated to mill villages from the farms. This labor was probably as illiterate and had as low a standard of living as the immigrant labor extensively employed in similar occupations in the North. During periods of active mill construction this supply sometimes proved inadequate, and organized efforts were made by some of the Southern manufacturing states to attract workers from Europe, but with only moderate success.[40]

In the North the employment of immigrants as factory operatives was most extensive in the large textile mills of New England. Among the 7,000 operatives of one great establishment at Lawrence, more than 30 nationalities were represented. These nationalities did not as a rule work together in the same departments and operations. The heavy labor was performed by Poles; unskilled Syrians worked in the picker room; the carding was done by Portuguese; the roving was done by Irish women who had worked for years at this occupation; French Canadians were employed in the spinning room and to a large extent as weavers, although English and Irish operatives still operated looms. In some departments of fine weaving, especially

---

[38] *Manufacturers' Record*, XVIII, 48, Jan. 3, 1891; American Iron and Steel Association, *Bulletin*, XLII, 53, June 1, 1908.

[39] *Manufacturers' Record*, XXIV, 130, Sept. 22, 1893; XXX, 410, Jan. 8, 1897; XXXI, 82, Feb. 26, 1897; XXXI, 420, July 16, 1897; XXXVIII, 176, Oct. 4, 1900; XLIX, 691, July 5, 1906; *South and Western Textile Excelsior*, VI, 10, Oct. 29, 1898; VI, 11, Dec. 10, 1898.

[40] *Cf.*, *South and Western Textile Excelsior*, VI, 9–14, Dec. 17, 1898; American Iron and Steel Association, *Bulletin*, XXXIV, 81, May 1, 1900; Thompson, *From the Cotton Field to the Cotton Mill*, 97–117.

of worsteds, French and Belgian operatives were employed. Meanwhile the print works were entirely run by skilled hands from England and Scotland. Italians, Greeks and Finns were also engaged in certain operations.[41] Turning now to the Baldwin Locomotive Works as representative of another field of industry, more than half of the men employed were native Americans, and well toward one-eighth were Irish. Next in point of numbers came Russians, Poles and Germans. Rather remarkably, in view of their aptitude and interest in engineering trades, there were only 299 Englishmen and 127 Scotchmen on the payrolls.[42] With the growing use of automatic machinery and the specialization of the metal-working industries, so that large departments in factories were devoted to a single operation, the employment of women and girls in this group of occupations increased.

While these twenty years had their full share of labor disturbances, it can hardly be said that labor troubles interfered seriously with the prosperity of industry. In 1894 a protracted coal strike crippled temporarily the operation of Eastern iron furnaces. A still more serious strike occurred in the anthracite coal fields about ten years later.[43] Several strikes occurred in the textile industries when the depression of 1894 with its pressure to lower wages caused trouble in the spinning mills of New England, especially at New Bedford and Fall River, where labor was particularly well organized. Strikes were recorded in the South in 1898, when the employes of the mills at Augusta made an organized protest against a lower wage scale. This contest was marked by the withdrawal of two or three employers, including perhaps the largest employer in the Augusta district, from the Manufacturers' Association, as a protest against what they considered an unfair attempt to depress the pay of the workers. Almost simultaneously a lock-out occurred at Fall River and New Bedford.[44] New England textile workers continued restless during the following year, when strikes were reported in a large number of establishments. The most dramatic and serious labor disputes that occurred in American textile mills during this period were among the woolen operatives at Lawrence and the silk workers at Paterson. These strikes cast vivid light upon some neglected social aspects of American industrial development, but they did not modify materially its course. In iron and steel making the two great labor battles of this period were the Homestead strike in Pittsburgh in 1892 and the strike of the Amalgamated Association in the same district in 1900. The latter conflict resulted in the defeat of the labor organization and the virtual end of trade unionism as an important factor in the steel industry.

[41] National Association of Cotton Manufacturers, *Transactions, 1913,* 114–115.
[42] *Manufacturers' Record,* LXV, 65, July 2, 1914.
[43] *Commercial and Financial Chronicle,* LIX, 52, July 14, 1894.
[44] *Commercial and Financial Chronicle,* LIX, 339, Aug. 25, 1894; LIX, 668, Oct. 30, 1894; LXVII, 1116, Nov. 26, 1898; LXVII, 1169, Dec. 3, 1898; LXVIII, 141, Jan. 21, 1899; LXVIII, 193, Jan. 28, 1899; LXVIII, 679, Apr. 8, 1899; LXVIII, 884, May 6, 1899; *Southern and Western Textile Excelsior,* Nov. 12, 1898.

CHAPTER II

MANUFACTURE OF PIG IRON

Domestic Ores, 15. Ore Imports, 16. Lake Superior Ores, 17. Organization of the Ore Trade, 19. Iron Smelting in the North, 22. Iron Smelting in the South, 24. Furnace Statistics, 28. Pig-Iron Output, 31.

DOMESTIC ORES

The geography of ore production did not change materially during these twenty years, except for the development of the Mesabi district in Northern Minnesota and the increasing proportion that came from the Lake Superior and the Alabama districts. In 1910 the Lake Superior region furnished four-fifths of the iron ore mined in the United States, and Minnesota alone more than one half.[1]

This did not imply, however, the exhaustion or an absolute decline in the amount of ore mined in the older iron-producing districts of the Union. The check to local mining in Pennsylvania and New Jersey, which had formerly been our leading producing states, was due largely to the substitution of steel for iron. The companies that made a specialty of foundry irons and iron products continued to use Eastern ores, exclusively or in part. In 1897 the Thomas Iron Company, one of the largest pig-iron producers for the general market in the United States, employed a mixture of New Jersey, Pennsylvania and Lake Superior ores. In 1901 the Cornwall Mines in Pennsylvania, which were still described as "the second most important source of iron ore supply in the United States,"[2] passed under the control of the Pennsylvania Steel Company. In 1914 the Warwick Furnaces in Pennsylvania drew their ore supplies from a remarkably wide area: Lake Superior, Northern New York, Spain, Sweden, Greece, Algiers and Cuba, as well as from their immediate neighborhood. Up to the close of this period ore continued to be mined for local furnaces, though in comparatively small quantities, in the Salisbury district of Connecticut.[3] The once promising deposits at Pilot Knob and Iron Mountain, Missouri, were exhausted before 1893, although leaner ores are found over approximately half the area of that state.[4] On the Pacific Coast there are scattered deposits of Bessemer ore, including a mine in Lyon County, Nevada, near the California line, belonging to the Western Steel Corporation of Seattle.[5]

---

[1] *Mineral Industry*, XIX, 404–405.
[2] American Iron and Steel Association, *Bulletin*, XXXI, 101, May 1, 1897; XXXV, 93, June 25, 1901.
[3] *Iron Age*, XCIV, 203, July 23, 1914; XCIV, 254–255, July 30, 1914.
[4] American Iron and Steel Association, *Bulletin*, XXIV, 188, July 2, 1890; XLVI, 111, Dec. 1, 1912.
[5] American Iron and Steel Association, *Bulletin*, XXXVI, 9, Jan. 29, 1902; XLIV, 94, Oct. 1, 1910.

In 1913 Texas shipped a few thousand tons of brown hematites to furnaces in Western Pennsylvania.[6] Carolina ores were occasionally worked, even at the disadvantage of having to be hauled by mule and ox wagons for five miles before they reached a railway.[7] No radical change occurred in the Birmingham district during this period. In a general way its deposits had been surveyed and tested before 1893. In the pioneer days of Alabama mining, their ores yielded from 40 to 50 per cent of iron, but the more important varieties eventually settled down to about 37 per cent. Meanwhile they changed as mining progressed to deeper levels from silicious to basic ores.[8] Between 1893 and 1913 the quantity of iron ore mined annually in the South rose from 3,000,000 to over 6,000,000 tons.[9]

ORE IMPORTS

During this period we both exported and imported iron ore. In 1895 there were some shipments by all-water routes from Port Henry, New York, to German furnaces on the Rhine. Such exports were not continuous and were small in quantity, however; while our imports steadily increased.[10] They came from widely separated points: Sweden, the Mediterranean, Cuba and South America. In 1895, when it was feared that the insurrection in Cuba might interfere with ore shipments from that Island, forty charters were reported to have been closed within two weeks for vessels to bring Bessemer ores to Philadelphia from Carthaginia, Spain, and adjacent ports. In 1896, a note regarding furnace outputs at Sparrows Point, Maryland, mentioned charges consisting of one-third Mokta, one-third Tafna, one-sixth Porman, and one-sixth Seriphos ore. Among the arrivals of iron ore and manganese in Philadelphia in 1899 were cargoes from Spain, Elba, the Black Sea, British India and Brazil.[11] In 1909 following a radical reduction in the duty of iron ore from 40 to 15 cents a ton, and to 12 cents under our tariff agreements with Cuba upon ores from that Island, accompanied by improvements in methods of handling and carrying, imports rapidly increased. The Cuban mines and the larger Swedish mines controlled their own ore fleets, and low freights—sometimes at little more than ballast rates—encouraged occasional importations from unexpected points. In 1909 the Western Steel Corporation of Seattle contracted for annual deliveries of 200,000 tons of ore from China. This was a very rich hematite containing 66 per cent of iron and practically no phosphorus, and was smelted in a mixture with equal amounts of British Columbia and Washington ores.

More than half of the ore we purchased abroad, however, ordinarily came from Cuba—Spain and Sweden sending the next largest quantities in

[6] *Mineral Industry*, XXII, 389.
[7] American Iron and Steel Association, *Bulletin*, XXXIV, 19, Jan. 22, 1900.
[8] *Mineral Industry*, XIX, 404–405; American Iron and Steel Association, *Bulletin*, XLIV, 21, Mar. 1, 1910.
[9] *Manufacturers' Record*, LXVI, 39, Oct. 15, 1914.
[10] American Iron and Steel Association, *Bulletin*, XXIX, 139, June 20, 1895; XXXVIII, 106, July 25, 1904.
[11] American Iron and Steel Association, *Bulletin*, XXIX, 213, Sept. 20, 1895; XXX, 66, Mar. 20, 1896; XXXIII, 139, Aug. 15, 1899; XXXIII, 197, Nov. 15, 1899.

the order named. Before the war with Spain, the Spanish-American Iron Company could deliver first-class Bessemer ores on shipboard, for about $1.25 a ton. The Pennsylvania Steel Company and the Tidewater Steel Company had large investments in Cuban mines. In 1901 the former corporation bought the stock of the Spanish-American Iron Company and a controlling interest in the Cuban Steel Ore Company. The former was one of the largest producers in Cuba; the second had not yet begun shipping. The Pennsylvania Company also owned jointly with the Bethlehem Iron Company the stock of the Juragua Company. Some of the Cuban ores were high in aluminum content, and therefore were for a time considered undesirable.[12]

Brazil had long been a source for manganese ore used in the United States; and copper ores had been imported from Chile for three-quarters of a century or more. Not long before the World War the Bethlehem Steel Company, probably having in view the early completion of the Panama Canal, acquired control of the Tofo Mines, an exceedingly important iron deposit in Chile, whose ore averages 68 per cent of metallic iron, with low sulphur, phosphorous and silicon content. This was a higher grade of ore than any mined in the United States, and higher even than the Swedish ores, of which we imported about half a million tons a year. Special steamers operating under the Swedish and Norwegian flag and capable of carrying 15,000 tons of ore, were built especially for this new trade, and the Bethlehem Steel Company prepared to bring a million and a half tons a year from Chile to Bethlehem, a distance of 4,500 miles.[13]

LAKE SUPERIOR ORES

But the great source of ore supply for the United States, and probably the largest producing iron-ore area in the world, continued to be the Lake Superior district. In Michigan, where the original discoveries were made, and in Wisconsin, the two states that produced practically all the Lake Superior ore mined prior to 1893, the ore is rocklike in texture and is quarried by drill and dynamite; in Minnesota it also exists in disclike deposits of fine red dust excavated with steam shovels. The development of the first of the Minnesota districts discovered, the Mesabi Range, was delayed by the fact that this fine ore could not be handled successfully by the methods and in the furnaces then existing. If confined during smelting, it was likely to "explode"; if loaded with mixtures of ordinary ore, it blew out of the furnace with the blast covering the whole countryside for a considerable distance around. Another obstacle to the immediate adoption of

---

[12] *Mineral Industry*, XVIII, 402; XXII, 391; American Iron and Steel Association, *Bulletin*, XXIX, 139, June 20, 1895; XXXV, 53, Apr. 10, 1901; XXXVII, 155, Oct. 25, 1903; XLIV, 106, Nov. 1, 1910; XLVI, 46, May 1, 1912; *Iron Age*, XCIII, 1338, May 28, 1914.

[13] American Iron and Steel Association, *Bulletin*, XXXIII, 85, May 15, 1899; *Iron Age*, XCIII, 1020, Apr. 23, 1914; XCIII, 1458, June 11, 1914; XCIV, 1448, Dec. 24, 1914; *Manufacturers' Record*, LXV, 37, June 25, 1914; *Mineral Industry*, XXIII, 418.

Mesabi ores on a large scale was the cost of transportation, the distance from the mines to Cleveland being some 300 miles greater than that from the Marquette and Menominee ranges of Michigan.[14]

In both districts the greatest care was observed in selecting ore in the stopes. In Michigan each set of timbers bore an iron tag showing the quality of the ore, whether Bessemer or non-Bessemer, and various qualities and grades were carefully sorted into different stock piles. Eventually the Lake Superior Iron Ore Association published an annual booklet of ore analyses, which became the basis of the guaranties for the succeeding year. These analyses stated the content of iron, phosphorous, silica, manganese, alumina, lime, magnesia and sulphur. In 1913, 296 ores from this region were listed.[15]

With the improvement and cheapening of transportation, the furnace area supplied by the Lake Superior District continued to grow larger. Some plants were situated immediately on the Great Lakes, or on waterways connected with them, at Toledo, Lorain, Cleveland, Buffalo, Tonawanda and elsewhere. Most of the iron ore shipped by water, however, was transshipped at Lower Lake ports for points further South and Southeast, such as Wheeling, Youngstown, Pittsburgh, and even the Susquehana, Lehigh, and Schuylkill Valleys, occasionally reaching destinations as distant as Southern Virginia, St. Louis and Alabama. Now and then a cargo went via the Welland Canal to tidewater points; for instance, to the Dominion Iron and Steel Company at Sidney, Cape Breton.[16]

In 1895 when the shipments from the Lake Superior district reached 10,500,000 tons, this was regarded an astonishing total. Indeed, the whole quantity of ore won in this region during the forty years from the beginning of mining until the close of 1895 was less than 100,000,000 tons. By the end of the century, however, annual shipments had nearly doubled, exceeding 19,000,000 tons, and they passed the 20,000,000-ton limit the following year. At this time the Lake Superior District produced 76 per cent of all the iron ore mined in the United States. In 1905, ten years after the "astonishing total" of 10,500,000 tons just mentioned, annual shipments from the Lake Superior region were over 34,353,000 tons. Five years later the figure had risen to 43,432,000 tons, and in 1913, when the total amount of iron ore mined in the United States was about 62,000,000 tons, the output of the Lake Superior region was almost exactly 50,000,000 tons, of which 70 per cent came from the Mesabi range.[17]

Improved methods of mining and of handling and transporting ore lowered its cost for Eastern furnace men. Cleveland was the great ore

---

[14] Gates, *The Truth About Mr. Rockefeller and the Merritts* (in *Oil Industry of the United States*), 4–5.

[15] *Iron Age*, xcIII, 1054, Apr. 23, 1914.

[16] American Iron and Steel Association, *Bulletin*, xxxvIII, 67, May 10, 1904; xxxvIII, 85, June 10, 1904.

[17] American Iron and Steel Association, *Bulletin*, xxx, 28, Feb. 1, 1896: xL, 34, Mar. 1, 1906; xLv, 30, Mar. 25, 1911; *Iron Age*, xcIv, 555, Sept. 3, 1914.

market of the United States. Prices at that point reached $18 in 1873, and averaged $12.17 throughout the season, the highest rate on record. After 1893, when they were based on much closer assays, rates for ores from different mines and for Bessemer and non-Bessemer uses naturally varied by a relatively wider margin than formerly. But the spread of prices during this latter period was generally below a five-dollar maximum for the highest grade, and at times ranged between two and three dollars. Price fluctuations from season to season occasionally amounted to 30 per cent. In 1894 prior to the ore pool era that was to begin the next season, contracts were made for $2.95 a ton for first-grade Bessemers, and $2.50 a ton for second grades. Twenty years later prices ranged from $3.50 to $3.75 a ton.[18]

While the old range ores of Northern Michigan and Wisconsin had the advantage of shorter hauls and slightly lower freights, the Minnesota ores which were coming into the market at this time and tended to keep down prices were mined at a minimum cost with steam shovels in open cuts. About 1890 ore was still unloaded from the vessels by means of tubs hoisted by a derrick, and it took a week to discharge the cargo of what were then considered large vessels in the ore trade, carrying about 2,000 tons. Twenty years later the largest carriers in the business had a capacity exceeding 13,000 tons, and 10,000 tons of ore could be taken out of a steamer's hold and put into cars in less than two hours. These improvements included the construction of special elevated docks with ore pockets, from which vessels could be loaded by gravity, and special receiving docks with clam-shell buckets and huge derricks for unloading. They involved further, the displacement of a great part of what had been considered modern shipping a few years before by vessels and barges of special design and large capacity.[19]

Land transportation also was specialized. Ore-carrying roads were constructed not only from the mines to the shipping ports, as in Northern Minnesota, but also from receiving ports to furnace centers, as between Cleveland and Pittsburgh. The mechanics of loading and unloading included facilities for handling trains with great rapidity. As early as 1901 the interval between trains in each direction on the Duluth and Iron Range Railway was but 45 minutes. Ore was ordinarily carried from Lake Superior ports to Cleveland and Buffalo for from 70 cents to one dollar a ton.[20]

ORGANIZATION OF THE ORE TRADE

In the early days Lake Superior mining companies maintained their own offices in Cleveland, and sold their own ore on a basis of occasional analyses.

[18] American Iron and Steel Association, *Bulletin*, xxviii, 54, Mar. 7, 1894; xxxi, 193, Sept. 1, 1897; xxxii, 37, Mar. 1, 1898; xlvi, 46, May 1, 1912; U. S. Geological Survey, *Mineral Resources of the United States, 1915*, i, 299.

[19] American Iron and Steel Association, *Bulletin*, xxviii, 201, Sept. 12, 1894; American Iron and Steel Institute, *Bulletin*, i, 162, May, 1913.

[20] American Iron and Steel Association, *Bulletin*, xxxv, 101, July 10, 1901; xlv, 54, June 1, 1911.

Subsequently brokers or factors acquired control of this business. Originally these agents merely chartered vessels and sold ore for the mines that were their clients, but eventually they extended their field of service so that they became the financial agents as well as the selling agents of the mine owners. They advanced funds for current operations and freights, passed upon credits, determined the movement of vessels, analyzed and appraised ores, and interested themselves in furnace and rolling-mill investments. They thus became a connecting link, so far as the financial and commercial side of the business was concerned, between the producer of raw materials and the consumer of raw iron and steel.[21]

The concentration of so large a part of the ore business at a single point, Cleveland, and in the hands of a few great factors, facilitated the formation of pools. The first of these was made in 1895, when the producers of Old Range Bessemer concluded an agreement as to prices and tonnage allotments. Usually Mesabi producers were not included, and during the early years of the association producers of non-Bessemer ores did not belong. These agreements, which were made at the beginning of each season, based prices on a theoretical ore containing at first 63 per cent of iron and definite proportions of phosphorous and moisture. The prices ranged from a minimum of $2.65 in 1897 to a maximum of $5.50 in 1900, the aim being to follow the iron market and to treat all buyers alike, so that furnace owners would have a stable foundation on which to operate. These pools continued practically without interruption until 1904, by which time their usefulness has been largely curtailed by the extensive acquisition of ore properties by great iron and steel-making companies in the East, who thus virtually dropped out of the market.[22]

While many ore consumers had thus become mine owners, others had adopted the policy of making long-term contracts running from five to ten years, the prices either being graded on a sliding scale in proportion to the market price of iron, or in some cases fixed at a low flat rate. The cessation of pool making did not terminate the organization that had been formed originally with the object of reaching price agreements, for it was continued for the purpose of gathering and distributing statistical and technical information to the members.[23]

The concentration of iron and steel making in the hands of great corporations, or vertical trusts, owning independent supplies of raw materials and controlling all the processes of production from winning the ore to the completion of the finished product, was not new in principle, for the first blast furnaces erected in New England and the larger works at Brady's Bend, Cambria and elsewhere, had been organized on this basis. But it was impressive and novel so far as the complexity, the vast scale of the

[21] *Iron Age*, LVII, 43–44, Jan. 2, 1896.
[22] American Iron and Steel Association, *Bulletin*, XXIX, 27, Jan. 30, 1893; XXXI, 78, Apr. 1, 1897, XXXI, 93; Apr. 20, 1897; XXXVIII, 74, May 25, 1904.
[23] American Iron and Steel Association, *Bulletin*, XXXIX, 42, Mar. 15, 1905.

operations and the large territory covered by those corporations, were concerned.

For a brief period, however, it was uncertain whether the initiative toward this form of consolidation would be taken by the miner or the manufacturer. Andrew Carnegie and his associates are commonly reputed to have been the first of the great modern steel makers in this country to have aggressively pursued this policy.[24] About the time they were building the Pittsburgh and Lake Erie Railway, buying coke ovens and coal fields and making investments in Lake Superior ore lands, the mining business was showing an independent tendency toward concentration within its own special field. This was particularly true of the newer ore districts in Minnesota, where farsighted capitalists bought up large tracts of land immediately after the first discoveries. In 1893, for instance, the Merritt family owned about two-fifths of the stock of the five companies operating on the Mesabi Range. They were also interested in the railway that tapped these fields. But they became financially embarrassed during the panic of 1893, and through a series of negotiations, which were later the subject of a protracted lawsuit, their property fell into the hands of the Rockefeller interests. The new owners proceeded to develop the business to the utmost, and soon were in possession not only of mines, railways and ore docks of the most modern character, but of a large fleet of ore-carrying vessels, so that they controlled all the operations of winning, transporting and selling ore. It was rumored that they contemplated also erecting furnaces to smelt it.[25]

In 1897, however, the Carnegie and Rockefeller interests reached an agreement, by which the Carnegie-Oliver group, representing the Carnegie properties and one of the largest independent mining companies in the Lake Superior region, agreed not to sell ore in the open market and thus become a competitor with the Rockefeller interests, while the latter contracted not to engage in the manufacture of steel. Naturally there were many other conditions in this agreement, but the essential point was the definition of the respective spheres of activity of the two enterprises.[26]

Meanwhile other large steel companies were following the example of the Carnegie Company. In 1899 the National Steel Company acquired important mines in the Lake Superior region, and a fleet of ore vessels. In 1901 the United States Steel Company bought out the Rockefeller ore and shipping interests on the Great Lakes. The same year the Jones and Laughlin Company purchased important Lake Superior mines. By the following year about two-thirds of all the ore produced in the Lake Superior region was mined directly by those using it. The shipments from the United States Steel Corporation properties were over 58 per cent of all the

[24] Bridge, *Inside History of the Carnegie Steel Company*, 169, 272; Mussey, *Combination in the Mining Industry*, 117-124.
[25] Gates, *The Truth about Mr. Rockefeller and the Merritts* (in *Oil Industry of the United States*), 3; Mussey, *Combination in the Mining Industry*, 115-117.
[26] *Iron Age*, Feb. 18, 1897, quoted in American Iron and Steel Association, *Bulletin*, xxxi, 50, Mar. 1, 1897.

ore raised in the Lake Superior region, and its holdings very soon reached three-fourths of a billion tons. In 1906 the same corporation entered into a contract by which it acquired on a royalty basis the ore on the Hill properties, the greatest single reserve outside of its own lands.[27]

By this time ore was raised and handled but twice from the mine in the far North until it went into the furnace at Pittsburgh. Machinery and gravity did the rest. Less than 35 per cent of the ore mined in 1903 was sold in the open market; the rest was mined directly by the companies using it.[28]

Nevertheless, this centralization of control and management from the mine to the finished product did not prove permanently economical. The United States Steel Corporation decided in 1911 to terminate its contract for the Great Northern ores at the first practicable date, January 1, 1915. In 1914 the Cambria Steel Company sold an important Lake Superior mine to a regular mining company. Steel manufacturers had reached the conclusion that the ore supply would take care of itself, and that the less their present resources were burdened with property upon which they could not realize before a distant future date, the more cheaply they could sell their products. Indeed, some large manufacturers of steel disposed of a portion of their ores in the open market, although when they purchased their properties they considered that they were merely safeguarding their future, and that all these reserves would be required for their own operations. They found in practice that an occasional ore sale helped them to meet bond interest, and sometimes to pay a dividend. Another consideration was the discovery that additional sources of ore and unanticipated extensions of existing fields made the likelihood of an ore famine within any period for which prudent provision required to be made, exceedingly improbable. Cuba and South America were shipping increasing quantities to our Eastern seaports. During the Federal suit against the United States Steel Corporation testimony was presented to the effect that the amount of iron ore available for American steel companies was practically inexhaustible. The Hill lease put a burden on every ton of steel the United States Steel Corporation produced, and handicapped it in meeting competition from Germany and elsewhere.[29]

IRON SMELTING IN THE NORTH

While an increasing proportion of the iron ore mined came from one group of states, an increasing proportion of the iron smelted was made in another group of states. Alabama was practically the only state where ore output and iron output increased *pari passu*. Furthermore the number of states

---

[27] American Iron and Steel Association, *Bulletin*, XXXIII, 138, Aug. 15, 1899; XXXV, 45, Mar. 25, 1901; XXXV, 93, June 25, 1901; XXXVII, 21, Feb. 10, 1903; XL, 150, Oct. 15, 1906; Michigan State Geological Survey, *Reports*, 1901, 128–131.

[28] *Mineral Industry*, 1902, 355–397.

[29] American Iron and Steel Association, *Bulletin*, XLV, 110, Nov. 1, 1911; *Iron Age*, XCIII, 1475, June 11, 1914.

making pig iron kept declining. In 1905 Pennsylvania, which made more than half the steel produced in the country, mined less than 2 per cent of the iron ore. Ohio, which came next to Pennsylvania as an iron maker, mined less than 1 per cent of the total.[30]

To be sure, many of the smaller furnaces in the East used mostly, or entirely, local ores. This was particularly true of those that made charcoal iron. It was not until 1891 that the manufacture of iron ceased at the old Principio Furnace in Maryland, erected in 1723. In 1899 the American Steel and Wire Company resumed operations at its furnaces at Crown Point, New York, employing ores from Port Henry in the same state. The following year the old Andover Furnace in New Jersey concluded an uninterrupted run of exactly five years. The Richmond Iron Company in western Massachusetts, and the Barnum Richardson Company of East Canaan, Connecticut, continued to make charcoal iron from local ores up to the end of the period we are discussing.[31] An interesting instance of the persistence of old processes was the opening of a new furnace in Allegheny County as recently as 1906, for the purpose of producing charcoal iron and hammered charcoal blooms and billets for boiler tubes and other special purposes. Four years later a group of charcoal furnaces in Columbia County, New York, where there is an extension of the ore beds of the Salisbury District, resumed operation under the control of a new company.[32]

Eastern furnaces at this time fell into two groups: comparatively small charcoal furnaces making special irons for car wheels, boiler tubes and other specific and limited uses from ores peculiarly suited for these purposes, and large furnaces vieing in size with the gigantic plants west of the Alleghenies and in the South, where imported and Lake Superior ores were smelted, sometimes in combination with ores from local mines, for the purpose of making steel. The greatest iron-smelting center of the United States was Allegheny County, which produced about one-fourth of all the pig iron made in the United States and a still larger proportion of its steel ingots, castings and rails. The Pittsburgh district also produced more than half the structural shapes rolled in the country and its iron and steel products found a market in all parts of the United States.[33] Nevertheless, a tendency was clearly manifested for furnaces and steel works to drift westward and to points having all-water communication with the ore docks on Lake Superior. There was a revival of the iron industry at Buffalo, and in 1902 the Lackawanna Steel Company dismantled all its furnaces at Scranton and transferred them to that city. Three other iron and steel-making companies of some importance were also in Buffalo or its

[30] *Cf. Commercial and Financial Chronicle*, LXVII, 203, July 30, 1899; American Iron and Steel Association, *Bulletin*, XXXIX, 90, June 15, 1905.

[31] American Iron and Steel Association, *Bulletin*, XXIX, 20, Jan. 18, 1895; XXXIII, 203, Nov. 15, 1899; XXXV, 13, Jan. 23, 1901; XXXVII, 105, July 25, 1903; *Iron Age*, XCIV, 257–258, July 30, 1914.

[32] American Iron and Steel Association, *Bulletin*, XL, 29, Feb. 15, 1906; XLIV, 19, Mar. 1, 1910; XLVI, 104, Nov. 1, 1912.

[33] American Iron and Steel Association, *Bulletin*, XXXVI, 190, Dec. 25, 1902.

immediate vicinity: the Buffalo and Susquehana Iron Company, The Buffalo Union Furnace Company and the Tonawanda Iron and Steel Company, each of which owned a group of modern blast furnaces. The Buffalo and Susquehana Company owned mines in the Mesabi Range in Minnesota, and coking and coal lands in Pennsylvania.[34] Cleveland, the greatest ore-receiving port in the United States, also made pig iron. Iron continued to be smelted on the Upper Peninsula of Michigan, where several charcoal furnaces were in operation; one of which, at Ashland, Wisconsin, was reputed to be the largest of its kind in the world. At Duluth, an attempt was made to smelt Bessemer pigs with coke brought in ore boats from lower Lake ports, or with coke manufactured locally from coal transported in the same manner. But the chief center of this industry in the West was in the Chicago district.[35]

Comparatively little iron was smelted west of the Mississippi, and states that at one time had been producers ceased to have active furnaces. No pig iron was made on the Pacific Coast in 1897, although it had been smelted in all three of the coast states at some previous date. During this year, Missouri, Colorado and Texas were the only states west of the Mississippi producing iron. In 1899 an attempt was made to revive the works on Puget Sound, which had been out of operation for several years. A new company was organized for this purpose, and for a time there seemed to be some promise that steel-making might become an established industry in this section. But the company failed, and in 1912 its property was taken over to satisfy the claims of its creditors.[36]

IRON SMELTING IN THE SOUTH

In the South, however, more substantial progress was made during these twenty years than in any previous period since iron making was first established in that section. The panic of 1893 had swept away most of the speculative and mushroom enterprises that had been promoted during the previous boom. Here, as in the North, progress was accompanied by geographical concentration. While iron making declined in the other Southern states, or made but little progress, it advanced by rapid strides in Alabama. During the years of depression immediately following the panic, Southern iron makers sought foreign markets. In 1894, 10,000 tons of cast-iron pipe were shipped to Japan from Birmingham; and this was followed by much larger shipments to the same country the following year.[37]

---

[34] American Iron and Steel Association, *Bulletin*, XXVIII, 93, May 2, 1894; XXIX, 37, Feb. 9, 1895; XXXVI, 107, July 25, 1902; XXXVII, 19, Feb. 10, 1903; XXXVIII, 18, Feb. 10, 1904; XXXVIII, 157, Oct. 25, 1904.
[35] American Iron and Steel Association, *Bulletin*, XXVIII, 133, June 23, 1894; XXXIII, 21, Feb. 1, 1899; XXXIII, 60, Apr. 10, 1899; XXXV, 13, Jan. 23, 1901; XLIV, 70, Aug. 1, 1910; *Mineral Industry*, XII, 195.
[36] *Mineral Industry*, VI, 401; American Iron and Steel Association, *Bulletin*, XXXIII, 162, Sept. 22, 1899; XXXVI, 125, Aug. 25, 1902; XXXVII, 139, Sept. 25, 1903; XLVI, 38, Apr. 1, 1912.
[37] *Manufacturers' Record*, XXVI, 235, Nov. 16, 1894; XXVIII, 20, Aug. 9, 1895; Aug. 6, 1895; American Iron and Steel Association, *Bulletin*, XXVIII, 101, May 12, 1894.

Manufacture of Pig Iron

The beginning of a trade in iron with Japan was partly responsible for the interest taken by Birmingham manufacturers in the completion of the Isthmian Canal. Before the Cuban Reciprocity Treaty was terminated, the same city was shipping iron and coal to Cuba. But this trade was brought to an abrupt end when the Gorman Bill was enacted and the first rumblings of the coming Revolution paralyzed the Cuban market.[38]

Between 1890 and 1896 the pig-iron production of Alabama after falling off by nearly one-third during the panic, increased by about one-eighth while that of Maryland decreased by nearly half. Tennessee, West Virginia, and indeed every other Southern state except Virginia and Kentucky, made less iron the latter year than the former. During this season, which marked the recovery of the South from the depression, the furnaces of that section kept more generally at work than those in other parts of the country, and the proportion of the total iron output of the Union credited to the South rose within a year from 18 to over 21 per cent.[39] Some of this iron continued to find a market abroad, shipments to England and Italy being recorded.[40] The following year, however, witnessed a marked decline in the iron output of Virginia, which brought down the South's share in the national output, although Alabama showed a substantial increase.[41]

The export market continued to grow. Over 150,000 tons of pig iron were shipped to Europe, South America and India, some Southern iron going even to Sweden.[42] In 1898 Birmingham was said to be the third largest iron shipping point in the world. During the eighteen months ending with January first of that year it had exported 297,000 tons of pigs to foreign countries. These figures were exceeded only by Middlesboro and Glasgow in Great Britain. The total shipments of iron, including those abroad and those to domestic points, averaged over 1,300,000 tons a year.[43]

In 1900 there were 120 furnaces in the South, or twelve fewer than ten years previously; but the total output of iron had practically doubled. This decline in the number of furnaces notwithstanding an increased output was due to the abandonment of old charcoal plants and the substitution for them, in furnace records, of modern coal and coke plants. Some observers were inclined to regard this progress as unsatisfactory. The Southern iron industry had not realized all the rosy hopes entertained by promoters and enthusiasts at the opening of the decade. Lack of capital and experience and bad management had precipitated many failures. Still the

---

[38] American Iron and Steel Association, *Bulletin*, XXVIII, 122, June 13, 1894; XXIX, 41, Feb. 20, 1895.
[39] *Commercial and Financial Chronicle*, LXIV, 217, Jan. 30, 1897; *Mineral Industry*, 1896, V, 332.
[40] *Manufacturers' Record*, XXIX, 341, June 19, 1896; XXX, 19, Sept. 18, 1896; XXX, 19, Dec. 11, 1896.
[41] *Mineral Industry*, VI, 401.
[42] *Commercial and Financial Chronicle*, LXV, 218, Aug. 7, 1897; *Manufacturers' Record*, XXXII, 223, Nov. 5, 1897; cf. American Iron and Steel Association, *Bulletin*, XXXIII, 178, Oct. 15, 1899.
[43] *Manufacturers' Record*, XXXIV, 136, Sept. 23, 1898; XXXIV, 300, Nov. 25, 1898.

industry was on a firm foundation, and from 1899 onward it attracted large amounts of outside capital.[44]

Between 1903 and 1914 the South's production of pig iron remained about stationary, while that of the United States as a whole increased more than 70 per cent. In 1893, when the pig-iron output of the whole country was somewhat over 7,000,000 tons, that of the South had just passed 1,500,000 tons. In other words, 22 per cent of the total output was credited to the latter section. Ten years later, in 1903, the United States made over 18,000,000 tons of pig iron, an increase of 152 per cent within a decade. Meanwhile, the South had increased its output to nearly 3,750,000 tons, which represented an addition for that section alone of only 106 per cent; and its proportion of the total quantity made in the country had consequently fallen to below 18 per cent. In 1913 the country's pig-iron output had risen to nearly 31,000,000 tons, the largest absolute increase made in any decade, though the percentage growth of the industry was less than between 1893 and 1903. In the last year mentioned, the South produced only about 50,000 tons more iron than it had ten years previously. Its percentage increase was practically nil, and the proportion of all the iron manufactured in the country credited to that section had fallen below 11 per cent.[45]

Turning to steel, relatively better progress had been made. Between 1901 and 1913 the output of the South doubled, rising from 900,000 to 1,800,000 tons. This rate of increase, however, did not equal that of the whole United States whose product rose during this period from approximately 13,500,000 tons to over 31,000,000 tons, or 132 per cent.

The stationary condition of the Southern iron industry during these ten or fifteen years was generally attributed to the facts that most of the pig iron manufactured in the South was marketed in the form in which it came from the furnace, without being converted into steel or finished products; and that consuming markets were relatively remote from the furnaces, so that their product was subject to heavy freight charges. Southern iron was always quoted at lower prices than similar grades of iron from Northern and Eastern furnaces. In respect to growth, the iron industry was in marked contrast to the other industries of the South, whose manufactured and agricultural products increased faster in value during this period than those of the country at large, as did also the volume of its banking business.

In 1914 the Interstate Commerce Commission handed down a decision that is interesting as showing the vital influence that freight rates may have upon the prosperity and growth of an industry. Between 1881 and 1907 the freight on pig iron from Birmingham and Chattanooga to Louisville and other Northern points was based upon a sliding scale varying with its market price. In 1907 a flat rate was established and maintained independ-

---

[44] American Iron and Steel Association, *Bulletin*, XXXVI, 36, Mar. 10, 1902; *Manufacturers' Record*, XLI, 106, Mar. 6, 1902.

[45] *Iron Age*, XCIV, 992–993, Oct. 29, 1914; *Manufacturers' Record*, LXVI, 58, Nov. 5, 1914.

ently of the price of iron. In 1914 the Interstate Commerce Commission lowered these rates appreciably, not only from the Alabama field, but also from Virginia, thereby removing certain discriminations made by Northern roads to encourage furnace development along their own lines and extending the area of profitable marketing from these districts farther North along the Atlantic Coast, and also farther West, than it had been for many years.[46]

Throughout this period the South produced mainly foundry iron, although as we have seen the local steel industry was growing, and with the extension of the open-hearth process in the North a new market was being created for basic pig. But it was in foundry irons and foundry products like cast-iron pipe, that the South at this time excelled. Southern pig was reputed to be more fluid, to make sharper, cleaner and softer castings with less internal shrinkage, and to produce a casting of a finer grain than most Northern irons. Castings made from Southern iron chilled slowly and retained a relatively smoother and softer surface.[47]

In 1899, when the movement toward industrial consolidation was under full headway, the South did not escape its influence. Among other large enterprises dating from this period was the Alabama Consolidated Iron and Coal Company, which purchased a number of furnaces in the Birmingham district. Measured by later standards it was a comparatively small corporation for this industry, the total capital being but $5,000,000; yet its property included 70,000 acres of mineral lands, 4 furnaces, and 200 coke ovens.[48] A second company, rather larger than those hitherto operating in the district, was the Alabama and Georgia Iron Company, which was incorporated at Trenton, New Jersey, with a capital of $1,300,000, to take over furnaces and mines in the states mentioned.[49] Two other companies of considerably larger dimensions were formed during this period, in addition to the Tennessee Coal and Iron Company, to which we have made earlier reference and which we shall have occasion to mention later. In 1899 several ore, coal and blast furnace properties, including one or two reproductive works, and the steel works erected some ten years before at Middlesboro, Kentucky, were acquired by a single corporation known as the Virginia Iron, Coal, and Coke Company. Some of the furnaces thus combined had been erected with British capital during the ill-considered boom of the late eighties and early nineties. Their owners had either become insolvent or had closed down their plants for other reasons and it was imagined that the new company would profit largely from acquiring these furnaces and their mineral holdings at less than their original cost. It purchased altogether 14 modern blast furnaces and 6 small charcoal furnaces, with a total capacity of over 700,000 tons of pig per annum, be-

[46] *Iron Age*, XCIV, 100–101, July 9, 1914; *Manufacturers' Record*, LXVI, 45, July 16, 1914.
[47] Cf. *Manufacturers' Record*, LXVI, 59, Nov. 5, 1914.
[48] *Commercial and Financial Chronicle*, LXIX, 227, July 29, 1899; American Iron and Steel Association, *Bulletin*, XXXIII, 180, Oct. 15, 1899.
[49] *Commercial and Financial Chronicle*, LXIX, 907, Oct. 28, 1899.

sides a steel plant, a horseshoe factory and foundries. These represented an investment of nearly $17,000,000, equally divided between stock and bonds. At the time the Company was organized the constituent works were producing annually about 400,000 tons of pig iron, 150,000 kegs of horseshoes, 40,000 tons of castings, besides coke and coal. Within less than two years of its formation, however, this corporation passed into the hands of a receiver and was reorganized. It continued to do business thereafter, but without conspicuous success.[50]

The second important combination in the Southern iron industry likewise occurred in 1899. This was the organization of the Sloss-Sheffield Steel and Iron Company, which took its name from the principal constituent firm, the Sloss Iron and Steel Company of Birmingham. It was incorporated in New Jersey with a capital $20,000,000 and acquired six or seven groups of furnaces and mineral properties in Alabama and the neighboring region of Tennessee. These included at the time they were acquired seven blast furnaces, 1,500 coke ovens, and about 100,000 acres of coal and iron land. The annual output of pig iron alone exceeded 200,000 tons. As soon as the new company was organized it proceeded to extend its plants and otherwise to develop its properties.[51]

FURNACE STATISTICS

On October 1, 1893, when the full effect of the financial panic of that year was being felt, only 114 furnaces with a weekly capacity of less than 74,000 tons of iron remained in blast in the United States. A slight revival occurred during the winter, which was checked, however, by the great coal strike the following spring.[52] There were at this time some 519 furnaces in the United States, of which 118 still used charcoal fuel. The average capacity of these furnaces exceeded 30,000 tons per annum, that of the charcoal furnaces being less than 11,000 tons, and that of the coke furnaces 37,000 tons.

During the ensuing year there was little improvement in the situation. The number of furnaces in blast on June 1, 1894, in the midst of the coke and coal strike, was only 88, or approximately one out of six of those capable of active operation in the country. After the strike was settled late in June a marked improvement ensued, especially in the Pittsburgh district, and by September first the number of furnaces in blast had risen to 171, with a weekly capacity of over 150,000 tons.[53] Production during 1895 remained fairly high, continuing throughout most of the season on a

---

[50] *Commercial and Financial Chronicle*, LXVIII, 675, Apr. 8, 1899; LXIX, 388, Aug. 19, 1899; American Iron and Steel Association, *Bulletin*, XXXIII, 59, Apr. 10, 1899; XXXV, 29, Feb. 23, 1901; XXXVI, 135, Sept. 10, 1902; XLI, 93, Aug. 1, 1907.

[51] *Commercial and Financial Chronicle*, LXVIII, 978–979, May 20, 1899; LXIX, 286, Aug. 5, 1899; LXX, 1200–1201, June 16, 1900.

[52] *Commercial and Financial Chronicle*, LVIII, 1008, June 16, 1894.

[53] American Iron and Steel Association, *Bulletin*, XXVIII, 133, June 23, 1894; XXVIII, 210, Sept. 22, 1894; *Commercial and Financial Chronicle*, LIX, 46, July 14, 1894.

basis of 8,000,000 tons or thereabouts per annum. Another year of depression followed in 1896, when only one-third of the furnaces in the country remained in blast throughout the season.

The furnace statistics of 1897 show that low prices were steadily forcing out of production the smaller and less advantageously situated plants. For instance, in July 1895, there were 185 furnaces at work, as compared with 153 furnaces in the spring of 1897, but the weekly output of pig iron was larger at the later date. This tendency, which is revealed even more clearly when longer periods are compared, was not altogether due to a depressed market; for furnaces continued to grow larger and fewer in good times as well as bad. In the autumn of 1897 the weekly production of pig iron rose to 226,000 tons, which was a new record. Two years previously, during a temporary boom in the iron trade, the country's output for the first time in its history had reached 200,000 tons a week.[54]

Between 1892 and 1898 the number of nominally active furnaces in the United States declined from 569 to 420; and of the latter some 50 were not expected to make iron again. But the capacity of the 370 furnaces in operation or likely to go into operation greatly exceeded the capacity of the 569 furnaces listed in 1892. In fact, the furnace capacity of the country in 1898 exceeded 19,000,000 tons and the current rate of production was about 12,000,000 tons a year.[55] It was at this time that the large steel companies generally adopted the practice of balancing their plants by providing ample means for supplying their own pig iron. Twenty-two furnaces were under construction in 1899 in connection with 9 steel works, and their capacity was expected to exceed 3,000,000 tons per annum.[56]

During the iron and steel boom at the end of the decade the subject of reserve capacity received much attention, some asserting that the furnaces of the country were wholly unequal to the maximum demand that iron and steel consumers were likely to make upon them. Those who differed from this opinion insisted that where a shortage developed it was due to the failure of the railroads to provide transportation for raw materials and finished goods. There was no serious scarcity of coke at the ovens and no lack of ore at Lower Lake ports. This controversy had merely speculative interest in 1900, since there was a sharp decline in the demand for iron and steel that year. In 1901, however, although an enormous increase occurred in the production of pig iron, steel works found difficulty in securing deliveries of pigs, and importations of foreign iron were not unusual. But 23 blast furnaces were under construction and were expected to begin producing during 1902 and 1903.[57]

[54] *Commercial and Financial Chronicle*, LXIV, 729, Apr. 17, 1897; LXV, 1145, Dec. 18, 1897; American Iron and Steel Association, *Bulletin*, XXXI, 285, Dec. 20, 1897.
[55] American Iron and Steel Association, *Bulletin*, XXXII, 98, July 1, 1898; *Commercial and Financial Chronicle*, LXVII, 202–203, July 30, 1898.
[56] *Mineral Industry*, VIII, 357.
[57] American Iron and Steel Association, *Bulletin*, XXXIV, 28, Feb. 1, 1900; XXXIV, 149, Sept. 1, 1900; *Mineral Industry*, IX, 388.

Although the formation of the United States Steel Corporation and of other large iron and steel combinations was characteristic of this period, many smaller independent companies erected plants. On the other hand, however, the Iron and Steel Directory of 1902 devoted seventeen pages to a list of iron and steel works that had been abandoned or dismantled since its previous edition four years before. The list embraced 61 furnaces and 118 rolling mills, Bessemer steel plants, open-hearth steel plants, crucible steel plants and special process plants, besides 5 forges and bloomeries. This was the largest mortality list ever compiled. But though it suggested many private losses in this branch of manufacturing, it also indicated rapid changes in the technology and organization of the industry, the survival of larger and more efficient plants at the expense of their smaller competitors, and the concentration of iron and steel making at the centers of most economical production. Bessemer steel was yielding ground rapidly to open-hearth steel at this time, though it still was used almost exclusively for rails. Only one of the Catalan forges, that half a century before had been such important sources of local iron supply, was still active and but 8 bloomeries were alive. The single Clapp-Griffiths converter steel works in existence had been idle for several years; the number of charcoal furnaces had declined from 79 to 55 since 1898, and the aggregate capacity of these furnaces was a quarter of a million tons less than four years previously; and for several reasons the crucible steel industry was practically stationary. Water power was still used to operate 8 blast furnaces, 13 rolling mills and 3 bloomeries. Six of these plants were in Pennsylvania. The number of iron and steel works using natural gas was 110; and 7 new plants to employ this fuel were in the course of construction. This was the largest number ever reported, the nearest approach being 104 works in 1889. The total annual capacity of the completed blast furnaces in the United States at this time was nearly 25,000,000 tons.[58]

After 1904 the number of furnaces in the United States ceased to decline; and indeed, four years later 20 had been added to the list of those either active or likely to become so later. But the tendency to concentration again manifested itself after 1910, and between that year and 1914 the number of active furnaces in the United States fell from 474 to 451. By 1910 the total furnace capacity of the country exceeded 40,000,000 tons per annum, or nearly double what it had been ten years before. During the previous three years 35 modern furnaces had been completed, of which 22, with an annual capacity of 3,500,000 tons, were operated by companies that consumed in their own steel plants virtually all the pig iron they made. The 13 remaining furnaces, with a capacity of a little more than 1,000,000 tons, were operated by companies that made pig iron for the general market.[59]

[58] American Iron and Steel Association, *Bulletin*, XXXVI, 60, Apr. 25, 1902.
[59] American Iron and Steel Association, *Bulletin*, XLII, 41, May 1, 1908; XLIV, 76, Aug. 15, 1910; *Mineral Industry*, XXIII, 407.

PIG-IRON OUTPUT

The largest annual production of pig iron prior to 1893 was in 1890, when more than 9,200,000 tons were made. This figure was not to be attained again for several years, the panic causing an abrupt decline in output. The principal cause of this lessened demand was the cessation of railroad building and the curtailment of railroad betterments, the market for steel outside of that required for the manufacture of rails remaining almost as active as during the period of great prosperity preceding the depression. During 1894 only about 2,000 miles of new track were laid; and in the first half of 1895 less than 700 miles. In 1895, however, our total production of pig iron again reached a new record, of almost 9,500,000 tons, largely in response to an extraordinary demand for Bessemer pig iron, due chiefly to the active demand for structural steel.[60] In 1896 the production of basic pig iron was for the first time reported separately. Most of this was made in Pennsylvania, although Virginia and Alabama supplied about one-fourth of the total, which was approximately 200,000 tons. From this time onward the output of basic iron rapidly increased, as its employment in making steel became more general.

The last two years of the century marked the culmination of a new era of prosperity, which found expression in the pig-iron and steel consolidations previously mentioned, and in a rapid increase of output. This period of unexampled production was distinguished from most previous periods of that character, at least during its earlier stages, by not bringing with it a decided rise in prices. Indeed, quotations of iron and steel and their products, as we shall see later, remained very low although output was advancing by leaps and bounds, suggesting that with the erection of new plants and the introduction of technical and general business economies the cost of production was sinking to a new level, which left an attractive margin of profit at prices that would have been considered insufficient a few years before.[61] It was not until the end of 1898 that iron quotations began to respond to the eagerness of the market. That year the country produced nearly 12,000,000 tons of pig iron. The following year this total was raised to over 13,620,000 tons—an increase of more than 5,000,000 tons within three years. During 1899, as we have previously observed, the impression became general and was sedulously cultivated by interested parties, that the capacity of American furnaces and steel works and of iron and coal mines, was no longer adequate to the country's needs. This helped to bring about a marked advance in prices, although it was not the sole cause of that movement. A similar increase occurred abroad, where quotations for iron and steel soon reached a point that checked American orders. It was true that the uses for iron and steel were multiplying and, as in previous

---

[60] American Iron and Steel Association, *Bulletin*, XXIX, 164, July 20, 1895; *Commercial and Financial Chronicle*, LXI, 135–136, July 27, 1895.
[61] *Cf. Commercial and Financial Chronicle*, LXVI, 104, Jan. 15, 1898.

periods of depression and low prices, the very fact of cheapened cost to consumers established new markets that were not entirely lost when prices rose again. The greatest expansion in consumption was for shipbuilding, bridge building and general construction. Nineteen Hundred was a year of less rosy prospects, although both consumption and production were slightly larger than even the previous season; and in 1901 our pig-iron output again made a rapid advance to 15,878,000 tons.[62]

This quantity was practically doubled by 1913, when the United States produced nearly 31,000,000 tons of pig iron. During these first thirteen years of the century the growth of output had been not only rapid, but practically continuous, each year with three exceptions marking an increase of production over any previous season. These exceptions were 1904, 1908 and 1911, when there were temporary declines in furnace output due to overstocked markets and low prices. The most notable of these setbacks was in 1908, when our pig-iron output fell from well toward 26,000,000 tons to less than 16,000,000 tons.[63]

During this period America's output of basic pig iron advanced relatively faster than that of Bessemer and low phosphorous iron. Between 1905 and 1913 the production of basic pigs increased three-fold, rising from something over 4,100,000 to more than 12,500,000 tons, while that of Bessemer iron actually declined by nearly a million tons. This was due to the rapid growth of the open-hearth steel industry. An increasing proportion of our iron was smelted with coke, the amount smelted with anthracite declining not only relatively but absolutely. The production of charcoal iron fluctuated, but upon the whole remained about stationary.[64]

Reviewing the history of iron production during the twenty years we are now describing, the period of minimum output was in the second half of 1893, when we made but 2,561,000 tons. In 1896 another low point occurred, followed by similar reductions in 1900, 1904, 1908 and 1911, suggesting a certain periodicity in demand, prices and production. During these years of minimum output our steel works operated at an average of about 50 per cent of their capacity, and possibly were working at not more than 40 per cent during brief periods. Soon after the turn of the century the United States began to make more pig iron than Germany and Great Britain combined.

Naturally our per capita consumption of iron and steel was also increasing. In 1907 it was estimated to be 675 pounds, or nearly double the domestic consumption of Great Britain or Germany after deducting exports. This represented an advance in consumption in seven years of 348 pounds per

---

[62] *Commercial and Financial Chronicle*, LXX, 150–151, Jan. 27, 1900; LXX, 1077–1078, June 2, 1900; LXXI, 161–162, July 28, 1900; American Iron and Steel Association, *Bulletin*, XXXV, 12, Jan. 23, 1901 (Supplement); XXXVI, 12, Jan. 25, 1902.

[63] *Manufacturers' Record*, LXVI, 39, Oct. 15, 1914.

[64] *Mineral Industry*, XXIII, 406; *Iron Age*, XCIII, 840–841, Oct. 8, 1914; American Iron and Steel Association, *Bulletin*, XLVI, 71, Aug. 1, 1912.

capita. In addition to the millions of tons of new iron produced annually, the re-use of old iron and scrap was naturally greater than before, partly because there was more iron and steel of this character in the market, and partly because the development of the open-hearth process created a demand for old iron and steel that otherwise might not have been economically utilizable.[65]

[65] American Iron and Steel Association, *Bulletin*, XXXI, 276, Dec. 10, 1897; XLII, April 1, 1898.

CHAPTER III

STEEL MAKING IN THE EASTERN STATES

Steel Works Geography, 34. Organization of the Steel Industry, 35. Influences Determining Plant Location, 36. Lackawanna Steel Company, 36. Tidewater Steel Makers, 37. Pennsylvania Steel Company, 38. Bethlehem Steel Corporation, 39. Cambria Steel Company, 41. Republic Iron and Steel Company, 42. National Steel Company, 43. Carnegie Steel Company, 43.

STEEL WORKS GEOGRAPHY

Although the manufacture of steel was fully established in the United States before 1893, its progress during the next twenty years was more than quantitative. It was characterized also by great technical and qualitative advances. But in respect to output its expansion not only kept pace with and accounted for the marvelous increase in the production of pig iron, but it advanced relatively faster than blast furnace output, partly because of the increasing use of scrap metal to which we have just referred. Both the iron and steel industries showed a tendency to increased geographical concentration. This is not explained solely by the growing absorbtion of plants and production by great corporations, although this influence was a powerful factor in producing that result. The promotion of small companies went on apace and some found a sphere of service that speedily placed them upon a profitable footing. But the successful small firms as a rule grew up almost in the shadow of their powerful rivals.

The manufacture of steel in New England made little, if any, progress, because the day had long since passed when it was profitable to import pig iron or to assemble the raw materials for steel making in that section of the country. Small works were established, to be sure, in the vicinity of Boston and at New Haven, principally for converting the scrap metal always fairly abundant in the neighborhood of these manufacturing cities into special steels for local machine shops and metal-working enterprises.[1] At Troy, one of the pioneer cities of Bessemer steel making in the United States, the industry languished, and in 1906 the works there were dismantled under the direction of the United States Steel Corporation and the machinery was shipped to western plants. Meanwhile new steel centers appeared west of Pittsburgh.[2] In 1894 the first works at Youngstown were erected by the Ohio Steel Company. Until February 1895, not a pound of Bessemer steel and only a little open-hearth steel from a single furnace had

---

[1] *Commercial and Financial Chronicle*, LXIX, 1017, Nov. 11, 1899; LXXI, 557, Sept. 15, 1900; American Iron and Steel Association, *Bulletin*, XXXV, 35, June 10, 1901.

[2] American Iron and Steel Association, *Bulletin*, XXVIII, 237, Oct. 17, 1894; XXX, 229, Oct. 10, 1896; XXXIV, 139, Aug. 15, 1900; XLI, 14, Feb. 1, 1907.

ever been made in the Mahoning Valley. But the displacement of rolled iron by rolled steel made it imperative for the local rolling mills, if they were to continue in operation, to provide for a supply of steel from their immediate neighborhood. Twenty years later there were four plants at Youngstown with a daily capacity of 5,000 tons of open-hearth steel and 6,000 tons of Bessemer steel. Most of these large works had erected their own blast furnaces, with the result that independent furnace owners saw the market for their product steadily contracting. This caused the latter to organize The Brier Hill Steel Company in order to secure an outlet for their product.[3]

About the time that the first steel works were erected in Youngstown, the Johnson Steel Company built an extensive plant at Lorain, Ohio, which was expected to tap the Shenango Valley furnaces for its raw materials. This company made its first steel in April 1895, with one of the most complete plants in the country, including blast furnaces, coke ovens and Bessemer converters. British capital was interested in this enterprise.[4]

ORGANIZATION OF THE STEEL INDUSTRY

Organization played such an important part, directly or indirectly, in deciding both the localization and the technology of the steel industry during this period, that it is a convenient container, so to speak, in which to store many miscellaneous and otherwise uncorrelated facts concerning this branch of manufacturing. These combinations were of two kinds: those that were organized more or less deliberately and usually by a single financial effort, for the purpose of bringing under unified control a number of existing plants of equal or approximately equal magnitude, often located in different sections of the country. Consolidations of the second type grew up as a rule around a single powerful parent company, as a result of organic growth, and represented extensions of the mother plant and business, branch plants, subsidiary plants and independent enterprises bought up and developed in alliance with the central firm, mines, railways, shipping lines and ancillary industries acquired in order to make the company independent and self-subsisting for raw materials. In 1894 several manufacturers of cast steel in Pennsylvania, Ohio and New York were consolidated under a single corporation, either through outright purchase by the financing company, or by an exchange of their stock for stock in the new concern. But the manufacture of Bessemer steel and of open-hearth steel, which was just beginning to become important, was in the hands of powerful parent corporations that had little motive, or at least little disposition, to unite. During the years that followed a number of smaller companies were formed to manufacture steel, and generally to make iron, especially in Eastern

---

[3] American Iron and Steel Association, *Bulletin*, XXVIII, 273, Dec. 5, 1894; XXIX, 115, May 20, 1895; *Iron Age*, XCIII, 840–841, Apr. 2, 1914.
[4] American Iron and Steel Association, *Bulletin*, XXIX, 13, Jan. 9, 1895; XXIX, 84, Apr. 10, 1895; XXXII, 59, Apr. 15, 1898; *Commercial and Financial Chronicle*, LXVI, 709, Apr. 9, 1898.

Pennsylvania. In 1899 the Diamond State Steel Company was organized to operate a plant at Wilmington; the Tidewater Steel Company was formed for the same purpose at Chester, Pennsylvania. Similar plants of moderate size were erected in the West and South. Most of these smaller companies made steel in connection with the manufacture of a particular line of finished shapes, such as sheets and galvanized iron, rods and bolts and other special products.[5]

INFLUENCES DETERMINING PLANT LOCATION

Geographical influences did more to determine the growth and eventual location of the large iron and steel making companies than their smaller and more highly specialized competitors, because the number of points where great plants such as began to characterize this period could be placed to best advantage was limited. In a general way, the big iron and steel industry of America tended to concentrate either in the immediate vicinity of raw materials, as in the Birmingham district, or at points where water carriage was available. The Pittsburgh district, which was the most important in North America, might seem an exception to this rule; but its expansion was as truly determined by the existence of a water route from the vicinity of the Lake Superior ore beds to within a comparatively short railway haul of its manufacturing plants, as was the growth of a great iron and steel-making center next to the wharfs at Chicago and Gary.

LACKAWANNA STEEL COMPANY

A striking illustration of this determining factor in the localization of the industry was the complete transfer of so old and prominent a corporation as the Lackawanna Iron and Steel Company from the site it had occupied for sixty years at Scranton, Pennsylvania, to the immediate vicinity of Buffalo. One of the first intimations of this move became public early in 1899, when the Company, which had done a prosperous business at Scranton for about sixty years, took the initiative in promoting what was understood to be a new and larger enterprise at Buffalo. This was followed by an increase of the original capital from $3,750,000 to $25,000,000, with which the erection of the new plant was undertaken on a tract of land having a Lake frontage of 3.5 miles just south of that city. During the period of development the original plan grew to double the proportions first proposed, so as to provide for an estimated production of 1,250,000 tons of steel per annum. In 1902 the first ore was brought by steamer to the Company's blast furnaces on the new site. By this time the original corporation, even with its enlarged capital, was found inadequate to handle the enterprise; and a new company, the Lackawanna Steel Company of New York, was

[5] American Iron and Steel Association, *Bulletin*, XXVIII, 69, Mar. 31, 1894; XXXIII, 189, Nov. 1, 1899; *Commercial and Financial Chronicle*, LXVIII, 826, Apr. 29, 1899; LXVIII, 926, May 13, 1899; LXIX, 178, July 22, 1899; LXIX, 335–336, Aug. 12, 1899; LXIX, 1014, Nov. 11, 1899; LXXI, 180, July 28, 1910.

incorporated with a capital of $40,000,000 thus multiplying by more than ten the resources of the parent firm that promoted the undertaking. In March 1902, the last rails were rolled at the old Scranton plant, only a few months after the first ore was received at the new furnaces in Buffalo. The Lackawanna Company controlled ore properties on Lake Superior, in Pennsylvania and in the Adirondacks. It owned coal mines and a terminal railroad on the new site which connected it with 28 railway lines. At Buffalo it had the advantage of both Lake and canal shipment. Iron ore from the Adirondacks was expected to come to Buffalo by canal as a backload in boats that would otherwise run empty after carrying grain to the seaboard. The President of the Company summarized the motives that induced his directors to embark upon this ambitious venture at a new location as follows:

"We came to Buffalo by a process of exclusion. We must remember that the Lackawanna Iron and Steel Company at Scranton had a line of customers that it did not want to lose. Any location that would not enable it to serve these customers as well as it could from Scranton would involve a very considerable loss. From Buffalo we can serve our large Eastern trade and our large trade in New England and the seaboard as advantageously as we can from Scranton. A large part of our Western business was going through Buffalo, and, of course, all that business we can serve better from Buffalo than from Scranton. The prospects of the future are for the West and the Orient. That trade we can serve from Buffalo as well as it can be served from South Chicago. At Stormy Point we can ship in vessels lying in our canal and have them go direct to Duluth. A few miles, more or less, on the Lakes counts for very little. It is the shipping and the unloading that are the great items in water transportation. . . . So much for distribution. . . . For the assembling of our material . . . there was no place that could equal [our present site]. The ore from Lake Superior, from the Adirondacks, and from Pennsylvania can be assembled at Buffalo more cheaply than at any other point, and our coal properties are within easy and economical reach."[6]

TIDEWATER STEEL MAKERS

Before considering further the inland companies, some of which, as we have just seen, were drifting farther westward, it may be well to describe the tidewater steel industry, as represented by great corporations. In a previous chapter we have noted the organization and early growth of the Pennsylvania Steel Company and the Maryland Steel Company, their eventual combination, and the period of financial distress and reorganization through which they passed during and following the panic of 1893. We have also mentioned the Bethlehem Iron Company, established on the eve of the Civil War. It was from these three centers that the larger tidewater steel industry was destined to develop.

[6] American Iron and Steel Association, *Bulletin*, XXXIII, 77, May 1, 1899; XXXV, 149, Oct. 10, 1901; XXXVI, 12, Jan. 25, 1902; XXXVI, 30, Feb. 25, 1902; XXXVI, 33, Mar. 10, 1902; XXXVI, 50, Apr. 10, 1902; XXXVII, 5, Jan. 10, 1903; *Commercial and Financial Chronicle*, LXX, 78, Jan. 13, 1900.

PENNSYLVANIA STEEL COMPANY

During the early nineties the Pennsylvania-Maryland Company was in process of convalescence. Its property was sold under foreclosure in May 1895, and bid in by a new Pennsylvania Steel Company having a total capitalization, including mortgages, of $12,550,000. The combined works consisted at this time of eight blast furnaces with a capacity of 558,000 tons of pig iron per annum, a rail mill and a shipbuilding and bridge-building plant, in addition to iron mines in Cuba and other mineral properties.[7]

During 1896 and 1897, which it will be recalled were a period of exceedingly low prices, the plants were not in full operation and lost money. In 1898 again scarcity of ore due to the war with Spain, which prevented shipment from the Company's Cuban mine, interfered with the output and prosperity of the Company. The Sparrows Point plant was able to work at about only half of its capacity for this reason. Nevertheless, during this period of depression, following so closely upon the heels of the reorganization of the Company, plant improvements were made, economies of organization were effected, and in general its efficiency as a producer was increased, notwithstanding the discouraging fact that during the four years immediately following the reorganization the combined plants were never running at full capacity.[8]

Then came the period of rapid expansion at the turn of the century. During the lean years that had preceded no dividends were paid and no surplus was accumulated. Consequently the Company lacked the liquid capital required to handle economically its rapidly increasing business. It was impossible to pay for supplies promptly so as to get the best cash prices, and at the same time to carry a volume of business that had more than trebled within a few months. A considerable part of the product of this company had always been shipped abroad. In 1900 it was sending bridges to all parts of the world—Norway, Australia, India and Japan. Half of the rails made at Sparrows Point were for foreign customers. Between 1896 and 1901 the annual sales of the Company rose from less than $7,000,000 to nearly $20,000,000, without any increase in capitalization. While the capital still stood at $13,000,000 the physical value of works, mines and other operating plant exceeded $20,000,000. Except for a small sum paid in dividends upon preferred stock all earnings had been turned back into the business, because this was imperative in order to handle the increased demands upon the liquid resources of the corporation.[9]

This situation led to the incorporation, in April 1901, of the Pennsylvania Steel Company of New Jersey with an authorized capital stock of

---

[7] *Commercial and Financial Chronicle*, LXI, 472, Sept. 14, 1895.
[8] *Commercial and Financial Chronicle*, LXII, 776, Apr. 25, 1896; LXVI, 662, Apr. 2, 1898; LXVIII, 568, Mar. 25, 1899; LXX, 582, Mar. 24, 1900; American Iron and Steel Association, *Bulletin*, XXXI, 61, Mar. 10, 1897; XXXIII, 53, Apr. 1, 1899.
[9] *Commercial and Financial Chronicle*, LXX, 1253, June 23, 1900; American Iron and Steel Association, *Bulletin*, XXXV, 9, Jan. 23, 1901; XXXV, 44, Mar. 25, 1901.

$50,000,000. Important plant improvements speedily followed. By 1903 the annual product rose to 751,000 tons of pig iron and 837,000 tons of steel. The shipyards were fully employed and a program of erecting by-product coke ovens had been begun that within two years made the Company independent of outside supplies of fuel. The ore properties owned in Cuba were developed and extended and 16,000 acres of coal lands in Pennsylvania were acquired.[10] At the close of the period we are discussing, when the Pennsylvania Steel Company was on the eve of being absorbed by its only great tidewater competitor, The Bethlehem Steel Company, it owned about 600,000,000 tons of iron ore in Cuba, or nearly as much as the United States Steel Corporation owned when it was organized. It possessed an established foreign market for many of its products and it was practically independent in respect to raw materials.[11]

BETHLEHEM STEEL CORPORATION

The Bethlehem Steel Company, which under the presidency of Charles M. Schwab was destined to acquire a practical monopoly of tidewater steel-making on a large scale, was organized in 1899 to lease the property of the old Bethlehem Iron Company at a fixed rental. This was a device adopted also by the Cambria Company, as we shall see, at the time of its reorganization, by which a new corporation with a greatly enlarged capital englobed, so to speak, a smaller parent corporation and eventually succeeded it. The shareholders of the Bethlehem Iron Company were entitled to subscribe pro rata according to their stock-holdings for all the shares of the new corporation. Since they had a guaranteed rental yielding 6 per cent on the par value of their old stock, they were practically assured an income upon their original investment regardless of the fate of the new enterprise. The primary object of the reorganization was to provide capital for a general enlargement of the Company's facilities for production. Thereafter the capital of the new corporation was $15,000,000, or three times the capital of the Bethlehem Iron Company as it stood before the reorganization began. In connection with that reorganization, however, a scrip dividend of 50 per cent out of accumulated earnings had been declared to the share-holders of the original company.[12]

Two years later the control of the Bethlehem Steel Company and the Bethlehem Iron Company was acquired by the Schwab interests and the rapid expansion already inaugurated continued apace. In 1905 the Bethlehem Steel Corporation was formed with a capital of $30,000,000. This was a successor to the United States Shipbuilding Company and its charter authorized it to build and repair ships, marine engines and the like, as well

[10] American Iron and Steel Association, *Bulletin*, XXXV, 69, May 10, 1901; XXXVIII, 59, Apr. 25, 1904; XXXIX, 70, May 1, 1905; XL, 78, June 1, 1906; XLII, 51, June 1, 1908.
[11] *Manufacturers' Record*, LXV, 49, Jan. 29, 1914.
[12] *Commercial and Financial Chronicle*, LXVIII, 821, Apr. 29, 1899; LXVIII, 975, May 20, 1899; American Iron and Steel Association, *Bulletin*, XXXV, 131, Sept. 10, 1901; *cf.*, Cotter, *The Story of Bethlehem Steel*.

as to manufacture and deal in iron and steel. The organization of this corporation brought under single control some of the largest individual consumers of steel as well as an important steel producer. In 1908 the Bethlehem Steel Corporation embraced the Bethlehem Steel Company, and through it the old Bethlehem Iron Company, the Union Iron Works at San Francisco, the Harlan and Hollingsworth Corporation, one of the largest shipbuilding enterprises upon the Delaware, and the Juragua Iron Company in Cuba, besides other subsidiary enterprises. The previous year the Bethlehem Steel Company, which had abandoned the manufacture of Bessemer steel rails several years previously, began to manufacture open-hearth steel rails. This corporation was a large producer of armor, ordnance, ammunition and naval supplies, as well as a builder of vessels.[13]

In 1915 at the close of the period we are discussing, the total assets of the Bethlehem Steel Corporation exceeded $145,000,000, or one thousand times what they were in 1862 when the Bethlehem Iron Company was just getting under headway as a producer. While the great expansion of this Company during the World War lies outside the period covered by this History, it may be referred to as the culmination of tendencies previously present in the evolution of the American iron and steel industry. Between 1913 and 1917 the shipbuilding interests of the Corporation were enlarged by the purchase of the Fore River Yards at Quincy, Massachusetts, by a deal with the Schneider interests in France which gave the Company control of the rich Tofo mines in Chile, by the acquisition of a number of minor companies, and last of all by the absorption of the Pennsylvania Steel Company, which was itself an amalgamation of the Pennsylvania and the Maryland companies and represented at the time of the actual transfer over $56,000,000 capital. This doubled the capacity of the Bethlehem Steel Corporation, raising its annual output of pig iron to 2,300,000 tons a year, to be increased to 4,000,000 tons a year by furnaces projected or under construction, and giving it a steel ingot capacity of 3,500,000 tons and a capacity for finished steel exceeding 2,000,000 tons. By the purchase of the Sparrows Point plant, moreover, the Bethlehem Corporation increased its shipyards to five. Furthermore, both the Bethlehem and the Pennsylvania Company, as we have seen, owned large quantities of ore in Cuba and depended largely upon this source for their supplies. The combination, therefore, was in several distinct respects a logical one, bringing under united ownership and direction plants working under similar geographical conditions, using imported ores from the same locality, deriving their coal and other raw materials from the same regions, and engaged in shipbuilding and the manufacture of steel for export.[14]

But while steel-making in the tidewater district had grown into a gigantic industry, serving special ends and working under conditions peculiar

[13] American Iron and Steel Association, *Bulletin*, xxxix, 19, Feb. 1, 1905; xli, 5, Jan. 15, 1907; xliii, 42, June 1, 1909; xliv, 38, Apr. 15, 1910.
[14] Cotter, *The Story of Bethlehem Steel*, 4–5, 31, 45–48.

to itself, the great steel-making center of the United States was in the Central West. In 1900 Allegheny County alone produced nearly one-fourth of the pig iron, one-half the open-hearth steel, and two-fifths of the steel of all varieties made in the country. Pennsylvania made more steel than Great Britain, one-sixth of the world's pig iron, and nearly one-fourth of the world's steel. The center of the industry in the United States at the beginning of the twentieth century was represented by the area enclosed by a line drawn from Pittsburgh to Wheeling, thence north to Lorain, southeast to Cleveland, and South again to Pittsburgh. The conditions that produced this concentration have previously been described. They were originally geographical. Ore, coke and limestone could meet most economically within this area, and could reach their market from it, upon the whole, more cheaply than from other points. To be sure there were certain exceptions which will be noted later, such as those already recorded in the tidewater district. But Pittsburgh and vicinity possessed another advantage—a population that had grown up in this branch of manufacturing. It was possible in that city or its vicinity to find men of all classes needed to organize and operate a plant. Slackwater navigation on the Alleghany, Monongahela and Ohio were some advantage in shipping to the West. Pittsburgh, in marked contrast to Birmingham, never sent pig iron to other districts, but always imported it, the consumption being much larger than the production. For many years Allegheny County had had but a single merchant blast furnace, the foundries and other iron consumers of its vicinity receiving their pigs from the Mahoning and Shenango Valleys, from western Pennsylvania furnaces, and from the South. By the time we are describing, however, it was in this region that the largest individual pig-iron producers and the largest steel corporations were to be found.[15]

CAMBRIA STEEL COMPANY

In 1898 the old Cambria Iron Company went through a transformation practically identical with that of the Bethlehem Iron Company; that is, it leased its properties to a new Cambria Steel Company for a fixed rental of 4 per cent upon its $8,500,000 capital. The share-holders in the old company had the privilege of subscribing for all the stock of the new company, which was $24,000,000. The assets of the Cambria Iron Company at the time this arrangement was made were estimated to be worth $20,000,000, or two and one-half times the nominal capital, an increase due to the turning back of profits into the enterprise.

The Cambria Steel Company at once inaugurated a policy of expansion. By-product coke ovens were erected and it began to make tar and asphalt roofing, as well as iron and steel. Two years later a new steel plant was built and plans were made for constructing four additional blast furnaces. By 1901, only three years after the reorganization and capital increase

[15] American Iron and Steel Association, *Bulletin*, xxxv, 18, Feb. 9, 1901; xxxv, 125, Aug. 25, 1901; xlii, 93, Sept. 1, 1908.

just noted, the still young Cambria Steel Company transferred its property through a temporary organization to a new Cambria Steel Company, with a capital of $44,000,000. This company had extended far beyond the territories occupied by the Cambria Company, vast as that enterprise had seemed when compared with its neighbors in the iron trade fifty years before. It now owned mines in Michigan and Minnesota and coal mines and coking ovens at Franklin, Pennsylvania.[16]

REPUBLIC IRON AND STEEL COMPANY

In 1899 a so-called "rolling mill trust," the Republic Iron and Steel Company, was incorporated to consolidate the leading rolling mills, with their attendant furnaces and steel works, in the Central and Southern States. The capital of the new enterprise was $55,000,000 and it embraced 36 plants for making bar and forge iron, or practically all such establishments West and South of Pittsburgh, 5 blast furnaces, mining properties on Lake Superior, and coal lands and coke plants in the Connellsville region. It also owned extensive tracts of ore and coal land and furnaces and rolling mills in the vicinity of Birmingham. The constituent works produced annually well toward a quarter of a million tons of pig iron, double that amount of rolled iron and shapes, 100,000 tons of steel bars, and many thousand tons of sheets, plates, bolts and other manufactured and semi-manufactured iron and steel. After its organization this Company proceeded to acquire additional plants and mines, especially in the Central West. It soon owned and operated open-hearth steel works at Birmingham, Alabama, and Minneapolis, Minnesota, and began immediately to erect a large steel plant at Youngstown, Ohio, which was supplied with pig iron from its own Ohio and Pennsylvania blast furnaces. Within three years after its organization, it increased its ownership of Bessemer mixture ores in the North from 2,500,000 tons to more than 14,000,000 tons. It also owned 70,000,000 tons of ore and 50,000,000 tons of coal in Alabama.[17]

During the years that followed, this Company abandoned several of its antiquated or badly located rolling mills. In fact it was burdened originally with more weak and poorly placed mills than most great consolidations formed at that period. Intelligent elimination enabled the Company to lift its works to a much higher plane of average efficiency and to reduce costs of production. In 1912 it produced, largely from its own ore, coke and limestone, more than a million tons of Bessemer and open-hearth steel and 980,000 tons of finished and semi-finished products.[18]

[16] *Commercial and Financial Chronicle*, LXVII, 427, Aug. 27, 1898; LXVII, 900, Oct. 29, 1898; LXVIII, 128, Jan. 21, 1899; LXXI, 1271, Dec. 22, 1900; American Iron and Steel Association, *Bulletin*, XXXII, 205, Dec. 20, 1898; XXXV, 101, July 10, 1901; XXXIX, 62, Apr. 15, 1905; XLII, 38, Apr. 15, 1908; XLIII, 42, June 1, 1909.

[17] *Commercial and Financial Chronicle*, LXVIII, 674, Apr. 8, 1899; LXIX, 339, Aug. 12, 1899; LXIX, 850, Oct. 21, 1899; LXIX, 1051, Dec. 2, 1899; LXX, 228–229, Feb. 3, 1900; American Iron and Steel Association, *Bulletin*, XXXIII, 91, June 1, 1899; XXXVI, 27, Feb. 25, 1902.

[18] American Iron and Steel Association, *Bulletin*, XL, 164, Nov. 15, 1906; XLVI, 79, Sept. 1, 1912.

NATIONAL STEEL COMPANY

Meanwhile, a second consolidation of existing companies, as distinct from great corporations developing from a single parent plant, was formed in the Central West. This was the National Steel Company incorporated in 1899, with a capital of $59,000,000. The plants thus consolidated included seven modern steel works with blast furnaces and rolling mills, advantageously situated in Ohio and Western Pennsylvania. Two of the largest of these establishments were at Youngstown. The total capacity of the plants controlled by the Corporation at the time it was organized was about 1,800,000 tons of steel per annum. It immediately proceeded to acquire extensive mining properties in the Lake Superior district, including the Chapin mines, the largest single producer of iron ore in the United States, and two fleets of steel ore vessels already in operation on the Great Lakes.[19]

CARNEGIE STEEL COMPANY

By far the largest steel corporation of the Pittsburgh district, however, was the Carnegie Company, whose earlier history has already been described. Its principal plants were even more concentrated than those of the National Steel Company, although the latter, as we have just seen, operated within a much narrower area than those of the Republic Iron and Steel Company. In 1895 the Carnegie interests purchased a mile of additional frontage on the Monongahela River between Homestead and Duquesne, thus acquiring control of 3.5 miles of river bank, including its Homestead and Duquesne plants and the intervening territory and facing directly across the River its extensive Edgar Thomson plant and blast furnaces. This was preliminary to a period of rapid extension, one item of which was the erection of 16 new open-hearth steel furnaces at its Homestead works. Meanwhile through an allied corporation, the Oliver Mining Company, the same interests acquired extensive tracts of ore lands in the Marquette, Gogebic and Mesabi ranges. In 1899 they purchased the property of the Lake Superior Iron Company, which made them also, for the first time, large vessel owners and the heaviest ore shippers from the Lake Superior region.[20] That year Andrew Carnegie endeavored to carry out the plan he realized two years later, to retire from the active management of his business. All the properties and interests of the Carnegie Steel Company Limited, which was a Pennsylvania copartnership, and the H. C. Frick Coke Company, with its subsidiary and allied organizations, were amalgamated without associating themselves with outside interests or taking in outside corporations. In the course of these negotiations, however,

---

[19] *Commercial and Financial Chronicle*, LXVIII, 672–673, Apr. 8, 1899; LXIX, 230, July 29, 1899; LXIX, 285, Aug. 5, 1899; LXX, 384, Feb. 24, 1900; LXX, 897, May 5, 1900.
[20] American Iron and Steel Association, *Bulletin*, XXIX, 285, Dec. 20, 1895; XXX, 93, Apr. 20, 1896; XXXIII, 77, May 1, 1899; Bridge, *Inside History of the Carnegie Steel Company*, 169, 255–257, 272.

disagreements arose that led to a lawsuit between H. C. Frick and Andrew Carnegie, and for a time blocked the completion of the reorganization. At this time the Carnegie Steel Company embraced the Edgar Thomson Works, the Duquesne Works, the Homestead Works, the Lucy Furnaces and the Upper Union Mills, all of which were at Pittsburgh or in its vicinity, the Carey Blast Furnaces, the Lorimer Coke Works, and the Allegheny Coke Works in Western Pennsylvania, a controlling interest in the Pittsburgh Bessemer and Lake Erie Railroad Company, the H. C. Frick Coke Company and its extensive holdings in the Connellsville region, five-sixths of the capital stock of the Oliver Mining Company, nearly 90 per cent of the stock of the Lake Superior Iron Company, besides a number of allied and accessory corporations including local railways, natural gas companies, dock companies and companies supplying limestone and similar raw materials. The Carnegie interests produced 17 per cent of the pig iron and 22 per cent of the Bessemer steel made in the United States. Their total output of finished material was about 2,500,000 tons per annum, and in prosperous years their annual profits exceeded $20,000,000.[21]

The following year an agreement was reached that settled the outstanding differences between Mr. Carnegie and Mr. Frick, and the interests they respectively represented. The incorporation of the Carnegie Steel Company with a capital stock of $160,000,000, of which Mr. Carnegie controlled over $86,000,000, and in which Charles M. Schwab, Henry Phipps, Henry C. Frick were the other stockholders, immediately followed. Its works already in operation or under construction had a capacity of 230,000 tons of pig iron and 240,000 tons of Bessemer and open-hearth ingots per month, or about one-fifth of the pig iron and more than one-fourth of the steel produced in the United States.[22]

[21] American Iron and Steel Association, *Bulletin*, XXXIII, 84, May 15, 1899; XXXIII, 90, June 1, 1899; XXXIII, 189, Nov. 1, 1899; XXXIV, 60, Mar. 20, 1900; *Commercial and Financial Chronicle*, LXVIII, 925, May 13, 1899; LXVIII, 1074, June 3, 1899; LXX, 330, Feb. 17, 1900; LXX, 533, Mar. 17, 1900.

[22] *Commercial and Financial Chronicle*, LXX, 586, Mar. 24, 1900; LXX, 635, Mar. 31, 1900; LXXI, 1168, Dec. 8, 1900; *Mineral Industry*, IX, 385; Bridge, *Inside History of the Carnegie Steel Company*, 170, 297.

CHAPTER IV

NEWER STEEL CENTERS AND THE GREAT CONSOLIDATION

Federal Steel Company, 45. Tennessee Coal, Iron, and Railroad Company, 47. Colorado Fuel and Iron Company, 52. United States Steel Corporation, 54.

FEDERAL STEEL COMPANY

Meanwhile, a parallel concentration of iron and steel making in the hands of a single giant corporation was occurring in the vicinity of Chicago. This continued to be the principal center of the industry west of the Pittsburgh-Lorain area already mentioned, although several efforts were made to establish a rival steel making site in the immediate vicinity of iron ore at the head of Lake Superior. The development of coal mining in Iowa and Kansas encouraged the erection of a basic-hearth steel plant at Minneapolis, midway between ore and fuel. This is the plant that was eventually acquired by the Republic Iron and Steel Company. The attempt to introduce the industry at Duluth and Superior was more ambitious and persistent. In 1899 the Lake Superior Steel Company was organized to purchase the Wisconsin Steel plant at West Superior, a structural steel plant at Ironton, and the West Duluth Car Works; but this enterprise, though backed by considerable capital, did not prove successful. In 1907 the United States Steel Corporation organized a new company to erect, own and operate a steel plant at Duluth which was finally built three years later.[1]

The Illinois Steel Company, with an invested capital of $33,000,000, was the principal western steel-making corporation in 1894. Notwithstanding the fact that the region which afforded the main market for its products was still suffering severely from the panic the previous year, the Company shipped during that season 563,000 tons of finished manufactures. In 1895 a new rail mill was added to its South Chicago Works and it started practically 4 new plants: open-hearth furnaces at South Chicago, a plate mill at the same point, the remodeled Union Works in the city of Chicago, which had been idle since 1892, and a sheet mill at Hammond, Indiana. It had 17 furnaces in blast, producing 4,000 tons of iron daily, all of which was made into steel and finished products in its own plants; and its output of pig iron for the year, which was the largest in its history, exceeded a million tons.[2]

[1] American Iron and Steel Association, *Bulletin*, XXIX, 77, Apr. 1, 1895; XXXIII, 25, Feb. 15, 1899; XXXIII, 44, Mar. 15, 1899; XXXIII, 181, Oct. 15, 1899; XLI, 77, June 20, 1907; XLIV, 109, Nov. 1, 1910; *Commercial and Financial Chronicle*, LXIX, 647, Sept. 23, 1899, LXIX, 757, Oct. 7, 1899; *Mineral Industry*, XV, 486.

[2] *Commercial and Financial Chronicle*, LVIII, 514, Mar. 24, 1894; LX, 299–300, Feb. 16, 1895; LX, 928–929, May 25, 1895; LXII, 316, Feb. 15, 1896; American Iron and Steel Association, *Bulletin*, XXXIX, 45, Feb. 20, 1895.

In 1896 dividends were resumed after an intermission of three years, but when only two quarterly instalments of 1.5 per cent had been paid they were passed again in September. This was due to a new period of stagnation in the iron and steel trade, caused largely in the opinion of the Company's officers by the political uncertainties of a presidential election. Though 40 per cent of the productive capacity of the Company was unemployed, it supplied one-third of all the rails used in the United States and shipped three-quarters of a million tons of finished products. The following year witnessed a sharp revival, and the quantity of manufactured steel sold, with every furnace in blast and the works operating at nearly full capacity, was about 1,000,000 tons. The Company shipped its products to Canada, Spanish America, Europe, the Orient, Africa and Australia, and reported "that its export business had grown to such proportions that it is almost a daily occurrence to bill goods to points varying from 5,000 to 15,000 miles distant."[3]

In 1898 reports were current in financial circles that the Illinois and the Cambria Companies were about to combine. Though this rumor proved groundless, it presaged a consolidation that was to make a corporation of which the Illinois Steel Company formed the nucleus, the rival, if not the superior, of the Carnegie Company, which at this time was easily the largest producer in the United States. The new merger included the Illinois Steel Company, the Minnesota Iron Company, and the Lorain Steel Company, with plants at Lorain, Ohio, and Johnstown, Pennsylvania, as well as the Chicago Outer Belt Line Railway. The new corporation, known as the Federal Steel Company, had a capital stock of $200,000,000. It controlled some of the richest ore lands in the Lake Superior district, transportation lines from the ore fields to its Chicago works and mineral lands and coke ovens in Pennsylvania.[4] The charter of the Company was broad enough to cover the most varied operations:

"Mining of all kinds, manufacturing of all kinds, transportation of goods, merchandize, or passengers upon land or water; building houses, structures, vessels, ships, boats, railroads, engines, cars, or other equipment, wharves or docks, or constructing, maintaining, and operating railroads, steamship lines, vessel lines, or other lines for transportation; the purchase, improvement or sale of lands."

An inventory of the new property of the Company included large investments in nearly every one of the branches of business here mentioned. Among its first sales were half a million tons of steel rails chiefly to western roads.[5]

---

[3] *Commercial and Financial Chronicle*, LXIII, 559, Sept. 26, 1896; LXIV, 327, Feb. 13, 1897; LXIV, 372, Feb. 20, 1897; LXVI, 332, Feb. 12, 1898; American Iron and Steel Association, *Bulletin*, XXX, 43, Feb. 20, 1896; XXXI, 43, Feb. 20, 1897; XXXI, 217, Oct. 1, 1897; XXXII, 35, Mar. 1, 1898.
[4] *Commercial and Financial Chronicle*, LXVI, 1089, June 4, 1898; LXVII, 633, Sept. 24, 1898; LXVII, 1008–1009, Nov. 12, 1898; American Iron and Steel Association, *Bulletin*, XXXII, 133, Sept. 1, 1898; XXXII, 139, Sept. 15, 1898; XXXIII, 195, Nov. 15, 1899.
[5] *Commercial and Financial Chronicle*, LXVII, 1160, Dec. 3, 1898; Tarbell, *Life of Judge Gary*, 90–97.

Of the $200,000,000 authorized capital, nearly half was issued at the outset, and represented some $45,000,000 in plants, according to actual book valuation, plus $31,000,000 additional investments not represented on the books, and an operating capital of $10,000,000. The Minnesota Iron Company was producing about 3,500,000 tons of ore a year. It owned the Duluth and Iron Range Railway, which could haul and put on shipboard at its own docks 5,000,000 tons a year. Its steamships could deliver at Chicago and lower lake ports 2,000,000 tons of ore annually. The Company manufactured in its own ovens 1,500,000 tons of coke a year and it planned to turn out upward of 2,000,000 tons of finished steel products.

The annual report for 1899, ten years after the parent company, the Illinois Steel Company, was organized, gave the prospective coke output of the corporation as 1,700,000 tons, or about 80 per cent of its furnace requirements. Practically all of its other raw materials were obtained from its own properties. The number of employes exceeded 21,000, and the actual output for the year was just under 3,000,000 tons of iron ore, more than 1,500,000 tons of pig iron, and equal quantity of Bessemer ingots, and 181,000 tons of open-hearth ingots. Among the miscellaneous products were slag cement and mineral wool. In their statement of policy the managers of the Company said:

"It has never been the intention or desire of the Company to secure a monopoly of any line of business. The plan is to own and control sufficient iron ore, coal, coke, limestone and other raw products to supply all of the mills of the constituent companies; to own and control adequate facilities for transportation, both on land and water; to manufacture and deliver finished steel, and to do all with the greatest economy."

The President and moving spirit of the new combination was Judge Elbert H. Gary, who later was so prominent in its successor, the United States Steel Corporation.[6]

Before proceeding to a consideration of the United States Steel Corporation, which represents the culmination of the combination movement in this industry, we shall pause to describe the development of steel making during this period in two other sections of the country: the South and the Far West. In both these regions a single corporation practically controlled this development.

TENNESSEE COAL, IRON, AND RAILROAD COMPANY

In the South this master corporation was the Tennessee Coal, Iron and Railroad Company, whose early history we have previously recorded. This Company emerged from the crisis of 1893 with some losses on operation and a check to its prosperity which it shared with its great rivals in the North and West. At this time the Company was not making steel, al-

---

[6] *Commercial and Financial Chronicle*, LXX, 684–685, Apr. 7, 1900; LXX, 1252, June 23, 1900; Tarbell, *Life of Judge Gary*, 88–94.

though as we have seen some basic open-hearth steel had been produced in Birmingham as early as 1888, and Bessemer steel had been made in small quantities elsewhere in the South;[7] but it was entering into a new era in its development. During the low prices of iron that had prevailed since the panic, many economies of operation had been introduced and a general tightening up of efficiency had occurred throughout the Company's properties. The use of convict labor ceased with the termination of the leases expiring in 1895. Early in 1894 experiments were undertaken with a process by which it was proposed to "treat the metal produced in the Company's blast furnaces under certain special methods protected by patent rights which have been acquired with a view to producing steel." The tests resulted satisfactorily and early in 1894 the officers of the Company reported that "several hundred tons of metal" had been made the previous year. It was not deemed expedient on account of financial conditions at this time, to erect a steel plant immediately; but the directors seem already to have decided that this was the next step to be taken as soon as expansion could be resumed. The President stated in his report:

"Our ownership of a well-equipped steel plant would furnish a welcome and profitable market for a large part of our iron, thus enabling us to obtain a readier sale and better prices for such pig iron as we might desire to dispose of on the general market."

At this time the assets of the Company, including more than $20,000,000 credited to "land account," amounted to over $33,000,000. They were therefore practically equal to those of the Illinois Steel Company. In comparing the inventories of the two corporations, however, it is evident that a much larger proportion of the investment of the Northern Company was represented by improvements, that is, by furnaces and manufacturing plant.[8]

Operating costs were lowered in 1895, apparently following a reduction of wages after the miners' strike that occurred that year. The Company's coke was marketed, in successful competition with English and Eastern coke, as far afield as Mexico. Meanwhile iron prices were advancing, and the Tennessee Company had established a joint selling agency with the Sloss Iron and Steel Company. At this time the Corporation owned 17 blast furnaces, of which 13 were in operation and making 65,000 tons of pig iron a month. No other pig-iron producer of equal magnitude sold its entire product in the open market. All the others, with the exception of the Thomas Iron Company of Pennsylvania, which was an older but less ambitious enterprise, converted a large share of the pig iron they produced into steel. In view of this situation, one of the Company's furnaces had been making basic pig since August 1895, which has been used with success

---

[7] Alabama State Geological Survey, *Iron Making in Alabama* (3d ed.), 213; *Commercial and Financial Chronicle*, LVIII, 752–753, May 5, 1894.

[8] *Commercial and Financial Chronicle*, LVIII, 715, 734–736, Apr. 28, 1894.

by some of the largest steel makers of the North. As a matter of fact, by 1896, 75,000 tons of basic iron suitable for open-hearth steel were made in the Birmingham district. The Tennessee Coal, Iron, and Railroad Company attempted to raise funds to build an open-hearth plant this season, but postponed the project on account of monetary conditions. A small independent plant in Birmingham began to manufacture basic open-hearth steel in July 1897, and succeeded in making commercially 25 to 30 tons a day.[9]

The acute depression in pig iron in the spring of 1897 caused the dissolution of many old alliances, both North and South, and promoted the new combinations of producers of ore, coke, iron and steel, and steamship and railroad lines which we have just described, with the result that production, especially in the Pittsburgh district, was stimulated and a lower cost level was reached than ever before. This development naturally impressed upon the iron makers of the South and investors in Southern mineral industries the importance of keeping abreast with the North and of securing a new market for their iron, since the old one seemed likely to disappear with the creation of the great self-contained corporations in that section. An added incentive was given to improvements that would economize production by the Semet-Solvay Corporation, which in 1898 erected its first by-product coke ovens at the Ensley furnace of the Tennessee Coal, Iron, and Railroad Company. Since the latter Company was already an exporter of pig iron, shipping abroad between July 1, 1896, and January 1, 1898, an average of over 16,000 tons a month, there seemed reason to believe that steel also might be exported from Birmingham; and it was argued that by manufacturing basic open-hearth steel the Company would be enabled to withdraw a large part of its product from unremunerative outlets in the North and in even remoter markets.[10]

These considerations induced the Tennessee Coal, Iron, and Railroad Company to build at Ensley, under the charter of the Alabama Steel and Shipbuilding Company, which it controlled, an open-hearth steel plant with a capacity of 1,000 tons a day. Simultaneously contracts were closed with the Alabama Steel and Wire Company to erect a rod, wire and wire-nail plant at the same place, and to supply it for a period of years with steel billets. The new works drew their pig iron, coke, ores, limestone and dolomite from the property of the Corporation. The Company's blast furnaces were at this time producing 50,000 tons of pig per month, or about one-fifth of all the non-Bessemer iron made in the United States; and its furnace capacity enabled it to add 50 per cent to this output without increasing its existing plant.[11]

[9] *Commercial and Financial Chronicle*, LX, 655, Apr. 13, 1895; LX, 746, Apr. 27, 1895; LX, 1106, June 22, 1895; LXI, 153, July 27, 1895; LXII, 632–633, Apr. 4, 1896; American Iron and Steel Association, *Bulletin*, XXIX, 195, Sept. 1, 1895; XXX, 101, May 1, 1896; XXX, 141, June 20, 1896; XXXI, 173, Aug. 1, 1897; *Mineral Industry*, v, 354–355.
[10] *Commercial and Financial Chronicle*, LXVI, 571, Mar. 19, 1898.
[11] *Commercial and Financial Chronicle*, LXVI, 1235, June 25, 1898; LXVIII, 567–568, Mar. 25, 1899; American Iron and Steel Association, *Bulletin*, XXXII, 105, July 15, 1898.

In 1899 the Company, whose stock had risen within three months from $17 to nearly its par value of $100, mined more coal and made more pig iron than all the other producers in the state of Alabama combined. The steel works, the plans for which had been enlarged to give them a capacity of 1,500 tons a day, were in actual operation, and many thousand tons of their future product had been sold in advance in Northern markets. Nevertheless, the main outlet for this steel was still expected to be abroad, where it could be shipped at low freights as ballast in corn and cotton cargoes. The first ingots were cast on November 30, 1899. These new works benefited by the experience of their predecessors in the North and contained practically all the labor-saving devices applicable to the special quality of steel they made. By the time they began operation, however, the domestic demand for pig iron had increased until it became, to quote the annual report of this Company, "insatiable." This led to a temporary cessation of exports, though it was expected that they would be resumed as soon as the existing high tide of prosperity began to ebb. Indeed, it was this abnormal activity in the iron and steel trade that delayed the completion of the steel works just mentioned, the contractors being constantly held back by inability to procure materials. During the month of December 400 heats were made, the analyses showing an average high quality of product. The annual report for that year says:

"The works have been the first to handle on a large scale the pouring of steel direct from the open-hearth furnace into the ingot moulds without the intervention of ladle practice."[12]

This new development attracted subsidiary industries to the vicinity. The Alabama Steel and Wire Company had commenced operation with a plant capable of using 300 tons of billets a month. The Birmingham Cement Company was consuming between 100 and 200 tons of blast-furnace slag a day; the Ensley Brick Company was manufacturing brick on a large scale from the shale underlying the Company's coal; and the gas from the Semet-Solvay coke ovens was used in the Company's reheating furnaces.

During this year the Corporation disposed of its local railway, which proved a source of expense because railroads running through Birmingham as common carriers refused to pro-rate charges with it. By selling the road to these lines and making it a common carrier, the Tennessee Coal, Iron, and Railroad Company obtained a cash consideration of $1,100,000, a reduction for a long term of years in the rates charged on materials brought to its blast furnaces, an agreement enabling it to ship coal, coke, iron and steel from the point of production to distant destinations at Birmingham rates and other advantages. Thus, at a time when the Company was adding to its mining properties, extending its existing plants and

---

[12] American Iron and Steel Association, *Bulletin*, XXXIII, 169, Oct. 1, 1899; XXXIII, 218, Dec. 20, 1899; *Commercial and Financial Chronicle*, LXX, 588–589, Mar. 24, 1900; *Manufacturers' Record*, LXVI, 56, Nov. 5, 1914.

acquiring new ones, it disposed of its transportation properties, in the latter respect departing from the policy of its great competitors in the North.

Another interesting feature in the history of this Company during 1900 was the adoption of a resolution authorizing the directors to change the status of the Company's preferred stock by reducing it to common, at the ratio of 180 shares of common for each 100 shares of preferred, plus accumulated dividends of 54 per cent upon the latter. The purpose was to remove the possibility of differences between the owners of the two classes of stock by making their interests identical. Partly as a result of this arrangement and partly in order to provide additional funds for acquiring new properties and extensions, the common stock was increased early in 1900 from $20,000,000 to $23,000,000. Immediately after this was accomplished the Company resumed dividends on its common stock. Previously it had paid no dividend on common since 1887—thirteen years before—and no dividend on preferred since 1893. The resumption of dividends had been held back to some extent by the fact that the Company had many long-term iron contracts to fill at low prices, so that it did not receive the benefit of the better prices that had prevailed for the previous 12 to 18 months to the same extent that otherwise would have been the case. At this time 17 of the Company's 19 completed furnaces were in blast, and it was shipping steel by the solid train load as far north as Worcester. It also erected a continuous billet and rail mill which enabled it to convert its entire steel output, above the quantity it was obligated by its contracts to deliver to the Alabama Steel and Wire Company, into finished forms salable in the South.[13]

In 1901 the Republic Iron and Steel Company, which already owned the small open-hearth furnace that had been operating in Birmingham since 1897, took steps to erect a new $3,000,000 steel plant in that city. A year later the Alabama Steel and Wire Company, which had been purchasing its billets from the Tennessee Coal, Iron, and Railroad Company, began to erect at its own works a steel plant consisting of 4 blast furnaces and 10 50-ton basic open-hearth furnaces. By this time the Tennessee Coal, Iron, and Railroad Company was operating its rail mill successfully. During 1903 the latter company made a small quantity of Bessemer pig iron from Cuban ores. The resumption of dividends in 1900 was of brief duration. They were discontinued in November of that year and were not resumed until 1905, the earnings of the Company, amounting to several millions of dollars, having been spent in betterments. That year the Alabama Steel and Wire Company combined with the Underwood Coal and Iron Company of the same city as the Southern Steel Company. The new corporation

---

[13] *Commercial and Financial Chronicle*, LXX, 483, Mar. 10, 1900; LXX, 554–555, Mar. 24, 1900; LXXI, 713, Oct. 6, 1900; American Iron and Steel Association, *Bulletin*, XXXIV, 21, Jan. 22, 1900; XXXIV, 77, Apr. 15, 1900; XXXV, 13, Jan. 23, 1901.

had an authorized capital of $16,000,000, and proposed to enlarge its existing steel-making facilities.[14]

Between 1904 and 1906 the steel output of the Tennessee Coal, Iron, and Railroad Company rose from 155,000 tons to 402,000 tons. During the same interval the Company's output of pig iron increased from 475,000 tons to 641,000 tons. This progress was accomplished in the face of certain untoward conditions, for the Corporation had been, to quote a conservative authority at that time, "the football of unscrupulous speculating and gambling in Wall Street."[15] But the day was approaching when this Company, although it continued the largest steel-making enterprise in the South, was to disappear as an independent corporation. Its absorption by the United States Steel Corporation, with the consent of the Federal Government, at a time when it seemed headed toward a financial catastrophe that threatened to shake the business confidence of the entire country, belongs to the annals of high finance rather than to the history of manufactures.

Up to this date, the progress of steel making in the South, hopeful as it was in many respects, had not kept pace with the unprecedented expansion in the North. In reviewing its vicissitudes just before the outbreak of the World War, a practical iron-maker of that section said:

"Up to 1907 no steel maker in the South had made a great financial success. The industry was considered a precarious one. Many problems had to be solved before cheap steel could be produced here. A tremendous investment of capital was required. To make steel cheap it must be made on a very large scale. . . . If the large output exists, a large demand is required to consume it. This consumption in the South did not exist before 1907, and does not exist today. . . . The Tennessee Coal, Iron, and Railroad Company before 1907 . . . had no working capital to spare. . . . It had to receive the highest prices for its products to subsist. Its mills were small and old fashioned. . . . It did not produce large tonnage. Its customers were comparatively few and were small buyers. It made but a small range of steel products. The flurry of 1907 was too great a financial strain for such a weak company."

We shall see that this situation rapidly changed when the principal producer in the Southern steel industry was coordinated with the steel industry of the North, with its abundant capital and highly developed marketing facilities.[16]

COLORADO FUEL AND IRON COMPANY

The only other steel-making center in the Union was in the Rocky Mountain region, where the Colorado Fuel and Iron Company made Bessemer steel rails in moderate quantities for western railroads. The depression of 1893 bore even more heavily upon this Company than upon its Eastern

---

[14] *Manufacturers' Record*, XL, 207, Oct. 17, 1901; XLII, 260, Oct. 30, 1902; XLVI, 500, Dec. 8, 1904; American Iron and Steel Association, *Bulletin*, XXXVI, 183, Dec. 10, 1902; XXXIX, 61, Apr. 15, 1905.

[15] American Iron and Steel Association, *Bulletin*, XLI, 59, May 15, 1907.

[16] *Manufacturers' Record*, LXV, 53–54, Apr. 16, 1914; LXVI, 55–58, Nov. 5, 1914.

competitors, because its market lay in a district directly affected by the depression of silver mining and of the smelting industry; and because the Eastern panic was coincident with a protracted coal strike in Colorado. The income of this Company was derived more largely from the sale of coal than from the sale of iron and steel. Its fortunes revived somewhat in 1895 when business in its market area improved. While silver mining did not recover, there was a large increase in the output of gold with a corresponding demand for coke. But the principal stimulus was given by the advance in the price of iron and of steel and the renewed demand for steel rails and merchant iron.[17]

In 1896 the manufacturing plant consisted of 857 coke ovens, 3 blast furnaces, 2 Bessemer converters, a rail mill, a merchant iron mill, a pipe foundry, a spike mill and facilities for general foundry and machine-shop work. The Company's iron and steel business was described as "in its infancy." It controlled the raw materials entering into the manufacture of its products, and could manufacture Bessemer pig cheaper than its nearest competitors; and it had the further advantage in the local market of the saving in freight from the nearest competing rail mills at Chicago, 1,000 miles away. Since the organization of the Company four years before, the capacity of its iron and steel plant had more than doubled, and costs had been reduced in some instances by 75 per cent.[18]

Nevertheless, the Company's advantage of location was not sufficient to compensate in all seasons the economies of lower costs and larger output enjoyed by its Eastern rivals. Its rail mill was idle from the autumn of 1896 until the middle of 1898 under an agreement with the Rail Makers Association, by which the Company was to receive $360,000 a year for withdrawing from the market. The Rail Makers Association was dissolved, however, without paying this obligation and the individual members refused to recognize their liability for a settlement. After that Association broke up, the price of steel rails was speedily reduced. Notwithstanding this the Company set about improving its rail mills, in order to lower operating costs, and resumed production.[19]

Up to the end of the century its maximum output of finished iron and steel products, including rails, was only 150,000 tons per annum. In 1899 however, $12,000,000 were added to the capital stock for the purpose of increasing this product to 550,000 tons a year. Hitherto the iron and steel business had been limited to the territory immediately tributary to the works, where the advantage of freight rates already mentioned enabled the Company to overcome the high production costs due to limited output, old-fashioned appliances and presumably higher wages.[20] During 1899 and

[17] *Commercial and Financial Chronicle*, LIX, 330, Aug. 25, 1894; LIX, 370, 373–374, Sept. 1, 1894; LX, 1144, June 29, 1895; LXI, 473–474, Sept. 14, 1895.
[18] *Commercial and Financial Chronicle*, LXII, 461–462, Mar. 7, 1896; LXIII, 400, Sept. 5, 1896; LXV, 365, Aug. 28, 1897.
[19] *Commercial and Financial Chronicle*, LXV, 365, Aug. 28, 1897; LXVII, 527, Sept. 10, 1898.
[20] Cf., Phillips, *Freight Rates and Manufacturers in Colorado*, 61.

1900 these improvements were pushed forward. They consisted of some 750 additional coke ovens, a new blast furnace and extensions to the steel plant that brought it abreast of Eastern works. Arrangements were made at the same time to construct auxiliary plants to manufacture wire rods, galvanized and barbed wire, poultry netting, wire nails, hoops, sheets and similar products. During this period of expansion dissensions arose in the management, and in 1903 the control of the Company fell into the hands of the Rockfeller interests, where it still remains.[21]

The only other steel works in the West were a small plant at San Francisco, where a 10 ton open-hearth furnace using oil fuel was put into operation in 1903 and those of the Irondale Steel Company, of Irondale, Washington, to whose blast furnace a basic open-hearth steel plant and subsidiary works were added in 1908. Three years later this Company was importing pig iron from the Orient.[22]

UNITED STATES STEEL CORPORATION

In 1899 the total capital of the largest companies producing iron and steel in the United States exceeded $900,000,000. This represented a tremendous increase within a short period. Between the first of September 1898 and the first of September 1899, eleven important consolidations occurred; and the reorganization of the Carnegie Steel Company, with a capital of $160,000,000, was on the eve of consummation. These included the Federal Steel Company, having its center in the Chicago district, with a capital of about $200,000,000, and such well-known trusts as the American Steel and Wire Company, the American Tinplate Company, the American Steel Hoop Company, the National Tube Company and the National Enameling and Stamping Company, all of which were large consumers of iron and steel, and some of which were also producers of their own raw materials.

These eleven companies included prior amalgamations of nearly 200 existing concerns, and probably an even greater number if we include still earlier consolidations. For instance, the Federal Steel Company had absorbed six previous companies, including the Illinois Steel Company, which was itself an amalgamation of several earlier corporations. The motives that dictated these consolidations were partly financial, in order to secure a larger working capital and funds for plant extension called for by the great growth of the market for steel and steel products, and partly to bring together under united control all the processes of production, eliminating both middlemen handling raw materials and original producers of raw materials.[23] To anticipate a moment, the Federal Steel Company

---

[21] *Commercial and Financial Chronicle*, LXIX, 592, Sept. 16, 1899; LXIX, 652, Sept. 23, 1899; LXX, 794, Apr. 21, 1900; American Iron and Steel Association, *Bulletin*, XXXV, 81, June 10, 1901; XXXVII, 101, July 10, 1903; XLIII, 106, Oct. 15, 1909.

[22] American Iron and Steel Association, *Bulletin*, XXXVIII, 139, Sept. 25, 1904; XLIII, 75, Aug. 10, 1909; XLV, 6, Jan. 1, 1911.

[23] *Cf.*, Berglund, *The United States Steel Corporation*, 33–40.

owned manufacturing plants at Joliet, Chicago, Milwaukee, Lorain, Ohio and Johnstown, Pennsylvania; iron mines in Minnesota; a railroad to carry the ore to the dock; steamships to convey it to the different plants; a railroad between Chicago and Joliet; coal mines in Pennsylvania, and other feeders and subsidiary enterprises. The American Steel and Wire Company, the Republic Iron and Steel Company, and the National Steel Company had the same variety of facilities.

Yet these consolidations did not define the full compass of the expansion that occurred at this time. Many important independent companies were growing rapidly. In reviewing this transformation a writer of the period said:

"First, there has been in recent months a remarkable concentration of interests in the steel and iron trade. Second, this concentration, to a large extent, has been of a kind to increase materially the effectiveness of the company as a producer of iron and steel articles at minimum cost. Third, the presumption is that in so far as the consolidated companies organized are complete units in themselves, and are so situated that they 'start at the bottom and have all the profits there are, from ore to finished materials,' it will prove difficult to make them see any advantage in surrendering their identity in favor of greater consolidations. Fourth, the enterprise shown in the case of the smaller companies indicates competition that would stand in the way of any would-be monopoly. Fifth, the most promising field for the union of large iron and steel companies seems to lie in the direction of an alliance of those that manufacture staple articles of the metal with those that can supply the iron and steel bars and plates."[24]

While the greatest of all consolidations that have occurred in the iron and steel industry up to date was formed after this was written, the combination movement practically matured at this time. Ten years later changes among iron and steel companies were comparatively few, though they continued occasionally to occur, as in case of the Bethlehem and the Pennsylvania corporations, where the interests and operating conditions of two neighboring concerns ran closely parallel.

The organization of the United States Steel Corporation was in the air during this period of consolidation. In December 1900, Charles M. Schwab gave a talk at a dinner attended by John Pierpont Morgan, Andrew Carnegie, and seventy or eighty prominent New York financiers, at the University Club in New York, which eventually led to Mr. Morgan becoming the financial patron of the new undertaking.[25] The rapid increase of production between 1870 and 1900 had, as we have seen, provoked ruthless competition. Pools, which were resorted to to prevent price cutting and unfair business practices, had repeatedly proved a failure. The first serious effort to prevent overcompetition by more efficient organization was the combination

---

[24] *Commercial and Financial Chronicle*, LXVIII, 899–901, May 13, 1899; *cf.*, American Iron and Steel Association, *Bulletin*, XXXIII, 212, Dec. 10, 1899; Berglund, *The United States Steel Corporation*, 55–57, 62–63.

[25] Tarbell, *The Life of Judge Gary*, 111–112.

of a number of companies producing different lines of finished steel. We have recorded how several of these came into being shortly before 1900. But these new industrial entities fought each other in the same spirit that their constituent companies had shown previously, and the only result was fiercer, more relentless and more powerful competition than before.

When Judge Gary organized the Federal Steel Company he is reported to have turned for financial assistance to J. P. Morgan, with a plan that would have embraced practically all the companies that eventually went into the United States Steel Corporation at the time it was formed. But the great financier was unresponsive, and nothing was done immediately. Andrew Carnegie presumably realized that the existing condition of the steel industry was perilous, and he was ready to sell out to a great combination because he felt that sooner or later his company might be exhausted by a life and death struggle with some powerful rival. This was the situation when the dinner mentioned occurred. Mr. Schwab's presentation of the subject proved so convincing that Mr. Morgan arranged with him to secure a price from Mr. Carnegie. The latter hesitated, but after some persuasion, named a sum slightly more than $492,000,000, the largest price that up to that time had ever been paid in the history of the world for a business enterprise. The United States Steel Corporation was chartered early in 1901, and began business with twelve of the largest companies then in existence and a capital of $1,404,000,000. Its properties included 73 blast furnaces, steel works, rolling mills, vast holdings of ore, coal and limestone lands, 112 steamships and a thousand miles of railroad; and its productive capacity was about 7,400,000 tons of pig iron, 9,400,000 tons of steel ingots, and 7,900,000 tons of finished steel per annum.[26]

More in detail, its ore lands embraced all the mines previously owned or controlled by Andrew Carnegie, the Federal Steel Company, the National Steel Company and the American Steel and Wire Company, to which the Rockefeller holdings were almost immediately added, giving the corporation a total practically from the outset of three-quarters of a billion tons of ore. Of the 20,000,000 tons, annually mined in the Lake Superior district, the United States Steel Corporation mined nearly 13,000,000 tons, in which was embraced 90 per cent of the output of Bessemer steel ore from this region. It owned five large docks at Two Harbors, besides extensive shipping facilities at other points. Its vessels could deliver at the ports nearest its works 13,000,000 tons of ore per annum, or substantially as much as its mines were producing. In fact, its steamers and barges constituted the largest fleet engaged in any one traffic under the American flag, and comprised all the largest vessels in this trade. The capacity of its larger carriers ranged from 6,000 to 9,000 tons.

---

[26] American Iron and Steel Association, *Bulletin*, xxxv, 34, 36, Mar. 10, 1901; xlv, 84, Sept. 1, 1911; Butler, *Fifty Years of Iron and Steel*, 82–88; Berglund, *The United States Steel Corporation*, 70–71; Cotter, *United States Steel*, 31–32.

The Corporation's manufacturing plants were situated at or tributary to most of the Great Lake ports, including Milwaukee, Chicago, Duluth, Lorain, Cleveland, Conneaut, Erie and Buffalo. At Conneaut immense automatic unloaders would clear a 9,000-ton cargo from a vessel within six or seven hours, and the ore sent inland from a single Lake port in one day was more than "all the farm wagons in the greatest agricultural state of the Union could transport in a month." From Conneaut solid trains carrying from 1,500 to 1,800 tons of ore, and pulled by what were reported to be the largest locomotives in the world, ran over the double track road of the Corporation directly to the furnaces at Pittsburgh.

Of the 47,000 coke ovens in the United States some 21,000 were in the Connellsville region of Pennsylvania. All but about 1,200 of the Connellsville ovens, producing more than half the coke made in the United States, belonged to the new Corporation. Its 78 furnaces, including some of the largest in the world, were one-third of the whole number in the country and had a capacity of 7,000,000 tons a year, or one-half the total output of the United States.[27]

Eight of the leading competitors of the United States Steel Corporation produced about 2,800,000 tons of pig iron, most of which they used in their own works, while the remainder was made by smaller companies. The Corporation had but one important rival producing steel billets west of the Alleghenies, the Jones and Laughlin Company, of Pittsburgh, and it rolled more than half of the Bessemer steel rails made in the United States. The old rail pool which had worked under varying agreements usually divided the tonnage so that the Illinois Steel Company, the Carnegie Company and The National Steel Company, all of which were now absorbed by The United States Steel Corporation, were entitled to about 68 per cent of the orders received from the United States, Canada and Mexico. After the consolidation, therefore, but four members remained in the Steel Rail Association, and one of them controlled two-thirds of the trade. The competing companies were the Allegheny Iron and Steel Company, the Pennsylvania Steel Company, the Maryland Steel Company, the Cambria Steel Company, the Tennessee Coal and Iron Company and the Colorado Fuel and Iron Company; but all of these were not included in the pool.

The proportion of other branches of the steel market supplied by the new corporation was about the same as in case of rails. It controlled 60 per cent of the structural steel product, a large fraction of the output of steel plates, sheets, bars, hoops and cotton ties; nearly the entire output of tinplates and tubes; 60 per cent of the output of wire and wire rods; 95 per cent of the output of wire nails, and practically all of the barbed wire and woven-wire fence business, of which it had a virtual monopoly through the ownership of patents. It built from 85 to 90 per cent of all bridges made in the country. And these facilities for producing finished products from

[27] Wilgus, *A Study of the United States Steel Corporation*, 35–48.

the raw materials could not be duplicated at any price. It was anticipated that the new corporation would save very large sums in distribution costs, and it was predicted that the Company would be capable of producing cheaper and better than any other firm in the world "nearly everything in iron and steel that is made."[28]

Hardly had the new Corporation organized its large and diversified business interests under a single general control, when it began to add to its investment by the purchase of outside properties. But the first and most notable effect of the consolidation was to stabilize the price of iron and steel. During the initial year of its operation, it manufactured more than 7,000,000 tons of pig iron, 6,000,000 tons of Bessemer steel, and well toward 3,000,000 tons of open-hearth steel, besides great quantities of finished products.[29] Though consumers anxious for immediate deliveries had voluntarily offered an advance upon the Corporation's fixed prices, a policy of not advancing quotations and of dealing with consumers without priority favors was strictly maintained. Possibly this was with a view to removing the suspicion and hostility with which a considerable portion of the public witnessed the formation of what it regarded as a monstrous and formidable trust; but the policy was no doubt inspired in part by a farsighted appreciation of business interest. By stabilizing the price of raw materials and finished products, the Corporation removed a speculative element from the market and contributed greatly to dispel the doubts of purchasers as to the future trend of own production costs. Prior to this, for example, an investor desiring to put up a large building was unable to induce a steel manufacturer to guarantee deliveries at a time further removed than six months from the date of the contract, unless he paid a premium of from 10 to 15 per cent upon the normal price. The manufacturer argued with reason that he could not predict his costs for more than six months ahead, and that by committing himself to deliveries more distant in time, he ran the risk of heavy losses. But a purchaser could contract with one of the subordinate companies of the United States Steel Corporation "for years in advance," if he so desired, upon the basis of existing figures, because the Corporation had virtually all its production costs under its own control.[30]

An analysis of the original investment of the Corporation, as shown by its own appraisals, indicated that of the $1,400,000,000 in round numbers represented by its properties, about $825,000,000 consisted of ore lands and mines, coal and coke fields, natural gas fields and limestone quarries; in other words, of raw materials. Of this sum $700,000,000 was represented by ore properties alone. Manufacturing plants, including the real estate upon which they were situated, were appraised at $348,000,000. The

---

[28] Wilgus, *A Study of the United States Steel Corporation*, 35–48; Berglund, *The United States Steel Corporation*, 96, 168.

[29] American Iron and Steel Association, *Bulletin*, xxxvi, 77, May 25, 1902.

[30] American Iron and Steel Association, *Bulletin*, xxxvi, 4, Jan. 10, 1902; xxxvi, 18, Feb. 10, 1902.

transportation agencies of the Corporation, including 1,500 miles of railway, 2,300 cars, 428 locomotives, 112 ships and terminals, docks, and accessories, were valued at $80,000,000. Nearly $150,000,000 consisted of cash and cash assets; in other words, of liquid operating capital. It will be seen, therefore, that the preponderant investment of the new corporation was in natural resources or raw materials, the ratio of fuel and ore property to plant and transportation equipment standing nearly two to one.[31]

No sooner had the consolidation become an accomplished fact than a careful campaign of education was inaugurated to prove to the people of the United States that it was not a monopoly. Figures were published showing that it mined but 44 per cent of the iron ore, and made but 43 per cent of the pig iron, 66 per cent of the steel ingots and castings, 50 per cent of the rolled products, and 66 per cent of the wire nails manufactured in the country. A list of twenty-five large independent companies and amalgamations was published in 1902 with a brief description of their plants, to show that the formation of this "trust" had not stifled competition. Meanwhile the fact that the price policy of the new Corporation was conservative and tended to stabilize the market at what were generally believed to be reasonable quotations contributed to mitigate the distrust and hostility with which its formation had been regarded in many quarters.[32]

In December 1902, the Union Steel Company with large interests on the Menominee and Mesabi Ranges was bought for $45,000,000. The Sharon Steel Company and the old Troy Furnace and Steel Works were also purchased at this time. Provision was made for the sale of the stock of the Corporation to its employes on a deferred payment basis, and the total number of share-holders on the Company's books was 53,894. By the end of 1903 when subscriptions from employes began to affect these figures, the number of share-holders rose to approximately 80,000.[33]

From its organization the Company undertook to consolidate its subsidiary interests. On April 1, 1903, the Carnegie Steel Company of Pennsylvania, the American Steel Hoop Company and the National Steel Company were merged under the charter of the National Steel Company as the Carnegie Steel Company of New Jersey. On the same date six coke companies owned by the Corporation were combined under the name of the H. C. Frick Coke Company. Later in the year the American Tinplate Company and the American Sheet Steel Company were combined. Consequently at the end of 1903 the number of subsidiary corporations was eight less than twelve months before. The Union Steel Company properties acquired the

[31] American Iron and Steel Association, *Bulletin*, xxxvi, 112, July 25, 1902; *cf.*, Berglund *The United States Steel Corporation*, 113–117.
[32] American Iron and Steel Association, *Bulletin*, xxxvi, 126, Aug. 25, 1902; Tarbell, *The Life of Judge Gary*, 131.
[33] *Mineral Industry*, xi, 370; American Iron and Steel Association, *Bulletin*, xxxvii, 10, Jan. 25, 1903; xxxviii, 44, Mar. 25, 1904; Berglund, *The United States Steel Corporation*, 82–83, 90–91; Tarbell, *The Life of Judge Gary*, 163–169; Cotter, *United States Steel*, 56–58.

previous year were leased to various other subsidiary companies operating similar lines of manufacture, so as to entail no additional administrative expense. In November 1903, the United States Steel Products Export Company, whose stock was held by the Federal Steel Company, was made the selling agent for all the subsidiary concerns. This resulted in an increase of the export trade.[34]

During the first few years the Corporation was in existence the percentage of ore mined and of coke, pig iron, steel and steel products produced by its constituent companies as compared with the total output of the United States fluctuated slightly, but continued approximately the same. Notwithstanding its immense holdings of ore and coal and other raw materials, and its large furnace properties, the Corporation was a large buyer of pig iron; for its converting and finishing capacity outran its ore smelting capacity. Whenever an important independent Company like the Lackawanna Steel Company entered the producing field, there was a slight decline in the percentage of the total amount of steel made in the country produced by the United States Steel Corporation. The growth of open-hearth steel making in the South also had a slight effect in this direction. At the close of 1904 all the Corporation's pig-iron furnaces were working to capacity, and 90 per cent of its open-hearth plants were in operation. Between the summer of 1903 and the late autumn of 1904 a widespread depression occurred in the iron and steel trade, which was reflected in decreased receipts; but the morbid market conditions, psychological depression, and other symptoms of acute disturbance that had characterized similar periods in the earlier history of the industry, were almost entirely absent.[35]

In 1905, with a revival of business activity and demand for its products, the Corporation took the first practical steps toward the most dramatic expansion of its manufacturing plant that it has up to the present undertaken. Approximately 2,500 acres of land were acquired on the south shore of Lake Michigan in the state of Indiana, for the purpose of erecting there a large steel plant and an industrial town. This work was carried out by the Indiana Steel Company, a subsidiary of the Illinois Steel Company. At this time the proportion of the total iron and steel output of the Union supplied by the Corporation was declining. Between 1902 and 1905 its percentage of Bessemer steel ingots fell between 6 and 7 per cent, and of open-hearth ingots and castings about 1 per cent. The Corporation did not manufacture crucible steel ingots or castings, that field remaining entirely in the hands of independent companies. Similar losses appeared in respect to almost every finished product that the Corporation manufactured. Although it greatly increased its absolute output of iron ore and

---

[34] American Iron and Steel Association, *Bulletin*, xxxviii, 44, Mar. 25, 1904; Berglund, *The United States Steel Corporation*, 86–88.
[35] American Iron and Steel Association, *Bulletin*, xxxviii, 149, Oct. 10, 1904; xxxix, 108, July 15, 1905; Berglund, *The United States Steel Corporation*, 96–97.

of all forms of iron and steel during these three years, it was not keeping pace with the expansion of the independent companies.[36]

Meanwhile, however, the export trade of the Corporation was making rapid progress. During 1905 it shipped abroad nearly 1,000,000 tons of manufactured products, at prices higher than previously received and approaching domestic prices. It was the policy of the Corporation to keep its furnaces, mills and transportation companies operating as nearly as possible at full capacity, because this lowered the cost of production, and eventually lowered prices to domestic consumers, and secured continuous employment for the Company's wage-earners. In order to attain these objects it was deemed "proper and desirable to sell for export what would otherwise be surplus products at prices lower than domestic prices. If a contrary policy should be adopted the general cost of production would be increased, the employes would at times be idle, and balances of trade between foreign countries and this country would be changed to the prejudice of the latter."[37]

Although the capacity of the Corporation's western furnaces and mills had been materially increased, it had not kept pace with the demands of the tributary market, a growing percentage of which was being supplied from eastern Mills. It was this situation that determined the Company to erect a plant at what was later to be known as Gary. This new construction, as well as the extensive additions to the Company's existing plants, was carried through without additional bond or stock issues. The only instance where new securities were floated for acquiring new property was when the Union Steel Company and the Sharon Steel Company were purchased in 1902. To build the Gary plant $50,000,000 were set aside and the new project was not affected in the slightest by the financial flurry of 1907. During that year the United States Steel Corporation, as already mentioned, acquired practically all of the common and preferred stock of the Tennessee Coal, Iron, and Railroad Company and of the Alabama Steel and Shipbuilding Company. It also purchased a site containing 1,580 acres in the vicinity of Duluth for the eventual erection of a new plant for one of its subsidiary corporations, the Minnesota Steel Company.[38]

If we are to believe the testimony of iron and steel men at this time, the inclusion of the Tennessee Coal, Iron, and Railroad Company in a larger corporation was a direct benefit to Southern consumers of steel, irrespective of whether it protected the acquired company from bankruptcy and the South from a business disaster, the effects of which might have shaken business confidence throughout the entire country. In 1914 a Southern iron manufacturer in describing the change brought about by this absorption,

---

[36] American Iron and Steel Association, *Bulletin*, xxxix, 190, Dec. 15, 1905; xl, 124, Sept 1, 1906.
[37] American Iron and Steel Association, *Bulletin*, xl, 53, Apr. 1, 1906; Berglund, *The United States Steel Corporation*, 144–147.
[38] American Iron and Steel Association, *Bulletin*, xl, 37, Mar. 1, 1906; xl, 53, Apr. 1, 1906; xli, 139, Dec. 1, 1907; xlii, 38, Apr. 15, 1908.

stated that previously a steel consumer in Birmingham paid the Tennessee Company the price of steel at Pittsburgh, Pennsylvania, plus freight from Pittsburgh to Birmingham, which added about 30 per cent to the prime cost. This 30 per cent was an extra profit to the Tennessee Company, and forced the Southern consumer to pay about that amount more for his raw material than a Northern competitor would pay. Before 1907, when steel bars sold for $30 a ton at Pittsburgh, they cost $37.60 delivered at Knoxville, whether shipped from Birmingham or Pittsburgh, although the actual freight from Birmingham was $2.60 a ton, and from Pittsburgh $7.60 a ton. In other words, the Tennessee Company pocketed five dollars per ton freight which it saved upon its shorter delivery distance. This practically confined Knoxville steel consumers to a market for their products limited to the vicinity of the city where they were manufactured. Seventy miles North from that point the Pittsburgh manufacturer was already at an advantage. These conditions kept steel consumers from erecting works in the South, and although the Tennessee Coal, Iron, and Railroad Company was directly interested in having them do so, it could not afford with its existing costs of production, to make low enough rates upon its steel billets and half-manufactured shapes to justify their locating inside its market area. Within a few years after the absorption of the Tennessee Company by the Steel Corporation prices to Southern consumers were reduced to below a parity with Pittsburgh prices plus freights. This was because plant improvements and abundant operating capital made it possible to produce steel in the South at lower prices than had hitherto prevailed.[39]

In July 1908, the first cargo of 12,000 tons of iron ore was delivered directly from the vessel to the new furnaces of the Corporation at Gary. Of the $50,000,000 appropriated for the construction of the new plant, more than $43,000,000 had been expended. This large addition to the Company's equipment came in the midst of a depression in the steel industry. In 1908 the decline in the Company's pig-iron output as compared with the previous year was nearly 4,500,000 tons. The decrease in its output of steel ingots was 5,500,000 tons, and the number of its employes had fallen within twelve months from 210,000 to 165,000. In spite of the recent acquisition of the Tennessee Coal, Iron, and Railroad Company, the proportion of the total iron and steel product of the Union credited to the Corporation was not increasing.[40]

The Corporation was primarily a maker of finished steel products. Its sales of other products were incidental. It had always been a buyer rather than a seller of pig iron, and when it acquired the merchant furnaces of the Tennessee Company it immediately set about converting them gradually

---

[39] *Manufacturers' Record*, LXV, 53–54, Apr. 16, 1914; this applied only to the Birmingham district, however; cf., *American Economic Review*, XIV, 509, 515, 516, Sept. 1924; Walker, *The Story of Steel*, 180.

[40] American Iron and Steel Association, *Bulletin*, XLII, 83, Aug. 15, 1908; XLIII, 42, June 1, 1909; XLIII, 97, Oct. 1, 1909.

from producers of foundry iron to producers of basic pig iron for its new steel works. In 1909 when its total output of finished steel was just under 10,000,000 tons, more than 10 per cent of its sales were to foreign purchasers. With the opening of the Gary plant and the extensions recently made at its Ensley, Alabama, works, the ratio of Bessemer steel to open-hearth steel declined. It was 67 per cent of the total steel output in 1907, and only 44 per cent two years later. At the close of the latter year the Company owned 143 separate manufacturing plants. Its iron ore properties included 42 developed mines in the Lake Superior region and 21 in Alabama. Its coal holdings covered more than 180,000 acres with 93 operating mines in the North, and 335,000 acres with 24 active mines in the South. Altogether it owned 82 coke plants, with approximately 26,000 beehive and 612 by-product ovens. Its transportation equipment included nearly 2,000 miles of railway, more than 1,000 locomotives, 45,000 cars, 77 steamers, and 121 barges.[41]

A comparison of the percentages of Corporation output and output by independent companies in the iron and steel business for 1902 and 1910 indicated that during these eight years the proportion produced by the Corporation generally declined. The falling off in pig iron was from 44.8 to 43.3 per cent, in steel ingots from 65.2 to 54.3 per cent, and in steel rails from 67.7 to 58.8 per cent. The figures for 1910 included the production of the Tennessee Coal, Iron, and Railroad Company, which was an independent corporation in 1902.[42]

Figures published in 1915 indicated a slight trend in the steel industry toward smaller corporations. New construction was light in any case, but that undertaken by relatively small interests was larger than at previous periods. This tendency was ascribed to changes in the character of the industry, particularly the growth of specialization in the kinds of steel produced. When the United States Steel Corporation was formed more than 90 per cent of all the steel made outside of rails was ordinary metal, interchangeable so to speak. By 1915 it was estimated that 50 per cent of the orders for finished steel products specified particular types and compositions of metal, or if the specification was not made, the seller, knowing the requirements of his purchaser, made it for him. The large steel mill, as well as the smaller plant, could make special steels, but it was easier for small plants than for large ones to gain an established reputation for particular brands.[43]

A review of the history of the United States Steel Corporation at the conclusion of the first decade of its existence showed that the Company had mined during these ten years more than 181,000,000 tons of ore, and that it had made 95,000,000 tons of pig iron, and over 86,000,000 tons of

[41] *Mineral Industry*, XVIII, 412–413.
[42] American Iron and Steel Association, *Bulletin*, XLV, 117, Nov. 15, 1911; *cf.*, Cotter, *United States Steel*, 308.
[43] *Iron Age*, XCIV, 98–99, July 9, 1914.

rolled and finished steel. Among its by-products during this period were 26,000,000 barrels of cement, the annual output of this commodity having increased sixteen fold to nearly 8,000,000 barrels during that period.[44] In 1912 the Corporation appropriated money to push to speedy completion its plant near the city of Duluth. In the suit brought by the United States Government to dissolve the Corporation the defense produced evidence in 1914 to show that during the existence of the Company the price of its products had decreased upon an average about $8 a ton, and that since 1903 domestic prices in the United States had been lower than in either England or Germany. The Corporation's percentage of all classes of finished rolled products had fallen from 50.1 per cent in 1901 to 45.7 per cent in 1911, and during that period its competitors had increased their production 67.8 per cent, while the Corporation's tonnage had grown but 40.6 per cent.[45]

Several large companies added to their output far more rapidly than the United States Steel Corporation. The Bethlehem Steel Company, which made but 18,000 tons of finished products in 1901, made over 700,000 tons in 1913, a growth of nearly 3,800 per cent. But these exceptional figures are hardly more impressive than those of the Jones and Laughlin Company, which was already one of the largest producers in the country in 1901, when it made nearly 486,000 tons of finished products. Ten years later its output had risen to 1,490,000 tons, a growth of over 206 per cent. The Cambria Steel Company, which had increased its product from 467,000 to 1,193,000 tons between 1901 and 1913, showed a growth of 155 per cent. Several other corporations, for instance the Lackawanna Steel Company, the Republic Iron and Steel Company, and the Colorado Fuel and Iron Company had increased their output in a far higher ratio than the United States Steel Corporation. Meanwhile, new independent works had arisen: The Youngstown Steel and Tube Company, which began operations early in 1902, had a production of steel ingots in 1913 of 849,000 tons, and its finished products amounted to 465,000 tons. Its capital during these eleven years had increased from $600,000 to over $22,000,000, with nearly $7,000,000 surplus.[46]

[44] American Iron and Steel Association, *Bulletin*, XLV, 34, Apr. 10, 1911.
[45] American Iron and Steel Association, *Bulletin*, XLVI, 62, July 1, 1912; *Manufacturers' Record*, LXVI, 43, Oct. 22, 1914.
[46] *Iron Age*, XCIII, 951–952, Oct. 22, 1914.

CHAPTER V

STATISTICAL AND TECHNICAL FEATURES OF THE IRON AND STEEL INDUSTRY

Steel Output, 65. The Open-Hearth Process, 67. Crucible Steel, 71. Charcoal Iron, 71. Furnace Fuels, 72. Blast Furnace Practice and Outputs, 73. Ore Treatment, 75. Electric Driving and Smelting, 75. Basic Steel, 77. Variants of the Bessemer Process, 77. Steel Furnace Capacity and Practice, 79. Alloys and Special Steels, 80. Wrought Iron, 82.

STEEL OUTPUT

During these twenty years the quantity of steel made annually in the United States increased nearly eight-fold, from about 4,000,000 tons to more than 31,000,000 tons. Our maximum production of Bessemer steel prior to 1893 had been in 1892, just before the panic, when we made 4,168,000 tons of ingots, and a comparatively small quantity of open-hearth and crucible steel. For several years subsequently the annual output of open-hearth steel, though growing rapidly, was a comparatively small fraction of the total product and annual fluctuations of output were determined mainly by the Bessemer figures.[1]

A notable feature of steel statistics during the nineties was the rapid growth in the use of steel for other purposes than making rails. Up to 1890 more steel was used for rails than for all other rolled shapes combined. The balance changed to structural and other shapes in 1891, and five years later more than twice as much steel was used for these purposes as was used for rails. Meanwhile, the quantity of open-hearth steel produced in the country had more than trebled, in 1895 exceeding a million tons. Practically all of the steel made by this process was used for miscellaneous purposes, only 1,085 tons being at this date rolled into rails. Indeed, our output of rails, while fluctuating, tended toward a lower annual average during the decade following 1887. That year we made more than 2,000,000 tons of Bessemer rails. In 1896 this product had fallen to 1,103,000 tons. In 1887 our total production of Bessemer ingots was well under 3,000,000 tons, while in 1895 it had risen to nearly 5,000,000 tons.[2]

During this decade several variants of the Bessemer process were in use, though they were confined as a rule to small plants and never became an important quantitative factor in the industry. The most prominent of these special methods were the Clapp-Griffiths and the Roberts-Bessemer processes. Later Tropenas plants began to appear as the Clapp-Griffiths

---

[1] *Commercial and Financial Chronicle*, LX, 373–374, Mar. 2, 1895; U. S. Geological Survey, *Mineral Resources of the United States, 1915*, I, 335.

[2] *Commercial and Financial Chronicle*, LX, 479–480, Mar. 14, 1896; LXIV, 402–403, Feb. 27, 1897.

process dropped out of the statistics, and the Roberts-Bessemer works dwindled to a single active establishment. In the late nineties the small Bessemer works seemed to be disappearing rapidly, but there was a revival of these special plants ten years later.[3]

In 1899 our output of Bessemer ingots was 7,586,000 tons. Our open-hearth output had by this time reached the neighborhood of 3,000,000 tons. It was not until 1899 that the quantity of rails made in the United States exceeded the record of twelve years before. But on the former date some 13,000 miles of new railway were constructed in the United States, while in 1899 the total of new track was less than 5,000 miles.[4]

A comparison of the steel statistics of the United States, Great Britain and Germany for the decade ending with 1899 indicated that we had more than held our own while Great Britain had steadily declined. In 1890 the United States made 42 per cent of the 10,000,000 tons then produced by the three countries, while Great Britain made 36 per cent and Germany 22 per cent. In 1899 the aggregate output of the three countries had more than doubled, reaching almost 22,000,000 tons. Of this the United States made about 48.6 per cent, Germany 28.5 per cent and Great Britain 22.8 per cent. While the growth of steel production in the United States had been irregular, and its progress was interrupted by marked declines in 1891, 1893 and 1896, and while the output of Great Britain had diminished between 1890 and 1896, Germany's product grew constantly throughout the period, advancing a few hundred-thousand tons with each successive season. During the decade the German output had grown well toward three-fold, while that of the United States had gained nearly 250 per cent.[5]

By this time American plants were mechanically among the most efficient in the world. They certainly operated the largest units. In 1901 we made more than 8,700,000 tons of Bessemer steel with 81 converters while the United Kingdom employed 78 converters to make 1,700,000 tons, and Germany with a product less than half our own used more than half again as many converters as our steel makers. In the open-hearth branch of the industry the same conditions prevailed, though to a less marked degree: 403 American furnaces made 4,700,000 tons of open-hearth steel, while 500 British furnaces made but 3,200,000 tons. In this case, too, Germany approached more closely to our practice, employing 239 furnaces for an output of 2,300,000 tons.[6]

In the open-hearth industry there was a marked difference of average capacity between the acid and the basic furnaces. Of the 403 furnaces reported in 1892, 167 made acid steel, their annual capacity being 1,874,000 tons, while 236 furnaces making basic steel reported an aggregate capacity

---

[3] American Iron and Steel Association, *Bulletin*, xxx, 53, Mar. 1, 1896; xxxii, 99, July 1, 1898; xxiv, 52, Mar. 10, 1900; xxv, 44, Mar. 25, 1901; xxxviii, 114, Aug. 10, 1904; Twelfth Census, *Reports*, x, 66.
[4] *Commercial and Financial Chronicle*, lxx, 507, Mar. 17, 1900.
[5] *Commercial and Financial Chronicle*, lii, 766–767, Apr. 21, 1900.
[6] Chapman, *Foreign Competition*, 89.

of 6,415,000 tons. The growth of individual works was as notable as the growth of the whole industry. For instance, the total output of the Edgar Thomson Steel plant of the Carnegie Company between 1875 and 1904, a period of thirty years, was something over 8,250,000 tons. The output during the first year of operation was less than 6,000 tons. It did not reach 100,000 until 1880, and in 1903 it approached three-quarters of a million tons. At this time no basic Bessemer steel was made in the country.[7]

The production of steel of all kinds about doubled between 1900 and 1905, and the latter year exceeded 20,000,000 tons. Of this, 11,000,000 tons were Bessemer and 9,000,000 tons open-hearth. While Pennsylvania was still the leading steel-making state, Ohio's output was increasing at a relatively faster rate, due to the erection of large furnaces at Youngstown and elsewhere in the territory between the Connellsville coke fields and Lower Lake ore ports.[8] In 1906, when we produced 23,000,000 tons of steel, the Bessemer process was still in the lead, accounting for 12,275,000 tons of the product. All of this was made by the acid process, while 88 per cent of the open-hearth output was basic.[9] During the next two years an abrupt decline in production occurred, due to the business depression; but there was a slight increase over 1906, three years later, when 23,955,000 tons were made. By this time the open-hearth process had taken precedence over the Bessemer process, the output of our Bessemer converters in 1909 being less than 9,500,000 tons, or nearly 3,000,000 tons below the figures of 1906.[10] In 1910 when our output rose to 26,000,000 tons, our Bessemer product remained approximately stationary, the immense increase in production being due entirely to the growth of our open-hearth output. The record year for Bessemer production remained 1906, with its maximum figure of 12,275,000 tons. These figures were reduced almost 50 per cent by 1914, when we made but 6,221,000 tons by the Bessemer process. Meanwhile the open-hearth output had risen to a maximum of over 21,500,000 tons in 1913, when the highest total steel output of the pre-war period was recorded, or 31,300,000 tons. That year our Bessemer output was 9,500,000 tons.[11]

THE OPEN-HEARTH PROCESS

Let us dwell a moment longer on the two transformations of first importance that occurred during these twenty years in the American steel industry: The first was the rapid development of the open-hearth process, which though introduced in the United States at about the same time as the Bessemer process, attained no appreciable importance until about 1890

---

[7] American Iron and Steel Association, *Bulletin*, XXXVI, 26, Feb. 25, 1902; XXXVIII, 68, May 10, 1904.

[8] *Mineral Industry*, XIV, 323; American Iron and Steel Association, *Bulletin*, XL, 20, Feb. 1, 1906.

[9] *Mineral Industry*, XV, 454–455.

[10] American Iron and Steel Association, *Bulletin*, XLIV, 60, July 1, 1910.

[11] *Mineral Industry*, XXIII, 408; U. S. Geological Survey, *Mineral Resources of the United States*, 1915, I, 335.

and lagged far behind its better established rival until nearly the close of the century. Then within a few years it outstripped the Bessemer method, so that the latter not only fell behind relatively, but came to a standstill and even entered upon a period of decreasing production. The second important change, which was associated intimately with the one just mentioned, was the rapid substitution of the basic for the acid process.

As early as 1894 it was noted in the annual review of the American Iron and Steel Association that during the previous few years the demand for open-hearth steel for boiler plates, ship-plates, armor plates, gun forgings, castings, tools and structural shapes had been growing rapidly. This steel, like Bessemer steel, had become a formidable competitor of puddled iron but, unlike Bessemer steel, it was also a formidable competitor of cast iron. At the beginning of the period we are discussing there were some 28 open-hearth plants that made castings.[12]

It was not unusual for the output of open-hearth steel to leap forward by 30 or 40 per cent from year to year during prosperous seasons. In 1896 it was the only branch of the steel trade that continued its expansion. The adoption of the basic process had made available a larger range of raw materials for its furnaces. Indeed, this fact was used to disparage this type of steel, the basic open-hearth furnace being called the "scavenger" of the trade. It could employ the greater part of any old material offered at a low price, and therefore throve when producers using methods demanding "closely-controlled and highly-priced" materials were unable to hold their markets. A second cause for the preference shown for the open-hearth process was that the plant unit might be relatively small as compared with the Bessemer converter. A Bessemer plant had to have a capacity of 8,000 to 10,000 tons a month to compete with its larger rivals. But an open-hearth plant could operate economically though it made only a few hundred tons a week, and as requirements increased it could be readily enlarged by adding small units. This gave the open-hearth method a decided advantage for isolated plants serving a limited local market, particularly if such plants also had local supplies of scrap.

Furthermore, consumers had begun to show a decided preference for open-hearth plates and structural shapes, and indeed many engineers already began to specify this material in contracts. That had practically forced some rolling mills to build open-hearth plants. In several markets a higher price could be obtained for such steel than for Bessemer. The premium on basic open-hearth billets demanded by makers who had an excess for sale after supplying their own requirements for producing rolled shapes forced outside manufacturers to build plants of their own. But the most potent stimulus in this transition was the discovery that steel could be made quite as cheaply by the open-hearth as by the acid Bessemer process; and that the former process seemed to promise growing economies

---

[12] American Iron and Steel Association, *Bulletin*, xxviii, 108, May 23, 1894.

in the future. Fuel consumption was being steadily reduced, the cost of repairs was falling, labor-saving appliances, especially the Wellman charging machine which alone gave a decided advantage to the open-hearth furnace over the Bessemer converter, were bringing about important cost reductions. Whenever a period of rising prices for select Lake Superior ores and for coke occurred—and the formation of the United States Steel Corporation, and of ore pools and big vertical corporations in general, were holding these prices to a uniformly high level—it encouraged recourse to the open-hearth process, which at this time seemed to promise salvation for the small independent producer.[13]

Consequently as early as 1896 shrewd observers predicted that open-hearth steel was destined to capture a large part of the market hitherto monopolized by Bessemer steel. It was supposed, to be sure, that Bessemer steel would always be employed exclusively or nearly exclusively for rails, barbed wire, wire nails and similar products; but two new and growing classes of consumers were insisting upon open-hearth steel in preference to Bessemer: manufacturers of tinplate and architects and structural engineers. Sheet and tinplate manufacturers were forced to demand open-hearth steel because of imperfections in Bessemer plates, and because their British competitors had adopted open-hearth steel entirely in order to capture the American market by the superiority of their product. Open-hearth steel was also displacing Bessemer for boiler plates, ship-plates, armor plates and machinery.[14] Moreover this steel was also employed for castings, where Bessemer steel was rarely used. Indeed, the expansion of the open-hearth process was rapidly displacing iron for castings and thereby working a great change in general foundry practice with the result that ingot statistics were no longer a close measure of total steel production.[15]

The fact that open-hearth steel could be manufactured economically in small plants, that makers using this process benefited by having their works in the vicinity of reproductive metal manufacturing establishments and factories whose waste materials and discarded machinery afforded large quantities of scrap, and that there was an appreciable economy in having open-hearth furnaces attached directly to works consuming their products, led to a wider geographical distribution of this branch of steel making than that of the Bessemer process. In 1900, 15 States and 82 active plants were making open-hearth steel as compared with 12 States and 33 active plants making Bessemer steel. This year our open-hearth steel production for the first time exceeded that of Great Britain, although the latter country's output was the largest in her history. While part of the open-hearth steel made in America was always produced by the acid process, the proportion made by this method steadily declined.[16]

[13] American Iron and Steel Association, *Bulletin*, xxx, 66, Mar. 20, 1896.
[14] American Iron and Steel Association, *Bulletin*, xxx, 276, Dec. 10, 1896.
[15] *Cf.*, American Iron and Steel Association, *Bulletin*, xxx, 53, Mar. 1, 1896.
[16] American Iron and Steel Association, *Bulletin*, xxxv, 76, May 25, 1901; xxxvi, 53, Apr. 10, 1902; xxxvii, 52, Apr. 10, 1903; Twelfth Census, *Reports*, x, 67, 69.

The tendency of the Bessemer industry to concentrate in large plants was due primarily to technical considerations already suggested. Bessemer steel was made from Bessemer pig, which could be most economically produced in blast furnaces directly connected with the converters. Indeed, as we have seen, the iron was not remelted from the smelting of the ore to the completion of the finished product. A plant, therefore, had to be large enough to use the output of a furnace. Production was cheaper in large converters, and above all in giant furnaces, than in smaller plants. Notable economies in administration costs and other charges were possible where several furnaces were operated together. Since special qualities of ore were required for making Bessemer pigs, a motive existed for controlling this raw material, and incidentally all raw materials used in the process of manufacturing. The difference between the two methods of steel-making in this respect is illustrated by the fact that in 1903 the United States Steel Corporation produced nearly 73 per cent of all the Bessemer ingots and less than 53 per cent of the open-hearth ingots made in the country. About this time there was an absolute decrease in the production of acid steel, although the output of basic steel continued to grow rapidly; and for several years in the first decade of the century the acid steel statistics show alternating plusses and minuses, though without any marked movement in either direction from year to year. Acid open-hearth steel was more extensively used than basic steel for castings.[17]

In 1905 it was stated that only one new Bessemer plant had been erected during the last ten years, though production had been largely increased by rapid driving. During the previous five years, however, open-hearth production had trebled, and basic steel had begun to be used for castings and even for rails.[18] We have already mentioned that the first steel plant of the Tennessee Coal, Iron and Railroad Company at Ensley, Alabama, was run exclusively on rail steel. Although this branch of the industry developed slowly and was not particularly profitable at first, basic open-hearth rails gradually secured a recognized place in the market.[19] In 1906 the Carnegie Steel Company of the United States Steel Corporation dismantled its Bessemer plants at Duquesne and Homestead, to replace them with open-hearth furnaces. At the Gary, Indiana, plant only open-hearth furnaces were installed. This was largely the result of the exhaustion of Bessemer ores. The size of open-hearth furnaces increased when big corporations began to adopt this process, the standard capacity rising from 50 to 60 or 70 tons.[20]

The growth in the manufacture of Bessemer steel during these years was almost wholly in the use of Tropenas and other modifications of the standard

[17] American Iron and Steel Association, *Bulletin*, xxxvii, 61, Apr. 25, 1903; xxxviii, 141, Sept. 25, 1904; xxxix, 44, Mar. 15, 1905; xl, 76, June 1, 1906.
[18] *Mineral Industry*, xiv, 350–351.
[19] *Manufacturers' Record*, xlvii, 517, June 15, 1905.
[20] *Mineral Industry*, xv, 480–481, 486–488.

Bessemer process. The number of converters showed a decrease, but their annual capacity was growing.[21] While the production of open-hearth steel exceeded that of Bessemer steel for the first time in 1908, five years later the open-hearth output was 126 per cent more than the Bessemer output.[22]

CRUCIBLE STEEL

The crucible steel industry was well established in the United States, dating as we have seen to the period before the Civil War, but the output of this metal was always comparatively small. In 1893 it was considerably less than 70,000 tons.[23] Nor was it destined to grow rapidly. With the improvement in other processes, especially the development of open-hearth steel making and the manufacture of alloyed steel, cheaper processes continued to invade the field hitherto monopolized by the crucible product. Nonetheless the industry was in a thriving condition, and in 1900 the Crucible Steel Company of America was formed with an authorized capital of $50,000,000, to combine thirteen of the principal works in the country. The plants thus acquired produced about 95 per cent of the steel made by this process in America.[24] At no time did our production of crucible steel reach 132,000 tons, and there were marked fluctuations in the quantity produced from year to year. We still imported steel of this kind, especially for manufacturing cutlery, from Sheffield, where Swedish iron was largely employed as a raw material.[25]

CHARCOAL IRON

Several aspects of the technical progress of the iron and steel industry in America between 1893 and 1914 have already been alluded to incidentally with other phases of the general subject. No revolutionary change was made in furnace construction or in raw materials during this period, but plant units were steadily enlarged and labor-saving devices were introduced to facilitate and cheapen their operation. Partly because machinery was thus substituted for human muscle, the rate at which furnaces were driven was increased so as to add rapidly to their output.

By the nineties the number of charcoal-iron furnaces in the country and their aggregate capacity were declining. Nevertheless in 1897 five states; Massachusetts and Connecticut in New England, Georgia and Texas in the South, and Michigan, made charcoal iron exclusively. Of these Michigan, where Lake Superior ores were used, was the largest producer, making

---

[21] American Iron and Steel Association, *Bulletin*, XLII, 44, May 1, 1908; XLII, 101, Oct. 1, 1908; *cf.* Walker, *The Story of Steel*, 54–56.
[22] American Iron and Steel Association, *Bulletin*, XLV, 28, Mar. 25, 1911; *Iron Age*, XCIV, 214, July 23, 1914; *Mineral Industry*, XXII, 403.
[23] American Iron and Steel Association, *Bulletin*, XXX, 53, Mar. 1, 1896.
[24] American Iron and Steel Association, *Bulletin*, XXXIV, 125, July 15, 1900; *Commercial and Financial Chronicle*, LXXI, 32, July 7, 1900.
[25] Chapman, *Foreign Competition*, 91; American Iron and Steel Association, *Bulletin*, XLIV, 53, June 1, 1910; U. S. Bureau of the Census, *Manufactures, 1914*, II, 237; U. S. Geological Survey, *Mineral Resources of the United States*, 1915, I, 335.

over 132,000 tons annually, or more than half the country's total product. In 1896 the average annual capacity of charcoal furnaces was over 12,000 tons; but the average capacity of furnaces using mineral fuel was more than four times as great, or 53,000 tons per annum.[26] In 1900 a large charcoal furnace with an annual capacity of 35,000 tons of iron was erected at Buffalo, and the following year what was reported to be the largest charcoal furnace in the world was under construction at Marquette, Michigan. The same year the Clergue interests which were making an ambitious attempt to develop a great manufacturing center at the Sault St. Marie, began preparations to make charcoal iron on a very large scale at that point; but this enterprise was never carried to completion.[27]

When the present century opened the United States and Canada were producing about 400,000 tons of charcoal iron per annum, which nearly equaled the total pig-iron product from all kinds of fuels fifty years before. We were by far the largest makers of this quality of iron, there being but one charcoal furnace in Great Britain, while Germany and France, a large share of whose iron was made with charcoal in 1850, produced but a few thousand tons a year. Most Swedish iron, to be sure, continued to be smelted with this fuel, and there was still a charcoal-iron industry in Russia.[28] The special uses for which charcoal iron was persistently demanded remained the same that they had been twenty or thirty years before. Certain tinplate makers insisted on charcoal-iron plates. Some boiler-tube specifications called for charcoal iron, and this demand seemed to be increasing. Car-wheel makers also used large quantities of the same material; and it was preferred by makers of harvesting machinery for certain malleable parts.[29] As recently as 1910 two new charcoal furnaces, producing about 1,000 tons of cold blast pig per year, were erected at Allentown, Pennsylvania. In 1912 a new process was developed near Philadelphia for making what was called charcoal wrought iron in an open-hearth furnace, which was first heated by oil or gas in order to economize the more expensive fuel. Alternate charges of charcoal and pig iron were used, so that the reduction partook of the nature of puddling or boiling to that extent, except that there was complete fusion of the material, which was tapped as from an open-hearth steel furnace and poured into ingots.[30]

FURNACE FUELS

The use of anthracite and bituminous coal, except in occasional mixtures with coke, was rapidly declining, and relatively more by-product coke as

[26] American Iron and Steel Association, *Bulletin*, xxx, 52, Mar. 1, 1896; *Mineral Industry*, vi, 400.
[27] American Iron and Steel Association, *Bulletin*, xxxiv, 27, Feb. 1, 1900; xxxv, 157, 158, Oct. 25, 1901.
[28] American Iron and Steel Association, *Bulletin*, xxxvi, 172, Nov. 25, 1902; Ashley, *British Industry*, 6.
[29] American Iron and Steel Association, *Bulletin*, xl, 171, Dec. 1, 1906.
[30] American Iron and Steel Association, *Bulletin*, xliv, 84, Sept. 1, 1910; *Mineral Industry*, xxi, 498.

compared with beehive-oven coke was used, although the latter was still by far the more common type of fuel. Natural gas was losing importance as a rolling mill and steel works fuel before the middle nineties, in spite of the recent discovery of the Indiana field: although it was still used extensively.[31] The employment of blast-furnace gases for the production of power was rapidly increasing; in 1904 and 1905 the new Lackawanna Steel Works at Buffalo generated 30,000 horsepower with them. In Texas oil was used as a fuel in local rolling mills. At the new steel works in Gary three open-hearth furnaces of from 90 to 100 tons capacity were heated in 1914 with coke-oven tar, with the result that better steel was made and output was increased. More attention was paid to the quality of fuel used in iron and steel furnaces than ever before. Some plants inspected each car of coke received to make sure that it was of the proper physical quality to resist the destructive action of the gases in the furnace, and much attention was also paid to careful screening.[32]

BLAST FURNACE PRACTICE AND OUTPUTS

By the middle nineties some of the large Pittsburgh furnaces had an output approaching 700 tons a day, increased by the end of the decade to over 800 tons, which far surpassed the capacity of any other furnaces in the world. While such records were being made, furnaces whose annual capacity did not exceed 5,000 tons per annum continued to operate, at least intermittently, in other sections of the country.[33] Advances in blast-furnace practice at this time were in the direction of employing internal combustion engines receiving their gas from the furnace stacks, and electric motors, to drive machinery, and of blowing with a larger number of tuyeres. In fact, the tuyere standard was raised from 8 to 12 within a few years. Yet in 1900 steam engines were still more generally used for blowing in the United States than abroad, and the Europeans were ahead of us in the employment of gas and turbines. This was partly due to the fact that in certain of our largest furnace districts, especially the vicinity of Pittsburgh, slack coal was used for generating steam at a far lower cost than prevailed in any foreign iron center. We worked our furnaces faster than our rivals across the Atlantic, 4,000 tons a week being a not unusual output in this country, while a thousand tons was considered a fair average in Great Britain. We wore out our furnaces faster, but reduced charges in other directions more than compensated for this element of expense.[34]

---

[31] American Iron and Steel Association, *Bulletin*, XXVIII, 109, May 23, 1894; XXX, 53, Mar. 1, 1896; XXXII, 99, July 1, 1898; XXXVI, 27, Feb. 25, 1902; XLII, 41, May 1, 1908.

[32] American Iron and Steel Association, *Bulletin*, XXXVIII, 33, Mar. 10, 1904; XLIV, 86, Sept. 1, 1910; *Iron Age*, XCIII, 1149, May 7, 1914; XCIV, 204, July 23, 1914.

[33] *Mineral Industry*, V, 336; Bridge, *Inside History of the Carnegie Steel Company*, 181–182; Ashley, *British Industry*, 31; American Iron and Steel Association, *Bulletin*, XXI, 269, Dec. 1, 1897; XXXIII, 130, Aug. 1, 1899.

[34] *Mineral Industry*, VII, 400; IX, 164; Chapman, *Foreign Competition*, 87–88.

Naturally labor costs were lowered to the utmost in the United States. It was estimated in 1900 that the average quantity of pig iron made per furnace employe ranged from 373 to 419 tons at the best German furnaces, as compared with 1,300 tons at the Carnegie Works. The larger output in America was attributed to three things: superior ore, labor-saving devices and "fierce blasting." The latter practice was defended by American metallurgists, who argued that results showed that the life of a plant was not thereby affected. In 1901 the large Pittsburgh furnaces made as much pig iron in a day as a cold-blast charcoal furnace had made in a year a half century before. The British Iron Trade Commission noted in 1902 that of the 21 blast furnaces visited by its members in America 18 were managed by college graduates. By this time both British and German iron masters were studying closely the development of furnace construction and furnace practise in America and adopting improvements from this country. Indeed, at least one large iron company in Great Britain at this time employed a general superintendent who had received his training in the United States.[35]

In March 1905, one of the furnaces of the Edgar Thomson Steel plant made 918 tons of pig iron in 24 hours. The large furnaces planned this year were designed to make about 600 tons a day, the 100-foot furnace stack having proved less profitable than the 85 or 90-foot stack. Increasing use of internal combustion engines, the extension of the air-drying process, improvements in mechanical chargers, and the growing employment of slag for useful purposes were conspicuous features of the development of this period. By 1907 the average output of American furnaces was 77,000 tons, as compared with 43,000 tons in Germany, and 36,000 tons in Belgium, 27,600 tons in England, and 25,500 in France. This was in spite of the fact that the American average was pulled down by including many small charcoal stacks.[36]

Reviewing briefly the steps in this progress toward high production—in 1850 a furnace that averaged 7 to 10 tons a day was regarded as doing good work; 25 years later a few of the larger Pennsylvania furnaces had reached an output of ten times that amount, or from 75 tons to a maximum of 100 tons a day. This was regarded as wonderful progress, as indeed it was, measured by the attainments of the iron industry up to that date. About 1880, with the introduction of rapid driving, output was increased, though at the cost of high-fuel consumption. The Census of that year reported that a yield of 100 tons a day was first attained in 1875, and that the maximum output up to 1880 was 130 tons a day. About 1885 furnace practice had been improved until production was maintained at the rate reached

---

[35] *Mineral Industry*, IX, 386; X, 400; Chapman, *Foreign Competition*, 81; British Iron Trade Commission, *Report*, American Industrial Conditions and Competition, 501; American Iron and Steel Association, *Bulletin*, XXXVI, 53, Apr. 10, 1902; XXXVI, 74, May 25, 1902.

[36] *Mineral Industry*, XIV, 347–350; XV, 482–483; Popplewell, *Iron and Steel Production in America*, 67.

five years before, but with slow driving and a low-fuel consumption; that is, by a much more economical process. By 1890 output was nearly doubled on a low-fuel consumption by rapid driving under new conditions. This change was brought about by lowering the boshes of the furnaces and strengthening the blowing equipment. By 1894 the output had risen to an average of 400 tons a day, with a coke consumption of less than 1,900 pounds. With the introduction of Mesabi ores still lower boshes were used and other modifications in the furnace outlines occurred, with the result that an output of 500 tons a day was easily attained. By 1905, as just mentioned, a maximum production of 918 tons had been reached by a single furnace at the Edgar Thomson Works. This remained the record up to 1914.[37]

ORE TREATMENT

The trend of development at this time, not only in the United States, but the world over, was not so much in the direction of new records of production and fuel consumption, as in ability to maintain the best results of the past in the face of greater handicaps in the shape of difficult raw materials. The manufacture of iron naturally begins with the best ores, so far as they have been discovered; that is, with those richest in iron and possessing a favorable physical structure. By 1914 ores were economically smelted that were formerly discarded. Wonderful strides had been made in smelting, grading and mixing ores, so that they were delivered to the furnace in a state of physical and chemical uniformity. Preliminary treatment of ores was very common. While briquetting had not been introduced to a large extent in the United States, as it had in Europe, washing to eliminate clay, gravel and sand was practised extensively, especially on the Mesabi range, where single plants had been constructed with a capacity for washing from 30,000 to 35,000 tons a day. By this operation ores with 45 per cent iron-content were enriched to 56 per cent and the silica they contained was reduced from 30 to 10 per cent. Improvements in blast-furnace practice also promoted the use of Cuban ores, very high in alumina, which had previously been considered an undesirable material.[38]

ELECTRIC DRIVING AND SMELTING

Electricity was employed not only to drive blowing machinery and to operate charging apparatus, cranes and other labor-saving devices, but also to smelt ore and refine steel. It was reported in 1903 that 4,000 men made three times as much steel at the Homestead Works of the Carnegie Company as 15,000 men made at the Krupp Works in Germany; and in partial explanation of this it was pointed out that at Pittsburgh three men with apparatus operated by electricity could charge twenty furnaces. Prior to the adoption of this improvement the labor of more than 200 men was

---

[37] American Iron and Steel Association, *Bulletin*, XLIII, 112, Nov. 1, 1909; *Iron Age*, XCIV, 32, July 2, 1914.
[38] *Iron Age*, XCIII, 1578–1579, June 25, 1914.

required.[39] A competent study of these economies made somewhat later showed that in filling furnaces, 5 men earning 27 cents an hour could, at a total labor cost of $13.50, charge for an output of 600 tons, whereas a few years before 36 men, whose services represented a total labor cost of $72 although they received only 14 cents an hour were required to charge furnaces for an output of 90 tons.[40] Electric smelting was introduced in Europe, however, before it was employed in the United States, and it had a larger development there throughout this period. Ore was smelted with electricity in Sweden, and in Germany some works performed all the processes from reducing ore to pouring steel ingots in electric furnaces. As early as 1905 extensive experiments in the same direction were conducted in Canada, where it was proposed to smelt ore with electricity generated by water power at Sault St. Marie. The first and most successful American furnace smelting ore by electricity was erected on the Pitt River at Reading, California, in 1907, and two tons of ferrosilicon, the first made in the United States, were drawn there in September of that year. Some pig iron had already been produced by electricity at this point. The output in 1908 was about two tons a day, made directly from the ore without any fuel or blast. This furnace was the only one of the kind in America, and it continued in successful operation throughout the period we are describing.[41]

The use of the electric current to refine steel was more general, though its employment in America was for super-refining; that is, for a final process after the iron had been smelted and had been partially refined by the open-hearth or Bessemer process. One of the largest plants of this kind was installed in 1909 at the South Chicago works of the United States Steel Corporation. It had a capacity of 15 tons and received its hot metal from a Bessemer converter. A similar plant was erected the same year at Worcester, Massachusetts. Hitherto the electric furnaces in use in the United States had been of relatively small capacity and were limited to making high-grade steel of crucible standard. In fact, the Crucible Steel Company of America began to employ electricity for refining the following year. In 1910 there were seven plants engaged in refining steel by electricity, and their aggregate output was over 52,000 tons. By 1914 electric steel castings began to compete with open-hearth steel castings, although at higher prices. That year the United States Steel Corporation made some 10,000 tons of electric steel rails, which were regarded as less likely to break than ordinary rails, especially in extremely cold weather. Such rails, however, were sold at $40 a ton, and more—a price that limited their use to points where exceptional specifications were required. There were at this time 15 electric furnaces in the United States, with an aggregate

---

[39] American Iron and Steel Association, *Bulletin*, XXXI, 257, Nov. 20, 1897; XXXV, 84, June 10, 1901; XXXVII, 38, Mar. 10, 1903.
[40] Reitell, *Machinery and its Benefits to Labor in the Crude Iron and Steel Industries*, 26.
[41] *Mineral Industry*, XIV, 354; XV, 499; XX, 443; American Iron and Steel Association, *Bulletin*, XLI, 114, Oct. 1, 1907; XLII, 26, Apr. 1, 1908.

daily capacity of 438 tons; quite a negligible figure, of course, compared with the capacity of our open-hearth furnaces, which was nearly 94,000 tons, or of our Bessemer converters, which exceeded 53,000 tons.[42]

BASIC STEEL

We have already mentioned the rapid expansion of the basic-steel manufacture in the United States. In 1895 it was confined to four works in Pennsylvania, three using the open-hearth and one using the Bessemer process. Outside of that State, steel had been made only experimentally, or on a very small scale by this method, which had made no progress whatever in the South. Two years later several open-hearth plants were producing basic steel. No Bessemer plants had as yet adopted this process, although the Troy Steel Company was preparing to do so.[43]

In all the large steel-producing countries a similar tendency for the basic process to grow at the expense of the acid process manifested itself. For instance, between 1902 and 1909 while the acid-steel output of Great Britain remained stationary the basic-steel output almost doubled. During the same period the acid-steel product of Germany, which was always small, actually declined, while the output of basic steel rose in round numbers from 7,250,000 to 11,500,000 tons. But in no other country was the change as marked as in the United States. Our acid steel product in 1902 and 1909 was practically the same, being both years between 10,250,000 and 10,500,000 tons. During this period, however, our total production of basic steel had risen from 4,500,000 to 13,500,000 tons. Great Britain had clung more closely to the acid process, because her furnaces depended so largely upon imported ore, where it was of first importance that the iron content should be as high as possible.[44]

VARIANTS OF THE BESSEMER PROCESS

Several modifications of the Bessemer method of making steel were introduced during these twenty years. Some of these have been mentioned. They included the Walrand-Legenisel process, and the Talbot process developed at the Pencoyd Iron Works in Pennsylvania. Certain modifications of the latter were perfected by Ambrose Monell of the Homestead Steel Works, patents for which were sustained after considerable litigation by the Court of Appeals of the District of Columbia in 1904. Talbot was associated with Percival Roberts of the Lackawanna Steel Company, whose name was sometimes given to a further modification of the process. In

---

[42] American Iron and Steel Association, *Bulletin*, XLIII, 46, June 1, 1909; XLIII, 121, Dec. 1, 1909; XLIV, 54, June 1, 1910; XLV, 28, Mar. 25, 1911; XLVI, 44, May 1, 1912; XLVI, 96, Oct. 1, 1912; *Iron Age*, XCIII, 1067, Apr. 30, 1914; XCIII, 1466, June 11, 1914; *Mineral Industry*, 1911, XX, 444; 1912, XXI, 997; U. S. Geological Survey, *Mineral Resources of the United States*, 1915, I, 334; cf. Walker, *The Story of Steel*, 49–52.

[43] American Iron and Steel Association, *Bulletin*, XXVIII, 108, May 23, 1894; XXX, 53, Mar. 1, 1896.

[44] American Iron and Steel Association, *Bulletin*, XLV, 5, Jan. 1, 1911.

1891 the so-called Tropenas process was first used in England, and was introduced into the United States seven years later. This method, which employed a very small converter, was preferred for making medium and small castings, which were employed as substitutes for drop and hand forgings in agricultural machinery and railway supplies, and for tools, gear wheels, crank-shafts and automobile parts. It was also used to some extent in armories.[45]

But the most important development of this period was the extension of the duplex process, by which iron was partially refined in Bessemer converters, and carried through the final stage of steel making in an open-hearth furnace. By this procedure, which had first been employed in Austria many years before, it was possible largely to dispense with the use of scrap. Naturally, therefore, it was in favor with steel makers in districts where ample supplies of scrap were not always to be had; as was the case with the Tennessee Coal, Iron and Railroad Company in Alabama, and the Colorado Fuel and Iron Company in Colorado. Several of the larger northern plants also equipped themselves for the same process. In fact at any point where large outputs were desired, and especially at times when the price of scrap iron was high, the duplex process was apt to be adopted. When the demand for steel was less active and scrap was cheap, it was frequently more economical to shut down the Bessemer converters and use the open-hearth furnaces alone. Where pig iron was made very cheaply, as in the South, the loss of metal in the Bessemer converter was overbalanced by the decrease in unit cost, due to the larger quantity of steel that could be made in a given time in a given plant by using pig metal instead of scrap. In other words, the process was economical in particular localities, usually those remoter from the main iron and steel producing and manufacturing areas, and in times of very active demand and high prices.[46] During 1909 when the trade was comparatively active, nearly 523,000 tons of steel were made by the duplex process. Five years later, during a period of depression, this quantity had fallen to 402,000 tons, although the total output of steel in both years was approximately the same—in the neighborhood of 23,500,000 tons.

With the gradual change from the Bessemer to the open-hearth process, the quantity of spiegeleisen used decreased. In many cases, where the Bessemer converter was still in use, it was employed for the duplex process, which required no carburizing and deoxidizing by the addition of this material, as in the straight Bessemer operation. Consequently imports of spiegeleisen, which at one time had exceeded 100,000 tons, declined to 1,000 tons in 1912, and domestic production fell from a maximum of 283,000

---

[45] American Iron and Steel Association, *Bulletin*, xxx, 68, Mar. 20, 1896; xxxiv, 107, June 15, 1900; xxxviii, 26, Feb. 25, 1904; xxxviii, 157, Oct. 25, 1904; xxxix, 17, Feb. 1, 1905.

[46] American Iron and Steel Association, *Bulletin*, xliv, 108, Nov. 1, 1910; *Iron Age*, xciii, 1284, May 21, 1914; xciii, 1519, June 11, 1914; xciv, 213, July 23, 1914; xciv, 882–884, Oct. 15, 1914.

tons in 1907 to 110,000 tons in 1913. Meanwhile, however, our output of ferromanganese, which was employed in the open-hearth process, rose within a decade from less than 60,000 tons to 125,000 tons, while our imports, which reached a maximum for this period during 1910, a year of very large steel production, increased from 20,000 to 114,000 tons. At the beginning of the century we used more than three times as much spiegeleisen as ferromanganese; in 1912 we used more than twice as much ferromanganese as spiegeleisen. The consumption of the former material in 1913 was approximately 224,000 tons, while the production of steel ingots and castings was over 31,000,000 tons. Until the middle of 1912 most of our imported manganese ores came from India and Brazil, but just before the War Russia took second place as a furnisher of this material.[47]

STEEL FURNACE CAPACITY AND PRACTICE

Reviewing some of the notable steps in the progress of the steel industry during these twenty years, the first and most striking change, if we except the substitution of the open-hearth for the Bessemer process, was the increased size of producing units. The development in this direction was relatively more pronounced than in case of blast furnaces. In 1892 Bessemer converters ranged from 3 to 20 tons capacity, and open-hearth furnaces from 5 to 35 tons. Ten years later there was no increase in the size of converters, but many open-hearth furnaces of 50 tons and one of 75 tons were in use. During that decade the output of Bessemer steel about doubled, that of open-hearth steel increased more than eight-fold, and that of crucible steel increased only one-third. In 1914 the largest converters were still of 20-ton capacity, while the largest open-hearth steel furnaces could produce 250 tons per heat. Of the 864 open-hearth furnaces in the country, 8 were of the latter capacity and 15 could melt over 100 tons at a time.

No improvement had been made in the quality of the finest grades of crucible steel for forty years, but the price had been reduced during that interval from 14 to 16 cents a pound to 6 cents a pound or even lower. Meanwhile, a marked development had occurred in the production of alloy and special tool steels. Simultaneously the competition of open-hearth steel had forced Bessemer steel makers to keep their product up to the highest standards of uniformity and quality. Open-hearth practice, however, had advanced with even greater rapidity than Bessemer practice, especially in the matter of handling large heats. Low-carbon steels had long been made with satisfactory uniformity. The progress, therefore, was largely in producing dependable high-carbon steels of uniform grade in the open-hearth furnace, where quantity production was possible. By the beginning of the present century our makers were able to produce steels in 50-ton furnaces with up to 1 per cent carbon-content and a variation in that

[47] *Iron Age*, xcIII, 913, Apr. 9, 1914; xcIV, 384–385, Aug. 13, 1914.

content of less than 0.1 per cent. This was a degree of uniformity that proved quite satisfactory in practice for metal used for car springs and similar purposes. This progress was one of the chief reasons for the increase in the output of open-hearth steel at the expense of crucible steel. While no open-hearth steel could replace the latter for fine lathe work, high-speed cutting tools and similar uses, it did compete with crucible steel in those fields where the consumption was largest.[48]

ALLOYS AND SPECIAL STEELS

In 1895 the Association of American Steel Manufacturers attempted to introduce uniform steel specifications, and in 1901 what are known as the American standard specifications, covering steel castings, axles, forgings, tires, rails, structural steel for buildings, bridges, shapes and open-hearth steels for boiler plates and rivets, were adopted. These specifications called for a degree of uniformity and an accuracy of composition that would have been impossible of attainment ten years before. Meanwhile steel was constantly being put to new uses. Its substitution for iron in the tinplate industry alone created a new market of great extent. During the last decade of the nineteenth century the substitution of municipal electric traction, which required heavy girder rails, for horse cars, and the construction of electric interurban lines, produced another large demand. Ten years later the growth of the automobile industry suddenly made still other and even more exacting calls upon makers, especially for alloy steels.[49]

The use of chromium and nickel for hardening and toughening steel was already known before 1890. During 1894, in the midst of the depression that followed the panic, manufacturers of alloy steel kept their works running full time in spite of general trade stagnation. This material was used for gear wheel, pinion and die castings, and for general machinery construction. It was also employed for burglar-proof safes and vaults. By 1897 nickel-steel axles were a standard specification for the heavy cars used upon some of the coal and ore roads. Before 1900 the Taylor-White process of making tool steel was developed by two engineers associated with the Bethlehem Steel Company. This metal would cut steel at a speed so great as to heat the tool to redness, a quality that immensely shortened the time used in cutting, shaping and tooling cold-worked steel.[50]

By 1900 nickel-steel rails were employed experimentally by the Pennsylvania Railroad Company on curves where traffic was exceptionally heavy and ordinary rails wore out with corresponding rapidity. In 1903 some 9,000 tons of such rails were made by the Carnegie Steel Company in 85

---

[48] American Iron and Steel Association, *Bulletin*, XXIX, 210, Sept. 20, 1895; XXXVIII, 154, Oct. 25, 1904.
[49] American Iron and Steel Association, *Bulletin*, XXIX, 89, Apr. 20, 1895; XXXVI, 54, Apr. 10, 1902.
[50] *Commercial and Financial Chronicle*, LVIII, 514, Mar. 24, 1894; American Iron and Steel Association, *Bulletin*, XXXI, 181, Aug. 10, 1897; XXXIV, 139, Aug. 15, 1900; *Mineral Industry*, VII, 432–433; IX, 390, 413, *et seq.;* British Iron Trade Commission, *Report*, 76.

and 100 pound sections, as a result of these earlier experiments.[51] By this date nickel, chrome and nickel-chrome steel were in demand for automobile parts. The principal steel-hardening metals in use in 1905 were nickel, chromium and manganese, tungsten, molybdenum, vanadium, titanium, cobalt and uranium; and about a thousand tons of these metals were annually produced in the United States for the use of steel makers. Most of our nickel, however, was reduced from matte imported from Canada and New Caledonia. In 1907 the Santa Fe Railroad laid five miles of track experimentally with vanadium rails. The same alloy was also employed in naval vessels and naval ordnance.[52]

Of the 182,000 tons of alloy steel produced in 1909, 120,000 tons were made in open-hearth furnaces, 42,000 tons in Bessemer converters, and 20,000 tons in crucible or electric furnaces. By the following year our output of alloy steels had jumped to 568,000 tons. The growing demand for these metals continued to be measured roughly by the increased production of automobiles. The total number of cars built in 1912 was 210,000, and although this was but a fraction of the output ten years later, the increase had been so rapid, rising from 20,000 cars eight years before, that the effect on the special steel market was prodigious. Of the alloy steels produced in 1910 more than 57 per cent were titanium, 19 per cent nickel, 9 per cent nickel-chrome, and the remainder chrome, manganese, vanadium and combinations of these metals. About 3,000 tons of tungsten steel were made. By this time nearly 196,000 tons of titanium-treated steel rails were rolled annually in the United States. That figure declined, however, to a little over 27,000 tons of alloy rails of all classes, in 1914, though the total quantity of this steel produced rose over 93 per cent in the preceding five-year interval. During this period also nickel-chrome steel rose to first place among these alloys.[53]

With the outbreak of the World War, American steel manufacturers suddenly discovered that our imports of alloy steel had been greater than was previously realized. Automobile manufacturers especially were eager inquirers for substitutes for the Krupp steels of which they were deprived by the outbreak of hostilities. The pursuit of tonnage had been pushed so energetically by our great steel makers that the production of special brands had been relatively neglected. Manufacturers of forgings and springs, particularly for automobiles, soon found, however, that domestic steels made to meet the analyses of the foreign steels previously employed were as satisfactory as those imported. It was also asserted that carbon steels could be produced under careful heat treatment capable of as good service as many alloy products.[54]

---

[51] American Iron and Steel Association, *Bulletin*, xxxiv, 190, Nov. 15, 1900; xxxviii, 26, Feb. 25, 1903.
[52] *Mineral Industry*, xiv, 356–357; American Iron and Steel Association, *Bulletin*, xl, 125, Sept. 1, 1906; xli, 89, Aug. 1, 1907; xli, 108, Sept. 10, 1907.
[53] American Iron and Steel Association, *Bulletin*, xliv, 53, June 1, 1910; xlv, 93, Oct. 1, 1911; *Mineral Industry*, xx, 446–447; U. S. Bureau of the Census, *Manufactures, 1914*, ii, 235.
[54] *Iron Age*, xciv, 1243, Nov. 26, 1914.

WROUGHT IRON

Naturally the unprecedented expansion of steel making was to some extent at the expense of manufacture of wrought iron, although the great increment in the steel market was a net addition to the previous metal demand of the country. Iron was still used for anchors, for instance, thousands of tons of scrap being forged for this purpose at Camden, Maine.[55] Bloomeries for making wrought iron directly from the ore continued in operation, as we have seen, up to the end of the century. In 1896 there were still one active forge of this character in North Carolina, one in Tennessee and seven in New York.[56] Occasionally a slight revival occurred in the manufacture of charcoal blooms from pig and scrap iron to meet a demand for this metal for conversion into plates, rivets and forgings. But such returns to old materials were temporary, and by the end of the century only two of the old type bloomeries making iron directly from the ore continued in operation, one in New York and one in North Carolina; and the latter was idle most of the time. By 1902 the last of these bloomery forges finally went out of use. It was situated at Plattsburgh, New York, and its last year's output was 2,310 tons.[57]

While puddling furnaces did not become as extinct as bloomery forges, their number and output declined. This, too, was due to the substitution of steel for forged and rolled iron. In 1895 it was estimated that it would have taken 60,000 skilled puddlers one year to refine sufficient iron to supply the country, had iron been used in place of steel. On the other hand, the same quantity of metal could be provided from Bessemer converters with the services of 3,000 men and those, with few exceptions, less skilled than puddlers.[58] The same year The Jones & Laughlin Company, of Pittsburgh, dismantled the last of its puddling furnaces, of which it had operated 92 as recently as January 1894.[59] This change was not peculiar to the United States. In Great Britain the quantity of puddled iron delivered by the firms connected with the Conciliation and Arbitration Board declined within five years from nearly 30,000 tons to less than 9,000 tons a month.[60] The number of puddling furnaces in the United States reached a maximum in 1884, when 5,265 were reported to the Iron and Steel Association; a decade later the number, after fluctuating from year to year, had declined to 4715; and in 1907, when puddled iron was produced only for a few special purposes, mainly to manufacture articles that were to be subjected to es-

---

[55] American Iron and Steel Association, *Bulletin*, xxx, 105, May 10, 1896.
[56] American Iron and Steel Association, *Bulletin*, xxx, 53, Mar. 1, 1896; xxx, 76, Apr. 1, 1896; xxxii, 99, July 1, 1898.
[57] American Iron and Steel Association, *Bulletin*, xxxvi, 27, Feb. 25, 1902; xlii, 41, May 1, 1908; xliv, 109, Nov. 1, 1910; *Mineral Industry*, xi, 366.
[58] *Mineral Industry*, iv, 451.
[59] American Iron and Steel Association, *Bulletin*, xxviii, 205, Sept. 12, 1894; xxix, 276, Dec. 10, 1895.
[60] *London Colliery Guardian*, quoted in American Iron and Steel Association, *Bulletin*, xxix, 154, July 10, 1895.

pecially severe corrosive influences, the number was 2,635. Between 1890 and 1910 the proportion of iron in the total quantity of rolled iron and steel produced in the country, fell from 43 per cent to 8 per cent.[61] The absolute decline was from 2,500,000 to less than 1,750,000 tons. Nevertheless certain firms, notably the old Tredegar Iron Works at Richmond, still specialized in wrought iron down to the eve of the World War.

[61] American Iron and Steel Association, *Bulletin*, xxx, 52, Mar. 1, 1896; xxxii, 99, July 1, 1898; xxxvi, 26, Feb. 25, 1902; xlii, 41, May 1, 1908; *Mineral Industry*, xx, 441; *Iron Age*, xciv, 196, July 23, 1914.

CHAPTER VI

MISCELLANEOUS FEATURES OF THE IRON AND STEEL INDUSTRY

Rolling Mills, 84. Foundries, 85. Forging, 85. Labor Conditions, 86. Pools and Consolidations, 87. General Organization, 89. Production Costs, 91.

ROLLING MILLS

Before the end of the century most rolling mills were equipped to handle steel. In fact one minor cause for the rapid displacement of rolled iron by steel was that the increasing use of the latter made it difficult to secure scrap entirely free from that metal. Between one-half and three-quarters of the wrought-iron tonnage was made by busheling and rerolling scrap. Since the latter almost invariably contained pieces of steel, which it was impossible to eliminate by any sufficiently inexpensive means, the product resisted rust less effectively than either wrought iron or steel alone, and therefore lacked the very quality for which the former was sought.

Steel rolling made rapid progress during this period. In 1894 the Wellman Iron and Steel mills at Chester, Pennsylvania, rolled a plate more than 37 feet long and 11 feet wide and 1.25 inches thick, which was supposed to be larger than any other works in the world except those of the Krupps at Essen could produce. Chester was the center of the principal platemaking district of the United States. This manufacture had been an established industry since the beginning of the century at Coatsville, on the neighboring Brandywine, where the first boiler plates produced in the United States were made. As recently as 1900 the two works at Coatsville were capable of producing one-third of all the plates rolled in America.

This change from wrought iron to steel for rolled products, which began with the use of Bessemer steel for rails before 1870, worked a revolution in that branch of industry. Indeed, the change from iron to steel itself was facilitated and encouraged by the fact that steel could be rolled more easily than iron. With the perfection of the reversing engine of great power, the three-high mill, which had been introduced at Cambria half a century before, was abandoned by many works, which returned to the improved two-high mill. Then came the electric motor to speed up this transition. In 1912 steam turbines were employed at Reading to drive rolling mills.[1] Meanwhile the whole lay-out of these mills was revolutionized by the introduction of new machinery, such as the electric traveling crane. Toward the close of the period we are describing the focus of interest in

---

[1] American Iron and Steel Association, *Bulletin*, XXVIII, 205, Sept. 12, 1894; XXXVII, 170, Nov. 25, 1903; *Iron Age*, XCIV, 1221, Nov. 26, 1914.

metallurgical progress shifted to some extent from mechanical devices to methods of bettering the composition of steel and perfecting control over heat treatment. In the sheet industry great advances were made in respect to surface finish. These apparently minor improvements enabled plates to be employed for uses for which they would have been considered undesirable or entirely inappropriate ten years before.[2]

FOUNDRIES

Many labor-saving devices were introduced in American foundries at this period, and our works were probably in advance of any others in the world in this respect. Mechanical sand mixers and temperers, sand conveyers, tumbling barrels, pneumatic hammers and chippers, sand blast for cleaning, and molding machines lightened labor, increased output and tended to standardize both processes and products. Molding machines began to be sold commercially about 1895. They soon developed into well-known types and keen competition arose between rival manufacturers.[3]

The steel-casting industry went through the same experience in respect to combinations as the producers of raw and half-finished products. In 1893 six plants in New York, Pennsylvania and Ohio were united as the American Steel Casting Company. This was the oldest trust in the steel business. It specialized in the manufacture of open-hearth steel castings, which at that time were just beginning to play an important part in the foundry market.[4] Five years later 47 open-hearth plants in the United States were prepared to make steel castings. The number rose to 56 three years later, and the capacity of many of the old plants had been increased. Many small Bessemer plants were also engaged in this business. Some 14 crucible steel works likewise manufactured castings. In 1902 the American Steel Foundries Company was chartered in New Jersey to acquire not only the works of the American Steel Castings Company, but also five large independent plants. It was estimated at this time that the foundry capacity of the United States had grown 30 per cent within two years. In fact, 20 new foundry companies were organized in 1902, adding more than one-fourth to the country's existing facilities for producing castings.[5]

FORGING

An equally spectacular increase occurred in the use of steel forgings, and the method of their manufacture was completely transformed during the period we are describing. In 1899 a shaft weighing 85 tons was forged

[2] *Iron Age*, XCIV, 37, July 2, 1914; cf., *Cassier's Magazine*, XXII, 567–582; Sept. 1902; *Engineering Magazine*, XI, 266–267, May 1896.
[3] *Engineering Magazine*, VIII, 1058, Mar. 1895; *Cassier's Magazine*, XXI, 292–305, Feb. 1902; *Mineral Industry*, XV, 495; *Iron Age*, XCIV, 99 July 9, 1914.
[4] American Iron and Steel Association, *Bulletin*, XXXI, 139, June 20, 1897; XXXV, 115, Aug. 10, 1901; *Commercial and Financial Chronicle*, LXX, 998, May 19, 1900.
[5] American Iron and Steel Association, *Bulletin*, XXXVI, 27, Feb. 25, 1902; XXXVI, 51, Apr. 10, 1902; XXXVI, 101, July 10, 1902; XXXVI, 125, Aug. 25, 1902; cf., *Cassier's Magazine*, XXI 292–305, Feb. 1902.

by the Bethlehem Iron Company. Not long afterward a shaft of almost equal size was forged at Milwaukee.[6] The great change in this branch of steel working, however, was the substitution of the forging press for the steam hammer. In 1893 the Bethlehem Steel Works built the largest steam hammer in the world for use in their own plant. It delivered a blow of 125 tons, and was intended to be used in making the heaviest classes of forgings produced in the world. This gigantic tool was completely supplanted, however, within two or three years by hydraulic presses, and after standing entirely idle for several seasons, it was finally scrapped nine years after its erection. It had been discovered during the interval that in forging large masses of metal the hammer failed to produce a uniform compression, and that therefore internal stresses were set up, which resulted in a tendency to form flaws in the interior of the forging. With a hydraulic press, on the other hand, the force is applied slowly and is as strong at the end of the stroke as at the beginning, so that a forging is made absolutely homogeneous, the interior being as thoroughly and effectively worked as the exterior. Furthermore, the press is a more convenient tool to operate and more cheaply maintained than a hammer.[7]

Another advantage was the greater exactness with which pressed forgings could be produced. For instance in 1893 the Niagara Falls Power Company required for its dynamos immense steel rings of absolute uniform density, having a diameter of more than 11 feet, a width exceeding 4 feet, and a thickness of more than 5 inches. Such a forging could not have been made satisfactorily even under the most powerful hammer in existence; but it was successfully produced by a Whitworth forging press. The problem and its solution appeared almost simultaneously.[8]

LABOR CONDITIONS

The labor history of the iron and steel industry between 1893 and the outbreak of the World War is marked by one historic strike. But upon the whole, this was a period of peace in industrial relations as compared with the previous two decades. The rapid introduction of labor-saving devices enabled iron and steel makers to reduce materially the number of employes per unit of output and to increase the compensation of those who remained. During the vicissitudes of the nineties reluctantly accepted reductions of wages and voluntary increases of wages accompanied in fairly regular rhythm the ups and downs of the industry.[9] Some reductions met the resistance of the workers and strikes—in nearly all cases unsuccessful—

---

[6] American Iron and Steel Association, *Bulletin*, XXXIII, 25, Feb. 15, 1899; XXXVI, 51, Apr. 10, 1902.
[7] American Iron and Steel Association, *Bulletin*, XXXVI, 65, May 10, 1902; cf., *Cassier's Magazine*, X, 83–98, June 1896.
[8] Franklin Institute, *Journal*, Jan. 1900; quoted in American Iron and Steel Association, *Bulletin*, XXXIV, 18, Jan. 22, 1900.
[9] E. g., American Iron and Steel Association, *Bulletin*, XXVII, 293, Oct. 4, 1893; XXIX, 157, July 10, 1895; XXXI, 133, June 10, 1897; XXXI, 139, June 20, 1897; XXXIV, 5, Jan. 1, 1900; Popplewell, *Iron and Steel Production in America*, 103.

ensued. During 1900 and 1901, however, the Amalgamated Association of Iron and Steel Workers was in almost constant conflict with the biggest employers in the industry; and the critical struggle of 1901 which finally wrecked the Amalgamated Association was not fought over wage rates or hours of labor. Had these issues been to the fore, presumably the differences would have been adjusted by arbitration, as had so often occurred before. The strike of 1901 was for the uniform closed shop throughout the plants of the United States Steel Corporation. Some of the shops were already union; others were non-union. After a protracted fight the men were defeated, and the open shop which has continued down to the present day was established throughout all the Company's works.[10]

POOLS AND CONSOLIDATIONS

We have already traced the growth of concentration in the iron and steel industry as illustrated in the history of the largest individual firms and combinations formed during this period; and we have pointed out that there probably was a direct connection between the era of abnormally low prices that began with the depression of 1893 and 1894 and the movement to control competition by giant corporations. This had been attempted much earlier, as we have seen, by temporary pools and agreements. The same devices were resorted to soon after the panic. In 1895, for instance, the Western Bar Iron Manufacturers' Association was organized at Cleveland to regulate prices in this field of trade.[11] In the autumn of the same year the Merchant Bar Iron Association and the Eastern Bar Iron Association took the occasion to form a national union of bar-iron manufacturers, largely with the same object in view. In 1896 a steel-billet pool was formed in the Pittsburgh district, which seems to have controlled for a time practically the entire billet output of that region so far as it found its way into the general market. The wire-nail manufacturers also had an association, but it was dissolved after an existence of less than eighteen months.[12] A succession of steel-rail pools was formed, as we have seen earlier. It was charged that the life of these associations was always dependent upon the support they received from the Carnegie interests, and that the reason the rail pools were not revived after the last failure in 1897 was the fact that the bigger producers, like the Carnegies, found that such agreements no longer served their purpose.[13] In 1898 the Bessemer pig-iron producers of the Central West agreed to bank their furnaces for thirty days between the first of June and the end of July, and each maker deposited $25,000 as a guaranty of good faith with the trustees of the pool. About the same

[10] American Iron and Steel Association, *Bulletin*, xxxv, 110, July 25, 1901; Tarbell, *Life of Judge Gary*, 152–160.
[11] American Iron and Steel Association, *Bulletin*, xxix, 77 Apr., 1, 1895.
[12] American Iron and Steel Association, *Bulletin*, xxix, 245, Nov. 1, 1895; xxx, 149, July 1, 1896; xxx, 277, Dec. 10, 1896.
[13] Singer, *Die Amerikanische Stahlindusrie und der Weltkrieg*, 63; *Commercial and Financial Chronicle*, LXIV, 302, Feb. 13, 1897.

time, however a combination of Southern pig-iron makers, formed at Birmingham, collapsed after a brief existence of two months, through the withdrawal of one of its principal members.[14] In commenting upon the failure of the Non-Bessemer Pig Iron Association at this time, the *Iron Age* said:

"The truth is that this country is too big to permit of an agreement of any kind being reached and respected by pig-iron manufacturers. There are too many of them, their interests are not identical, their financial necessities differ, and mutual confidence must always be lacking."[15]

There was also a Bessemer Pig Iron Association embracing the blast furnaces of the Mahoning and Shenango Valleys, and there were other local groups of a similar kind. None of these associations of furnacemen, however, except the first mentioned, has left a record of significant success.[16] In 1903 the independent sheet manufacturers of Youngstown and vicinity formed a permanent organization.[17]

In a word, voluntary associations held together by more or less informal agreements or short-term contracts, often ambiguous in their interpretation and possessing no adequate sanction for their enforcement, never proved of more than temporary and questionable benefit to their members. Evidently a firmer and more permanent type of combination was destined to deal with the problem which these looser associations had failed to solve. We have already seen the outcome in the organization of the great Tidewater Steel companies, and the still more gigantic combinations in the Pittsburgh and Chicago districts. At the same time that these big corporations were taking shape, a number of combinations, some of which have already been mentioned, were formed by producers of finished goods. Among these horizontal trusts were the American Steel Hoop Company organized in 1899 with a capital of $33,000,000; a consolidation of a number of cast-iron pipe foundries the same year under the name of The United States Cast Iron Pipe and Foundry Company; the American Iron and Steel Manufacturing Company, which was a combination of several iron companies principally engaged in making nuts, bolts and rivets at Lebanon and Reading, Pennsylvania; and the American Sheet Steel Company with a capital stock of $52,000,000, which was national in extent. This Company owned 27 plants in Pennsylvania, Ohio, Indiana and Kansas, and almost immediately made an agreement with the Republic Iron and Steel Company, the great rolling-mill combination which we have previously described, whereby it withdrew from the merchant bar trade and the latter withdrew from sheet production. This led to an exchange of plants, the

---

[14] American Iron and Steel Association, *Bulletin*, xxxii, 69, May 1, 1898; xxxii, 93, June 15, 1898.
[15] Quoted in American Iron and Steel Association, *Bulletin*, xxxii, 108, July 15, 1898.
[16] American Iron and Steel Association, *Bulletin*, xxxii, 165, Nov. 1, 1898; xl, 13, Jan. 10, 1906.
[17] American Iron and Steel Association, *Bulletin*, xxxvii, 141, Sept. 25, 1903.

sheet mills of the Republic Iron and Steel Company passing to the American Sheet Steel Company, and the bar mills of the latter company passing to the former corporation. About the same time a smaller combination, the National Roofing and Corrugating Company, was formed, including a majority of the manufacturers of metal roofing, metal ceiling, eaves-troughs and conductors, most of whose plants were in the Middle West. The principal product of the Company was metal ceilings, the manufacturing of which was a comparatively new industry, having been introduced into the United States from Germany in the middle eighties.[18] About this time the American Locomotive Company, a $50,000,000 trust which owned every important locomotive plant in the United States and Canada except one, purchased through the International Power Company, a sort of catalytic corporation that bought up independent companies and then combined them, a controlling interest in the Alabama Consolidated Coal and Iron Company, thus becoming a producer of part of the raw materials it used.[19]

Meanwhile, local combinations were springing up here and there. In 1900 the three largest producers of pig iron for the general market at Buffalo consolidated under the name of the Buffalo Union Furnace Company, owning three stacks, all new and of large capacity, one of which made charcoal iron. A little earlier a group of four rolling mills at Bridgeport and Mingo Junction, Ohio, was consolidated under a single company, which was engaged largely in the manufacture of tin plates. As recently as 1911 the Pacific Coast Steel Company at San Francisco acquired several plants in California, Washington and Oregon.[20]

GENERAL ORGANIZATION

During this period a number of associations were organized in different branches of iron and steel manufacturing for promoting the general welfare of the industry. These societies were semi-social and semi-technical. They held conventions at which papers upon subjects of professional interest to the members were read by experts in various fields of manufacturing and merchandizing, and in some cases they exchanged statistical information and maintained trade and technical publications. The charcoal-iron manufacturers had such a society; the American Foundrymen's Association, organized in 1896, had a similar purpose, and in 1908 all branches of the industry were brought together for the purposes just mentioned in the American Iron and Steel Institute, which grew out of the Old Iron and Steel Association originally organized in 1855 and revived in 1864.[21]

[18] American Iron and Steel Association, *Bulletin*, xxxiii, 38, Mar. 1, 1899; xxxiii, 75, May 1, 1899; xxxiii, 138, Aug. 15, 1899; xxxiv, 45, Mar. 1, 1900; xxxiv, 74, Apr. 15, 1900; xxxiv, 133, Aug. 1, 1900; xxxiv, 149, Sept. 1, 1900; xxxiv, 165, Oct. 1, 1900; *Commercial and Financial Chronicle*, lxix, 227, July 29, 1899; lxx, 332, Feb. 17, 1900; lxxi, 183, July 28, 1900.
[19] American Iron and Steel Association, *Bulletin*, xxxix, 38, Mar. 1, 1905.
[20] American Iron and Steel Association, *Bulletin*, xxxi, 141, June 20, 1897; xxxiv, 189, Nov. 15, 1900; xlv, 78, Aug. 1, 1911.
[21] American Iron and Steel Association, *Bulletin*, xxx, 125, June 1, 1896; xlii, 35, Apr. 15, 1908; xliv, 108, Nov. 1, 1910; xlvi, 119, Dec. 31, 1912.

Naturally centralized control was accompanied by both geographical and plant centralization. Not only did the larger enterprises grow at the expense of smaller producers, but in many instances they bought up and dismantled minor competing plants. This movement toward concentration was more rapid in the United States than in either Great Britain or Germany, and it expressed itself not only in large plants, but also in the greater average size of iron and steel furnaces, rolling mills and other producing units.[22] At the same time, however, primitive plants and primitive organizations survived into the present century. In 1897 a charcoal furnace in Ohio still combined iron making with farming and grazing, as had colonial furnace owners two-hundred years before. Presumably this furnace frequently blew out during the hot season, leaving its laborers free to work in the fields.[23]

Commenting upon the general organization of the American Iron and Steel industry in 1902, the British Iron Trade Commission pointed out that American companies were managed by "industrial men," and not by "commercial men" as in Great Britain and Germany. They attributed the rapid technical progress of the industry in our country in part to this condition. Commercial men are inclined to avoid present expenditures, while industrial men are "mainly concerned in economizing production almost regardless of present outlay." The same Commission noted that furnaces and foundries in the United States were often conducted as separate establishments, because it was impossible to predict what kind of iron would be run from a furnace until it was examined cold. Indeed, a German observer noted as recently as 1915 the important place that merchant furnaces filled in our iron economy. At the close of the period we are discussing, they produced more than 8,500,000 tons of the 30,000,000 tons of pig iron made in the United States. The remainder was made by firms that worked the product of their smelting furnaces directly into steel and steel products. In Germany a far greater proportion of the iron produced was made in works that converted the iron directly into steel castings and finished or semi-finished shapes.

The fact that these merchant furnaces continued important was due partly to the wider dispersion of our iron industry, to the great distances separating fuel and ore in many instances, and to the larger area served by producers. These merchant furnaces sold some of their output to the great steel works, which made most of their own pig iron, and thus formed an elastic reserve upon which the larger companies drew in time of maximum production. Still the growth of the basic open-hearth industry tended to lessen the importance of merchant furnaces as a source of supply for steel makers, because other reserves—especially scrap—were drawn upon to the utmost in periods of great activity.[24]

[22] *Mineral Industry*, IV, 389; VI, 354; American Iron and Steel Association, *Bulletin*, XXXII, 35, Mar. 1, 1898.
[23] American Iron and Steel Association, *Bulletin*, XXXI, 218, Oct. 1, 1897.
[24] British Iron Trade Commission, *Report*, 61, 236; Singer, *Die Amerikanische Stahlindustrie und der Weltkrieg*, 65–66.

PRODUCTION COSTS

Between the crisis of 1893 and the World War iron was made cheaper and was sold cheaper than at any other time in our history. Indeed, it is not unlikely that these years marked a turning point in cost and price conditions and inaugurated a new period in which the cheapening of processes of production through technical improvements and quantity output will not reduce costs rapidly enough to compensate for the growing scarcity of high-grade ores and the increased demands of labor.

The era of low prices after the panic of 1893 enabled the United States for the first time since its existence as an independent nation to export iron and steel extensively. Until 1893 our foreign sales formed a rather negligible item in the iron trade of the world. With the development of the Mesabi district, the rapid introduction of labor-saving devices and other furnace economies, and with the fall of wages and general operating costs that followed the panic, the United States was able to produce iron for less than any of its great competitors. In 1899 Charles M. Schwab, at that time President of the Carnegie Steel Company, stated in a letter to H. C. Frick, that the Edgar Thomson Works in Braddock, Pennsylvania, could manufacture steel rails for $12 a ton, or $7 a ton less than the cost of making similar rails in England. Although these figures were disputed later, Mr. Carnegie reaffirmed them in 1903:

"There have been made and sold without loss hundreds of thousands of tons of four-inch steel billets at three pounds for a penny. Surely, gentlemen, the limit has been reached here. It is doubtful if ever a lower price can be reached for steel. On the contrary, there is every indication that period after period the price of steel is to become dearer owing to the lack of raw materials. To make that three pounds of steel at least nine pounds of material were required— three pounds of coke, mined and transported sixty miles to the works, one and one-half pounds of lime, mined and transported one hundred and fifty miles, and four and one-half pounds of iron stone, mined at Lake Superior, and transported nine hundred miles to Pittsburgh, being transferred twice, once from the cars to the ship and again from the ship into the railway cars. . . . This was done during the day of depression, when everything was at the lowest."[25]

Notwithstanding this remarkably low cost of production, considering the great amount of transportation involved in that item, American iron and steel did not flood foreign markets. This was partly because the cost of carriage from the producing centers to tidewater added materially to export prices and partly because, averaged over a period of years, the effects of high capitalization, high wages, and perhaps an accumulation of minor burdens on production and marketing natural in a new country where petty economies have never been considered, tended to push up normal prices even though it was possible to produce at remarkably low cost in periods of emergency. Furthermore, American steel makers always had a

---

[25] Singer, *Die Amerikanische Stahlindustrie und der Weltkrieg*, 53–54; American Iron and Steel Association, *Bulletin*, XXXVII, 137, Sept. 25, 1903.

vast protected market at their door, ready to take the greater share of their output at liberal rates. Last of all, primary costs of production, such as the expense of mining coal and making coke, were rising. The cream of the newly discovered ore ranges had been skimmed off, and furnaces were compelled to use leaner ores. Speculation in ore lands added further to the capital burden that must be borne by raw materials. All these influences began to make themselves felt during the opening years of the twentieth century.

The period of minimum costs was probably in 1897 and 1898. A British expert after studying conditions in our country reported in 1897 that Bessemer pig could be made in America under the most favorable circumstances for $2.50 or $3 a ton less than in Great Britain, and that the difference in the cost of producing steel was equally in favor of the United States. In some cases the labor cost of a ton of billets or rails was from one-fourth to one-third less than the lowest labor costs in England or Scotland, although wages were materially higher in the United States. Coke cost about one-third in Pittsburgh what it cost in Great Britain. Though Lake Superior ores were transported a long distance, the cost of carriage was not materially greater than that of Spanish ores imported into Wales, which in a way controlled the level of the ore market in England itself. In 1898 a British observer reported, on the basis of a labor comparison of production costs in Europe and the United States, that England could make iron cheaper than any of her continental competitors, but that the cost of fuel was less in America than in any European country, and that though the cost of iron ores was more nearly the same in England than the United States, the total cost of making pigs was less in our country than anywhere else in the world. A ton of iron according to this comparison, which did not take into consideration depreciation and renewals, could be made for less than $9.50 at Pittsburgh, while it cost to produce about $12 in Great Britain, nearly $13 in Germany, a shade more than this in Belgium, and considerably higher—approaching $14—in France.[26]

This represented a radical revolution within a generation. During the Civil War it had cost about $75 a ton to make crucible steel in the United States. The greater part of this charge was represented by the item of labor. At the close of the century the labor cost of making crucible steel in America did not exceed $2.50 a ton. Within twenty-five years the cost of Lake Superior ore and of fuel had declined one-half, and the labor cost of making a ton of pig iron had declined with equal rapidity. At the earlier period profits, especially on ore, were several times as high as in 1900. Large-scale production and the recovery of by-products also helped to account for these declining charges.[27]

[26] American Iron and Steel Association, *Bulletin*, XXXI, 249, Nov. 10, 1897; XXXII, 3, Jan. 1 1898; cf. Popplewell, *Iron and Steel Production in America*, 86–87.
[27] American Iron and Steel Association, *Bulletin*, XXXII, 185, Dec. 1, 1898.

In 1899 an American metallurgical engineer ascertained from a comparison of statistics from identical furnaces that at a typical establishment in the South the following changes had occurred between 1889 and 1898: increase in output, 68 per cent; decrease in fuel cost per ton, 36 per cent; decrease in fuel consumption per ton, 9 per cent; decrease in cost of ore 21 per cent; decrease in cost of limestone, 60 per cent; decrease in cost of labor, 48 per cent. The only offset against this was the item including maintenance, general office expenses and taxes and insurance, which had increased 13 per cent. Summarizing all the items and giving proper weight to each in the total, the cost of making a ton of iron at this furnace had declined 36.6 per cent. During the same period, however, the selling price of iron at the furnace had fallen 38.8 per cent. This furnace was selected because it was situated in the immediate vicinity of its raw materials and freight played a minor part in its production costs. The change in the labor factor in production, at least as measured in terms of human effort, is indicated by the fact that the average annual output of iron and steel per wage-earner in the United States rose from 56.7 tons in 1899 to 74.3 tons in 1914.

Transportation charges by land and by water had fallen with equal rapidity. At one of the best furnaces in the North during the same period, output had risen 63 per cent, fuel consumption had fallen 3 per cent, while ore consumption had risen nearly 4 per cent. There had been heavy declines in wages and costs of raw material, so that the total cost of production had declined over 34 per cent. A similar study of costs at other furnaces and in other branches of iron and steel making gave approximately the same results.[28]

[28] *Commercial and Financial Chronicle*, LXVIII, 402–403, Mar. 4, 1899; Bureau of the Census, *Manufactures, 1914*, II, 229.

CHAPTER VII

COMMERCIAL FEATURES OF THE IRON AND STEEL INDUSTRIES

Low Prices, 94. Price Recovery of 1899, 98. Some Causes of Price Instability in America, 99. The New Century's Prosperous Beginning, 101. Depression of 1907, 104. The Pre-War Dullness, 105. Marketing Methods, 107. Our Foreign Iron Trade, 108. International Comparisons, 115.

LOW PRICES

The statistics of iron and steel production given in a preceding chapter measure as accurately perhaps as any other group of data the fluctuations of the industry between 1893 and 1914. The conditions they indicate are substantially corroborated by price statistics and general descriptions of market and trade conditions from year to year.

World prices did not reach the lowest level for the decade during or immediately following the financial panic of 1893. The year after the crisis, to be sure, the *London Economist* reported that the general price level was "the lowest that has been recorded for the past fifty years;"[1] but this was only preliminary to a still further decline. In 1893 Lake Superior ore had fallen to $3.75 a ton delivered at Lake Erie ports, which was at that time the lowest price ever known. The following season it fell to $2.75, with a result that the market for these ores extended farther East. Bessemer pig iron sold at the end of 1894 at $10.24 a ton.[2] It was reported from Birmingham that southern foundry iron could be made with washed coke for less than $6 a ton.[3] On the New York Metal Exchange in midsummer charcoal iron was selling for $7 and $8 a ton, plus transportation charges from the furnace.[4] Naturally the price of steel followed the price of iron. In 1892 a steel-billet pool was formed to hold prices at $25. Less than two years later the price was between $16 and $17.[5]

The effect of the panic recorded itself in prices somewhat later than in market demands, output and employment conditions, which were probably at their worst, averaging these three elements of the industry together, in the autumn of 1893 and the early winter of the following year. At Pittsburgh out of nearly 60,000 men normally employed in the principal iron-working industries of the city, only about half were on the payrolls in January 1894. Between the fall of 1892 and of 1893 the number of men employed in the six largest rolling mills at Youngstown fell from 6,700 to

---

[1] Quoted in American Iron and Steel Association, *Bulletin*, XXVIII, 155, July 18, 1894.
[2] *Mineral Industry*, III, 371.
[3] *Iron Age* quoted in *Manufacturers' Record*, XXV, 322, June 15, 1894.
[4] American Iron and Steel Association, *Bulletin*, XXVIII, 141, June 30, 1894.
[5] *Mineral Industry*, II, 361; cf., American Iron and Steel Association, *Bulletin*, XXIX, 4, Jan. 2, 1895.

less than 500. Never in the history of the American iron trade, according to current reports, were there so few furnaces in operation as in October. Less than half of the furnace and rolling mill capacity was employed, and the steel rail mills, which were hardest hit, were running at only one-fifth of their capacity. The low prices just mentioned in 1894 were concurrent with a slight improvement in employment and production figures. This price decline was general throughout all branches of the iron and steel market. For instance, old iron rails, which were already becoming rare, particularly in the East, and were in demand for special uses, fell to $12.50 a ton in March 1894, or to about half the price for which they sold in 1892.[6]

By the autumn of 1894 the situation, except as to prices, had again completely changed. Within the area of production of cheap pig iron from Lake Superior ores and Connellsville coke, the country's furnace capacity was practically all employed. Very few modern plants were out of blast at Buffalo, Pittsburgh, in the Mahoning and Shenango Valleys, or in the Wheeling and upper Ohio region. This revival in output was in the face of a practically stagnant market for rails and railway equipment, and was conditional upon the very lowness of prices that was so marked a feature of this period; for the cheapness of iron and steel was rapidly extending their use in new directions.[7] Nonetheless, producers remained timid, doubtless because they felt that the market remained too sensitive to tolerate an increase of prices that would have restored their old hopefulness and prosperity. After the depth of reaction that year, however, a gradual recovery, delayed by currency uncertainties, ensued, so that by the middle of 1895 confidence was restored and there was a regular boom in demand. A speculative market was created for billets and Bessemer pig, the former rising from $14.75 in January to $24.50 the following September, while Bessemer pig rose from $9.88 to $17.25. Naturally, this sky-rocketing was followed by a sudden recession, though by no means to the low level of the previous year.[8]

Meanwhile, the general level of prices showed no sign of improvement. The average for staple commodities was the lowest ever known. Prior to 1893 the minimum price level, according to Dunn and Company's index number for the period since 1860, had been reached in 1887, when prices were less than 74 per cent of those for the same articles in the same markets in 1860. During the panic this average fell to 72.76 per cent. It continued to sag, and at the close of 1894 was at 68.73 per cent. The phenomenally

[6] *Commercial and Financial Chronicle*, LVII, 393, Sept. 9, 1893; American Iron and Steel Association, *Bulletin*, XXVII, 269, Sept. 6 and 13, 1893; XXVII, 297, Oct. 11, 1893; XXVII, 308, Oct. 18, 1893; XXVIII, 21, Jan. 20, 1894; XXVIII, 50, Mar. 7, 1894.
[7] *Iron Age* quoted in American Iron and Steel Association, *Bulletin*, XXVIII, 260, Nov. 14, 1894; *Commercial and Financial Chronicle*, LX, 151–152, Jan. 26, 1895.
[8] American Iron and Steel Association, *Bulletin*, XXIX, 173, Aug. 1, 1895; XXIX, 204, Sept. 10, 1895; *Mineral Industry*, IV, 399–400.

low prices of iron that year were attributed partly to the low cost of ores; but during 1895 ore rates steadily advanced.[9]

A competent review of the iron trade the following year contained this observation:

"There has been no year on record when pools and combinations had so strongly marked and unfavorable an effect as during 1896."[10]

Other contemporary authorities referred to the iron and steel industries as in the most demoralized condition in their history. So marked was the depression that in the midst of the season twelve big steamers went out of the ore-carrying trade and were tied up for the remainder of the year. The docks at Lake Erie ports were piled high with ore that could not be sold. Several of the Carnegie plants shut down in September, owing to scarcity of orders.[11] This sudden cessation of activity was attributed largely to currency uncertainties, accentuated by the Presidential campaign. The pools, to which reference has been made, failed to stand up under the strain. Late in 1896 the wire-nail pool came to an end and prices dropped rapidly; the steel-billet pool was terminated, and steel billets at once fell several dollars a ton; steel-rail makers were forced to follow suit, and in February 1897 occurred one of the most sensational and least expected events in the iron trade for many years. The steel-rail pool was suddenly dissolved and the price of standard rails fell within a week from $25 to $17 a ton. In May the beam pool, which had been revived in December 1897, went to pieces with a similar break in prices.

In summing up the causes of this demoralization, James M. Swank, speaking for the American Iron and Steel Association, said:

"Some of these causes may be occult and intangible, as industrial and commercial influences often are, but one cause that is plainly visible is distrust of the country's future in many financial circles at home and abroad . . . while another cause has been operative for many years, certainly since 1890, and may briefly be defined to be the pressure upon prices and profits of a capacity of production in mining, manufactures and agriculture that is greatly in excess of our consuming capacity, even in so-called good times."[12]

As earlier noted, this era of low prices encouraged exports of iron and steel and its manufactures, while imports declined. The falling off of the latter was partly due to the decreased demand for foreign tin plates, but the increase of the domestic market thus implied and the growth of exports did not noticeably relieve the excess of iron and steel produced at home. In 1896 some 40,000 tons of Southern pig iron were sold in England at 38

---

[9] American Iron and Steel Association, *Bulletin*, XXIX, 19, Jan. 18, 1895; XXX, 116, May 20, 1896; *Iron Age*, LV, 483, Mar. 7, 1895; *Mineral Industry*, IV, 405; *Commercial and Financial Chronicle*, LXII, 157–159, Jan. 25, 1896.
[10] *Mineral Industry*, V, 327–349.
[11] American Iron and Steel Association, *Bulletin*, XXX, 181, Aug. 10, 1896; XXX, 189, Aug. 20, 1896; XXX, 205, Sept. 10, 1986.
[12] American Iron and Steel Association, *Bulletin*, XXXI, 124, June 1, 1897.

shillings a ton delivered at Liverpool. In 1897 a small lot of Birmingham iron was sold in the domestic market as low as $5.50 a ton, though this was probably under the price at which a larger quantity could have been bought.[13] The result of this new period of abnormally low prices was not only to stimulate exports, but to encourage railroads to make liberal purchases in spite of their still embarrassed finances. Furnaces and rolling mills seized hopefully upon the promise of better times following McKinley's election and overstocked the market. Thus production, anticipating a revival of demand, depressed prices to the point where they irresistibly attracted buyers. Yet in July a single iron firm bought 100,000 tons of pigs from the Tennessee Coal, Iron and Railroad Company for deliveries extending over several months at prices ranging from $5.75 and $6.25 a ton net at the furnace for foundry irons of different grades. Part of this was for export to Europe. It is significant that even at a time when such prices were possible, our pig-iron output was approaching a million tons a month. Indeed, 1897 was characterized as a year of large output and of increasing consumption, but of low prices and free competition.[14]

The following year opened with a more hopeful spirit. In April 1898, representatives of pig-iron interests from the South and West gathered at Pittsburgh for the purpose of fixing the prices of non-Bessemer iron, but failed to come to an agreement. The outbreak of the War with Spain a few months later brought the steel makers of Pennsylvania large orders from the War Department, and by the end of March the *Iron Age* reported that there never was a time when, generally speaking, the iron and steel plants of the United States were so fully employed. Even some of the largest producers had been obliged to go into the open market to supply their own needs for finished products. But while Government orders piled in upon manufacturers, building operations were for a time checked or suspended, and some of the leading steel makers doubted whether the total effect of hostilities was beneficial to the trade. The silver issue and the tariff issue were thought to be disposed of for a considerable time to come, in view of the new problems likely to face the country when the War was over, and this was regarded as of hopeful portent for the business world.[15]

By the autumn of 1898 the pig-iron and steel market were reported to be "getting excited," and cool-headed buyers and sellers were urging caution. At the same time considerable foreign orders were being placed, among the most notable at this date being a single purchase of 33,000 tons of steel plates for the great water pipe 380 miles long from the coastal district to the gold fields of Western Australia.[16] In general, the year was one

[13] *Mineral Industry*, v, 339–342; *Manufacturers' Record*, xxxi, 239, Apr. 30, 1897.
[14] *Commercial and Financial Chronicle*, LXIV, 1110, June 12, 1897; LXV, 948, Nov. 20, 1897; American Iron and Steel Association, *Bulletin*, xxxi, 157, July 10, 1897; *Mineral Industry*, vi, 410.
[15] American Iron and Steel Association, *Bulletin*, xxxii, 40, May 1, 1898; xxxii, 78, May 15, 1898; xxxii, 84, June 1, 1898; xxxii, 125, Aug. 15, 1898.
[16] *Iron Age*, LXII, 18 & 25, Dec. 15, 1898.

of active business at prices that fluctuated little, and the war alone was not responsible for this. Two years of good crops and steady recovery had produced their results.[17] The lowest price for steel billets ever recorded, $13.85, was in May 1897. Steel rails were down to $17 and $18. Such prices were the result of world-wide conditions. They were one of the incentives in America for the formation of the great combinations in the iron and steel industry that we have already described.[18]

PRICE RECOVERY OF 1899

An abrupt change for the better occurred in 1899 when prices covered a greater range than had ever been known before since there was an organized iron market in the United States. All grades of pig iron and varieties of finished steel sold in December for more than double the prices quoted the previous January. The rise began in December 1898 and was accelerated by an excited market the following February; then after a period of slackness there was another quick ascent which by the end of June brought Bessemer pig iron, for instance, to quotations just double those at the beginning of the year. Steel billets rose from $16.25 a ton in December 1898 to $33.50 a ton the following July. Meanwhile, European orders continued in spite of these prices, the active demand for iron, beyond productive capacity, being world-wide. By October Bessemer pig iron was $24 a ton. Steel billets were $43 a ton at the mills and steel rails $33. The Federal Steel Company bought 80,000 tons of pig iron in the autumn of 1899 at $22.50 a ton. It had purchased iron a year before for $9.50 a ton. This advance ceased, with a slight recession in prices in case of some commodities, at the end of the year, but the boom, as we shall see, was destined to continue.[19]

Naturally this prosperity was due to an exigent market. In the first place, as just observed, prosperity was world-wide. The great colonial powers and countries having undeveloped territory within their immediate frontiers competed with each other in their haste and eagerness to exploit their natural resources. Our own railways, which had made good profits in 1898, looked forward to a heavier business in the future and placed large orders for rails and equipment. The United States and other Governments were buying great quantities of steel for armaments and war vessels. An active call for ocean and fresh-water tonnage created an unusual demand from the shipyards. Building was active throughout the country. This comparatively new market was calling for steel in quantities that alone would have been able to sustain the prosperity of the industry a few years previously.[20] Protectionists were careful to point out that the rapid rise

[17] *Engineering and Mining Journal*, Jan. 7, 1899.
[18] American Iron and Steel Association, *Bulletin*, XXXII, 124, Aug. 15, 1898.
[19] *Mineral Industry*, VIII, 359; American Iron and Steel Association, *Bulletin*, XXXIII, 92, June 1, 1899; XXXIII, 124, July 15, 1899; XXXIII, 172, Oct. 1, 1899; XXXIII, 206, Dec. 1, 1899; *Commercial and Financial Chronicle*, LXIX, 745, Oct. 7, 1899; LXIX, 1081, Nov. 25, 1899.
[20] American Iron and Steel Association, *Bulletin*, XXXIV, 4, Jan. 1, 1900; XXXIV, 51, Mar. 10, 1900; *Commercial and Financial Chronicle*, LXVIII, 299, Feb. 18, 1899.

of prices was not due to the tariff, for our exports of iron and steel continued heavier than ever before. Indeed, American makers were refusing foreign orders because their works were too fully employed to fill them.

This was also a period of industrial concentration, as we have previously mentioned. Not only were price advances among the most sensational in our industrial history, but the efforts at consolidation stimulated during the preceding era of low prices suddenly bore fruit.[21] Another new feature accompanying this revival was the conclusion of heavy long-term contracts between large corporations for the delivery of raw materials and half-finished products. For instance, the Carnegie Steel Company contracted to furnish the Pressed Steel Car Company 30,000 tons of plates a month for a period of ten years. Naturally these market conditions and the gambling spirit that was abroad in the business world at the time encouraged some purchasing and carrying of iron and steel for a strictly speculative profit; but the exigencies of the trade did not permit extensive operations of this character.[22] Minor declines occurred the following year, but prices remained higher than they had been even during the prosperous seasons immediately prior to 1899. British manufacturers were still importing pig iron from the United States, and a marked drop in quotations would presumably have led to heavy orders from that source. In any case the decline was checked by the middle of the year, when Bessemer pig prices showed signs of stabilizing around $18. At no time was there a serious check to the general prosperity of the country. The boom, which was of far larger proportions and longer continuance then even the celebrated iron and steel boom which began the latter part of 1879 and ended suddenly in 1880, was over, but a satisfactory market at remunerative prices continued.[23]

Indeed, the market had been expanding rapidly at the old price level before the leap upward in 1899. Raw materials did not fall with the decline in the price of finished products. Iron ore and coke were higher in 1900 than in 1899, and Bessemer steel rails retained their former level. In brief, this boom was distinguished from its predecessors by an unprecedented change in prices, by the sustaining of prices at a relatively high level after the apex of the boom was over, by the associated fact that foreign competition was at no time a factor in determining domestic prices or bringing the boom to an end, by a steady expansion of output, and by the rapid concentration of the industry in the hands of powerful combinations.

SOME CAUSES OF PRICE INSTABILITY IN AMERICA

Such phenomena were more marked and more significant in the iron and steel industry than in most other branches of manufacturing. The fluc-

[21] *Cf.*, Berglund, *The United States Steel Corporation*, 100–103.
[22] *Commercial and Financial Chronicle*, LXIX, 181, July 22, 1899; American Iron and Steel Association, *Bulletin*, XXXIII, 148, Sept. 1, 1899; XXXIII, 204, Dec. 1, 1899.
[23] *Mineral Industry*, IX, 393; American Iron and Steel Association, *Bulletin*, XXXIV, 86, May 1, 1900; XXXIV, 100–101, June 1, 1900; XXXIV, 148, Sept. 1, 1900.

tuations in its prosperity were perhaps more sudden and violent in the United States than in any other great industrial country. If we divide iron and steel consumption into two classes, consumption for maintenance and consumption for development, the latter was relatively more important in the domestic market of the United States than in that of any other important iron-producing nation. It is this class of consumption that always fluctuates most. When capital is abundant, business optimism prevails, and there are no artificial checks to initiative and enterprise, the demand for iron and steel for railway extensions and rolling stock, for bridges and buildings, for vessels and docks, for machinery and for other instruments to increase production, expands rapidly, as it did between 1899 and 1905. Furnaces and rolling mills are pushed to the limits of their capacity to supply this need. Such developmental uses are, of course, important in older countries like Great Britain, Belgium and Germany. Moreover, the iron and steel producers of those nations supply great quantities of development materials to less fully exploited parts of the world. But it is probable that the ratio of maintenance consumption to consumption for development was at this time higher in those countries than in the United States. In other words, the constant factors in the market there were relatively more important than in America.[24]

Whenever liquid capital showed signs of exhaustion in America, as it did after the great wave of speculation and trust promotion between 1899 and 1903, a sharp curtailment of new enterprises was certain to occur. That happened in 1904, 1908, 1911 and 1914. Statistics show, however, that the production and demand for rails was less affected at these dates than the demand and production of other finished steel products. This was due partly to the fact that our national railway system was approaching completion so far as the construction of new trunk lines and other far-reaching enterprises were concerned. In this particular respect conditions in the United States were drawing closer to the more stable conditions of Western Europe. But new fields of consumption, some of them of a strictly developmental sort, were constantly being opened to the steel makers of the United States, who were exceptionally well prepared to supply such demands on account of their experience in serving domestic consumers, and who consequently pushed their wares eagerly into the pioneer markets of other new countries and continents. Those markets, tended, however, to be somewhat more stable than those of the United States, partly because of their greater diversity, partly because they drew their capital from the great financial reservoirs of Europe, and partly because foreign marketing conditions taken as a whole were not affected by the legislative policy of any single country in the way that our domestic market for developmental machinery was affected by tariff and currency legislation in the United States.

[24] *Cf.*, Singer, *Die Amerikanische Stahlindustrie und der Weltkrieg*, 17–18.

THE NEW CENTURY'S PROSPEROUS BEGINNING

As we have just suggested, the period of good times in the steel industry lasted until late in 1904. There were temporary reactions, but none of those was serious enough to affect the general character of the period. Certain stabilizing factors were at work that had not previously existed. The influence of the United States Steel Corporation, after its formation in 1901, was thrown into the scale in favor of conservative price policies. This company was able to determine to a considerable extent the base price of Lake Superior ores, and of certain staple products like rails and billets. It was the largest individual consumer of Bessemer pig iron in the United States, buying lots of 100,000 tons at a time from the Bessemer Iron Association, and this patronage tended to extend its influence beyond the confines of its own works.[25]

In 1901 the strike of the Amalgamated Association of Steel Workers already mentioned embarrassed the industry in certain localities, but prices remained steady and production increased. Toward the close of the year a condition arose that was repeatedly to embarrass the business of the country during the following decade. This was the lack of railway facilities. When the sudden expansion of the iron trade occurred in 1899, it became manifest that the railroads, which hauled most of the raw materials it used and the finished products it produced did not have adequate equipment to perform that service satisfactorily. Heavy orders for cars and locomotives given to supply this need did not bring facilities to the point where they fully met the industry's needs for two or three years later, though meanwhile they added to the already heavy demand for iron and steel. When hundreds of new locomotives and thousands of new cars were in service, it was suddenly discovered that the railroads did not have tracks and yard facilities to accommodate their increased equipment. As a result of this transportation crisis coke and ore could not be supplied to the furnaces, and pig iron and finished products could not be delivered to customers with sufficient regularity and promptness. Furnaces were obliged to bank for want of raw materials, and customers were compelled to send abroad orders that otherwise would have been placed at home because they could not depend on deliveries from domestic producers. It was not until the spring of 1903, when the market was on the verge of another decline, that this situation was even temporarily remedied. Naturally such conditions discouraged exports, while they encouraged imports.[26]

In 1903 precisely ten years after the preceding panic, there was a marked subsidence of the boom that had then lasted more than four years. By autumn producers believed that they were facing a new depression. Labor troubles, curtailed and cancelled orders, and the symptoms of a period of

---

[25] *Cf.*, American Iron and Steel Association, *Bulletin*, xxxv, 190, Dec. 25, 1901; xxxvi, 12, Jan. 25, 1902; xxxvi, 29, Feb. 25, 1902.

[26] American Iron and Steel Association, *Bulletin*, xxxvi, 4, Jan. 10, 1902; xxxvii, 76, May 25, 1903; *Mineral Industry*, x, 384–385; xi, 374.

contracting consumption added to this pessimistic mood. The great anthracite coal strike of 1903 had left its impression. The absorption of floating capital by the big consolidations and combinations formed during the past few years was felt by investors. In order to meet foreign competition, and because production had more than overtaken consumption, prices were lowered in several districts. But the cost of raw materials did not follow the decline in finished products, especially pig iron.[27] Among the disturbing factors this year was the failure early in the season of the Consolidated Lake Superior Company, projected to manufacture iron and steel and a variety of other products at Sault Ste. Marie. Almost simultaneously the United States Shipbuilding Company collapsed, and William Cramp and Sons were forced to undergo reorganization. The dividends of the United States Steel Corporation were reduced and a dividend of its common stock was passed entirely. At the same time some business interests were inclined to attribute their troubles in part to the vigorous action that the Roosevelt Administration was taking against the trusts.[28]

Nevertheless a resumption of activity occurred early in 1904, and before the spring was well advanced a slight upward movement of prices foreshadowed a speedy return to the old prosperity. After a summer lull business again became active in the autumn months, and by October confidence was fully restored. Railways, which even now were not abreast of the country's marvelous industrial development, entered the market for large quantities of rails, bridges and equipment. Bessemer pig iron advanced between September and December from $12.69 to $16.72 a ton.[29]

At the close of 1905 the American Iron and Steel Association reported that this had been "not only the most productive and the most prosperous year in the history of the American iron trade, but the most uniformly prosperous year." Prices were kept within reasonable bounds and, indeed, the price of rails was held at the same figure as in 1904 in spite of a market that would have tolerated a decided advance. Exports were steadily increasing, rising from $128,000,000 in 1904 to $142,000,000 the following year. We shipped abroad iron and steel and its manufactures to more than five times the value of our imports.[30]

By this time the production and price of steel billets began to be recognized as a more accurate measure of the condition of the iron and steel industry than the production and price of pig iron. The four-inch billet is an American invention. It had long been recognized that a piece of crude steel with a cross-section four inches square could be put to a more varied use in the rolling of finished materials than any other form. Bil-

[27] American Iron and Steel Association, *Bulletin*, XXXII, 53, Apr. 10, 1903; XXXVII, 140, Sept. 25, 1903; XXXVII, 165, Nov. 10, 1903; *Mineral Industry*, XII, 188, 203–204.
[28] American Iron and Steel Association, *Bulletin*, XXXVI, 191, Dec. 25, 1902; XXXVII, 188, Dec. 25, 1903; XXXVIII, 162, Nov. 10, 1904.
[29] American Iron and Steel Association, *Bulletin*, XXXVIII, 13, Jan. 25, 1904; XXXVIII, 44, Mar. 25, 1904; XXXVIII, 162, Nov. 10, 1904; XXXIX, 84, June 1, 1905; XXXIX, 113, Aug. 1, 1905.
[30] American Iron and Steel Association, *Bulletin*, XL, 52, Apr. 1, 1906.

lets of various dimensions were regularly produced and dealt in, a two-inch billet being the usual size taken by wire-rod mills, and various sizes both larger and smaller than these were regularly produced; but where no size was specified, the four-inch billet was understood to be meant. Such a billet weighed roughly 150 pounds per yard.[31]

The market for billets is more uniform than the market for pig iron. The latter is sold on open quotations with different prices in different districts. Moreover, pig iron is of varying qualities and grades, sufficiently unlike each other to cause definite gradations of prices and fluctuations of demand for different qualities within a single market area. While there was no general agreement as to prices of steel products, billets were customarily sold throughout the country on fixed quotations, the Pittsburgh price being taken as a base and the freight from Pittsburgh added. In a majority of billet sales if the market declined before delivery the buyer refused to permit the shipment to be made. Since the price was uniform and well-established, mills seldom ventured to cut it. Furthermore, a general market decline was likely to impair the validity of contracts already on the books. As a rule, therefore, these mills did not cut established prices as long as they had sufficient business to operate to full capacity, even though their future orders became very light. The reverse was often the case in the pig-iron market.

The recovery of 1905 from what may be described as the gentle depression of 1903 and the previous year continued throughout 1906, which was a period of remarkable activity. Some leading steel plants started the season with orders enough on hand to employ them for more than a year. The United States Steel Corporation, which was making 35,000 tons of finished and semi-finished steel a day, had enough business booked to keep its mills in operation for seven or eight months, with new orders coming in at about 1,000 tons a day in excess of the capacity of the Corporation's plants. Naturally this led to a rapid stiffening of prices. Bessemer pig iron rose at Pittsburgh from $18 to $23.75 a ton. Steel billets rose from $26.50 to $29.50 a ton. Rails were held at their standard price of $28.[32]

The year continued uniformly prosperous throughout. Crops were good and the prices received for them satisfactory. The railroads were taxed to capacity. There was a scarcity of labor in many industries. Wages were maintained at their high level, and in many instances advanced. Exports of iron and steel and its manufactures, which had first assumed large proportions in 1904, reached a total of $172,500,000 three years later. At the same time imports of iron ore and of pig iron rose rapidly. Average quotations of iron and steel in 1907 were higher than they had been since the marked advance that terminated almost a decade of exceed-

[31] American Iron and Steel Association, *Bulletin*, XL, 83, June 15, 1906.
[32] American Iron and Steel Association, *Bulletin*, XXXIX, 113, Aug. 1, 1905; XL, 5, Jan. 15, 1906; XL, 93, July 1, 1906.

ingly low prices at the opening of the century. Steel billets averaged throughout the year over $29, approaching their record price of $30.57 in 1902. The price of rails remained at $28, and they could be purchased in the United States cheaper than anywhere else on the globe. Sales were made in Germany this year for $35 a ton, and in England for $32 a ton.[33]

DEPRESSION OF 1907

But 1906 marked the culmination of a period of prosperity that had lasted without serious interruption, despite the minor relapses mentioned, since the beginning of the century. In March and October 1907 stock-market panics occurred at New York. By midsummer the pig-iron market was duller than it had been for several years. In December the United States Steel Corporation discharged about 20,000 men, and was working only three-fourths its capacity instead of being pushed with future orders as it had been the previous season. This depression, which lasted well toward two years, resulted in the most abrupt shrinkage of production in our history. The quantity of Bessemer steel and of steel rails produced decreased 47 per cent within twelve months. A still more marked falling off was recorded in case of railway equipment, the total number of locomotives built in the United States declining from 7,098 in 1907 to 2,124 in 1908. Exports, which had approached $200,000,000 in 1907, fell to $151,000,000 the following year. In June, the United States Steel Corporation and the largest producers held a conference at which they agreed upon a radical reduction of prices.[34]

This move did not materially stimulate demand at the moment, but it may have accelerated recovery, which was proceeding slowly throughout the following season. By the autumn of 1909 demand was again abnormally active and prices had begun to rise. It was estimated in December that the various steel companies had an aggregate of more than 10,000,000 tons of orders on their books, which represented the capacity of their works for six months.[35] This prosperity was of brief duration, however, and conditions during 1910 were upon the whole less satisfactory than the previous season. Indeed, the country had not fully recovered from the effects of the secondary panic of 1907. Fear of Government intervention and control was said to be checking investments. Falling prices and a general depression in the iron and steel market continued until 1911. After a sharp break in May of that year prices reached lower levels than they had touched for many seasons. When a revival began in 1912 it was characterized at first by an expansion of production rather than by a rise of prices, which were about equal in America and Europe. Steel works were crowded to

[33] American Iron and Steel Association, *Bulletin*, XLI, 38, Apr. 1, 1907; *cf.*, Berglund, *The United States Steel Corporation*, 138.
[34] American Iron and Steel Association, *Bulletin*, XLI, 141, Dec. 1, 1907; XLII, 4, Jan. 1, 1908; XLII, 59, June 15, 1908; XLII, 75, Aug. 1, 1908; XLIII, 22, Mar. 1, 1909; XLIII, 36, May 1, 1909.
[35] *Mineral Industry*, XVIII, 415–416; American Iron and Steel Association, *Bulletin*, XLIII 98, Oct. 1, 1909.

their capacity, but Bessemer pig iron for instance, which had sold above $24 in 1907, was selling below $16, and Bessemer billets were but $24 as compared with $30 five years before. Yet the prospect for a long period of prosperity seemed bright. Prices in Germany and in England were advancing quite as rapidly as in the United States, and in some instances were higher than in this country.[36]

THE PRE-WAR DULLNESS

But this promise of settled prosperity was not fulfilled. During the first three or four months of 1913, to be sure, an active demand existed for iron and steel, and a high rate of production continued until autumn, even after buying had been sharply checked. In November and December, however, a tremendous shrinkage in output occurred. Although the period of high demand had been so brief, it stimulated construction of new plants. Additional open-hearth furnaces with a capacity of about 3,000,000 tons a year were rushed to completion, although a few months earlier iron makers were protesting that the existing capacity was in excess of any probable demand.[37]

During 1914 pig-iron prices fell more rapidly than those of steel, especially during the first weeks of the downward cycle. Basic pig which was quoted at about $13 at the furnaces, or $13.90 delivered at Pittsburgh, commanded two to three dollars more than scrap iron at that market. This was a new condition, the margin between the two ordinarily ranging below a dollar. Indeed, on rare occasions scrap had commanded more than pig. The difference was due partly to the economy of employing molten pig iron direct from the smelting furnace for making steel, partly to the fact that steel makers were producing a large share of their own pig, and partly to the policy of retrenchment enforced by the rapid lowering of prices for finished products, which caused producers to use up their stocks of ore and iron in hand, rather than spend money for raw materials.[38] Prices for iron and steel in general were not much, if any, lower than in 1913, although the year was characterized by less than normal demand. Railroads refused to buy, agricultural implement makers had overstocked, and optimism where it existed was rapidly abating when the European War came to upset all normal calculations. During the first two months of hostilities buying nearly ceased and Southern pig iron dropped below $10 a ton for the first time since 1904.[39]

Thus the period of two decades ends with a depression, relieved by no immediate promise of the extraordinary stimulation that all our metallurgical industries were soon to receive from the War abroad. The decline in trade activity that preceded the brief rise of 1912 had been a compara-

---

[36] American Iron and Steel Association, *Bulletin*, XLV, 4, Jan. 1, 1911; XLVI, 60, July 1, 1912; XLVI, 92, Oct. 1, 1912; XLVI, 101, Nov. 1, 1912.
[37] *Iron Age*, Jan. 1, 1914, cited in *Mineral Industry*, XXII, 382–383; *ibid.*, 392–394.
[38] *Iron Age*, XCIII, 782, Oct. 1, 1914.
[39] *Mineral Industry*, XXIII, 399–400.

tively long one, at least much longer than the preceding advance. The rise of 1909 lasted 8 months, the increase in production about 9 months, the subsequent sagging of prices occupied almost 2 years, while the decline in production continued for 17 months. The low points immediately prior to 1912 were July 1911 for production, and the last week in November 1911 for prices. From July to November the rate of production increased nearly 27 per cent, while prices continued to decline, the divergence reflecting a principle well-recognized in the steel trade that prices often fall when demand appears, because there are large orders in the market worth competing for.[40]

A foreign observer rated the year 1914 the most unfavorable for the American steel industry in its history, probably worse than the period following the panic of 1893. He based this opinion on the abrupt decline in output from 16,500,000 tons in the first half of 1913 to 11,750,000 tons in the second half of 1914, and the fall of the price of steel billets within a year from $28 to $20 a ton.[41] In April 1914, a compilation of cost and price statistics gathered from more than 85 per cent of the merchant pig-iron furnaces North of the Ohio indicated that their average loss on sales during February was $1.15 a ton, or over half a million dollars. The Commissioner of Corporations in his report upon the steel industry in the spring of 1913 found the average cost of making Bessemer and basic iron for the entire country to be slightly over $14 a ton. This estimate covered the five years from 1902 to 1906 inclusive, and did not include marketing costs, interests, or profits. The average selling price of iron in 1914 was $13.30 a ton. It was assumed in this computation that costs of production were quite as high as at the earlier period mentioned, since wages, fuel and other items of expense had risen enough during the interval to compensate for mechanical economies.[42]

During the depression of 1903 and 1904 the capacity of our furnaces and steel works was clearly in excess of the country's normal requirements. During the depression that began toward the close of 1907 the country was recovering from a period of obvious overbuying. In 1913 and 1914, however, capacity did not appear to be much above our normal needs, and the condition of the market during the previous period of activity had not been speculative or unhealthy. Steel could be produced more cheaply than ten or fifteen years before, because the output per unit of equipment and per man employed had greatly increased. These economies had accompanied higher prices for supplies and labor, measuring labor in terms of actual effort expended.[43]

In April 1914, not over two-thirds of the steel works' capacity of the Union was employed.[44] In the South, where exports were relied upon to

[40] *Iron Age*, XCIII, 1080–1081, Apr. 30, 1914.
[41] Singer, *Die Amerikanische Stahlindustrie und der Weltkrieg*, 11.
[42] *Iron Age*, XLIII, 1072, Apr. 30, 1914.
[43] *Iron Age*, XCIII, 912, Apr. 9, 1914.
[44] *Iron Age*, XCIII, 1020, Apr. 23, 1914.

give tone to the market in periods of low prices, foreign demand suddenly ceased with the outbreak of the War. But the interruption was a brief one. During December well toward 200,000 tons of Southern pig iron were sold on foreign orders, at $10 a ton or less at the furnace. The Pacific Coast, which ordinarily procured its iron from China, also came into the market. These sales alone exceeded the average total output of the Alabama furnaces during the early months of 1914. Southern iron makers were for a time inclined to attribute their difficulties partly to the low duties levied on iron by the Underwood Tariff Bill. They had been shipping iron to New England and to the Pacific Coast. Under the previous duty their margin of profit was sufficient to give them virtual control of the New England market; but China iron was always cheaper than Alabama iron on the Pacific Coast, even under the previous higher duties, whenever the Chinese producers had pig to sell. Since southern furnaces found an outlet, however, for both pig and castings in Europe and the Orient this complaint was hardly tenable.[45]

MARKETING METHODS

No radical change in marketing methods occurred during these two decades, except so far as the formation of great trusts and combinations tended to consolidate the agencies for disposing of their products. The American Pig Iron Storage Warrant Company, which was formed shortly before the period we are describing for the purpose of warehousing iron against storage certificates, much as grain is warehoused in the Northwest or as pig iron had been stored and dealt in for half a century or more in Scotland, continued in business, but it never became a marketing agency of the first importance. The maximum amount of pig iron it ordinarily held in storage did not exceed a quarter of a million tons, while the unsold iron on the market was often three times or more that amount. To be sure, a small quantity of iron manipulated for the purpose of affecting prices under speculative control might have been a factor of some importance in the market; but this seems never to have occurred, although one argument used by the promoters of the Company was that it would enable furnace owners to store their stocks in periods of low prices and to negotiate their storage warrants so as to be relieved of the necessity of forced selling on a falling market in order to obtain cash for operating expenses and other urgent needs.

The same conditions that have been described in an earlier chapter continued to prevent a system from thriving in the United States that had worked well in Scotland. Our domestic iron market was very large; our pig-iron consumers were scattered; they were not economically served from a single center or a limited group of storage yards, no matter how strategically these might be placed; practically all our Bessemer iron and a considerable proportion of the basic iron we used in steel making was produced

[45] *Manufacturers' Record*, LXV, 49, May 28, 1914; LXV, 62, July 2, 1914; LXVI, 57, Dec. 31, 1914.

directly by the consumers, that is, by the great steel-making corporations. Even when the latter entered the open market for merchant iron, they usually made large contracts for 100,000 tons or more, involving deliveries at different plants and different dates, and did not need to use the services of brokers in such transactions. Still another condition that discouraged the growth of this institution in the United States was the further fact that even smaller consumers bought their iron as a rule by specific grades and brands, which they were not sure of procuring from a general yard; and they were prejudiced in favor of direct dealings with the furnace owner by their desire to have the product guaranteed immediately by its maker. Nevertheless, the Warrant Company struggled on with varying success. Its warrants were dealt in to some extent upon the New York Produce Exchange and its advocates hoped for a time that a speculative iron market within rather limited confines might be created. But the general sentiment of iron makers and iron buyers was adverse to the institution.[46]

We have already mentioned the numerous associations, pools and similar organizations formed to maintain prices and adjust output to consumption. Not a single pool agreement, according to some authorities, was ever honestly kept. According to the statements of men who themselves were members, it was no uncommon thing for an iron maker to station a salesman outside the building where a pool conference was being held, and as soon as a price had been agreed upon, to stroll casually to a window, and by pre-arranged signals indicate what it was. Thereupon the latter would hasten away to undercut the price which his employer was even then pledging himself to maintain.[47]

Several studies of the American iron and steel industry were made by foreign students during this period, betokening the interest that its recent progress had awakened in other countries. The British Iron Trade Commission in its report of 1902 made many pertinent observations regarding our industrial methods and the technical status of our works. The latter were recognized as embodying the latest improvements in plant and processes, although these improvements were by no means invariably of American origin. High wages, high outputs and low labor costs were the result.[48]

OUR FOREIGN IRON TRADE

The decline in imports of iron and steel and their manufactures, and the accompanying increase of exports that characterized this period as a whole, were most noticeable during the era of abnormally low prices that followed the panic of 1893. A reaction set in toward the turn of the century, when

[46] *Cf.*, American Iron and Steel Association, *Bulletin*, XXVIII, 85, Apr. 21, 1894; XXX, 273, Dec. 10, 1896; XXXI, 19, Jan. 20, 1897; XXXI, 213, Sept. 20, 1897; XXIX, 19, Feb. 1, 1905.
[47] Cotter, *Authentic History of the United States Steel Corporation*, 5–6.
[48] *Cf.*, also Popplewell, *Iron and Steel Production in America* (1906), Foster, *Engineering in the United States* (1906), and Singer, *Die Amerikanische Stahlindustrie und der Weltkrieg* (1917).

the domestic market was again active and a relative depression occurred abroad; and this was followed by another increase of exports and fall of imports, in spite of higher prices at home, during the years immediately preceding 1914. A brief depression shortly before the World War was soon converted into a tremendous boom for foreign trade by the military market in Europe.

In 1895 James Bowron, Treasurer of the Tennessee Coal, Iron and Railway Company, who was an Englishman by birth and training, and a successful promoter of markets for Southern iron in Great Britain, completed arrangements by which sales in the latter country and elsewhere abroad were greatly facilitated. Furnace practice had improved so as to reduce costs of production at the Alabama furnaces, and special export rates had been procured on the railroads between Birmingham and tidewater. In 1895 Bowron was able to report that his Company had already made two shipments to Liverpool and one to Genoa, in spite of advancing domestic prices.[49] But this trade did not at first give much promise of becoming important. Even its most active promoters regarded foreign markets merely as a safety valve that would afford an outlet for accumulations in time of overproduction and relieve the domestic market of their weight. American furnaces, as we have seen, had long exported charcoal iron in small quantities and for special purposes, even to England, and in 1895 had begun to ship to the same class of customers malleable iron from Pennsylvania. Such special lots, however, were never likely to bulk large in the foreign trade of a country like the United States.[50]

In 1896 it was reported that iron could be shipped from Birmingham, Alabama, to Liverpool at less cost than to New York, the rate to North Atlantic ports being $3.75 a ton, while freights to Liverpool did not average above $3, and were frequently below that figure. This condition, plus favorable prices abroad, led to shipments of from 10,000 to 11,000 tons a week, during the active season, from Birmingham to Europe. The *London Ironmonger* reported in March of that year that American iron could be sold in the Midland counties cheaper than either English or Scotch pig, and predicted that a determined effort on the part of American producers to establish a market in England would be severely felt by British furnace men. But James Bowron, emphasized in a published statement that large sales of Alabama iron were not likely to be made in England even though it could be put down at British ports a little below quotations for English iron. The profit margin was not large enough to justify cultivating the market. It was just possible at existing prices for Alabama iron to make a reasonable profit at South European and North German ports. Tokyo and Melbourne would be still better paying outlets, but American producers were excluded from them because they could not control ocean tonnage.

[49] American Iron and Steel Association, *Bulletin*, XXIX, 170, Aug. 1, 1895.
[50] American Iron and Steel Association, *Bulletin*, XXIX, 181, Aug. 10, 1895.

An awakening interest on the part of manufacturers in overseas trade was beginning to make itself felt in regard to shipping policies.

"It is in this respect that the English system of subsidized mail steamers gives a great advantage to English commerce and industry, as it opens the way for certain shipments at stated schedules and reasonable freights to every important market."

Alabama iron was not in quite as favorable a position abroad, in view of comparative prices, in 1896 as in 1895, but a concerted effort of Southern furnace men to produce up to capacity and employ all their idle plants might easily have enabled them to deliver their product at competitive foreign ports at prices that England could not meet. Thomas Seddon, President of the Sloss Iron and Steel Company, of Birmingham, the second largest iron producer in the South, in advancing this opinion, however, stated that his own firm had shipped small lots of iron to England when freights were peculiarly favorable, that is when cotton vessels were going eastward with light cargoes and wanted iron for ballast, but that only under such circumstances was the foreign market attractive.[51]

Nevertheless single shipments of 2,000 tons or more via Mobile to Europe were recorded in 1896. It was estimated that these shipments had aggregated 25,000 tons during the first nine months of the year, and that the total for the season would pass 40,000 tons. Both foundry and forge iron were included in these consignments, but mainly the former. Cautious iron men continued to predict that these exports would never reach a large volume, and that they would be checked as soon as business revived in America. The main advantage of this new outlet was to set "a limit to the depression of prices in the United States." Lack of tonnage continued to be a trouble. For instance, it was not possible to ship iron to Argentina, Brazil, Chile, or the Pacific Coast without first forwarding to England and thus incurring double freights. Toward the end of the year orders grew larger and the Tennessee Coal, Iron and Railroad Company and the Sloss Iron and Steel Company booked several thousand tons for European points and Calcutta.[52]

During the first years of the transition of the United States from an iron and steel importing to an iron and steel exporting country, this Southern pig iron formed the principal item in our foreign shipments—in weight at least, if not in value. Foundry iron outward bound from the Gulf ports for England and inward bound from Glasgow to our North Atlantic ports doubtless passed in mid-ocean on more than one occasion. But American steel makers had already placed some orders abroad. In 1896 they shipped rails to Japan and Brazil. The machinery for a locomotive plant of considerable size was shipped intact to Nijni Novgorod, Russia. For the first time in the country's history aggregate iron and steel exports overtopped

[51] American Iron and Steel Association, *Bulletin*, xxx, 81, Apr. 10, 1896; xx, 97, May 1, 1896; xxxi, 1, Jan. 1, 1897.
[52] American Iron and Steel Association, *Bulletin*, xxx, 221, Oct. 1, 1896; xxx, 274, 277, Dec. 10, 1896.

imports. During the four years ending with 1896 our total exports of iron and steel and its manufactures amounted to nearly $144,000,000 as compared with imports of less than $96,000,000. Part of the decline in the latter, as we have observed, was due to a heavy falling off in our purchases of tin plates abroad.[53]

By the beginning of 1897 the larger iron companies of the Birmingham district were selling more iron abroad than they were at home, and their foreign markets were widely distributed, including England, Italy, Germany, Holland, Belgium, Canada, Japan, Austria and Mexico. The British were importing small lots of steel as well as considerable quantities of pig iron—in 1897 the former totalled approximately 26,000 tons and the latter 91,000 tons. Japan attracted growing attention as a market for Southern iron, partly because her own merchant vessels were beginning to appear at Southern ports, primarily as cotton carriers to the growing textile mills of Osaka and Kobe, but also incidentally as carriers of pig iron.[54]

The steady dwindling of our imports and the equally steady, if less rapid, growth of our exports were now a matter of general popular interest. It was pointed out that prior to 1887 we had purchased abroad annually between a 1,500,000 and 2,000,000 tons of iron and steel and their manufactures. Ten years later this figure had fallen to the neighborhood of 150,000 tons. Meanwhile, our foreign shipments of pig iron had risen from almost nothing to a quarter of a million tons, and if to these were added shipments of steel, and iron and steel manufactures in their bulkier forms alone, the total would reach 650,000 tons.[55] The trade with Japan was steadily growing, a single order of 10,000 tons of Alabama iron for Yokohoma being recorded in the December business of 1897. During the fiscal year ending June 30, 1898, we exported in round numbers 235,000 tons of pig iron and 232,000 tons of iron and steel rails. Birmingham had become the third largest point of export of pig iron in the world, Middlesborough, England, being the first and Glasgow, Scotland, the second. It was pointed out that this constituted a very remarkable condition, since Birmingham unlike Middlesborough and Glasgow was not situated upon the sea, but was 200 miles from tidewater. But it enjoyed one compensating advantage in the concentration of all the raw materials employed for making iron, often within a mile or a mile and a half of the furnace where the ore was smelted. Birmingham's principal shipping ports were Pensacola and Mobile, the rate to either point being one dollar a ton. Iron, as already mentioned, was shipped in connection with cotton and also with coke, for which there was a steady demand abroad. In 1898 a specific instance was mentioned of a

[53] American Iron and Steel Association, *Bulletin*, xxx, 125, June 1, 1896; xxx, 196, Sept. 1, 1896; *Commercial and Financial Chronicle*, LXIV, 1163, June 19, 1897.
[54] American Iron and Steel Association, *Bulletin*, xxxi, 45, Feb. 20, 1897; xxxi, 66, Mar. 20, 1897; xxxi, 285, Dec. 20, 1897; xxxii, 29, Feb. 15, 1898.
[55] *Commercial and Financial Chronicle*, LXVI, 210, Jan. 29, 1898; *Statistical Abstract of the United States, 1923*, 265.

combined cargo of iron with coke that was carried from Pensacola to Yokohoma for $5 ton, the through rate on the iron from Birmingham to its destination being $6.[56]

In spite of the activity of the domestic market in 1898 the export trade was well maintained. During the latter half of the year the Tennessee Coal, Iron and Railroad Company averaged sales to foreign customers of about 1,000 tons a day, or about 65 per cent of its output.[57] The same year recorded a new development in our export trade, inaugurated with an order for 3,000 tons of American steel ship plates for a shipbuilding firm at Belfast. The Carnegie Company also sold over 5,000 tons of deck plates to shipbuilders on the Clyde. American rails were contracted for in lots of 30,000 tons and above for the trans-Siberian Railway at Vladivostock, and large orders were placed with our makers by the Railway Commissioners in Australia. Exports of steel rails alone now approached 300,000 tons per annum while exports of pig iron were about a quarter of a million tons. Our heavy sales to England were explained in part by the inability of British iron and steel masters to supply the extraordinary demand of their own customers. An engineer's strike in England and a coal strike in Wales had aggravated this situation.[58]

The year 1899 opened with conditions unfavorable for foreign shipments. There was a short supply of pig iron for domestic needs and a marked lack of ocean tonnage. Between 1895 and 1898 the annual foreign sales of iron by the Tennessee Iron and Steel Company had risen from 25 tons to over 190,000 tons; those of the Sloss Iron Company had risen during the same interval from 100 tons to 67,000 tons. Some of the steel-rail orders received by our makers this year were, in the opinion of the time, imposing. The Maryland Steel Company contracted to supply 120,000 tons to the trans-Siberian railroad, and 35,000 tons to the Victorian railways of Australia.[59]

Returning from a trip abroad in the spring of 1900, the Treasurer of the Tennessee Coal, Iron and Railroad Company reported that he had sold 25,000 tons of pig iron to one customer in England, and was negotiating for two other sales of 100,000 tons each. He also had been able to take orders for steel, bar iron, rails, coal and coke, the demand from Italy alone running into hundreds of thousands of tons of the latter fuel. So active was the foreign iron trade at this time that Germany had purchased the entire output of important new Swedish ore fields for twelve years in advance. The appearance of orders for manufactured shapes given by foreign consumers to Southern producers marked a new step in the development of

[56] American Iron and Steel Association, *Bulletin*, XXXII, 125, Aug. 15, 1898; XXXII, 145, Oct. 1, 1898; XXXII, 163, Nov. 1, 1898.
[57] American Iron and Steel Association, *Bulletin*, XXXII, 201, Dec. 20, 1898.
[58] American Iron and Steel Association, *Bulletin*, XXXII, 61, Apr. 15, 1898; XXXII, 69, May 1, 1898; XXXIII, 19, Feb. 1, 1899; XXXIII, 76, May 1, 1899; *Commercial and Financial Chronicle*, LXVIII, 1000–1001, May 27, 1899.
[59] *Manufacturers' Record*, XXXV, 34, Feb. 10, 1899; American Iron and Steel Association, *Bulletin*, XXXIII, 5, Jan. 1, 1899.

this business. The Tennessee Coal, Iron and Railroad Company made its first commercial shipment of bar iron to London in 1900. The same year it exported the first steel ever sent abroad from the South to Copenhagen and Glasgow, where it undersold the foreign product. A novel feature in the market this year was a marked decline in the demand for scrap iron, thousands of tons of which had recently been imported only to be shipped abroad again for want of a market in the United States. We made our first delivery of steel rails to Norway this year.[60]

In 1901 the Carnegie Steel Company was awarded a contract for 20,000 tons of steel ship-plates by a shipbuilding company at Belfast, Ireland. Clyde shipbuilders also purchased plates in the United States; and the Lorain Steel Company sold rails and other tramway material to the municipal roads at Glasgow and Dundee. Nonetheless, 1901 saw a decline in the total value of our iron and steel exports, due to the growing demand at home accompanied by a slackening request abroad, particularly for pig iron, rails, plates and structural steel. The principal falling off was in exports of pig iron, which decreased from 287,000 tons in 1900 to 81,000 tons the following year. By 1902 the tide of iron and steel shipments had so far ebbed that we were importing both pig iron and billets in small lots from Europe. This, as we have mentioned, was attributed at the time to the failure of railways to deliver raw materials to our furnaces in sufficient quantities to keep them in full operation. Baltimore imported over 8,000 tons of pig iron from London in two shipments, and our iron makers were also buying English hematite in Great Britain. Between 1901 and 1902 imports of iron and steel in unmanufactured and partly manufactured forms rose from 141,000 tons to 733,000 tons. Simultaneously imports of iron ore rose from 725,000 tons to 895,000 tons.[61]

To be sure, our iron and steel makers still held many of their foreign markets and retained practically unimpaired their foreign trade in some classes of material. The charge that they dumped their surplus products abroad—that is, sold them to foreign customers at a lower price than they charged domestic consumers—was made at this time, and the practice was defended on the ground that the sale of a surplus which the domestic market could not take, even at little or no profit, lowered average cost of production and enabled manufacturers to serve their domestic customers more cheaply than they could otherwise. Furthermore our tariff gave our manufacturers a drawback on the duties paid on raw materials when the goods manufactured from these materials were shipped abroad. It was this provision that accounted mainly for the recent importations of pig iron from Great Britain. The margin between the average price at which steel rails were sold in foreign markets and the average price charged

---

[60] American Iron and Steel Association, *Bulletin*, xxxiv, 107, June 15, 1900; xxxiv, 125, July 15, 1900; xxxiv, 125, July 15, 1900; xxxiv, 139, Aug. 15, 1900; xxxv, 18, Feb. 9, 1901.
[61] American Iron and Steel Association, *Bulletin*, xxxv, 70, May 10, 1901; xxxvi, 29, Feb. 25, 1902; xxxvi, 42, 45, Mar. 25, 1902; xxxvi, 76, May 25, 1902; xxxvi, 166, Nov. 10, 1902.

domestic consumers ranged from 20 cents to $1.71 a ton in different years, the lower price being received for foreign shipments. The Secretary of the British Iron Trade Association, to be sure, asserted in a report of that body on American industrial conditions, that differences of 60 to 90 per cent against our consumers and in favor of foreign consumers sometimes existed, but if this occurred it was not in case of staple commodities like those just mentioned.[62]

In spite of the revival of activity at home, however, and perhaps in part on account of it, our exports on the whole continued to increase. In 1905 The Pennsylvania Steel Company imported 30,000 tons of British Bessemer pig to convert into steel rails for export under the drawback to South America, where it had contracts calling for deliveries of 12,000 tons a month. Foundry iron, which formerly came so largely from Scotland, was rarely imported. The give and take character of our iron trade was illustrated by the fact that in 1910 we bought abroad 453,000 tons of iron and steel and its heavier manufactures and 2,600,000 tons of iron ore; yet we simultaneously shipped to foreign customers 1,536,000 tons of iron and steel in unmanufactured and manufactured forms. During a single week in 1912, 35,000 tons of southern pig iron were sold on foreign orders.[63]

The United States now ranked third among the iron and steel exporting nations. Germany stood first, her foreign shipments of both manufactured and unmanufactured iron and steel during the first half of 1912 reaching almost 3,000,000 tons; Great Britain followed with over 2,300,000 tons for the same period; and the United States exported 1,428,000 tons. Our years of maximum export prior to the World War were 1912 and 1913. In 1913 we shipped abroad 277,000 tons of pig iron, 460,000 tons of rails, 463,000 tons of sheets and plates, 403,000 tons of structural steel and vast quantities of bars, pipes and fittings, wire and finished shapes. Our imports were comparatively small, except in case of pig iron, of which we took 165,000 tons, presumably to manufacture for foreign markets under the drawback provisions already mentioned. Some pig iron, however, especially that used on the Pacific Coast, was imported for final consumption in this country. By 1914 the iron works at Hankow, China, had completely displaced Alabama pig iron in our Far Western markets, and had even shipped steel to Brooklyn at prices which could not be met by our producers. The same year—not long before the War cut off that source of supply—German basic-steel billets were used to some extent by New England manufacturers. It was also reported that a considerable tonnage of German bars and angles was in transit to American warehouses; and steel rails from India were expected to enter the San Francisco market.[64]

---

[62] American Iron and Steel Association, *Bulletin*, XXXVI, 156, Oct. 25, 1902; Ashley, *British Industries*, 29; U. S. Industrial Commission, *Reports*, XIII, 454, 464.
[63] American Iron and Steel Association, *Bulletin*, XXXIX, 69, May 1, 1905; XLV, 25, Mar. 25, 1911.
[64] American Iron and Steel Association, *Bulletin*, XLVI, 14, Feb. 1, 1912; XLVI, 88, Sept. 15, 1912; *Manufacturers' Record*, LXV, 57, June 11, 1914; *Iron Age*, XCIII, 1346, May 28, 1914; *Mineral Industry*, XXXIII, 412.

INTERNATIONAL COMPARISONS

As the appearance of American iron and steel and heavy steel products in the world market would imply, the United States acquired during these two decades an entirely new position in the international industry. It will be recalled that our pig-iron output exceeded that of Great Britain for the first time in 1890. We did not hold the position then won uninterruptedly during the next few years; and in 1894 the United Kingdom again forged ahead of us. But we speedily recovered from this temporary setback and took a lead that never again was wrested from us. It was during the first years of this period that Germany made her spectacular advance in iron and steel production. Until the late eighties the furnace men and steel makers of that country had been behind those of England and the United States in economy of methods and appliances, so that their cheaper labor did not alone give them an absolute advantage. By 1895, however, Germany had modernized her plants and brought them up to the same standards as those of her great competitors. Within less than ten years the average output of her furnaces had doubled, and the average output per man employed had nearly doubled. She already excelled either of her competitors in the utilization of waste materials, especially in the recovery of by-products from coal. This saving of secondary products, for which Germany's growing chemical industries afforded profitable uses, affected powerfully her ability to compete with English and American makers in international markets.

During the decade ending with 1894 England's pig-iron production practically stood still. Indeed, it was less the latter year than it had been more than ten years previously. During this interval Germany had increased her production from less than 3,700,000 tons to nearly 5,560,000 tons. In 1894 England, as we have just seen, had resumed, after losing it for three seasons, her old position as the largest producer of pig iron in the world. The United States ranked second, and Germany third. Twelve years later the United States produced considerably more than twice as much pig iron as any of her competitors and nearly 3,000,000 tons more than Germany and the United Kingdom combined.[65]

Accompanying our step forward to the first place among iron and steel producing countries came a recognition of the superiority of our processes and plants. At the 1897 meeting of the British Iron and Steel Institute, it was freely acknowledged that American blast-furnace practise had made such strides within the last few years as to be ahead of that in Great Britain herself. Leading English firms were adding equipment to their plants that would enable them to follow American methods. A Manchester correspondent said:

"These American improvements will before long be found to have brought about almost a revolution in the making of pig iron in this country. But American

---

[65] *Commercial and Financial Chronicle*, LX, 733–734, Apr. 27, 1894; LXII, 1116, June 20, 1896; *Mineral Industry*, XIV, 339.

ingenuity and energy are also leading the way in lessening the cost, by increasing the amount of the out-turn, in the production of steel rails and billets, and in this respect also their example is not likely to be neglected on this side the Atlantic."

We also enjoyed certain other advantages. While our railway hauls were, of course, longer than those of Great Britain, our rates were much lower; and the cost of fuel was materially less in the United States.[66]

Before the end of the century, therefore, we had already established our undisputed leadership among the nations of the world so far as output was concerned; and we were somewhat in advance of other countries in furnace practice and plant equipment. Not only was our output as a country greater than that of England or Germany, but we possessed the largest individual establishments. The Carnegie Steel Company was by far the largest producer of both pig iron and steel in the world, exceeding the Krupps enterprises, which were often thought by Europeans to hold this position.[67] While several elements of cost were rising abroad, they continued to fall in the United States. For instance, Lake Superior ore was delivered at Eastern furnaces for half its price twenty years before. Improvements not directly related to the iron and steel industry, such as heavier cars and roadbeds cheapening transportation, had relatively more influence upon export possibilities in America than they had in Great Britain or Germany, where plants were comparatively near tidewater. Our supplies of raw material were probably more elastic. At least in both Great Britain and Germany temporary scarcities of coke, and often of ore, hampered iron and steel makers in periods of unusual activity. The cost of raw materials was advancing rapidly in Europe toward the close of the century, and the fact that some of these materials were purchased abroad in competitive markets, where iron makers of different countries bid against each other, tended to prevent the same continuity of control from the first to the last stage of production that was being worked out in the United States.[68]

In 1901 the United Kingdom was estimated to consume more iron and steel per capita than any other country in the world, or nearly 419 pounds per person. Belgium ranked next with over 414 pounds, the United States third with 379 pounds, and Germany fourth with 359 pounds. This was a German estimate. No other country approached these figures; Sweden ranked fifth with a per capita consumption of 218 pounds per annum.[69]

A British comparison of blast-furnace conditions and cost of production in the United Kingdom and the United States in 1902 gave the average annual output per furnace in Great Britain at 25,000 tons and in our country

---

[66] *Commercial and Financial Chronicle*, LXIV, 1026–1027, May 29, 1897.
[67] American Iron and Steel Association, *Bulletin*, XXXII, 189, Dec. 1, 1898.
[68] American Iron and Steel Association, *Bulletin*, XXXIII, 81, May 15, 1899; XXXIII, 156, Sept. 15, 1899.
[69] *Mineral Industry*, X, 140.

at 60,000 tons, the respective blast pressures being from four to six pounds in England and ten to twenty pounds in the United States. The average labor cost of pig iron at furnaces was about a shilling a ton more in Great Britain than in this country, and the average amount of iron in our domestic ores was 50 per cent as compared with 38 per cent in British domestic ores.[70]

In comparing relations among iron and steel makers in the United States and in foreign countries respectively marked differences appeared. In Germany, for instance, producers of steel blooms and billets for the general market sold their products abroad at lower prices than they charged domestic manufacturers, who bought steel in these forms for working it into finished products. This was a handicap for German manufacturers of finished products made from purchased blooms and billets selling in the German home market, and an almost insurmountable obstacle in the way of cultivating foreign markets.[71] This condition seems not to have existed, at least to the extent of becoming a matter of serious complaint, in Great Britain, probably because foreign blooms and billets were admitted to the country without a customs duty. In the United States there was a strong tendency, as we have seen, for all the processes of production to come under the control of single companies; but the billet pools which were intended to regulate prices of finished products to manufacturers who did not make their own steel never succeeded in controlling the market for a long period; and their members probably did not sell abroad at materially lower prices than they sold to domestic manufacturers. Furthermore, a comparatively open market for coal, coke, natural gas and petroleum, and for iron ore and pig iron, made it possible for any manufacturer of finished goods who felt himself aggrieved by the selling policy of billet makers to set up furnaces of his own.

[70] American Iron and Steel Association, *Bulletin*, XXXVII, 11, Jan. 25, 1903.
[71] Ashley, *British Industries*, 33–34.

CHAPTER VIII

IRON AND STEEL SHAPES

Rails, 118. Structural Shapes, 119. Wire and Wire Products, 122. Nails, 125. Pipes and Tubes, 127. Tin-plate, 129.

RAILS

Even after other forms of steel acquired in the aggregate relatively greater importance, the rail business continued to be the largest single branch of the industry. The outstanding features of its history during these twenty years were the rolling of rails of heavier weight and greater length than heretofore, the rapid increase in the production of heavy girder rails for electric lines, the remarkable increase in the use of open-hearth steel in preference to Bessemer steel, especially for rails of the heavier type, and the increasing employment of nickel, vanadium and other alloy rails, as already described, on track exposed to unusually heavy service. Meanwhile the geography of this industry did not change materially. Colorado continued to manufacture rails in considerable quantities for Western roads. With the growth of our export trade in iron and steel, beginning in the middle nineties, and with the application of drawbacks to steel manufactures made from imported iron for export, the rolling of rails for export markets, especially in the tidewater district, was encouraged. As previously mentioned, American steel plants shipped girder rails and heavy rails for railway service even to Great Britain, and contributed largely to the needs of builders in South America, Japan, Australia, India, South Africa and nearly every colony and rail-importing country where construction was at this time active. The most notable addition to our producing districts was Alabama, which for a period was our largest manufacturer of open-hearth rails; though rails of this material were also made in Colorado and Pennsylvania, and ultimately in large quantities in Illinois and elsewhere.

We have seen previously that the rail business was controlled during most of this period by a pool, which fixed prices and allotted output to its constituent firms. This organization, which dated back to 1885, had a stormy career and was temporarily terminated on various occasions.[1] Prior to the organization of the United States Steel Corporation it was dominated by the Carnegie Steel Company and the Illinois Steel Company, which usually worked under an agreement that made them virtually a pool within a pool. When they fell out the pool was disrupted, as happened in 1897, and this dangerous rivalry was one motive for organizing the United States Steel Corporation, thus bringing together under single management the two most powerful competitors in this industrial field.

[1] American Iron and Steel Association, *Bulletin*, xxxi, 44, Feb. 20, 1897.

In 1894 the Pennsylvania Railway increased the standard weight of steel rails on its main line from 85 to 100 pounds per yard.[2] With the introduction of heavier locomotives and rolling stock and of larger rail sections, rail tests became more exacting. It was this condition that speeded up the transition from Bessemer to open-hearth steel as soon as it was discovered that the latter material was likely to prove the more reliable and uniform when worked in large masses.[3] Yet as recently as 1900 more than two-thirds of the rails made in the United States weighed less than 85 pounds per yard; and of nearly 2,400,000 tons produced that year, only 1,333 tons —and these in lighter sections—were made of open-hearth steel. Iron rails had practically disappeared, less than a thousand tons being made that year.[4] In 1907 the Harriman lines placed their largest orders, amounting to 150,000 tons, with the Tennessee Coal, Iron and Railroad Company, which made only open-hearth rails.[5] Two years later the increase of rails of this character was the most notable feature of the season. For years the defects of Bessemer rails had been discussed by engineers and railway men, and the result was a general turning to the open-hearth furnaces for materials. Even at that date the greater part of the open-hearth rails produced in the United States were made at the Ensley, Alabama, works of the Tennessee Coal, Iron, and Railroad Company.[6] In 1910 when we rolled 3,636,000 tons of rails in this country—a figure not exceeded prior to the World War except in 1906, when we produced just under 4,000,000 tons—Bessemer steel still out-ranked open-hearth steel, though by only 135,000 tons. By 1914 we produced well toward five times as many open-hearth as Bessemer rails, and the Bessemer output had sunk within four years from nearly 2,000,000 tons to 324,000 tons—though it should be observed there was a heavy decline of 50 per cent in our total output of rails during this period. A new item in rail statistics at this time recorded a modest beginning in the production of rails from electric steel.[7]

STRUCTURAL SHAPES

The use of cast-iron beams and pillars, rolled-iron beams, and eventually rolled-steel plates and beams, in structural work for buildings, bridges, elevated railways, ships and other similar employments, which had gradually extended during the half century or more before 1890, prepared the way for the subsequent rapid expansion of the use of steel, and especially of open-hearth steel, for these purposes, so that actual consumption multiplied over and over again during the twenty years that followed. This was not due so much to the discovery of new fields of usefulness for struc-

---

[2] American Iron and Steel Association, *Bulletin*, xxviii, 253, Nov. 3, 1894.
[3] *Cf.* American Iron and Steel Association, *Bulletin*, xxxi, 245, Nov. 1, 1897.
[4] American Iron and Steel Association, *Bulletin*, xxxv, 116, Aug. 10, 1901.
[5] American Iron and Steel Association, *Bulletin*, xli, 61, May 15, 1907.
[6] *Mineral Industry*, xviii, 406.
[7] American Iron and Steel Association, *Bulletin* xlv, 20, Feb. 20, 1911; *Mineral Industry*, xix, 413; xxiii, 410.

tural shapes—although their employment in car building added very largely to the market for such materials—as to the growth of consumption within fields already explored.

Bridge building early attained a high degree of development in America because necessity, represented by the great demand for such structures to span our numerous rivers and valleys, was not only the mother of invention in this branch of engineering, but also the patroness of sustained progress. The result was that we established an export market for bridges of American design and construction at a comparatively early day. By 1895 foreign contractors called regularly for American tenders whenever they had an important enterprise of this sort in hand. In 1895 the Phoenix Iron Company, of Pennsylvania, designed, built and delivered for shipment at New York within five weeks of receiving the contract a steel bridge weighing over a thousand tons and nearly a quarter of a mile long, to span the Santa Maria River in California. The ability to fill contracts with such surprising speed counted heavily to the advantage of American makers in foreign markets.[8] But in addition to this, American firms sometimes underbid British bridge builders, as they did British manufacturers of ship-plates, at their own ports. The Pencoyd Works supplied under competitive bids a large steel bridge to the Netherlands Government, to be erected in that country, and several thousand tons of bridge material for the Imperial Railways of Japan.[9]

Among the notable incidents of the early nineties was the erection of the first skyscrapers in Chicago and New York City and this field of construction alone was soon to draw heavily upon the capacity of our steel works. Already large orders for beams and angles were being given for buildings of more moderate height. For instance, in 1895 a tobacco company at St. Louis placed a single order for 5,000 tons of structural steel to be employed in erecting a manufacturing plant. At this time the Homestead Steel Works, one of the most important in the country, considered a monthly shipment of 12,600 tons of structural shapes a record breaker. This company was rolling beams up to 24 inches in depth, from ingots of about 20 by 30 inches cross-section, by a single continuous process. These beams were rolled in 110-foot sections, cut cold to standard length and straightened by a special hydraulic press.[10] In 1897 the Colorado Fuel and Iron Company, which had hitherto depended mainly upon the rolling of rails to employ its plant, added a structural steel department.

Although the market was expanding rapidly, competition held prices down, especially during the years when they were abnormally low throughout the whole steel industry. The result was the formation of steel beam

[8] American Iron and Steel Association, *Bulletin*, XXIX, 125, June 1, 1895.
[9] American Iron and Steel Association, *Bulletin*, XXXI, 219, Oct. 1, 1897; XXXI, 228, Oct. 10, 1897; XXXI, 277, Dec. 10, 1897.
[10] American Iron and Steel Association, *Bulletin*. XXIX. 141, June 20, 1895; XXIX, 261, Nov. 20, 1895; XXX, 19, Jan. 20, 1896.

pools under what often proved to be ephemeral agreements.[11] In 1898 the six largest beam manufacturers in the United States, the Pencoyd, Passaic, Phoenix, Cambria, Carnegie, and Jones and Laughlin Works joined in such an effort to regulate the market. Within two or three years the consumption of steel beams had increased from 100,000 tons to over 300,000 tons per annum. About this time our facilities for promptly filling orders gave our makers preference even over British contractors in supplying bridges, locomotives and other structural material for the Sudan Railway.[12] In 1899 the American Bridge Company was incorporated to combine under a single control twenty-five of the largest bridge-building firms, including some plants manufacturing other forms of structural material. The amalgamation was completed the following year, with a capital of $70,000,000, and was reported to control about 90 per cent of the bridge tonnage of the country.[13]

Although an output of 300,000 tons of beams per annum had been the record in 1898, the quantity of structural iron rolled in 1899, including beams, girders, channels and angles, but not plate girders, exceeded 850,000, tons, 93 per cent of which was produced in Pennsylvania. This was but the beginning of a period of even greater growth that was to carry output ten years later to over 2,250,000 tons.[14] In 1902, 67 works were engaged wholly or partly in this branch of steel making, and it rivaled the production of steel castings as a department making rapid progress. So heavy was the demand for structural shapes early in the century, that conversion contracts, by which a steel-making company equipped to roll shapes let out a part of its rolling to other firms to which it supplied ingots for this purpose, became very common. This year two "monster works" were erected by the American Bridge Company, one at Economy, Pennsylvania, and the other at Chicago. Individual contracts were constantly becoming larger; that for the Blackwell's Island bridge at New York, awarded to the Pennsylvania Steel Company in 1903, called for 50,000 tons of steel, as compared with less than 4,000 tons for the original Brooklyn bridge.[15]

Production of structural shapes made a sudden leap forward in 1905— perhaps one of the most spectacular increases in the history of the business—from less than 1,000,000 tons to 1,660,000 tons. This was an addition of approximately 75 per cent to the output within a single year. Moreover, these figures did not tell the whole story of the increased employment of steel for structural purposes; for in the earlier records the use of plates for fabricated structural work was relatively small. Large girders and columns were built up with I and Z bars, riveted together with very little

[11] *E.g.*, American Iron and Steel Association, *Bulletin*, xxxi, 125, June 1, 1897.
[12] American Iron and Steel Association, *Bulletin*, xxxii, 13, Jan. 15, 1898; xxxiii, 68, Apr. 20, 1899.
[13] *Commercial and Financial Chronicle*, lxix, 696, Sept. 30, 1899; lxxi, 86, July 14, 1900.
[14] American Iron and Steel Association, *Bulletin*, xxxv, 156, Oct. 25, 1901; xliv, 60, July 1, 1910.
[15] American Iron and Steel Association, *Bulletin*, xxxvi, 27, Feb. 25, 1902; xxxvi, 45, Mar. 25, 1902; xxxvi, 69, May 10, 1902; xxxviii, 165, Nov. 10, 1904.

plate material. As the science of steel construction advanced, many heavy girders and columns were built mainly of plates, with relatively light angles connecting them. Statistics of the trade did not show this material under the heading of structural steel.[16] The total output of structural shapes reached 2,275,000 tons in 1909, which was an increase over the previous year of more than 110 per cent, or even greater than that recorded in 1905. Among the important improvements in structural shapes during this period was the steel section invented by Henry Grey, that enabled big beams used in erecting buildings to be rolled in a single piece instead of fabricating them by riveting together a number of different pieces. Grey's patents were purchased by the Bethlehem Steel Company, which erected an immense structural mill for the special purpose of rolling them.[17]

WIRE AND WIRE PRODUCTS

Another branch of steel making that experienced a wonderful growth during these twenty years was the manufacture of wire and wire products, especially fencing and nails. This was a well-established department of the industry, as we have seen, before 1893. In 1894 over a quarter-million tons of steel was used for wire nails alone, and the consumption for fencing nearly equaled that figure. The manufacture of wire rope was another leading branch of the steel wire industry. Large quantities were also employed in connection with telegraphs and telephones and electric railways. A single company, Washburn & Moen, manufactured in 1895 168,000 tons of wire. Our makers shipped this product from Pittsburgh to Great Britain, via the St. Lawrence River. In 1897 the output of wire rods in the United States exceeded 970,000 tons, an increase over the previous year of more than 55 per cent. While we exported heavy wire to Great Britain, we still imported considerable quantities of finer iron and steel wire rods, chiefly from Norway and Sweden.[18]

In 1897 steps were taken toward combining the principal wire works in the United States under the ownership of a single corporation. During the early months of that year the market for finished products in iron and steel had been singularly free from pools, combinations and other agencies of price control. The original effort to combine the wire works of the whole country proved unsuccessful, differences of opinion having arisen as to the appraisal of certain plants. This led some Eastern works to withdraw from the undertaking, whereupon the Western plants formed a combination of their own. They made chiefly fence and nail wire and coarse wire products. This first company, known as the American Steel and Wire Company, of Chicago, was chartered in Illinois in January 1898, with a

---

[16] American Iron and Steel Association, *Bulletin*, xl, 76, June 1, 1906; xl, 90, July 1, 1906.
[17] Cotter, *The Story of Bethlehem Steel*, 44.
[18] American Iron and Steel Association, *Bulletin*, xxx, 3, Jan. 1, 1896; xxxi, 219, Oct. 1, 1897; xxxii, 51, Apr. 1, 1898; xxxiii, 68, Apr. 20, 1899.

capital of $87,000,000. John W. Gates and Elbert H. Gary, later prominent in the Federal Steel Company and the United States Steel Corporation, were among the promoters. After the withdrawal of the Eastern firms the capital was fixed at $24,000,000 and the combination embraced fourteen plants, all of them West of the Alleghenies.[19] Meanwhile the Alabama Steel and Wire Company was incorporated the same year to erect a rod and wire mill at Ensley. This enterprise, as already noted, was closely identified with the Tennessee Coal, Iron, and Railroad Company and proposed to manufacture entirely for export.[20]

The following year, however, the American Steel and Wire Company of Illinois was dissolved and a New Jersey corporation was chartered, embracing all the plants of the old company, the three Washburn and Moen plants at Worcester, Waukegan and San Francisco, and twenty-four other companies engaged in manufacturing steel rods and wire, or in mining and smelting. The new corporation also controlled by stock ownership five other large corporations, including one zinc plant and large coal and coking properties. The plants were so distributed as to be immediately accessible to all the important markets. Barbed wire was made at Lawrence, Kansas, for the Western prairies, and also manufactured at Worcester, Massachusetts, for export. The Company owned some of the best ore lands in the Mesabi range, coal mines and coke furnaces as already mentioned, and before the end of the year had acquired a fleet of Lake steamers to convey its ore to its Great Lakes plants. It had entered the Southern field by purchasing extensive holdings in Northern Alabama and Southern Tennessee.[21]

In 1900 the Alabama Steel and Wire Company commenced operations, and both the Carnegie Steel Company and the Jones and Laughlin Company erected rod mills, the former reported to be the largest ever built.[22] The tendency of the big steel makers to go into the manufacture of wire rods, wire and wire products doubtless explains the eagerness of the American Steel and Wire Company to extend its operations backward to mining its raw materials and producing its own iron and steel. Whatever the motive, there was a rapid expansion of wire-making facilities at this time. In 1914 wire rods were the largest single item, except the capacious category of merchant bars, in the 25,500,000 tons of rolled, forged and other classified iron and steel products produced in the United States. They totaled 2,378,000 tons; sheets and tin-plates which came next exceeding structural shapes, rails, black-plates for tinning, and all other finished products.

[19] *Mineral Industry*, VI, 410–411; *Commercial and Financial Chronicle*, LXV, 1172, Dec. 18, 1897; LXVI, 519, Mar. 12, 1898; LXVII, 632, Sept. 24, 1898; U. S. Commissioner of Corporations, *Summary of Report on the Steel Industry*, I, 6; Tarbell, *Life of Judge Gary*, 82.
[20] *Commercial and Financial Chronicle*, LXVII, 1001, Nov. 12, 1898; American Iron and Steel Association, *Bulletin*, XXXII, 171, Nov. 10, 1898.
[21] *Commercial and Financial Chronicle*, LXIX, 543, Sept. 9, 1899; LXIX, 646, Sept. 23, 1899; LXIX, 1013, 1017, Nov. 11, 1899; U. S. Industrial Commission, *Reports*, I, 1005–1006, 1019–1020, 1028.
[22] *Commercial and Financial Chronicle*, LXX, 533, Mar. 17, 1900; LXXI, 184, July 28, 1900; LXXI, 866, Oct. 27, 1900.

The most important uses for wire during this period were for the manufacture of fencing and of nails. Great changes had occurred in the industry since the Civil War, when the Washburn Company in Worcester, at that time the leading wire makers of the United States, regarded a freak of fashion, that created a temporary annual demand for 1,500 tons of crinoline wire, a boon to the industry.[23] This wire was manufactured of cast steel. In 1876 the adoption of Bessemer steel had created a revolution in the business, coming happily just at the time when a market for barbed wire was being established. It was estimated that the use of Bessemer steel for this purpose not only furnished a stronger wire than could be made from the Swedish iron previously in use, but represented a saving of four to five million dollars annually to the farmers of the United States. The history of the barbed-wire industry has been given elsewhere.[24] Another new market for wire was as a substitute for bale rope and twine for binding hay and cotton, and to some extent for use in the harvesting field. An incidental saving from the introduction of wire for binding purposes was the increased security against loss by fire, as wire-bound bales remained solid and were nearly incombustible. Iron, and later steel, were used for telegraph wires for many years. Galvanizing steel wire to protect it from rusting did not become common until after telegraph lines covered a large part of the Eastern section of the country. Copper was not generally introduced until the middle eighties, just about the time when the great expansion of the electrical industries that followed the perfection of the dynamo as a source of light and power occurred. Previously, copper wire did not possess the requisite strength for telegraph and transmission lines; but about this time the introduction of hard-drawn copper wire, which was much lighter than iron and a vastly better conductor, led to the practical displacement of steel for this purpose. "In January, 1884, there were probably not more than one or two hundred miles of hard-drawn copper wire in use in this country. In 1889 there were at least 50,000 miles."[25] But these new industrial uses were secondary, at least from the quantitative point of view, to the two great fields of consumption—fencing and nails.

By the end of the century woven-wire fencing, which had been more or less familiar but not widely used previously, began to be substituted in many places for barbed wire, though without diminishing the sales of the latter product. While the shipments of barbed wire of the American Steel and Wire Company increased 16 per cent during the fifteen years ending 1914, their shipments of woven-wire fencing, reckoned in tons, increased more than 1,000 per cent. The latter year the quantity of barbed wire sold was 194,000 tons, and of woven-wire fencing 293,000 tons.[26] During the South African War, in 1900, barbed wire was extensively used for military entanglements. It was still more generally employed for this purpose in the

---

[23] Washburn, *Industrial Worcester*, 151–153.
[24] *Cf.*, Washburn, *Industrial Worcester*, 154–157.
[25] Washburn, *Industrial Worcester*, 159.
[26] Washburn, *Industrial Worcester*, 163.

war between Russia and Japan a few years later. The tremendous market afforded by the World War does not come within the limits of this survey.[27]

The geography of wire making was naturally influenced by the steady westward movement of the steel industry as a whole, and by the development of markets for nails and fencing in the prairie states. This was indicated in 1891 when, as already recorded, the Washburn and Moen Company, of Worcester, erected their large plant on the shores of Lake Michigan. The introduction of cable lines upon the heavy grades in San Francisco caused wire works to be erected in that city, which were acquired by the Washburn and Moen Company soon after they erected their Waukegan works. Although electric construction soon displaced cable lines, the use of wire for other purposes, especially for aerial cable ways, in the Far West soon compensated for the loss of this earlier market. Wire making also moved Southward. Among the minor instances of Northern firms establishing plants in the South is that of the Mohawk Valley Steel and Wire Company, of Portland, Maine, which in 1903 erected an open-hearth steel plant and extensive nail works at Brunswick, Georgia.[28] This drift of the manufacture of standardized products to new market areas encouraged greater attention to specialties in the older wire drawing centers, a development illustrated by the experience of the Washburn and Moen Company.

"Little by little, the manufacture of the more common products has been transferred to other districts, and the Worcester plants have long since come to be known as the specialty producing plants of the Company. Notwithstanding the fact that the tonnage of many of these specialties is light when taken separately, it is by no means small when viewed in the aggregate. Some idea of the volume of business in normal times may be obtained from the fact that the maximum output of the Worcester plants in a single year approximates 200,000 tons. . . . In no other city in the world are so many different kinds of wire and wire products manufactured as are produced in Worcester by the American Steel and Wire Company."[29]

In 1885 the Washburn & Moen Company built at Worcester one 12-ton stationary furnace for making open-hearth steel, and this plant was subsequently expanded into a group of eight furnaces with an annual capacity of 170,000 tons of ingots.

NAILS

It will be recalled that two important changes occurred in the nail-making industry between 1880 and 1890: the substitution of steel for iron and the rapid introduction of wire nails for uses hitherto monopolized by cut nails. No such radical changes occurred between 1893 and 1914, although the manufacture of cut nails steadily declined and the manufacture of wire nails more than correspondingly increased. America also began to

---

[27] American Iron and Steel Association, *Bulletin*, XXXIV, 69, Apr. 1, 1900.
[28] *Manufacturers' Record*, XLIII, 27, Jan. 29, 1903; cf., *ibid.*, LXV, 61, Jan. 15, 1914.
[29] Washburn, *Industrial Worcester*. 165.

export wire nails in quantities during the period of low prices in the middle nineties. Indeed, nails could be manufactured at such low cost that a computation made in 1895 showed that if a carpenter dropped a nail it was considerably cheaper for him to let it lie than to take the time to pick it up.[30] A rapid concentration in large establishments and under central control occurred in the wire-nail industry as it did in the wire industry. Indeed the two branches of manufacture were more or less associated. The cut-nail manufacturers formed an association as late as 1897, with a membership of 21 firms, for the purpose of advancing prices; but wire nails were displacing cut nails so rapidly that the latter already ruled the market.[31]

In 1898 the Oliver Wire Company of Pittsburgh, the strongest competitor of the American Steel and Wire Company, reduced wire nails to $1.35 per keg. Yet two years later, in the midst of a severe depression in the nail business, said to be due to a series of strikes in the building trades, prices were $2.20 a keg for both wire and cut nails. During the late nineties the country's output of steel-wire nails averaged between 7,000,000 and 8,000,000 kegs per annum, reaching nearly 9,000,000 kegs in 1897. In 1900, when 7,234,000 kegs of wire nails were made, the output of cut nails was 1,573,000 kegs, a decline from 8,161,000 kegs in 1886. By 1913 the output of cut nails had fallen to 740,000 kegs, while the product of wire nails and spikes approached 13,000,000 kegs and had reached nearly 14,000,000 kegs the year of maximum production.[32]

The manufacture of wood screws had always been highly centralized because a few firms controlled the patents for the automatic machinery employed in making them. For the same reason the American Screw Company at one time owned large plants in Great Britain and Canada. These properties were disposed of in 1898 and the following year the National Screw Company, absorbing the old American Screw Company and a number of its competitors, was organized with a capital of $10,000,000. This manufacture was carried on chiefly in New England although the Company acquired plants at Philadelphia, Cleveland, and Pullman, Illinois.[33]

Another branch of steel manufacturing that had segregated itself from the general industry by this time was rolling hoops and cotton ties, a business that was likewise centralized during 1899, the great trust-building year. The company organized on that date was closely allied with the National Steel Company and controlled not only plants for rolling hoops but also blast furnaces. The new corporation, known as the American Steel Hoop Company, started with a capital of $33,000,000, and took over the works

---

[30] American Iron and Steel Association, *Bulletin*, XXVIII, 227, Oct. 10, 1894; XXIX, 17, Jan. 18, 1895.
[31] American Iron and Steel Association, *Bulletin*, XXXI, 253, Nov. 10, 1897.
[32] American Iron and Steel Association, *Bulletin*, XXXII, 122, Aug. 15, 1898; XXXIV, 85, May 1, 1900; XXXV, 156, Oct. 25, 1901.
[33] *Commercial and Financial Chronicle*, LXIV, 607, Mar. 27, 1897; LXVII, 735, Oct. 8, 1898; LXVIII, 572, Mar. 25, 1899.

of nine existing companies. It immediately purchased an interest in ore properties in the Mesabi Range and manufactured pig iron for the open market as well as hoops. In 1900 the Company owned a large part of its coke, as well as its ore supplies, and made about 300,000 tons of Bessemer and foundry iron annually. The finished products that it manufactured included hoops, bands, cotton ties, iron and steel bars, bolt and nut iron, angles and many other shapes.[34]

PIPES AND TUBES

Among the most important foundry products, measured by tonnage, is cast-iron pipe, the use of which has expanded very rapidly with the growth of cities in America and the adoption of modern plumbing throughout the world. Alabama with its superior foundry irons, low production costs and limited range of local iron and steel manufactures, rapidly took the lead in this industry, and by 1894 was exporting pipe as well as pig iron to foreign countries. The first important contract recorded was for 10,000 tons of cast-iron pipe for the Tokyo Water Works, followed the next year by contracts aggregating 30,000 tons for the neighboring city of Yokohoma.[35]

Naturally, however, the principal market for such pipe was at home, and the fact that the principal purchasers were municipal and other public corporations with less flexible bargaining powers than private buyers, opened the way for an abuse that, though not peculiar to this industry, was conspicuously associated with it by a famous lawsuit. This was the so-called Addyston Pipe case, brought by the Government against six cast-iron pipe companies, including the firm mentioned, for violating the Sherman Anti-Trust Law. It was shown that these companies had by agreement divided the United States into what was technically known as "pay territory" and "free territory." In the free territory the members were permitted to sell at such prices as they pleased. This included New England and the North Atlantic states as far South as Maryland and Virginia, where there was active competition from independent plants and potential competition from abroad. The pay territory embraced all the rest of the country and was handled on a non-competitive basis. Whenever a municipal corporation, a water company, or a gas company, advertised for pipe an Executive Committee of pipe manufacturers met to determine the price at which a bid was to be put in by one of the members of the Association. This price was determined by a sort of auction among the members. The Company which agreed to pay the highest bonus was awarded the right to bid and to the order in case the bid secured it, the bonus measuring approximately the margin of profit over what the latter would have been under free competition. After the right to a contract was thus determined, it

---

[34] *Commercial and Financial Chronicle*, LXVIII, 616–617, Apr. 1, 1899; LXVIII, 721, Apr. 15 1899; LXIX, 852, Oct. 21, 1899; LXIX, 1064, Nov. 18, 1899; LXX, 77, Jan. 13, 1900.
[35] American Iron and Steel Association, *Bulletin*, XXVIII, 269, Nov. 24, 1894; XXIX, 189 Aug. 20, 1895.

was protected by the other companies, who graded their bids so as to have them higher than the bid of the company to whom the contract was to go. There was also a fixed bonus paid to the Association upon all contracts in certain territories reserved exclusively to one or another of the members. The proceeds of the bonus were distributed pro rata among the members from time to time. The Court compelled the companies to dissolve the Association and to discontinue the practice described.[36]

The year the Federal supreme court handed down its decision in the Addyston case the Central Foundry Company was organized, consolidating in the ownership of a single corporation a large number of pipe foundries in all parts of the country, controlling about 95 per cent of the soil-pipe trade of the United States.[37] In 1913 more than 1,000,000 tons of cast-iron pipe and fittings were made. The leading states, on a tonnage rating were Alabama, New Jersey, Pennsylvania and Ohio in the order named, this being one of the few instances where Pennsylvania failed to take precedence in a branch of iron and steel production.

During the great popularity of bicycles just prior to the general introduction of the automobile a large market arose for weldless steel tubing, which was largely employed in the manufacture of these vehicles. This tubing, it will be recalled, was made under special patents and the manufacture soon fell largely into the hands of men connected with the bicycle business. In 1897 these tube manufacturers combined as the Shelby Steel and Tube Company, which controlled nearly 90 per cent of the output of unwelded steel tubing. A majority of the capital of the new company was owned by Englishmen. Two years later the capital stock was doubled, and additional works were purchased, giving the Company practically a monopoly in the United States. The seamless tube it made at this time did not exceed four inches in diameter and the market for it was limited to a few fields of which the chief—the manufacture of bicycles just mentioned—was speedily to decline. After paying one or two dividends the Company began to show evidence of precarious prosperity. To be sure, it still had a large field for its products in certain types of boilers, but the great future quantity market was to be for larger sizes than those in which the Company specialized. This required a modification of its plants and brought it into conflict with a gigantic rival that was soon to merge in the United States Steel Corporation.[38]

The National Tube Company, with a capital stock of $80,000,000, was incorporated in 1899, embracing many of the largest wrought steel, iron tube and pipe-making plants in the United States. It was at the time of

---

[36] American Iron and Steel Association, *Bulletin*, XXXI, 93, Apr. 20, 1897; *Commercial and Financial Chronicle*, LXVI, 362–363, Feb. 19, 1898; LXIX, 1080, Nov. 25, 1899; LXIX, 1171, Dec. 9, 1899; U. S. Industrial Commission, *Reports*, II, 41–47.

[37] *Commercial and Financial Chronicle*, LXIX, 178, July 22, 1899.

[38] American Iron and Steel Association, *Bulletin*, XXXI, 125, June 1, 1897; XXXI, 261, Nov. 20, 1897; *Commercial and Financial Chronicle*, LXVIII, 1026, May 27, 1899; LXVIII, 1183, June 17, 1899; LXX, 331–332, Feb. 17, 1900; LXX, 949, May 12, 1900; LXXI, 1074, Nov. 24, 1900.

its formation the largest tube concern in the world and the third largest steel and iron corporation, the Krupp and the Carnegie companies alone exceeding it. It included iron furnaces and other subsidiary properties, as well as rolling mills and pipe works, the aggregate capacity of its plants being more than 1,100,000 tons per annum, and it manufactured all grades of steam, gas and water pipes, boiler tubes, oil and artesian-well tubes, electric conduits, trolley poles, shells and projectiles, hand rails, "and innumerable other varieties of pipe for hundreds of purposes." Not only did the Company practically control the domestic business in these products, but it was also a powerful factor in foreign markets. It supplied pipes for the oil fields of Russia, Bulgaria, Java and Canada; irrigation pipes for Australia and South Africa, and hydraulic equipment for mines and industrial works in every part of the world. The range of sizes manufactured by the Company extended from one-sixteenth of an inch to thirty-six inches diameter, and three distinct processes of manufacture were employed: butt welding, lap welding and solid drawing. The last was the process used by the Shelby Steel and Tube Company, with which the National Tube Company was a competitor. About 40 per cent of the finished products made by the Company were manufactured directly from the ore.

It was estimated that the economies this amalgamation realized through better coördination of production and the elimination of competitive selling and office forces and other duplicated expenses, totalled fully $3,000,000 per annum.[39] Notwithstanding the presence of this dominant corporation, new corporations were organized from time to time to compete with it. Shortly before the formation of the United States Steel Corporation, the Carnegie Company planned to erect immense tube works at Conneaut. In 1900 the Wheeling Steel and Iron Company, which already operated blast furnaces and a Bessemer steel plant, erected tube works at a cost of a half million dollars; and a plant of nearly this size was built about that time at Norfolk.[40]

The demand for steel tubing grew at a remarkable rate. In 1905 when the industry had already made what was considered record progress, the total output of steel pipe in the United States was somewhat under a million tons. Eight years later, in 1913, it was 2,190,000 tons. While the production of steel rails increased less than 4 per cent during this period, the production of steel pipe grew more than 120 per cent.[41]

TIN-PLATE

Another rapidly expanding market for steel was created by the demand for plates and sheets for structural requirements, in shipyards, and in the tin-plate industry. In addition to considerable quantities of ship plates

[39] *Commercial and Financial Chronicle*, LXIX, 131, July 15, 1899; LXX, 384, Feb. 24, 1900; LXX, 744–745, Apr. 14, 1900; American Iron and Steel Association, *Bulletin*, XXXIII, 129, Aug. 1, 1899.
[40] *Commercial and Financial Chronicle*, LXXI, 1274, Dec. 22, 1900; American Iron and Steel Association, *Bulletin*, XXXV, 9, Jan. 23, 1901.
[41] *Manufacturers' Record*, LXVI, 40, Dec. 10, 1914.

exported to Belfast and the Clyde during favorable seasons, our own shipyards, especially on the Great Lakes, called for large quantities of these materials. The tin-plate industry, which became firmly established subsequent to 1890, gave birth to what was practically a new domestic market, the consumption of steel for tin and terne plate increasing from less than a thousand tons in 1891 to approximately 900,000 tons in 1914.

We have previously described the earlier adventures into tin-plate manufacturing in the United States and their ultimate failure, and the beginning of a permanent industry shortly before the opening of the period we are now to describe. In 1892, just previous to the panic, 20 works in the United States either were making or were equipped to make tin-plates or terneplates, and 10 additional tin-plate works were in course of construction. Two years later, the number of such establishments had risen to 56.[42] At this time the tendency of the industry was toward plant dispersion, many old firms in the iron and steel industry and new firms organized for this purpose being eager to reap the large profits which were promised, at least in the imagination of promoters, by the tariff levied on this product by the McKinley Bill. In 1894 the first tin-plate mill south of Maryland was established at the old Dominion Iron and Mill Works in Richmond.[43]

At this time American makers were by no means able to meet Welsh competition at every point. Low through rates by water and rail to interior points, as well as lower wages and the advantage of long experience and an established business good will, gave Welsh mills the ascendancy on the Pacific Coast, where the canning industry offered a large market for their products. They also supplied firms like the Standard Oil Company, that re-exported plates in the form of containers and collected a drawback on this material. Only part of the black-plates used by American makers were of domestic manufacture. Large quantities were still brought into the country from Great Britain, paying a duty that partly countervailed the protection afforded by the tariff on the plates when tinned. The latter condition was but temporary, however, the proportion of foreign black-plates used for tinning falling from nearly 32 per cent of the total consumed in the country in 1891, to a fraction of 1 per cent six years later. The displacement of foreign black-plates was accelerated by a provision in the Wilson Tariff, levying a higher duty on them than on tin-plates.[44]

How rapid the progress of the new industry was is illustrated by the fact that Welsh plates had a monopoly of the American market until 1890; in 1896 domestic production for the first time exceeded imports; two years later the Welsh product had been driven from our markets, except where it was imported for re-exportation under a drawback of 99 per cent of the duty. In 1911 American manufacturers captured this re-export trade, and

---

[42] American Iron and Steel Association, *Bulletin*, XXVIII, 109, May 23, 1894.
[43] American Iron and Steel Association, *Bulletin*, XXVIII, 269, Nov. 24, 1894.
[44] American Iron and Steel Association, *Bulletin*, XXIX, 29, Jan. 30, 1895; Dunbar, *The Tin Plate Industry*, 21.

Iron and Steel Shapes 131

thereafter the amount of foreign tin-plate consumed in the United States was relatively negligible. The brief period of active Welsh competition did not seriously check the growth of the industry, as the dates just recorded sufficiently prove; but it stimulated mechanical improvements, the adoption of labor-saving processes and administrative economies, which later redounded to the benefit of the industry as a whole.[45]

The geography of tin-plate making was influenced by the same general conditions that determined the geography of the iron and steel industry and, subject to this controlling influence, by proximity to heavy consumers of its products. We have already seen that some of the earliest plate-dipping works, notably those at Baltimore, were founded largely with the local canning industry in view. In case of the latter city, however, there was the additional motive that it was a long-standing center for rolling sheet iron, and was in the immediate neighborhood of the first district in the United States where the manufacture of galvanized iron became a local specialty. Pennsylvania from the first became the principal site of the industry. Indiana speedily took second rank, partly because of its supply of natural gas.

Domestic output multiplied so rapidly that by 1897 price cutting and other competition were felt to be an evil, and manufacturers organized to regulate the distribution of their product, "so as to realize a reasonable profit to the makers," and to defend their tariff privileges. For instance, one of the first moves made was to appoint a committee to confer with the Standard Oil Company regarding its attitude toward the new tariff bill, with a view to repealing the drawback provision that permitted this powerful corporation to use imported plates.[46] About the same time labor became restive. Many of the tin-plate workers were Welshmen, trained in collective action in their own country. During the negotiations between the employees and their employers there was a general suspension of work, which was terminated by an advance in wages and an agreement on the part of tin-plate makers not to manufacture sheet iron for the general market in the event of the market for tin-plate becoming depressed.[47] New mills were being built so rapidly that overproduction was feared, and some of the hastily erected, poorly located and uneconomically conducted plants were forced to suspend operations. Efforts to control prices by agreement were ineffective in face of the difference in cost of production at different works.[48]

These conditions led in 1898 to the organization of the American Tinplate Company, through the purchase, by a corporation having an authorized capital of $50,000,000, of 39 plants in different parts of the country, repre-

[45] Dunbar, *The Tin-Plate Industry*, 23–24.
[46] American Iron and Steel Association, *Bulletin*, xxxi, 61, Mar. 10, 1897; xxxi, 93, Apr. 20, 1897; Dunbar, *The Tin-Plate Industry*, 77–78.
[47] American Iron and Steel Association, *Bulletin*, xxxi, 157, July 10, 1897.
[48] American Iron and Steel Association, *Bulletin*, xxxi, 235, 237, Oct. 20, 1897.

senting, it was said, over 90 per cent of the productive capacity of the United States.[49] It is not our purpose to trace the history of this combination during its brief independent existence. It succeeded in advancing prices and maintaining them at a steadier level than hitherto. In 1899 it was embarrassed for a short period by inability to secure sufficient supplies of steel, and shipments of tin-plates were temporarily delayed for that reason. This led to the organization of the National Steel Company, already described, by the same interests that were in control of the American Tinplate Company, partly for the purpose of supplying the latter with billets or sheet bars. The new organization dismantled its inadequate and poorly located plants and concentrated its operations at points where costs of production and marketing charges were at a minimum. It also encouraged mechanical improvements that speedily reduced the labor costs per unit of output, in spite of an increase of wages in many departments of the mills. Centralized control probably hastened the complete conquest of the domestic market and the successful invasion of certain foreign markets.[50]

In 1899 the National Enameling and Stamping Company was incorporated at Trenton, with a capital of $30,000,000, to combine the four principal manufactories of enamel and tin-plate goods in the United States, situated respectively at St. Louis, Milwaukee, New York and Baltimore. This Company was regarded as a competitor of the American Tinplate Company—at least in certain lines—and the latter promptly incorporated three allied concerns, the National Tinplate Company, the United States Tinplate Company, and the National Tinplate and Stamped Ware Company to fight the former. At least, this was one of the alleged motives for their organization. The National Tinplate Company proposed to employ a new method of manufacture, known as the Rogers Process, from the name of its inventor, W. H. Rogers, of Wheeling.[51]

With the organization of the United States Steel Corporation, the American Tinplate Company became part of the larger concern and later was combined, as previously mentioned, with the American Sheet Steel Company under the same control. In 1904 the United States Steel Corporation made a shipment of 25,000 boxes of tin-plate to the Canadian Canneries, which had previously used Welsh plate entirely.[52] The following year they wrested from their Welsh competitors the California market, which was of immensely more importance, their contracts with the Pacific Coast canneries this season amounting to well toward 2,000,000 boxes.[53] Meanwhile, however, many competing plants were springing up in all directions, and the

[49] *Commercial and Financial Chronicle*, LXVII, 1065, Nov. 19, 1898; LXVII, 1261, Dec. 17, 1898; U. S. Industrial Commission, *Reports*, I, 866; Dunbar, *The Tin-Plate Industry*, 79–83. XXXIII 69, Apr. 20, 1899; XXXIII, 130, Aug. 1, 1899; XXXIII, 153, Sept. 15, 1899.
[50] Dunbar, *The Tin-Plate Industry*, 78–104; American Iron and Steel Association, *Bulletin*, XXXIII, 69, Apr. 20, 1899; XXXIII, 130, Aug. 1, 1899; XXXIII, 153, Sept. 15, 1899.
[51] *Commercial and Financial Chronicle*, LXVIII, 187, Jan. 28, 1899; American Iron and Steel Association, *Bulletin*, XXXIII, 25, Feb. 15, 1899; XXXIV, 53, Mar. 10, 1900.
[52] American Iron and Steel Association, *Bulletin*, XXXVIII, 77, May 25, 1904.
[53] American Iron and Steel Association, *Bulletin*, XXXIX, 158, Oct. 15, 1905.

percentage of the tin and terne plate made in the United States supplied by the United States Steel Corporation was steadily decreasing, although there was an absolute growth in its output. In 1900 it was practically a complete monopoly; in 1913 it produced only 50 per cent of the country's total product. In 1910 the American Sheet and Tinplate Company erected one of the largest mills in the world at Gary, the new city founded by its parent corporation.[54]

At no time was independent production completely extinguished, although the American Tinplate Company and later the United States Steel Corporation were probably in a position to control market conditions. Among the old independent plants, for example, was the N. & G. Taylor Company of Philadelphia and Cumberland, Maryland, an enterprise that had been handed down from father to son through four generations. It was in its 105th year when the World War broke out. Naturally it had not manufactured tin-plates during most of this period, its business during the greater part of its existence having been rolling sheet iron and allied products. This Company, however, had Welsh connections, and after 1893 removed its tinning equipment to Philadelphia, where it operated dipping works on black-plates mostly imported. Later it purchased a sheet mill at Cumberland and ultimately concentrated all its operations at that point.[55]

Since 1898 the United States has imported very little tin-plate, and since 1911 practically none, although occasionally between the former and the latter date some Welsh plates were still brought into the country for re-export with kerosene, canned goods, or packing-house products, under the draw-back clauses of the tariff. Indeed, the prices of tin-plates in America and Wales for the years immediately preceding the World War were practically on a level, and domestic producers naturally took the re-export trade from their former competitors. In doing this, certain interesting arrangements were entered into between employers and their workers. The United States Steel Corporation at one time had an agreement with its skilled employes, by which the latter yielded a rebate of 25 per cent of their wages for making tin-plates sold to exporters in competition with the Welsh. Today the period when such devices were necessary has long since passed. Indeed, America exports tin-plate in considerable quantities to competitive markets outside of Canada. In the latter country our makers possess certain geographical advantages, especially in regard to shipments to interior points, that make it tributary territory. In 1912 exports reached the maximum for any year before the World War, or 81,000 tons. These shipments went to South America and Asia, as well as Canada—at prices somewhat lower than were given to domestic consumers. The re-export and export business together amounted to 150,000 tons of tin-plate, or about 15 per cent of the total output, and naturally this quantity was not sold

[54] American Iron and Steel Association, *Bulletin*, XLIV, 6, Jan. 1, 1910; Dunbar, *The Tin-Plate Industry*, 96.
[55] *Iron Age*, XCIV, 73, 78, July 9, 1914.

below cost, although presumably at a narrower margin of profit than was expected from sales to domestic consumers. America is now the largest producer of tin-plates in the world.[56]

The manufacture of galvanized iron was established in the United States long before that of tin-plate, although there is a legend that makes terne-plate, or plate coated with a lead and tin mixture and used for much the same purposes as tin-plate in certain applications, an American invention and dates its manufacture at Philadelphia back to the earlier decades of the last century. The manufacture of galvanized iron, especially plates and wire, has already been mentioned, as well as its concentration in the district between Philadelphia and Baltimore. Galvanized iron was not made at Pittsburgh, the great steel manufacturing center, until 1898.[57] In this branch of manufacture we enjoyed one advantage that we did not have in case of tin-plate making; the raw materials were produced at home.[58]

In 1908 a new process for employing zinc and iron was introduced into this country from England, where it had been invented a short time before. It was accidentally discovered that when steel and zinc dust are heated to a temperature somewhat below the fusing point of the latter metal in an annealing furnace, the zinc forms a silvery coating of alloy on the surface of the steel, the resulting product being unlike that obtained by either electro or heat galvanizing. Steel protected by this treatment is largely employed for electrical conduits and fittings, and in certain plumbing and household fixtures.[59]

This by no means exhausts the instances where metals are used in alloy or in surface combinations for purposes that widely extend the uses that may be made of iron and steel; but from the quantitative standpoint tin, terne-plate and galvanized iron are the most important products of the latter class. Between 1904 and 1914 the quantity of steel converted into black-plates for dipping increased from about half a million to more than a million tons. The quantity of pig tin used for coating plates increased during the five years ending with 1914 from some 14,000 to 18,000 tons. The use of lead compounds was apparently decreasing, the consumption of lead in terne mixtures having declined during this period. Most tin-plate made in the United States in 1914 was rolled and dipped in the same establishment. In fact, of 1,050,000 tons of steel used for tin-plate, 1,042,000 tons was rolled in the works where the plate was dipped.[60]

The American tin-plate industry is often referred to as a creation of the McKinley Tariff. This is denied, apparently on good grounds, though unquestionably the duty imposed upon tin-plates by that law came at the psychological moment to produce the maximum effect. Our steel industry

---

[56] Dunbar, *The Tin-Plate Industry*, 63, 110–114.
[57] American Iron and Steel Association, *Bulletin*, XXXII, 157, Oct. 15, 1898.
[58] *Mineral Industry*, IX, 659; XIV, 654; XV, 755.
[59] *Iron Age*, XCIII, 1189, May 14, 1914; XCIV, 191, July 23, 1914.
[60] U. S. Bureau of the Census, *Manufactures, 1914*, II, 259.

had been expanding with remarkable rapidity and, as we have seen elsewhere, the cost of making steel in this country in practically all its finished shapes had fallen to the level prevailing in the principal competing countries on the other side of the Atlantic. Our canners and other tin-plate using industries afforded us a very large and steady market. We had successfully manufactured sheet steel in almost every form except black-plates for a considerable period prior to 1890. When the manufacture was once begun, the technical traditions of the steel industry were immediately applied to it, with the result that labor-saving devices of every kind were rapidly devised or adopted from less progressive countries, and quantity production was introduced.[61]

[61] Dunbar, *The Tin-Plate Industry*, 115–118; Taussig, *Tariff History of the United States*, 347–348.

CHAPTER IX

ENGINEERING INDUSTRIES

Locomotives and Rolling Stock, 136. Shipbuilding, 141. Agricultural Machinery, 146. Ordnance and Armor, 147. Hardware, 148. Tools and Cutlery, 148. Stoves and Furnaces, 150. Prime Movers, 150. Machine Tools, 153. Bicycles, 155.

LOCOMOTIVES AND ROLLING STOCK

No branch of our engineering industries suffered more from the panic of 1893 than the manufacture of locomotives, cars and other railway equipment. During the years immediately preceding, American works had made over 2,000 locomotives annually; in 1894 the number fell abruptly to 695, of which more than 80 were built for export. The number of railway cars constructed declined from over 50,000 to some 17,000 in a single year. The latter figure is still more striking if we recall that the number of cars built in 1890 well exceeded 100,000. The year 1894 was marked further by a dramatic strike at Pullman, Illinois, where a number of standing grievances were brought to a head by measures taken by the Company to reduce costs of production in order to keep their plant at least partially employed. The earnings of the Michigan-Peninsular-Car Company, probably the largest manufacturer of rolling stock other than locomotives in the United States, fell within twelve months from $867,000 to $36,000.[1]

Recovery from this depression was very gradual, though the building of locomotives for export was fairly active, especially at the Baldwin Works. In 1894 the number completed in the country increased to 1,109, while the number of freight cars nearly doubled. An agreement was entered into between the Baldwin Works of Philadelphia and the Westinghouse Company of Pittsburgh for the manufacture of electric locomotives, the former firm making the bodies of the engines, the latter the electrical machinery to supply the motive power.[2] In 1896 the Baldwin Works completed eight electric locomotives for the Chicago Elevated Railway.[3] Steel cars, whose introduction was to be one of the most notable improvements of this period, first began to attract attention this year. Steel was first employed in the form of channel under-frames for flat cars, although practically at the same time that this construction was introduced the Carnegie Company made hopper bottom cars of steel throughout, as well as composite flat cars with

---

[1] American Iron and Steel Association, *Bulletin*, XXIX, 10, Jan. 9, 1895; XXIX, 108, May 10, 1895; *Commercial and Financial Chronicle*, LIX, 28–29, July 7, 1894; LIX, 717, Oct. 27, 1894; LIX, 778, Nov. 3, 1894.

[2] American Iron and Steel Association, *Bulletin*, XXIX, 107, May 10, 1895; XXX, 10, Jan. 10, 1896; XXX, 29, Feb. 1, 1896; *Commercial and Financial Chronicle*, LXI, 1132–1133, Dec. 28, 1895.

[3] American Iron and Steel Association, *Bulletin*, XXIX, 181, Aug. 10, 1895; XXX, 77, Apr. 1, 1896; cf., *Boston Journal of Commerce*, XLII, 262, July 29, 1893.

steel frames and wooden floors. Iron continued to be used for car wheels, although charcoal iron was no longer employed to the same extent as a few years previously. This was due to the fact that steel makers found that the tested mixtures used in old car wheels were an even more reliable material than the pigs fresh from the furnace, and therefore much scrap was employed in this branch of foundry work.[4]

By 1897 the worst of the depression was over. American firms were exporting locomotives to China, South America and Europe. The Baldwin Works closed orders within a single week for fifty-nine locomotives to be delivered to five countries outside the United States. Output was still far below the record figures prior to the panic, however, the number built in 1897 being 1,251 as compared with some 2,300 in 1890. Compound locomotives were becoming more common, and the export business steadily gained upon the domestic business. The number of cars built was less than 44,000, as compared with 103,000 in 1890. The low price of steel hastened the adoption of all-steel cars, cost having been the principal obstacle to its earlier use. In 1880 a steel car cost several times as much as a wooden car; by 1897 it could be built for about the same sum as a wooden car per ton of carrying capacity. Naturally, steel cars were most rapidly adopted upon the roads running out of Pittsburgh, where they were used for carrying ore.[5]

In 1898, when 1,875 locomotives were built by works outside of carshops, it was noted that 20 per cent were compounds, as compared with but 11 per cent even a year before. Twelve electric locomotives were made this season; and exports continued to grow. The average size of locomotives was increasing, as it had been consistently since the first railways were constructed in this country, and the largest now weighed 115 tons. The Baldwin Works still shipped locomotives to Russia, which had been a customer of American makers from the time her first railways were built. The same works also supplied locomotives for British railways, partly because they could make prompter deliveries than English firms. The two leading establishments building steel cars were rushed with orders; and the assertion was repeated with significant insistence that these could be built as cheaply per ton of carrying capacity as wooden cars. The Carnegie Company erected a large plant at Homestead especially for this branch of manufacture.[6]

In 1899 the number of locomotives made in the United States exceeded the number in 1890 for the first time since the panic. Within five months British operated railways in England and India ordered 130 locomotives

[4] American Iron and Steel Association, *Bulletin*, xxx, 11, Jan. 10, 1896; xxx, 153, July 10, 1896; xxxiii, 5, Jan. 1, 1899.
[5] American Iron and Steel Association, *Bulletin*, xxxi, 75, Apr. 1, 1897; xxxi, 109, May 10, 1897; xxxi, 261, Nov. 20, 1897; xxxii, 11, Jan. 15, 1898; *Boston Journal of Commerce*, xlix, 232, Jan. 9, 1897.
[6] American Iron and Steel Association, *Bulletin*, xxxii, 42, Mar. 15, 1898; xxxii, 155, Oct. 15, 1898; xxxii, 189, Dec. 1, 1898; xxxiii, 11, 13, Jan. 15, 1899; *Commercial and Financial Chronicle*, lxviii, 57–58, Jan. 14, 1899; *Boston Journal of Commerce*, liv, 318–319, July 29, 1899.

of American makers, partly because they could be bought for less money in the United States than at home. This was also a record year for the manufacture of freight cars, the total number approximating 124,000.[7] Naturally car building did not escape the movement toward consolidation that was so marked in most industries at this time. In 1899 the American Car and Foundry Company was organized under the laws of New Jersey to combine thirteen of the most important plants in the United States. During the first five months of its existence the new Company, whose capacity was about 7,500 cars a month, made over 26,000 cars, in addition to a very large quantity of replacement parts and car findings.[8] Another consolidation brought together the two largest makers of pressed steel cars in the United States, the Schoen Pressed Steel Company and the Fox Pressed Steel Equipment Company, as the Pressed Steel Car Company with a capital of $25,000,000. The new amalgamation controlled important patents registered in the United States and abroad, and its annual capacity was 12,000 steel cars per year, plus truck frames, bolsters and smaller articles which were used on wooden cars. The Company at once added to its plant at Joliet, increasing the capacity by 30 cars a day, and extended its business in other directions.[9] It had competitors, however, the Carnegie Company filling single orders for as high as 2,000 steel hopper and gondola cars. The Southern Car and Foundry Company had extensive works in the South. The same year the International Car Wheel Company, the American Switch Company and the American Railway Equipment Company, each embracing a group of firms engaged in the manufacture of certain special lines of railway equipment, were organized, and the Pullman Palace Car Company and the Wagner Palace Car Company were consolidated.[10]

With the beginning of the century a new era of large output for all classes of railway rolling stock began. In 1900 the number of locomotives built abruptly rose to 3,153, of which the Baldwin Locomotive Works alone made 1,217. Steel-car making, though still less than four years old in America, was already a prominent industry. Similar cars had been employed in Europe for twenty or thirty years, but new principles of construction and, above all, much larger units were used in the United States. In 1900 the Pressed Steel Car Company erected separate works near Pittsburgh for making wooden cars on steel frames, thus raising the capacity of its plants to 180 cars a day; and its orders on hand at the close of the year aggregated nearly 18,000 cars. The Cambria Company also made steel cars in considerable quantities. The American Car and Foundry Company, the

---

[7] American Iron and Steel Association, *Bulletin*, XXXIII, 33, Mar. 1, 1899; XXXIII, 84, May 15, 1899; XXXIV, 12, Jan. 15, 1900.
[8] *Commercial and Financial Chronicle*, LXVIII, 280, Feb. 11, 1899; LXVIII, 668, Apr. 8, 1899; LXVIII, 1029, May 27, 1899; LXIX, 542, Sept. 9, 1899; LXIX, 908, Oct. 28, 1899.
[9] *Commercial and Financial Chronicle*, LXVIII, 131, Jan. 21, 1899; LXVIII, 188, Jan. 28, 1899; LXIX, 745, Oct. 7, 1899.
[10] American Iron and Steel Association, *Bulletin*, XXXIII, 25, Feb. 15, 1899; *Commercial and Financial Chronicle*, LXVIII, 826, Apr. 29, 1899; LXVIII, 974, May 20, 1899; LXIX, 130, July 15, 1899; LXIX, 227, July 29, 1899; LXIX, 854, Oct. 21, 1899.

enormous organization with $60,000,000 authorized capital formed the year before, made street cars at some of its plants. Last of all, the Southern Car and Foundry Company, an amalgamation of several works, erected a plant at Birmingham, in close alliance with the Tennessee Coal, Iron, and Railroad Company, with a capacity of 10 wooden and 10 pressed steel cars a day.[11]

By 1902 the number of locomotives made in the United States for the first time exceeded 4,000, of which 47 were electric. Early this year the Baldwin Works celebrated their seventieth anniversary and the completion of their twenty-thousandth locomotive. The number of steam railway cars built by independent plants, that is, not including railroad shops, was nearly 165,000, of which 15 per cent were steel. This year the Pressed Steel Car Company had completed its 60,000th car, five years after the first modern steel car was made in the United States. At this time two types of steel car construction had been introduced—that covered by the patents of the Pressed Steel Car Company, in which the parts were shaped with the aid of hydraulic presses, and fabricated cars employing ordinary structural shapes, such as flat plates and beams. Cars of the latter type were made by the Cambria Company and by the Sterlingworth Company, of Easton, Pennsylvania.[12]

Rapid as had been the increase of rolling stock during the first years of the century, it was estimated in 1905 that while the number of locomotives in the country had increased from 31,000 to nearly 45,000 in 15 years, or about 40 per cent, and the number of cars had risen from 1,100,000 to 1,550,000 or in about the same proportion as the locomotives, the volume of freight moved during the same period had increased 153 per cent. While locomotives and cars were of heavier construction and capacity in 1905 than in 1890, these figures seem to show a decided decline in equipment as compared with the service rendered by it. This year the Baldwin Locomotive Works for the first time in their history made more than 2,000 locomotives. It will be recalled that this was about the maximum output for the entire country ten years before. Of these locomotives 85 were operated by electricity and 300 were compound.[13]

By this time all the locomotive works in the United States, with the exception of the Baldwin Company, were combined under the control of the American Locomotive Company, a fifty-million dollar corporation, which owned establishments at Paterson, New Jersey; Providence, Rhode Island; Manchester, New Hampshire; Schenectady and Dunkirk, New York; Pittsburgh and Scranton, Pennsylvania; Richmond, Virginia; and Montreal, Canada. At Paterson the Company owned two plants, the Cook Locomo-

[11] American Iron and Steel Association, *Bulletin*, XXXIV, 115, July 1, 1900; XXXV, 5, Jan. 10, 1901; XXXV, 11, Jan. 23, 1901; *Commercial and Financial Chronicle*, LXX, 1000, May 19, 1900; LXXI, 1273, Dec. 22, 1900; LXXI, 1312, Dec. 29, 1900.
[12] American Iron and Steel Association, *Bulletin*, XXXV, 45, Mar. 25, 1901; XXXVI, 29, Feb. 25, 1902; XXXVI, 50, Apr. 10, 1902; XXXVII, 3, Jan. 10, 1903; XXXVII, 53, Apr. 10, 1903.
[13] *Manufacturers' Record*, XLVII, 263, Apr. 13, 1905; American Iron and Steel Association, *Bulletin*, XXXVIII, 21, Feb. 10, 1904.

tive and Machine Company and the Rogers Locomotive Works. These nine plants made only a few more locomotives than the Baldwin Works alone, the total output of the United States and Canada in 1905 aside from those built at railway shops being 5,491.[14]

By 1906 about 45 per cent of the cars made in the United States were either entirely of steel or had steel under-frames, and the total consumption of steel for this single purpose was estimated at more than 600,000 tons. Indeed, an even larger proportion of the cars made would have been of this material had it been possible to obtain steel promptly. Of course the proportion of steel cars in the total freight equipment of the country was not so large, because the older wooden cars formerly exclusively in use were still in service; nevertheless, all-steel or part-steel equipment was now about 12 per cent of the total. Simultaneously the size of cars had increased rapidly, those of fifty-ton capacity being the standard of the Pennsylvania Road, and largely employed on the Harriman system, while forty-ton cars were in common use on other lines. It was now possible to build wooden cars of the latter capacity by careful body trussing, and since such cars could be delivered several months earlier than steel cars, on account of the scarcity of steel just mentioned, many roads that were pressed for rolling stock ordered the latter. Furthermore, the fabricated or structural steel under-frame car was gaining upon the pressed steel car, because of the waste of material in forming the larger members by pressing and the difficulty of repairing them. Even the wooden car of this period often contained light steel sections in place of wood.[15]

During 1906, also, the Pennsylvania Railway Company ordered the first all-steel passenger coaches regularly contracted for in the United States. The next year the same company placed orders for 200 steel passenger cars, since only steel coaches were to be used in the tunnels of the New York terminal, which were at this time approaching completion. Three years later the number of such cars in service was 1,228. The United States Steel Corporation, through the American Car and Foundry Company, erected one of the largest steel-car plants in the United States at Gary, Indiana. During 1907 the Baldwin Works built 2,663 locomotives. This equalled numerically the entire output for the first thirty years of the firm's history and, measured by traction power, of course, greatly exceeded it. The Company completed its thirty-thousandth locomotive that year, and within a quarter of a century it had raised the capacity of its works from 300 locomotives per annum to nine locomotives a day.[16]

This period of extraordinary activity was followed by a sudden setback in 1908, when the car works of the United States built only 27 per cent as many cars as the previous year, while the number of locomotives constructed

[14] *Manufacturers' Record*, XLVII, 25, Jan. 26, 1905; American Iron and Steel Association, *Bulletin*, XXXIX, 5, Jan. 5, 1905.
[15] American Iron and Steel Association, *Bulletin*, XXX, 13, Jan. 10, 1906.
[16] American Iron and Steel Association, *Bulletin*, XL, 90, July 1, 1906; XLI, 18, Feb. 22, 1907; XLI, 61, May 15, 1907; XLII, 14, Feb. 1, 1908; XLIII, 3, Jan. 1, 1909.

fell from 7,362 to 2,342. This depression continued into 1909. During the spring of that year but two of the ten plants of the American Locomotive Company—those at Schenectady and at Montreal—were in operation. The Baldwin Works were at this time incorporated, having hitherto existed as an unlimited partnership, under which form they had operated since 1832.[17]

Between 1900 and 1913 the tonnage carried by the railways of the United States more than doubled, exceeding in the latter year 300,000,000,000 tons. This tonnage was naturally transported with far fewer locomotives, cars and trains than at the earlier date, and the possibility of this development was due, to a very large extent, to the progress in steel making, which had made it practicable to use heavier rail sections, larger locomotives, and steel cars. In the manufacture of rolling stock, as well as of rails, alloys were now used to some extent. Seventeen roads employed vanadium steel frames in locomotive construction, and ten used chrome-vanadium more or less experimentally for piston rods, axles, crank pins and other machinery parts.[18]

SHIPBUILDING

Although wooden ships and steamers had by no means disappeared either from salt or fresh-water navigation, and the construction and repair of wooden vessels continued to be a large business, shipbuilding was by 1893 a recognized branch of the steel industry, and some of the largest shipbuilding plants in the country were directly or indirectly connected with steel works. The increasing interest exhibited by steel men in this business was illustrated by the action of Charles M. Schwab, the former president of the United States Steel Corporation, in becoming president of the largest enterprise of this kind in America.

This period did not open propitiously for shipbuilders. In 1894 the important works of the Delaware River Iron Shipbuilding and Engine Company at Chester, associated with John Roach and Sons, were practically idle. The tonnage of iron and steel vessels launched was only a little more than 50,000 tons, as compared with 94,000 tons the previous year. Yet the Cramps Yards, which had Government and private contracts carried over from the period before the panic, were partly occupied, and the *St. Louis* and *St. Paul*, the first two transatlantic boats of the new American merchant line, left the ways this year.[19]

But if the shipyards of the Coast were idle, this was not equally true of those on the Great Lakes. In 1895 there were under construction between Buffalo and Duluth 35 vessels with a total tonnage of 74,000 tons. Lake shipping made high profits this year, and steel steamers of the 6,000-ton

[17] American Iron and Steel Association, *Bulletin*, XLIII, 3, Jan. 1, 1909; XLIII, 14, Feb. 1, 1909; XLIII, 62, July 1, 1909.
[18] *Iron Age*, XCIV, 186, July 6, 1914; XCIV, 273, July 30, 1914.
[19] American Iron and Steel Association, *Bulletin*, XXVIII, 93, May 2, 1894; XXVIII, 237, Oct. 17, 1894; XXIX, 108, May 10, 1895.

class were already in operation. The large mining companies had begun to make themselves independent of the fluctuations of Lake business by building and operating their own ore carriers. This year the Standard Oil Company launched its first steel tanker, a vessel with a capacity of a quarter of a million gallons. It was built at the Nixon Shipyards, at Elizabeth, New Jersey, and represented the first unit of a large fleet already under contract. But, upon the whole, the year was not a prosperous one for shipbuilders. Indeed, the merchant tonnage constructed was even less than during the dull season of 1894.[20]

A change for the better came the following year. The Newport News Shipyards doubled their capital to $6,000,000, and were awarded contracts for $7,000,000 worth of vessels, mostly for the Government. Late in 1895 the Rockefeller interests ordered twelve ore carriers of the largest size from Great Lakes shipyards. Most of these were completed before the end of the ensuing season, and their construction brought prosperity to the larger builders of that district. The following year the Rockefeller interests, which were known as the Bessemer Steamship Company, placed contracts for three other vessels, one steamship and two consorts, each having a capacity of 6,500 to 7,000 tons.[21]

In 1898 the Spanish-American War created a sudden and unanticipated demand for shipping. The Government purchased a large number of merchant vessels for transports and for scouting service. Some yards were already engaged upon new steamships for the Cuban and South American trade before war was declared. Soon after hostilities began the Morgan Line contracted for four new ocean vessels to replace steamers sold to the Government. When Hawaii, the Philippines and Porto Rico were brought under the provisions of the coastal shipping law, the market for American built vessels was still further widened.[22] In 1899 the Cramps contracted to build three freight and passenger steamers for a line operating between San Francisco and Australia, via Honolulu and Pago Pago. The same year the Newport News Shipyards began work upon two 18,000-ton passenger vessels for the Pacific Mail Line, and the Union Iron Works of San Francisco secured a contract for two of the largest steamers ever built in this country, for the American Hawaiian Steam Navigation Company. On the whole the stimulation of interest in American Shipping, as a result of the War, was at first largely in the Pacific, though new vessels for the Porto Rican trade were built about the same time. This year also, the New York

---

[20] American Iron and Steel Association, *Bulletin*, XXIX, 35, Feb. 9, 1895; XXIX, 101, May 1, 1895; XXIX, 213, Sept. 20, 1895; XXIX, 250, Nov. 10, 1895; XXIX, 281, Dec. 20, 1895; *Mineral Industry*, IV, 406.

[21] American Iron and Steel Association, *Bulletin*, XXXII, 13, Jan. 15, 1898; XXXII, 109, July 15, 1898; XXXII, 122, Aug. 15, 1898.

[22] *Manufacturers' Record*, XXVIII, 340, Jan. 3, 1896; XXVIII, 19, Jan. 17, 1896; American Iron and Steel Association, *Bulletin*, XXX, 217, Oct. 1, 1896; XXXI, 237, Oct. 20, 1897; *Cassier's Magazine*, XV, 499–507, Apr. 1900.

Shipbuilding Company began the construction of a large shipbuilding plant at Camden, opposite Philadelphia.[23]

This industry did not escape the wave of consolidation that swept over the country at this time. A combination of eight of the largest shipbuilding concerns on the Great Lakes was formed with a capital stock of $30,000,000. It was known as the American Shipbuilding Company and remained one of the largest firms in this business. Indeed, it competed occasionally with tidewater companies in the construction of tonnage for ocean traffic. In the autumn of 1899 the Carnegie Steel Company ordered seven steel steamers of the 8,000-tons class of the American Shipbuilding Company, while the American Steel Barge Company of West Superior, an independent builder, took contracts for building two steel barges of the same capacity for the Rockefeller interests. It should be noted parenthetically, that Great Lake ore carriers were customarily measured by their tonnage capacity for that commodity, which was larger than ordinary registered gross or net tonnage, since 100 cubic feet of ore weigh considerably more than a ton.[24]

In 1900 William Cramp and Sons enlarged their plant and took over, through a subsidiary company, a rival establishment adjoining their Philadelphia yard. In addition to two United States battleships and two battleships for the Russian Government, this firm had under construction or under contract in the spring of this year ten merchant steamships, two of which were of 12,000-tons gross register, the total merchant tonnage amounting to nearly 70,000 tons. A rumor was current at this time that the Cramps were to amalgamate with the Midvale Steel Company and the British firm of Vickers, Sons and Maxim.[25] Not far distant from their yards the plant of the New York Shipbuilding Company was approaching completion. Its land rights covered 130 acres, and even before the yards themselves were finished it had begun the construction of three vessels, the largest of which was one of 11,000-tons capacity for the American-Hawaiian Steamship Company. The Newport News Yards were reported to be the most perfectly equipped shipbuilding plant in the world. The Eastern Shipbuilding Company, which had yards on the Thames River in Connecticut, opposite the city of New London, was building two steel steamships for the Great Northern Railway, to operate upon the Pacific, and of larger tonnage than any vessels hitherto constructed in the United States. New shipyards were begun in San Francisco this year by the Risdon Iron and Locomotive Works.[26] On the Great Lakes, likewise, shipbuilding continued remarkably active, and The American Shipbuilding Company built

[23] American Iron and Steel Association, *Bulletin*, XXXIII, 45, Mar. 15, 1899; XXXIII, 61, Apr. 10, 1899; XXXIII, 122, July 15, 1899; XXXIII, 157, Sept. 15, 1899.
[24] *Commercial and Financial Chronicle*, LXVIII, 471, Mar. 11, 1899; LXIX, 853, Oct. 21, 1899; American Iron and Steel Association, *Bulletin*, XXXIII, 43, Mar. 15, 1899; XXXIII, 53, Apr. 1, 1899.
[25] *Commercial and Financial Chronicle*, LXX, 999, May 19, 1900; LXXI, 234–235, Aug. 4, 1900; LXXI, 1313, Dec. 29, 1900.
[26] American Iron and Steel Association, *Bulletin*, XXXIV, 69, Apr. 1, 1900; XXXIV, 189, Nov. 15, 1900; *Engineering Magazine*, XIX, 498, July 1900; *Commercial and Financial Chronicle*, LXXI, 915, Nov. 3, 1900; LXXI, 970, Nov. 10, 1900.

four steel steamers of 3,000-tons gross burthen each for the Atlantic coastal trade. When the season closed this Company had contracts on its books for twenty new steel vessels to be completed during the coming year.[27]

In 1901 the Atlantic Transport Company placed contracts with the New York Shipbuilding Company for four vessels at a total cost of about $5,000,000. The Bath Iron Works entered the steel shipbuilding industry after a long experience in building wooden vessels, of timber brought from the South and from the Pacific Coast, with a contract for a 5,000-tons seven-mast steel schooner to carry coal. The American Shipbuilding Company constructed at Duluth two vessels of 7,000-tons gross burthen for the ocean trade. The aggregate value of the vessels built and contracted for this year on the Great Lakes exceeded $16,000,000, and the combined capacity of the sixty-three freight carriers in this list was 267,000 tons.[28]

The Sparrows Point Works at Baltimore also became active. In 1902 they launched for Kidder, Peabody and Company of Boston, two of the largest tramp steamers ever placed in this branch of the trade, having capacity for 10,000 tons of cargo. This year was also marked by the formation of an unfortunate shipbuilding combination promoted by Lewis Nixon. The new corporation absorbed eight companies building vessels and manufacturing vessel supplies at points as distant from each other as San Francisco and Bath, Maine. The American Bridge Company provided at its new works at Economy, Pennsylvania, facilities for building steel river barges on a large schedule. The American Shipbuilding Company, with its headquarters at Cleveland, closed a single contract for eleven cargo steamers to cost more than $2,000,000, which it was proposed to employ in freight traffic on the St. Lawrence. Every berth at the Lake yards was filled for the entire winter and contracts for new tonnage to be completed in that district during the ensuing season were estimated to total $10,000,000.[29]

In 1903 the *Minnesota* and *Dakota*, the vessels previously mentioned as under construction in Connecticut for the Great Northern Steamship Company to engage in the Seattle and Oriental trade, were launched. Each could carry 28,000 gross tons of coal or 280,000 barrels of flour, and had 50 per cent more dead-weight capacity than the largest freighters then plying on the Atlantic, the *Cedric* and the *Celtic* of the White Star Line. The American Shipbuilding Company closed contracts in 1903 for two vessels 550 feet long by 57 feet beam, to carry 11,000 tons of ore.[30]

The following season was marked by the failure of the United States Shipbuilding Company, organized by Lewis Nixon two years before, and the

[27] *Commercial and Financial Chronicle*, LXXI, 493, Sept. 8, 1900; American Iron and Steel Association, *Bulletin*, XXXIV, 181, Nov. 1, 1900.
[28] American Iron and Steel Association, *Bulletin*, XXXV, 21, Feb. 9, 1901; XXXV, 25, 29, Feb. 23, 1901; XXXV, 126, Aug. 25, 1901.
[29] American Iron and Steel Association, *Bulletin*, XXXVI, 41, Mar. 25, 1902; XXXVI, 85, June 10, 1902; XXXVI, 91, June 25, 1902; XXXVI, 101, July 10, 1902; XXXVI, 127, Aug. 25, 1902.
[30] American Iron and Steel Association, *Bulletin*, XXXVII, 61, Apr. 25, 1903; XXXVII, 133, Sept. 10, 1903; *Cassier's Magazine*, XXVI, 601–602, Oct. 1904.

sale of the constituent plants at auction for very low prices. The Eastern Shipbuilding Company's property at New London, where the *Minnesota* and the *Dakota* had been built, passed into the hands of the reorganization committee of the larger company for $145,000. It was at this time that Charles M. Schwab entered the scene as one of the salvagers of the wrecked enterprise. None of the plants of the first rank on the Atlantic Coast, however, Cramps, Sparrows Point, or Newport News, belonged to this corporation. The Newport News Yards had a world-wide reputation and were resorted to by merchant and war vessels from all parts of the globe, partly because they made a specialty of repair work, although they also built a large amount of tonnage.[31]

On the Great Lakes the transition from wood to steel, which had been going on rapidly for many years, was fast being completed. During 1904 fifty-two wooden ships passed out of existence by being wrecked or condemned and no new ones were built. A cargo steamer sailed on her maiden trip to the upper lakes with 10,250 tons of coal in her holds, the largest lading ever carried by a fresh-water vessel. This steamer alone brought back about ten times as much ore as passed through the Sault Ste. Marie Canal during the entire season of 1855, when that waterway was first opened to commerce. Within five years, according to the President of the American Shipbuilding Company, $125,000,000 had been invested in new vessels on the Great Lakes. In 1905 of the twenty-two ships under contract at Great Lake yards, twelve were of 10,000-tons capacity and over; and the carrying capacity of the ships launched during two successive seasons exceeded the entire Lake tonnage engaged in the ore trade ten years before. Among orders placed with Lake shipbuilders in 1906 were four for 12,000-ton vessels for the United States Steel Corporation. The smallest of eight of the vessels on the ways at the beginning of this year was 600 feet long, while the largest had a net cargo capacity of 13,500 tons; and in 1911 two ore vessels were laid down at the Detroit Yards, having a carrying capacity of 14,000 tons of ore on a 19-foot draught.[32]

The total tonnage of merchant vessels built annually in the United States toward the close of this period, according to the Bureau of Navigation, varied from 250,000 to 300,000 tons. The census figures are somewhat lower than this and show a decrease in 1909, 1914 and 1916, as compared with 1904, when the net tonnage was in round numbers 251,000 tons. In 1914 it had fallen to 156,000 tons. On the Great Lakes, at least, the decline was chiefly in vessels of less than 1,000 tons, and was attributed to the general business depression, which made it more difficult for small concerns to finance their enterprises than for big corporations whose resources per-

[31] American Iron and Steel Association, *Bulletin*, xxxviii, 139, Sept. 25, 1904; xxxviii 149, Oct. 10, 1904; xxxviii, 155, Oct. 25, 1904; xxxviii, 165, Nov. 10, 1904.
[32] American Iron and Steel Association, *Bulletin*, xxxviii, 10, Jan. 25, 1904; xxxviii, 94, June 25, 1904; xxxviii, 122, Aug. 25, 1904; xxxix, 149, Oct. 1, 1905; xl, 110, Aug. 1, 1906; xlv, 37, Apr. 10, 1911; *Mineral Industry*, xiv, 338.

mitted them to take advantage of a quiet season to carry through projected construction. The ratio of wooden to steel vessels was largest on the Pacific Coast and the Western Rivers, where wooden tonnage exceeded the steel tonnage by nearly 40 per cent. Wood was least used relatively on the Great Lakes, where it constituted considerably less than one-tenth of the total new construction. On the Atlantic Coast about one-third of the new tonnage consisted of wooden vessels, the remainder being of steel.[33]

AGRICULTURAL MACHINERY

During this period the agricultural machinery industry entered into a new phase, in which questions of organization and markets became relatively more important than individual patents and inventions. Indeed, no invention of the first order revolutionizing either the machines made or the method of making them occurred during these twenty years. The internal combustion tractor was being developed, but as an outgrowth of the automobile industry, which constitutes a field by itself. Moreover, this type of tractor did not become an element of first importance in farm equipment nor did it influence the general design of agricultural machinery before the World War. Two unanswered problems had not yet been solved: the perfection of machinery for picking cotton and for cutting cane. The technology of this industry was subject to the same influences as the machine making and engineering industries in general. Steel castings supplanted iron castings, where the latter continued to be used up to 1890. Steel alloys were employed to lessen the weight and increase the strength of parts subjected to unusual strain, minor attachments and devices were perfected, and the economies of quantity production were introduced to the fullest possible extent.

The most notable incident in the history of the organization of this industry was the formation of the International Harvester Company in 1902, with a capital of $120,000,000. This was a combination of the five principal firms making harvesters, mowers and similar agricultural machinery in the United States, partly for the purpose of controlling the market and introducing economies usually associated with such undertakings, and partly to promote the sale of American agricultural machinery abroad. Here, as in the case of the United States Steel Corporation, a union of resources was sought for the purpose of a foreign campaign; and that function of the new company was in this instance clearly specified in its name. Like several other large iron and steel consumers, it proceeded to make itself independent so far as possible in respect to raw materials. In 1902 it erected a steel plant and a rolling mill at its Deering Works at Chicago to supply its factories with bars and shapes.[34]

[33] *Iron Age*, XLIV, 177, July 16, 1914.
[34] American Iron and Steel Association, *Bulletin*, XXXVI, 157, Oct. 25, 1902; Jenks and Clark, *The Trust Problem*, 372–382.

The formation of this great corporation by no means eliminated competition in many fields in which the so-called monopoly nominally controlled, nor did it prevent a number of new and small companies springing up in different parts of the country to manufacture up-to-date specialties or standard implements and machinery not made by the Trust. Indeed, there were combinations for the manufacture of special classes of agricultural machinery outside the International Harvester Company. In 1893 the Standard Harrow Company was incorporated to acquire the property of twenty-one existing companies and firms producing some 85 per cent of the spring tooth harrows made in the United States.[35] Small factories making cotton planters, cultivators and plows were established at a number of points in the Southern and the prairie states.

Between 1899 and 1914 the total value of the agricultural machinery and implements manufactured in the United States increased from $101,000,000 to $164,000,000, while the number of establishments decreased from 640 to 601, and the average number of employes from 50,000 to 48,000. More than 68 per cent of the products of these establishments, as measured by value, were manufactured in plants whose output was rated at more than $1,000,000 a year. Illinois was credited with over $65,000,000 of the $164,000,000 worth of machinery reported; the other important states engaged in this industry, ranked according to product, were Wisconsin, Michigan, New York and Indiana. The four adjacent states of Illinois, Wisconsin, Michigan and Indiana produced about three-fourths of the farm machinery made in the country.

ORDNANCE AND ARMOR

No branch of the iron and steel industry made more exacting demands upon the technical skill of steel makers, engineers and mechanics, than the manufacture of heavy ordnance and armor plate. It has been pointed out in an earlier chapter that these were products subject to careful Government inspection throughout all the stages of manufacture and submitted to searching tests before they were accepted by the purchaser. Elaborate experiments were repeatedly made to verify and improve the quality of the output. Therefore the production of ordnance and armor plate was far more important as a gage to the progress of the country's iron and steel and engineering industries than its value of product would indicate. By 1893 we had caught up with the steel makers of Great Britain, Germany and France in this branch of manufacturing. We were able to turn out as heavy ordnance or armor plate as any country, and in quality our products compared favorably with the best made abroad; but in respect to costs European makers still had the advantage over us. In 1894, when the country was waking up to the importance of modern coast defenses, we produced our first 13-inch guns. The armor plants at Bethlehem and Homestead were

---

[35] *Commercial and Financial Chronicle*, LXXI, 1170, Dec. 8, 1900.

reported to be the best equipped in the world, and during that year the Bethlehem Company secured a contract for the armor for two Russian battleships over fourteen competitors, including the best armor-plate manufacturers of England, France, Germany and Italy.[36]

HARDWARE

At the other extreme of the metal-working trades was the manufacture of hardware, in which Americans had excelled, as they had in making light tools and farm implements, for many generations. No radical change occurred in that industry during this period, although it experienced a growth comparable with that of allied lines of manufacturing and steadily extended its foreign markets. Having attained a high degree of efficiency in methods of production and business organization, hardware manufacturers began to devote themselves to a larger extent than hitherto to the ultimate refinement of progress in any industry—the perfection of design. Building hardware especially profited by higher artistic standards. This industry was not influenced as much as most other branches of metal-working by the tendency toward consolidation. Geographically it was centered in Connecticut, which produced nearly $29,000,000 worth of product out of less than $40,000,000 for the entire United States. Illinois, with about one-third the output of Connecticut, ranked second, and Ohio followed close upon Illinois. Pennsylvania, New York and New Jersey came next in order. Both New York and Illinois had more establishments than Connecticut, though neither state employed one-fourth as many operatives as the latter.

TOOLS AND CUTLERY

American tools and cutlery practically controlled the domestic market from the beginning of this period, although tool steel was imported from England and occasionally from other countries, especially for high-grade cutlery. This industry still employed more manual labor relatively to output than most branches of iron and steel working, a condition that favored foreign competitors with their lower wage rates. Nevertheless, American makers of standard products, many of which had a world-wide reputation, suffered little from this fact. Their works were constantly abreast, and were perhaps ahead, of the best works abroad, and their products were distributed in competition with those of British and continental makers to nearly every country. This was notably true, for example, of Disston saws and Douglas axes.

In 1898 the American consul in Edinburgh reported that wholesale dealers in that city carried regularly in stock American axes, forks, hoes, picks, spades, hay knives, lawn mowers, saws, files, wheels, washing machines, wringers and even bolts and nuts. Lightness and convenience of design

---

[36] American Iron and Steel Association, *Bulletin*, xxviii, 61, Mar. 21, 1894; xxviii, 261, Nov. 14, 1894; xxviii, 289, Dec. 28, 1894; *Engineering Magazine*, xv, 371–386, June 1898.

still accounted for no small part of this popularity. The consul quoted said, upon the authority of British dealers:

"American tools are preferred by workmen to either English or German. They are tempered harder, are more serviceable, and have a finish that is lacking in the others. Tools of German make are somewhat cheaper, but are softer and do not stand use as well as the American. Moreover, . . . there is just now a lively prejudice here against anything German."[37]

This industry, like most branches of steel manufacturing that produced varied, highly finished quality goods in small units and minor patented articles or novelties made by patented processes, was not highly integrated or centralized under monopolistic or semi-monopolistic control. At the same time, however, it showed a marked tendency toward geographical concentration in the vicinity of the skilled labor so essential for its success. The cost of raw materials and of freight upon materials and products was a relatively small fraction of the selling price of finished goods, and therefore little or no tendency manifested itself to place works in the immediate vicinity of coal and iron mines. How far tradition and the presence of a skilled operative population determined the location of these industries— even those producing comparatively heavy articles like machine tools—is illustrated by the continued prosperity of great tool-making centers like Providence and New Haven, Philadelphia, Cincinnati and Cleveland.

To be sure, independent works were occasionally combined, sometimes in an effort to control a special department of the trade. In 1899 four establishments, two of which were in Philadelphia and the others respectively in Plainfield, New Jersey, and Hamilton, Ohio, united as the Niles-Bement-Pond Company. The statement was made at the time that these companies controlled the heavy machine trade of the country, but the usual methods of trust making had not been employed to bring about this consolidation. There had been no promoter's fees and no underwriting. The stock in the new company was taken up by members of the constituent concerns and no immediate change in management was made.[38] The American Ax and Tool Company had been incorporated as early as 1889 to combine 12 ax works—including eventually the famous establishment at East Douglas, Massachusetts—several of which it transferred to a new plant near Pittsburgh.[39] The National Shear Company, incorporated in 1898 to combine five important works in New England, New Jersey and Ohio, proved unsuccessful, and two years later its properties were disposed of at a receiver's sale, most of the works passing into the hands of a new combination known as the International Cutlery Company.[40]

[37] American Iron and Steel Association, *Bulletin*, XXXII, 185, Dec. 1, 1898; cf., Foster, *Engineering in the United States*, 78.
[38] *Commercial and Financial Chronicle*, LXIX, 388, Aug. 19, 1899.
[39] *Commercial and Financial Chronicle*, LXX, 998, May 19, 1900.
[40] *Commercial and Financial Chronicle*, LXX, 1052, May 26, 1900; U. S. Industrial Commission, *Reports*, I, 1041, 1043–1044.

STOVES AND FURNACES

One of the oldest differentiated branches of the iron trades is stove making, which had developed into an independent business early in the Nineteenth Century. While the number of stoves made in America did not decline absolutely, the industry developed allied and subsidiary branches that eventualy rivaled it in importance. This was due to the substitution of furnace, steam and hot-water heating for direct heating by stoves. While Pennsylvania and New York continued to hold a respectable position in the production of stoves and hot-air furnaces, their output was dwarfed by that of a group of central western states headed by Ohio, followed closely by Michigan and Illinois. Together the latter three states produced about 40 per cent in value of products of all the stoves and ranges made in the country. Furthermore, nearly half of the gas and oil stoves manufactured in the United States were made in the State of Ohio.

Several attempts to consolidate this industry finally resulted in the incorporation of the American Radiator Company in 1899. This company had affiliations with the National Steel Company and merged nearly every heating apparatus concern of first importance in the United States, including the American Radiator Company of Illinois. Altogether it controlled about 75 per cent of the output of steam and water heating apparatus. The same year the Pittsburgh Stove and Range Company was organized to consolidate nine stove works in the Pittsburgh District.[41] Stove making, however, required a comparatively simple plant and was not protected by patents to the same extent as the manufacture of more modern heating devices. Consequently it was more widely dispersed than the younger but more vigorous and progressive sister industry, and suffered from over-competition. In 1899 it was reported that there were 218 stove works in the country, with a total invested capital of $30,000,000. An effort was made to consolidate them in one great organization, but this did not discourage erection of numerous independent local plants.[42]

PRIME MOVERS

Writing upon international competition, early in the present century, an English economist said:

"A country might be expected to manifest the greatest efficiency in producing that which it used itself most largely. . . . We should be prepared to find England exporting large quantities of cotton and linen machinery and also woolen machinery . . . and America exporting mining machinery, general pioneering machinery, agricultural implements; and since American industrialism is a world of specialization, standardization and cheap production in large quantities . . . and machine tools also. . . . Since the division of labor is conditioned by the scope of the market indirectly, and directly by the size of the business, it was in America with its large scale of production com-

---

[41] *Commercial and Financial Chronicle*, LXVIII, 329, Feb. 18, 1899; LXIX, 388, Aug. 19, 1899.
[42] American Iron and Steel Association, *Bulletin*, XXXIII, 189, Nov. 1, 1899.

bined with the restriction of the output to a few types . . . that the highly specialized machine tool was to be looked for."[43]

This generalization points to facts increasingly confirmed by subsequent history. It would lead us into a labyrinth of details, however, to follow out even in the most summary way the growth of the manifold branches of the engineering industries thus alluded to, each of which had its independent development and independent history during the time we are describing. Certain general features characterized most of them. One of these was the trend toward consolidation, toward the formation of "horizontal" trusts. Thus, the manufacture of stoves, soda-water apparatus, steam pumps, and as we shall see a little later, electrical machinery, was rapidly grouped under the control of a few great producing companies. Not all of these enterprises prospered, and there was the usual tale of receiverships and reorganizations. In many branches of the engineering industry individual firms continued placidly an independent career that dated back for several generations, deeming their established reputation more valuable than the advantages any combination, no matter how efficient and powerful, could offer. New firms were constantly formed to undertake the manufacture of specialties for the first time presented to the market, and a few gigantic industries like the manufacture of automobiles sprang up *de novo*, and speedily acquired a momentum of progress and expansion that defied all efforts to bring them under the mastery of a single man or financial group.

The development of the internal-combustion engine ranked with the growing use of electric power as the most important feature of the history of prime movers during this period. Up to 1914, however, this type of motor was seldom used in larger units. In 1905 the International Power Company received a contract from the Baldwin Locomotive Works, to build two of the largest size Diesel stationary engines then in the market and part of the Cramp Shipyards was operated with an engine of the same character. Hopeful predictions that a modification of the Diesel principles applicable to locomotives would come into general use were not realized. As in case of steam engines, increased economy was found to lie in the use of higher pressures. By the close of the last century the Westinghouse Company was building gas engines of over 600 horse-power for electric plants. Another notable advance in the field of power generation was the increasing employment of steam turbines, frequently in very large units, both for propelling ships and for driving dynamos.[44]

Pennsylvania held an easy lead in the building of marine engines and also in the manufacture of high-pressure engines, while Wisconsin stood far ahead of all other states in the construction of the heavier type of engine, classed in the census as "low speed, variable automatic cut-off." That

[43] Chapman, *Foreign Competition*, 122, 124.
[44] *Manufacturers' Record*, XLVII, 218, Mar. 30, 1905; *Commercial and Financial Chronicle* LXIX, 802, Oct. 14, 1899; *American Machinist*, XXI, 157, Mar. 3, 1898.

state owed its rank chiefly to Milwaukee, where there were several large establishments that specialized in building engines of this class. As recently as 1900, before the expansion of the automobile industry, Pennsylvania led in the manufacture of internal combustion engines, especially of the larger type. Wisconsin held second rank, and indeed turned out a greater number of engines, though of a much smaller aggregate horse-power, than Pennsylvania. At this time their main use was for the propulsion of small boats—"naphtha launches." No new principle was adopted in steam boilers or in the reciprocating steam engine during the last decade of the century, though there was a decided tendency to increase steam pressures and much progress was made in popularizing the compound engine, especially in expensive fuel areas.[45] In 1914 Wisconsin ranked first and Michigan second in the value of engines, "steam, gas, and water," manufactured, Pennsylvania having fallen to third place.[46]

The largest steam turbine constructed in the United States before 1900 was of 3,000 horse-power and turned the dynamos of the Electric Light Company at Hartford. Its advantages for that particular service were minimum friction, there being but two bearings, absence of lubrication, and a perfect balance that reduced vibration to a minimum. These qualities tended to minimize wear, increase life, and reduce the chance of interruption in service, all especially important considerations in the electric-light industry. The use of turbines for propelling ships began in England in the nineties.

The rapid growth in the consumption of electricity for light and power naturally influenced the development of water motors as well as steam motors. In water-driven plants ability to produce power capable of wide distribution naturally led to an increase in the size of units and a special effort to attain a reliability in functioning that would insure users against interruptions of service. New methods of arrangement, notably the horizontal wheel, whose bearings were at all times available for inspection, and the suspended turbine, where the water is admitted from beneath so that the vast weight of the wheel-shaft and the dynamo upon its upper end is sustained by water pressure, thus reducing the element of friction to a nominal point, where the results of this influence. The wider use of turbine water wheels to generate electricity also necessitated the development of sensitive governors to regulate the supply of water according to the changing load upon the dynamo. In the West, where tremendous water heads of 1,000 feet and upward were available, the impact wheel, a California invention, was perfected.

The internal combustion engines built prior to 1900 were in comparatively small units. The largest gas engine exhibited at the Chicago Exposition was of 35 horse-power, while the largest at the Paris Exposition in

---

[45] Twelfth Census, x, 394–395; cf. *Boston Journal of Commerce*, XLII, 8, Apr. 8, 1893.
[46] U. S. Bureau of the Census, *Manufactures, 1914*, II, 948–949.

1900—seven years later—was capable of developing 1,000 horse-power. It was not until the latter year that internal combustion engines, utilizing furnace gases were employed in the United States to drive blowing engines, although they had been used in Germany, Belgium and Great Britain before this date.[47]

One of the best evidences of the maturity of our engineering industries was the important position that machinery held in our exports of manufactures. Between 1911 and 1913 the value shipped abroad increased from less than $103,000,000 to approximately $128,000,000. We were excelled in this branch of foreign trade only by Great Britain, whose exports in 1913 were approximately $185,000,000. We sent abroad engines to the value of over $20,000,000, an increasing share of this total representing internal combustion motors; metal working machinery to the value of $15,000,000, and sewing machines, typewriters and mining machinery to the value of well above $10,000,000 each. Our exports of machine tools rose from less than $10,000,000 prior to 1910 to $16,000,000 in 1913. Three-fourths of these exports went to Europe and one-eighth to Canada.[48]

MACHINE TOOLS

A number of causes coöperated during these two decades to draw our machine-making establishments farther west and to increase their specialization. One was the vicinity of iron and steel works and cheap fuel; another was the neighborhood of an extensive western market for their products at works manufacturing or repairing railway rolling stock, agriculture machinery, automobile and mining machinery, and at the Great Lake Shipyards. The trend toward specialization was powerful enough to overcome any tendency that otherwise might have existed toward industrial concentration, such as was occurring in so many related branches of manufacture. During the nineties Ohio for the first time took the lead in the manufacture of metal-working machinery and was the state where the tendency toward specialization was strongest. Until the late eighties the leading manufacturers of machine tools were in New England or Pennsylvania, and they produced a variety of machines—in many cases nearly everything required for the equipment of a shop. The new tendency was toward the production of a single type of machine, often containing improvements protected by patent rights or by a reputation almost as effective. By 1900 there were large establishments that made nothing but engine lathes; others were devoted exclusively to planers, and still others made milling machines their specialty.

Characteristic of this general situation was Cincinnati's rise to first rank among American cities in the manufacture of metal-working machinery. During the census year of 1899 its 30 establishments turned out an aggregate

[47] Twelfth Census, *Report*, x, 398–400; U. S. Bureau of the Census, *Manufactures, 1905*, IV, 635–637.
[48] *Iron Age*, XCIII, 1434, May 28, 1914; XCIV, 189, July 23, 1914.

product of $3,375,000. Philadelphia, one of the oldest centers of this industry, reported 11 establishments and an aggregate product of $3,095,000. The Philadelphia works, like those of most other eastern cities with the possible exception of Worcester, Massachusetts, produced a wide range of tools, with much less specialization than was characteristic of Cincinnati and other new sites of the industry. Providence, with 14 establishments, mostly diversified, followed Philadelphia with an aggregate product falling but a little below $3,000,000. In a broad way, perhaps, the Providence industry might be said to be specialized, as it tended toward the production of automatic and semi-automatic machinery, such as screw machines, turret lathes, gear cutters, and milling machines, for which its makers had long held a high reputation. Hartford followed closely after Providence and Worcester, with more independent shops than any of the cities previously mentioned except Cincinnati, and held fifth place in this industry. One of its specialties was engine lathes.[49]

Among the influences that shaped the development of the machine-tool industry at this time, the most important was unquestionably the introduction of new modes of locomotion calling for the cheap production in large quantities of new machine elements, possessing great accuracy of dimension, uniformity of quality, reliability and strength, combined with the utmost lightness and simplicity of design. This influence first made itself felt with the sudden popularity of the bicycle, to which we shall have occasion shortly to recur. For instance, the forming tool, which was one of the most notable recent improvements in metal-working machinery, while known prior to 1890, was used chiefly if not entirely at that time for making articles of very soft composition such as caps of salt and pepper boxes. The application of the tool to harder material was brought about by its use in making the steel hubs of bicycle wheels, and if this were not its first employment on that metal, it at least familiarized the mechanical public with the principle and led to its extended application. Parallel with the general introduction of the forming tool in the bicycle industry came the use of the oil-tube drill, in which oil is constantly fed to or near the point of a drill to lubricate and cool the cutting edges and wash away the chips. Such drills were not a novelty, having been used to a limited extent before 1890, especially for drilling gun barrels. But their general use was due to the fact that the time economized in machining the outside of the bicycle wheel hubs by the use of the forming tool was lost, because the simultaneous drilling of the hole required more time than did the work upon the outside of the piece. This led to the adoption of the oil-tube drill for this operation, and its application in an important and widely extended industry resulted in a multitude of new uses being found for it. Many of these were in the machine-tool industry itself, and followed the increased use of hollow-spindle lathes and automatic and hand-operated turret lathes, in which the spindles

[49] Twelfth Census, *Report*, x, 385–386; Roe, *English and American Tool Builders*, 278.

are necessarily hollow, and where rapid and accurate boring is needed for economical production.

In fact, the growing employment of automatic and semi-automatic machines for shaping steel and other hard metals was one of the notable advances of the decade ending with the century. From this decade, also, dates the more general use, if not the absolute beginning, of compressed air tools, electrical driving and high-speed steel cutting tools. The electrical industries which, as we shall see, were in the hey-dey of youthful progress and expansion at this time, are to be credited with the increased use of power presses. The advent of the laminated armature for electric generators and motors demanded accurately made punchings of sheet metal of a size and in numbers previously unknown. Power presses solved the problem thus presented to manufacturers, and this demonstration of the capability of such machines led to their employment for still other purposes. The electrical industry also brought into use the system of heavy portable machine tools attached to a massive iron floor plate. In this instance it not only created a demand but helped to satisfy it. Such heavy tools were first used to machine the rings or magnet frames of large electric generators, where it was at times important to bring the machine to the work rather than carry the work to the machine. Yet such portable tools did not become practicable until the electric drive had been developed. Among other significant steps in the progress of the industry at this time was the growing use of large grinding machines, which proved a source of economy as well as a means of securing superior workmanship, and a revolutionary betterment in crane facilities. This last step again was rendered possible by the use of electricity for driving; indeed, the fact that an electric generating plant must be installed to operate cranes encouraged many a machine shop to employ the electric drive for other purposes.[50]

BICYCLES

No other single industry has exercised more influence upon the development of machine tools, and particularly of special tools, than the manufacture of automobiles. This young giant in the sphere of metal-working industries was not regarded as important enough to have a special heading in the census classification until 1905. Prior to that, however, the manufacture of bicycles and tricycles had been well-established and this country had attained a position in that branch of vehicle making that prophesied its later preeminence in the larger development that was to follow.

Although the bicycle was the product of a protracted evolution, having emerged by hesitating and painful steps from clumsy devices introduced nearly a century before, the improvements that so abruptly converted it from a plaything into a serviceable vehicle were made within a short period.

---

[50] Twelfth Census, *Reports*, x, 386–388; *Engineering Magazine*, VIII, 1057–1058, March 1895; XI, 264–267, May 1896.

At the time of the Centennial Exposition in 1876 a few high-wheel bicycles were brought to this country from England and suggested their manufacture in this country. The first factory was established by Colonel Albert Pope of Boston at Hartford, Connecticut, in 1878, and 92 wheels were marketed that season.[51] But for ten or fifteen years thereafter most of the improvements were made abroad, particularly in England. The rubber tire, which had been used on vehicles experimentally as early as the eighteen-thirties, was replaced about 1890 by the pneumatic tire, and for a brief period by the cushion tire invented in 1891. The suspension wheel which goes back, it is said, to the days of Leonardo da Vinci, was perfected, ball bearings were introduced, the bevelled gear was slowly substituted for the chain gear previously employed, and the coaster brake was invented. The key inventions were not made in the United States, but they were modified and improved in this country. After 1893, as we have seen, America began to manufacture its own seamless tubing.[52]

The result of the establishment of the manufacture of bicycles on a large scale in America was to train a great number of mechanics in operations that were later employed in the manufacture of automobiles, and to introduce into our shop equipment and practice devices and methods that had a wide application in the latter industry. Our exports of bicycles rose in value from less than $2,000,000 in 1896 to $3,500,000 in 1900; only to fall to about $700,000 thirteen years later. Imports were negligible, their value seldom exceeding $50,000 per annum. This industry declined with the growing popularity of the automobile, the number of bicycles manufactured in the United States falling from 1,113,000 in 1899 to 299,000 in 1914.[53]

[51] Depew, *One Hundred Years of American Commerce*, II, 550.
[52] Twelfth Census, *Report*, x, 331–335.
[53] U. S. Bureau of the Census, *Manufactures, 1914*, II, 753.

CHAPTER X

THE AUTOMOBILE AND THE DYNAMO

Pioneer Motor Cars, 157. Early Promoting, 158. First Manufacturing Companies, 160. Motor Shows, 160. Status of the Industry in 1910, 162. Culmination of Pre-War Development, 163. Electrical Industries, 165. Electric Generators, 166. Industrial Consumption, 167. Company Organization, 168.

PIONEER MOTOR CARS

The idea of using mechanical power to propel vehicles on public highways is older than the invention of the railway. It was eventually realized by the parallel development of new methods of vehicle construction and new motors. For a time it was doubtful whether the internal combustion engine, the steam engine, or electricity would prove the most successful method of propulsion. The first vehicle run by an internal combustion engine was built by Carl Benz, a German, in 1885. It was a tricycle and its engine copied closely the type developed in Germany by Otto nine years earlier. The first automobile imported into the United States was a Benz car brought to the Chicago World's Fair in 1893.[1] Six years before Benz built his tricycle, however, George B. Selden of Rochester, New York, applied for a patent for a gasoline motor, designed essentially like those already employed as stationary engines,[2] to drive a road vehicle. This patent was not granted, however, until 1895, sixteen years after the application was filed. It later became, as we shall see, a source of litigation and affected to some extent the subsequent organization of the automobile industry.[3] Electricity was regarded at first as a more promising source of power and the first electric automobile was built in Chicago in 1891. It appeared on the streets of that city in 1893, the year that Charles E. Duryea built the first American gasoline car. By this time all the fundamental problems of automobile construction had been solved with two exceptions—a method of cushioning wheel rims and a way to prevent motor injury by shock and vibrations.[4]

Before either of these pioneer machines was built, however, S. H. Roper of Massachusetts had constructed in 1889 the first steam automobile made in America. During the following ten years steam propulsion gave promise of taking precedence in this country, for up to 1900 the gasoline motor was not reversible, and the steam engine excelled it not only in that respect, but also in flexibility and speed. In fact the gasoline engine did not finally

---

[1] Barber, *Story of the Automobile*, 69; *cf.*, however, U. S. Bureau of the Census, *Manufactures, 1905*, Part IV, 277–278.
[2] *Cf.*, U. S. Commissioner to the Paris Exposition of 1889, *Reports*, III, 142, 146, 147.
[3] Barber, *Story of the Automobile*, 65–66, 69.
[4] Barber, *The Story of the Automobile*, 71–73.

come to the front until 1905.[5] Henry Ford built his first car in 1893, and in 1896 there were but four gasoline-driven automobiles in America, the pioneer cars built by Duryea and Ford, a car built by Elwood Haynes at Kokomo, Indiana, in 1894, and the imported Benz car already mentioned. Perhaps we should add to this number a gas car built by Charles B. King, with the completion of which, in 1894, Detroit is said to have made her bow to the world as the country's largest center of this manufacture. No gasoline automobiles were made for sale in the United States until 1896 or 1898, by which time steam and electric cars were already on the market and electric cabs were running in New York City and elsewhere.[6]

In fact Altman and Company of New York put several electric delivery wagons into service in 1898, not solely as an advertisement but because they were considered more economical than horse-drawn vehicles. They cost $2,000 and were operated at an expense of two cents a mile for power.[7] The following year there were said to be a hundred motor hansom and coupe cabs in public service in New York City, besides 20 motor wagons and between 30 and 50 private motor carriages. Over 90 per cent of these were propelled by electricity, the others by gasoline engines. In Boston, where local causes had affected development, steam took about an even place with gasoline.[8]

EARLY PROMOTING

The manufacture of automobiles first appears in the records of industrial promotion with the formation of what were called electric-vehicle companies, which were operating enterprises generally fathered by the Electric Storage Battery Company, a concern organized to own and operate electric conveyances in Chicago, New York and other cities. In 1899 the International Automobile and Vehicle Tire Company was formed to manufacture pneumatic tires for automobiles. This company purchased rubber works in Boston and vicinity and in New York, including patents owned by them covering the processes of manufacture. The same year the short-lived Lewis Motor Vehicle Company, with $5,000,000 authorized capital, was incorporated to make a patented gasoline motor to be used by subsidiary companies manufacturing vehicles under royalty throughout the United States.[9] The Wood's Motor Vehicle Company, incorporated the same year, was to erect "the largest manufactory of electric carriages in the world." The Riker Electric Vehicle Company, with $7,000,000 capital, was formed to build electric vehicles at Elizabeth, New Jersey,

---

[5] American Society of Mechanical Engineers, *Transactions*, XXI (41st meeting), 1900, quoted in *American Machinist*, XXIII, 505, May 24, 1900.

[6] Barber, *The Story of the Automobile*, 75–76; Ford, *My Life and Work*, 30–31; Catlin, *The Story of Detroit*, 710; U. S. Bureau of the Census, *Manufactures, 1905*, IV, 278.

[7] *New York Tribune*, quoted in American Iron and Steel Association, *Bulletin*, XXXII, 179, Nov. 20, 1898.

[8] *Cassier's Magazine*, XVI, 599, Sept. 1899.

[9] *Commercial and Financial Chronicle*, LXVIII, 927, May 13, 1899; LXX, 999, May 19, 1900.

under patent rights owned by Andrew L. Riker. The International Power Company, a New Jersey corporation capitalized at $8,000,000, proposed to operate thousands of auto-trucks propelled by compressed air, thereby displacing 110,000 horses used in the trucking business in New York City alone. An even more ambitious enterprise, with $75,000,000 prospective capital planned to consolidate the automobile industry of the world.[10]

Of these and a half score other companies formed during this speculative boom, one of which owned 49 foreign and domestic patents, only a few left a permanent record in the automobile business, and those were for the most part firms that had had previous experience in this or allied industries. For instance, Colonel Albert Pope, long associated with the manufacture of Columbia bicycles, successfully established the manufacture of the Columbia Electric automobile at New Haven, an old carriage-making center.[11] Indeed, at this time the financial world was much more interested in the formation of the American Bicycle Company, with a capitalization of $40,000,000, combining 45 firms and 56 separate plants engaged in the manufacture of bicycles and bicycle parts, than in the ambitious promotions both in the East and in the West associated, on paper at least, with the automobile manufacture. This corporation was closely associated with the Shelby Steel Tube Company which was, as we have seen, one of the larger organizations in the secondary steel industry. At this time it was estimated that the number of bicycles sold in the United States annually was nearly 850,000, while automobiles were for the most part luxuries or sporting toys out of reach of the popular market. Only a year later, however, the automobile fever caught the American Bicycle Company also.[12]

To judge by press reports, a large share of the energy devoted to building up an automobile industry at this time was expended upon vast and visionary financial projects to monopolize patents in what was already seen to be a promising but uncertain new field of enterprise. Perhaps no industry in American history has started out with more seeming likelihood than this one of falling immediately into the hands of a small clique of financiers. Happily, however, the practical exigencies of the industry defeated the intentions of these promoters and brought their schemes to nought. The real foundations of automobile making were not laid in banks and counting rooms, or indeed in the large factories already engaged in making bicycles, engines and other allied products, nor were they being laid by inventors who hastily assembled odds and ends of experience with the propulsion of road vehicles and with novel motors from all quarters of the globe and tried

[10] *Commercial and Financial Chronicle*, LXVIII, 282, Feb. 11, 1899; LXVIII, 671, Apr. 8, 1899; LXVIII, 726, Apr. 15, 1899; LXVIII, 1227, June 24, 1899; LXIX, 1064, Nov. 18, 1899; cf., ibid., LXVIII, 574, Mar. 25, 1899; LXIX, 181, July 22, 1899; LXIX, 493, Sept. 2, 1899; LXIX, 796, Oct. 14, 1899; LXX, 999, May 19, 1900.

[11] *Commercial and Financial Chronicle*, LXVIII, 926, May 13, 1899; LXIX, 850, Oct. 21, 1899.

[12] American Iron and Steel Association, *Bulletin*, XXIX, 227, Oct. 10, 1895; XXXI, 107, May 10, 1897; *Commercial and Financial Chronicle*, LXIX, 177–178, July 22, 1899; LXIX, 286, Aug. 5, 1899; LXIX, 696, Sept. 30, 1899; LXIX, 908, Oct. 28, 1899; LXXI, 391, Aug. 25, 1900; LXXI, 750, Oct. 13, 1900.

to combine them into a new scheme of construction. The true foundations were being laid in small work shops where all the problems involved in making a successful car were being worked out through practical experience. For the question to be solved was not one of motors or tires or gears or any other single element or group of elements; it was one of patient and painstaking improvement of a thousand minor details, not among the least of which were problems of materials, machinery and processes of manufacture—problems that rested with the mechanic and the engineer rather than with the financier and the industrial organizer to solve.

THE FIRST MANUFACTURING COMPANIES

We have seen that early attempts to organize the automobile industry on a large scale were by operating companies that designed to manufacture and control the operation of electrical and in one instance compressed-air vehicles. The first general manufacture of automobiles for private use to attract wide attention was that of steam cars by the Mobile Company and the Locomobile Company, which erected a large plant on the Hudson River north of New York City for their manufacture, and produced in 1900 about 95 per cent of all the steam carriages built in America. This plant was capable of turning out, when working to full capacity, 90 locomobiles per week. The Electrical Vehicle Company attempted to control the entire manufacture of gasoline cars under the patent granted in 1895 to George B. Selden, covering the operation of road vehicles by motors of the compression type using "a liquid hydrocarbon gas" as a fuel.[13] Two years later Ransom E. Olds, who had been experimenting since 1895 with gasoline carriages, organized the Olds Motor Vehicle Company of Detroit, which completed its first car in 1898. A new model perfected the next season was for a time one of the most popular cars in the world, the output rising from 1,400 in 1901 to 2,500 the following year. In 1904, when Henry Ford made 1,708 automobiles, 4,500 Oldsmobiles were placed in the market. They were exported to all parts of the world; and we are even told that Sir Thomas Lipton, the tea magnate, and Queen Helena of Italy, owned and drove them.[14]

MOTOR SHOWS

In 1900, 57 establishments in the United States were devoted entirely to the manufacture of automobiles; and their product was less than $5,000,000. Five years later the number of establishments had more than doubled, increasing to 121, and the value of product exceeded $27,000,000. Most of the factories reported in 1900 were engaged largely in experimental work.[15] Both the McCormick and the Deering Companies placed motor-

---

[13] *Commercial and Financial Chronicle*, LXXI, 1015, Nov. 17, 1900.
[14] Catlin, *The Story of Detroit*, 714–715; Barber, *Story of the Automobile*, 94.
[15] Bureau of the Census, *Manufactures, 1905*, Part IV, 269.

driven mowing machines on exhibition that year;[16] and in November the first annual motor show in the United States was held in Madison Square Garden under the auspices of the Automobile Club of America. Steam cars, both domestic and imported, held the center of the stage, although electric vehicles were well represented. A few machines still had the body and the machinery separated by springs, the differentiation of touring cars from runabouts had just begun, and motors of from three to five-horsepower were common.[17] At the annual show the following year electric carriages, despite improvements in the direction of lighter and longer-lived batteries, were losing ground relatively to steam and gasoline carriages. The most striking general feature of the latter was that they were now built lower. "Horse-drawn vehicles are placed high in order that the occupants may see over the horses. This reason does not pertain to automobiles, and mechanical considerations naturally lead to them being placed as near to the ground as possible." In adopting the latter practice, American builders were copying the French, who had already adopted lower models. The rapid change in design at this time was summarized by one observer in the statement: "Last year the exhibition was one of horseless carriages; this year the automobile makes its appearance." The status of the internal-combustion motor is sufficiently indicated by the observation that gasoline cars were "being fitted with two-cylinder engines to an increasing extent," the one-cylinder motor having been hitherto the rule. Commercial vehicles had appeared, including light steam delivery wagons and omnibuses as well as heavy trucks.[18] The automobile market was already very active, and purchasers willingly paid more for cars than the anticipated prices later, for their cost was steadily falling. Already people had begun to worry about the supply of fuel, since the Standard Oil Company had a virtual monopoly of gasoline, and the possibility of employing alcohol, which was already used to some extent in Germany, was under discussion.[19]

By 1905 Michigan held the lead in this industry which it has maintained consistently since that date. The automobile was "not yet perfected," but was "at least reliable." Standardization was making rapid progress and commercial vehicles had won a secure place in the country's transportation mechanism. A few automobile stage lines had been established, especially in the West, where there was one operating between Roswell and Torrance, a distance of 101 miles. Auto busses were in use in several cities. Costs were being lowered and the expansion of the industry was felt to depend largely upon the extension of good roads.[20]

At the New York Automobile Show of 1905 French and American vehicles to the value of nearly $12,000,000 were sold and the same year

[16] *American Machinist*, XXIII, 1087, Nov. 15, 1900.
[17] *American Machinist*, XXIII, 1120–1121, Nov. 22, 1900; cf., U. S. Bureau of the Census, *Manufactures, 1905*, IV, 168.
[18] *American Machinist*, XXIV, 1277, Nov. 14, 1901.
[19] *American Machinist*, XXV, 1206, Aug. 21, 1902; XXVI, 164, Jan. 29, 1903.
[20] U. S. Bureau of the Census, *Manufactures, 1905*, Part IV, 280.

$4,000,000 of orders were placed at the Chicago Show.[21] Before 1909 the industry had emerged from the experimental stage; so that the Madison Square show that year was notable for the entire absence of freak ideas either in construction or design and for the great number of accessories exhibited. During this period two shows were regularly held, the National Exhibition of Licensed Automobile Manufacturers at Madison Square Garden, limited to American cars manufactured under the Selden patents, and the International Show held at Grand Central Palace, which included foreign cars as well as several makes of domestic cars, notably those of the Ford Company which was contesting the patents in question. Thirty different exhibitors had displays at the former exhibition, and the prices of the cars shown ranged all the way from $350 for a Waltham buckboard to $7,300 for the most expensive limousines. By this time the steam car had practically vanished from the picture. Electric cars held their place for limited uses; and heavy trucks with capacities up to ten tons were among the vehicles displayed. Most gasoline engines were of the four-cycle four-cylinder type although six-cylinder cars were coming into use. Notwithstanding the declining popularity of steam automobiles the Stanley Company of Newton, Massachusetts, had sold its entire product to date, some 7,000 cars, within 50 miles of its factory.[22]

By this time the automobile industry had absorbed many of the skilled workers and mechanical devices and processes developed by the declining bicycle manufacture. It also made invasions into carriage making, which as recently as 1900 had employed 80,000 wage-earners and a capital of $118,000,000. Prominent carriage builders, discovering that the automobile had captured their market, turned to the manufacture of automobile bodies and in some cases to producing entire cars.[23]

STATUS OF THE INDUSTRY IN 1910

By 1910 the new industry had already acquired the prominent position among American manufactures that it has subsequently held. An increase of nearly 200 per cent in the population of Flint, Michigan, within a decade was ascribed to its growth at that center.[24] Henry Ford had introduced his system of producing automobiles within the reach of the masses, which was to prove such a remarkable success during the following decade. In 1909 his annual output for the first time passed the 10,000 mark; the next season it was 18,664.[25] In 1909 the number of establishments engaged in making automobiles was 265, employing 58,000 wage earners and turning out a product valued at $194,000,000. The number of cars manufactured that year was 126,593. At the two automobile shows in New York the following season, the windshield was noted as having recently come into

---

[21] *Manufacturers' Record*, XLVII, 90, Feb. 16, 1905.
[22] *American Machinist*, XXXII, 151, Jan. 28, 1909; XXXII, 962, June 10, 1909.
[23] *American Machinist*, XXXII, 845, Nov. 11, 1909.
[24] American Iron and Steel Association, *Bulletin*, XLIV, 86, Sept. 1, 1910.
[25] Barber, *The Story of the Automobile*, 94.

popular favor, and many manufacturers supplied it with their regular equipment. The left-hand drive and continuous mud-guards, "including a step between the wheels," were likewise recorded among recent improvements. Trucks and other business vehicles occupied more space than at any previous show. The licensed manufacturers displayed 42 makes of pleasure vehicles including a few electrics, 12 makes of commercial vehicles and 33 models of motorcycles. Pleasure cars ranged in price from $750 to $7,500. Magnetos had largely supplanted batteries to supply the ignition current.[26]

Until the close of this year, when the United States Circuit Court of Appeals, reversing the decision of the lower courts, declared the Selden patents invalid, the American automobile industry had labored under the incubus of a threatened monopoly. To be sure the existence of this patent, and of the association of Licensed Automobile Manufacturers who sheltered themselves behind it, helped to protect the domestic market from foreign competition; although the growth of the Ford Company outside of the combination, and indeed in a constant legal struggle with it, suggested that this protection was not indispensable. Nevertheless, the voiding of the Selden patents was a favorable factor for the industry as a whole.[27]

CULMINATION OF PRE-WAR DEVELOPMENT

By 1913 the automobile of substantially the type familiar today had arrived. Most of the cars had adopted the self-starter, which had first appeared the previous year. The center control was gaining ground and the unit power plant had almost entirely supplanted the old system of assembling the motor on a sub-base. Six cylinders were becoming more common and the price of the cheapest four-cylinder car fully equipped had fallen to $395. Worm drives had begun to be employed on trucks, although the majority still used the chain drive. Very heavy trucks were in the market, and one of these carried with ease a load of substantially 45 tons, or the weight of a modern locomotive, up a 4.5 per cent grade at Bowling Green, New York. Caterpillar tractors, built by the Holt Manufacturing Company of Stockton, California, practically identical with the tractors so extensively employed during the World War, were already in the market.[28]

An English estimate of the number of motor vehicles in the principal countries of the world in 1914, including motorcycles which were more common in Great Britain than elsewhere, credited the United Kingdom with 426,000, France, the cradle of the automobile industry, with 91,000, Germany with 77,000, and Italy with 20,000. In the United States there were about 1,200,000 motor cars of all kinds or nearly twice as many as in all these countries combined.

[26] Thirteenth Census, *Reports*, x, 807; *American Machinist*, xxxiii, 90–91, Jan. 13 1900; xxxiii, 181, Jan. 27, 1910.
[27] *American Machinist*, xxviii, 370, Sept. 14, 1905; xxix, 550, Oct. 25, 1906; xxxiv, 135–136, Jan. 19, 1911; xxxvi, 598, Apr. 11, 1912; Ford, *My Life and Work*, 60–63.
[28] *American Machinist*, xxxviii, 167, Jan. 23, 1913; xxxviii, 209, Jan. 30, 1913; xxxviii, 910, May 29, 1913; xxxix, 505, Sept. 25, 1913.

Specialization was making rapid headway in the industry at this time. It reached its culmination in firms like the Continental Motor Manufacturing Company, which devoted itself exclusively to building automobile motors in large quantities with inter-changeable parts, at factories especially equipped for this purpose.[29] In fact the census for 1914 listed 971 establishments engaged in the manufacture of automobile bodies and parts and only 300 establishments making automobiles. More than 569,000 cars were turned out by American factories that year and their total value exceeded half a billion dollars. During the preceding five years this manufacture advanced in rank among the industries of the country from twenty-first to the sixth place in respect to value of products, and from twentieth to fourteenth place with respect to the number of wage-earners employed. The relatively more rapid growth in value of products as compared with the number of operatives was due to the increasing use of highly specialized automatic machinery.

Michigan employed 53 per cent of the wage-earners and turned out nearly 63 per cent of the product, while Ohio, which ranked second, manufactured only 13 per cent of the total product and employed 15 per cent of the wage-earners. Detroit was the largest automobile-making center in the country, producing complete cars and parts to the value of over $164,000,000.[30] That year the Ford works alone turned out nearly a quarter of a million cars.[31] Only ten years before the Olds Motor Vehicle Company of Detroit, which in 1905 had just substituted a two-cylinder for a single-cylinder engine, felt justified on the strength of an output of 6,500 cars in claiming to have the largest automobile factory in the world.[32]

During the twelve years preceding the outbreak of the War, the industry as a whole had not taken a single backward step. More cars had been made every year, and sales had correspondingly increased. Of the 450 listed manufacturers of motor vehicles in 1914, disregarding firms that made only parts, 170 made gasoline passenger cars; 245, gasoline commercial cars; 18 made electric pleasure cars; and 24, electric commercial vehicles. The number of business vehicles, however, while increasing rapidly, did not yet hold the prominent position in the total trade that it holds today. In 1914 of the 569,054 automobiles made in the United States only 25,375 were delivery wagons, trucks, and similar conveyances used for other than passenger service.[33] Our imports of automobiles have never been large. In 1907 when they reached a maximum, they totaled 1,176 cars, worth something over $4,000,000. Thereafter they declined to 322 cars, worth $525,000, in 1915. Meanwhile our exports rose from 2,862 cars valued at less than $5,000,000 in 1907, to nearly 38,000 cars valued at over $60,000,000 in 1915.

---

[29] *American Machinist*, XL, 629, Apr. 9, 1914.
[30] *Census of Manufactures, 1914*, I, 681; II, 732–733.
[31] Ford, *My Life and Work*, 145; Barber, *Story of the Automobile*, 44.
[32] Catlin, *Story of Detroit*, 715.
[33] *Iron Age*, XCIV, 1052, Nov. 5, 1914; Bureau of the Census, *Manufactures, 1914*, II, 739–740, 742.

ELECTRICAL INDUSTRIES

We have already traced the history of the electrical industries from their beginning with the electric telegraph in the forties through the expansion that began with the invention and improvement of the telephone and the electric light between 1870 and 1890 and the beginning of electric traction shortly before the latter date. While the telegraph, the telephone and electric lighting extended incomparably faster than previously during the two decades and a half that followed, these branches of the industry were overshadowed by the even more rapid growth of electric traction and electric power transmission and by the employment of electricity to operate machinery.

Remarkable technical advances characterized this progress and gave its history a dramatic character. Within two decades electricity revolutionized the living conditions of a large fraction of the population. The telephone became a household convenience. When the twentieth century opened there were 3,620 electric-light stations, representing an investment of over half a billion dollars, in the United States, and more than 18,000,000 incandescent lamps and 386,000 arc lamps were manufactured annually. Both lamps and electricity were rapidly reduced in cost. The inclosed arc lamp, which was introduced in the early nineties, lessened the consumption of electricity for street lighting, and economies in the method of manufacturing incandescent lamps and the substitution in them of cellulose and metallic filaments for carbon, lowered both their price and the amount of current they consumed.[34]

In 1890 electric traction was confined to urban districts and was employed on less than twenty-five hundred miles of road. Twelve years later electric lines had extended into the suburban districts and nearly 22,000 miles, or over 94 per cent, of all the street railway trackage in the United States used this power.[35] That remarkable development was made possible by the invention of alternating-current dynamos generating high-tension currents, which could be transmitted without loss of power for long distances and transformed to lower voltages at sub-stations.[36] American manufacturers of electric-railway equipment were leaders in this field. In 1897, when they were given the contract to supply cars, locomotives and machinery for the London Central Underground Railway, the decision of that Company to go outside of Great Britain for its equipment was defended on the ground "that the greater use of electrical traction in the United States has brought its manufacture to a higher degree of perfection and made it far less expensive than in England." Six years later the Lorain Steel Company secured

---

[34] U. S. Bureau of the Census, *Special Reports, Electrical Industries, 1902*, 6, 94, 95, 96, 98; U. S. Bureau of the Census, *Manufactures, 1905*, Part IV, 184–187.

[35] *Cassier's Magazine*, XV, 241, Jan. 1899; XVI, 518–526, Aug. 1899; XXIII, 506–507, Oct. 1903; U. S. Bureau of the Census, *Special Reports, Electrical Industries, 1902* (Street and Electric Railways), 172.

[36] U. S. Bureau of the Census, *Manufactures, 1905*, IV, 163.

the contract to put in the entire electric trolley system of the city of Wolverhampton, England.[37]

As early as 1895 electric locomotives were employed more or less experimentally on the Nantasket Beach branch of the Old Colony Railroad, in the Baltimore and Ohio tunnel at Baltimore, on the Mount Holly branch of the Pennsylvania Railway, and in the new workshops of the Westinghouse Company at East Pittsburg. The latter firm was reported at the time to have entered into negotiations with the Baldwin Locomotive Company with a view to promoting this form of traction. Several years before this, in 1887, an electric locomotive had been installed in a Pennsylvania colliery; and in 1893 the General Electric Company had built a locomotive of this type for use at Chicago.[38] It was not until nearly ten years later, however, that the first important step was taken toward the substitution of high-speed electric traction for steam by a large railway system. In 1904 the New York Central Railroad placed its initial order for 30 to 50 electric locomotives, to be built by the General Electric Company and the American Locomotive Company, for use in its suburban service out of New York. Four years later steam traction, except to a limited extent on one or two outlying freight sidings, had become "as extinct on the island of Manhattan as the dodo."[39]

ELECTRIC GENERATORS

This progress was conditioned by improvements in the machinery and methods employed for generating and transmitting electricity. The dynamo, after calling forth great improvements in the reciprocating steam engine, virtually brought into being the steam turbine, which speedily proved to be the most efficient prime mover for producing electricity with coal, oil or furnace gases. The latter became virtually an integral part of the generater wherever electricity was produced on a large scale by steam power and the whole machine with this improvement was known as a turbo-generator. The number of dynamo revolutions was increased approximately ten-fold, or from 300 to 3,000 per minute.[40] Simultaneously the water turbine was applied to the generation of electricity, and the great era of hydro-electric development began.

The largest contract ever made for electrical apparatus up to 1893 was that awarded for the plant at Niagara Falls, where ten 5,000-horsepower generators, each mounted on its respective turbine shaft, were installed to deliver electricity to neighboring manufacturing establishments and to the city of Buffalo. Ten years later the capacity of this station was more than

---

[37] American Iron and Steel Association, *Bulletin*, XXXI, 181, Aug. 10, 1897; XXXVII, 181, Dec. 10, 1903.

[38] *Boston Journal of Commerce*, XLII, 262, July 29, 1893; XLVI, 312, Aug. 17, 1895; *Cassier's Magazine*, XVI, 461–486, Aug. 1899.

[39] American Iron and Steel Association, *Bulletin*, XXXVIII, 177, Dec. 10, 1904; XLII, 85, Aug. 15, 1908; U. S. Bureau of the Census, *Manufactures, 1905*, Part IV, 172.

[40] U. S. Bureau of the Census, *Special Reports, Electrical Industries, 1902*, 95; U. S. Bureau of the Census, *Manufactures, 1905*, Part IV, 163–165.

PLATE 1

FIG. 1.—First Direct Connected Dynamo (1881)

FIG. 2.—Modern Connected Turbine Generator

Courtesy General Electric Company

doubled, and generators of 10,000-horsepower, each delivering a current of 12,000 volts were installed on the Canadian side of the river.[41] The growth of these huge central stations, of which there were several in the country by the latter date, was rendered possible by improvements in transmission that that made it possible to deliver power economically over a wide area. Some of the earliest of these long-distance transmission lines were in the West. One opened in southern California in 1892 delivered a 10,000-volt current to points 28 miles away, where it was used for lighting. Another in Colorado supplied power for operating stamp mills at a mine 13,000 feet above sea-level and 14 miles from the generating station. In 1896 the Niagara plant began to supply power to the Buffalo Street Railways 22 miles distant.[42] By 1902 a transmission line carrying 40,000 volts and more than 200 miles long was in constant and successful use between the mountains and San Francisco. This was the greatest distance over which power was delivered at this date, though the Niagara station was supplying electricity to consumers 185 miles away. At this time currents with a potential of 80,000 volts were sometimes used.[43]

INDUSTRIAL CONSUMPTION

Cotton mills were among the earliest large manufacturing establishments to employ electricity for driving machinery. The first such instance was probably at the weave shop of the Ponemah Mills, at Taftville, Connecticut, in 1893, where the power used was generated more than five miles away. The Columbia Mills, at Columbia, South Carolina, were the first to depend entirely upon electric motors to operate their machinery, but the electricity itself was generated at a power-house in a valley only 600 feet from the main building. Early in 1894 the Pelzer Manufacturing Company of Pelzer, South Carolina, introduced the same system but took its power from a source three miles away. From this beginning the use of electricity spread rapidly, especially throughout the South, and it speedily modified both the design and location of cotton mills. The new power, which could be delivered easily and economically at any point, made it possible to build single story factories of large floor area without employing long lines of shafting; to select mill sites with a view to cheap foundations, convenient access to transportation and good lighting, and to obviate much of the risk of fire or accident incurred in establishments of older design.[44]

[41] *Boston Journal of Commerce*, XLIII, 72, Nov. 4, 1893; Bureau of the Census, *Manufactures, 1905*, Part IV, 163–164; *Engineering Magazine*, X, 407–417, Dec. 1897; XVI, 255–268, Nov. 1898.
[42] New England Cotton Manufacturers' Association, *Transactions*, Apr. 24, 1905; 248–249; *Commercial and Financial Chronicle*, LXIII, 923, Nov. 21, 1896; *Cassier's Magazine*, XXVI, 137, June 1904.
[43] *Cassier's Magazine*, XXII, 653–654, Oct. 1902; U. S. Bureau of the Census, *Manufactures, 1905*, IV, 634–635.
[44] New England Cotton Manufacturers' Association, *Transactions*, Apr. 24, 1895, 235–238; *Cassier's Magazine*, XVI, 203–206, July 1899; XXI, 394–401, Mar. 1902; *Boston Journal of Commerce*, XLIV, 69, May 5, 1894; XLIV, 280, Aug. 4, 1894.

Nevertheless the chief industrial consumers of electric power were iron and steel works. In 1905 these employed over half a million horsepower produced by electric generation as compared with 65,000 horsepower in cotton mills. This difference was due in part to the greater force required to move the heavy machinery employed in the metallurgical industries. While much of the electricity used in textile mills was of hydro-electric origin, iron works generated their power by steam made with furnace gases, or directly by gas engines. All the machinery at the great Gary plant was driven electrically. Its rail mills were turned by the largest electric motors in the world which at maximum capacity were capable of exerting 6,000 horsepower. Referring to the first half decade of the century an authority said:

"It may be safely asserted that practically all the newer factories and shops in the United States of any size, constructed within the past five years, have an electric drive either exclusively or for most purposes."

The amount of electric power generated in America had increased more than 100-fold during the previous fifteen years, or from 15,569 horsepower in 1890 to 1,592,000 horsepower in 1905; indeed by the latter year the quantity of electric power and of water power developed in the United States was approximately equal.[45] Naturally the use of electricity was not confined to the industries mentioned. It was extensively employed in the printing trades, in the clothing industries, in the manufacture of paper, and wherever large urban power stations or neighboring water heads afforded convenient sources of supply. Electricity was also employed in the primary metallurgical and chemical industries, particularly in the production of aluminum, ferro-alloys, electrolytic copper commercial alkalis and abrasives.[46]

COMPANY ORGANIZATION

Although the manufacture of electrical machinery and apparatus was dispersed in a large number of plants widely scattered throughout the country, this industry was dominated by two firms of first importance, the General Electric and the Westinghouse companies. Both controlled essential basic patents that placed them in a position to prevent powerful competitors from growing up beside them. To be sure, new companies of some importance controlling independent patent rights were organized, and numerous firms were engaged in special branches of electrical manufacture. Some of these were corporations of first rank. The Electric Storage Battery Company, organized in 1888 with $10,000,000 capital, practically controlled the manufacture of storage batteries for electric vehicles and traction companies in the United States, and although the storage battery soon

---

[45] U. S. Bureau of the Census, *Manufactures, 1905*, IV, 169, 631–635; *Cassier's Magazine*, XV, 442, Apr. 1899; XXII, 117–136, June 1902; XXV, 148, Dec. 1903; *Engineering Magazine*, XX, 858–876, Feb. 1901.

[46] U. S. Bureau of the Census, *Manufactures, 1905*, Part IV, 22–24, 162; Pring, *Some Electro-Chemical Centers*, 7, 14–33, 93–95.

went out of use for feeding motors, it found a growing application in connection with the lighting of railway and street railway cars and motor cars. The Electric Boat Company, organized in 1899, controlled important patents for launch and torpedo and submarine machinery. The same year the principal manufacturers of carbons for electric furnaces and battery electrodes, arc lamps and similar uses consolidated under the name of the National Carbon Company.[47]

No radical change was made in the plant arrangements of the General Electric Company during this period. Its principal works continued to be at Lynn, Massachusetts; Schenectady, New York; and Harrison, New Jersey. Gradually its management withdrew from the promotion of local lighting and traction companies, which had been so actively pursued by the Edison and the Thomson Houston Companies that had fused to form it. The consolidated enterprise no longer underwrote or bought up stocks and bonds in such undertakings and ceased to accept their securities except for license rights. Some of these subordinate companies had extended unduly during the period of commercial activity preceding the panic of 1893, and it was necessary to scale down their assets, with the result that the financial statement of the General Electric Company was temporarily, though not seriously, affected. On January 31, 1894, the latter owned stocks and bonds in nearly eighty such companies, amounting to approximately $14,000,000.[48]

In 1897 the General Electric Company concluded an arrangement with the Westinghouse Electric and Manufacturing Company for an exchange of licenses under patents owned and controlled by these two organizations. Before the end of the century its business had extended remarkably, largely on account of hydro-electric development, which had become a powerful influence in the progress of the industry. In 1898, when the successful transmission of electric power over an 80-mile line terminating at Los Angeles was still the record of long-distance delivery, the General Electric Company had in operation some 40 long-distance distributing plants, employing potentials of from 10,000 to 40,000 volts, and transmitting power of from 10 to 80 miles. The amount annually expended for new patents and in patent litigation approached $350,000.[49]

Meanwhile the Westinghouse Company continued to develop its great plant at East Pittsburgh, twelve miles from the latter city. Like the General Electric, it was involved in almost constant litigation. It controlled the Tesla patents, which it was found necessary to defend from various infringements, as these were the only inventions by which extensive electric traction systems could be successfully operated. The Company built the 50,000-horsepower hydro-electric plant at Niagara, and carried out the early electrification program of the Pennsylvania Railway.[50]

[47] *Commercial and Financial Chronicle*, LIX, 1007, Dec. 8, 1894; LXVI, 1187, June 18, 1898; LXVIII, 85, Jan. 14, 1899; LXIX, 697, Sept. 30, 1899; LXX, 175, Jan. 27, 1900.
[48] *Commercial and Financial Chronicle*, LVIII, 600–602, Apr. 7, 1894; LX, 82, Jan. 12, 1895.
[49] *Commercial and Financial Chronicle*, LX, 561, Mar. 30, 1895; LXIV, 849, May 1, 1897; LXVI, 858, Apr. 30, 1898; LXVIII, 822, Apr. 29, 1899.
[50] *Commercial and Financial Chronicle*, LXI, 25–26, July 6, 1895.

After the Westinghouse and General Electric Companies pooled their patents, in March 1896, they controlled all the power transmission apparatus used in the United States. The East Pittsburgh works began to export equipment heavily to England and other foreign countries, and in 1899 the parent company inaugurated the policy of organizing subsidiary companies throughout Europe. Most of its establishments abroad were financed partly by itself and partly by local investors. In 1899 a steel foundry and steel forge plant was erected, which made the Company independent of everything required for its machinery except pig iron. The British Westinghouse Electric and Manufacturing Company, Ltd., organized in 1899 with a capital stock of 1,500,000 pounds sterling, took over the Corporation's British business, which was already very large.[51]

Between the census years of 1889 and 1914, which correspond most closely with the limits of the period we are now discussing, the value of electrical machinery, apparatus and supplies manufactured in the United States increased from $19,000,000 to $335,000,000. During the last fifteen years of this period the value of dynamos made rose from $11,000,000 to $23,000,000. At the latter date nearly 44 per cent of the generators manufactured, as distinguished from motors driving machinery with current received from other sources, were designed for direct connection with steam turbines. The next step forward in steam engineering after the development of the turbine came during the following decade with radical boiler improvements making it possible to deliver steam to prime movers at higher pressures and temperatures and in greater volume than before; and this progress, like that which immediately preceded it, was intimately associated with the advance of the electrical industries.[52]

[51] *Commercial and Financial Chronicle*, LXIV, 1222, June 26, 1897; LXIX, 232–233, July 29, 1899; LXIX, 1198, Dec. 9, 1899; American Iron and Steel Association, *Bulletin*, XXXII, 189 Dec. 1, 1898; XXXIII, 19, Feb. 1, 1899.

[52] Bureau of the Census, *Manufactures, 1914*, II, 275, 283–284.

CHAPTER XI

COTTON MANUFACTURE

Cotton Consumption, 171. Spindle Statistics and Geography, 172. North and South, 173. Technical Progress, 177. Organization, 180. Trade Conditions, 184. Exports of Cotton Goods, 187. Labor, 188.

COTTON CONSUMPTION

During the decade ending with 1890 cotton manufacturing had expanded with exceptional rapidity in all industrial countries. Of nearly 13,000,000 bales spun the latter year, the Continent of Europe took about 4,500,000; Great Britain about 4,250,000, and the United States well under 3,000,000. All the cotton consumed in America was of domestic origin except for a relatively small quantity from Egypt, never exceeding 4 per cent of the total amount spun in our factories, which was used by New England mills for making fine knitting yarns.[1] The spindle statistics of the three great cotton manufacturing areas just mentioned did not correspond with their respective consumption quotas, because Great Britain spun finer numbers than did either Europe or America. The Continent with 27,000,000 spindles consumed more cotton than Great Britain with nearly 45,000,000 spindles, while the United States with between 15,000,000 and 16,000,000 spindles used three-fourths as much cotton as that country.[2]

A similar disproportion existed between the average consumption per spindle in the Northern and the Southern States. In 1890 the South spun nearly one-fourth of all the cotton manufactured in the country. Five years later she spun more than one-third of the cotton consumed in domestic plants. During the period we are discussing, from 1893 to 1914, the takings of cotton by mills in the thirteen Southern States rose from 718,000 bales to 3,000,000 bales, or considerably more than four-fold; while the increase for mills in the rest of the country was only 57 per cent. Between 1894 and 1914 the American cotton crop almost doubled, rising from 7,500,000 to 14,500,000 bales. Our consumption of cotton rose during the same period from 2,300,000 to well toward 5,600,000 bales. On the former date Southern mills spun 718,000 bales and Northern mills 1,600,000 bales. Twenty years later Southern mills spun 3,000,000 bales and Northern mills but 2,500,000 bales.[3]

[1] *Boston Journal of Commerce*, XLII, 88, May 13, 1893; L, 24, Apr. 10, 1897; American Iron and Steel Association, *Bulletin*, XXXII, 163, Nov. 1, 1898; Twelfth Census, *Reports*, IX, 37; U. S. Bureau of the Census, *Manufactures, 1914*, II, 30.
[2] *Commercial and Financial Chronicle*, LIX, 633–634, Oct. 13, 1894; *cf.* however, U. S. Bureau of the Census, *Manufactures, 1905*, III, 11.
[3] *Manufacturers' Record*, LXVI, 39–40, Sept. 17, 1914.

This period closes with a crisis in the raw-cotton market, due to the sudden cessation of demand with the outbreak of hostilities between the Central Powers and the Entente. That condition was transient, but during its continuance several devices were adopted to increase the demand for cotton, some of which had a temporary and perhaps to some extent a more enduring effect upon manufacturing. This is especially true of the studied effort— which did not originate at this time, however—to substitute cotton for jute and other materials in sacks for shipping flour, sugar, fertilizers, grain, coffee and other commodities.[4]

SPINDLE STATISTICS AND GEOGRAPHY

During the twenty years ending with 1914 the number of cotton spindles in the United States about doubled, rising to nearly 31,000,000, but the growth was mostly in the South. In 1890 that section of the country had much less than 2,000,000 spindles; in 1914 it had well toward 13,000,000, or nearly as many as had been in operation in the North twenty years before. Meanwhile the increase in the North was less than 4,000,000.[5] During these years Great Britain increased her spindles from 44,000,000 to 56,000,000, and the total number in the world rose from 85,000,000 to 142,000,000.[6]

Nowhere else in America is there even today such concentration of cotton spinning as in Rhode Island, Southeastern Massachusetts, and the Merrimac Valley. As late as 1900 the two adjoining counties of Bristol in Massachusetts, where Fall River and New Bedford are located, and Providence in Rhode Island contained over 30 per cent of the spindles in the United States. In 1906 Fall River had 3,300,000 spindles and 83,000 looms, and produced well toward 1,500 miles of cloth every working day, besides a large amount of yarn, thread and other cotton products.[7]

Though losing ground relatively to some of her competitors, Massachusetts continued to increase her spindle capacity, and to lead by a large margin all the other cotton-manufacturing states. She had nearly 6,000,000 spindles in 1890, as compared with about one-third that number in Rhode Island, her nearest rival; and twenty-five years later she had well toward 11,000,000 spindles when South Carolina, which since 1905 had ranked second among the cotton spinning states, had slightly over 4,500,000. None of the New England or Central Atlantic states except Pennsylvania showed an absolute decline of spindles during this quarter of a century, and in the aggregate they exhibited a large increase, but the great expansion of that period, both relatively and absolutely, occurred between the Potomac and the Gulf.

---

[4] *Cf., Manufacturers' Record*, LXVI, 44, Oct. 22, 1914.
[5] *Commercial and Financial Chronicle*, LXIII, 436, Sept. 12, 1896; Twelfth Census, *Reports*, IX, 45; Bureau of the Census, *Manufactures, 1914*, II, 36.
[6] Burkett, *Cotton*, 308; Scherer, *Cotton as a World Power*, 349.
[7] Burkett, *Cotton*, 307; Fenner, *History of Fall River*, 75; Twelfth Census, *Reports*, IX, 30.

NORTH AND SOUTH

So notable was the development in that section that northern manufacturers viewed it with no little alarm, and the number of those who predicted that cotton manufacturing would eventually concentrate almost entirely in the Southern States grew larger. This possibility was most actively debated during the last years of the century, when the spindle capacity of the South was overtaking that of the North by rapid strides. While the average increase of spindles for the whole United States between 1890 and 1898 was between 32 and 33 per cent, it was less than 1 per cent in the Middle States, 20 per cent in New England, 38 per cent in the West and 151 per cent in the South. In the last year mentioned the Massachusetts Bureau of Labor Statistics and the Boston Arkwright Club dealt with this subject in their reports. They found that in the South labor costs were decidedly lower, fuel was cheaper, and water power, which was more largely used than in northern mills, cost less than in New England. On the other hand the latter section enjoyed certain compensating advantages. Contrary to popular opinion, freight charges, taking into consideration those both on raw cotton and on finished goods, were not appreciably lower for southern than for northern mills. Indeed they were sometimes higher than those paid by New England manufacturers. The business was better organized in the North, and mill owners there benefited from economies in marketing. When all elements of production and distributing cost were totalled neither section had a marked advantage over the other. Moreover a tendency existed for conditions to equalize themselves in the older and the newer manufacturing region. For instance, the labor cost of production was steadily rising in the South, while it was declining somewhat in New England.[8]

But this net equality, or approximate equality, in the relative manufacturing advantages of the two sections was a broad statistical conclusion for which it might be difficult to discover confirmation in the concrete conditions surrounding individual establishments and particular lines of manufacture. Unquestionably the South could produce coarse goods cheaper than New England and, as we shall see, New England companies engaged in this line of cotton manufacturing were establishing branch mills in that section. On the other hand, New England, and especially the Fall River district, could make fine goods cheaper than competitors farther South. These differences, in the class of goods for which conditions in each locality were adapted, were reflected in their varying prosperity. When only export markets, particularly in China, fell off, and the demand for sheetings, drills and other coarse cotton goods was dull, the Southern industry was depressed, while that of the North continued relatively prosperous. On the other hand, when as sometimes happened there was an

[8] *Commercial and Financial Chronicle*, LXVI, 786–788, Apr. 23, 1898; National Association of Wool Manufacturers, *Bulletin*, XXVIII, 64–67, Mar. 1898; Ashley, *British Industries*, 90–91; U. S. Industrial Commission, *Reports*, VI, 171–186.

active market for coarse cottons and little demand for finer goods, the situation was reversed, and Southern mills were running full capacity while the mills of New Bedford and Fall River were curtailing production and reducing wages.

Naturally, therefore, southern competition affected the coarse-cotton spinning area of New England, mainly in the Merrimac Valley and northward, more than it did mills and factories in the Providence-Fall River region. Furthermore mills in the latter vicinity had certain advantages in the shape of cheaper freights on coal over their neighbors farther north.[9] Consequently, the principal New England firms establishing factories in the South during this period were Merrimac Valley corporations. In 1894 the Massachusetts Mills of Lowell organized a sister corporation with a capital of $600,000 to build a mill in the South; and the Dwight Manufacturing Company of Chicopee Falls appropriated half a million dollars to erect a mill in Alabama. The following year the Whittier Cotton Mills of Lowell planned to spin all their yarns in a branch establishment at Atlanta. In 1896 the American Net and Twine Company of Canton, Massachusetts, erected a mill at Anniston, Alabama. The Merrimac Company of Lowell built a large mill for spinning and weaving at Huntsville in the same state. This by no means exhausted the list of northern companies that found it economical to erect branches in the South, or to transfer their business entirely to that section.[10]

While southern competition thus compelled some northern companies to change their location or to extend their operations to new localities, it also stimulated the adoption of mechanical improvements and the production of finer goods in the older manufacturing centers. One reason why the rush of competition from the South was so formidable in the early nineties was that the new mills there were better equipped in many respects than their longer established rivals. By driving New England to the manufacture of fine fabrics and specialties, this new development compelled factory owners in that section also to install the latest and the best machinery.[11] It probably accelerated also the elimination of small and uneconomically located mills both in the North and in the South, but more markedly in the former section. On the whole, therefore, the geographical changes occurring in the industry were part of a process of differentiation that resulted in its increased centralization in large establishments and the greater diversification of its products.[12]

[9] Copeland, *The Cotton Manufacturing Industry in the United States*, 29–30.
[10] *Boston Journal of Commerce*, XLIV, 408, Sept. 29, 1894; XLV, 136, Dec. 1, 1894; XLV, 232, Jan. 12, 1895; XLV, 248, Jan. 19, 1895; *Manufacturers' Record*, XXVIII, 180, Oct. 18, 1895; XXIX, 324, June 12, 1896; XXXIV, 31, Aug. 12, 1898; XXXV, 173, Apr. 7, 1899; XLI, 188, Apr. 3, 1902; *Commercial and Financial Chronicle*, LXXI, 33, July 7, 1900.
[11] *Boston Journal of Commerce*, XLIII, 408, Mar. 31, 1894; LIV, 25, Apr. 8, 1899; LXVI, 11, Mar. 25, 1905; LXVI, 270, June 24, 1905; *Manufacturers' Record*, XLVII, 267, Apr. 13, 1905; Uttley, *Cotton Spinning and Manufacturing in the United States*, 44; Thompson, *From the Cotton Field to the Cotton Mill*, 78; Mitchell, *The Rise of Cotton Mills in the South*, 246.
[12] Cf., *Boston Journal of Commerce*, XLVII, 418, Mar. 28, 1896.

During these years of active expansion mills were sometimes started in the South, in the same way that iron furnaces had been erected during the previous decade, to boom a new town or to put new life into an old one. This stimulus to the growth of the industry was transient and unimportant, however, and was oftentimes more of a handicap than an advantage.[13] In the main the geography of the industry in the South was determined by the presence of water power, and there was a tendency to concentrate in the vicinity of the older manufacturing centers. Charlotte, North Carolina, became the hub of a spinning district which by the close of the century embraced within a radius of 100 miles 2,238,000 spindles and more than 62,000 looms. Columbia, South Carolina, speedily became one of the most important spindle centers of the South. Greenville in the same state, which in the Centennial Year was simply a country market town where "occasional apple, cabbage, and chestnut wagons driven in from the mountain country to the primitive stores mired to the hub in the soft and sticky street," multiplied its population ten-fold by the end of the century, and had within a radius of 20 miles 665,000 spindles, employing nearly 12,000 operatives. Spartanburg County had 26 cotton mills with nearly half a million spindles. Old spinning towns like Augusta and Columbus, Georgia, and Huntsville and Florence, Alabama, continued to make progress. Meanwhile, smaller mills began to dot the lower Mississippi and Southern prairie states. Mississippi and Arkansas had a number of these little establishments, employing a capital of $100,000 or less, and operating at the maximum not to exceed 10,000 spindles and a few hundred looms. Several such enterprises were established in Texas, especially in the northern region around Dennison and Sherman, and even appeared in Oklahoma and what was then known as the Indian Territory.[14]

During this period southern mills made mostly coarse plain fabrics, largely for export. Indeed some establishments sold all their product in China and colonial markets. The rapid increase in spindles in the South during the nineties actually lowered the average count of all yarns spun in the United States. Nevertheless the same progress toward the production of print cloths and finer goods that was occurring in the North was repeated, with two or three decades delay, south of the Potomac. Bleacheries and print works became familiar sights in the South Appalachian textile districts, and gray cloths from that section were eagerly taken by northern converters to the renewed alarm of New England spinners. During the first decade of the century yarns as fine as 100s and 120s were spun in old textile towns like Columbus, Georgia.[15]

[13] e. g., *S. and W. Excelsior*, 10, May 27, 1889; Thompson, *From the Cotton Field to the Cotton Mill*, 87–88; cf., however, Mitchell, *The Rise of Cotton Mills in the South*, 127–137.
[14] *Manufacturers' Record*, XXXV, 310, June 4, 1899; XLVII, 423–424, May 25, 1905; American Iron and Steel Association, *Bulletin*, XXXIX, 98, July 1, 1905; *Commercial and Financial Chronicle*, LXXI, 1245–1246, Dec. 22, 1900; *Georgia, Historical and Industrial*, 337, 810–811; Landrum, *History of Spartanburg County*, 164–165.
[15] *Boston Journal of Commerce*, XLVII, 400, Mar. 21, 1896; LXIV, 511, Sept. 17, 1904; LXX, 10, Mar. 23, 1907; Twelfth Census, *Reports*, IX, 48; American Cotton Manufacturers' Association, *Proceedings, Richmond Meeting, May 1908*, 180–181; Uttley, *Cotton Spinning and Manufacturing in the United States*, 58; Thompson, *From the Cotton Field to the Cotton Mill*, 80.

Many of the mills in the South lacked working capital and were therefore compelled to pay a high rate for banking and factor accommodation. In this respect they were more or less the victims of conditions and practices inherited from the plantation system. Commission agents charged them 4 and 5 per cent for selling their yarns and cloths, and 6 per cent upon funds advanced them.[16] Operatives continued to be drawn almost exclusively from the native white population, and the revolution in social conditions brought about by the advent of manufactures in the old cotton kingdom was one of the moot questions of the day. Some abuses naturally attended this rapid transfer of workers from the farm to the factory; but no evidence exists that conditions in the South were worse than they had been among the native white workers in the southern New England mill villages during the corresponding stage of the industry there. Nevertheless southern mill owners were on the defensive. Working hours were longer in their establishments than in those of the North and they continued to employ children after child labor had been abolished in similar occupations elsewhere. Yet bad conditions where they existed were not static, but were gradually ameliorated, and families appear to have been better off as a rule in the mill towns than on the tenant farms from which a majority of them came.[17]

Southern factories were increasing in size and by the close of the century many establishments operating from 50,000 to 70,000 spindles were erected. In 1900 South Carolina had two establishments with over 100,000 spindles, and the plant of the Merrimac Company in Alabama employed twice that number.[18]

Nevertheless a remarkable revival of small mill building occurred about this time, though it was not pronounced enough to affect the general tendency to group more spindles under a single roof. The erection of small establishments in the older manufacturing regions in the South was due partly to the effort to bring the mill as close as possible to its supply of cotton; but by the beginning of the century, North Carolina was already manufacturing 50,000 bales a year more than its cotton fields produced. Another important object was to tap the local labor markets, found among the town and village population of the rural districts. In general the placing of a mill on a small water power in one of these out-of-the way localities was determined by the size and constancy of the stream, and by the neighborhood supply of labor and cotton. A Georgia manufacturer operating three small mills of this kind, reported that during 1899 "one made a profit of 40 per cent, one 54 per cent and one 100 per cent." Naturally this was partly due to an exceptional season when the demand for cotton fabrics

---

[16] Young, *American Cotton Industry*, 117; Thompson, *From the Cotton Field to the Cotton Mill*, 89–90; Mitchell, *The Rise of Cotton Mills in the South*, 249–253.

[17] Mitchell, *The Rise of Cotton Mills in the South*, 168–191; Thompson, *From the Cotton Field to the Cotton Mill*, and Kohn, *The Cotton Mills of South Carolina, passim;* National Child Labor Commission, *Reports,*

[18] U. S. Industrial Commission, *Reports,* vi, 155, 161, 162.

was exceptionally active and the price of raw cotton was rising, so that mills that had contracted for their year's supply of cotton early made a large profit on the increased value of their raw materials.[19]

Indeed it has been suggested that a cycle of low cotton prices was a special incentive to spindle expansion in the South because it diverted both capital and labor in that section from raising the staple to manufacturing it, while simultaneously the cheapening of coarse fabrics that usually attended a lowering in the cost of raw materials encouraged consumption in the Asiatic and colonial markets to which many Southern mills at this time catered.[20]

TECHNICAL PROGRESS

Technical progress was not confined to any single department of the cotton industry during these twenty years, but in a general way the great modern improvements in spinning machinery, which were American inventions, were perfected shortly before 1890, and the marked advances in weaving machinery, which were likewise of American origin, came during the following decade. Still metal drawing rolls were adopted in the nineties, and spindle output continued to increase so rapidly that the number of spindles in the country at successive dates ceased to measure accurately expansion of manufacturing capacity.[21] It was estimated in 1903 that improvements in ring spinning alone represented a saving of $64,000,000 in the factory investments of the United States required to produce the output at that time, compared with what they would have been with spindles of the older type; that the lighter running of the new machinery enabled manufacturers to dispense with 160,000 horsepower that would otherwise have been required, and that the labor cost of attending nearly 16,000,000 spindles had been saved. So much for the economies of invention in a single department of one industry within a generation.[22] By 1905 as high as 20,000 revolutions a minute had been secured with reasonable steadiness, a speed at which light machinery almost ceases to remain in mechanical suspension, but 10,000 revolutions were still the maximum normal rate.[23]

Although mules had also been improved until they carried 1,300 spindles and required but two persons to operate them, frame spinning steadily gained on mule spinning. Between 1890 and 1900, when nearly 5,000,000 spindles were added to the nation's equipment, the increase in mule spindles was only 200,000; and by 1914 they had actually decreased nearly 2,000,000, a decline of over one-third since the beginning of the century. Most of the

---

[19] *Commercial and Financial Chronicle*, LXXI, Supplement, 6, Sept. 8, 1900; Thompson, *From the Cotton Field to the Cotton Mill*, 90–95; *cf.*, however, Mitchell, *The Rise of Cotton Mills in the South*, 185.

[20] *Cf.*, Thompson, *From the Cotton Field to the Cotton Mill*, 69–71; Mitchell, *The Rise of Cotton Mills in the South*, 144, 173.

[21] Twelfth Census, *Reports*, IX, 43; X, 819; Bureau of the Census, *Manufactures, 1905*, III, 39; *Boston Journal of Commerce*, XLIV, 40, Apr. 21, 1894; XLVIII, 276, July 25, 1896.

[22] Southern Cotton Spinners' Association, *Proceedings, Charlotte Meeting, May 1903*, p. 58.

[23] Twelfth Census, *Reports*, X, 819; Copeland, *The Cotton Manufacturing Industry in the United States*, 67; 62d Cong., 2d sess., *Document 643*, vol. II, 670–682.

mule spindles were in the North, where they were used for making yarns for knitting and for weaving exceptionally fine fabrics; but at the very close of this period, despite their falling off in the country as a whole, a small increase was recorded in Alabama.[24]

The economies and refinements of cotton manufacturing, if we begin with the fiber on the seed, extend even farther back. For example during the twenty-five years following 1870 the cost of ginning and baling was reduced four-fifths.[25] Toward the close of the period we are describing, conditioning and the scientific testing of textile fibers began to occupy the attention of progressive manufacturers, but they did not assume the importance in cotton spinning that they did in the silk and woolen industries.[26] Combing was added to carding in the preparation of cotton for spinning finer yarns, and cotton combing machinery, which originated and was first made in Europe, began to be manufactured in the United States.[27]

But the great step forward during these twenty years was in weaving. Between 1889 and 1895 the Northrop loom was invented and perfected by James H. Northrop and George A. Draper, at Hopedale, Massachusetts. It embodied two fundamental improvements upon existing looms: a filling-changing mechanism by which the time hitherto lost in replacing exhausted shuttles was wholly saved, and a perfected warp-stopping device that stopped the loom instantly when a single warp thread broke. The importance of these inventions may be measured by the fact that within a decade the number of looms a weaver could attend increased from eight to twenty-four, and that the latter produced better cloth than the smaller number did previously.[28] Other inventors immediately entered this field with detailed improvements that widened the application of the automatic loom to colored goods and still further increased its output. These culminated in the development of the Crompton and Knowles looms between 1905 and 1910.[29] The last hand operation in the whole process of cotton manufacturing disappeared from the more modern establishments between 1882 and the end of the century with the invention of a practical machine to draw the warp through the loom harnesses and reed preparatory to weaving.[30] These improvements, especially the Northrop loom, were adopted in the South somewhat faster than in the North, partly because the industry was expanding

---

[24] Bureau of the Census, *Manufactures, 1905*, III, 42; *Manufactures, 1914*, II, 37–38; *Boston Journal of Commerce*, XLV, 40, Oct. 20, 1894; Burkett, *Cotton*, 305; *S. and W. Textile Reporter* 11, Nov. 26, 1898.

[25] New England Cotton Manufacturers' Association, *Transactions, Atlanta, 1895*, 213.

[26] National Association of Cotton Manufacturers, *Transactions, 1913*, 165–167.

[27] *Boston Journal of Commerce*, XLV, 136, Dec. 1, 1894; Copeland, *The Cotton Manufacturing Industry in the United States*, 61–62.

[28] Twelfth Census, *Reports*, IX, 44, New England Cotton Manufacturers' Association, *Transactions, Atlanta, 1905*, 89–91, 100–101; National Association of Cotton Manufacturers, *Transactions, Boston, 1906*, 125; Uttley, *Cotton Spinning and Manufacturing in the United States*, 6–7; *cf.*, *Boston Herald*, Nov. 1, 1923.

[29] Twelfth Census, *Reports*, X, 820–821; Copeland, *The Cotton Manufacturing Industry in the United States*, 85–89.

[30] Twelfth Census, *Reports*, X, 820–821; *Commercial and Financial Chronicle*, LXVIII, 569 Mar. 25, 1899.

Fig. 1.—Cotton Weaving Room in the Thirties

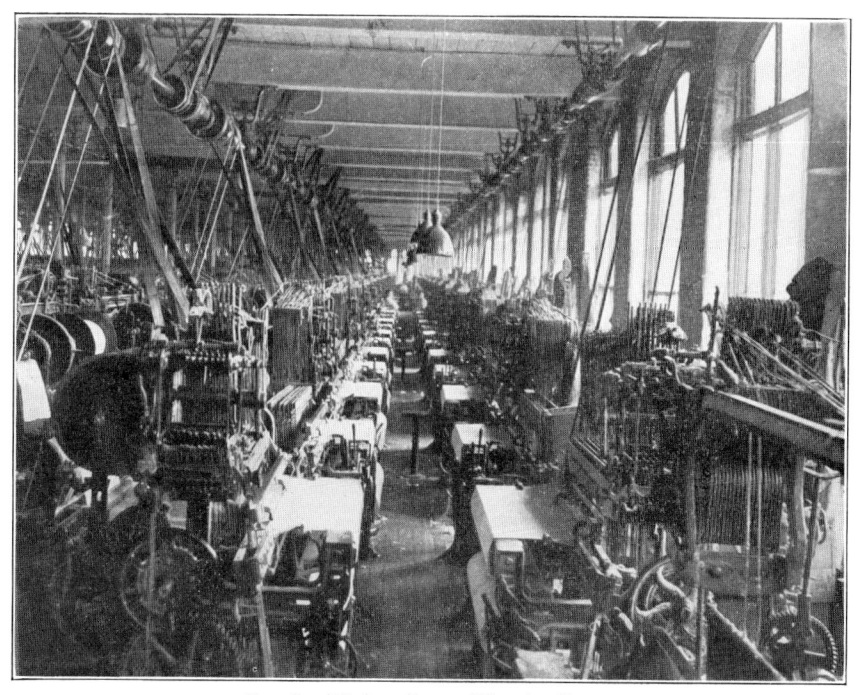

Fig. 2.—Modern Cotton Weaving Room

faster in that region and partly because the class of goods manufactured and the character of the labor employed there placed a premium on automatic processes.[31] Curious backwaters existed beside the current of progress, however, and as recently as 1912 spinning and weaving machinery sixty years old was still in use in some American mills.[32]

In 1906 the Presidential address delivered before the National Association of Cotton Manufacturers, contained the following statement:

"It may without boastfulness be said that in almost every class of cotton fabrics there are some mills in this country producing goods equal in texture and novelty of design to any foreign productions."

About the same time an English expert who visited a number of cotton mills in the United States reported that our fabrics were inferior to those of Lancashire, and that there were as many faults in one yard of American cotton as in a whole piece of English cotton. In speaking of prints, he remarked that only one or two works made goods equal to those manufactured in his own country; but that printing machines in America turned out 75,000 yards a week as compared with 20,000 yards in Great Britain.[33]

This merely records the persistence of conditions that had characterized cotton manufacturing in America and Europe respectively since the industry was established in this country. New England mills probably could make as perfect and as fine fabrics as the best produced abroad. Yarns as high as number 600 had been spun in some of them. The factor determining the character of the goods made on this side of the Atlantic was economic, not technical.[34] Diversification of products was proceeding apace; indeed, as already mentioned, the expansion of cotton manufacturing in the South compelled Northern factories to specialize increasingly in finer and more varied goods. Between 1890 and 1914 the number of looms employed on fancy weaves multiplied nearly five fold, while the total number of looms but little more than doubled.[35] Meanwhile, as far as the incomplete records show, after 1900 the quantity of fine yarns spun, above number 40, increased rapidly, while notwithstanding the great growth of total product the quantity of coarse yarns manufactured actually declined.[36] No new fabrics of notable importance were devised or popularized during this period. Mercerized goods had a brief vogue during the nineties, which was reflected in a demand for Egyptian and Sea Island cotton, since upland staples did not lend themselves to this process. About the same time a

---

[31] *Cf.*, Uttley, *Cotton Spinning and Manufacturing in the United States*, 68.
[32] 62d Cong., 2d sess., *Document 643*, vol. II, 416, 472.
[33] National Association of Cotton Manufacturers, *Transactions*, Boston, 1906, p. 126; *Boston Journal of Commerce*, LXVIII, 110–111, Apr. 28, 1906; Young, *American Cotton Industry*, 121, 123.
[34] *Boston Journal of Commerce*, LXXI, 368, Jan. 25, 1908.
[35] Twelfth Census, *Reports*, IX, 51; Bureau of the Census, *Manufactures, 1914*, II, 39.
[36] Bureau of the Census, *Manufactures, 1905*, III, 38; *cf.*, however, Copeland, *The Cotton Manufacturing Industry of the United States*, 21.

wonderful growth occurred in the weaving of cotton upholstery goods and similar fabrics at Philadelphia.[37]

New England manufactured relatively more print cloths, twills, sateens and fancy woven, napped and pile fabrics than the South; the latter section made more sheetings, shirtings, duck, drills and cottonades; and both regions were about equal in ginghams, ticks, denims and stripes. In New England the production of the last-mentioned fabrics was more common north of Boston, in the Merrimac Valley, while the finer goods and print cloths were made in the vicinity of Fall River and the Sound.[38]

During the nineties textile education received more attention than hitherto, and extended beyond the field of design, to which the pioneer institutions at Boston and Providence had confined their instruction. Following the example of the Philadelphia Textile School, founded in 1884, the three schools established at Lowell, Fall River and New Bedford under the Massachusetts law enacted in 1895, offered courses in cotton manufacturing, chemistry, dyeing and textile engineering, as well as in designing, and catered especially to the needs of operatives. Several institutions in the South opened textile departments about the same time, more particularly to train experts and men for managerial positions.[39]

ORGANIZATION

The movement toward consolidation in certain branches of cotton manufacturing, already referred to as having occurred during the trust-building epoch of the late nineties, resulted in the formation of the American Thread Company, incorporated in New Jersey in 1898 with a capital of $18,000,000. Sixty per cent of the common stock was taken by English investors previously interested in the same manufacture in their own country.[40] During the years immediately preceding excessive competition had developed in this business, with the result that few if any American mills had earned dividends.[41] About two years previously the J. and P. Coats Company, the largest thread manufacturers in Great Britain, had absorbed four competing firms in that county together with their important American branches, thus facing the mills that subsequently entered the new combination with a powerful rival which they could not individually meet on equal terms.[42] The new corporation combined fourteen companies and factories, coördinated their operations, transferred the machinery of some establishments to more favorably situated plants and centers and put the joint enterprise on a profitable basis. It appears to have controlled, however, only about one-third of the thread production of the United States. This company was an

[37] Twelfth Census, *Reports*, IX, 51, 52–53.
[38] Copeland, *The Cotton Manufacturing Industry in the United States*, 146–149.
[39] Copeland, *The Cotton Manufacturing Industry in the United States*, 135–138.
[40] *Cf.*, Copeland, *The Cotton Manufacturing Industry in the United States*, 169–170, 340; U. S. Industrial Commission, *Reports*, XIII, 353–354.
[41] U. S. Industrial Commission, *Reports*, XIII, 346; *Commercial and Financial Chronicle*, LXVII, 1158–1159, Dec. 3, 1898.
[42] *Boston Journal of Commerce*, LI, 392, Mar. 19, 1898.

interesting example of a great industrial consolidation inspired, at least in part, by a parallel development in another country.[43]

A year later a number of mills manufacturing cotton yarn in southeastern Massachusetts were combined under the control and ownership of a corporation known as the New England Cotton Yarn Company. Nine factories operating about 600,000 spindles and having an annual output of between 40,000,000 and 50,000,000 pounds of yarn entered this combination. Like the American Thread Company it closed down less profitable plants and transferred their machinery to factories where the cost of operation was lower. This amalgamation did not prosper, however, partly because its highly capitalized mule mills could not compete with those equipped with the new spinning frames, and four years later it was reorganized with a reduction of capital; and in 1910 it was virtually absorbed, under a ninety-nine year lease of all its properties, by the Union Mills of New York, a group of knitting mills that consumed its products.[44] About the time this Company was formed new yarn mills were organized in New England and in the South, partly as a direct result of the displacement of personnel and the promise of higher prices attending the appearance of the combination.[45]

This movement toward consolidation in the southern New England textile district resulted in another attempt the same year to bring an important branch of production under unified control. It was an enterprise more ambitious in its conception than either of the others and was destined to fail in its initial stages. Three groups of promoters, at least one of which claimed to be backed by British capital, tried to purchase or combine in a single corporation thirty of the largest print-cloth factories of Fall River and New Bedford, operating about 2,250,000 spindles. Their rivalry provoked mutual criticism of the different plans submitted, however, and made mill owners exceptionally cautious; some companies declared high dividends, which disinclined shareholders to sell their stock, and a spirit of local pride was aroused, hostile to the intrusion of outsiders into the affairs of an old experienced and wealthy manufacturing community. Consequently the project was dropped, and though it was revived in a half-hearted way five years later it was never carried to a point where it influenced, even indirectly, the organization of the industry.[46]

The advantages of such a combination for the manufacturers had been somewhat discounted by the organization of a print-cloth pool in 1898. Under this arrangement all cloths of certain descriptions made in the city

---

[43] *Commercial and Financial Chronicle*, LXVI, 519, Mar. 12, 1898; LXVI, 899, May 7, 1898; LXX, 179, Jan. 27, 1900; U. S. Industrial Commission, *Reports*, XIII, 343–347, 348, 356; Copeland, *The Cotton Manufacturing Industry in the United States*, 169–170, 339–341.

[44] *Boston Journal of Commerce*, LIV, 88, May 6, 1899; LIV, 120, May 20, 1899; LIV, 198, June 17, 1899; LIV, 218, June 24, 1899; *Commercial and Financial Chronicle*, LXIX, 28, July 1, 1899; LXXI, 345, Aug. 18, 1900; Copeland, *The Cotton Manufacturing Industry in the United States*, 166–168; U. S. Industrial Commission, *Reports*, XIV, 546.

[45] *Boston Journal of Commerce*, LIV, 88, May 6, 1899; LIV, 338, Aug. 5, 1899.

[46] *Boston Journal of Commerce*, LIV, 136, May 27, 1899; LIV, 378, Aug. 19, 1899; LIV, 418, Sept. 2, 1899; LIV, 458, Sept. 16, 1899; LXV, 270, Dec. 24, 1904; *Commercial and Financial Chronicle*, LXIX, 452, Aug. 25, 1899; Fenner, *History of Fall River*, 74.

of Fall River, as well as all surplus stock of special cloths not included within the schedule, were placed in the hands of two trustees, and at the end of every quarter the prices received were averaged and each mill reimbursed pro rata. An advisory committee of five was appointed to control the production of the four classes of goods specified in the schedule attached to this agreement. Fifty-two mills, operating about 2,500,000 of the 3,000,000 spindles in Fall River, joined this selling combination. Although this proposition for pooling goods for sale seemed very promising for a time, difficulties were encountered in prosecuting it and it was discontinued August 3, 1901.[47]

Several Southern mills attempted in 1899 to form a similar combination. Their plan was to put the control of their product into the hands of an executive committee of three, with a forfeiture of five dollars per loom in case any mill failed to hold goods at the price made by the committee. This project received but apathetic support, however, and seems never to have been put into practical operation.[48]

Only one permanent, though not entirely successful, consolidation was formed among manufacturers of cotton fabrics, and that was originally confined to producers of a cloth almost as highly standardized as thread and yarn. This was the United States Cotton Duck Corporation, organized in 1901 to combine some twenty mills making duck, especially sail cloth. Most of these establishments were in the vicinity of Baltimore, the old clipper ship city, and were family enterprises manufacturing their goods under brands that had been known not only in America but in foreign markets for several generations. Six years later the Company was reorganized as the Consolidated Cotton Duck Company, at which time it completely absorbed the Mount Vernon-Woodberry Cotton Duck Company, an earlier consolidation which was one of the largest producers in the country, which it had previously controlled as a separate corporation. This reorganization was accompanied by a reduction of the capital stock to a little over $21,000,000, a shrinkage of considerably more than a third in the original amount. Nevertheless there was another slight capital reduction in 1910, when the Company was reincorporated as the International Cotton Mills Corporation. It then controlled 22 mills and 2 selling houses and made and distributed about 3,000 varieties of cotton fabrics. In 1913 still another reorganization occurred, which resulted in divorcing the Mount Vernon-Woodberry Cotton Duck Company, which had never entirely lost its identity, from the other mills, though under a joint stock-holding arrangement.[49]

[47] *Commercial and Financial Chronicle*, LXVII, 858, Oct. 22, 1898; LXIX, 708, Sept. 30, 1899; Fenner, *History of Fall River*, 74.
[48] *Commercial and Financial Chronicle*, LXVIII, 778, Apr. 22, 1899; LXVIII, 833, Apr. 29, 1899.
[49] Copeland, *The Cotton Manufacturing Industry of the United States*, 161–164; *Boston Journal of Commerce*, LIV, 198, June 17, 1899; LIV, 258–259, July 8, 1899; LIV, 338, Aug. 5, 1899; *Commercial and Financial Chronicle*, LXIX, 129, July 15, 1899; *Manufacturers' Record*, XLVII, 390, May 11, 1905; Moody, *Manual of Railroads and Corporation Securities, 1920* (Industrial Section), 714, 1150.

A number of so-called "co-operative mills" were organized in the South during the middle nineties. These were regular corporations financed by small local subscriptions, the instalments being in some cases as low as 25 cents a week.[50] Another experimental development, recalling a similar practice in the silk industry at Lyons, was inaugurated at Durham, North Carolina, just before the World War. A manufacturing company owning a chain of eight hosiery mills in that state placed looping machines run by electricity in the homes of some fifty of its best-trained operatives, who had married and whose time was partly absorbed by household duties. A wagon from a central factory delivered materials and collected finished goods.[51]

Although cotton manufacturing as a whole escaped the trust-forming movement that captured so many industries toward the end of the century, concentration in larger establishments and the formation of important mill groups controlled by single families or corporations went on at a fairly rapid rate. Moreover the interownership and community of interest that had always characterized the textile business, especially in New England, continued virtually unimpaired. A student of this industry says:

"The stock of the New England cotton mills is in many cases closely held. In a few instances the stock of one company is all in the hands of a single family, but more frequently a large proportion of the stock is owned by the members of a few families. A number of these families hold stock in several mills, and a network of such interrelations extends over the greater part of the New England cotton-manufacturing district. At one point one set of interests comes in contact with another set, at the next point with still another, and the weaving in and out of these controlling interests makes it much easier to secure a uniform policy."[52]

As at earlier periods in the history of the industry, groups of mills sometimes integrated around selling houses, or those dependent on a single water power combined to insure its economical and harmonious development to the maximum capacity. Units operating in the vicinity of half a million spindles, with a corresponding quota of looms and sometimes bleacheries and print works in addition, were not uncommon. A more novel feature of this period was the acquisition of cotton mills by large merchandising houses like the H. B. Claflin Company and Marshall Field and Company; but this had little effect upon the general organization of the industry. During the quarter of a century ending with 1914 the average number of spindles in an American cotton mill rose from 18,000 to 23,000.[53]

In 1906 the New England Cotton Manufacturers' Association became the National Association of Cotton Manufacturers, without any further

[50] *Manufacturers' Record*, xxv, 289, June 1, 1894; xxvii, 208, May 3, 1895; xxviii, 22, Aug. 9, 1895; xxviii, 188, Oct. 18, 1895; xxviii, 200, Oct. 25, 1895; Thompson, *From the Cotton Field to the Cotton Mill*, 82–85; Mitchell, *The Rise of Cotton Mills in the South*, 236–237.
[51] *Manufacturers' Record*, lxv, 54, Feb. 12, 1914.
[52] Copeland, *The Cotton Manufacturing Industry of the United States*, 159.
[53] Copeland, *The Cotton Manufacturing Industry of the United States*, 172–175; Thompson, *From the Cotton Field to the Cotton Mill*, 82; Fenner, *History of Fall River*, 75–76; *Boston Journal of Commerce*, liv, 88, May 6, 1899; *Commercial and Financial Chronicle*, lxx, 1098, June 2, 1900.

change of management and functions than that implied in the enlarged area of membership indicated by the new title. A similar body, the American Cotton Manufacturers' Association, had been founded in 1903, including principally Southern manufacturers. Various local and state associations were also formed, especially in the South, to influence labor legislation or to regulate output. An older and more important, but less formal, organization of a somewhat similar kind was the Arkwright Club of Boston, which included a majority of the important mills in New England. It acted as a clearing house for current information of practical interest to its members and as an organ for formulating general policies. In 1906 it established a transportation agency, the New England Cotton Freight Claim Bureau, which secured substantial benefits for the industry in that section by obtaining concessions and adjustments from railroad companies and effecting joint economies in other directions.[54]

TRADE CONDITIONS

During the quarter of a century between the panic of 1893 and the outbreak of the World War, cotton manufacturers naturally shared the ups and downs of the country's prosperity. In their case the panic itself projected its effects throughout the ensuing year. The average dividends of the Fall River corporations fell from over 8 per cent in 1893 to 5.25 per cent in 1894, only four mills maintaining the dividends of the previous season and one mill increasing them. In fact dividends were lower in 1894 than in any of the ten years preceding. Fall River companies were hardly representative of those in the country as a whole, however, because the price of print cloths, which declined 24 per cent during the last nine months of 1893, fell more than the prices of other cotton fabrics. Indeed coarser goods held up in several cases to within 4 per cent of their previous quotations, and many southern mills paid dividends throughout the depression at a rate of from 8 to 16 per cent per annum.[55] In the autumn of 1894 a brief recovery occurred, only to be followed by a second sag in prices following a fall in the raw cotton market. Consequently in January 1895 print cloths reached 2.5 cents a yard for "extras," the lowest point they had ever touched. This decline was accompanied, however, by an increasing volume of trade, and when the mills resumed at full capacity they found raw materials lower and earnings higher than the previous season, so that the year was described as "fairly satisfactory to the cotton manufacturing corporations of the United States as a whole, and to those located at Fall River in particular." Many new plants and plant extensions were recorded this year, and average dividends at Fall River again rose to over 8 per cent, or higher than they had been since 1889.[56]

[54] Copeland, *The Cotton Manufacturing Industry of the United States*, 157–159.
[55] *Commercial and Financial Chronicle*, LIX, 857–858, Nov. 17, 1894; *Boston Journal of Commerce*, XLIII, 248, Jan. 20, 1894; XLIV, 88, May 12, 1894.
[56] *Commercial and Financial Chronicle*, LIX, 350, Sept. 1, 1894; LIX, 390, Sept. 8, 1894; LIX, 1087–1088, Dec. 22, 1894; LX, 102, Jan. 19, 1895; LXI, 900–901, Nov. 23, 1895; *Boston Journal of Commerce*, XLVII, 200, June 29, 1895.

A remarkable reversal occurred during 1896 from the promise of an unusually prosperous season early in the year to an autumn of overstocked markets, idle machinery and uncertain prospects. By summer curtailments of production were in order in both the North and the South, and in the latter section several companies passed into the hands of receivers, among them the Eagle and Phoenix Mills at Columbus, Georgia, one of the oldest and largest factories in that section of the country. Nevertheless the South probably suffered less than the North, because the coarse white goods its mills so largely manufactured were sold in foreign markets, which were more stable than the domestic market at this time.[57]

This era of low prices continued throughout 1897 and culminated the following year in a crisis that is historical in the American cotton-manufacturing industry. It was precipitated by a sudden and unexampled decline of nearly one-third in the price of raw cotton within three months. This was due to the fact that world consumption fell one or two million bales behind production, and that the principal crop excess was in the South. The result was felt earliest and most keenly in New England, whose factories produced goods from six to eight months ahead of the market and held them in stock. Buyers finding that raw cotton had fallen from 8 cents a pound to under 6 cents naturally expected a corresponding reduction in the cost of cotton manufactures, although the goods in the warehouses of the New England mills and commission houses had been made from high-priced materials. Consequently sales immediately stopped in the North, and Southern mills, which manufactured to a larger extent for the current market, supplied the demand until the Northern mills were compelled to yield. This breaking of the cotton-cloth market to a low raw-material level, when manufacturers held unusually large stocks of higher cost goods, involved the loss of millions of dollars to factory owners. Naturally the situation was rendered more acute by the recent rapid growth of spindles in the South, and pessimists thought the cotton industry in New England doomed.[58]

This was the period when the legislative investigations into Southern competition and the special reports upon that subject already mentioned in an earlier connection occupied the attention of the industrial world. It was also the time when Fall River manufacturers agreed to pool their goods and place the control of sales and prices in the hands of a board of trustees. During this period of stress New England factories adopted a common policy of curtailing production, under the initiative of the Arkwright Club. Similar agreements to shorten hours or to shut down mills were discussed in the South, but the geographical dispersion of the industry in that section, and

[57] *Boston Journal of Commerce*, XLVIII, 228, July 4, 1896; XLVIII, 244, July 11, 1896; XLVIII, 260, July 18, 1896; XLVIII, 276, July 25, 1896; XLIX, 8, Oct. 3, 1896; *Commercial and Financial Chronicle*, LXIII, 434, Sept. 12, 1896; LXVI, 1140, June 11, 1898, *Manufacturers' Record*, July 3, 1896.

[58] *Commercial and Financial Chronicle*, LXV, 390, Sept. 4, 1897; LXVII (Supplement), 6, Sept. 3, 1898; American Iron and Steel Association, *Bulletin*, XXXII, 26, Feb. 15, 1898; National Association of Wool Manufacturers, *Bulletin*, XXIX, 13–14, Mar. 1899.

perhaps the individualist traditions of mill owners and managers where no such community of interest existed as in New England, rendered such measures less effective there than in the North.[59]

Early in 1899, however, the business sky brightened, especially in New England. Demand suddenly became active, surplus stocks decreased and prices rose. Some mills that had been shut down for two or three years resumed operations. Gloomy predictions of the final decline of the industry in New England were no longer heard and the spindle capacity of the country was found to be no greater than the market could employ. Lowell mills put on night shifts, especially in their spinning departments, which were feeling the draft for yarn made upon them by the new automatic looms. As early as October 1898, when 52 mills signed the pooling agreement just mentioned, the price of print cloths was marked up to two cents a yard; but general signs of improvement were not visible until the beginning of 1899. In February employers restored the wage scale prevailing before the depression. Although this activity received a slight set-back late in the summer, the year as a whole was the most prosperous for several seasons.[60]

We have recorded in some detail the vicissitudes of cotton manufacturing between the panic of 1893 and the close of the century because the price level of both raw cotton and cotton fabrics declined throughout that period and in 1898 reached the lowest point in the history of the industry. Thereafter conditions were reversed and prices, while fluctuating from season to season and experiencing temporary recessions, consistently moved upward. The spread of the boll-weevil and other unfavorable influences occasionally caused raw cotton to soar on a speculative market, and in 1904 mill owners were as agitated over the high cost of raw materials as they had been over their low cost six years earlier. Periodical curtailments of production continued to occur, and while there was no depression during the sixteen years that followed 1898 quite as acute as the one that season, temporary crises cast passing shadows over the manufacturing world. Cotton-mill owners shared the embarrassments of the financial stringency of 1907, and four years later a drastic curtailment of production was necessary in New England. When the World War broke out in 1914 mills were running at about 80 per cent of their capacity.[61]

This record of the embarrassments and solicitudes of the industry, however, while an essential part of a complete picture of its history, is only the rough obverse of a pattern that viewed from another side presents a much pleasanter aspect. The expansion of capital invested in cotton manufacturing from $467,000,000 in 1899 to $890,000,000 in 1914, a growth due in

---

[59] *e. g.*, Rhode Island, *Acts, Resolves, and Reports*, Jan. 1898, Document 31; National Association of Wool Manufacturers, *Bulletin*, XXVIII, 61, Mar. 1898.

[60] *Commercial and Financial Chronicle*, LIX, 191, July 22, 1899; LIX (Supplement, 4), Sept. 9, 1899; LIX, 814, Oct. 14, 1899; *Boston Journal of Commerce*, LIV, 238, July 1, 1899; LIV, 258, July 8, 1899.

[61] *Boston Journal of Commerce*, LXIV, 190, May 28, 1904; LXIV, 230, June 11, 1904; LXVIII, 150, May 12, 1906; LXXI, 150, Nov. 9, 1907; American Iron and Steel Association, *Bulletin*, XLV, 94, Oct. 1, 1911; *Manufacturers' Record*, LXVI, 42, Aug. 13, 1914.

no small part to the reinvestment of profits, is sufficient testimony to its average prosperity. Many cotton-manufacturing corporations were undercapitalized, because they had not issued stock to represent earnings put back into the business, but this does not affect the census totals just quoted which record actual capital invested. A compilation made in 1912 indicated that the average dividends of seventy-six representative New England companies, for a period of over twenty years preceding, was 7.7 per cent on their share capital. Another compilation, made somewhat earlier, was not so favorable. It showed that thirty-eight companies averaged 5.87 per cent upon their average capital during the ten years ending with the termination of the low-price cycle in 1898; and that they earned 6.70 per cent on their average capital stock during the ten years of rising prices that followed.[62] No corresponding figures exist for Southern mills, but dividends were probably higher in that section than in the North. Stock ownership there was not concentrated to the same extent in the hands of old manufacturing families who had no motive for thus distributing profits that they would reinvest in any case in the ancestral firm. One Northern corporation, that like many mills in the South exported all its product, paid dividends of 12 or 14 per cent annually for fourteen years besides aggregate bonuses of 125 per cent upon its capital. Other New England corporations made even higher distributions to their shareholders.[63]

EXPORTS OF COTTON GOODS

During these years export trade played little part in the prosperity of our manufacturers. Great Britain's supremacy in that field remained unchallenged. Her vast army of permanent textile workers, with their inheritance of special skill and knowledge, her abundant capital and cheap interest rates, her established position as the world's largest cotton market, her banking system which extended to the remotest consuming centers, her merchant marine whose ships took her goods from the mill doors to all ports of the world, were advantages that no change then forseen was likely to impair. The United States ranked second among cotton-manufacturing nations; yet when the World War broke out her spindles numbered but slightly over half those of Great Britain. While 75 per cent of the British product was exported, only 5 per cent of the output of our mills sought foreign markets.[64]

Yet as we have seen there were establishments in America that depended largely or exclusively upon customers abroad for the disposal of their product. Some of these owed their hold upon these consumers to the reputa-

[62] Copeland, *The Cotton Manufacturing Industry of the United States*, 262–264; National Association of Wool Manufacturers, *Bulletin*, xxxix, 119–120, Mar. 1909; Twelfth Census, *Reports*, ix, 31.
[63] Young, *American Cotton Industry*, 43; Copeland, *The Cotton Manufacturing Industry of the United States*, 395–397.
[64] Scherer, *Cotton as a World Power*, 349; American Cotton Manufacturers' Association, *Proceedings, Richmond, 1909*, 158; cf., *Boston Journal of Commerce*, LXVI, 370–371, July 29, 1905; U. S. Bureau of the Census, *Manufactures, 1914*, II, 45.

tion of the familiar brands of sheeting, duck or other standard fabrics that they manufactured. In 1895 Biddeford mills shipped to Vancouver a special train of twenty-nine cars loaded with cotton goods to fill Shanghai orders. At that time more American drills and sheetings were sold in China than those of British manufacture. When the railway from Mombasa to Lake Victoria in East Africa was constructed American cottons were used to pay the laborers, although the work was done by English contractors under the British flag. The contractors pursued this policy, against the protests of the Lancashire spinners, because goods made under American trade-marks commanded the confidence of the natives to a greater extent than those of other manufacture. During the interruption of trade with China at the time of the Boxer outbreak in 1900 some Southern mills suffered seriously from the loss of their market in that country. This particular outlet for American cotton goods was on the eve of permanent curtailment, however, on account of growing Japanese competition, which began to make itself felt about the beginning of the century, and of the establishment of cotton mills in China itself. In 1905 we shipped to the latter country 563,000,000 yards of cotton cloth. Two years later the quantity had fallen to 38,000,000 yards. The former year the Chinese market took 70 per cent of all the cotton textiles we exported; in 1907 it took but 18 per cent.[65]

Between 1890 and 1910 the value of the cotton cloth manufactured in America rose from $192,000,000 to $428,000,000, while exports of these cloths increased from something over $8,000,000 to nearly $20,000,000. In 1913, when the value of the cotton cloths woven in the United States reached $490,000,000 we exported nearly 445,000,000 yards valued at over $30,000,000. These figures show that a small but growing percentage of the total product was sold in foreign markets. While we ranked second among cotton manufacturing countries, we ranked fourth among exporters of cotton goods. Moreover this growth was not uniform. Our maximum exports before the World War were in 1906, when we shipped abroad cotton manufactures of all descriptions, except apparel and knit goods, to the value of $48,605,000.[66]

LABOR

Naturally the depression that followed the panic of 1893, and continued with only temporary alleviation in New England for several years thereafter, was accompanied by wage unsettlements and labor difficulties. Strikes were especially numerous and protracted during the cotton-mill crisis of 1898. This was not a period of uniformly declining wages, however, but rather of successive reductions and increases repeated so frequently as to be almost seasonal. After an obstinate strike at Fall River in 1905 a

---

[65] American Iron and Steel Association, *Bulletin*, XXIX, 77, Apr. 1, 1895; *Boston Journal of Commerce*, XLVIII, 132, May 23, 1896; *Commercial and Financial Chronicle*, LXII, 1017, June 6, 1896; LXXI, Supplement, 5, Sept. 8, 1900; American Cotton Manufacturers' Association, *Proceedings, Richmond, 1908*, 141–142.

[66] 62d Cong., 2d sess., *Document No. 643*, I, 180 (chart); U. S. Bureau of the Census, *Manufactures, 1914*, II, 33, 45; *Textile World Record*, XLVII, 186–188, May, 1914; *cf.*, Copeland, *The Cotton Manufacturing Industry of the United States*, 220–226.

sliding scale for the payment of weavers was tried, but without success. Collective bargaining made little headway and both piece-work rates and time wages varied from point to point and even at different mills in the same city. A constant influx of unskilled foreign operatives with a low standard of living kept wages down in some branches of the textile trades. But the increasing proportion of men and of adults employed, and such fragmentary data as we have of actual earnings, both point to a steady improvement in the general condition of the workers. Although the Fall River mills paid their weavers practically the same rate per cut for print cloths in 1908 as in 1892, the output per operative was much higher at the later date on account of loom improvements.[67]

An upward movement of wages also occurred in the South. During the early nineties the low price of cotton drove many tenant farmers into the mills and labor was abundant; but ten years later the growth of the industry had created a demand for operatives that exceeded the supply. Foreigners were not welcomed—at least they did not enter the Southern labor market in appreciable numbers. For a time "stealing" workers from other mills became an "abuse" in certain localities, such was the call for their services; in other words eager employers outbid each other to get hands. At the meeting of the American Cotton Manufacturers' Association, which represented Southern spinners, held at Nashville in 1906, one Southern mill owner boasted:

"When I started my last addition of thirty-thousand spindles, I entered into a contract with myself that I would not take help from other mills, and of the one-thousand hands we are employing today, eight hundred are East Tennesseeans who have been educated to manufacture velvets, corduroys and fancies; and if we can train the mountain people to do this class of work, they can certainly be taught to turn out drills for the China market."

But in the older manufacturing regions many of the local operatives were leaving the mills to go into other pursuits. In the small village of Graniteville, South Carolina, sixty employes left the factory within a year for "higher lines or grades of employment, where there is more call for brains."[68]

Mechanical improvements steadily reduced the quantity of labor required in a mill of given spindle and loom capacity. As early as 1896 there were 12 weavers in a cotton factory in Vermont who each attended 20 Northrop looms, and one weaver who attended 28, working on 64 by 64 print cloth; and in the Merrimac Manufacturing Company's mills the average number of looms was 16 per operative. Where 100 weavers were required for 743 ordinary looms, 134 weavers attended 2,000 Northrop looms. Naturally the earnings of labor rose, though not in proportion to their increased output. In a comparison of cotton manufacturing in

[67] Cf., Copeland, *The Cotton Manufacturing Industry of the United States*, 113–133; Uttley, *Cotton Spinning and Manufacturing in the United States*, passim; Kohn, *The Cotton Mills of South Carolina*, 37–50; Thompson, *From the Cotton Field to the Cotton Mill*, 151, 279–280; Mitchell, *The Rise of Cotton Mills in the South*, 229.

[68] Southern Cotton Manufacturers' Association, *Proceedings, Knoxville, 1905*, 193; American Cotton Manufacturers' Association, *Proceedings, Asheville, 1906*, 300–301.

Great Britain and the United States, an expert from the former country wrote in 1903, that while 2,500 operatives were required in a specified factory in Manchester to run 135,000 spindles and 3,000 looms, 2,700 operatives at Fall River ran over 266,000 spindles and 7,660 looms. In other words, the machinery tended per employe in the United States was about double that in Great Britain. One result of this was to change the relative labor cost of weaving in proportion to the total labor cost of making cotton goods. For some time prior to the invention of the Northrop loom, weaving cost had been growing relatively greater on account of recent improvements in carding and spinning. Indeed, it was estimated that on plain goods they had risen from 50 per cent to 60 per cent of the entire labor cost of manufacturing. On fancy fabrics they naturally ran higher. The introduction of the Northrop loom and other improved weaving machinery checked this tendency, and indeed reversed it.[69]

These figures, which though from authoritative sources have scarcely the validity of broader statistical comparisons, might suggest the inference that labor costs were lower in this country than in Great Britain, despite our higher wages, on account of the greater productivity of American operatives. This was not generally true, however; for spinning costs and the cost of weaving finer and fancy fabrics were lower in England than in the United States. Plain coarse cottons could be woven cheaper in this country on account of the more general adoption of the automatic loom; and charges for bleaching, dyeing, printing, mercerizing and other finishing processes seem also to have been less in America, perhaps because those branches of industry were closely organized in Great Britain. But on the whole most classes of cotton goods could be produced more cheaply on the other side of the Atlantic.[70]

Whatever advantage foreign manufacturers enjoyed in the way of lower production costs, however, were more than counterbalanced by our customs duties, which averaged over 40 per cent upon most fabrics, and gave American mills a virtual monopoly of the domestic market. To be sure a few million dollars worth of cotton goods were imported annually, but this competition never threatened seriously the prosperity of the industry. Excepting laces, embroideries and similar specialties, we always shipped to foreign countries more manufactured cotton than we bought from them.[71]

During the early years of the century this industry made the largest growth in its history and it ranked an easy first among our textile manufactures. In 1889 our output of woolens, which was valued at $270,000,000, slightly exceeded our output of cotton goods. Twenty-five years later our cotton mills turned out a product valued at $701,000,000, as compared with $464,000,000 for the woolen industry.[72]

[69] Young, *American Cotton Industry*, 6, 23; Levasseur, *The American Workman*, 68, footnote 38; New England Cotton Manufacturers' Association, *Transactions, Atlanta, 1895*, p. 88; Copeland, *The Cotton Manufacturing Industry of the United States*, 296–304.
[70] 62d Cong., 2d sess., *Document No. 643*, I, 9–13; II, 502.
[71] *Cf.*, Copeland, *The Cotton Manufacturing Industry of the United States*, 236–246; 62d Cong., 2d sess., *Document 643*, I, 174–181; Bureau of the Census, *Manufactures, 1914*, II, 45.
[72] Bureau of the Census, *Manufactures, 1914*, II, 12.

CHAPTER XII

WOOL MANUFACTURE

Wool Production, 191. Wool Substitutes, 194. Geography of the Wool Manufacture, 195. Fabrics, 196. Technical Aspects, 197. Trade Conditions, 199. Foreign Competition, 202. Labor, 203. Exports, 204. Organization, 205. Carpets, 207.

WOOL PRODUCTION

Both graziers and wool manufacturers suffered from the depression that followed the panic of 1893. The latter, like their colleagues in the cotton industry, faced a falling raw-material market that caused a sharp shrinkage in the value of their inventories and discouraged cloth buyers, who postponed purchases in the hope of still lower prices. But the cotton crop maintained its normal level while the domestic wool clip experienced a notable decline.[1] In 1895 Eastern farmers delivered sheep at the Pittsburgh market for fifty cents a head, and dealers reported refusing tenders at thirty-three and one-third cents a head. Between 1893 and 1897, which embraced the period of free wool, the number of sheep in the country diminished by about two-fifths. This falling off was not permanent and between 1897 and 1902 American flocks rose from less than 3,500,000 head to well toward 4,250,000 head; but the decline of wool growing in the East proved final, and toward the end of the period we are describing closer settlement and competing rural industries began slowly but surely to curtail production even in the West. Our total clip, which repeatedly exceeded 300,000,000 pounds during the eighties and nineties, and reached a maximum of 316,000,000 pounds in 1911, never after 1912 attained those figures.[2]

In fact the wools of the world were tending to become, like cotton, the product of two or three countries, such as Australia, the Argentine and the South African Union. The annual clip of the wool-manufacturing nations of Europe, like that of the United States, was steadily declining; so that the production of raw materials, and of the finished goods into which they were converted, were becoming entirely separated geographically. Simultaneously the method of dealing in wool, at least in America, was changing. The wool buyers of the seventies and eighties still traveled about the country inspecting and purchasing fleeces on the spot. An attempt was made in 1894 to establish a wool exchange at New York for the purpose of concentrating sales, though Boston was the chief wool market of the country.

---

[1] U. S. Department of Commerce and Labor, *Statistical Record of the Progress of the United States*, 1800–1907, 27.

[2] Wright, *Wool Growing and the Tariff*, 298–312; American Iron and Steel Association, *Bulletin*, XXIX, 147, July 1, 1895; XXX, 245, Nov. 1, 1896; U. S. Bureau of the Census, *Manufactures, 1914*, II, 64; *Manufacturers' Record*, LXV, 56, Feb. 5, 1914; *Statistical Abstract of the United States, 1923*, 172.

But this enterprise collapsed two years later, together with its associated undertakings, including a wool warehouse, a newspaper and a bank. Nevertheless with the shifting of wool growing westward and the increasing concentration of manufacturing in the East, the city warehouseman took the place of the itinerant buyer. Yet in no other country of equal importance was the domestic trade in so chaotic a condition. Wool reached the mills carelessly packed, unskirted and uneven in quality. Every farmer and every ranchman was a law to himself in respect to breeding and sorting for market. Wool-handling centers existed at certain points, such as San Francisco and Pendleton, Oregon, where country wools were graded and baled for shipment; but the motive for this was to save freight, and shippers' classifications carried little weight with Eastern consumers. Up to the very end of the period we are considering no decided improvement occurred to remedy these faulty methods, although other phases of wool marketing progressed *pari passu* with the demands of the industry. Manufacturers regularly discounted the prices they paid for domestic fleeces by enough to compensate them for its inferior packing and grading as compared with foreign wool. This lack of organization, uniformity and standardization reacted upon both grazing and manufacturing. The individual wool grower remained a victim of his own unprogressive habits, and mills that used domestic wool were obliged to adapt their machinery and their products to poorer raw materials as well as to their markets.[3]

By 1900 the world's sheep husbandry had virtually ceased to be an adjunct of farming and had become a distinct occupation. The quality of wool was changing with changes in methods of manufacture and popular taste. For several years after the Civil War most of the wool imported and grown in the United States was pure or nearly pure merino, which was admirably adapted to make the finest woolen goods. Later merino sheep were rapidly converted into mutton crossbreed types on account of the better adaptation of these wools to the worsted manufacture and the rise of the export trade in frozen mutton from the great grazing countries of the Southern Hemisphere. The result was something approaching a wool famine, and manufacturers were forced to produce from medium long wools goods that would have been deemed impossible a few years before. Simultaneously in the great wool-producing countries the classification of wools into definite and minute grades reached an accuracy that approached a science. Indeed technical courses were established to teach this art. But, as we have just seen, the United States, which might have been expected to adopt the best way of doing things as early as any other nation, still clung to the old haphazard gradings.[4]

[3] National Association of Wool Manufacturers, *Bulletins*, XXVIII, 140–141, June 1898; XXVIII, 361–364, Dec. 1898; XLIV, 230, July 1914; National Association of Cotton Manufacturers, *Transactions, Boston, 1906*, 271; U. S. Industrial Commission, *Reports*, VI, 327–328, 330, 335–336; Cole, *The American Wool Manufacture*, II, 73–78.

[4] S. N. D. North, in American Association of Wool Manufacturers, *Bulletin*, XXXIII, 7–13, Mar. 1903; U. S. Industrial Commission, *Reports*, VI, 327–328; Cole, *The American Wool Manufacture*, II, Jan. 1870, 63–65.

During the last quarter of the nineteenth century the average price of wool pretty steadily declined. Indeed it was estimated that the fall abroad exceeded 50 per cent, and that it was largely due to the increase in the supply of cross-breed wools. In America the depreciation in wool values was not so marked, amounting probably to something less than 25 per cent. One factor in this price decline was the remarkable increase in the supply of cotton and the adaptation of that fiber to uses for which it previously had been thought unsuitable.

After a brief season of acute demoralization in 1900, however, prices recovered rapidly from the low level of the nineties, in sympathy with the upward trend of most commodity quotations that followed the turn of the century. Fine territory wools, upon which prices are based, rose from 38 cents a pound in 1901 to 70 cents and more in 1905; and substantial though less-marked changes occurred in the price of unscoured Eastern wools. While the high level of the latter year was not maintained throughout the ensuing decade, quotations never sank to even approximately the low points reached ten or fifteen years earlier.[5]

Domestic fleeces supplied a decreasing share of the total spindle consumption of the country, as was natural in view of the steady growth of manufacturing at a time when wool production was stationary or declining. Between 1889 and 1914 the proportion of native wool used by American mills fell from 68 to 55 per cent. These figures naturally varied with different classes of fabrics. For example carpets, which are made of the cheapest grade of fiber, consisted almost exclusively—to the extent of 99.7 per cent—of foreign wool. During these twenty-five years the proportion of domestic wool employed in the worsted manufacture fell from 61 to 57 per cent, and the quantity used in the production of carded fabrics declined from 91 to 79 per cent.[6]

Since manufacturers used enough imported wool to make them dependent in a degree upon the world market for raw materials, and since foreign quotations affected the price of domestic wool, mill owners were forced to deal with a more complex group of production costs than did producers of cotton goods, or indeed of silks or other textiles. This situation was reflected in the tariff controversies that were a perennial feature of the industry's history for over a century and that continued unabated up to the World War. The only novel episode of this period, so far as raw material duties were concerned, was the three-year era of free wool between 1894 and 1897, when the Wilson Act was in force. That innovation was not accompanied by sensational developments, however, partly perhaps because its temporary character was anticipated.

[5] Twelfth Census, *Reports*, IX, 77; Thirteenth Census, *Reports*, X, 106, table 27; National Association of Cotton Manufacturers, *Transactions*, Boston, *1906*, 244 et seq.; Wright, *Wool Growing and the Tariff*, 348–349; 62d Cong., 2d sess., *House Document 342*, I, 36, 37; National Association of Wool Manufacturers, *Bulletin*, XLIII, 66–67, Mar. 1913.
[6] U. S. Bureau of the Census, *Manufactures, 1914*, II, 64.

WOOL SUBSTITUTES

Another aspect of the raw-material question, that perturbed wool growers and consumers of woolen goods alike, was the use of shoddy and other substitutes. Nevertheless these were not employed in the United States to the same extent as in countries making goods for export. It is difficult to follow through the shifting classifications of the census the proportion of shoddy, or "recovered wool fiber" as it was eventually termed, used in the wool manufacture at different dates. It formed together with cotton and other substitutes a larger fraction of the materials from which carded cloths were made than of those employed in worsteds, but it was used in both fabrics.[7] In 1914 about nine-tenths of the fiber consumed in the latter branch of the industry was pure wool and most of the remainder consisted of animal hair added to give special qualities to the fabric and not to cheapen it. On the other hand only 29 per cent of the materials in carded goods were scoured wool. To this should be added some 17 per cent of noils and waste, which were virtually new wool mechanically discarded during the preparatory processes for making other goods. But nearly one-third of the fiber used in the production of carded cloths consisted of shoddy, and 12 per cent was cotton.

Shoddy was made to a considerable extent in the factories that consumed it, though in 1914 sixty-four establishments were engaged independently in its production. An undeservedly bad reputation hung over this material, and it was as unpopular with wool growers as with cloth consumers. Several efforts were made to levy an internal revenue tax upon it or upon fabrics containing it, and prohibitive duties prevented its importation. In 1909 manufacturers of shoddies and wool extracts formed a national association to protect their mutual interests and to "disseminate information for the general understanding of their products." A portion of the relatively moderate amount made in the United States was exported, nearly 2,000,000 pounds being shipped annually to Great Britain.[8]

The outstanding facts in the development of the wool manufacture during this period were the expansion of the worsted at the expense of the carded-wool industry, and the invasion of certain fields of consumption hitherto occupied by carded woolens by the products of the knitting mill. These changes were merely the culmination of tendencies previously existing and already remarked in connection with the history of the period immediately preceding. Between 1889 and 1914 the value of carded cloths made in the United States declined, in round numbers, from $134,000,000 to $104,000,000, and the machinery employed in their production was probably

---

[7] *Cf.*, Committee on Ways and Means, 54th Cong., 2d sess., *Tariff Hearings*, II, 1672–1675.
[8] Twelfth Census, *Reports*, IX, 94–95; Thirteenth Census, *Reports*, X, 107; Bureau of the Census, *Manufactures, 1914*, II, 68, 90; Wright, *Wool Growing and the Tariff*, 296; 62d Cong., 2d sess., *House Document 342*, I, 72; National Association of Wool Manufacturers, *Bulletin*, XXXII, 289, Sept. 1902; XXXIII, 14–15, Mar. 1903; XXXIV, 269–273, Sept. 1904; XXXIX, 359, June 1909; *Textile World Record*, XLVII, 267–271, June 1914; Cole, *The American Wool Manufacture*, II, 69–71; 205–206.

less in 1914 than in 1870. During the same quarter of a century the value of the worsted goods manufactured in this country rose from $79,000,000 to $276,000,000 and the machinery used in this branch of the industry increased from about 750,000 to well toward 2,250,000 spindles.[9]

GEOGRAPHY OF THE WOOL MANUFACTURE

No marked shift in the geography of the wool manufacture accompanied these changes, though Massachusetts supplanted and eventually drew well ahead of Pennsylvania as the leading state in this industry. Indeed in 1914 her product approached in value the combined products of Pennsylvania and Rhode Island, which ranked third in this manufacture. New York ranked fourth at the latter date, followed by New Jersey, which had risen from thirteenth to fifth place during these twenty-five years, thanks to the establishment of large worsted factories there under German auspices. Maine, Connecticut and New Hampshire also occupied a respectable position in woolen-mill statistics. Though there were some worsted mills west of the North Atlantic seaboard, the relative decline of the carded-wool manufacture was attended in the other states by a corresponding falling off of the industry as a whole. Indeed with one or two immaterial exceptions those states employed less machinery and turned out a smaller product in 1914 than they had previously.[10]

During this period Lawrence succeeded Philadelphia as the greatest producer in the country of woolen cloths and worsteds. Including carpets, which she made to the value of over $20,000,000 per annum, Philadelphia still held the primacy; but at the close of this period Lawrence produced annually a greater value of other woolen fabrics. Providence ranked third, and these three cities accounted for about one-fourth of all the goods of this character made in the Union.

Notwithstanding this centralization, which, especially in the worsted industry, applied to the concentration of production in larger manufacturing units as well as in restricted geographical areas, many small woolen mills in all parts of the country continued to make yarns and cloths from local materials for a limited neighborhood market. Of the total number of establishments in the United States, which decreased from over 1,400 to less than 1,000 between 1889 and 1914, only forty at the latter date were west of the Mississippi and sixty south of the Potomac. Nevertheless thirty-two states reported woolen or worsted mills of some description.[11] While the inland and western manufacturer did not command the skill which was at the disposal of the manufacturer of the northeastern seaboard, his labor was cheap and unorganized and many of his other expenses were relatively lighter than those of mill owners in the latter region. He did not turn out

[9] Twelfth Census, *Reports*, IX, 99, 102; Bureau of the Census, *Manufactures, 1914*, II, 82, 83, 87.
[10] 62d Cong., 2d sess., *House Document 342*, I, 220–222; Bureau of the Census, *Manufactures, 1914*, II, 85.
[11] Bureau of the Census, *Manufactures, 1914*, II, 52, 53.

many fashion goods, but confined himself to producing plain fabrics for which there was a stable market in his vicinity. In 1910 a leading newspaper in Iowa reported that not a new woolen mill had been built in that state for twenty-five years, and that during this period several had gone out of existence.[12] Nevertheless the erection of new woolen mills in the West and South was occasionally recorded. These were usually small establishments employing in the neighborhood of $100,000 capital, and presumably some of them manufactured mixed cotton and woolen goods. Of the twenty-four new establishments reported for the whole country in 1913, one was in Indiana, one in Wisconsin and one in California. In 1898 the last of these states has six or seven mills making tweeds, cheviots, kerseys, blankets, flannels and other carded fabrics. Only one of these remained in operation sixteen years later.[13]

This tendency to geographical concentration also applied to the distribution of mills within single states as well as within the Union as a whole. Notwithstanding the remarkable expansion of the industry in Massachusetts, Berkshire County, which was an ancient seat of this manufacture, had but twelve mills in 1914 as compared with eighteen mills thirty years before. During that period only two new mills were erected, while eight had gone out of business or been converted to other uses. At the same time small establishments such as were typical of the industry almost a century before survived in some localities. As recently as 1906 a little mill operated all the year round by water power was running near Lancaster, Pennsylvania, whose entire complement of employes consisted of four persons. It bought much of its wool from neighboring farmers and made a wide variety of fabrics, ranging from cassimeres, flannel shirtings and even women's dress goods to horse blankets and heavy hosiery yarns.[14]

FABRICS

The trend of textile manufacturing was steadily toward finer and lighter weight fabrics without regard to the nature of the materials used. With increasing wealth, luxury and refinement of tastes and occupations, the demand for better goods constantly increased. These better goods were really more durable as well as handsomer in appearance than many of the coarser and rougher factory products of an earlier period, and they were in no wise inferior to foreign fabrics of the same general class. Shortly before the outbreak of the World War, when the lower duties levied by the Underwood Tariff and general trade conditions encouraged heavier importations of foreign worsteds than for some years preceding, it was dis-

[12] National Association of Wool Manufacturers, *Bulletin*, xxv, 16–17, Mar. 1895; xl, 280, Sept. 1910; American Iron and Steel Association, *Bulletin*, xliv, 97, Oct. 15, 1910.
[13] *S. & W. Textile Recorder*, p. 9, Dec. 10, 1898; *Manufacturers' Record*, Dec. 10, 1903; *Textile World Record*, xlvi, 299, Dec. 1913; Bureau of the Census, *Manufactures, 1914*, i, 87, footnote 7; Cole, *The American Wool Manufacture*, ii, 182–188.
[14] National Association of Wool Manufacturers, *Bulletin*, xliii, 69–70, Mar. 1913; Lancaster County Historical Society, *Publications*, x, 298–299.

covered that American serges not only had faster colors but stood tension and tear tests better than imported goods of comparable grades and prices.[15]

Nevertheless the traditional old-fashioned fabrics popular with an earlier generation were still manufactured and sold to some extent long after they had disappeared from common consumption. Even jeans, which it was expected would vanish from the market "as civilization advanced," continued to be made in considerable quantities, the principal buyers being manufacturers of cheap garments. No longer were they exclusively blue as in the days when they were almost universally employed for men's ordinary attire throughout the country districts of the United States. They were made in blacks, browns and combinations, their variety being one of the features that kept them in demand. They ranked among the cheapest woolen goods, ranging in price about 1900 from six to thirty cents a yard. Flannels, another American staple, yielded to the inroads of knit underwear and fashion changes, the quantity made annually declining between 1889 and 1914 from 9,000,000 yards to 2,000,000 yards. Even Germantown knitting yarns, familiar to most American households for a century or more, gave place to worsted yarns spun on French machinery.[16]

Occasionally a caprice of fashion revived the popularity of some carded fabric and started rumors that woolens were coming back at the expense of worsteds. The vogue of cheviots in the late nineties, and an attendant increase in the call for other goods of an allied character, were so interpreted in some quarters. But the worsted industry was now supported by conditions of such a basic nature that its continued ascendancy was assured. Two-thirds or more of the spindles and looms employed in the wool manufacture were adapted to making fabrics of the latter class. Improvements in combing machinery, which constantly added to the kinds of wool that could be employed in worsteds, and the introduction of the French system of spinning, made it possible for our manufacturers greatly to extend their worsted production without changing their sources of raw materials. Furthermore the organization of the woolen industry was rapidly accommodating itself to this form of manufacture.[17]

TECHNICAL ASPECTS

A report on the American wool manufacture made in 1912 stated—

"The distinctive features of the present organization of the worsted industry are the large average size of the mills and the specialization in processes."

The value of products per establishment was more than five times that of the average factory making carded cloths.[18] In 1896 the Arlington

---

[15] National Association of Wool Manufacturers, *Bulletin*, XLIV, 272–275, July 1914.
[16] *S. & W. Textile Reporter*, p. 3, May 27, 1899; Bureau of the Census, *Manufactures, 1914*, II, 78; National Association of Wool Manufacturers, *Bulletin*, XXXIX, 241–242, Mar. 1909; Cole, *The American Wool Manufacture*, II, 150–151.
[17] National Association of Wool Manufacturers, *Bulletin*, XLI, 224, June 1911.
[18] 62d Cong., 2d sess., *House Document 342*, I, 220.

Mills began to comb worsted tops on commission or for sale to spinners. This was the first attempt made in this country to specialize in that process for outside consumers. Combing mills were very expensive, and many manufacturers were prepared to spin and weave worsted yarns who lacked the capital, or found it uneconomical, to erect a complete plant. Between 1899 and 1914 the quantity of tops purchased by spinners increased from 5,500,000 to over 29,000,000 pounds. At the latter date nearly 88 per cent of the yarns used by manufacturers of woolens were spun in the establishment where they were woven into cloth, as compared with 58 per cent of those used by worsted manufacturers. In other words the British and European system of distributing different processes among different establishments, instead of combining them under a single roof and management, was more common in the worsted branch than in the woolen branch of the industry.[19]

Foreign precedents in this respect were possibly encouraged by the large use of imported machinery and labor. For many years nearly all the preparatory and spinning machinery in our worsted mills was of foreign make. It was not until 1898, for example, that the Lowell Machine Shops, which had been building other textile machinery for fifty years, began to make equipment for worsted mills. In 1911 a representative of a German firm, which after manufacturing worsteds for just a century in Germany had established a factory in New Jersey, testified that when the American works were built their owners were obliged—

"In order to be able to compete not only as to price but also with respect to quality and technical perfection with the best European mills, to import most of its machinery because a great deal of American spinning, weaving, dyeing and finishing machinery is not yet so highly developed as the European. This is especially true of the machinery used in what is known as the French system of worsted spinning, which is being adopted more and more each year."

The same company had to import all its woolen spinning machinery in order to compete with the highest grade fabrics made by European manufacturers. Most looms could be bought from American makers, but after paying duties they were almost as expensive as those imported. In a word, according to this authority, "domestic machinery, especially that used for the production of finer goods, has not the same efficiency as the European and consequently proves more costly in the long run."[20] In 1912 all the combs and drawing frames used in America for manufacturing upon the French system were imported. In fact 23 per cent of the looms and 78 per cent of the other machinery employed in all branches of the woolen industry were of foreign manufacture, and American makers were undis-

[19] Bureau of the Census, *Manufactures, 1914*, II, 66, 67; National Association of Wool Manufacturers, *Bulletin*, XXXIII, 176–178, June 1903; XXXIX, 183, Mar. 1909; *cf.*, also Committee on Ways and Means, 54th Cong., 2d sess., *Tariff Hearings*, II, 1700–1701; Cole, *The American Wool Manufacture*, II, 201.
[20] National Association of Wool Manufacturers, *Bulletin*, XXVIII, 177–178, June 1898; XLI, 416–417, Sept. 1911.

puted masters of the field only in respect to carding machines and mules for spinning carded wool.[21]

As already suggested this period witnessed a gradual transition from the older English or "Bradford" system of worsted combing and spinning to the French or Continental method, though to be sure the earlier system still remained in more common use. The two did not differ radically in principle. In both the wool passed through virtually the same processes in the same succession, though there was somewhat more manipulation in the French method and mules were used instead of frames for spinning. But the telling advantages of the latter were its ability to handle satisfactorily shorter staple wools than the Bradford system, and the softer appearance and feel of dress goods manufactured by it.[22]

Large worsted mills were the order of the day. The Arlington Mills operated more than 80,000 worsted spindles, 62,000 cotton spindles and 2,400 looms; the Washington Mills, also at Lawrence, had 78,000 worsted spindles and 1,400 looms; and in 1906 the Wood Worsted Mill in the same city started with 1,000 looms supplied by spinning and preparatory machinery using the Bradford system, and also a second department of somewhat smaller extent using the French method. The first of these three establishments, in addition to inaugurating the manufacture of tops as a separate industry in America, was the first to introduce the so-called solvent process for cleaning wool, by which valuable by-products, such as lanoline oil and carbonate of potash, are recovered.[23]

TRADE CONDITIONS

During the two decades that elapsed between the panic of 1893 and the opening of the World War the wool manufacture experienced the usual alternations of activity and depression, such as had characterized its history throughout the previous century. An unexpected revival followed the enactment of the Wilson Law in 1894, quite out of accord with the predictions of those who fancied that a lower tariff was bound to depress the industry. The market was stripped of goods, partly because the panic had forced many factories to close down wholly or partially the previous seasons. Simultaneously wool prices throughout the world were rising, and the prospect that yarn and cloth would advance to correspond stimulated buying. The Wilson tariff gave manufacturers free wool, where they had been paying theretofore from 32 to 60 per cent duty upon their imported raw materials.[24]

But after this brief revival a second wave of depression overtook the wool manufacture which seemed to confirm all the prophecies of evil that had

[21] 62d Cong., 2d sess., *House Document 342*, II, 1042–1044.
[22] Committee on Ways and Means, 54th Cong., 2d sess., *Tariff Hearings*, II, 1732–1733.
[23] National Association of Wool Manufacturers, *Bulletin*, XXXIII, 157–160, June 1903; XXXVII, 2–4, 6–12, Mar. 1907.
[24] National Association of Wool Manufacturers, *Bulletin*, XXV, 22–23, Mar. 1895; XXVI, 40–41, Mar. 1896; cf., Taussig, *Tariff History of the United States*, 291–292; American Iron and Steel Association, *Bulletin*, XXIX, 77, Apr. 1, 1895.

greeted the enactment of this law. Between 1893 and 1895 less new machinery was added to the woolen and worsted mills of the United States than during any other preceding three years since the Civil War. Such growth as occurred was mostly in the West. Altogether twenty-three mills were erected during these three years, the largest of which was a six-set woolen factory in South Dakota. Imports of woolen goods after a moment of hesitation rose rapidly. From 1891 to 1893, when the tariff averaged 91 per cent, they amounted to $38,000,000 per annum; under the Wilson tariff, which averaged 49 per cent, they reached $47,000,000 annually. When the high duties were restored imports fell off, and between 1900 and 1907, under the Dingley tariff, they declined to $19,000,000. Worsted manufacturers were particularly gratified by a decision of the United States Supreme Court, in 1898, reversing a Treasury definition that had been in force since 1836, classifying worsteds in a distinct category from manufactures of wool and depriving their makers in a measure of the protection accorded producers of the latter goods.[25]

During the depression of the nineties wool was shipped from the United States to Great Britain and Europe, thus reversing the usual movement of this commodity. In the summer of 1896 of 246 mills reporting, 131 were running full time, 61 were operating part time and 64 were closed entirely. In contemporary opinion this was in many respects the worst year in the recent history of the industry. Unusually heavy imports of goods from Europe, a general business stagnation, an unsettled currency and a presidential campaign combined to discourage manufacturers.[26]

Such optimism as greeted the election in the autumn of that year of a president and congress having the confidence of the business world was of brief duration so far as wool manufacturers were concerned. Disputes and uncertainties arose over the new wool and woolen schedule in the Dingley Bill. In addition to the usual controversies over adjusting the respective rates upon raw materials and their manufactures, makers of carded goods demanded a revision of the duties in force prior to the enactment of the Wilson Law, because improvements in machinery since the original compensatory arrangement of 1867 was adopted enabled manufacturers of worsteds to use what had been until recently exclusively carding wools, and thus placed them at an unfair advantage over producers of other classes of fabrics. In other words, instead of two parties in interest, the wool growers and the wool manufacturers, appearing on the scene, three parties now had the floor, the grower, the worsted spinner and weaver, and the hard-pressed maker of carded cloths.[27] In fact some manufacturers op-

[25] National Association of Wool Manufacturers, *Bulletin*, xxvi, 92–95, Mar. 1896; xxxviii, 130, June 1898; Wright, *Wool Growing and the Tariff*, 288; Committee on Ways and Means, 54th Cong., 2d sess., *Tariff Hearings*, ii, 1537–1539, 1636–1637; cf., Cole, *The American Wool Manufacture*, ii, 33–34, 44–45.
[26] American Iron and Steel Association, *Bulletin*, xxix, 243, Nov. 1, 1895; xxix, 257, Nov. 20, 1895; xxx, 93, Apr. 20, 1896; xxx, 131, June 10, 1896.
[27] Committee on Ways and Means, 54th Cong., 2d sess., *Tariff Hearings*, ii, 1691–1696; S. N. D. North, *The Revision of the Wool and Woolen Schedule*, 12–14.

posed restoring any duty on wool. Roland Hazard, a veteran Rhode Island mill owner and free-wool advocate, argued that the era of the Wilson Law, which admitted wool free, had not witnessed a marked falling off in the domestic clip. Producers must be able to sell their goods at a price within the means of consumers—

"The consequence is that if the manufacturer is forced to pay a higher price for the foreign wool which enters into his fabrics, he must pay less for the domestic wool which is mixed with the foreign."[28]

With the enactment of the Dingley tariff in 1897 and the improvement of business that accompanied it, woolen and worsted manufacturing picked up for a time; but this revival was at first largely speculative. The sudden rise in wool prices following the passage of the law created a fictitious demand for woolen goods, in anticipation of a still greater advance in the price of manufactures, that outran the legitimate wants of consumers. As a result many hastily given orders were subsequently canceled, and when a war with Spain was seen to be inevitable, buying practically ceased and several mills were forced to shut down. The number of failures that ensued among woolen manufacturers was said to be larger and to involve more important establishments, than in any equal period since the panic of 1857. The seriousness of the crisis was attributed to a gradual impairment of capital, reaching back in many cases to the depression of 1893. Happily, however, one of those sudden reversals so characteristic of the American industry occurred the following season, and in 1899 practically all the woolen and worsted machinery in the United States was fully employed and many mills could not meet their orders. It was indicative of the soundness of this recovery that wages were restored to the standard prevailing in 1892, prior to the panic.[29]

While 1899 had been a year of rising prices for manufactured goods, following an advance of 75 per cent in quotations of Australian wool and a more moderate increase of those of domestic fleeces, 1900 witnessed a sudden collapse of the market both at home and abroad, which forced many mills to shut down or to curtail their production and caused the failure or liquidation of several large concerns. Nevertheless somewhat less machinery was idle during this census year than ten years before, and the closed establishments were mostly in the South and West where the industry was already declining. Production was less than normal, however, because the large Eastern factories under whose roofs the bulk of the country's output was concentrated were not operating to full capacity. The stress under which the wool manufacture labored at this time was said to be "largely instru-

---

[28] National Association of Wool Manufacturers, *Bulletin*, XXVII, 352–353, Dec. 1897; Taussig, *Tariff History of the United States*, 328–332.
[29] *Commercial and Financial Chronicle*, LXVI, 590, Mar. 26, 1898; National Association of Wool Manufacturers, *Bulletin*, XXIX, 12–13, Mar. 1899; XXX, 13, Mar. 1900.

mental in bringing about consolidations of establishments under one management."[30]

Another period of prosperity began the next season which lasted until 1903, when a great scarcity of Australian wool embarrassed worsted manufacturers, whose raw-material costs advanced faster than the prices their goods commanded in the general market. At the same time the war between Russia and Japan caused a sharp advance in coarse wools, which were in demand for army clothing, to the temporary distress of American carpet manufacturers.[31] Seasonal fluctuations of prosperity responding to the pulse of general business activity occurred during the years that followed. Makers of carded cloths usually had more difficulty than worsted manufacturers in keeping their machinery fully employed. For example in December 1908, 36 per cent of the looms and 39 per cent of the cards engaged on woolen goods in New England were idle, as compared with only 10 per cent of the looms and 3 per cent of the combs in the worsted industry.[32]

With the election of a Congress in the autumn of 1909 known to be hostile to the high duties on wool and its manufactures levied under the Payne-Aldrich Act, a new period of tariff uncertainty began. Other disturbing influences followed, such as the bitter and protracted strike at Lawrence in 1912, and similar troubles the same year at Passaic, which had also become an important worsted manufacturing center. Altogether these were seasons of worry and uncertainty for manufacturers, even when their machinery was active. Another labor dispute in 1913, which brought the garment-making industry of New York and other Eastern centers to a standstill, interfered with cloth sales and again lessened production. When the control of the national Government passed into new hands the following year a low-tariff era was assured; and with the enactment of the Underwood Law providing for free wool and a radical reduction in duties on all kinds of woolen goods, it seemed likely that the conditions prevailing during the operation of the Wilson Act twenty years before would be repeated. But the enforced curtailments of the previous season, plus underproduction in anticipation of lower prices during the time that the Underwood bill was being debated in Congress, left the market seriously understocked. As a result mills were very busy during the autumn of 1913 and January of the following year. Nevertheless nearly one-fourth of the woolen and worsted machinery in the country was idle during the twelve months prior to the outbreak of the World War.[33]

FOREIGN COMPETITION

Notwithstanding these vicissitudes, which were partly tariff begotten and psychological, between 1893 and 1914 the industry continued to expand at about the normal rate. By the turn of the century the American people

---
[30] Twelfth Census, *Reports*, IX, 77, 85–86.
[31] Bureau of the Census, *Manufactures, 1905*, III, 85–86.
[32] *Textile World Record*, XLVI, 392–393, Jan. 1914.
[33] National Association of Wool Manufacturers, *Bulletin*, XLIV, 110–113, Jan. 1914; XLIV, 371, Oct. 1914.

used more domestic woolens in proportion to their total consumption of goods of this material than they did in the case of any other group of textiles. Nine-tenths of those they consumed were the product of their own mills. Measured by value, more than twice as many cotton goods as woolen goods were imported. Between 1868 and 1904 the country's imports of raw wool multiplied about eight-fold. Meanwhile the foreign value of imports of woolen manufactures declined one-half, despite the fact that during these thirty-six years the population more than doubled. By 1909 less than 3 per cent of the woolen and worsted cloth and of the blankets and flannels consumed in the United States came from abroad, and the proportion of all other manufactures of wool except rugs, of which a slightly larger fraction was imported from Asia, was well under 10 per cent.[34]

Practically all production costs, from those of raw materials to those of marketing finished goods, were decidedly higher in the United States than abroad. In 1911 the labor charges of turning wool into tops and tops into yarn were respectively about 80 and 100 per cent more in America than in competing countries. The difference in the cost of converting yarn into cloth varied widely for different fabrics, but was in extreme cases 170 per cent higher in this country than in Great Britain and Europe. Consequently American manufacturers did not enjoy as wide a market as their transatlantic competitors, and for lack of an export outlet were exposed to the full force of seasonal fluctuations of demand at home. If a European mill owner turned out a set of patterns that did not take with the buyers for whom they were originally designed he could shift the goods to a more promising market elsewhere. The American maker had no such alternative. Our traditions, looking to quantity production more than to specifically artistic qualities, still militated against our manufacturers in spite of the increasing attention devoted to textile designing and other phases of industrial art in the United States; and the old prejudice in favor of imported fabrics had not entirely died out. Indeed a factory sometimes invited losses by its very effort to reduce costs of production through increasing output. Our most consistently prosperous mills were those making such standard cloths as flannels and serges.[35]

LABOR

American manufacturers have always contended that the high cost of producing woolen goods in the United States as compared with Great Britain and Europe was largely due to the lower quality and the higher wages of labor. In 1911 a German worsted manufacturer, who had previously owned and operated mills in his native country, testified that the average wages paid in American woolen and worsted factories were almost

---

[34] National Association of Wool Manufacturers, *Bulletin*, xxxv, 16–17, Mar. 1905; 62d Cong., 2d sess., *House Document 342*, I, 190–191.

[35] 62d Cong., 2d sess., *House Document 342*, II, 639–704; National Association of Wool Manufacturers, *Bulletin*, XLIII, 168–173, June 1913; 63d Cong., 1st sess., *Senate Document 167*, 7–8, 10.

125 per cent higher than those customary in Germany. He further maintained that the high rates paid in this country were usually to operatives of inferior training and experience as compared with their European fellows. In Germany both employers and employes were often the children and grandchildren of their predecessors in the same establishment. Operatives in American woolen mills were largely drawn from the ranks of unskilled labor, usually of immigrant origin, but not as a rule trained in the industry before coming to the United States.[36]

A Government investigation made in 1911 showed that textile labor in America was curiously unstable. In woolen mills less than half of the operatives had been employed in the industry for five years, and less than 30 per cent had been employed in the same mill for five years. Consequently employers were constantly breaking-in new and untrained workmen. The immigrant operatives of the United States had formed few home and neighborhood ties in the country of their adoption, and consequently they shifted restlessly from place to place. Moreover, great inequality in wages prevailed in different American industries. Some of these were more prosperous than others, and consequently afforded greater profits and higher wages. The woolen industry did not belong to the latter class. It had no single advantage not enjoyed in equal or greater degree by the same industry abroad. Its prosperity was so largely dependent on tariff protection that intelligent workers instinctively sought fields of employment that rested on a securer foundation, leaving the thoughtless, the indifferent and the more nomadic workers to man the woolen mills. Possibly this picture was slightly overdrawn, so far as the analysis of motives determining the quality of the workers found in this occupation was concerned, but the statistical evidence of the transitory character of this labor, with all that implies as to its deficient skill and efficiency, was irrefutable.[37]

EXPORTS

We have just seen that despite these handicaps, and thanks largely to tariff protection, American manufacturers steadily gained ground at home over their foreign competitors, and the consumption of imported fabrics constantly decreased. But they won no corresponding victories in export markets. To be sure the value of the domestic wool manufactures that we exported multiplied about eight-fold during the twenty years preceding the World War. But at the end of this period it was still well under $3,000,000 and of this amount two-thirds was accounted for by ready-made clothing sold to our two immediate neighbors, Canada and Mexico. A small quantity of carpets was shipped abroad under the encouragement of a drawback upon the duties paid upon the raw wool of which they were made. Occasionally a little flurry of interest was aroused in the woolen

[36] National Association of Wool Manufacturers, *Bulletin*, XLI, 418–420, Sept. 1911.
[37] 62d Cong., 2d sess., *House Document 342*, II, 955–984; National Association of Wool Manufacturers, *Bulletin*, XLIII, 172–173, June 1913; Cole, *The American Wool Manufacture*, II, 114–116, 118–123.

trade by the announcement that a consignment of American fabrics had found its way to a foreign market. But the status of the industry was accurately described in a statement, written in 1912, to the effect that, "as far as the rest of the world is concerned, the wool manufactures of the United States are isolated." In general the tariff "confined the American consumer to woolen goods of American manufactures, and it also confines the domestic producer to the home market."[38]

ORGANIZATION

It was long contended that a trust or monopoly was impossible in the wool manufacture, because the diversity of woolen products was so great, the influence of fashions upon the demand for goods was so decisive, and the opportunity for individual skill and enterprise was so broad, that a shrewd manufacturer could always invade any field he desired, regardless of monopolistic competition, by creating a specialty that appealed to the public taste. And in fact the tendency toward centralization, which had already manifested itself in case of firms making certain standardized cotton products, did not appear in this industry until 1899, when rumors of a great approaching consolidation began to agitate mill owners and in some cases to unsettle their plans. That year witnessed the formation of three large corporations in different branches of this manufacture: the American Felt Company, which was organized by Eastern makers after the Chicago packers entered the field and which controlled a majority of the felt mills in the country with about seventy-five sets of cards; the American Woolen Company, embracing plants making nearly all varieties of fabrics except women's wear; and the United States Worsted Company, whose establishments were confined to the group of products indicated by its name.

The most important of these new organizations, and the one destined to play the largest part in the subsequent history of the industry, was the American Woolen Company, incorporated under the laws of the state of New Jersey in 1899, with an authorized capital of $65,000,000, of which nearly $50,000,000 was immediately issued in exchange for properties purchased. The latter consisted of twenty-six mills, of which one was dismantled and its machinery removed to other plants. Most of these were situated in Massachusetts, Rhode Island and Maine, and altogether they operated 541 sets of cards, 166 combs, 300,000 spindles and 5,400 looms. This represented the largest capital and plant ever brought together under one management for the manufacture of any textile fiber. The Company professed not to be a monopoly, although it controlled a very large proportion of the machinery in the country devoted to men's wear, especially in the worsted branch. While this control was not complete enough to exclude effective competition, it was expected that it would enable the manage-

---

[38] 62d Cong., 2d sess., *House Document 342*, I, 191; National Association of Wool Manufacturers, *Bulletin*, XXXIII, 61–63, Mar. 1903; XLIV, 173, Apr. 1914; *Boston Journal of Commerce*, XLV, 392, Mar. 23, 1895.

ment to standardize contracts between manufacturers and cloth merchants, where serious abuses existed, especially in respect to unwarranted cancelations of orders.[39]

The new corporation started out with the policy of confining its individual plants to the production of single lines or closely allied lines of goods, for which they were especially equipped, and of selling its products through its own agent, thus liberating its component firms from some sixty commission houses. Two years after the Company was organized its president testified as follows regarding the advantages realized from the consolidation up to that time: the selling of our goods direct is a great feature in economizing; the facility afforded the different managers to compare notes has brought about happy results; by the centralization of our business we are able to buy our supplies more economically; to be able to make a comparison of the mill costs in the various departments is invaluable; economies arise from the transfer of materials from one mill to another, the waste of one mill being used as a raw material in another mill producing different goods; we have also saved a great deal in freights.[40]

So despite the scepticism with which the experiment was greeted in many quarters this consolidation proved successful, although it was not imitated. Ten years after its organization it controlled nearly 12 per cent of the woolen machinery in the country. During this period its annual sales had risen from $20,000,000 to $60,000,000, and it had paid uninterruptedly upon its preferred stock dividends at the rate of 7 per cent. In the meantime it had added to its original equipment four new mills, some of which were among the largest in the world.[41]

Considerable difficulty had been experienced in organizing the United States Worsted Company, which was a combination of yarn mills, including a subordinate consolidation incorporated in Pennsylvania; and the subsequent history of this enterprise was not as prosperous as that of the American Woolen Company, partly because it lacked equally competent management. In 1906 five Southern mills in Kentucky, Tennessee and Georgia combined as the American Textile Woolen Company. Some of the largest establishments in the country, like the Arlington Mills, remained outside these combinations, and indeed vied with them in efficiency and economical production, if not in quantity of output. Nor did this temporary gravitation toward large industrial units, which speedily expended itself without further results than those already mentioned, materially affect the fortunes or the organization of independent mills. It was in response to a different group of influences that during the last decades of the century corporations

[39] U. S. Industrial Commission, *Reports*, XIV, 239, 513–514; *Boston Journal of Commerce*, LIV, 56, Apr. 22, 1899; *Commercial and Financial Chronicle*, LXVIII, 472, Mar. 11, 1899; LXIX, 77, July 8, 1899; LXXI, 1316, Dec. 29, 1900; National Association of Wool Manufacturers, *Bulletin*, XXVIII, 420, Dec. 1898; XXIX, 203–212; 271–273, Sept. 1899; XXIX, 398, Dec. 1899; XXX, 16–17, Mar. 1900; Cole, *The American Wool Manufacture*, II, 231–232.

[40] U. S. Industrial Commission, *Reports*, XIV, 514.

[41] National Association of Wool Manufacturers, *Bulletin*, XXXVIII, 418, Dec. 1908; XXXIX, 597, Dec. 1909; cf., Cole, *The American Wool Manufacture*, II, 233–235.

rapidly replaced individual ownership and co-parnerships even in regions that clung most obstinately to old forms of conducting business.[42]

Simultaneously a change occurred in the technical management of manufacturing plants. Until within a generation this had been largely in the hands of members of the firm who had grown up in the industry. Gradually, however, young men trained in textile colleges at home or abroad found a place in the business. As their number increased they became an increasingly important factor in the general management of the mills as well as in the supervision of special departments. Soon they were occupying official positions, particularly in establishments owned by corporations. This placed the control of operations to a larger extent than previously in the hands of salaried employes who had little or no capital in the business. With the advent of theoretically trained men, also, a rapid breaking away from routine occurred, accompanied by more readiness than heretofore to adopt new processes and mechanical improvements. The scientific mind is essentially experimental, and young men trained scientifically in the textile trades were more likely to retain this attitude, with its eager acceptance of new ideas and results, than were men who had grown up in the business and knew it only by rule of thumb.[43]

Plant specialization was not confined to mills within the larger consolidations. It was becoming so marked a feature of the industry as a whole that in 1898 the National Association of Wool Manufacturers found it necessary to recommend that the old method of assessing dues against its members upon a machine-unit basis be changed to a payroll basis. At that time nine groups of establishments were enumerated among the Association's members, all differing from each other in respect to the processes or groups of processes they performed, and naturally varying correspondingly in their equipment. But this specialization had not been carried as far in America as in Great Britain, particularly in its commercial aspects; nor was there, naturally, the same interchange of partially manufactured goods with other countries that went on between England and the Continent, to the great advantage of manufacturers on both sides of the Channel.[44]

CARPETS

The most important developments in the manufacture of carpets during this period were the displacement of cheaper weaves like ingrains by more expensive fabrics and the substitution of rugs for continuous floor coverings. These changes were due to mechanical improvements which made it possible to weave pile carpets in large dimensions more cheaply than before,

[42] National Association of Wool Manufacturers, *Bulletin*, xxxvii, 437, Dec. 1907; *Boston Journal of Commerce*, liv, 120, May 20, 1899; liv, 299, July 22, 1899; liv, 378–379, Aug 19, 1899; *Commercial and Financial Chronicle*, lxix, 29, July 1, 1899; lxix, 339, Aug. 12, 1899; Cole, *The American Wool Manufacture*, ii, 251–254.

[43] National Association of Wool Manufacturers, *Bulletin*, xxxv, 259–261, Sept. 1905; *cf.*, U. S. Industrial Commission, *Reports*, xiv, 222–229.

[44] National Association of Wool Manufacturers, *Bulletin*, xxviii, 6–7, Mar. 1898; Ashley, *British Industries*, 98–99, 109, 115, 117; U. S. Industrial Commission, *Reports*, xiv, 247.

to the growing popularity of hardwood floors, and to a higher standard of living accompanied by more exacting canons of good taste. They affected both the geography and the plant distribution of the industry, because ingrain carpets were made largely in Pennsylvania and by comparatively small establishments, while pile carpets were also made extensively at large factories in New York State and Massachusetts. In fact so many ingrain-weaving shops went out of business as a consequence of this changing vogue, that the number of carpet factories in the United States fell from 139 in 1909 to 97 five years later. During the fifteen years preceding 1914 the annual output of ingrain carpets declined from about 40,000,000 yards to less than 6,000,000 yards, and though the quantity of Brussels, Axminster, moquette, velvet and other more expensive types, and of domestic Smyrna and other rugs, increased very rapidly, the total amount of carpeting made in the United States at the latter date was 10,000,000 square yards less than it had been in 1899. Meanwhile Pennsylvania, which produced more than 56 per cent of the country's output at the beginning of this period, or twice as much as New York and nearly six times as much as Massachusetts, the states next to her in rank, made in 1914 less than New York and only two and a half times as much as Massachusetts. While the number of spindles employed in spinning carpet yarns in the United States increased from 209,000 to 252,000 during the decade ending with 1909 and the number in New York from 90,000 to 131,000, the number in Pennsylvania fell from 43,000 to 30,500.[45]

This industry, which was favored by high protective duties, supplied the domestic market except for a comparatively small importation of expensive oriental rugs and occasional purchases of strictly luxury goods from Europe. It was reported in 1900 that with one exception no carpets were made in the United States that cost more than $2.25 a yard, while most of the rugs imported cost over $2.50 a yard and the Berlin and India carpets occasionally brought in on special order were priced at $3.50 or more at the place of manufacture. Neither was the export trade of appreciable importance, though during the free-wool era of the Wilson Act, and before American moquette looms had been introduced in England, our manufacturers sent some goods to that country. While the American product was for the most part of medium grade, such as the popular market demanded, the average value per yard was steadily rising; it was about 64 cents a yard in 1899 and over one dollar a yard fifteen years later. The former year, which is the first for which comparable statistics exist, only about 9,000,000 of the more than 75,000,000 square yards of carpeting manufactured in the country were in the form of rugs; while in 1914 rugs constituted over 49,000,000 yards of our somewhat diminished output of 66,000,000 yards.[46]

[45] Twelfth Census, *Reports*, IX, 107; Thirteenth Census, *Reports*, X, 128–130; Bureau of the Census, *Manufactures, 1914*, II, 75–76, 79.

[46] Twelfth Census, *Reports*, IX, 106–107; Bureau of the Census, *Manufactures, 1914*, II, 76; U. S. Industrial Commission, *Reports*, XIV, 708–709, 711; 62d Cong., 2d sess., *House Document 342*, I, 171–172.

No radical changes occurred in the organization of the industry during this period. Manufacturers were hard hit by the crisis of 1893, and during the subsequent decline in the demand for ingrains some efforts were made to form a combination in that branch of the business. In 1899 the Lowell Manufacturing Company and the Bigelow Carpet Company in Massachusetts consolidated as a $4,000,000 corporation, but without assuming any of the features of a trust or inaugurating a further movement toward centralization.[47]

[47] *Boston Journal of Commerce*, XLIII, 136, Dec. 2, 1893; LI, 360, Mar. 5, 1898; *Commercial and Financial Chronicle*, LXIX, 1195, Dec. 9, 1899.

CHAPTER XIII
SILK MANUFACTURE

Rapid Growth, 210. Geography, 210. Specialization of Process, 211. Technical Progress, 212. Fabrics, 213. Organization, 215.

RAPID GROWTH

Silk manufacturing made relatively more rapid progress than either wool or cotton manufacturing during the fifty years between the end of the Civil War and the beginning of the World War. During the last three decades of the century the value of its product multiplied nine-fold, while that of the cotton manufacture scarcely doubled and that of the wool manufacture increased by less than one half. Although it remained the smallest industry of the three, with an output valued at but $254,000,000 in 1914, as compared with the $464,000,000 worth of woolen goods and more than $700,000,000 worth of cotton goods turned out by our mills annually, it had started in 1870 with a product of but $12,000,000 as compared with well toward $200,000,000 and $177,000,000 respectively for wool and cotton. In 1870 two-thirds of the silk goods consumed in the United States were imported; by 1914 this proportion had fallen to a little over 10 per cent.[1]

GEOGRAPHY

No radical change occurred in the localization of the industry between 1893 and 1914. The movement of throwing mills to the Susquehanna, Schuylkill and Lehigh Valley coal and iron towns, where there was a large supply of otherwise unemployed woman and child labor, continued throughout this period; and this was followed by a rapid extension of ribbon and plain broad-silk weaving in Pennsylvania. As a result that State outranked New Jersey, which had heretofore led in this industry, at the time the last pre-war census was taken. But the manufacture remained concentrated in a few localities. More than half of the silk machinery in the country, producing about two-thirds of the total output, was in Paterson, New York City, Allentown, Philadelphia and Scranton. Nearly all the mills in New Jersey were in Passaic County, and four-fifths of them were in Paterson itself, and the latter city manufactured silk goods annually to the value of over $44,000,000, or more than the other four cities combined.[2]

Since all the raw silk consumed in America came from abroad, mills were never dispersed, like cotton factories, in order to place them near their raw

---

[1] Twelfth Census, *Reports*, IX, 5; Bureau of the Census, *Manufactures, 1914*, II, 11, 142.
[2] Bureau of the Census, *Manufactures, 1914*, II, 128; Mason, *The American Silk Industry and the Tariff*, 50–55.

materials. Between 1899 and 1914 our imports of unmanufactured silk, in the state in which it is unwound and reeled from the cocoon, rose in round numbers from 13,000,000 pounds to over 40,000,000 pounds, of which at the latter date well toward 3,000,000 pounds were artificial.[3] While the mills between the Delaware and the Connecticut profited some by being near the principal ports of entry, their proximity to New York and Philadelphia was more important to them on account of the markets these cities afforded than on account of the materials they supplied. A few establishments were attracted to the South by cheap labor, and the mills in New England derived some advantage from the neighboring demand for silk yarns to use in connection with other fibers in the highly developed textile industries of that region.[4]

Not only was silk manufacturing highly centralized geographically, but it was also specialized by localities. Pennsylvania produced most of the tram and organzine thrown for use in other states, especially by the Paterson weavers. Its mills also led in the production of most classes of broad goods. Pennsylvania and New Jersey wove more than two-thirds of the ribbons made in the country. The latter state and New York made most of the laces, nets and veils; and New York alone made most of the silk fringes, braids and bindings. Connecticut on the other hand, which ranked third in the value of products and had some of the largest factories in the country, produced almost the entire output of velvets and more than half of the plushes, and also led in the production of machine twist, sewing and embroidery silk and spun silk yarn.[5]

SPECIALIZATION OF PROCESSES

No other branch of the textile industry, not even the manufacture of worsteds, showed so marked a tendency to conduct different processes in separate plants; and this practice became more common as time went on. In 1889 contract throwers, whose establishments performed that operation alone, converted into tram or organzine about half, or nearly 5,000,000 pounds out of slightly under 10,000,000 pounds, of the raw silk manufactured. Twenty-five years later they handled nearly 14,000,000 pounds out of somewhat over 22,000,000 pounds thus prepared for weavers. Quite naturally under such conditions weaving itself, as well as finishing and printing, was often done in plants devoted to that single operation.[6] This specialization was most common in Pennsylvania and New Jersey, where it was also a feature of other textile manufactures, and was rarer in New England where the older textile industries more frequently conducted all their operations under one roof. For example, of the 142,000 producing silk spindles in Connecticut only 29,000 were in mills devoted exclusively to throwing, while of the one and one-third million spindles in Pennsylvania

[3] Bureau of the Census, *Manufactures, 1914*, II, 138.
[4] *Cf.*, Bureau of the Census, *Manufactures, 1905*, III, 166–167.
[5] Bureau of the Census, *Manufactures, 1914*, II, 139–140.
[6] Bureau of the Census, *Manufactures, 1914*, II, 137, 142.

well toward 900,000 were in such establishments. This explains partly why the latter state, although it contained more than half the producing spindles in the country, accounted for only 34 per cent of its finished goods.[7]

TECHNICAL PROGRESS

Many notable technical improvements marked the progress of the industry during these years. A majority of them were American inventions, designed to compensate our manufacturers for the relatively high wages paid in this country, and also for the migratory habits and imperfect training of their operatives. New machinery was designed for throwing, which is the process of twisting and doubling the raw silk filament, unwound from the cocoon and reeled in the country of its origin, into the slack-twisted tram or woof and the tight-twisted organzine or warp of the future fabric. These innovations began to have an observable effect upon the industry during the eighties, when importations of tram and organzine dwindled rapidly and throwing mills started to migrate to Pennsylvania, where cheap, unskilled labor was competent enough to operate the new automatic machines. They enabled spindle speeds to be increased to eleven and twelve thousand revolutions a minute, and yet demanded less attention from the operative and turned out a much better product than the older equipment. Consequently the American manufacturer found himself, for the first time in the history of the industry, upon about an equal footing with his European competitors so far as the cost of this operation was concerned. Other improvements followed in rapid succession during the early nineties, such as the adoption of endless friction belts for driving spindles and devices for combining what had previously been distinct stages of throwing, so that spinning, doubling and twisting became virtually a single process. It was estimated that the improvements introduced between 1890 and 1900 effected a saving of about 40 per cent in floor space and 20 per cent in labor cost in this single department of the silk manufacture. Within the lifetime of men still active in the industry the cost of throwing a pound of raw silk into tram or organzine fell from $4.50 to less than 75 cents.[8]

Corresponding progress was made in weaving machinery. By 1900 less than 200 of the 44,000 silk looms in the United States were still operated by hand. The high-speed automatic ribbon loom, which was invented in this country in 1889, soon displaced the German and Swiss machinery previously in use, while broad looms simultaneously developed into a distinct American type under the double urge toward higher speeds and toward devices that would produce mechanically the most varied weaves and patterns. These looms combined the apparently contradictory features of structural simplicity and versatility of product, qualities demanded by labor conditions in America, where the untrained operative must learn

---

[7] Bureau of the Census, *Manufactures, 1914*, II, 137, 143.
[8] Twelfth Census, *Reports*, IX, 218, 222–223; Bureau of the Census, *Manufactures, 1905*, III, 165–166; Mason, *The American Silk Industry and the Tariff*, 113–115; *Boston Journal of Commerce*, LXX, 50, Apr. 6, 1907.

quickly to understand the unfamiliar mechanism he used, and nevertheless the machine must accomplish automatically many things that in other countries were entrusted to the skill and the individual oversight of the weaver.[9]

FABRICS

American manufacturers excelled in the production of substantial medium grade goods, which were those most largely consumed in the domestic market. They could not compete with the older industry of Europe, with its skilled and settled operative population, in turning out luxury fabrics, whose elaborate patterns were oftentimes used for only a limited yardage. But these high-priced silks were not infrequently less durable and serviceable than those of more moderate cost made in this country. Neither did American mills find it profitable to make the cheap and heavily weighted silks, whose defective and adulterated materials could not be manufactured by automatic machinery, that foreign manufacturers employing hand labor were able to produce at a very low cost. In a word, the industry continued to be conditioned in America by the same factors that had influenced its earlier growth; machine production requiring substantial materials for economic handling, and a prosperous middle-class market, whose purchasers demanded fabrics of good quality, but were less exacting in respect to novelty and exclusive styles than were a small elite of wealthy consumers. The same reason that induced the American broad-silk manufacturer to use only the best grade of raw material likewise caused him to employ only coarse sizes of tram and organzine. His aim, besides perfection in his goods and small waste of materials, was to obtain the best possible results from his looms in yardage, since high yardage reduced his average of wages and general expenses.[10]

Nevertheless the stimulus given to the manufacture of broad silks about the turn of the century, by a combination of high duties, general prosperity and labor-saving machinery, resulted in overproduction, low prices and the other results of excessive domestic competition. In 1901 dress silks retailed at New York for from 39 to 95 cents a yard. Many manufacturers were tempted by these conditions to cheapen the quality of their goods, so that consumers protested against this deterioration and began to place orders abroad. Naturally this abuse soon corrected itself in large measure, because, as we have seen, it had the economics of the industry against it.[11]

Fashion has always ruled the silk manufacture, as it has the manufacture of worsteds and other fabrics which are generally either worn for adornment as well as warmth or else are employed as upholsteries and draperies for decorative effects. Indeed fashion changes extended even to such stand-

[9] Twelfth Census, *Reports*, IX, 223–224; Mason, *The American Silk Industry and the Tariff*, 124, 130–133; U. S. Industrial Commission, *Reports*, XIV, 673.
[10] U. S. Industrial Commission, *Reports*, XIV, 672; Mason, *The American Silk Industry and Tariff*, 118–120, 122, 170–175.
[11] Mason, *The American Silk Industry and the Tariff*, 134–136, 139–140; U. S. Industrial Commission, *Reports*, XIV, 682, 730.

ardized and unobtrusive products as machine twist and sewing silk, which were spun in much finer numbers than formerly as time went on and were dyed to harmonize with the colors in vogue. By the end of the century domestic producers had captured the home market for piece dyed and printed silks, and also for warp-print fabrics, for which two American exhibitors were awarded gold medals at the Paris Exposition of 1900. Between 1890 and 1900 the manufacture of velvets, which had been begun in a small way previously, became firmly established, and the manufacture of plushes, though handicapped by the bad reputation incurred by the inferior quality of the goods produced during their popularity and by undue tariff stimulation of this branch of the industry just before the panic of 1893, passed through a period of depression without succumbing entirely to these adverse influences and expanded rapidly during the closing years of the period we are describing.

Fashion alone, therefore, did not account for the fact that the production of velvets consistently increased while the output of plushes, after declining for ten years, rose abruptly between 1909 and 1914 from well under 3,000,000 yards to more than 9,000,000 yards. Indeed, though both velvets and plushes are made in the same general way and are classed together as pile fabrics, they illustrate in the silk manufacture a rule that has been repeatedly noted in this history as applying to other textile manufactures. Velvets were turned out in large quantities of uniform grades while plushes were diversified. Moreover velvets of the kind chiefly made in the United States were used mostly for carpets and upholstery, where defects are not as obvious as in the case of plushes, which at this time were used mainly for cloaks and other garments.[12]

Fashion accounted largely, however, for the increase of the silk hosiery knit in American from 12,572 dozen pairs in 1899 to 2,354,648 dozen pairs fifteen years later. But here also the quality of domestic goods had a large influence in extending the market for them, as they were more durable than those imported. What was practically a new branch of the industry, though in a minor field, was developed about 1903 in the manufacture of silk labels; and by 1914 its product was valued at nearly a million dollars, or more than that of cravats and neckties.[13]

Since fashions and patterns continued to be copied from abroad, American producers were compelled to turn out goods at a much greater speed than their European competitors in order to keep up with the market. A Swiss account of the American industry written about 1900 stresses particularly the point that the whole practice and organization of the manufacture was adapted to this requirement of quick deliveries.

[12] Mason, *The American Silk Industry and the Tariff*, 75–77, 155; Twelfth Census, *Reports*, IX, 205–206; Bureau of the Census, *Manufactures, 1914*, II, 138, Table 21; *cf.*, U. S. Industrial Commission, *Reports*, XIV, 730–731; 56th Cong., 2d sess., *Document 232*, IV, 228.
[13] Mason, *The American Silk Industry and the Tariff*, 159; Bureau of the Census, *Manufactures, 1905*, III, 171; Bureau of the Census, *Manufactures, 1914*, II, 137, 138, 139.

"It is astonishing to an impartial observer to note the facility with which the American mill changes from light to heavy, from simple to complicated, from plain to faconné goods, and from yarn to piece-dyed weaves."[14]

During these twenty-five years the value of the sewing silk and machine twist made in the United States remained about stationary, at between nine and ten million dollars. This failure of the oldest and best established branch of the manufacture, and of the only one which had ever captured export markets, to keep pace with other departments of the industry was due partly to the substitution of mercerized cotton thread for silk by makers of ready made clothing and boots and shoes, who ordinarily used more than one-half of the domestic output.[15] During the same period the value of narrow goods, such as ribbons, braids and trimmings, less than doubled; while the value of the broad silks produced in the country, including dress goods, velvets, plushes and tapestries, increased nearly six-fold. In 1889 the values of the narrow and of the broad silks made in America were not far from equal, being in both cases somewhat below $30,000,000. Twenty-five years later the value of narrow goods had risen to a little over $45,000,000 but the value of broad goods had mounted above $157,000,000.[16]

Except at Paterson and vicinity the labor history of this period was uneventful. At that city the foreign weavers, who had enjoyed a privileged position among textile workers as long as their skill was a monopoly and could not be replaced by automatic machinery, were under constant pressure from the cheaper female labor of the Pennsylvania coal and iron towns and resisted violently efforts to reduce their wages or otherwise to worsen their conditions of employment. Relatively more native labor was used in New England and these troubles seldom extended to the factories of that section. One or two silk mills in the South employed negro operatives. With the perfection of automatic machinery, especially in the throwing department, the number of children engaged in the industry, after declining for a time, increased; and the vogue of plain fabrics in the nineties, assisted by loom improvements, facilitated the change from male to female weavers just mentioned, and resulted in an increasing proportion of women on the payrolls. Not only were the employes in this industry, particularly in New Jersey and Pennsylvania, largely of foreign birth, but several of the leading mill owners of that section were Europeans.[17]

ORGANIZATION

It was not unusual for a single firm to own two or three plants at different points, generally for carrying on distinct stages of the manufacture or for

---

[14] U. S. Industrial Commission, *Reports*, XIV, 672–673.
[15] Bureau of the Census, *Manufactures, 1905*, III, 167.
[16] Twelfth Census, *Reports*, IX, 203, Table 5; Bureau of the Census, *Manufactures, 1914*, II, 138, Table 21.
[17] *Manufacturers' Record*, XLVII, 482, June 8, 1905; American Iron and Steel Association, *Bulletin*, XXXI, 245, Nov. 1, 1897; National Association of Wool Manufacturers, *Bulletin*, XXXIX, 610, Dec. 1909; U. S. Industrial Commission, *Reports*, XIV, 669, 677–678, 695, 702; Mason, *The American Silk Industry and the Tariff*, 114.

producing different classes of goods; and some silk mills, like some thread factories, were virtually links in an international chain of establishments. But the two or three attemtps made to form large combinations in this industry failed. The Silk Association of America exercised no control over the business operations of its members. Manufacturers were at the same disadvantage in dealing with buyers that caused complaint in the worsted and print-goods industries, especially in respect to the cancelation of contracts. Since nearly all the raw silk used in America came from Japan and China, or else from Italy, mill owners had to buy their materials a considerable time ahead. But they were not able to insure themselves against falling markets by equally firm contracts for the goods made from those materials. Sometimes, it is true, they realized an unanticipated commercial profit out of a sudden rise in raw silk, the price of which was ruled by world demand although America was the largest single consumer. Current discussions of the condition of the industry, which had its annual and seasonal ups and downs—though they were not as marked as some of those that afflicted the cotton and wool manufacture—nearly always turned on the fluctuation of raw-silk prices. Motives like those that persuaded the print-goods makers of Fall River and New Bedford to combine for the disposal of their product therefore existed in the case of the Paterson silk manufacturers, but on account of fashion changes their fabrics were not standardized and could not be held for better prices or rationed out gradually to the market. Consequently silk-mill owners never entered into even a loose union to control sales or output.[18]

Silk duties formed one of the most complicated schedules of our tariff acts; and it would be of little interest to analyze them here. Those upon the most important groups of manufactures were graduated to the weight of the fabric, to the percentage of pure silk it contained and to the color; and for part of the period were both specific and ad valorem on the same articles. Comparatively little interest was taken in this schedule by members of Congress, because silks were regarded as a luxury upon which heavy taxes were justifiable. Even Southern free traders found it difficult to reprehend checking a flood of importations that would compete directly with the product of their cotton fields. Consequently silk manufacturers secured a ready hearing for any arrangement they cared to suggest. Seldom did the aggregate duties average less than 50 per cent of the domestic price of the article taxed, and at times or in special instances they considerably exceeded that amount.[19]

Artificial silk was first made in Europe, where it began to be produced commercially about the beginning of the present century. Its manufacture in the United States did not begin until 1910, when an English firm com-

---

[18] U. S. Industrial Commission, *Reports*, XIV, 674–675, 580, 683, 702, 734; *Boston Journal of Commerce*, LXX, 90, Apr. 20, 1907.
[19] Mason, *The American Silk Industry and the Tariff*, 63–109; Taussig, *Tariff History of the United States*, 336–338, 388–390.

pleted a mill at Marcus Hook, near Chester, Pennsylvania, which remained the only plant in the country up to the beginning of the World War. At the latter date this establishment had a capacity of about ten tons of fiber a week.[20]

[20] *Textile World Record*, XLV, 644–645, Sept. 1913; Bureau of the Census, *Manufactures, 1914*, II, 136.

CHAPTER XIV

MINOR TEXTILES AND ALLIED INDUSTRIES

Flax Manufactures, 218. Hemp and Other Fibers, 219. Knit Goods, 220. Dyeing and Finishing, 221. Hats, 221. Clothing, 222.

FLAX MANUFACTURES

Although the people of the United States consumed more linen goods than any other nation, and more than half of all those exported from Great Britain were shipped to this country, no flax was manufactured in America except some 10,000 tons of imported fiber, spun principally into thread and twine. Throughout the world the manufacture of linens was declining on account of the encroachment of cotton and woolen fabrics upon their former markets. This progress began to reveal itself in European spindle statistics about the middle seventies, when the boom that began during the cotton shortage of the Civil War passed its culmination. It was not strange, in view of this world-wide contraction, that the manufacture made relatively little progress in the United States.[1] But American manufacturers occupied an exceedingly humble position in this industry even when we make allowance for the slight promise of future expansion it afforded. In 1914 the number of flax spindles in America was less than 9,000, as compared with over 18,000 in little Sweden, and well toward 1,200,000 in the United Kingdom.[2] Evidently this was a manufacture that failed to respond to the largest home market in existence, except in the single department of thread spinning, where American mills had an output equal to that of all the remaining establishments in the world combined.[3]

American boot and shoe factories were heavy consumers of linen thread, and American carpet mills took large quantities of linen yarns. These were steady sources of demand for the highly standardized products, sold mostly under familiar trade-marks, that our thread mills turned out. Domestic makers were well enough protected by the tariff, despite a duty on their raw material, to control the home market. Part of the flax they used came from just across the border, in Canada. Very little fiber was prepared for manufacture within the country, notwithstanding the extensive cultivation of this crop for seed. Four of the principal thread mills in the United States were controlled by a single corporation, but they were operated independently and without sacrificing the identity of the constituent companies. Several leading manufacturers had originally followed the

---

[1] National Association of Wool Manufacturers, *Bulletin*, XXVIII, 344–345, Dec. 1898; Ashley, *British Industry*, 128–129.
[2] *Textile World Record*, XLVI, 474, Feb. 1914.
[3] U. S. Industrial Commission, *Reports*, XIV, 724.

same business abroad, and some American establishments were virtually branches of British companies.[4]

Coarse toweling was the only linen fabric successfully produced in the United States, and it was woven to some extent in cotton mills which bought their yarn from outside spinners. Well toward 7,000,000 square yards of this material were woven in 1899, and a decided increase occurred during the following decade. Measured by value of product, flax manufacturing made consistent progress during the twenty years before the World War, but its output probably never reached $10,000,000.[5]

HEMP AND OTHER FIBERS

The hemp manufacture was relatively more important than that of flax, especially if we embrace within this category cordage and binding twine made from sisal, Manila hemp and other imported fibers. Attempts to organize the industry on a quasi-monopoly or trust basis were attended by many vicissitudes. In 1894, the old National Cordage Company already described in an earlier chapter was reorganized as the United States Cordage Company. The new corporation owned or controlled some twenty-four factories scattered all the way from Boston to Galveston. Almost immediately it encountered difficulties and dissensions arose among its security holders. As in the case of several trusts formed about this time, large sums were lost through speculation in raw materials. For example the Company's hemp purchases in 1894 were about 50 per cent greater than its sales of manufactured goods. A reorganization committee promptly assumed control of the corporation's affairs and sold its property to a new concern, the Standard Rope and Twine Company, which took over only the more profitable mills.[6] None of these combinations ever monopolized output and only one of them, the original National Cordage Company, at any time controlled a majority of the country's spindles. The Standard Rope and Twine Company was simply the second in size, ranking after the Plymouth Cordage Company, of several large firms engaged in this business. Although it may have owned more machinery than any of the others, so many of its mills were idle and in part definitely abandoned, that its output never measured up to its theoretical plant capacity. In one of the two nearly equal fields of production, cordage and binder twine, the great agricultural machinery makers of the West, like the McCormicks and the Deerings, were a controlling influence.[7]

No important changes occurred in the geography of this industry. The principal Eastern factories, which made the most of the cordage manufactured in the country and employed mainly Manila hemp, were in the vi-

[4] U. S. Industrial Commission, *Reports*, XIV, 723–725; Twelfth Census, *Reports*, IX, 241; Committee on Ways and Means, 54th Cong., 2d sess., *Tariff Hearings*, II, 1283, 1307.
[5] Twelfth Census, *Reports*, IX, 240–241; Thirteenth Census, *Reports*, X, 183; *Boston Journal of Commerce*, L, 8, Apr. 3, 1897.
[6] *Commercial and Financial Chronicle*, LVIII, 820–821, May 12, 1894; LX, 80–81, Jan. 12, 1895; LX, 1106, June 22, 1895.
[7] U. S. Industrial Commission, *Reports*, XIII, 119, 120, 124, 144, 152, 157, 163.

cinity of seaports, like Boston, New York and Philadelphia, while many important binder twine works, which used sisal from Yucatan imported through Mobile and New Orleans, were in the West. Some of those in the prairie-grain states were operated at state prisons with convict labor. Other varieties of fiber, especially New Zealand flax, were imported in considerable quantities and American hemp was still used to some extent for cordage; but Manila hemp and sisal formed over 96 per cent of the materials employed in this industry.[8]

KNIT GOODS

During this period the manufacture of knit goods made great quantitative progress, but otherwise its history was uneventful. The principal features of its development were the encroachment of cotton and wool in combination upon fields previously occupied by wool alone; the increasing use of machines for making full-fashion goods, especially at Philadelphia; the establishment of knitting mills in the South to make cheaper grades of cotton hosiery and underwear; and its extension to the Central West, where other branches of the textile industry were stationary or declining, and where relatively more woolen and merino goods were made. The United States outranked Great Britain more than three-fold in this branch of manufacture, and probably led even Germany, at that time the principal producer of knit goods on the Continent. More establishments were engaged in this manufacture than in any other single line of textile production; but the total output, although it was growing in value faster than the output of cotton, woolen, or silk fabrics, did not overtake the latter. During these twenty-five years, however, that value nearly quadrupled, rising, in round numbers, from $67,000,000 to $250,000,000.[9]

No such revolutionary improvements were made in knitting machinery during these years as had marked certain earlier stages of the industry, but numerous auxiliary machines and devices were perfected that in the aggregate had an important effect upon manufacturing methods. As a result most of the hand operations that survived until the nineties were practically eliminated during the following two decades.[10] New York, Pennsylvania, Massachusetts and Wisconsin, in the order named, continued to be the leading states in this manufacture, and New Hampshire still made more woolen and worsted—and latterly merino—hosiery than any of its rivals. By 1890 cotton had already supplanted wool as the principal material used in knit goods. During the next twenty-five years the quantity of wool and worsted, together with certain allied materials such as mohair, consumed in this industry, rose in round numbers from 42,000,000 pounds to 43,000,000 pounds, while the amount of cotton similarly employed in-

---

[8] Bureau of the Census, *Manufactures, 1914*, II, 151; Committee on Ways and Means, 54th Cong., 2d sess., *Tariff Hearings*, II, 1291–1293; U. S. Industrial Commission, *Reports*, XIII, 150.
[9] Bureau of the Census, *Manufactures, 1914*, II, 111, Table 21; Copeland, *The Cotton Manufacturing Industry in the United States*, 346–347.
[10] Copeland, *The Cotton Manufacturing Industry in the United States*, 109–110.

creased from 65,000,000 pounds to 360,000,000 pounds. The relatively faster growth in the use of cotton continued up to the end of this period; but toward its close an invasion of silk—which was not infrequently used in combination with wool, especially for underwear—began to cause a new shift in raw-material statistics. By 1914 well toward one-third of the hosiery made in the United States, as measured by value, was silk, and quantitatively the output of cotton hosiery had fallen within five years from 91 per cent to 82 per cent of the total product.[11]

DYEING AND FINISHING

Dyeing and finishing were conducted both in separate establishments and in departments of spinning and weaving factories, something over half of the dyestuffs consumed in America being accounted for by the latter. About two-thirds of the silk goods and four-fifths of the cotton prints produced in the country passed through these final stages in independent works, but the large extent to which regular textile mills finished their own goods was characteristic of the United States as compared with Great Britain and Continental countries. New Jersey, Massachusetts, New York, Pennsylvania and Rhode Island did nine-tenths of the dyeing and finishing reported in the census, and New Jersey, with its large silk and worsted mills, outranked the other states in this branch of the industry. Practically all our dyestuffs were imported, most of the skilled and unskilled labor employed in dyeing and finishing were immigrants, and much of the machinery used was either brought from abroad or copied, generally with modifications, from foreign models. Though these operations were as long established in America as the other stages of textile manufacturing, and though a distinct American practice had developed in respect to them, we still followed instead of led in this department of the industry.

This was because quantity production and a rapid rate of output still took precedence of perfect workmanship and variety of patterns in a majority of our works, though one or two of them turned out goods comparable with high-grade foreign fabrics. Some important American inventions, such as the cell dryer, which dates from this period, were designed mainly to accelerate output. In this case as in so many others, the technique of the industry responded to the character of our domestic market.[12]

HATS

Several industries associated with the textile trades need detain us but briefly, for although they were individually important, they illustrated no significant or novel manufacturing process or condition. Fur-felt hats were made much as they had been ever since American ingenuity substituted machinery, and with it the factory system, for hand processes and village

[11] Bureau of the Census, *Manufactures, 1905*, III, 66; Bureau of the Census, *Manufactures, 1914*, II, 108, Table 17; III, 112, Table 22.
[12] Higgins, *Dyeing in Germany and America*, 38–58; Bureau of the Census, *Manufactures, 1905*, III, 195, IV, 456; Bureau of the Census, *Manufactures, 1914*, II, 165.

workshops. Some establishments migrated to new centers, mainly as a result of labor controversies; but this did not appreciably affect the concentration of the industry. Five cities, in order of output Philadelphia, Danbury, New York, Newark and Orange, made nearly four-fifths of all those manufactured in the country. Soft hats, which required a somewhat finer grade of fur than stiff hats, gained in popular favor soon after the turn of the century; but this was of little profit to manufacturers, as such hats were worn on an average longer than the old-fashioned derby. Moreover the growing popularity of the automobile and of outdoor sports caused the substitution of cloth caps and hats for those made of felt, so that a slight decrease occurred in the value of output before the close of the period we are describing.[13]

CLOTHING

Labor conditions have influenced the geography and organization of the clothing industry about as much as power and machinery have influenced those of metal-working and textile manufactures. Measured by value of product, or even by the value added to materials by manufacture, the total of the half-score branches included under this general head reached an imposing figure. In 1914 the gross output of garments made in factories and contract shops was well over $1,250,000,000, but this presumably included duplications of work done in contract shops and delivered to factories.[14]

Home work, where garments were sewn in the living room of the operative who was paid by the piece, the task or sweat-shop system, where the processes of making a garment were divided among the members of a team of three or five operatives who worked in shops run by contractors, and the Boston or factory system, where the subdivision of labor was carried to so fine a point that as many as one-hundred persons might be employed in the manufacture of a single garment and time wages were paid, survived, as more or less general usages, into the period we are describing. During the nineties the states where this industry was most important, beginning with Massachusetts, enacted laws regulating the conditions under which clothing could be made, partly in the interest of the workers and partly to protect the health of the public, which encouraged the extension of the factory system. This industry, which is largely in the hands of immigrant employers and operatives, has been the scene of numerous labor conflicts; and the workers, who include a large proportion of women and children, have probably been the object of more solicitude upon the part of welfare agencies than those in any other branch of employment of equal magnitude.[15]

Legislation and inspection had begun to banish the manufacture of clothing from the tenement house before the end of the century, although home-

[13] Bureau of the Census, *Manufactures, 1914*, II, 158; American Iron and Steel Association, *Bulletin*, XXVIII, 21, Jan. 20, 1894; Fenner, *History of Fall River*, 88.
[14] Bureau of the Census, *Manufactures, 1914*, II, 174, 179.
[15] *Cf.*, Pope, *The Clothing Industry in New York*, 156 et seq.; U. S. Industrial Commission, *Reports*, XV, 328–331.

work in various guises lingered until much later. Moreover many contractor's shops, which by this time occupied the center of the picture, were as unsanitary and crowded as the domestic quarters of the operatives. Nevertheless they were easier to keep under scrutiny, and they made it easier for the workers to better their own condition and incidentally to improve the conditions under which their trade was carried on. Many of these shops developed into factories, a process that occurred more rapidly outside New York City than within that principal center of the industry. But factory did not mean in the clothing manufacture primarily a mechanical plant, as it did for example in the textile industries, but rather a labor system characterized by such a minute subdivision of operations that from 50 to 200 workers might be employed in making a single type of garment without duplicating the most quickly performed task in the series.[16]

Naturally this expansion of the labor unit made it necessary to provide correspondingly extensive plant facilities, and with specialized plants came the same economic inducements to enlarge still further that existed in other industries. These inducements were stronger perhaps in other cities than they were in New York, where premises were usually leased. Be this as it may, by 1914 there were twenty-four clothing factories in the United States that employed more than 1,000 operatives. The appearance of the factory hastened the mechanization of the industry, and this in turn brought about a great saving of labor. Between 1890 and 1914 the amount of mechanical power used in the manufacture of men's clothing increased between six and seven-fold and the value of product about doubled, while the number of employes rose by only about one-fifth. Corresponding changes in the manufacture of women's clothing, which grew relatively faster during this period, were even more marked. To be sure occasional back currents manifested themselves in the movement toward factory organization. In making women's cloaks, for instance, the small manufacturer gained ground for a time upon the large manufacturer, partly on account of the highly seasonal character of the branch of the industry, which made it difficult to keep a large plant and corps of workers continually employed, while the small establishment could shift with facility to other lines of production.[17]

Most branches of the clothing industry were highly centralized in the great cities, and especially in New York, the principal factor determining its geography being the presence of cheap labor. Indeed so important was this that suburban factories in Brooklyn found it necessary to transfer their operations to crowded and otherwise less desirable quarters in the center of the city. Even the pin-money clothing makers of rural New England were unable to compete with urban immigrants, and the old homework

[16] U. S. Industrial Commission, *Reports*, xiv, 254, 284–285; xv, 348–351.
[17] Pope, *The Clothing Industry in New York*, 290; Twelfth Census, *Reports*, ix, 299–300; Bureau of the Census, *Manufactures, 1914*, 177, Table 9.

industry of that section drifted to New York. The localization of collar and cuff making was even more striking, Troy producing over four-fifths of those manufactured in the United States.[18]

Between 1890 and 1914 the value of women's clothing classed as factory product rose from $68,000,000 to well toward half a billion dollars; at the earlier date it was not a third the value of the men's clothing similarly manufactured, and at the later date it exceeded that value by nearly $20,000,000. Although these figures are subject to some interpretative qualification, the movement they indicate was very significant; for it represented in a most striking way the transfer of labor from the home to the factory that has been going on in America, and in all civilized countries, for the last century and a half, and that has affected the kitchen, with its substitution of the tin can and the pasteboard carton for the market basket, almost as much as it has the sewing room. Simultaneously the quality of factory goods has improved. In case of men's clothing, an industry that at first catered almost exclusively to slaves and sailors, and to the least exacting class of common laborers, now competes with the best custom tailors.[19]

[18] Pope, *The Clothing Industry in New York*, 290–291; Bureau of the Census, *Manufactures, 1914*, II, 185.
[19] Twelfth Census, *Reports*, IX, 301–302, Table 24; Bureau of the Census, *Manufactures, 1914*, II, 174; Pope, *The Clothing Industry in New York*, 292.

CHAPTER XV

LEATHER AND RUBBER MANUFACTURE

Tanning Technology, 225. Geography and Organization, 226. Leather Varieties, 228. Leather Exports and Hide Imports, 229. Boot and Shoe Making, 230. Boot and Shoe Exports, 231. Geography of Boot and Shoe Making, 232. Shoe Machinery Business, 233. Glove Making, 234. Organization of the Rubber Manufacture, 235. Rubber Tire Manufacture, 236.

TANNING TECHNOLOGY

Of the two great divisions of the tanning industry, the manufacture of sole and heavy leather and the manufacture of upper and light leather, the former was the older and more firmly established in America. It used tannages from our own forests and had established a market for its products in Europe. Light leathers, especially those of better quality, were still imported to some extent in the early nineties, and the manufacturers producing them did not have the natural advantages over their transatlantic competitors that tanners of heavy leathers enjoyed. Both departments of the industry made marked technical progress during this period, but the advance was much more striking in case of the manufacture of light leather.

Although the first tannery in the United States regularly to employ a chemist was erected on the banks of the Schuylkill as long ago as 1855, that example was not imitated, and indeed seems to have contributed nothing to the success of the establishment in question. As recently as 1890 only about half a dozen American tanneries had chemists on their staffs. Fifteen years later this number had risen to nearly 150. Indeed, the Association of American Leather Trade Chemists, organized in 1893, made its bow to the public almost simultaneously with the general introduction of chemical control in the tanning business. What this meant in the economics of the industry is suggested by a statement published in 1897 to the effect that a single large establishment estimated its savings in by-products alone, which were wasted ten or fifteen years before, at $400,000 annually, or between 6 and 12 cents for every hide it handled.[1]

Oak and hemlock bark, or a combination of the two, were still used almost exclusively by heavy leather manufacturers; but these materials were growing more expensive, if not appreciably less abundant in the consuming market, and the incentive to economize in their use increased. Within a few years the maximum quantity of leather that could be tanned with a ton of bark rose from two hundred pounds to three hundred pounds; so that despite its increasing price, its cost per pound of leather remained about the

---

[1] *The Leather Manufacturer*, IV, 120, Sept. 1894; VIII, 35, Sept. 1897; XV, 62–63, Mar. 1904; *cf.*, however, XVIII, 206, Sept. 1907.

same. Canaigre, which came from our western plains, was added to native tannages at this time. But quebracho wood or extract from Argentina, and gambier, an extract from the leaves of an East Indian shrub, began to be imported extensively to supplement domestic materials, thus reversing conditions a generation before, when bark and bark extracts were exported. Some large tanneries brought their extracts from the forests to the works in tank cars, and the custom of taking the tannery to the bark supply had ceased. Toward the end of this period chrome tanning, which had hitherto been confined to lighter grades of leather, began to be employed for sole leather.[2]

No radical improvement occurred in chrome tanning, except the revival in 1893, under new patents, of the one-bath process, which was simpler than the two-bath process invented in America nine years before but did not supplant it. Patents for the two-bath process were the subject of protracted litigation, and when they expired, in 1901, the opinion was expressed that they anticipated rather than inaugurated the new era in leather manufacturing. "The real development of what was known as the chrome tannage was during the last decade of the nineteenth century," which witnessed "more progress in the art of leather manufacturing than any other decade in the history of the world."[3]

By the close of this period nearly half of the hides, two-thirds of the sheep skins, and practically all of the goat skins tanned in the United States were imported, and a monopoly of the manufacture of heavy leather seemed imminent through the increasing control exercised over the raw-hide supply by the great packers, with their plants not only in this country, but also in South America, which furnished most of the cattle hides imported. The supply of sheep and goat skins came from more varied sources and was not so easily engrossed. No control over tanning materials was attempted. Most of the native bark came from lumber companies, which were interested in the tanning business only as a market for a valuable byproduct.[4]

GEOGRAPHY AND ORGANIZATION

Centralization in larger plants, within narrower geographical limits, and under the control of fewer companies, characterized in a marked degree the development of this industry. At the outbreak of the World War there were less than one-tenth as many tanneries in the United States as there had been when the Civil War began, despite the vast increase in leather output during the intervening years. Well toward three-fourths of the leather made in the country was credited, in 1914, to Pennsylvania, Massachusetts, Wisconsin, New York, New Jersey and Michigan; and 47 per cent

[2] *The Leather Manufacturer*, v, 150, Oct. 1895; viii, 55, Oct. 1897; ix, 28–29, Feb. 1898; x, 46, Apr. 1899; xii, 221–222, Dec. 1901; xviii, 274, Dec. 1907; xix, 11, Jan. 1908; Twelfth Census, *Reports*, ix, 715.
[3] *The Leather Manufacturer*, v, 72–73, May 1895; v, 89, June 1895; x, 74, July 1899; xi, 22, Jan. 1900; xii, 1, Jan. 1901; Bennett, *The Manufacture of Leather*, 210–211.
[4] Federal Trade Commission, *Report on the Leather and Shoe Industries*, 1919, pp. 156–159, 161, 163; *The Leather Manufacturer*, iv, 129, Oct. 1894.

of the total was made in the three states first mentioned. Milwaukee remained the great tanning city of the interior, and competed on virtually equal terms with Philadelphia for first rank among American tanning centers. Chicago, aided by her great packing houses, ranked fourth. These two interior cities produced for the most part heavy leathers and calf-skin uppers from native hides, while Philadelphia, Newark, and Peabody, Massachusetts, the three leading centers of the East, converted imported goat and sheep skins into light and fancy leathers for ladies' footwear, upholstery, and for a great variety of miscellaneous uses.[5]

Consolidation of ownership, or horizontal trust building, made more progress in the heavy leather than in the light leather branch of the manufacture. Even the patent rights in chrome tanning did not promote appreciably the consolidation of that business. Indeed rapid tanning, by lessening the amount of capital tied up in stock, made it somewhat easier for small establishments to survive. But the comparatively heavy investment and slow turn-over of the sole-leather manufacture, aided by the growing control of cattle slaughtering by a few large companies, encouraged amalgamations. In 1893 the United States Leather Company was formed with a capital stock of $80,000,000 for the purpose of combining the principal tanning plants making sole leather in the United States. There were already large corporations engaged in this industry, especially in Pennsylvania, where three companies were absorbed, each with a capital stock of $10,000,000. The property of the new trust, as it was popularly called, included great areas of timber lands, and incidentally to the production of bark these lands supplied large quantities of timber, so that the United States Leather Company was a manufacturer of lumber as well as of sole leather and belting.

This company was organized in the year of the panic and its history, during the seasons immediately succeeding, illustrates the vicissitudes of a business that from the nature of its processes was obliged to carry large stocks of raw materials and of goods in process of tanning. During the decline of prices following the panic high cost hides were in liquor to make leather that when marketed did not command enough to pay for the raw materials and labor used to produce it. Later, however, when leather rose again the tables were turned to the advantage of the Company, which was able to collect a very heavy margin between the low price of raw materials and the high-priced products made from them and marketed some months later. The Company continued to extend its properties, especially its bark-land holdings, and invested large sums in bringing its less efficient plants up to the standard of its best tanneries. In this respect the effect of consolidation was to raise the average technical efficiency of the industry. In 1900 the United States Leather Company purchased a large group of tanneries in the West, including extensive bark lands in Wisconsin.[6]

[5] Bureau of the Census, *Manufactures, 1914*, II, 674–675.
[6] *Commercial and Financial Chronicle*, LVII, 23–24, July 1, 1893; LX, 390–391, Mar. 2, 1895; LXII, 411–412, Feb. 29, 1896; LXXI, 557, Sept. 15, 1900.

Five years later this consolidation was absorbed by the Central Leather Company, another New Jersey corporation, which combined with it several other concerns, mostly engaged in the lumbering and transportation business, but including one rival tannery company with a capital of over $34,000,000. Nevertheless at the end of the period we are discussing the Central Leather Company produced only about one-third of the sole leather made in the United States; and the larger packers, who slaughtered three-fourths of the cattle and calves killed annually by wholesale dealers, had entered the tanning business upon so large a scale, and with such superior strategic advantages, that they were virtually the determining influence in the industry.[7]

In 1899 the American Hide and Leather Company was formed, by the direct or indirect merger of twenty-three companies, which were said to manufacture three-fourths of the upper leather produced in the United States. This corporation made a small amount of sole leather, from the heavier portions of hides converted mainly into lighter grades, but the special character of the bulk of its products prevented its being a competitor of the United States Leather Company. Its capital, including both stock and bonds, was less than $35,000,000, or but a little more than one-third that of the latter corporation; but on account of the nature of its business, which was chiefly chrome tanning, it had relatively little money invested in bark lands and allied enterprises, or in leather in process of manufacture.[8]

It is highly improbable, however, that either this or any other company ever controlled as high a proportion of the light leather output of the United States as was just indicated. About the end of the World War it was estimated that the five largest corporations engaged in this branch of the industry produced from approximately a quarter to half of the principal grades of light leather made in this country, the fraction varying according to the character, quality and uses of the kind in question, and generally being highest in case of the less important specialties. Centralized control was most complete in the manufacture of upholstery leather, and least so in the production of shoe leathers.[9]

LEATHER VARIETIES

A far greater variety of leather was manufactured at the close of this period than had been made even a few years before. This was due not only to the use of new tannages and treatments, but also to new fields of employment opened by the growing diversification of manufacture and to the increasing influence of fashion upon consumption. To be sure some

---

[7] 61st Cong., 1st sess., *Sen. Doc. No. 72*, 4–5; Federal Trade Commission, *Report on the Leather and Shoe Industries*, 1919, 164–165.

[8] *Commercial and Financial Chronicle*, LXVIII, 522, Mar. 18, 1899; LXX, 77, Jan. 13, 1900; *The Leather Manufacturer*, x, 97, Sept. 1899; 61st 1st sess., *Sen. Doc. No. 72*, 9–10; Twelfth Census, *Reports*, IX, 718.

[9] Federal Trade Commission, *Report on the Leather and Shoe Industries*, 1919, 161–162.

hopeful attempts to find new uses for this material, such as employing chrome-tanned pig skin to cover automobile tires, failed; but simultaneously the growing popularity of the motor car vastly increased the demand for upholstery leather.[10] For many years light leathers were finished on the flesh side only; and it was the discovery that such leathers could be finished equally well or better on the hair, or "grain," side that enabled the Milwaukee tanners to build up a vast trade, first in "pebbled calf" and later in "velours calf" and other special types of shoe leather. The almost complete conquest of the domestic market by American light leathers and the popularity that they, and shoes made from them, enjoyed abroad were due quite as much to the variety and perfection of their finish as to their low price. Improved technique thus compensated for our diminishing advantage over Europe in respect to raw materials. Although some adulterated sole leather found its way into foreign markets, by the middle eighties the superiority of American chrome-tanned leathers was recognized by British and Continental consumers, thus reversing the situation of only a few years before.[11]

LEATHER EXPORTS AND HIDE IMPORTS

American machinery for manufacturing leather was exported and expert American tanners were employed in British and German tanneries. In 1905 the United States exported more sole leather than all the other great leather-producing countries of the world combined. Nine-tenths of the leather used in Leicester, the principal boot and shoe-making town of England, was said to come from this country; and in some cases raw hides were sent to America from British slaughter houses for tanning. In 1913, when our exports of leather were valued at over $42,000,000, nearly half of these shipments went to the United Kingdom.[12]

During this period goat skins and practically all the materials used in the manufacture of lighter leathers were on the free list; but between 1897 and 1909, while the Dingley tariff was in force, cattle hides were subject to a duty of 15 per cent ad valorem, with a proviso that a drawback should be given of an equal amount upon leather made from imported hides when shipped abroad. This duty, which had been condemned by Secretary Blaine when proposed in 1890, and which was adopted against the wishes of the manufacturing interests in order to placate members of Congress from the grazing states, was very unpopular in the East, and was rumored to redound chiefly to the advantage of the Chicago packers. It did not

[10] *The Leather Manufacturer*, XVI (unpaged), July 1905.
[11] *The Leather Manufacturer*, V, 8, Jan. 1895; V, 189, Dec. 1895; VIII, 24, July 1897; X, 64, June 1899; XII, 237, Dec. 1901; XV, 60, Mar. 1904; XVI, 149, Sept. 1905; XVIII, 67, Mar. 1907; XVIII, 119, May 1907.
[12] *Boston Journal of Commerce*, L, 420, Sept. 25, 1897; *The Leather Manufacturer*, IX, 25, Feb. 1898; XV, 251, Sept. 1904; XVI (unpaged), July 1905; National Association of Wool Manufacturers, *Bulletin*, XXXVI, 374–375, Oct. 1906; *Yorkshire Post*, quoted in American Iron and Steel Association, *Bulletin*, XL, 154, Nov. 1, 1906; U. S. Industrial Commission, *Reports*, XIII, 747–748.

materially check importations, however, which rose from 206,000,000 pounds, for hides and skins together, in 1898, the first full year after the duty was imposed, to nearly 246,000,000 pounds the following year. Among the skins that escaped this duty were Indian buffalo hides, of which we imported more than a million and a quarter annually. The extent to which the manufacture of light leathers was centering in America is suggested by the fact that of 14,130,000 goat skins shipped through the Calcutta customs house in 1899, 13,352,000 came to the United States.[13]

In 1914 less than one-fourth of the hides and skins converted into leather in the United States were of domestic origin. During the preceding quarter of a century the value of the leather manufactured in the country had more than doubled, rising from $172,000,000 to $367,000,000. Imports had not entirely ceased; for that is not the nature of international trade. After the removal of the duty on heavy leather in 1913 they increased slightly, especially from Canada, which enjoyed the advantage of cheaper tan bark.

BOOT AND SHOE MAKING

No such changes occurred in the technology and organization of boot and shoe making during this period as had characterized its progress during the preceding twenty-five years. Some survivals of the unintegrated industry of earlier days still lingered in the steadily diminishing number of contract shops, performing such operations as stitching, heeling and working button holes for manufacturers, which had once been a prominent feature of the business in certain sections of New England, especially at Haverhill and Lynn.[14] On the other hand the manufacture in separate establishments of cut stock, such as soles, heels and tips, increased faster than the industry as a whole. Shoemaking companies varied greatly in size, some having a daily output of nearly 30,000 pairs and others of less than 250 pairs; but as a rule the larger firms operated several factories. No great consolidations occurred in this industry, the only corporation approaching monopolistic dimensions being the United Shoe Machinery Company, which did not make footwear directly, and of which we shall have more to say later. But average plant capacity was steadily increasing, and in 1914 more than half of the boots and shoes made in the United States were manufactured in establishments having an annual product of a million dollars or more.[15]

Naturally new inventions and mechanical improvements were constantly appearing, but they did not create new types of footwear or modify profoundly the distribution of labor and the division of operations in the manufacturing process, as did the machines introduced during the decades

---

[13] Taussig, *Tariff History of the United States*, 332, 378–379; American Iron and Steel Association, *Bulletin*, XXXI, 99, May 1, 1897; *The Leather Manufacturer*, X, 53, 57, May 1899; XI, 46, Mar. 1900; XII, 222, Dec. 1901; XV, 326, Nov. 1904; U. S. Industrial Commission, *Reports*, XIII, 747–749; XIV, 507, 509.

[14] Twelfth Census, *Reports*, IX, 741; Bureau of the Census, *Manufactures, 1914*, II, 686.

[15] Bureau of the Census, *Manufactures, 1914*, II, 691, 700; *The Leather Manufactures*, XV, 112, Apr. 1904; XVIII, 72, Mar. 1907.

immediately preceding. The technical progress of the period lay rather in a growing refinement and diversification of products. In 1914 the number of welted shoes, which were those of the highest quality, for the first time exceeded the number of the less elaborately and comfortably constructed McKay sewed shoes made in America. Shoes with sewed soles, which probably constituted a minority of those worn a decade before, were in almost universal use, less than one-tenth of the annual output of our factories consisting of the coarse footwear, with soles attached by pegs or metal fasteners, that had still been considered satisfactory by a majority of the preceding generation. The development of new tanning processes brought with it a great variety of new finishes and colors, especially for upper leathers, which encouraged a multiplication of styles. Naturally this affected ladies' footwear chiefly, but by no means exclusively, and shoe designing, for which the last and the pattern makers were ultimately responsible, became an art—one of the few artistic phases of manufacture in which America was recognized to lead the world.[16]

BOOT AND SHOE EXPORTS

This development naturally resulted, first, in a rapid increase of exports and, second, in the adoption of American machinery and manufacturing methods by the more advanced countries to which we sold our goods. Between 1887, when the American system of manufacture was still in its earlier stages, and 1908 the number of pairs of boots and shoes exported annually rose from 351,000 to over 6,500,000; and it is significant of the quality of these goods that although Great Britain still sold to foreign customers a larger quantity of footwear than we did, our exports considerably exceeded in value those of the United Kingdom. Between 1890 and 1914 the value of boots and shoes exported from the United States rose from $663,000 to well over $18,000,000.[17]

The growth of this export business was largely spontaneous at first, and it did not assume proportions that engaged seriously the interest of the industry until toward the middle nineties. To be sure some enterprising manufacturers had previously worked up a trade in the West Indies and in other adjacent countries that regularly resorted to our markets for a share of their general merchandise. With the growth of large shoe factories in the West, also, some Eastern manufacturers, finding their former market partially supplied by their new competitors, turned abroad for additional outlets for their goods. But western makers also produced for export. Some manufacturers, either individually or in association with other firms in the same business, set up agencies in Europe and elsewhere, which supplied foreign dealers directly, without putting them to the delay and trouble of sending individual orders to America to be filled.[18]

[16] Bureau of the Census, *Manufactures, 1905*, III, 232, 244; *Manufactures, 1914*, II, 695; U. S. Industrial Commission, *Reports*, XIV, 344–345.
[17] American Iron and Steel Association, *Bulletin*, XLIII, 3, Jan. 1909; Bureau of the Census, *Manufactures, 1914*, II, 696, Table 45.
[18] U. S. Industrial Commission, *Reports*, VII, 675, 676, 677; XIV, 343, 501.

Shoe-making machinery followed in the wake of the American footwear shipped abroad, thus repeating the history of the manufacture of leather, watches, firearms and other articles, where labor-saving devices developed in our country under the stress of high wages and inadequate industrial training first reversed production costs in our favor, so that our factories captured a foreign market and then forced competitors abroad to adopt our methods. To be sure American machinery did not always prove as successful in other countries as it was in the land of its invention. It failed utterly, at least for a time, in Spain, where it had been imported in an effort to recover the West Indian market which our manufacturers had captured. Even in Great Britain old habits and trade-union opposition detracted from its benefits. Nevertheless it revolutionized the technique of the industry in that country, as it did in Germany, and even to some extent in a land of such fixed trade traditions as France.[19]

GEOGRAPHY OF BOOT AND SHOE MAKING

No radical change occurred in the geography of this industry, although New England, with the pessimism that has characterized her discussion of her relations with the marginal political or industrial sections of the Union ever since the days of federation, and that we have already seen illustrated in case of the cotton manufacture, occasionally professed to see portentious possibilities in western competition. And indeed St. Louis, where a few large manufacturers of great enterprise and initiative monopolized this business, forged ahead remarkably, and in 1909 ranked third among the shoe towns of America—only to fall back to fifth place, however, five years later. Between 1909 and 1914 New York made a sudden spurt forward, with a larger relative increase than any other state. But none of these changes measurably affected the predominance of Massachusetts, which in 1914 made 40 per cent of all the shoes manufactured in the country —or a still larger fraction if computed in quantity instead of value—and contained the three largest shoe-making centers in the Union: Brockton, Lynn and Haverhill. New York City, St. Louis, Cincinnati and Rochester, outside of New England, were next in rank; but more than one-fifth of all the shoes manufactured in the country were made within thirty miles of Boston.[20]

To be sure some of the advantages that had originally favored the centralization of shoe-making in this region had disappeared. With the introduction of machinery, trade skill and traditions, which are among the least mobile elements of an industry, lost part of their former importance. How persistent a factor these may be in determining the geography of a manufacture is illustrated by a division of work that still survives in the shoe factories north and south of Boston, respectively. The making of

[19] U. S. Industrial Commission, *Reports*, VII, 680, XIV, 343–344, 489; *The Leather Manufacturer*, XVII, 71, Mar. 1906; XVII, 137, June 1906; XVIII, 97, Apr. 1907.
[20] Bureau of the Census, *Manufactures, 1914*, II, 688.

women's shoes, which was established at Lynn in the middle of the eighteenth century, remains the dominant business of that city and its neighborhood; while the manufacture of men's shoes, which is said to have been taught to the "South Shore" farmers in the vicinity of the present town of Brockton by British prisoners at the time of the Revolution, is today the chief branch of this industry in that section of the state—

"Due to the absence of good harbors the South Shore men did not follow the sea. The men being at home all the time, there was no need for their women-folk to seek accessory income. Furthermore, the sewing on men's shoes was a heavier job than the women wanted. So the women of the North Shore around Lynn made women's shoes while the men of the South Shore specialized on men's shoes. Today almost half of the working force in Lynn's factories are women, while at Brockton hardly a quarter are women."[21]

Certain other advantages which New England shoemakers formerly enjoyed to the exclusion of most other sections of the country, such as a highly developed tanning industry in their vicinity, they now shared on equal terms with their competitors elsewhere. But their designers still set shoe styles for the United States and all shoe-importing countries; their operatives were upon the whole more highly skilled than those of the newer and smaller shoe-making centers, and their establishments were in the midst of a community prepared to supply promptly all the machinery and other equipment, the shoe findings and the shoe parts they used. Indeed, as we have already intimated, some manufacturers in this section were largely assemblers of cut leather shapes made by specialists in different subdivisions of the industry, who could supply such shoe parts cheaper than a factory performing many distinct operations.

SHOE MACHINERY BUSINESS

New England was the home of the United Shoe Machinery Company, which was formed in 1899 by the consolidation of the most important firms already in the business. In this way conflicting patents were eliminated and patents supplementing each other were brought under united control so as to permit their prompt combination in a single machine or process. Since this Company continued the practice previously followed by its constituent firms, of renting instead of selling its machinery, the expense of keeping repair men on the rounds of customers' establishments was also reduced by combination. The authorized capital of the new corporation was $25,000,000, and it controlled branch companies in several foreign countries. In this case the organization of a "trust" in the machinery trades may have discouraged consolidation in the industry employing that machinery, for it did not take as much capital to engage in shoe-making as in most other large lines of manufacturing, since a rented loft and rented machinery driven by electric current taken from a public main were all that

[21] Malcolm Keir in the *Boston Herald*, Sept. 23, 1922; cf., the same author, *Manufacturing Industries in America*, 225–226.

was required in the way of a plant. To be sure competing machine companies existed, and some machinery was eventually sold outright, but the rental system nevertheless continued to characterize the industry—and to encourage, or at least to facilitate, plant dispersion.[22]

In 1895, when the mechanical system of manufacture was fully matured, an investigation indicated that it took about one-ninth as much time to make a pair of shoes by machinery as by the hand method in use thirty years before; and that the labor cost of producing them had sunk to correspond. At that time the average cost of manufacturing a pair of substantial shoes at Chicago, including rent, power and plant maintenance as well as wages, was approximately fifteen cents.[23]

The boot and shoe industry is one of the rare branches of manufacture in America that has liberated itself from psychological as well as economic dependence upon protective duties. A Philadelphia shoe manufacturer testifying before the Industrial Commission in 1900 thought a tariff unnecessary because; "there are no foreign shoes that could come here anyhow." Twenty-two years later, a writer describing the industry in New England declared:

"There never has been any reason for placing a tariff on shoes except as an offset to the import duties on hides and leather. Of all the articles of common consumption, shoes are the only ones that can be made better and cheaper in the United States than any other place in the world."

Evidently the writer overlooked automobiles, and one or two other articles in universal use.[24]

GLOVE MAKING

Other branches of the leather manufacture were of great and growing importance, but they illustrated no unique or characteristic feature of development that was not exhibited equally well, or better, by another line of industry. Glove making continued to be a typical example of geographical concentration in response to neighborhood labor traditions, inherited skill, habit and business organization. More than half of the leather gloves or mittens made in the United States were manufactured in Fulton County, New York, and more than one-fourth of them in the town of Gloversville. But ladies dress gloves were largely imported, the domestic industry being confined almost exclusively to men's wear and short, heavy gloves of the coarser sort for women.[25]

[22] U. S. Industrial Commission, *Reports*, XIV, 482–491, 503–504; *Commercial and Financial Chronicle*, LXVIII, 333, Feb. 18, 1899; LXVIII, 430, Mar. 4, 1899; LXIX, 797, Oct. 14, 1899; LXX, 1053, May 26, 1900.

[23] 55th Cong., 3d sess., *House Document No. 301*, I, 28–29, 123; U. S. Industrial Commission, *Reports*, VII, 678.

[24] U. S. Industrial Commission, *Reports*, XIV, 343; Malcolm Keir, in *Boston Herald*, Sept. 23, 1922.

[25] *Twelfth Census, Reports*, IX, 790–791; Bureau of the Census, *Manufactures, 1914*, II, 705; Committee on Ways and Means, 54th Cong., 2d sess., *Tariff Hearings*, II, 1928, 1931.

ORGANIZATION OF THE RUBBER MANUFACTURE

The manufacture of rubber goods had reached technical maturity before 1893, at which date it was on the eve of developing new fields of utility of the first importance. Like many industries at this period it experienced an era of consolidation, although the formation of large corporations controlling many plants never reached the stage where the market was monopolized by a single firm. The United States Rubber Company, whose organization was mentioned in an earlier chapter, embraced a majority of the companies making rubber footwear, and its history records an interesting struggle between the dispersive forces represented by old establishments accustomed to operate under independent management and central control seeking to localize the industry in plants situated at the most economical points of production. In 1896 this Company operated eighteen factories, several of which were run against the better judgment of the directors, who declared in their annual report that the manufacture of a large number of brands of goods in isolated establishments, when there was not a sufficient demand for each brand to utilize fully each plant's organization and the machinery, added very largely to the cost of production. The loss due to this dispersion was estimated to be 8 per cent upon the selling price of the goods produced. Simultaneously the Company endeavored to concentrate purchases and sales, believing that it could buy raw rubber through a single agency cheaper than its constituent establishments could buy it. At this time rubber was rising rapidly because new demands, particularly for bicycle tires, had increased consumption faster than the supply. The economies effected by unifying the sales organization, which bore all marketing charges including freights from the factory to the distributor, were estimated to be $150,000 yearly.[26]

In 1897 the Corporation began to apply its theories of plant specialization in earnest, by discontinuing entirely the manufacture of footwear at one of its factories, which was devoted exclusively to making bicycle tires, and by employing another factory wholly to reclaim rubber. The following year the consolidation absorbed the Boston Rubber Shoe Company, one of the largest manufacturers of footwear in the country, and two years later it added to its plant capacity to take care of its growing export business. At the close of the century the total output of the company was over 150,000 pairs of rubbers daily, besides other products of increasing importance in the rubber-goods market. It supplied about 70 per cent of the footwear produced in the country.[27]

Nevertheless several new companies entered the field, three such establishments having at their head former directors of the United States Rubber Company. Soon their aggregate product was estimated to be 60,000 pairs of rubber shoes a day, new consolidations were mooted among the

---

[26] *Commercial and Financial Chronicle*, LXI, 114, July 20, 1895; LXII, 951–952, May 23, 1896; LXIII, 1160, Dec. 26, 1896; *cf.*, however, U. S. Industrial Commission, *Reports*, XIII, 36, 81.
[27] *Commercial and Financial Chronicle*, LXIV, 998, May 22, 1897; LXVII, 905, Oct. 29, 1898; LXX, 743; Apr. 14, 1900; U. S. Industrial Commission, *Reports*, XIII, 34.

independent producers, and more or less community of interest existed between these producers and their big competitor.[28]

RUBBER TIRE MANUFACTURE

Turning now to the tire business, which was the outstanding branch of the industry from 1900 onward, we meet a new situation—one in which the very exuberance of a manufacturing specialty's growth defeated attempts to confine it within the compass of a single corporation. In this respect the early history of tire making and of automobile making are strikingly similar. In 1899 the Rubber Goods Manufacturing Company, a New Jersey corporation having an authorized capital of $50,000,000 like its sister corporation, the United States Rubber Company, and like the latter actually issuing only about half of this amount, was formed to manufacture all classes of rubber goods made in the United States except footwear. It absorbed among other firms the Mechanical Rubber Company, which has already been mentioned as an earlier consolidation in this branch of manufacture. But more significant was the inclusion in the original group of the Morgan and Wright Company, manufacturing tires as a specialty, and the acquisition the same year of a controlling interest in the Dunlop Tire Company of the United States, which was the most important maker of bicycle and vehicle tires in America. The following year it also acquired the three tire factories owned by the American Bicycle Company, which was a customer for two-fifths of its tire output. By these purchases the Rubber Goods Manufacturing Company secured control not only of the most important plants making bicycle tires, but also of most of the patents relating to them. Yet it did not have an absolute monopoly of the rubber-tire business as a whole, as was testified by the organization in 1899 of the Rubber Tire Company of America, backed by the Locomobile Company, then one of the largest producers of motor vehicles in the country.[29]

In 1868 the Edinburgh *Scotsman* published an account of a cross-country trip made by a patent road steamer, manufactured in that city, which drew four loaded wagons of coal with a total weight of 32 tons over hilly country roads. The road steamer weighed 8 tons. This tractor was provided with solid vulcanized India rubber tires, 12 inches wide and 5 inches thick, and it was noted that in passing over newly broken metal, they did not sink into the roadbed and the broken flints did not leave a mark on the India rubber.[30] Little attention appears to have been paid to this demonstration, however, and it remained for the bicycle to familiarize the public with the advantages of rubber as a tire material and the superiority of the pneumatic tire for vehicles where vibration was to be avoided. The various steps by which the design, fabrics and construction of tires were accommo-

[28] *Commercial and Financial Chronicle*, LXVIII, 574, Mar. 25, 1899; LXXI, 37, July 7, 1900; LXXI, 1317, Dec. 29, 1900.

[29] U. S. Industrial Commission, *Reports*, XIII, 34, 37, 47, 48, 83–84; *Commercial and Financial Chronicle*, LXVIII, 872, May 6, 1899; LXIX, 231, July 29, 1899; LXIX, 964, Nov. 4, 1899; LXIX, 1015, Nov. 11, 1899; LXIX, 1066, Nov. 18, 1899.

[30] *Scientific American*, XIX, 226–227, Oct. 7, 1868.

dated to the exacting demand of the modern automobile need not detain us here. Between 1909 and 1911 these features seemed to have become standardized and stabilized, though naturally great progress in detail was made after those dates. By the close of the period we are describing the annual consumption of automobile tires in the United States had probably passed the six-million mark. Akron, Ohio, was the greatest center of this manufacture, and this fifteen-year old industry, which now accounted for well toward half of the value of all the rubber goods we manufactured, had created a group of great companies whose brands and trade-marks alone were worth fortunes, but whose names were unknown when the big trusts of the nineties were formed.[31] To be sure the United States Rubber Company which had acquired control of most of the stock of the Rubber Goods Manufacturing Company, a corporation allied with it from the first, was one of our largest tire producers. It had factories devoted to this specialty in seven states and in Canada. But in 1912 a combination of the B.F. Goodrich Company and the Diamond Rubber Company, both of Akron, Ohio, faced even that giant combination with a formidable rival in this branch of the industry.[32]

Our exports of rubber goods expanded rapidly, and their manufacture, like that of boots and shoes, was hardly dependent upon tariff protection for its prosperity. Now and then a mild protest was raised when duties were lowered, as they were by the Wilson Law, but this was mostly perhaps by way of testimony to a doctrine. A number of foreign rubber manufacturers established factories in this country, behind the shelter of our tariff wall; but on the other hand some American manufacturers erected works abroad. Except in case of waterproof garments, our rubber goods were equal or superior to those made in other countries, and they were better adapted to local tastes and conditions. During this period the manufacture of mackintoshes was successfully introduced from Great Britain.[33]

Already our great rubber manufacturers were reaching out for plantations that would enable them to control at least part of their raw materials. The production of guayule rubber, chiefly in Mexico, was promoted by the International Rubber Company, an American corporation which produced nearly half of the ten or eleven million pounds extracted annually during the latter part of this period. The United States Rubber Company owned a plantation in Sumatra. In fact plantation rubber came into the market just in time to make possible the great expansion of the industry that followed the popularization of the automobile.[34] We have no accurate measure of that expansion; but recorded in money the value of our rubber manufactures in 1889 was, in round numbers, $43,000,000; twenty-five years later it was $301,000,000.[35]

[31] *India Rubber World*, xxxix, 143, Jan. 1909; xliii, 155, Feb. 1911; xlix, 56, Nov. 1913.
[32] *India Rubber World*, xlvi, 416, 417, June 1912.
[33] *India Rubber World*, xliii, 76, Dec. 1910; xlviii, 449, June 1913; xlix, 56, Nov. 1913; U. S. Industrial Commission, *Reports*, xiii, 82, 83.
[34] *India Rubber World*, xlv, 51–52, Nov. 1911; xlvi, 416–417, June 1912.
[35] Bureau of the Census, *Manufactures, 1914*, ii, 794.

CHAPTER XVI

MANUFACTURES OF WOOD

Lumber Industry, 238. Technical Development, 239. Organization, 241. Miscellaneous Timber Manufactures, 242. Naval Stores, 243. Furniture, 244. Paper Making, 245.

LUMBER INDUSTRY

This period witnessed the culmination of the American lumber industry, which after expanding consistently for three-hundred years reached its maximum output and started on its decline about the end of the first decade of the present century. That decline had begun considerably earlier in the older forest areas of the Union. In 1889, 70 per cent of the country's lumber cut came from the Great Lakes and the Northern Appalachian regions; in 1914 only 20 per cent came from those sections. During these twenty-five years the South and the Pacific Northwest increased their aggregate annual output from less than a fourth to approximately half the total. Timber was the first of our great natural resources to be taxed beyond the limit of replacement or new development.[1]

This fact overshadowed all other features of the industry's history during the years we are now describing. This shifting geography of sawmilling, the accompanying changes in the kind and class of timber converted into lumber, and other significant phases of its development, merely continued processes well under way prior to 1890. In general the migration to new forest areas resulted in the erection there of larger and more efficient plants by highly capitalized and elaborately organized undertakings. Topographical and timber conditions influenced logging operations more than they did sawmill practice; but a very different plant was required to convert into merchantable forms the giant redwoods and Douglas firs of Washington, Oregon and California, from the mills that were still running on the small streams of Pennsylvania, New York or New England.[2]

With the exhaustion of the white-pine areas in their vicinity some lumber companies of the Great Lakes region transferred their capital and enterprise either to the yellow-pine areas of the South, especially the less-exploited sections of the Gulf States, or else to the fir forests of the North Pacific Coast. In 1895 it was estimated that the South cut annually 7,000,000,000 feet of yellow pine—an amount that was doubled twenty years later when the output reached its maximum, 4,000,000,000 feet of oak and other hard wood and half a billion feet of cypress, besides large quantities of less

[1] U. S. Dept. Agriculture, *Lumber Cut of the United States, 1870–1920*, 3.
[2] Twelfth Census, *Reports*, ix, 811.

valuable timber. In 1909, when the lumber output of the United States reached its highest point, or over 44,000,000,000 feet, the South accounted for about 54 per cent of the soft woods and 60 per cent of the hard woods cut in the country.[3]

This wholesale invasion of the Southern forests, therefore, marked the culmination of sawmilling in America. Room still remained for expansion on the Pacific Coast, especially if we include Alaska, but no other intact forest area was left large enough to increase materially, or even to maintain at its existing level, the country's lumber output. How quickly the geographical center of the industry shifted is suggested by the fact that the three leading lumber-producing states in 1899 were Wisconsin, Michigan and Minnesota; in 1905, Washington, Wisconsin and Louisiana; in 1910, Washington, Louisiana and Mississippi; and in 1915 again, Washington, Louisiana and Mississippi.[4]

With the gradual exhaustion of better timbers, attention was turned to those formerly considered worthless or held in light esteem. In Indiana and Ohio the white oak was cut first and the red oak was left. In the South, the gum was considered so unserviceable as to have no commercial value. On the Pacific Coast the Western hemlock was not thought worth transporting from the forests to the mill. As timber grew scarcer, however, even these inferior varieties were heavily drawn upon. When Canada retaliated for the duty of two dollars a thousand feet levied upon imported lumber under the Dingley Law of 1897, by prohibiting the export of saw logs, Michigan mill owners, having exhausted the white-pine stumpage in the Lower Peninsula, turned to the manufacture of local hemlock and hard woods, which they had hitherto neglected. With the expansion of the paper industry in northern New York spruce became more valuable for pulp wood than for lumber, and sawmills were obliged to resort to hemlock and cheap pine in its stead. Of more than 540,000,000 feet of logs of all timbers cut in the Adirondacks in 1898, nearly 230,000,000 feet were consumed by pulp mills. In 1910 it was reported that the old cedar rail fences of middle Tennessee were furnishing the world's main supply of cedar pencils, and farmers were selling these fences for what their fathers would have considered fabulous sums. Indeed the price received for a cedar fence would build four wire fences of equal length.[5]

TECHNICAL DEVELOPMENT

Until the end of the last century American lumbermen had not advanced much beyond the wasteful technique of the pioneer. They sawed their logs green, usually in or near the forests from which they came, converting them directly from the freshly felled timber into boards. Abroad it was

---

[3] Bruce, *Rise of the New South*, 88–89; *Manufacturers' Record*, LXV, 45–46, Apr. 16, 1914.
[4] U. S. Dept. Agriculture, *Lumber Cut of the United States, 1870–1920*, 30–33.
[5] *Manufacturers' Record*, XLVII, 74, Feb. 9, 1905; American Iron and Steel Association, *Bulletin*, XLIV, 73, Aug. 15, 1910; *Curiosity Shop*, 322–323; Fox, *History of the Lumber Industry in the State of New York*, 41–42.

customary merely to slab or square the logs at the forest mill, and to saw them into boards subsequently, after they were partly seasoned, at central establishments. The waste of timber by this double reduction process was only about one-twelfth, as compared with one-third in the United States where the single reduction method was used. Indeed sawing waste probably increased for a time in this country, as a result of mechanical improvements looking primarily to speed and high output. The old sash saw of colonial days, and also the lighter and faster-moving muley saw that succeeded it about the middle of the last century, were fixed at both ends and made an even cut. But the circular saw which followed them, while it ran about ten times as fast as a muley saw, or at the rate of from 6,000 to 9,000 feet a minute, was fixed only at the center and therefore wobbled and made a wide cut in the log. This evil was aggravated when a double circular saw was used, as was necessary for logs more than two feet in diameter. As long as timber was abundant and cheap this waste was compensated by the greater cutting speed, the comparative cheapness, and the portability of circular saw mills. But the more economical band saw, which was introduced from France in 1869 to cut valuable woods like mahogany, was perfected in this country until it made a narrower cut than even the muley saw at a speed about equal to that of the circular saw. By the end of the century it was generally employed by the larger mills to square logs, which were then cut into boards by gang saws at a single operation.[6]

A growing proportion of the lumber sawed was manufactured in large establishments. More than half of the total in 1914 was produced by mills cutting more than 10,000,000 feet annually, and some plants had a maximum output of a million feet a day. These naturally employed highly improved machinery in carefully adjusted combinations, and could use economically mechanical devices that smaller establishments had less inducement to install. Consequently concentration in large plants encouraged technical progress. Such establishments generally adopted kiln drying and turned out upon the whole a product somewhat superior to that of the smaller mills. But these giant undertakings were profitable only in the neighborhood of great areas of virgin timber. The largest of them consumed the equivalent of from 50 to 300 acres of forest a day, and manufactured 180,000,000 feet of boards a year. Steam had long since supplanted water as a source of power, partly because it was an economy rather than an expense for most mills to consume their sawdust and other waste under their boilers, and partly because the newer timber areas, especially in the South, were in the coastal plains. Between 1899 and 1914 the steam-engine capacity employed in the industry increased from 1,400,000 to 2,100,000 horse-power, while the water-wheel capacity declined from 201,000 to 84,000 horse-power. Even in smaller mills internal combustion

[6] *Engineering Magazine*, XVI, 932–946. Mar. 1899.

engines and motors driven by rented electric current were displacing water wheels.[7]

Water played a diminishing rôle, not only as a source of power but also as a medium of transportation. Timber adjacent to logging streams was the first to be exhausted, and relatively to the total amount of lumber marketed the quantity shipped by lake and river was decreasing. This explains the decline of old-time national lumber markets, such as once existed at Albany and later at Chicago. Their function, except to supply the local trade, ceased when it became possible to ship lumber by rail directly from the mill to the consumer. Another result of this change in transportation methods was to encourage the manufacture of planed lumber at the original establishment, since dressed boards could be shipped to advantage by rail but not by vessels.[8]

ORGANIZATION

Several attempts were made to form great sawmill amalgamations, though never on a national scale. During the late nineties measures were taken to organize a trust among North Carolina pine producers, including several mills in the adjoining states, but this project failed of realization. Efforts to effect a big mill merger about ten years later among the yellow-pine producers of the Mississippi Valley were equally unsuccessful, partly on account of public hostility. Not long afterward a plan to consolidate the "cargo," or coastal mills of Washington and Oregon, which ship most of their product by sea, came to naught; and several similar proposals among the redwood and the sugar-pine millers of California never advanced beyond their initial stages. Local consolidations occurred, however, among makers of sash and doors and other finished mill products. To be sure large lumber corporations, some of which owned mills and vast areas of timber land in different sections of the country, at times acquired trust dimensions; but they owed their growth to the expansion of a single parent firm and not to the amalgamation of many companies. Some of these enterprises, besides logging immense stretches of forest and operating large sawmills, also owned or controlled fleets of lumber schooners, conducted wholesale distributing yards and even maintained chains of retail yards, so that they took a profit at every stage of the business from the stump to the consumer. But market control, which was the sole object of the suggested combinations, since few manufacturing economies would result from such mergers, was secured by concentrating timber-land ownership in

---

[7] Depew, *One Hundred Years of American Commerce*, I, 202–203; Cochrane, *Modern Industrial Progress*, 284–285; U. S. Dept. Agriculture, *Lumber Cut of the United States, 1870–1920*, 25–27, and legend Plate I; Twelfth Census, *Reports*, IX, 894; Bureau of the Census, *Manufactures, 1905*, III, 620; *Manufactures, 1914*, II, 987; U. S. Bureau of Corporations, *The Lumber Industry*, IV, 250; *Curiosity Shop*, 221–222.

[8] U. S. Industrial Commission, *Reports*, IX, 431–432; *American Lumberman*, June 1, 1907, p. 31; cf., U. S. Bureau of Corporations, *The Lumber Industry*, IV, 382.

fewer hands, and by trade associations, which were apparently more successful in the lumber industry than in most other branches of manufacture.[9]

These associations were regional and confined as a rule to producers of a single class of lumber; and they were generally promoted and dominated by the larger and more powerful firms in the geographical area where they existed. Each employed a secretary or manager, who was its executive head. Several, but not all, of these associations were incorporated, but not for the purpose of acquiring their member companies. Mergers of associations sometimes occurred, and in 1902 the principal bodies of this character were finally banded together in a federation, known as the National Lumber Manufacturers' Association.

One of the first functions of these associations was to standardize products, after which price fixing followed, if not exactly automatically, at least as a comparatively easy step. Naturally the price lists thus established were sometimes disregarded; it was difficult to reconcile the often conflicting interests of large and small mills; and more or less competition existed between the products of different associations. But upon the whole these organizations succeeded in imposing their law upon the lumber market, not always perhaps to the immediate advantage of consumers and the general public, but with great benefit to the producing interests. They formed clearing houses of statistical and trade information, supported an able press of their own, disseminated technical knowledge relating to their branch of manufacture, and in the final outcome probably assisted industrial progress. They seem never to have embraced, at least during the period we are describing, producers of more than about one-third of the country's total lumber output; but they included a majority of those who manufactured primarily for the national market. After all, this industry continued to be dispersed in a great number of establishments, several thousand of which sold their product in their immediate vicinity, and still did custom work—that is, sawed on shares or for a fee logs brought to them by local patrons.[10]

MISCELLANEOUS TIMBER MANUFACTURES

Coincident with the rise of the lumber industry to primary importance in the South, other branches of timber manufacturing developed in that region. A great demand for boxes, crates and other containers was occasioned by the extension of market gardening and fruit growing in these milder latitudes after the invention of the refrigerator car, so that within twenty years this branch of woodworking tripled its output. The manufacture of woodenware was introduced, and cooperage stock was made on a large scale. Many of these industries employed timber that was not

---

[9] *Commercial and Financial Chronicle*, LXX, 283, Feb. 24, 1900; LXXI, 136, July 21, 1900; LXXI, 1124, Dec. 1, 1900; *American Lumberman*, June 22, 1907, p. 46; U. S. Bureau of Corporations, *The Lumber Industry*, IV, 5, 74–75, 254.

[10] U. S. Bureau of Corporations, *The Lumber Industry*, IV, 4–6 50–52, *et passim;* Thirteenth Census, *Reports*, X, 487.

suitable for ordinary lumber. Arkansas became the leading stave-making state of the Union, and with the neighboring state of Tennessee supplied great quantities of white-oak barrel stock to Spain, Portugal, Italy and France, where it was used, as it had been since colonial times, to make casts for wine and oil. Red-oak staves were chiefly used in this country for whisky and molasses barrels. The old employment of oak containers for storing and shipping pickled pork and beef and other packing house and dairy products had practically ceased with improved methods of curing and refrigeration. The Southern cypress first came into extensive use for the manufacture of tanks, vats and cisterns, which were sold from Maine to Colorado, and only later acquired its present reputation as a building timber.[11]

NAVAL STORES

With the decline of wooden shipping, the manufacture of naval stores might have been expected likewise to wane. This did not occur, however, because new industrial demands arose for pitch, tar and turpentine which greatly exceeded these older requirements. The center of the industry had previously shifted southward, from North Carolina to Florida and Georgia, with Louisiana and other states farther west increasing their production rapidly. The output of turpentine and rosin, like the lumber cut, attained its peak during these years; but as its expansion depended upon the supply of a single timber, the long-leafed pine of the southern coastal plain, this point was reached about a decade earlier than it was in lumbering. At the date of maximum production, about the beginning of the century, well toward 38,000,000 gallons of turpentine and over 4,250,000 barrels of rosin were manufactured, nearly half of which was exported. Comparatively little pitch and tar, so important in the days of oakum calked vessels and tarred ship's cables, was now made, the tappings being converted almost entirely into turpentine and rosin to be used in the manufacture of paints, varnishes, soap and in the other industrial arts. Except for the adoption of more economical methods of tapping as the supply of timber grew scarcer, no radical changes occurred in the technology of the industry.[12]

Some turpentine to be sure, was produced by wood distillation, which was a process distinct from the distillation of the natural pitch tapped from the tree; but the newer industry was conducted primarily with other purposes in view. It employed kilns, ovens, or retorts to convert the wood itself into charcoal and a variety of products, of which the most important were wood alcohol and acetate of lime. Incidentally this process was likewise a source of formaldehyde, creosote and several other distillates of minor but growing importance. Most of these were obtained from the hard woods

[11] Bruce, *Rise of the New South*, 89–90; *S. and W. Textile Excelsior*, VI, 5, Apr. 29, 1899; Bureau of the Census, *Manufactures, 1905*, III, 612; Thirteenth Census, *Reports*, X, 487.

[12] Twelfth Census, *Reports*, IX, 1003–1006; Bureau of the Census, *Manufactures, 1905*, III, 654–656; Thirteenth Census, *Reports*, X, 685–689; Bureau of the Census, *Manufactures, 1914*, II, 597, 602–603.

of the North, except the turpentine, which even in this branch of the industry came from the South, where pine was the principal wood distilled. Consumers had a prejudice, however, against turpentine manufactured in this manner, similar to that cherished a century or more earlier by shipbuilders and riggers against pitch and tar made from pitch-pine stumps. But the quantity of wood-distilled turpentine was not large; in 1914 it was no more than 575,000 gallons, or about 2 per cent of the total output of the country. The same year over 7,000,000 gallons of wood alcohol were distilled, and 82,000 tons of acetate of lime were manufactured.[13]

FURNITURE

Probably more household, school and office furniture was manufactured in the United States during this period than in any other country in the world. Measured in value, New York, followed closely by Chicago, turned out the largest product, but Grand Rapids, which ranked third in this industry, was still the most prominent center of manufacture. Several other cities in the Central West were large furniture producers; but the distinctive feature of the geography of the industry at this time was its marked expansion in the South, whither makers were attracted by the same influences that drew the lumber business in that direction. North Carolina, which still had an abundant supply of hardwood timber, developed an important furniture manufacturing center at High Point, which by the opening of the century had 30 factories engaged in this line of production, all of them established within a decade. Their output was shipped to every part of the world and had attracted to the vicinity several subsidiary industries. Thomasville, in the same vicinity, had become a chair-making town, like some New England villages near Worcester at an earlier date. Other factories were clustered in smaller places in the neighborhood of High Point, where the first Southern Furniture Exposition was held in 1913, in imitation of the biennial furniture displays at Grand Rapids. Farther west, in Arkansas, where the pine woods and the prairie meet, factories were established at Pine Bluff, Little Rock and Fort Smith, to make cheaper grades of furniture for the western market. Some of these establishments also turned out ready-made and portable houses. An even larger business grew up at Portland, Oregon, and Los Angeles, on the Pacific Coast, to supply the local market, which was protected from eastern competition by high freights. But the principal centers of the industry were Illinois, Indiana and Michigan, tributary to the northern hardwood forests, and New York, Pennsylvania and Massachusetts in the East, accessible to ports receiving cabinet woods from abroad.[14]

[13] Twelfth Census, *Reports*, x, 556–559; Bureau of the Census, *Manufactures, 1905*, IV, 436–437; Bureau of the Census, *Manufactures, 1914*, II, 523, 602.

[14] Thirteenth Census, *Reports*, x, 619, 622; *Curiosity Shop*, 250–255; *Manufacturers' Record*, XLVII, 395, May 18, 1905; LXIV, 58, Dec. 18, 1913; Bureau of the Census, *Manufactures, 1914*, II, 958–961; Federal Trade Commission, *Summary of Report on Household Furniture*, 27.

No giant corporations were formed in this industry, although in 1897 three large manufacturers of rattan furniture in Massachusetts and at Chicago consolidated in a $6,000,000 company. A still more ambitious project carried out in 1899 was the amalgamation of twelve important plants making school furniture, most of which were in the Central West, as the American School Furniture Company. Another group of establishments, whose business lies rather in the margin of this branch of manufacture, combined the same year as the National Casket Company. But the tendency in this industry, as it was in the lumber industry, was to attain the ends of corporate union through trade associations. A Federal investigation made somewhat later than the period we are now describing revealed the fact that 90 per cent of the furniture output in the South was produced by members of the Southern Furniture Manufacturers' Association; that a National Association of Chair Manufacturers controlled 85 per cent of the production of wooden chairs; that a third association occupied a similar position among table manufacturers; and that a fourth group of a similar kind, known as the National Alliance of Case Goods Associations, embraced most producers of other ordinary types of household furniture. Besides these national or general bodies, local associations existed in New England and on the Pacific Coast. On account of the great variety of design, materials and workmanship employed in household furniture, standardization and price-fixing were very difficult. Indeed price agreements of the kind attempted by the steel rail pool, for example, were never made. Standardization, so far as it was enforced, was designed to maintain quality and to prevent the deception of customers as much as it was to stabilize markets and obviate undue competition. But naturally the total effect of these organizations was to enable the trade in a broad way to maintain more uniform and remunerative sales conditions than would otherwise have prevailed.[15]

PAPER MAKING

The roll call of other wood-using industries might be extended indefinitely. By far the most important of them was paper making, which in respect to its demand upon the timber supply and the value of its product ranked second to lumbering itself among this group of manufactures. To be sure the total output of paper, including that made from all materials, was valued at less than half the lumber cut, or at $332,000,000 as compared with $715,000,000, and the 4,250,000 cords of pulp wood it annually consumed did not loom large beside the mountains of saw logs required to make thirty or forty million feet of rough lumber. Nevertheless, next to this major industry it was the most responsive to the wastage of our forest resources.

---

[15] *Commercial and Financial Chronicle*, LXIV, 423, Feb. 27, 1897; LXVIII, 668, Apr. 16, 1899; LXIX, 131, July 15, 1899; Federal Trade Commission, *Summary of Report on Household Furniture*, 6, 28–40.

No revolutionary change occurred at this time in either the technology or the geography of paper-making, although this industry was on the eve of the gradual drift to Canada that was to characterize the next decade. Machinery and processes were improved in detail, mainly in the direction of producing a larger output with existing plants and methods. Europe probably retained the lead in chemical progress and manufacturing economies as applied to the production of wood pulp, but all the mechanical operations of paper making were conducted on a larger scale, and apparently with more efficient machinery, on this side of the Atlantic. In the production of mechanical pulp a magazine device that automatically fed logs to the grinders, and an arrangement for shredding the wood longitudinally so as to produce a longer fiber, were experimentally introduced, though they had not been generally adopted when the period we are describing closed. But the great advance was in the paper-making machine itself, which was increased in width to a maximum of 186 inches and in the best mills turned out news-print paper at the rate of 650 feet a minute.[16]

Hydro-electric power was used increasingly in paper mills, and water wheels, while still the main reliance for driving their machinery and not actually diminishing, supplied a constantly lessening proportion of the primary power they employed. On the other hand the use of steam increased relatively as well as absolutely, partly because machinery driven by it could be run at a more even speed, an essential condition for producing paper of uniform quality, and partly because steam was used in any case to heat the drying cylinders and the digestors in which chemical wood pulp was manufactured. The proportion of mechanical pulp, which was ground by stones usually affixed directly to the shafts of turbine water wheels, declined, while that of the superior sulphite pulp increased. The latter was made somewhat more cheaply than it had been in the past, and its higher cost as compared with ground pulp was partly compensated by the increased output that could be obtained from machinery when stock strengthened by a larger admixture of it was employed. Moreover, several causes combined about this time to create a demand for a better quality of news-print paper. A change in the contracts between paper makers and publishers threw the loss from press waste upon the latter; high-speed modern presses require for economical operation a paper capable of resisting uniformly a certain tension; and the vogue of newspaper illustrations, especially half-tones, made it necessary to employ a better-faced paper than formerly.[17] Contrasting with the larger establishments of this period, some of which had an output of over 300 tons of paper daily, were numerous small mills scattered over the country, at two of which hand-made paper was manufactured until the close of the last century. In fact the last mill

---

[16] Federal Trade Commission, *Report on the News-Print Paper Industry*, 27–30; Weeks, *History of Paper Manufacturing*, 295–296; Committee on Ways and Means, 54th Cong., 2d sess., *Tariff Hearings*, II, 1758; Bureau of the Census, *Manufactures, 1905*, III, 684; *Manufactures, 1914*, II, 618

[17] *Cf.*, Twelfth Census, *Reports*, IX, 1026; Bureau of the Census, *Manufactures, 1905*, III, 680, 683; Thirteenth Census, *Reports*, X, 754, 756; Bureau of the Census, *Manufactures, 1914*, II, 611, 614; U. S. Industrial Commission, *Reports*, XIII, 433.

retaining the hand process continued in operation at Adams, Massachusetts, until 1906.[18]

Nearly three-fourths of the news-print paper manufactured in the country was made in New York and in the three New England States adjoining the Canadian border. An increasing share of the pulp wood and wood pulp they consumed came from beyond that border; but their location was determined primarily by proximity to the spruce forests just south of the boundary. At first this timber constituted three-fourths of that employed for paper making, poplar being a poor second; but with the approaching exhaustion of the spruce supply an increasing amount of hemlock, and also of southern long-leaf pine, was used. Timber resources account for the prominence in this industry of Wisconsin, which ranked fourth among the paper-making states; and also for the presence of large paper mills in Oregon and Washington.

Yet wood pulp was by no means the only material used for making paper. Massachusetts, which ranked second only to New York in this industry and owed her position chiefly to her fine paper manufacturers, consumed two-fifths of the three or four hundred thousand tons of rags annually converted into these products in the country. Indiana made more straw paper than any other state, and with her neighbors, Illinois and Ohio, produced 70 per cent of the country's output. But this branch of the industry was declining, partly because sulphate wood pulp was supplanting straw in the manufacture of wrapping paper.[19]

Maine, which ranked third among our paper-making states, was the chief consumer of pulp wood, as Massachusetts was the chief consumer of rags and miscellaneous paper stock. In 1897 its governor reported that no new cotton and woolen mills had been erected in the state during the preceding three years and several of those already built had been compelled to suspend operation, but that meanwhile several large pulp and paper mills had been erected and others were in contemplation. These included what were probably then the largest establishments of the kind in the world.[20] So rapid was the exhaustion of the pulp wood in the vicinity of the mills that manufacturers sought new forest areas. In 1914 one of the largest pulp mills in the country, supplying a parent paper mill in Ohio, was situated in North Carolina.[21] With the extension of pulp and paper making into Canada some American companies acquired a controlling interest in establishments operating in the Dominion.[22]

Paper makers began to reforest their cut-over pulp wood lands before lumber manufacturers took corresponding action; and had it not been for the proximity of the Canadian spruce forests they might have shown in-

[18] Weeks, *Paper Manufacturing in the United States*, 302.
[19] Bureau of the Census, *Manufactures, 1914*, II, 614, 615.
[20] Maine, *Journal of the Senate, 1897*, 39–40; *Commercial and Financial Chronicle*, LXIX, 79–80, July 8, 1899; LXXI, 1015, Nov. 17, 1900.
[21] *Manufacturers' Record*, LXV, 55, May 21, 1914.
[22] Federal Trade Commission, *The News-Print Paper Industry* 31.

terest in such a policy earlier than they did. Reforestation appealed to them more forcibly than it did to sawmill operators, because young second-growth timber was better suited for paper making than it was for lumber; and because a modern pulp and paper mill represents a much larger fixed investment than a sawmill. The farther afield paper-makers were forced to go for their raw materials, moreover, the greater the inducement to develop finer lines of manufacture employing high-grade sulphite pulp and rags. When the migration toward Canada set in, the mills in the Dominion devoted themselves almost entirely to the production of news-print paper. Nevertheless the percentage of sulphite pulp employed in this branch of manufacture was higher in Canada than it was in the United States. Probably this is explained in part by the fact that the Canadian mills were upon an average more modern and larger than those in the United States, and ran their machinery at a higher rate of speed.[23]

In 1898, after a long period of preliminary negotiation and failure, the principal mills manufacturing news-print paper in New York and New England were consolidated as the International Paper Company. Twenty-one establishments, having an aggregate daily capacity of about 1,400 tons of wood pulp, and a somewhat larger paper tonnage, entered the new combination. It owned well toward half a million acres of spruce land in New England, New York and Michigan, and Government licenses to cut timber on more than twice that area in the Province of Quebec. The developed water power associated with its properties exceeded 150,000 horse-power, besides two-thirds as much again not yet developed. This was mostly on the Hudson and the Androscoggin Rivers. Soon after its organization the Company extended its timber holdings until they included by the summer of 1899 about 1,000,000 acres of owned or leased lands in the United States and 2,500 square miles of forest in Canada.[24]

Subsequently this Company continued to extend the capacity of its mills, though not their number, and to enlarge its timber holdings. It also erected plants for special purposes, including a factory capable of manufacturing 10,000,000 paper bags a day, and engaged heavily in making Manila paper. Besides selling agencies in the principal cities of the United States, it established an office in England. At the time it was organized this Company probably controlled about 70 per cent of the news-print paper output of the United States, a proportion that declined somewhat during the next decade and a half.[25]

Newspaper publishers actively opposed the organization of this company, or at least used its existence as an argument in favor of removing the duty

---

[23] U. S. Industrial Commission, *Reports*, XIII, 444–445, 447; Federal Trade Commission, *The News-Print Paper Industry*, 38.

[24] *Commercial and Financial Chronicle*, LXVI, 288, Feb. 5, 1898; LXVII, 428, Aug. 27, 1898; LXVII, 1359, Dec. 31, 1898; LXIX, 281, Aug. 5, 1899; U. S. Industrial Commission, *Reports*, XIII, 415–416, 420, 431–433; Weeks, *Paper Manufacturing in the United States*, 302–304.

[25] *Commercial and Financial Chronicle*, LXIX, 494, Sept. 2, 1899; LXX, 742, Apr. 14, 1900; U. S. Industrial Commission, *Reports*, XIII, 435.

from wood pulp and paper, and it soon had to meet formidable rivals, not only in the West and Pacific Northwest, where large mills were built that supplied markets as far east as the Great Lake cities, but also in the district where its mills were situated. In 1899 the Great Northern Paper Company was formed, which erected in Maine the largest paper mill in the world, capable of making 300 tons of paper daily. This company owned over a quarter of a million acres of spruce land tributary to its plants.[26]

In 1899 the American Writing Paper Company was formed for the purpose of consolidating most of the mills making writing paper in New England, New York, Pennsylvania, Ohio and Michigan. The output of these mills was about three-fourths of the total for the whole United States and 85 per cent of the total in New England. The previous year the United States Envelope Company had been organized to absorb ten firms making more than 90 per cent of the commercial envelopes manufactured in America. This merger movement was soon communicated to almost every branch of paper manufacturing. In 1899 the Union Bag and Paper Company was organized for the purpose of taking over plants representing 90 per cent of the paper-bag business of the country. This trust almost immediately encountered a competitor in the United States Paper Bag Manufacturers' Association, which was organized by a group of independent companies including two or three in the South, having a daily output of between 12,000,000 and 15,000,000 bags. In addition, as we have seen, the International Paper Company had erected a large bag-making plant in Maine.[27]

Manufacturers of straw board, who suffered from periods of overproduction and excessive competition, and had no difficulty in procuring an abundance of raw materials wherever they started new enterprises, formed several unsuccessful pools during the eighties in an effort to regulate output and prices. At length, in 1889, a relatively strong combination with a capital of $6,000,000 emerged from the conflict. It was known as the American Straw Board Company and controlled about one-third of the plant capacity of the country. During its early history it leased competing mills and shut them down, but this proved unwise and in 1897 the directors decided that it was better to do a competitive business than to subsidize competitors. Two years later the Company's mills, which were reported to be among the best in the country, had a daily capacity of 400 tons; but as the straw-board business, partly on account of its markets and partly because it used a raw material more abundant in the later than in the earlier months of the year, was more or less seasonal, their annual

[26] Committee on Ways and Means, 54th Cong., 2d sess., *Tariff Hearings*, II, 1753; U. S. Industrial Commission, *Reports*, XIII, 407, 409–410, 412, 414–415; *Commercial and Financial Chronicle*, LXIX, 79–80, July 8, 1899; Weeks, *Paper Manufacturing in the United States*, 309–310; *Boston Journal of Commerce*, LIV, May 20, 1899.
[27] *Commercial and Financial Chronicle*, LXVI, 1003, May 21, 1898; LXVIII, 333, Feb. 18, 1899; LXVIII, 1130–1131, June 10, 1899; LXIX, 128, July 15, 1899; LXIX, 182, July 22, 1899; LXIX, 909, Oct. 28, 1899; Weeks, *Paper Manufacturing in the United States*, 304–305, 308–309.

product was considerably less than these figures might indicate. In addition the Company's output fluctuated greatly from year to year, falling from 90,000 tons, for example, in 1892, to 37,000 tons in 1896. In 1899 its directors viewed with complacency, if they did not actually encourage, a project to unite the principal competing mills in a single combination. Their annual report stated:

"It will be easier for us to maintain trade relations with one company than with fifteen or sixteen scattered small concerns."

The new consolidation, which was to be known as the National Straw Board Company, would have been approximately as strong as its older rival, its annual product being 70,000 tons. Most of the mills it was proposed to combine were modern plants of practically uniform construction, and an iron-clad contract was contemplated between the existing and the proposed amalgamation, dividing territory between them and regulating output and prices. This scheme fell through, and several others like it had short and uneventful careers; but they serve to illustrate competitive conditions in a typical field of paper-making and the forces that drove toward concentration.[28]

This by no means completes the list of mergers in different branches of this industry. None of them illustrates novel or significant features important enough to detain the reader. Some of these consolidations after existing for a few years voluntarily disbanded. That occurred, for example, in case of the National Wall Paper Company, organized in 1892 and dissolved in 1900. It had done a large business, but its profits had not been "commensurate with the expectations of the stockholders." This was ascribed to the fact that the existence of the trust had stimulated competition, so that the number of plants engaged in the manufacture of wall paper had practically doubled during its lifetime. Moreover, the successful manufacture of wall paper was found to depend so largely upon designs, individual taste and personal attention to the requirements of different customers that independent plants could be operated to better advantage than a group of plants under a single management.

In both the news-print paper and the straw-board manufacture several firms sometimes joined hands to maintain a separate sales agency incorporated as an independent company.[29] These two branches of the industry represented its opposite poles in every respect except refinement of manufacturing processes. As time went on the news-print industry required a larger and larger capitalization, which was invested in expensive plants and

[28] *Commercial and Financial Chronicle*, LXII, 317, Feb. 15, 1896; LXIV, 841, May 1, 1897; LXVI, 333, Feb. 12, 1898; LXVII, 1108, Nov. 26, 1898; LXVIII, 327, Feb. 18, 1899; LXVIII, 572–573, Mar. 25, 1899; LXX, 278, Feb. 10, 1900; LXXI, 238, Aug. 4, 1900; Weeks, *Paper Manufacturing in the United States*, 305–307, 312.

[29] Committee on Ways and Means, 54th Cong., 2d sess., *Tariff Hearings*, II, 1761, 1765; Weeks, *Paper Manufacturing in the United States*, 307; Federal Trade Commission, *The News-Print Paper Industry of the United States*, 42–43.

in timber lands and transportation equipment. Its market was a relatively stable one. Its site was necessarily in the forest states. On the other hand the straw-board manufacture required a comparatively inexpensive plant and necessitated no investment in lands to provide it with raw materials. It employed simpler processes and seasonal and semi-skilled labor. Its mills were for the most part in the central prairie states, close to one of their largest markets. Notwithstanding these apparent advantages, however, the straw-board and straw-paper manufacture was the less uniformly prosperous of the two, partly because it was more exposed to overcompetition. And where there was an overlapping margin between the markets served respectively by straw paper and by wood-pulp paper producers, the more highly capitalized and more elaborately organized pulp users gained ground on their rivals.

Paper making, like sawmilling, was responsible for certain controversies with Canada, whose authorities naturally preferred that their timber should be manufactured into pulp and paper within the borders of the Dominion rather than shipped to mills in the United States. Ontario prohibited the export of logs, thus pretty effectively crippling the growth of a great paper-making center on the American water power at Sault Ste. Marie, and Quebec collected a much higher royalty upon timber cut on public lands, which included the greater part of the supply there, when it was exported than when it was manufactured within the country. But irrespective of such artificial encouragements, the advantage that Canadian mills derived from the juxtaposition of water power and spruce timber, plus cheaper labor than in the United States, insured the rapid growth of the industry in her territories. The American duty on paper was never high, being equivalent to about 15 per cent ad valorem on news-print, and less than 10 per cent upon wood pulp. After 1913 the cheaper grades of printing paper and wood and rag pulp of all descriptions were admitted free.[30]

Imports of both wood pulp and paper increased after 1900. Prior to that moderate quantities of spruce soda pulp and bleached sulphite pulp were imported from Europe, principally from Sweden and the Baltic countries. All cheaper grades of pulp from other than domestic sources came from Canada. These importations, especially those from our northern neighbor, continued to grow and in 1914 exceeded half a million tons and were about one-third of the total consumption. Between 1906 and 1916 our imports of news-print paper rose in value from $64,000 to more than $16,500,000, of which practically all came from Canada. Three years after the abolition of the duty in 1913 the quantity imported had risen from 57,000 tons to 439,000 tons. Between 1899 and 1914 our imports of paper increased in value nearly seven-fold, our imports of wood pulp and other raw materials rose between three and four-fold; but our exports of paper only doubled.

[30] Federal Trade Commission, *The News-Print Paper Industry*, 45, 148–151; U. S. Industrial Commission, *Reports*, XIII, 425, 439, 442; Taussig, *Tariff History of the United States*, 380–382.

Until 1906 we sold more paper abroad than we bought abroad; eight years later our imports were nearly twice our exports.[31]

Thus all three of the major industries of the country that were based on forest resources passed through a critical phase of development caused by the partial exhaustion of their raw materials during the quarter of a century we have just considered. Two of them, lumbering and the manufacture of turpentine and rosin, experienced what promises to be a permanent decline in output, while the third, paper making, became increasingly dependent on imported raw materials for its expansion and supplied a steadily diminishing share of domestic consumption.

[31] Committee on Ways and Means, 54th Cong., 2d sess., *Tariff Hearings*, II, 1769–1770; Bureau of the Census, *Manufactures, 1914*, II, 613, Table 15, 619, Table 25; Federal Trade Commission, *The News-Print Paper Industry*, 43–47.

CHAPTER XVII

CEMENT, CLAY AND GLASS

The Cement Age, 253. Clay Manufactures, 256. Glass Making, 259.

THE CEMENT AGE

While the lumber industry was reaching its maximum output and beginning to decline, a new building material, and one better suited than timber for the constructions of a nation fast becoming a people of city dwellers and factory workers, was beginning to take its place. This was cement, the rapidly expanding manufacture of which during the first years of the century was attributed "in no small part to its substitution for wood in public works and for structural purposes;"[1] and indeed we may say that the nineties witnessed the true dawn in America of the age of both cement and structural steel, although there had been earlier premonitions of its coming.

In 1894 the United States produced about one-fifth of the forty million barrels of cement of all kinds made annually in the world, but stood a poor third to Great Britain and Germany in this industry. Thirty years later it manufactured about half of the world's output, and four times as much as Great Britain, its nearest rival. Notwithstanding a duty of 32 cents a barrel, large quantities were imported throughout the early nineties, partly because buyers had a pronounced preference for the foreign article. In 1892, just before the panic, American plants made only 547,000 barrels of Portland cement, while five times that amount was brought from abroad, and during the years immediately preceding several works had been either abandoned or had run at a loss. The foreign product was brought to the United States practically at ballast rates, so that the European producer often enjoyed lower freights than his American competitors to our coastal markets. Natural or hydraulic cement commanded only 25 cents a barrel in bulk in some sections of the country and there was a marked depression in the entire industry.

At this time the old-fashioned high kilns were still used in many places for burning cement, and a large amount of labor was necessarily employed in handling materials. But the rotary kiln, which was to accomplish so much in lessening labor costs, and eventually in economizing fuel and accelerating production, had recently been installed successfully at several plants. Indeed what was to be the American system of cement manufacture was already foreshadowed, although not yet generally adopted or fully perfected.[2]

---

[1] *Mineral Industry*, xv, 100, 107.
[2] U. S. Geological Survey, *Mineral Resources of the United States*, 1892, 739–745; *Mineral Industry*, III, 90; Committee on Ways and Means, 54th Cong., 2d sess., *Tariff Hearings*, I, 182–183.

By 1896, when there were twenty-four Portland cement works in the United States, half of which had rotary kilns, costs had been so far reduced that both the importation of Portland cement and the manufacture of natural cement were decreasing. During this and the following year plants to make cement from furnace slag were installed at the North Chicago Works of the Illinois Steel Company and at the steel works at Sparrows Point, Maryland.[3]

By this time the rapid growth of the industry was foreseen, although the proportions it was to assume within a very few years could hardly have been anticipated. The rotary kiln, which had been handicapped ever since its introduction in 1889 by expensive fuel, had been improved ten years later so as to permit the use of powdered coal instead of crude petroleum, which had cost at the works from 30 to 40 cents a barrel. The effect of this was to reduce the cost of production in America to less than that in England, and practically to the level in Germany. With the cheapening of the product, a rapid expansion of its use occurred. Railways were its earliest large consumers. During 1899 New Jersey nearly doubled its product, and Michigan appeared for the first time as a large producer. The total output of Portland cement made in the country rose from slightly over 3,500,000 barrels in 1898, to well toward 6,000,000 barrels the following year. The output of natural cement, which was shipped in somewhat smaller containers, again increased, and rose the latter year to more than 10,000,000 barrels. About this time the industry was established in Kansas, where natural gas was used as fuel and caused a great expansion of both cement and brick-making in that section. Indeed in 1910 the largest individual plant in the United States was in this state.[4]

At the turn of the century the output of Portland cement for the first time exceeded that of natural cement, which entered upon a permanent decline after the peak of 1899, and the era of startling growth began that was to carry the product from about 3,000,000 barrels to about 80,000,000 barrels within a decade. The two largest manufacturers of Portland cement at this time were the American Cement Company, organized as a Pennsylvania corporation in 1884 and as a New Jersey corporation in 1899, which operated six mills in the former state and in New York and turned out 1,200,000 barrels a year, and the Atlas Company, which also had its seat in the Lehigh Valley, where most of the Portland cement works of the country were situated. These two companies accounted for nearly half of the total production of the United States. By the opening years of the new century American manufacturers had virtually conquered the home market and the domestic product was generally considered better than that imported. Contemporary records of the industry consist of little else than statistics of its marvelous expansion. Slag cement, though relatively

---

[3] *Mineral Industry*, v, 64; American Iron and Steel Association, *Bulletin*, xxx, 157, July 10, 1896; *Manufacturers' Record*, Aug. 1, 1897.

[4] *Mineral Industry*, vii, 113–114, viii, 83–85; *Commercial and Financial Chronicle*, lxxi, 1015, Nov. 17, 1900.

less important in tables of output, occupied a prominent place in contemporary technical discussion.[5]

This period of growth was accompanied by the erection of many new plants in the West and South, near the great consuming markets afforded by the numerous engineering and construction enterprises of these rapidly developing sections, and also by a marked decline in prices. In 1900 the industry was alarmed because Portland cement quotations had fallen to $1.40 a barrel; five years later an average price of 90 cents a barrel was not considered ruinous and natural cement sold as low as 50 cents a barrel.[6] The trend of the industry toward the West and South reduced the lead of the Lehigh Valley as a producing center. Between 1887 and 1914 the proportion of the country's output manufactured in that region fell from 75 per cent to 28 per cent, notwithstanding the fact that in the meantime the output of the Lehigh Valley mills had quadrupled and was larger at the later date than that of the whole country eleven years before.[7] The growth of individual concerns is illustrated by the Universal Cement Company, which employed Bessemer slag and limestone as its raw materials and increased its output from 32,000 barrels in 1900 to about 6,000,000 barrels eight years later.[8]

The technical advance of the industry was in two directions—better machinery and better chemical control of products by the careful selection and combination of raw materials. The early rotary kilns were 30 feet long. They had doubled in average length by 1905; and Thomas Edison had installed two kilns 150 feet long, which reduced coal consumption per barrel of cement by more than half,[9] and in 1914 46 kilns of this length or longer were in use. More powerful grinding machines and finer grinding lowered the cost of production and simultaneously raised the quality of the product. With the employment of this material in large buildings, bridges and engineering works, new methods of testing and new reliability standards had to be devised. It was necessary to create a science of cement construction parallel with the science of cement manufacture.[10]

In 1914 the total output of cement of all kinds was more than 87,000,000 barrels. It had reached nearly 90,000,000 barrels, its maximum for this period, the previous year. The amount of natural cement made had declined from the 10,000,000 barrels mentioned at an earlier date to three-quarters of a million barrels; and the production of Puzzolan cement, which was made from slag and lime, was small and decreasing. Pennsylvania still manufactured well toward one-third of the country's output, followed at a long interval by Indiana, which had the largest individual

[5] *Mineral Industry*, x, 80–82, 89; xi, 85–87; xii, 41; *Commercial and Financial Chronicle*, LXIX, 1249, Dec. 16, 1899.
[6] *Mineral Industry*, ix, 77; xiii, 49–50.
[7] U. S. Geological Survey, *Mineral Resources of the United States*, 1915, ii, 198.
[8] American Iron and Steel Association, *Bulletin*, xlii, 130, Dec. 1, 1908; *cf.*, *Mineral Industry*, xx, 440; U. S. Geological Survey, *Mineral Resources of the United States, 1915*, ii, 205.
[9] *Mineral Industry*, xv, 112–113.
[10] *Cf.*, Willis and Byers, *Portland Cement Prices*, 76–82.

plants in the United States. But the industry was widely distributed, its geography being determined largely by the presence of cheap fuel. Coal was chiefly used, but nearly 8,000,000 barrels were made with oil and a quarter of a million barrels with natural gas.[11] In 1900 the United States produced about one-tenth as much cement as pig iron; ten years later this proportion had risen to 47 per cent. In several states the consumption of Portland cement exceeded one barrel per capita annually.[12]

No trusts or corporations exercising monopoly control were formed in the cement business; but about 1904 manufacturers organized a national body known as the Portland Cement Association. The purpose of this society resembled in a general way that of the associations formed among lumber producers. It standardized commercial practices and attempted to establish standards of product. The latter function eventually necessitated setting up a great research and testing laboratory at Chicago, which contributed largely to the technical advance of the industry.[13]

CLAY MANUFACTURES

The aggregate value of the clay products manufactured in the United States surpasses that of all other materials except coal and iron, and their consumption has increased rapidly with the industrial development of the country, which is constantly creating new markets for such articles and commodities. The chemical industries employ them; electricity for traction and lighting has created a large demand for insulators and conduits. The use of sanitary porcelain in dwellings, factories and business buildings, the employment of glazed bricks in subways and tunnels, and a multitude of other new uses, added to the expansion of consumption in the older fields, also helped to explain the great growth of this manufacture.[14]

Naturally this industry was widely distributed, for it embraced the greatest variety of products from brick and coarse stoneware to porcelain, artistic pottery and terra cotta. As recently as 1896 a special report on Missouri clays mentions the existence of forty-nine potteries manufacturing stoneware in that state, mostly in out of the way places inaccessible by rail and depending entirely upon local trade. Most of these establishments had but a single kiln and the neighborhood market seldom justified running the plant more than part of the year. The survival of these small potteries employing half-skilled labor and turning out crude products was due to the wide distribution of the materials they consumed, the high cost of transportation and the universal use of their products. At the other extreme of the industry were potteries that likewise manufactured for a comparatively limited market and did not seek quantity production, but for a very differ-

[11] U. S. Geological Survey, *Mineral Resources of the United States, 1915*, II, 195, 205.
[12] U. S. Geological Survey, *Mineral Resources of the United States, 1915*, II, 202; Willis and Byers, *Portland Cement Prices*, 18.
[13] Willis and Byers, *Portland Cement Prices*, 23–53; Hungerford, *Observations on an Outstanding American Industry*, 30–36.
[14] *Mineral Industry*, VI, 153; VIII, 101.

ent reason. Such works sometimes had the character of studios rather than factories and turned out art products exclusively. One of the most prominent of these establishments was the Rockwood Pottery near Cleveland, whose exhibit received a gold medal at the Paris Exposition of 1900. The commercial manufacture of pottery and porcelain continued to be concentrated geographically in the vicinity of Trenton, New Jersey, and East Liverpool, Ohio, which had been the principal sites of this manufacture for several decades. In 1899 Trenton manufactured pottery and porcelain to the value of five or six million dollars a year, and East Liverpool to the value of $4,000,000; these two places reporting nearly 40 per cent of the total value in the United States.[15]

This manufacture was said to be affected adversely during the middle nineties by a reduction of duties to about half their former rate under the Wilson Law, although imports did not increase remarkably at that time. Between 1890 and 1900 the value of the pottery made at Trenton, whose works were most exposed to foreign competition, remained about stationary, but that of the wares produced at East Liverpool approximately doubled.[16] Altogether the increase in the country's total output between 1890 and 1905 was very moderate. East Liverpool, which used natural gas as a fuel and domestic clays, ceased to manufacture Belleek ware and decorated bone china, which it formerly had produced to some extent, and concentrated entirely upon coarser wares, while Trenton continued to make finer goods.[17] By 1910, however, a marked increase in the value of pottery and allied products was recorded, especially at Trenton. Though that city produced less common white ware in 1910 than it had in 1900, it doubled its output of porcelain, delft and other high-quality goods, and increased by still higher percentages its output of sanitary ware and porcelain electrical supplies. East Liverpool, meanwhile, owed its progress chiefly to the expansion of its white crockery and other coarse ware manufactures. The value of pottery products reported for the country as a whole more than doubled between 1899 and 1914, rising in round numbers from $17,000,000 to $35,000,000. Well toward half of this was common white ware and only about 7 per cent finer grades of porcelain and china. Ohio was the leading pottery-making state, followed in the order named by New Jersey, West Virginia and New York.[18]

The pottery industry shrinks into relative insignificance, however, so far as statistical measurements are concerned, when compared with other clay-working industries, notably the manufacture of brick. While brick yards have always existed in the vicinity of the cities and many of the medium-

[15] *Mineral Industry*, v, 134; U. S. Commissioners to the Paris Exposition of 1900, *Reports*, v, 534–535; American Iron and Steel Association, *Bulletin*, XLIII, 106, Oct. 15, 1909.
[16] Committee on Ways and Means, 54th Cong., 2d sess., *Tariff Hearings*, I, 196–211; Twelfth Census, *Reports*, IX, 908, Tables 12 and 13.
[17] Bureau of the Census, *Manufactures, 1905*, III, 888–889.
[18] Thirteenth Census, *Reports*, X, 867, Table 31, 871, Table 34; U. S. Geological Survey, *Mineral Resources of the United States, 1915*, II, 881; cf., Ries and Leighton, *History of the Clay-Working Industry in the United States*, 141–144, 185–187.

sized and smaller towns of the United States, the tendency to concentrate at favorable production centers began to manifest itself distinctly by the end of the century. Naturally there were important brick-making establishments adjacent to every large city, the market in this case determining the local concentration of the industry. Notable examples of this were the Hudson River region, tributary to New York, which by 1914 made about a billion brick annually, and Cook Country, Illinois, which produced about three-fourths that number. But with the discovery of natural gas, the employment of petroleum for burning brick, the opening of new coal fields near excellent clay deposits, and cheaper transportation, especially in the West, brick-making centers of importance were developed away from large urban areas. Among the more prominent of these were Galesburg, Illinois, and Coffeyville, Kansas, at both of which towns paving brick was extensively manufactured. At the close of the century, Illinois ranked first in this particular branch of brick-making, with large establishments at Springfield, as well as Galesburg, and Iowa ranked second, its industry at that date being centralized at Des Moines. The growth of the industry in Kansas and Oklahoma was notable in the following decade.[19]

Among the new types of brick introduced during this period were those made from sand and lime, burned under pressure, a process invented in Germany about 1880. Their manufacture began at Michigan City, Indiana, in 1901 and four years later some 50 establishments in the United States were producing them, either exclusively or in connection with clay brick. Before the end of this period common brick were giving way to pressed, faced, vitrified, enameled and fire brick and other special varieties; so that between 1905, when the maximum number was made, and 1915 the output declined by more than three billion.[20]

Some branches of clay manufacturing experienced an era of consolidation about the end of the century. These combinations were of two kinds, local and national. The local groups embraced mainly brick works tributary to a single large city. For instance, in 1900 25 brick-making concerns operating 34 plants in the immediate vicinity of Boston were combined as the New England Brick Company. A similar consolidation, incorporated as the Illinois Brick Company, was formed the same year by the leading brick-makers tributary to Chicago.[21] Trusts embracing the plants in a larger territory were organized by manufacturers of sewer pipe and similar products. In 1900, after more than a year of preliminary negotiation some 27 makers of vitrified drain pipe in the Ohio Valley, Michigan, New York and Pennsylvania, incorporated as the American

[19] U. S. Geological Survey, *Mineral Resources of the United States*, 1892, p. 733; *ibid.*, 1915, II, 859, 877; Bureau of the Census, *Manufactures, 1905*, III, 894–895; *Mineral Industry*, VII, 145–146; *Engineering Magazine*, IV, 883–897, March, 1893.
[20] Bureau of the Census, *Manufactures, 1905*, III, 893; U. S. Geological Survey, *Mineral Resources of the United States, 1915*, II, 7–8, 866.
[21] *Commercial and Financial Chronicle*, LXX, 383, Feb. 24, 1900; LXXI, 1123, Dec. 1, 1900; Ries and Leighton, *History of the Clay-Working Industry in the United States*, 12.

Clay Manufacturing Company, whose plants were reported to turn out more than 80 per cent of the country's product of this commodity. A year previously the American Potteries Company was promoted, to combine the leading makers of the United States; and shortly afterward what was sometimes called "the bath-tub trust," but was known in serious business circles and the advertising pages of popular magazines as the Standard Manufacturing Company, was organized to bring under central management the principal producers of porcelain sanitary goods in the West.[22]

GLASS MAKING

Until about the end of the century the technology of glass making lagged behind that of the chemical and metallurgical industries. Tank furnaces were not generally introduced until the nineties, and during that decade there was a decrease of only 20 per cent in the number of pot furnaces, although most new installations were of the newer type. Yet, as not infrequently happens after a manufacture has marked time for a period, an era of rapid development ensued. All bottles were blown by hand until 1896. "Then came the one-man, one-boy machine, followed by the one-man, no-boy machine, and then came the no-man, no-boy, automatic machine," which took the molten glass directly from the tank and converted it into bottles at the rate of 165 a minute without other human attendance than the occasional attention of an oiler. Between 1905 and 1914 the number of Owens automatic glass-blowing machines in use increased from 1 to 164; and they reduced the cost of making milk bottles, for instance, from 75 cents to 10 cents a gross. Indeed the multiplication of glass containers, with the sanitary advantages as well as the convenience they afford, is partly due to this cheapening of production. Nevertheless a large percentage of the bottles made in the United States, if we include those of all sizes and designs, were still blown by hand.[23]

Corresponding progress had been made in the application of machinery to the manufacture of common window glass. In this case, as in the manufacture of pressed glass three-quarters of a century before, the key inventions were of American origin. They date from about 1904 and multiplied the product of an operative more than eight-fold. In the production of plate glass the substitution of continuous annealing in lehrs, or a series of kilns and annealing ovens, for the old kiln process, shortened the time required for this operation from three days to as many hours, with a corresponding reduction in cost, and enabled manufacturers to make thinner plates than formerly. Some of these improvements, especially the introduction of machines for making window glass, caused distress among skilled operatives. During the years immediately preceding the World War,

[22] *Commercial and Financial Chronicle*, LXVIII, 229–230; Feb. 4, 1899; LXX, 86, Jan. 13, 1900; LXX, 383, Feb. 24, 1900; LXX, 482, Mar. 10, 1900.
[23] *Mineral Industry*, IX, 310; Twelfth Census, *Reports*, IX, 957; Bureau of the Census, *Manufactures, 1905*, III, 978, 988–990; *Quarterly Journal of Economics*, XXXIX, 546–551, Aug. 1925; U. S. Tariff Commission, *Glass and Glassware, 1921*, 11, 36.

piecework rates were reduced to such an extent in the latter branch of the industry that the earnings of hand blowers fell from $50 to $15 a week. Between 1899 and 1914 the output of window glass about doubled in value, but the proportion made by hand fell from 100 per cent to 40 per cent.[24]

Pittsburgh was the leading glass-making center of America, but the discovery of natural gas in Indiana attracted some of her factories to that state. This shifting was not permanent in all cases, and certain establishments returned to their original sites when the wells upon which they depended showed signs of exhaustion. But Indiana for a time ranked second only to Pennsylvania in this industry, a place she later yielded to Ohio. Indeed these three states and West Virginia made well toward three-fourths of the glass produced in the country. For many years the drift had been steadily westward from the north Atlantic seaboard to the Ohio Valley in response to the attraction of cheap fuel, excellent glass sands and local supplies of soda ash.[25]

Between 1889 and 1914 the value of the glass of all kinds produced in the United States trebled, rising from $41,000,000 to $123,000,000. This increase was shared by all departments of the industry, but it was more marked in case of bottles and other containers than of either building glass or glassware. The output of plate glass increased more rapidly than that of window glass, because as costs of production in America were reduced it was substituted for the latter and also displaced the imported article, and because it was applied to many new uses, such as automobile windows and shields, which eventually—though not within the period we are now describing—absorbed the greater part of the total output.[26]

Exports of glass more than doubled in value between 1899 and 1914, but at the latter date, when they approached $4,000,000, they were less than half that season's exceptionally high imports. This condition was completely reversed during the World War, when imports fell to less than $2,000,000 annually, while exports reached ten-fold that figure. Foreign shipments during the period we are considering included some pressed-glass tableware, and also lamps and lamp chimneys. The production of the latter declined, however, with the increasing encroachment of gas and electricity upon the illuminating field.[27] Several varieties of patterned and art glass were made in the United States. This branch of the industry was naturally centered in the East, especially around the old glass-making center in the vicinity of Boston, and at New York City, where the opalescent "Tiffany" glass, which was for some years a unique product which Europe sought—

---

[24] Twelfth Census, *Reports*, IX, 962–963; Bureau of the Census, *Manufactures, 1905*, III, 846; U. S. Tariff Commission, *Glass and Glassware, 1921*, 12, 77, 106; U. S. Committee of Ways and Means, 60th Congress, *Tariff Hearings*, Schedule B, 1122.

[25] *Manufacturers' Record*, XLVII, 571–572, July 6, 1905; Bureau of the Census, *Manufactures, 1905*, III, 958; *Manufactures, 1914*, II, 828.

[26] Bureau of the Census, *Manufactures, 1905*, III, 858; *Manufactures, 1914*, II, 833.

[27] Twelfth Census, *Reports*, IX, 988; Bureau of the Census, *Manufactures, 1914*, II, 835; U. S. Tariff Commission, *Glass and Silverware, 1921*, 13, 16–23.

and at last successfully—to imitate, was invented.[28] Until America entered the World War the manufacture of optical glass, which represents perhaps the highest refinement of the industry, hardly existed in the United States, but in 1910 lighthouse lenses equal to those imported were made for the Government by an American firm, and a step thus taken toward this final achievement.[29]

From a comparatively early date various associations existed among the makers of particular kinds of glass, which exercised more or less control over output and prices. One of the first amalgamations to attract attention occurred in 1892, when four important works manufacturing window glass at Bellaire, Ohio, combined. Several years elapsed, however, before a serious attempt was made to consolidate all the principal works in any branch of the industry. In 1895 the American Glass Company, a selling pool for four-fifths or more of the manufacturers of window glass, was formed, and was succeeded in October 1899 by the American Window Glass Company, a $17,000,000 corporation, controlling about three-fourths of the plant capacity of the country. The new corporation immediately announced a cut of one-third or more in the price of its product, as the first move in a campaign against independent and coöperative producers. The first annual report stated that the Company embraced forty-one individual firms, and indicated that several establishments which contemplated joining the combination had failed to do so. This probably explains the reduction in prices put through, ostensibly "in order to discourage further building of factories and to diminish importations." At this time the Company had a capacity of 1,737 pots but could operate only 70 per cent of them because it could not get sufficient blowers. Glass making is to some extent a seasonal occupation, and the plants of the trust, being shut down during the hot season, were open only six months of the ten and one-half months covered in this report. The corporation owned gas wells and pipe lines, as well as the plants for furnishing sand. Among the interesting features of the new company, perhaps due to the fact that it embraced certain former coöperative factories, was a provision that one of the directors should be named by the Window Glass Workers' Association, and putting in trust for this Association five thousand shares of common stock to be delivered when accumulating dividends had paid for it.[30]

Plate-glass manufactures suffered severely from the panic of 1893, when the sudden cessation of building operations curtailed their market so abruptly that sales fell from 15,000,000 square feet to 9,000,000 feet within twelve months. This caused two of the eight companies in the United States to fail, and forced the remaining plants to run at reduced capacity. In 1895 the principal works, including all those in the Pittsburgh district,

---

[28] Bureau of the Census, *Manufactures, 1905*, III, 872–874.
[29] Macbeth-Evans Glass Company, *Fifty Years of Glass Making*, 73.
[30] American Iron and Steel Association, *Bulletin*, XXVI, 69, Mar. 9, 1892; U. S. Industrial Commission, *Reports*, XIII, 565; *Commercial and Financial Chronicle*, LXIX, 744, Oct. 7, 1899; LXIX, 1249, Dec. 16, 1899; LXXI, 810, Oct. 20, 1900; LXXI, 912, Nov. 3, 1900.

which was the leading center of this manufacture, combined as the Pittsburgh Plate Glass Company. This corporation proceeded at once to organize the sales end of the business, which had hitherto been controlled by jobbers' associations to the detriment of manufacturers, by establishing its own distributing agencies and dealing directly with consumers. In 1900 there were only three independent plants in the country, and they sold almost exclusively in the western market. At this time the Pittsburgh Plate Glass Company operated ten plants, with an aggregate yearly capacity of about 26,000,000 square feet, or double its actual output; the independents produced over 5,000,000 square feet per annum. By 1914 the product for the whole country had trebled, rising to over 60,000,000 square feet of polished glass.[31]

Another important branch of glass making, the manufacture of lamp chimneys, of which more than 7,000,000 dozen were used in the United States, was controlled by a combination of the leading manufacturers, who owned jointly the patents for blowing, by machinery, chimneys, reflectors and globes. The new apparatus, which was perfected during the late nineties, reduced the cost of making lamp chimneys from 15 cents to 5 cents a dozen.[32]

Another consolidation of first importance, among others that might be mentioned, was the National Glass Company, or tableware combination, which was formed in 1899, and included over two-thirds the plant capacity of the country engaged in the production of this class of goods. Only one establishment of first rank remained outside the new corporation, which embraced nineteen firms operating a total of 678 pots. The eight concerns outside the combination had 280 pots, of which 150 belonged to the United States Glass Company, a large Pittsburgh corporation, which was apparently run in harmony with the new enterprise.[33]

The outstanding facts in the history of American glass-making during these twenty-five years, therefore, were the introduction of improved machinery, which displaced hand work especially in the production of blown-glass goods, the drift of the industry toward the furnace-fuel area of the Central West, and the consolidation of plants under unified management. This was accompanied by a rapid expansion of output and increasing control of the domestic market; but not by important extensions of the export trade.

[31] U. S. Industrial Commission, *Reports*, XIII, 226–243; Bureau of the Census, *Manufactures, 1914*, 833, Table 13; American Iron and Steel Association, *Bulletin*, XXVIII, 276, Dec. 5, 1894; *Commercial and Financial Chronicle*, LXVIII, 525, Mar. 18, 1899; LXX, 1094, June 2, 1900
[32] *Commercial and Financial Chronicle*, LXVII, 123, July 16, 1898; LXXI, 866, Oct. 27, 1900.
[33] *Commercial and Financial Chronicle*, LXIX, 1015, Nov. 11, 1899; LXIX, 1304, Dec. 23, 1899.

CHAPTER XVIII

MANUFACTURE OF FOOD, DRINK AND TOBACCO

Food Manufacture in General, 263. Meat Packing, 263. Flour Milling, 266. Cereals, Bakery Goods, and Miscellaneous Grain Products, 268. Canning, 270. Cane Sugar, 272. Beet Sugar, 272. Sugar Refining, 274. Alcoholic Liquors, 275. Tobacco, 278.

FOOD MANUFACTURE IN GENERAL

During the decades immediately preceding and following the turn of the century, the preparation of food was transferred to an increasing extent from the kitchen to the factory, and the factory became in so many cases a unit in a larger consolidation, that we may speak without exaggeration of the substitution of the "trust" for the household in this group of manufactures. In 1914 the gross value of products, including the cost of raw materials and certain unavoidable duplication, reported by these industries exceeded $3,500,000,000, divided in round numbers approximately as follows: slaughtering and meat packing, $1,454,000,000; flour and grist-mill products, $878,000,000; sugar, including sugar refining, $374,000,000; dairy products, $364,000,000; miscellaneous food preparations, such as cereals, starch—partly used for food—macaroni, glucose and syrups, and compound lards, $249,000,000; and canning, except canned meats and milk, $243,000,000. In all these branches of manufacture, except the production of butter and cheese, large corporations were the rule; and the list does not include baking and the manufacture of yeast and baking powder, which were also to a considerable extent in the hands of large companies, and which in the aggregate would add many million dollars to the above totals.

MEAT PACKING

Chicago remained the great packing center of the United States throughout this period, followed in value of products by Kansas City, New York, Indianapolis and St. Louis, in the order named. So unimpaired was its primacy that in 1914 it accounted for nearly one-fourth of the country's output, while the other four cities, taken together, accounted for less than one-fifth. But the industry was widely distributed, and the growth of secondary centers, while not affecting materially its larger geography, was at times remarkable. Between 1897 and 1900 a notable development occurred at South Saint Joseph, Missouri, and during the ten years ending with 1913 the number of animals annually slaughtered at Fort Worth increased from 60,000 to 1,200,000.[1] The latter city was a market for

---

[1] Twelfth Census, *Reports*, IX, 416; *Manufacturers' Record*, LXVI, 50, Aug. 27, 1914.

Mexican as well as Southern ranch and range cattle, which were no longer driven north after the exhaustion of free grazing along the route. The establishment of packing houses farther south than formerly was rendered possible by mechanical refrigeration, and was encouraged by the practice of fattening cattle on cottonseed meal and hulls, a business sometimes carried on in connection with the cottonseed-oil manufacture.[2] Texas and Oklahoma were the only states south of Maryland and Missouri, however, that figured prominently in output statistics. Although packing and distilling were not formally associated, distillery mash was used to fatten livestock, and this fact probably cooperated with more important influences to give the two industries the same geographical center. Illinois led the Union in the value of her packing-house products, with an output in 1914 more than three times that of Kansas, her nearest rival. New York, Nebraska and Missouri ranked next in order, while Ohio, which once held the primacy, stood eighth in the list of states.[3]

No improvement as revolutionary as artificial cooling, the refrigerator car and modern canning, occurred during this period; but the substitution of mechanical refrigeration for natural ice refrigeration, about 1890, enabled the packing house to dispense with its enormous ice house in favor of a more compact and efficient power plant, and freed it from the climatic limitations that had previously prevented, in some cases, the choice of what would otherwise have been the most convenient and economical site for operation. Meanwhile the movement toward concentration of ownership and management that these earlier advances had so conspicuously fostered continued apace. Simultaneously scientific research was called in to assist in the technical progress of the industry, and soon made itself an indispensable aid in discovering and preparing by-products, and in perfecting and controlling preserving processes. Division of labor and organization of operations in packing houses had already reached a degree of efficiency and economy not likely to be radically bettered. For a few years following the Spanish-American War, to be sure, sanitary and labor conditions in these establishments were under public attack. This criticism subsided, however, after certain reforms had been adopted, only to be aroused in a new direction a few years later by the growing power of monopoly in this business.[4]

Pork was the packers' principal product, the dressed weight slaughtered annually exceeding five billion pounds. The quantity of beef handled varied widely from year to year, fluctuating half a billion pounds or more above and below a four-billion median; while the consumption of mutton and veal, although it increased relatively faster than that of beef or pork, never reached in the aggregate one billion pounds.[5]

[2] *Engineering Magazine*, III, 824–825, Sept. 1892.
[3] Bureau of the Census, *Manufactures*, 1914, II, 321.
[4] Twelfth Census, *Reports*, IX, 417–420; Institute of American Meat Packers, *The Packing Industry*, 101, 268–271; Committee on Agriculture, 59th Cong., 1st sess., *Hearings on the Beveridge Amendment*, passim.
[5] Bureau of the Census, *Manufactures, 1914*, II, 329, Table 21.

Five great corporations acquired a controlling position in the packing industry. These firms worked in agreement so as to exclude effective competition either in purchasing live-stock or in selling products. A Government report published immediately after the World War states that Armour and Company, Swift and Company, Morris and Company, Wilson and Company, and the Cudahy Packing Company, together with their subsidiary and affiliated organizations, not only exercised "a monopolistic control over the American meat industry," but that they had secured control, "similar in purpose if not yet in extent, over the principal substitutes for meat, such as eggs, cheese, and vegetable-oil products," and were rapidly extending their power "to cover fish and nearly every kind of food stuff."[6] Such a development was natural enough, because all these branches of food preservation and marketing were centered around the cold-storage warehouse and the refrigerator car; and in some cases the products mentioned were the logical backload for highly specialized transportation equipment that would otherwise have been partly idle and would have collected an unemployment dole from the consumer.[7] But the public was peculiarly sensitive to attempts to monopolize the food trade, and farmers and graziers naturally resented being forced to sell to a solitary buyer. Moreover powerful industrial interests were aroused against some of the packers' operations. Independent cottonseed-oil men resented their entering this industry; tanners witnessed with a jealous eye their growing domination of the domestic raw-hide and heavy-leather market, and manufacturers of fertilizer viewed with disfavor their operations in this particular field. Some of the largest soap manufacturers in the country found their products imitated under new names by packers controlling direct supplies of raw materials. Altogether the array of forces hostile to the intrusion of packers into other lines of business was imposing but helpless. To be sure an attempt to form a great merger of the three leading companies, in 1902, was relinquished in face of a threatened Government suit and public opposition. But seventeen years later these three firms, together with two associates which had grown in the meantime to something approaching equal stature, were reported to control the production and distribution of about three-fourths of the fresh meats entering into general trade in the United States, and in addition to possess "a very great competitive advantage in more than a hundred products and by-products—ranging in importance from hides and oleomargerine to sand paper and curled hair." They also controlled more than half of the export meat production of the Argentine, Brazil and Uruguay, and were heavily interested in Australian packing enterprises. They were the largest distributors of butter, eggs and canned goods in the country, and either individually or jointly were the country's largest rice merchants and extensive manufacturers of breakfast foods and staple groceries. The Government report earlier quoted asserted that—

[6] Federal Trade Commission, *Report on the Meat-Packing Industry*, Summary and Part I, 31.
[7] Collins, *The Story of Canned Foods*, 155.

"Wisconsin, the leading state in the production of butter and cheese, is covered by their creameries, condensaries and buying stations, and a similar process of concentration and control is already evident in the other principal dairy states."[8]

This interest in the dairy business was partly due to the use of milk and cream in the manufacture of butter substitutes, just as the original motive of the packers in entering the cotton-oil business was to procure raw material for vegetable shortening. Oleomargarine was manufactured in the United States before 1880, but the first reliable statistics regarding its production date from that year. So bitter was the opposition of the dairy interests to this new food product that in 1886 Congress levied a tax of two cents a pound upon it, and several states enacted legislation to discourage its manufacture. The total effect was to cause the value of output to decline between 1880 and 1890 from nearly $7,000,000 to less than $3,000,000, after which it gradually rose to $15,000,000 just before the World War. The principal ingredients used in the manufacture of oleomargarine were oleo oil, neutral lard and milk or cream, with occasionally some cottonseed oil, which had to be employed discriminatingly because it gave a peculiar flavor to the product. The residues from refining oleo oil and cottonseed oil were employed for soap stock, and one motive that induced the packers to engage in the soap manufacture was to find a profitable use for these by-products.[9]

Notwithstanding this development the factory production of butter, cheese and condensed milk was dispersed in a large number of establishments, though it showed a tendency to centralize geographically in the upper Mississippi Valley. In addition to the control exercised by the packers, its most rapidly growing branch, the manufacture of condensed milk, fell into the hands of a few companies. In 1914 three corporations produced more than 56 per cent of the total output, and the two largest of these were working in close agreement.[10] Among the minor industries that became well established during this period was the manufacture of casein. In 1900 a corporation with a capital stock of $6,500,000 was organized in New Jersey to take over a large enterprise engaged in this business. Its product was used extensively in paper making, calico printing and the manufacture of waterproof veneers, glues and paints. The same material formed the basis of egg powders, which were also manufactured by this concern.[11]

FLOUR MILLING

Although our wheat lands have by no means reached the stage of maximum production and threatened progressive exhaustion that apparently has

[8] Clement, *American Live Stock and Meat Industry*, 747–748, 761, 765; Federal Trade Commission, *Report on the Meat-Packing Industry*, Summary and Part I, 31–38.
[9] Twelfth Census, *Reports*, IX, 517, 521–524; Bureau of the Census, *Manufactures, 1914*, II, 998; Industrial Commission, *Reports*, XI, 141–142, XIX, 194–195.
[10] Bureau of the Census, *Manufactures, 1914*, II, 344; Federal Trade Commission, *Report on Milk and Milk Products, 1914–1918*, 13–16; cf., Hunziker, *The Dairy Industry*, 19–21, 46–47.
[11] *Commercial and Financial Chronicle*, LXXI, 965, Nov. 10, 1900; Twelfth Census, *Reports*, IX, 441–442.

arrived in case of our forest resources, it is significant that during the first two decades of this century the wheat flour output of the United States increased only half as fast as the population, despite the stimulation of war markets and of a growing demand in all consuming countries. Nevertheless the milling industry showed a steady growth and the quantity of wheat ground increased faster than that of corn, oats and the minor grains that contributed to its total product. Minnesota far outranked any other state in value of output, although New York, which held second place in this manufacture, ground more corn, oats and buckwheat than its northwestern rival; and early in the century Kansas advanced within five years from the tenth to the third position among flour-making states. Establishments increased steadily in size as well as number, their average capacity much more than doubling during the half century before the World War.[12]

No such radical improvement as the introduction of the roller process in the seventies marked the technical advance of the industry at this time; nor was its geography affected by new influences like the extension of wheat raising into the northwestern prairies during the preceding decades. Our great merchant-milling areas were the tier of states next to the Canadian border from Minnesota to the Pacific Coast, and the cluster of states tributary to Kansas City in the heart of the Union, both of which regions manufactured far more flour than they consumed. On the other hand important and populous sections of the country, like New England and the Central Atlantic states, and the cotton-growing district from North Carolina to Texas, produced less flour than they used. In general the greatest excess of production above local consumption was in the hard-wheat area of the Northwest, which manufactured about nine barrels per capita, as compared with less than one-tenth of a barrel per capita in New England or in the cotton region.[13] A matter of historical rather than statistical interest was the continued prosperity of Richmond, Virginia, as a flour-milling center, a rather unique instance of the survival of an important industry drawing its raw materials from the farm on the same site for well over a century. In 1914 the Gallego Mills of that city were filling the largest export orders recorded in their 116 years of active operation.[14]

About the time the roller process was introduced in the United States, conflicting patents for flour-mill machinery burdened the industry with so much litigation that the leading producers formed a protective association to defend themselves against this flood of lawsuits. Eventually the original motive for the existence of this society, which was known as the Millers' National Association, lost its former importance, and it assumed other functions, such as looking after railway charges and claims for its members,

---

[12] Twelfth Census, *Reports*, IX, 357; Bureau of the Census, *Manufactures, 1905*, III, 345; Thirteenth Census, *Reports*, X, 406–407; Bureau of the Census, *Manufactures, 1914*, II, 395, 401; Federal Trade Commission, *Commercial Wheat Flour Milling*, 7.

[13] Federal Trade Commission, *Commercial Wheat Flour Milling*, Map I.

[14] *Manufacturers' Record*, LXVI, 44, Oct. 8, 1914.

standardizing products and maintaining prices. Local mill consolidations occurred at Minneapolis, which was the country's greatest flour-manufacturing center, and elsewhere, but never acquired national importance until 1899, when some twenty-four important mills, at points as far apart as New York City, Minneapolis and Superior, were brought together in a single corporation. This combination, the United States Flour Milling Company, had an output of 40,000 or 50,000 barrels a day when its mills were running to capacity; but it did not exercise an appreciable control over prices. In general the big milling companies were the most extensively engaged in the export trade; while custom flour mills or gristmills, and the small local merchant millers, supplied a relatively larger share of the domestic consumption.[15]

CEREALS, BAKERY GOODS, AND MISCELLANEOUS GRAIN PRODUCTS

Closely allied with flour milling in respect to raw materials and markets, and sometimes associated with the latter industry under common ownership, was the manufacture of breakfast foods, which attained large proportions during the decades we are describing. But this manufacture had a distinct technique and its marketing methods, particularly in respect to intensive advertising and the featuring of brands and trade-marks, were at first different from those of the flour business. In 1899 an attempt was made to combine the larger companies into a single corporation, including about 95 per cent of the mill capacity of the country, which was estimated to be between 14,000 and 15,000 barrels a day. Although this project was not realized as originally planned, great firms, utilizing patented processes and formulas and controlling widely advertised brands, were characteristic of the industry. Most of the more important plants were in the Central West, between Niagara Falls and Minneapolis; but there were also large establishments in Canada.[16]

Consolidation was also the order of the day in the baking industries. By the middle nineties several large companies, representing for the most part combinations of plants associated by their location or by common sources of capital, occupied conspicuous positions in this business at New York City and at other important population centers. In 1898 the New York City Biscuit Company, The American Biscuit and Manufacturing Company, The United States Baking Company, and the United States Biscuit Company consolidated as The National Biscuit Company with a total capital of $55,000,000. There had been severe competition in the industry for some time previously, and the combined companies from the first operated as one. The new corporation controlled the cracker and biscuit trade between the Atlantic Ocean and the Rocky Mountains, operating

[15] U. S. Industrial Commission, *Reports*, IV, 240–246; *Commercial and Financial Chronicle*, LXIX, 1010, Nov. 11, 1899.
[16] *Commercial and Financial Chronicle*, LXVIII, 328–329, Feb. 18, 1899; LXVIII, 821, Apr. 29, 1899; LXXI, 1273, Dec. 22, 1900.

139 plants, or about 90 per cent of all the larger bakeries in the country. It started out with a settled policy of reducing its percentage of profit but of simultaneously increasing its total profit by multiplying its sales. In spite of the large share of the commercial baking business, at least in certain lines, that the consolidation controlled, the first report of the President said:

"We have no monopoly. . . . We always expect to have a great deal of competition. We purpose to get the business and to hold it by selling better goods, by furnishing them in a better condition to consumers and at lower prices . . . than our competitors are able to do."[17]

A very large increase in sales testified to the wisdom of this policy—so large, indeed, that it was at times impossible to fill the demand for goods. This was accounted for partly, however, by scientific advertising and the distribution of products in attractive sanitary packages. Within two years the combination's annual consumption of flour exceeded 2,000,000 barrels. At this time the National Biscuit Company was said to have a working agreement with the Pacific Coast Biscuit Company, which was organized almost simultaneously and controlled the biscuit, cracker and cake trade of the three Coast states, not to operate west of the Rocky Mountains, while the Pacific Coast company shipped none of its products east of that boundary. Notwithstanding the existence of these large corporations, however, many small cracker-manufacturing companies were formed during the next few years, particularly in the South.[18]

Starch, like casein, is employed in the industries as well as for food, but its manufacture falls into the category we are now considering because it is made largely from Indian corn in America, and because other food products, like glucose and maize oil, are usually produced in connection with it. Little need be added to what has been said in previous chapters concerning the statistics and technology of its production; but a certain degree of interest attaches to the fact that this industry, like so many branches of the food manufacture, fell into the hands of two large corporations, which united in 1900 to form the National Starch Manufacturing Company. The United States Glucose Company, which was in turn a large stockholder in the United States Sugar Refinery, also joined this combination, which two years later became the Corn Products Company, controlling about 84 per cent of the starch output of the country. Two other reorganizations followed before this amalgamation emerged as the present Corn Products Refining Company.

The manufacture of glucose was a well-established industry before 1890, but until the late nineties it was dispersed in relatively small establishments

[17] *Commercial and Financial Chronicle*, LX, 348, Feb. 23, 1895; LXII, 363, Feb. 22, 1896; LXVI, 82–83, Jan. 8, 1898; LXVI, 288, Feb. 5, 1898; LXVII, 274, Aug. 6, 1898; LXVIII, 327, Feb. 18, 1899; U. S. Industrial Commission, *Reports*, I, 959; XIII, 719–720.
[18] *Commercial and Financial Chronicle*, LXVIII, 928, May 13, 1899; LXIX, 442, Aug. 25, 1899; LXIX, 796, Oct. 14, 1899; LXX, 326, Feb. 17, 1900.

scattered throughout the corn belt. The quantity of sugar obtained per bushel of corn was comparatively small, and many valuable by-products were lost on account of the technical imperfections of the plants and lack of expert scientific control of processes. In 1898, several of the more important companies formed a consolidation known as the American Glucose Sugar Refining Company, later incorporated in the Corn Products Company. This new combination, or trust, set chemists at work perfecting processes and investigating new products and their possibilities. A hopeful essay was made in the direction of producing artificial rubber from corn oil, and a fairly successful rubber adulterant or dilutant was discovered. The products of the trust, which used over 20,000,000 bushels of corn in its operations, consisted of more than 500,000,000 pounds of glucose, 100,000,000 pounds of sugar, 120,000,000 pounds of starch, 2,500,000 pounds of dextrine, and 160,000 tons of residue. Altogether, the glucose companies turned out over thirty commodities entirely derived from corn, and the demand for glucose itself from confectioners, brewers, fruit driers and preservers was described as practically unlimited. Within a few years improvements in machinery and processes nearly doubled the quantity of glucose secured from a bushel of corn.[19] In few industries was the concentration of production in large plants more marked than in this one. Though the two were closely associated, the manufacture of glucose made much faster progress than that of starch. The value of their product was about equal in 1889; but twenty-five years later the output of the former was worth nearly three times that of the latter.[20]

CANNING

Among the outstanding developments in the canning industry, which increased the value of its output from $99,000,000 to $243,000,000 during the twenty-five years ending with 1913, were the establishment of pineapple canning in Hawaii; additions of the first importance, like condensed soups, to the older range of products; increased specialization of plants and processes; and the extension of scientific control to all stages of production, from the vegetable field and the orchard to the warehouse for finished goods. Unlike so many other food manufactures, canning did not fall into the hands of a few great corporations, although certain packing firms entered this field on a large scale; and in some localities, like Alaska, California and Hawaii, where the business was highly standardized and was centralized geographically, big company control was the rule. In addition to these large corporations, trade associations of canners were organized, which performed numerous services, such as standardizing prices, securing favorable

[19] *Commercial and Financial Chronicle*, LXV, 327, Aug. 21, 1897; LXV, 729, Oct. 16, 1897; LXVI, 182, Jan. 22, 1898; LXVII, 272, Aug. 6, 1898; LXVII, 319, Aug. 13, 1898; LXVII, 484, Sept. 3, 1898; LXVII, 1263, Dec. 17, 1898; LXVIII, 1134, June 10, 1899; U. S. Industrial Commission, *Reports*, XIII (Testimony), 73–79; Vogt, *The Sugar Refining Industry in the United States*, 65–69.
[20] *Commercial and Financial Chronicle*, LXX, 742–743, Apr. 14, 1900; U. S. Industrial Commission, *Reports*, XIII, 66–80, 671–674; Twelfth Census, *Reports*, IX, 576–579; Bureau of the Census, *Manufactures, 1914*, II, 412.

freight rates, and conducting joint publicity campaigns for their members. In 1907 a National Canners' Association, embracing companies in all parts of the country, was formed, which in addition to the usual functions of such a body maintains a laboratory to study problems of practical interest to the industry. A similar association, also with a special research department, was organized by canners using glass containers.[21]

Among the largest corporations in the business were the Alaska Packing Company, whose chief product was canned salmon, and the California Fruit Canners' Association. The latter company was organized in 1899, with a capital of $3,500,000, to consolidate the principal plants in that state canning fruits and vegetables. When in full operation throughout the season its output was more than 50,000,000 cans annually, or three-fourths the total product of California, which was the leading state in this industry. Although the growth in the West was relatively greater than in the older sections of the country, the canning of certain products, like oysters, lobsters and shrimps, was of necessity confined to sections of the Atlantic seaboard where these abounded. Maine, which had many lobster and sardine canneries, was also a leading vegetable canning state, sweet corn being its principal product. As late as 1901 many Maine canners still made their own cans, but the American Can Company, which had plants in the vicinity of the principal canning districts and controlled patents for can-making machinery, speedily dominated the latter business. Maryland, which was a great oyster-canning center, also packed large quantities of tomatoes, which were the most popular canning vegetable, taking precedence even of sweet corn. Wisconsin, on the other hand, was a leading pea-packing state.[22]

Peaches, which were canned largely in Maryland and California, and pineapples, which began to be packed extensively in Hawaii during the first decade of the present century, were the most popular canned fruits. By the end of this period growers raised certain fruits and vegetables, like pineapples, peaches and tomatoes, of uniform size to fit standard containers. Plant selection had also enabled the grower to produce crops that ripened simultaneously, as in case of peas, where it is important that all the pods on a vine should mature at the same time for easy harvesting. During the period we are discussing, machinery was invented to shell peas without taking the pods from the vine, to husk corn, to peel tomatoes, and to perform other preparatory cannery operations that previously required manual labor. Notwithstanding these technical improvements, however, the greatest advances in this branch of food preparation were due to the chemist and the bacteriologist, whose labors insured a more wholesome and palatable product than before.

[21] Collins, *The Story of Canned Foods*, 24, 26, 165–166, 186–187; Bureau of the Census, *Manufactures, 1914*, II, 364.
[22] American Iron and Steel Association, *Bulletin*, XXXV, 139, Sept. 25, 1901; XXXIX, 197, Dec. 30, 1905; XL, 174, Dec. 1, 1906; XLII, 5, Jan. 1, 1908; Maine, State Board of Agriculture, *Annual Report, 1900*, 198–199; *Commercial and Financial Chronicle*, LXIX, 284, Aug. 5, 1899.

CANE SUGAR

No important change occurred during this period in the production of cane sugar upon the mainland of the United States, but the annexation of Hawaii and the acquisition of Porto Rico after the Spanish-American War brought under our jurisdiction areas destined to produce, with the assurance of a protected market, well toward 1,000,000 tons of sugar annually. The Philippines contained sugar lands of great potential capacity, although they were but superficially developed, and Cuba secured preferential treatment in our market that encouraged large investments of American capital in her plantations. Altogether the effect of the War, therefore, was to make the United States an important cane-sugar producing country, and to give it a direct interest in the largest single cane growing area in the world. This new situation did not materially affect the industry in Louisiana, whose crop, except for seasonal fluctuations, remained about stationary.[23]

It would take us too far afield to record with sufficient detail to be intelligible the technical improvements made in the manufacture of sugar during this quarter of a century. They consisted in refinements of existing processes and machinery rather than in radical changes in methods of manufacture. More powerful and elaborate mills increased the proportion of juice extracted, and perfected apparatus and treatment added largely to the quantity of sugar recovered per unit of juice. So efficient are the crushers used in a modern mill that more than 98 per cent of the sugar in the cane finds its way to the juice tanks, and so completely is the crystallized sugar taken from the molasses that the latter is no longer a palatable food product. These improvements were accompanied by increasing centralization in large establishments many of which manufactured sugar from cane grown by outside planters.[24]

BEET SUGAR

Simultaneously with this great expansion of cane-sugar production under the folds—or at least under the shadow—of our flag, the output of domestic beet sugar also rapidly increased. It will be recalled that this industry, which had made several futile starts at earlier periods, finally showed signs of stable prosperity in California during the eighties. By 1893 there were seven establishments in the United States, making about 20,000 tons of beet sugar annually, of which three-fourths was produced in the state just mentioned.[25] Despite some discouragement when the sugar bounty, which had been in effect since 1890, was repealed by the Wilson Law four years later, the output continued to increase. In 1897 it had acquired sufficient importance to induce the American Sugar Refining Company to conclude

---

[23] Rolph, *Something about Sugar*, 174, 181, 188.
[24] Rolph, *Something about Sugar*, 24; Vogt, *The Sugar Refining Industry in the United States*, 77–80.
[25] American Iron and Steel Association, *Bulletin*, XXVIII, 75, Apr. 1894; *Engineering Magazine*, VII, 85, Apr. 1894.

an arrangement with Claus Spreckels, the principal manufacturer in this country, for an amicable elimination of competition between their respective products, and ten years later the refiners were said to control more than one-third of the beet-sugar output of the country. The Watsonville Factory, in California, for several years averaged 8 and 10 per cent per annum profit on its investment; and it was argued in behalf of beet farmers that three dollars worth of beets made ten dollars worth of sugar, thus opening a debate upon the outcome of which the future of the industry was to depend even more, perhaps, than upon the tariff.[26]

Several states offered bounties, which they by no means invariably paid, to encourage the erection of beet-sugar factories within their limits; but such artificial inducements had little influence upon the ultimate geography of the manufacture. This legislation, however, combined with the high duties upon sugar imposed by the Dingley Act in 1897, caused several factories to be built in Michigan and elsewhere in the Central West, comparatively few of which were immediately successful. It is significant that when the American Beet Sugar Company was organized, in 1899, to take over enterprises whose proved earning power had won the confidence of financiers, the only factories it acquired were in California and Nebraska. To these it promptly added a new plant of large capacity at Rocky Ford, Colorado.[27]

Notwithstanding a temporary reaction after the activity of the late nineties, to which agitation in favor of a preferential tariff upon Cuban and Philippine sugars contributed, the quantity of beet sugar made in the United States increased from about 80,000 tons in 1900 to over a quarter of a million tons five years later. By this time a small but growing market had been established for beet pulp and molasses, by-products which were used as stock food. During the decade following 1905 the output of our beet sugar factories increased at the rate of about 50,000 tons per annum, passing the three-quarters of a million mark in 1914 and reaching 874,222 short tons the following season. Colorado, California and Michigan were the principal contributors to these figures. During this progress the quality of beets had been improved so as to add about 2 per cent to their sugar-content and to supply a juice purer and more easily and economically worked than that with which the pioneer establishments had been forced to deal. Thus within a little more than a quarter of a century a new in-

[26] *Cassier's Magazine*, VII, 504–515, Apr. 1895; American Iron and Steel Association, *Bulletin*, XXVIII, 203, Sept. 12, 1894; XXVIII, 245, Oct. 27, 1894; XXXI, 11, Jan. 10, 1897; XXXI, 147, July 1, 1897; *Commercial and Financial Chronicle*, LXIV, 841, May 1, 1897; Vogt, *The Sugar Refining Industry in the United States*, 61–63.
[27] Rolph, *Something about Sugar*, 155; American Iron and Steel Association, *Bulletin*, XXXI, 243, Nov. 1, 1897; XXXII, 45, Mar. 15, 1898; *Commercial and Financial Chronicle*, LXV, 1070, Dec. 4, 1897; LXVI, 132–133, Jan. 15, 1898; LXVIII, 280, Feb. 11, 1899; LXIX, 1149, Dec. 2, 1899; LXIX, 1249–1250, Dec. 16, 1899; LXXI, 700, Oct. 6, 1900; *Cassier's Magazine*, XVII, 348–349, Feb. 1900; Twelfth Census, *Reports*, IX, 546–547, 550–551; Bureau of the Census, *Manufactures, 1905*, III, 451–452.

dustry was created, which employed a capital of nearly $150,000,000 and turned out an annual product valued at well toward $60,000,000.[28]

SUGAR REFINING

In 1914 the eighteen refineries in the United States reported a product of three and a third million pounds of refined sugar and 36,000,000 gallons of sirup and molasses, over 57 per cent of which was the output of six establishments.[29] This concentration was due largely to the control which one great corporation, The American Sugar Refining Company, exercised over the industry. We have already described the earlier history of that combination, whose antecedents and inception date from the eighties and early nineties. No other important "trusts," to use a popular but incorrect term, was less liked by the public or more vigorously attacked in the courts. The result is that its operations are recorded so voluminously as almost to be obscured in the minutes of numerous legislative and judicial hearings.

This testimony contributed little that is novel or significant to the general history of manufacturing. We learn how unified control accelerated the adoption of technical improvements and business economies; how obsolete refineries were scrapped and new ones erected to do their work; and how dependence upon an imported raw material encouraged the industry's concentration in highly capitalized establishments situated at strategic seaports. On the other hand this evidence records a long tale of overcapitalization, exorbitant promotion profits that became a permanent burden on consumers, railway rebates and other unfair commercial practices, and even admitted frauds against the Government.[30] The Company's history was enlivened at times by struggles with powerful and aggressive rivals, but these "sugar wars" were invariably followed by a period of profitable peace.[31] Between 1894 and 1914 the proportion of the country's annual consumption supplied directly by this corporation declined from over 75 per cent to the neighborhood of 40 per cent.

In respect to economic doctrine the founders of the American Sugar Refining Company were out of alignment with most of their contemporaries in the world of great consolidations. Although as insistent as the others upon adequate protection for themselves, they were not enthusiastic supporters of high duties upon raw sugar, such as were demanded by the planters of Louisiana and Hawaii; albeit, to be sure, their attitude on this subject

[28] Rolph, *Something about Sugar*, 159–162; American Iron and Steel Association, *Bulletin*, XL, 70, May 15, 1906; XLIV, 106, Nov. 1, 1910; Bureau of the Census, *Manufactures, 1905*, III, 450, 451; *Manufactures, 1914*, II, 429–431; Thirteenth Census, *Reports*, X, 472, 475; cf., also, Blakey, *The United States Beet-Sugar Industry and the Tariff*, and U. S. Dept. Agriculture, *Special Report on the Beet-Sugar Industry in the United States*, 1898, passim; Vogt, *The Sugar Refining Industry in the United States*, 64–65.
[29] Bureau of the Census, *Manufactures, 1914*, II, 435, 437.
[30] Cf., Van Hise, *Concentration and Control*, 13, 147–150.
[31] *Commercial and Financial Chronicle*, LXIII, 1008, Dec. 5, 1896; LXVII, 632, Sept. 24, 1898; LXIX, 441, Aug. 26, 1899; LXX, 1096, 1098–1099, June 2, 1900; LXX, 1151, June 9, 1900; U. S. Industrial Commission, *Reports*, I (testimony), 141, 158; American Sugar Refining Company, *Conditions in the Sugar Market, January–October, 1917*, 31; Vogt, *The Sugar Industry in the United States*, 49–54, 82–106.

grew slightly less heretical after 1901, when their Company began to acquire an interest in beet-sugar factories. At one time, indeed, Congressmen and Government investigators were astonished to hear this Company's president trace the paternity of all trusts but his own to the tariff.[32]

While a modern refinery is as a rule a much larger and better equipped establishment than its predecessor of 1890, and many labor-saving devices have been introduced during the interval, processes and machinery are the same in principle that they were at the earlier date. The most notable innovation has been in packing. Refined sugar, instead of being sold to household consumers from bulk containers—usually barrels—as was the custom only a generation ago, is now distributed in sanitary cartons, like breakfast foods and innumerable other table products. Furthermore a greater variety of sugars than formerly, ranging from wrapped cubes to the finest types of pulverized, is now supplied to the general public; and with the introduction of containers that go directly to the purchaser the advertising importance of special brands has vastly increased.[33]

ALCOHOLIC LIQUORS

In a country like our own, where the tariff has always occupied a prominent place in economic discussion, the prosperity or depression of an industry has often been attributed to legislation; but rarely has the fiat of the lawmaker decreed the abolition of a manufacture of first statistical rank, as occurred with the adoption of the Eighteenth Amendment. In 1914 the manufacture of alcoholic liquors in the United States employed a capital of more than $900,000,000, and its annual product was valued at over two-thirds of a billion dollars. Moreover it was far from being a decadent industry, notwithstanding the spread of state prohibition in the West and South; for during the preceding quarter of a century the annual per capita consumption of these beverages had increased from less than 15 gallons to over 26 gallons, an increment of 55 per cent. Nearly 2,000 establishments were engaged in this manufacture, and they had well toward 90,000 employes upon their payrolls. These figures were fairly complete for the production of wine and beer, but the unreported output of illicit distilleries was always large. For example, the number of illegal stills seized by Federal officers in 1898 was 2,391, and ten were said to escape detection for every one captured by the authorities.[34]

New York and Pennsylvania were the leading brewing states, and at the close of this period Illinois and Kentucky held first rank in distilling.

---

[32] U. S. Industrial Commission, *Reports*, I (testimony), 101; *cf.*, *Commercial and Financial Chronicle*, LXVI, 132, Jan. 15, 1898.

[33] Rolph, *Something about Sugar*, 74–75; U. S. Industrial Commission, *Reports*, I (testimony), 91, 106, 141; American Sugar Refining Company, *A Century of Sugar Refining in the United States*, 1816–1916, pp. 16–21.

[34] Twelfth Census, *Reports*, IX, 616; Bureau of the Census, *Manufactures, 1914*, II, 982–985; *Statistical Abstract of the United States, 1923*, 841; U. S. Industrial Commission, *Reports*, I, 231, 843.

California far outstripped any of her sister commonwealths in the production of wine. Indian corn was the principal raw material used by both the brewer and the distiller, its consumption for alcoholic beverages exceeding half a billion bushels annually.[35] Of the three branches of the liquor manufacture, distilling was the most highly speculative and was more largely monopolized by great corporations. No historical continuity existed between the early whisky pools of the seventies and eighties and later combinations in this business, but both were begotten by similar conditions and the precedents of the pools doubtless influenced the practices of the trusts. The Distilling and Cattle Feeding Company, which took over the business of the Distillers and Cattle Feeders Trust in 1890, like its predecessor fell into financial difficulties five years later and passed through a receivership and a stormy reorganization. Competition, the prejudice of customers against its alleged monopoly, and unsatisfactory distributing arrangements, interfered with its sales and profits. Moreover the Supreme Court of the State of Illinois handed down a decision declaring that the Company had exceeded its powers under its charter because it had purchased or leased distilleries, not to operate them, but to shut them down in order to eliminate competition.[36]

In 1896, soon after the Company was placed in the hands of receivers and this court decision was delivered against it, the American Spirits Manufacturing Company was organized under the laws of New York State, to take over the principal distilleries of the old company; but only sixteen or seventeen of the eighty-four establishments originally controlled by the former corporation were retained and the remainder were either sold or dismantled.[37] Two years later, a second combination, The Standard Distilling and Distributing Company, was incorporated under the laws of New Jersey to unite the distilleries outside of those controlled by the American Spirits Manufacturing Company. The establishments owned by each combination were widely distributed geographically, and the two groups, operating under an amicable agreement, produced about the same quantity of corn spirits annually. In 1899 The Kentucky Distilleries and Warehouse Company was incorporated, also under the laws of New Jersey, to combine the Bourbon or Kentucky whisky manufacturers of the United States, and the Standard Distilling and Distributing Company was represented on its directorate. This combination was said to embrace at the time of its organization fifty-seven firms. The same year The American Spirits Manufacturing Company, The Kentucky Distilleries and Warehouse Company, The Spirits Distributing Company, The Standard Distilling and Distributing Company, and The Distilling Company of America

[35] Twelfth Census, *Reports*, IX, 601–602, 614–615; Bureau of the Census, *Manufactures, 1914*, II, 983.
[36] U. S. Industrial Commission, Reports, I (testimony), 167–169; *Commercial and Financial Chronicle*, LIX, 1103–1104, Dec. 22, 1894; LX, 259, Feb. 9, 1895; LX, 1058, June 15, 1895.
[37] *Commercial and Financial Chronicle*, LXIII, 152, July 25, 1896; U. S. Industrial Commission, *Reports*, I, 832–833.

formed a new consolidation, The Distilling Company of America, with an authorized capital stock of $125,000,000. Powerful as was this group, however, it at once encountered formidable opposition from the independent distillers of Kentucky, who were organized as an association and controlled half the Bourbon output. At no time, therefore, did the trust or group of trusts have a complete monopoly on the trade.[38]

Peoria, Illinois, which was favored by its situation in the midst of the corn belt and near a coal supply, and possessed an abundance of cold water of uniform temperature throughout the year for cooling mash, was one of the principal distilling centers of the United States. While most of the spirits distilled in America were made from corn, considerable rye whisky was manufactured in Kentucky and the East, especially Pennsylvania and Maryland. Corn spirits were the quantity-output product of the business, and one Peoria distillery had a capacity of 60,000 gallons a day, while Kentucky whiskies were sold almost exclusively under brands. Outside of the more important producing centers were several hundred small distilleries, mostly scattered through the South, which sold their output in their immediate neighborhood. Rum was still made principally in New England.[39]

While the manufacture of distilled liquors thus fell increasingly under the control of combinations operating throughout the whole country, the brewing industry showed a tendency to fall into the hands of local consolidations. An exception was the American Malting Company, another trust of precarious prosperity which was organized in 1897 and acquired malt houses and elevators throughout the territory from Atlantic tidewater to the grain fields of the Northwest. The earnings of this combination proved disappointing. The report of the company in 1900 stated:

"The maltsters owning the plants your company acquired made money for themselves, and when your company was organized there was in the trade generally a fair margin of profit. From the inception of your company, although it sells about 60 per cent of all the malt consumed by brewers in the United States who do not make their own malt, the prices at which its product have been sold were not judiciously established with reference to cost, or firmly maintained with reference to competitors."

The result was an increase of competition and unprofitable price-cutting.[40] Among the local brewery consolidations formed at the turn of the century were the United Breweries Company of Chicago, embracing 13 of the leading establishments in that city, the Cleveland and Sandusky Brewing Company, combining 13 breweries in Cleveland and Sandusky, the Maryland Brewery Company, comprising 16 of the 20 breweries in Baltimore, the

---

[38] *Commercial and Financial Chronicle*, LXVI, 1190, June 18, 1898; LXVII, 957, Nov. 5, 1898; LXVIII, 232, Feb. 4, 1899; LXVIII, 1224, June 24, 1899; LXIX, 494, Sept. 2, 1899.
[39] U. S. Industrial Commission, *Reports*, I (testimony), 201–204, 217, 231, 836, 837.
[40] *Commercial and Financial Chronicle*, LXIX, 908, Oct. 28, 1899; LXX, 478–479, Mar. 10, 1900; U. S. Industrial Commission, *Reports*, XIII, 932.

Boston Breweries Company, later known as the Massachusetts Brewery Company, producing about 50 per cent of the total product of Boston in 10 establishments, and the Schuylkill Brewing Company, combining the brewing interests in Schuylkill, Northumberland and Montour Counties, Pennsylvania, and controlling the 12 largest plants in the anthracite district.[41]

The production of malt liquor increased faster than that of spirits, and notwithstanding the fact that consumption was also expanding rapidly this business was subject to keen competition. Breweries were widely distributed throughout the country and most of them served a strictly local market, although some large firms sold nationally advertised brands of bottled beer in all parts of the United States and abroad. As a result of this competition, not only among establishments in the same city but also between local and outside establishments, brewers entered the retail trade and controlled in some instances hundreds or thousands of saloons for the distribution of their products. We shall see directly that somewhat similar conditions of production and marketing caused the largest manufacturers of tobacco to adopt a similar device.

TOBACCO

A word remains to be added about the tobacco manufacture, chiefly because its history during this period confirms strikingly the tendency of industries producing comestibles to fall into the hands of monopolies or near monopolies. Such industries had an assured, stable, expanding and suggestible market. The last qualification is particularly important, because mass response to advertising suggestion, and the possibility this offered of creating a brand habit among large bodies of consumers, gave purveyors of standardized and easily recognized package goods a national market, with all the attendant economies of quantity production and highly systematized methods of distribution.

Until about 1890 all branches of the tobacco manufacture were in the hands of small producers, or of larger firms operating independently among their equals. That year the five principal cigarette factories of the country were combined as the American Tobacco Company. Cigarette making was the youngest department of this industry and the one in which machinery was most extensively employed and products were most highly standardized. Within a few years, although at the cost of a bitter struggle, the Company succeeded in virtually monopolizing this branch of the business. Simultaneously it extended its operations to other lines by purchasing several large establishments making plug and smoking tobacco. The latter interests were for a time combined in an allied organization, the Continental Tobacco Company, with which the American Tobacco Company

[41] *Commercial and Financial Chronicle*, LXVI, 471, Mar. 5, 1898; LXVII, 323, Aug. 13, 1898; LXVII, 1358, Dec. 31, 1898; LXVIII, 331, Feb. 18, 1899; LXVIII, 1074, June 3, 1899; LXX, 384, Feb. 24, 1900; LXXI, 289–290, Aug. 11, 1900; U. S. Industrial Commission, *Reports*, XIII, 105.

ultimately consolidated. The manufacture of snuff and of cigars passed under the control, or at least the partial control, of the men who dominated the older combination, although separate companies were organized to handle these departments. Even the retailer was supplanted in large population centers by the United Cigar Stores, a chain of distributing agencies selling directly to consumers, which formed part of this great alliance.[42]

Machines for making cigarettes, cutting and granulating smoking tobacco, and pressing plug tobacco, of which only the first-mentioned were at all elaborate, had been invented before 1890, but much of the present mechanization of the industry dates from the period we are now describing. The advent of the "trust" was marked by the consolidation of plants and the erection of larger factories, and by the rapid adoption of modern manufacturing economies. Among the latter was machinery for making cheap cigars containing a chopped filler. Upon the whole, however, cigar making remained a manual occupation conducted in small shops, which outnumbered all other establishments engaged in the manufacture of tobacco by more than six to one. While the number of cigars made annually in the United States remained about stationary, fluctuating around the seven-billion mark, the number of cigarettes made in the country rose from 3,000,000,000 to nearly 18,000,000,000 during the first fifteen years of the century.[43]

The powerful group of allied companies that dominated the tobacco industry was one of the earliest American organizations to inaugurate an aggressive campaign to capture foreign markets from their national producers. One of the first overseas fields thus invaded was Japan, where the American Tobacco Company organized and bought up cigarette factories and acquired such a preponderant position that the authorities, either alarmed by this foreign usurpation or anxious to pocket the profits foreigners were making in its territories, converted the business into a Government monopoly. Factories were also established in Canada and Australia to evade the high tariff on imported cigarettes. Mexico came into the folds of the trust, and Germany was invaded. Several Havana cigar factories were taken over. But the most spectacular campaign was in Great Britain, where a long struggle ended in a compromise with British producers and the creation of what was virtually an international tobacco trust.[44]

In 1904 the American Tobacco Company of New Jersey was organized to merge the earlier company of the same name with its associate combinations. Three years later an investigator wrote:

"Besides controlling about 75 per cent of the entire American trade in cigarettes, plug, chewing and smoking tobacco, and snuff, and about 25 per cent of

[42] Jacobstein, *The Tobacco Industry in the United States*, 104–112; U. S. Industrial Commission, *Reports*, XIII, 317, 329.
[43] Jacobstein, *The Tobacco Industry in the United States*, 85–93; Twelfth Census, *Reports*, IX, 672; *Statistical Abstract of the United States, 1923*, p. 352.
[44] Jacobstein, *The Tobacco Industry in the United States*, 112–115; U. S. Industrial Commission, *Reports*, XIII, 322.

the cigar industry, it also possesses its own licorice plant, tin-foil factory, pipe manufacturing company, machine company and retail as well as wholesale agencies and controls directly some tobacco land in Cuba and in the United States. Since 1904, its activities have expanded. The real magnitude of this $450,000,000 Trust will be more fully appreciated when we consider, in another connection, its financial operations. The circle of the Trust organization is now practically complete from the ownership or control of tobacco lands to the manufacture of products and the marketing of goods. In no other industry has there been developed so complete and so splendid an organization as the Tobacco Trust."[45]

To be sure this great industrial structure had been built up with brutal energy upon ruthless competition and unfair practices. But it was a typical product of an age from which we have by no means emerged as yet, and admirable in its way.

[45] Jacobstein, *The Tobacco Industry in the United States*, 115–116.

CHAPTER XIX

INDUSTRIAL FUELS AND MISCELLANEOUS MANUFACTURES

Industrial Fuels, 281. Mineral and Vegetable Oils, 283. Chemical Industries, 284. Fertilizers, 289. Miscellaneous Industries of the Chemical Group, 291. Cultural Manufactures, 293.

INDUSTRIAL FUELS

In 1899 the United States passed Great Britain in coal output, and took first rank among the countries of the world in both the production and the consumption of industrial fuel. Between 1893 and 1913 the amount of coal mined in the United States increased more than three-fold, and in 1914 our industrial establishments used 180,000,000 tons of coal, 32,000,000 tons of coke, nearly 50,000,000 barrels of fuel oil, and 285,000,000,000 cubic feet of gas.[1] The natural-gas belt extended during this period from the territory tributary to Pittsburgh to Indiana and farther West, and, as we have seen, the development of new wells in the prairie states encouraged the growth of an important group of fuel-using industries like the manufacture of vitrified and paving brick and tile, cement, glass and certain classes of metal goods in their vicinity.[2] Nevertheless in 1915 West Virginia and Pennsylvania were the two largest producers, although Oklahoma ranked third among the states in output. Taking the country as a whole the amount of natural gas marketed annually continued to increase, and after 1910 a growing proportion of this product, especially in Oklahoma, was used as a source for gasoline. Meanwhile a remarkable increase occurred in the use of artificial gas for fuel, the amount thus consumed rising from 2,500,000,000 cubic feet in 1898 to 185,000,000,000 feet in 1915. The consumption of illuminating gas increased from 16,000,000,000 cubic feet in 1898 to over a 109,000,000,000 feet ten years later; but it decreased thereafter, declining in 1915 to less than 81,000,000,000 feet.[3]

Between the early nineties and the outbreak of the European War, the annual production of coke in the United States more than quadrupled, rising from an average of less than 10,000,000 tons a year to over 46,000,000 tons in 1913. This expansion occurred without a notable shifting of centers of production. Pennsylvania was the leading coke-producing state, and was credited with about two-thirds of the country's output.[4]

---

[1] *Statistical Abstract of the United States*, 1923, 272, 290; cf., *Cassier's Magazine*, x, 298–304, Aug. 1896.
[2] *Commercial and Financial Chronicle*, LXVII, 126, July 16, 1898; *Cassier's Magazine*, XVIII, 58–64, May 1900; American Iron and Steel Association, *Bulletin*, XXXVIII, 169, Nov. 25, 1904; *Statistical Abstract of the United States*, 1923, 277.
[3] *Mineral Resources of the United States*, 1915, Part II, 1033, 1038–1039.
[4] *Mineral Resources of the United States*, 1915, 520–523; cf., *Cassier's Magazine*, XIX, 197–206, Jan. 1901.

By-product coke ovens were still more or less experimental in the early nineties, having been used with marked success in Europe for only a little more than a decade, and though their adoption was actively advocated in the United States, it took a considerable period to overcome the prejudice of industrial consumers against coke made by this method; and a symmetrical demand for the by-products themselves had not been developed. Moreover, beehive-oven practice had recently been improved so as to increase materially the quantity of coke obtained from a given quantity of coal. Indeed the first by-product plant in America, which went into operation at Syracuse early in 1892, was erected by the Solvay Process Company to make ammonia for its soda manufacture; and the ovens were of the type developed by the parent Solvay Company in Belgium ten years before. The first by-product works designed primarily to make coke for blast furnaces were a battery of sixty Otto-Hoffmann ovens erected in 1894 by the Cambria Steel Company at Johnstown, Pennsylvania. Tar and sulphate of ammonia were recovered at this plant. Before it was built a small consignment of Connellsville coal was shipped to Germany for an experimental test in the furnaces already in operation there.[5]

After this progress was rapid, although by far the greater part of the coke produced in America continued to be made in beehive ovens. The extension of the new method tended to shift the coking industry to points where there was a market for fuel gas and the other by-products recovered. By the close of the century the quantity of coke thus manufactured in the United States was about 1,500,000 tons, or approximately 5 per cent of the total output; by 1913 it had risen to nearly 13,000,000 tons, or over 27 per cent of all the coke produced in the country, nearly half of which was made by the United States Steel Corporation. The total value of by-products recovered at the latter date was over $16,000,000, but nearly $80,000,000, worth of equally good materials was still wasted in beehive ovens. In the five coke-producing states of the South the percentage of the total output made in by-product ovens was nearly half, a much larger proportion than for the country as a whole. Since the method was introduced from Europe, average oven capacity had been increased from less than five tons to twenty tons a day, and the amount of coal a unit crew of men was capable of coking had multiplied more than ten-fold. In no other department allied with the metallurgical industry had there been an equal growth in tonnage efficiency.

Just before the outbreak of the World War, the Carnegie Steel Company contracted for the construction of benzol works at Farrell, Pennsylvania. This was a new departure in by-product production in the United States, although the process was already familiar in Europe. A less novel enter-

[5] American Iron and Steel Association, *Bulletin*, XXVIII, 257, Nov. 14, 1894; XXVIII, 235, Oct. 17, 1894; Twelfth Census, *Reports*, x, 691; Bureau of the Census, *Report on Manufactures*, 1905, IV, 534, 537; U. S. National Museum, *Bulletin*, 102, Part 4, pp. 11–12; *Engineering Magazine*, XXII, 49–50, Oct. 1901.

prise was a large creosoting plant established in connection with a new battery of by-product coke ovens erected in 1914 at Woodward, Alabama. While the total coke output of the country increased less than five-fold between 1893 and the latter date, the output of by-product coke multiplied nearly one-thousand-fold. Several plants designed primarily for the recovery of chemicals, or already making this an important feature of their operations, were erected or planned shortly before the World War. We were still dependent upon Europe, however, for part of our supply of creosote, benzol and similar coal derivatives, notwithstanding the fact that we had an abundance of raw materials in the United States for their production.[6]

MINERAL AND VEGETABLE OILS

Mineral oil plays such an important rôle in our modern civilization that it is difficult to realize that it is a comparatively recent arrival upon the industrial stage. Between 1889 and 1914 the value of petroleum products produced in the United States rose from $85,000,000 to $396,000,000. The principal item in this increase was fuel oils, whose output rose from 6,000,000 barrels to 160,000,000 barrels; next in order of growth were lighter petroleum products, including gasoline, for which a rapidly expanding demand existed on account of its use in internal-combustion engines, which multiplied five-fold; this was followed by lubricants, which increased about three-fold. Meanwhile the growth in the production of illuminating oils was but moderate, testifying to the increasing use of gas and electricity for lighting.[7]

No new discoveries of revolutionary importance marked the progress of the vegetable-oil industry, although new uses for its products were constantly being discovered. In the case of cottonseed oil several of these were in the food manufacture. The consumption of cottolene, crisco and similar products grew rapidly. "Refined lard," a compound of lard and cottonseed oil, with suet added to harden it, became a recognized packing-house commodity. As early as 1892, 300,000 barrels of cottonseed oil were used annually at Chicago, mostly in the manufacture of food fats, and about two-thirds as much at Omaha, Kansas City, and St. Louis. Twenty-thousand barrels were shipped annually to the Maine coast for packing sardines, and ten times that amount was exported to Rotterdam where it was used for making butterine.[8]

[6] *Mineral Industry*, IV, 216; V, 94; X, 135; XI, 158; XV, 173–176; XIII, 103; *Engineering Magazine*, XI, 211, May 1896; XXII, 41–59, Oct. 1901; *Iron Age*, XCIII, 915, Apr. 9, 1914; XCIII, 1395, May 28, 1914; XCIII, 1462, June 11, 1914; XCIV, 235, July 23, 1914; XCIV, 1349, Dec. 10, 1914; *Manufacturers' Record*, LXV, 49–50, Jan. 15, 1914; LXVI, 41, July 23, 1914; LXVI, 45, Sept. 24, 1914; American Iron and Steel Association, *Bulletin*, XXXII, 193, Dec. 15, 1898; U. S. National Museum, *Bulletin*, 102, Part 2, 12; U. S. Department of the Interior, *Technical Paper 89*, 6, 11–13; Federal Trade Commission, *Report on the Fertilizer Industry, 1916*, 39–44.

[7] Bureau of the Census, *Manufactures, 1914*, II, 582, table 16.

[8] *Engineering Magazine*, III, 821–831, Sept. 1892; *Boston Journal of Commerce*, XLIII, 328, Feb. 24, 1894.

For several years this manufacture was dominated by the two great corporations described in an earlier chapter: the American Cotton Oil Company and the Southern Cotton Oil Company. In 1894 the properties owned by the former corporation included 72 oil mills, 15 refineries, 4 lard and cottolene plants, 9 soap factories, 15 cotton gins, 3 compressors and 2 fertilizer plants—an enumeration that suggests the industry's chief products and by-products. In 1901 the plants of the Southern Cotton Oil Company and a number of other seed mills in the South were purchased by the Virginia-Carolina Chemical Company. Smaller corporations operating several establishments were also organized in different parts of the South and large packing companies, such as Armour, Swift and Morris, controlled important mill groups. Combinations, however, did not monopolize the business. Independent mills sprang up on every side, some of which were of first rank although the majority were small establishments near local shipping points. These were encouraged by the higher freight on seed as compared with oil, and by the existence of a neighborhood market near the mills for the seed-cake and meal that they produced.[9]

While cotton seed became the principal source of vegetable oil in the United States after 1880, the longer established manufacture of linseed oil was also a growing business. The National Linseed Oil Company, which was the principal combination in this industry, became involved in financial difficulties during the 1893 depression through an attempt to corner the seed market and, after several years of discord among its shareowners and security-holders, was reorganized and combined with several previously independent companies in 1898. At that time the properties included nearly 40 different oil mills, about the same number of flaxseed elevators and warehouses, a castor-oil mill, several tank stations, and a number of tank cars. The quantity of linseed crushed annually in the United States was about 16,000,000 bushels, yielding in the neighborhood of 40,000,000 gallons of oil and 300,000 tons of linseed cake. A duty of 20 cents a gallon was levied on imported oil, although the domestic product sometimes sold as low as 25 cents a gallon. Flaxseed was also protected, for the benefit of the prairie farmers, by a duty of 25 cents a barrel. Since the flax crop of the country was limited, however, manufacturers competed against each other for seed, the price of which fluctuated widely, causing a corresponding instability of oil prices. At the time the National Linseed Oil Company was reorganized as the American Linseed Company, it controlled about 85 per cent of the business in the United States.[10]

CHEMICAL INDUSTRIES

In no branch of manufacturing was progress more marked during this period than in the production of chemicals. Some branches of this in-

[9] *Commercial and Financial Chronicle*, LIX, 795–796, Nov. 3, 1894; *Manufacturers' Record*, XXXIX, 429, June 27, 1901; XL, 245, Oct. 31, 1901; Federal Trade Commission, *Report on the Fertilizer Industry, 1916*, 62–68; 189–190.
[10] *Commercial and Financial Chronicle*, LX, 712, Apr. 20, 1895; LXII, 275–276, Feb. 8, 1896; LXVII, 1161, Dec. 3, 1898; LXVII, 1206, Dec. 10, 1898

dustry dated back for many years, as the earlier chapters of this history indicate; but during the two decades preceding the World War both the variety and the quantity of chemicals manufactured in the United States increased remarkably. At the beginning of this period our manufactures included alum and sulphate of aluminum, bichromates of potassium and sodium, borax, bromine, calcium carbide, potassium cyanide, the various sodas, sodium peroxide, sulphuric acid, superphosphates, copperas and blue vitriols, besides, naturally, a great number of minor chemicals and drugs. The production of some of these was still in its infancy, and indeed, began after 1890.[11]

Of the raw materials employed in the chemical industries, sulphur is one of the most important. Domestic production in 1893 was confined to a small amount from mines in Utah, and a few hundred tons obtained in an experimental way in Louisiana. During the next few years output did not materially increase, and at the end of the century the country produced considerably less than 5,000 tons, of which only 50 tons came from Louisiana. Two years later the product of the latter State rose to over 8,000 tons; and the following year our national product was just under 40,000 tons. This was but a fraction of our consumption, which reached 570,000 tons per annum, of which well over half was obtained from pyrites which we largely imported. Within twelve months, however, the production of Louisiana alone increased by a single bound to nearly 200,000 tons.[12] The output of pyrites declined rapidly, and Sicilian sulphur ceased to compete in the American market.

The use of sulphur in connection with the heavy-chemical industry was principally in the manufacture of sulphuric acid, which was centered largely on the Atlantic Coast. This was partly because sulphuric-acid works had hitherto employed imported raw materials, and partly because their product was largely used in branches of manufacture for which the raw materials were either imported or were found mainly on the Atlantic seaboard. Baltimore had eleven firms engaged in this industry in 1897, producing 340 tons daily, the greater part of which was used in the manufacture of superphosphates from southern rock. The remainder was employed in chrome works, copper works, and soda-water— carbonic acid gas—factories. About this time chemical works drifted inland, partly on account of the development of phosphate mining in Tennessee, and several of the largest concerns in the South and West substituted pyrites for sulphur in making acid. Another great sulphur and pyrites consuming industry was the preparation of sulphite liquor for digesting and bleaching wood pulp. This encouraged the extension of the industry to regions where it would not otherwise have established itself. In 1905 the Lake Superior Power Company at Sault St. Marie was using its own pyrites to make bleaching liquor for its paper

[11] *Mineral Industry*, v, 92–93.
[12] *Mineral Industry*, iv, 62; xii, 314; xiii, 382–383.

mills. Other establishments were erected in the West, where there was a demand for sulphuric acid in connection with the mining industry; and in 1914, Swift and Company of Chicago erected a large plant in New Orleans, the product of which was used in making fertilizers.[13] Three-fourths of the pyrites used for making sulphuric acid in the United States came from abroad, principally from Spain, and this material was generally preferred to sulphur by manufacturers. Many plants which had previously employed sulphur had been equipped to use pyrites, because the former was too expensive to be used. Sulphur was worth at the outbreak of the War about $22 a ton. Sulphuric acid could be made for $7 a ton from pyrites, because the copper and other metals in that material made it valuable to mine without reference to the sulphuric acid that it yielded. In fact, owners of pyrites mines could give away their sulphuric acid if forced to do so. This substitution of pyrites for brimstone began in the early eighties, when 85 per cent of the acid manufactured in America was made from the latter material. By 1914 nearly three-fourths was made from pyrites; 13 per cent was derived as a by-product from zinc smelters, 10 per cent from copper smelters, and only about 2 per cent was still made from sulphur.[14]

It is indicative of the rapid growth of this industry that during the five years ending with 1913 the amount of pyrites mined in the United States increased from 247,000 to 341,000 tons; while the amount imported rose from 689,000 to 851,000 tons. By the outbreak of the World War the total production of sulphuric acid of all grades in the United States, including by-product acid obtained in the smelter industry, was rapidly approaching 4,000,000 tons per annum. Most of this was used in the manufacture of fertilizers from phosphate rock, of sulphate of ammonia in connection with the destructive distillation of coal, and of alum. Large quantities were also used in the steel industry for pickling purposes, and the concentrated acid was employed for refining petroleum and in the explosives industry.[15]

Ammonia ranks next to the acids as the principal reagent employed in the heavy chemical industry. It was obtained largely as a by-product from coke, and originally was produced at municipal gas works. With the introduction of by-product coke ovens during the early nineties, the first of which, as we have seen, were erected expressly to make ammonia, output rapidly expanded. A very large demand was created for anhydrous ammonia by the rapid growth of cold storage, but the principal increase of consumption was in the manufacture of fertilizers. As a result production rose from less than 28,000 tons in 1899 to 130,000 tons thirteen years later. Meanwhile the proportion made by coke ovens enlarged from 31 per cent

---

[13] *Mineral Industry*, VI, 125; 559–560; XIV, 521; *Manufacturers' Record*, LXV, 50, Jan. 29, 1914.
[14] *Manufacturers' Record*, LXVI, 53, Sept. 3, 1914; *Chemical and Metallurgical Engineering*, XXXIII, 269, May 1926.
[15] *Mineral Industry*, XXIII, 701–702; Federal Trade Commission, *Report on the Fertilizer Industry, 1916*, 104–106.

to 79 per cent. Even at the latter date, however, the domestic output failed by more than 100,000 tons to meet the country's annual requirements.[16]

Another great group of heavy or industrial chemicals was the alkalis, the modern manufacture of which may be said to have been established in this country in 1884 when the works of the Solvay Process Company at Syracuse, New York, began to manufacture soda ash. Early in the period we are discussing the output of soda in the United States had risen to 160,000 metric tons a year, and in addition to the works at Syracuse, which employed the Solvay or ammonia process, alkalis were already made by the electrolytic method at Saltville, Virginia.[17]

It was the successful introduction of the Solvay process and the development of the electrolytic process in this country that promoted the American chemical industry from a local, comparatively unimportant and technically backward branch of manufacturing to a leading position in the chemical industry of the world. Naturally this manufacture concentrated in the vicinity of raw materials—near the salt wells at Syracuse, in the neighborhood of Detroit, where Wyandotte became a great alkali-producing center, and in Southwestern Virginia. With the introduction of the electrolytic process, the presence of water power also became a determining factor in the localization of this industry, and for this reason large works were established at Niagara Falls and Sault St. Marie. The United States was blessed beyond most European countries with cheap and abundant water power and had ample supplies of coal, salt, lime and sulphur. Its only handicap as compared with the older industries of Europe was the high cost of labor and, for a time at least, the relative scarcity of experienced industrial chemists.[18]

Once introduced, the manufacture of soda ash extended rapidly. In 1899 works for manufacturing bicarbonate of soda were established as far West as Laramie, Wyoming. The carbon dioxide previously wasted from the various breweries of Milwaukee was likewise used for this manufacture. Glass makers also had begun to produce the soda ash they required, to some extent, in their own establishments. By this time the electrolytic process was a proved success, and two great companies were organized in 1899 to make caustic soda and chlorine by this method. The American Alkali Company was formed with a capital of $30,000,000, and planned to manufacture at Sault Ste. Marie in Northern Michigan 170,000 tons of caustic soda and 93,000 tons of bleaching powder per annum, thus supplying well toward half of the domestic consumption of these chemicals, which were used for paper making, soap making, oil refining, cotton finishing, bleaching and disinfecting, laundry and cleaning purposes, and a variety of minor purposes. The following year a smaller

[16] Mineral Industry, x, 160–161; xix, 30; xxi, 32; Federal Trade Commission, *Report on the Fertilizer Industry, 1916*, 43.
[17] Mineral Industry, iv, 60.
[18] Mineral Industry, iv, 57; vi, 119–120; viii, 518–519; 530–532.

rival corporation, the Castner Electrolytic Alkali Company, was formed, with its principal plant at Niagara Falls.[19]

The accidental discovery in the middle eighties that calcium carbide when brought into contact with water produced a gas that might be used for heating and lighting started a new industry in this country. During the early nineties burners were perfected for using this illuminant, and by 1897 four establishments with a total output of 4,000,000 pounds per annum were engaged in manufacturing carbide. The following year a single corporation, the Union Carbide Company of Chicago, secured control of the business in America, and for a time concentrated production at Niagara Falls, the chief seat of the electro-chemical industry in this country, where works were erected which had a capacity of about 8,000 tons per month. Later another plant was established at Sault Ste. Marie.[20]

Another development of this period was the commercial manufacture of compressed or liquefied gases, the sales of which more than tripled during the first decade of the century. In 1909 a chemical manufacturer of Wyandotte, Michigan, made the first delivery of liquid chlorine in cylinders, thus reducing to its simplest terms the principal bleaching agent produced in the country.[21] Some branches of the chemical industry were particularly sensitive to the effects of customs legislation: for example, sodium cyanide, which is extensively used in the reduction of gold and silver, and of which 16,000,000 to 18,000,000 tons per annum were at one time manufactured in the United States, virtually ceased to be produced here after it was placed upon the free list. The manufacture of certain plastics, and particularly of artificial silk, was retarded by the heavy excise on the grain alcohol extensively employed, directly or indirectly, in this branch of manufacture.[22] The principal episode in the manufacture of miscellaneous and minor chemicals during this period was the organization of the General Chemical Company at Albany, New York, in 1899, with a capital of $25,000,000, to take over the business hitherto conducted by twelve of the leading companies in the country.[23]

It would lead us into confusing detail to follow all the ramifications of this rapidly expanding group of industries through these twenty years. Its aggregate product rose in value from $48,000,000 in 1899 to $158,000,000 in 1914; and though these figures contain duplications and may not represent absolute measures of output, they record with reasonable truthfulness the rate of growth. This expansion, however, was chiefly in the production of heavy chemicals, of which typical examples have just been given,

[19] *Mineral Industry*, VIII, 518–519, 530–532; *Commercial and Financial Chronicle*, LXIX, 1194, Dec. 9, 1899; LXXI, 344, Aug. 18, 1900.
[20] Mineral Industry, VI, 67; VII, 99; XV, 89.
[21] *Chemical and Metallurgical Engineering*, XXXIII, 300, May 1926; Thirteenth Census, *Reports*, X, 546.
[22] Bureau of the Census, *Manufactures, 1905*, IV, 476–477; *Mineral Industries*, XXIII, 165.
[23] *Commercial and Financial Chronicle*, LXVIII, 330, Feb. 18, 1899; LXVIII, 571, Mar. 25, 1899; United States Industrial Commission, *Reports*, XIII, 674–676.

for in this branch of the industry the advantage of domestic raw materials and power and proximity to markets were determining factors in international competition.[24] Germany is to be credited with most of the industry's laboratory progress, but its mechanical advance owed much to the United States. This was particularly true of applied electrolytic processes, a feature of the manufacture that suddenly became prominent at this time. In 1899 less than 3 per cent of the chemicals made in the United States, as measured by value, were produced by the aid of electricity; twenty years later this proportion had risen to more than 15 per cent.[25]

FERTILIZERS

With the increasing employment of domestic raw materials, especially the phosphate rocks in the South, in the manufacture of fertilizers the principal seat of this industry drifted from Baltimore, where it was first established in America about 1850, toward South Carolina and Georgia. By 1900 the importation of guano, upon which the industry was largely based at first, had almost ceased.[26] Phosphate rock was imported at this time from Germany and Spain, although the principal sources of this material were already in our South Atlantic states. German potash and Chilean nitrates, which eventually contributed largely to this manufacture, began to come into the country in quantities during the next five years.[27] As recently as 1905 only two-thirds of the ammonium sulphate produced by our by-product coke ovens, and less than 10 per cent of the cottonseed meal and cake made by our oil mills, were employed in this manufacture.[28] The situation changed rapidly, however, for the amount of cottonseed meal thus used nearly quadrupled and that of ammonium sulphate multiplied fifteen-fold during the following decade. Nevertheless phosphate rock, of which over 2,000,000 tons were manufactured into fertilizer in 1914, continued to be the principal material employed.[29] All three of these substances were produced in the South; indeed the growth of the fertilizer industry in that section partly accounts for the rapid introduction of by-product coke ovens in the Birmingham District, as well as for the expansion of sulphuric-acid production in the same region. The result was that Maryland lost its old primacy as a fertilizer manufacturing state, taking second rank after Georgia and being immediately followed by South Carolina and Virginia. The growing centralization of the manufacture in the South, however, was due to a neighboring market as well as to the possession of raw materials, for more fertilizer was used in the cotton fields of that section than in any other part of the country.[30]

[24] Twelfth Census, *Reports*, x, 528–529; Bureau of the Census, *Manufactures, 1914*, II, 458, Table 4.
[25] Thirteenth Census, *Reports*, x, 538, Table 18.
[26] Twelfth Census, *Reports*, x, 562–563; *Mineral Industry*, III, 252.
[27] Bureau of the Census, *Manufactures, 1905*, IV, 440, Table 70; *Mineral Industry*, IV, 513.
[28] Bureau of the Census, *Manufactures, 1905*, IV, 440.
[29] Bureau of the Census, *Manufactures, 1914*, II, 487–488.
[30] Bureau of the Census, *Manufactures, 1914*, II, 482.

In 1895 the first great combination was formed in this industry with the organization of the Virginia-Carolina Chemical Company, which acquired ten of the most successful factories in the South. This corporation speedily increased its holdings and by the end of the century owned some 31 works along the Atlantic coast, from Baltimore to Atlanta and Savannah, Georgia; extensive phosphate beds in South Carolina, and a steam vessel of 2,500 tons used for transporting phosphate rock from its mines to its reduction works. Only two or three establishments of first rank in the Southern States remained outside the combination. It was powerful enough in 1905 to defy the German Kali Syndicate, and to purchase important potash concessions in that country in order to render itself independent of the trust. This finally led to an agreement by which the Virginia-Carolina Company received special consideration from the German producers.[31]

In 1899 a second corporation, the American Agricultural Chemical Company, was formed with a capital of $30,000,000, to acquire some 24 of the largest fertilizer plants in the Northern and Eastern states. These companies not only manufactured fertilizers, but also bone black, gelatine, glue, sulphuric, muriatic and phosphoric acid, sulphate of ammonia, sulphate of potash, and soda and various heavy chemicals.[32] Several other large corporations, including great packing companies like Armour and Swift, were also engaged in this manufacture.

In 1895 two German scientists found that when nitrogen gas is conducted through a hot mass of calcium carbide, a compound known as cyanamid is produced, which is very rich in nitrogen, and possesses great value as a fertilizer. Its manufacture soon developed into an important industry, and on January 1, 1910, a plant to produce this product began operations on the Canadian side of the River at Niagara Falls.[33]

Shortly before the outbreak of the World War phosphate fertilizer began to be manufactured from the slag of the open-hearth furnaces of the Tennessee Coal, Iron and Railroad Company, at Ensley, Alabama, and elsewhere. This was a source of phosphates that had long been exploited abroad, but had hitherto been neglected in this country, although southern basic slag contained about 17 per cent of soluble phosphoric acid and 48 per cent of lime.[34] Another undeveloped but promising source of fertilizers was the flue dust of Portland Cement plants.

At this time Charleston, South Carolina, was one of the chief fertilizer manufacturing cities of the world. It had 14 plants in active operation, giving employment to 3,000 people, and turning out annually a product

[31] *Commercial and Financial Chronicle*, LXVIII, 431, Mar. 4, 1899; LXIX, 964, Nov. 4, 1899; *Mineral Industry*, XIV, 499–500; Federal Trade Commission, *Report on the Fertilizer Industry, 1916*, 184–194.

[32] *Commercial and Financial Chronicle*, LXVIII, 974, May 20, 1899; Federal Trade Commission, *Report on the Fertilizer Industry, 1916*, 176, 194–217.

[33] *Manufacturers' Record*, LXV, 60–61, May 21, 1914; Federal Trade Commission, *Report on the Fertilizer Industry, 1916*, 35–36.

[34] *Mineral Industry*, XXIII, 437; *Manufacturers' Record*, LXV, 48, June 18, 1914; LXVI, 60, Dec. 3, 1914; cf., however, Federal Trade Commission, *Report on the Fertilizer Industry, 1916*, 90; U. S. National Museum, *Bulletin 102*, Part 2, 17–18.

valued at $8,000,000. In 1914 the South made more than two-thirds of the commercial fertilizers produced in the United States, and consumed nearly that proportion of all those manufactured. The country's total output was well over 8,000,000 tons per annum, a three-fold increase since the beginning of the century.[35]

MISCELLANEOUS INDUSTRIES OF THE CHEMICAL GROUP

A number of industries are so closely allied with the chemical manufacture that they are usually grouped with it in official statistics. These include the production of dyes, pigments and tanning materials, many of which at the period we are describing were vegetable extracts; for aniline dyes, though produced to some extent in the United States, were not as yet an important article of manufacture. On the other hand American makers largely controlled the domestic market for paints and varnishes; the imports of the former but slightly exceeded the exports, while more varnishes were shipped abroad than were purchased from foreign producers. Some of the most important pigments used in paints were manufactured by improved processes invented in America.[36] Incidentally it may be noted here that the celluloid manufacture is also based upon the American discovery, made in 1869, that pyroxylin is soluble in camphor. Like Goodyear's lucky discovery several decades before, that rubber could be converted into a valuable industrial commodity by adding sulphur at certain temperatures, it was patented, and largely as a result of this the production of celluloid was concentrated in a single large plant at Newark, New Jersey.[37]

Notwithstanding the fact that the country was at peace, except for the brief interruption of the Spanish War, from 1865 to 1914, the value of the explosives it produced multiplied more than tenfold during that period, thus emphasizing the fact that the industrial function of these commodities is immensely more important than their war function.[38] Nitroglycerine, guncotton and dynamite were manufactured extensively in the United States before 1890; but smokeless powder, though it was made in America about 1850, was not produced on a commercial scale until 1890, when the Government built a factory at Newport, Rhode Island, expressly to make it. By 1914 well toward 13,000,000 pounds were manufactured annually.[39] The output of explosives in the United States during the calendar year 1913, was nearly 232,000 tons, of which more than half were so-called "high" and "permissible" explosives, and the remainder black powder, the production of which was steadily decreasing. Just before the outbreak of

[35] *Manufacturers' Record*, LXV, 47–48, June 18, 1914; LXVI, 40, July 9, 1914; Bureau of the Census, *Manufactures, 1914*, II, 489, Table 55.
[36] *E. g.*, Bureau of the Census, *Manufactures, 1905*, IV, 464–465; U. S. Department of the Interior, *Technical Paper 89*, 13.
[37] Twelfth Census, *Reports*, X, 599–600; Van Gelder and Schlatter, *History of the Explosive Industry in the United States*, 785–789.
[38] *Cf.*, Thirteenth Census, *Reports*, X, 567.
[39] Twelfth Census, *Reports*, X, 596–597; Bureau of the Census, *Manufactures, 1914*, II, 510; *Commercial and Financial Chronicle* LXX, 1098, June 2, 1900.

the World War the E. I. du Pont de Nemours Powder Company completed one of the largest works in this country for making dynamite at Hopewell near Petersburg, Virginia, on a tract of land nearly three square miles in extent.[40]

Although the electric switch and central heating made the match box much less of a household necessity than formerly, the manufacture of matches in the United States was a highly capitalized and concentrated industry. This was largely owing to the development of patented machinery, mostly of American invention, for making matches and match containers. The Diamond Match Company, which was organized in 1881, was the dominant firm in this industry, and to it were due in no small part the improvements in processes of manufacture that enabled American factories to compete successfully with those of Sweden and Japan, notwithstanding the fact that labor was so cheap in those countries and that many of the materials used in match-making were imported. This corporation organized a corps of mechanical experts, chemists and inventors to study ways of simplifying and cheapening processes of production and marketing. In 1895 it was estimated that the Company's patents were worth fully as much as its capital stock, and during the previous year new machinery had reduced appreciably the cost of manufacture. In order to profit to the fullest possible extent from its mechanical inventions, the Company promoted plants abroad in countries where it had acquired patent protection, usually on a basis of retaining a controlling interest in the foreign enterprise. Thus it erected the largest match factory in the world at Liverpool in 1896, at a time when its general appliances and system of manufacturing enabled it to make matches not only at its new factory but at its older plants in the United States "with 25 per cent of the manual labor of any other known processes in the world."[41]

The Diamond Match Company was a vertical trust to the extent of controlling its own raw materials so far as they were produced in the United States. Like the International Paper Company and the United States Leather Company it owned large timber areas. Of course, this condition did not necessarily apply to plants in foreign countries, nor did the Diamond Match Company attempt to retain administrative control over its establishments abroad. Although it owned a majority of their common stock, it was usually considered advisable to let natives of the country have a majority on the board of directors. In 1898 a branch company was organized on this plan in Switzerland; another began operation in Brazil, and still other plants were projected or in operation in Germany, Peru, Canada and Capetown.[42]

In 1899 the Diamond Match Company established a community of interest with the Continental Match Company, controlled by Edwin Gould,

[40] *Manufacturers' Record*, LXVI, 43, July 9, 1914; LXVI, 46, Oct. 22, 1914.
[41] *Commercial and Financial Chronicle*, LXII, 317, Feb. 15, 1896; LXIV, 285, Feb. 6, 1897; LXIV, 1088, June 5, 1897.
[42] *Commercial and Financial Chronicle*, LXVI, 286, Feb. 5, 1898; LXVIII, 228, Feb. 8, 1899.

which had three large factories in this country. At the same time it purchased three other plants in Michigan, Indiana and Maine. The result was that the price of matches was almost doubled, and powerful competing companies, controlling independent patents for making matches and match boxes, entered this field.[43]

CULTURAL MANUFACTURES

This term may be permissible to designate a group of manufactures that has first appeared, or has attained unprecedented importance, in our mechanical and inventive age. These manufactures are distinct from those basic industries that directly or indirectly afford us sustenance or shelter, in that they minister primarily to intellectual or esthetic needs. They include printing and the other graphic arts, photography, musical instruments and mechanical agencies for communicating intelligence, and they have possibilities of expansion which the older and socially primary manufactures do not possess; for there is a limit to what we can eat and wear and employ in material pursuits, but the demands of the intellect and the taste are infinite. Their capacity for amazing growth is illustrated by the fact that two of those which bulk largest in the statistics of today did not exist at the beginning of the century, and have won their position among great industries within a decade. These are the manufactures grouped around the cinema and the radio.

Printing is the oldest of the cultural manufactures and the only one for which statistical comparisons can be made for the half-century compassed by this volume. Between 1860 and 1914 its product increased in value from less than $35,000,000 to more than $900,000,000, or nearly nine times as rapidly as the population. It would be straining the definition to credit all this growth to the cultural balance sheet of the nation, even if we disregard the cynical—but doubtful—objection that the popularization of the printed page has resulted in its depreciation as a cultural agency. The enormous growth of advertising, the increased employment of printed forms in business, and the larger margin of waste that accompanies the multiplication and cheapening of products, discounted heavily the strictly cultural import of the figures quoted. On the other hand, however, during this period artistic progress was as marked as quantitative expansion in the printing trades.

The generation of the Civil War congratulated itself upon the wonderful improvements in the mechanics of printing that began in 1847, with the invention of the revolving cylinder press, by Richard M. Hoe of New York. By 1860 this press was in general use in the larger newspaper offices of both the United States and Europe. It printed directly from the type, was fed by hand, and had a maximum output of about 25,000 impressions an

[43] *Commercial and Financial Chronicle*, LXVIII, 873, May 6, 1899; LXVIII, 1075, June 3, 1899; LXIX, 79, July 8, 1899; LXIX, 335, Aug. 12, 1899; LXX, 793, Apr. 21, 1900.

hour. During the Civil War, which made a demand unprecedented up to that time upon the printing facilities of metropolitan newspapers, stereotyping from papier-mache molds was introduced, and the web-perfecting press, which printed a complete newspaper directly from the rolls without requiring men to feed it, was developed. During the next twenty years pressroom progress consisted mainly in detailed improvements. In 1880 the "most perfect and rapid printing machine in the world," recently erected at St. Louis, had a capacity of 30,000 papers per hour, printed, cut, folded and pasted ready for delivery. About this time, rather oddly, there was a temporary tendency to return to presses printing directly from the type instead of from stereotyped plates.[44]

During the last two decades of the century another great advance was make in printing machinery. Presses were perfected which could produce 100,000 impressions per hour, printed in twelve colors, and the best of them turned out the finest typographical work and illustrations as rapidly as though printing newspapers. These mechanical improvements rendered possible the production of cheap illustrated magazines and newspaper supplements.

Typesetting and distributing machines, which were still experimental devices at the beginning of the period we are now describing, were successfully employed for book composition in 1880; and before the end of the century the Mergenthaler linotype, the Lanston monotype, and other machines had successfully overcome the difficulties that long prevented their general use for newspaper work. Simultaneously automatic type-casting machines were perfected, type was standardized, and the half-tone process and other modern methods of illustration were introduced. By the beginning of the present century, therefore, the printing trades were mechanically in about the same position they occupy today. The subsequent period has been one of detailed improvement rather than of radical innovation.[45]

This progress was conditioned by a simultaneous advance in other industries, like paper making, by increased facilities for gathering news and distributing printed matter to readers, and by new forms of business organization. It was most rapid in those fields of publication where the time element is important—in the manufacture of newspapers more than of books, and in the reproduction of half-tones, which carry graphic representations of current events to the multitude, rather than of engravings, which reach a smaller and more select circle. Nevertheless, as in all other fields of mechanical production, the intrinsic difference between standardized mass output and restricted quality output was steadily diminishing.

Mechanical progress has had far-reaching effects upon the economics of the printing industry, especially the publication of newspapers and periodicals. The manufacture of "patent insides," or partially printed sheets, for

[44] *History and Present Condition of the Newspaper and Periodical Press of the United States;* Tenth Census, *Reports*, VIII, 100–104.
[45] Twelfth Census, *Reports*, IX, 1086–1100.

PLATE 3

FIG. 1.—Hoe 10-Cylinder Newspaper Press of the Seventies
(20,000 papers an hour)

FIG. 2.—Modern Hoe Perfecting Newspaper Press
(320,000 papers an hour)

Courtesy R. Hoe and Co., Inc.

the country press, which probably had its heyday in the eighties, yielded to the competition of plate matter with the cheapening of stereotyping and the increasing efficiency of small office presses, thus giving the local editor better control of his contents and make-up. More recently, with the growing use of typesetting machinery, many comparatively small journals have emancipated themselves altogether from their former dependence on such sources of material. Improved machinery and better facilities for distribution account for that doubtful blessing—the huge Sunday newspaper, with its numerous feature sections; and likewise for the virtual disappearance of the old weekly editions of the metropolitan dailies, which summarized the contents of six or seven issues for leisurely rural readers. The early nineties witnessed the appearance of the 10-cent magazine, beginning with the reduction of *Munsey* to that price in October 1893, followed by *McClure's* and the *Cosmopolitan* two years later. This innovation enlarged immensely the reading circle reached by monthly periodicals, and made them for a time a powerful agency for molding public opinion. Their circulation as a group increased almost eight-fold between 1880 and 1905, or relatively much faster than that of either dailies or weeklies.[46]

While printing presses were almost as widely distributed as the population, the publishing business, as measured by larger figures of production, was concentrated in great cities, especially New York, Philadelphia and Boston in the East, and Chicago in the Middle West. During the late eighties a large magazine industry grew up in Maine, chiefly in the city of Augusta, where periodicals printed on the cheapest grade of paper and making small expenditure for literary matter were produced in enormous editions, and were so largely supported by advertising that they throve upon subscription rates ranging from 10 cents to 25 cents per annum. In 1904 approximately 1,000,000 pounds of such publications were mailed in that state each month. Happily, however, periodicals of higher grade, and reaching an even larger circle of readers, came to the fore about this time, in the popular literary weeklies, of which the most widely circulated was the *Saturday Evening Post*. The first illustrated daily paper ever published was the *New York Graphic*, founded in New York in 1873, which was immediately successful thanks to recent improvements in the art of photo-lithographic printing. The cheap pictorials, which have acquired such popularity with a sub-intelligent public within the last few years, are entirely a product of a later period.

Many aspects of the publishing business transcend the sphere of industrial history and are part of the cultural and political annals of the nation. Even some of its economic aspects, like newspaper consolidations, the influence of advertising upon policies and make-up, the decline of personal editorship, and the virtual disappearance of the old-time party organ, are determined as much by social as by economic forces. Of the total product

[46] Bureau of the Census, *Manufactures, 1905*, Part III, 747.

of the printing trades in 1914, which amounted in value to over $810,000,000, more than half was represented by newspapers and periodicals, whose receipts were derived roughly in the proportion of $3 from advertisers for every $2 from subscribers. Nearly 23,000 newspapers and periodicals were printed in the United States that year, and their average combined circulation was well above 200,000,000 copies per issue.

About 1890 photography changed from a studio profession to a popular pastime. The dry plate had been invented in 1881, and in 1888 the Eastman Kodak, the first camera to take pictures on a film roll, was placed on the market. The latter invention caused a revolution in the attitude of the public toward photography, which became first a vogue among amateurs, and then an almost universal avocation. This created virtually a new industry; for as soon as light, unbreakable, easily manipulated material for negatives was perfected other improvements followed in rapid succession. Within a few years many new types of printing paper had been invented and processes of developing and printing had been greatly simplified. The effect of this was statistically recorded in an increase of the value of photographic apparatus and materials manufactured in the United States from $165,000 in 1880, to nearly $3,000,000 in 1890, and to more than $39,000,000 in 1914. During the first fifteen years of the century the output of photographic apparatus and materials grew about twenty-three times as fast as the population. Of the product in 1914 less than $2,225,000 were represented by motion picture films and apparatus. Seven years later these items exceeded $77,000.000.[47]

Aside from the constantly accelerated growth of the manufacture of musical instruments, which increased in value of output from less than $14,000,000 in 1870 to nearly $120,000,000 in 1914, the most important developments in this industry were the invention of automatic players and of the phonograph. The first piano player made in America was patented as early as 1860, but it was not until the late nineties that manufacturers began to put such devices on the market with confidence. In case of organs, to which similar attachments were applied about this time, this innovation had no observable influence on output statistics, the annual product remaining about stationary in the neighborhood of $6,000,000. On the other hand, a rapid increase occurred in the production of pianos, whose value rose from $35,000,000 in 1899 to $89,000,000 five years later.[48]

After 1904 the expansion of the piano manufacture was checked, probably by the increasing popularity of machines for reproducing music mechanically. The first phonograph was put on the market by Thomas Edison, its inventor, in 1877–1878; the graphophone, with whose develop-

---

[47] Tenth Census, *Report on Manufactures*, 74; Bureau of the Census, *Manufactures, 1914*, II, 1005; Committee on Ways and Means, Fifty-first Congress, First Session, *Hearings*, 730–733; U. S. Industrial Commission, *Reports*, XIII, 173–205; *Statistical Abstract of the United States, 1923*, 305.

[48] Twelfth Census, *Reports*, x, 448, 454–455; Bureau of the Census, *Manufactures, 1905*, IV, 248–249; Bureau of the Census *Manufactures, 1914*, II. 808.

ment Alexander Graham Bell was associated, was invented in 1886; and the gramophone was invented two years later by Emile Berliner, who likewise had contributed to the improvement of the telephone. But the introduction of these machines was slow at first, and in 1890 only two establishments in the United States were engaged in making them. During the following decade, however, they were improved in detail and began to take with the public; so that by the close of the century they were manufactured to the value of over $2,000,000. But the great expansion of the industry came later, with a jump of the product to $10,500,000 in 1904 and to more than $27,000,000 in 1914.[49]

[49] Twelfth Census, *Reports*, x, 181, 183–184; Bureau of the Census, *Manufactures, 1914*, II, 824; *North American Review*, CXLVI, 641–650, June 1888; *Harper's Weekly*, XXX, 458, July 17, 1886; Wile, *Emile Berliner, Maker of the Microphone, passim.*

CHAPTER XX
THE WORLD WAR EPISODE

Some Historical Parallels, 298. The Government and Business, 300. Iron and Steel, 306. Non-ferrous Metals, 310. Engineering Industries, 312. Chemical Industries, 315. Textiles, 318.

SOME HISTORICAL PARALLELS

Comparisons between events so fundamentally different as the American Civil War and the World War are in most respects of curious rather than scientific interest. Nevertheless, they present coincidences worthy of passing notice. Both began in periods of subnormal prosperity. In 1860 the United States was still convalescing from the business depression of three years before. The Bank Commissioners of Massachusetts, a State fairly representative of the manufacturing section of the Union, reported that the demand for bank accomodation by many branches of manufacturing had materially diminished.

"The manufacture of boots and shoes, one of the great staples of our manufacturing industry, which in years past has proved to be the prolific source from which so many of our banks have derived sustenance, is now measurably depressed. Iron manufacturers, failing to prosecute the business as successfully as in former years, are reducing operations as far as possible. On the other hand, the manufacture of cotton and woolen fabrics has been in so marked a degree prosperous that it has been far less dependent than usual on bank favors."

Fifty-four years later on the eve of the World War, the Bureau of Statistics of the same State reported:

"Conditions in our industries as a whole were considerably below normal in 1914, the rate of increase not only in value of product but in the other factors taken into account in the returns falling far below the average at any time for nearly a score of years . . . ."

But that year, likewise, the increase in value of product over 1913 was "pronounced in the woolen and worsted goods industries."

In 1914, however, the country was descending into the trough of a depression and not emerging from one. Moreover, the influences checking business progress were partly of a kind unfamiliar a half century before. After a period of comparative quiescence following President Roosevelt's "trust-busting" campaign, an administration had come into power which was accounted in higher industrial and financial circles hostile to the consolidation and integration of manufacturing. The Clayton Act had just been passed, placing big business under the surveillance of the Federal authority. A tariff law construed to be less friendly to industrial interests than its predecessors had been placed on the statute books. Consequently a spirit of hesitation and distrust was prevalent.

How rapidly this situation changed, both in the early sixties and in the years following the outbreak of the World War, is abundantly indicated in the commercial literature of the two periods. In 1862 the Bank Commissioners of Massachusetts reported:

"Seldom if ever has the business of manufacturing been more active or profitable than during the past year. The war has brought into activity many mechanical employments for which there is little occasion in times of peace."

Besides the production of munitions and military equipment, the Commissioners noted that the war had "also greatly stimulated the manufacture of boots and shoes and of woolen goods." Fifty-two years later the Massachusetts Bureau of Statistics, after reporting "an exceptionally quiet year in 1915," described the following season as finding,

"Massachusetts in the busiest period of our manufactures and in a position of greatest advantage as regards the development of our export trade. Greatly increased home consumption—the unfailing accompaniment of a general rise of wages—as well as the military consumption of all kinds of Massachusetts goods, have called out the resources of every shoe factory and textile mill, every tannery and machine shop in the State."

Within two years—and this was before inflation had played as prominent a part as later in the increase of prices—the value of the State's manufactured products had risen from $1,000,641,000 to $2,000,350,000, and the value of her exports from less than $40,000,000 to approximately $165,000,000.

What was true of Massachusetts was more nearly true of the entire nation in 1916 than it was in 1862, but at both periods the general tendency was the same. During the decade ending with 1870, the value of the country's manufactured products and the wages paid manufacturing operatives more than doubled, while the number of employees engaged in manufacturing increased a little over one-half. During the decade ending with 1925, disregarding the effects of inflation which were roughly equal in both instances, the value of manufactured product and the wages paid manufacturing operatives increased over 160 per cent; but the number of employees engaged in manufacturing rose less than 22 per cent. Comparisons of the three major industries common to both periods present roughly similar results, except that during the Civil War decade our iron and steel industries increased their product relatively more rapidly than they did during the ten years following the outbreak of the World War. The output of pig iron, for example, more than doubled between 1860 and 1870, while it increased less than two-fifths between 1914 and 1925. On the other hand, the growth of the manufacture of cotton goods and of woolen and worsted goods was considerably greater during the decade of the World War than during that of the Civil War. In case of cotton manufacturing this may be explained by shortage of raw materials at the earlier period. But that period has commonly been considered an era of exceptionally rapid growth in the wool manufacture. Nevertheless, the product of the latter increased in value by only 170 per cent between 1860 and 1870 as compared with 248 per cent during the decade ending with 1925.

THE GOVERNMENT AND BUSINESS

Even without the cataclysm of the World War, the years which it so abundantly fills in history would probably have inaugurated a new era in our manufacturing annals; for the stage was already set for the great expansion of industry, the revolution in industrial processes and organization, and the changed relation of the Government to business, which we are wont to associate with the exigencies of our nation's great military effort. A new policy toward industry had been gradually taking shape in the public mind, and to some extent in governmental practice, ever since the Interstate Commerce Commission was established in 1886. Men began to recognize that purely punitive or inhibitory measures for checking dominant and spontaneous business developments are either futile or injurious. The establishment of the Federal Trade Commission in the autumn of 1914 was soon followed by the announcement of a new policy. Some eighteen months after its organization, and as soon as it had reconnoitred its field of action, its vice-president, speaking before the Boston Better Business Club, stressed the Government's desire to cooperate with business men and not to hamper them. He dwelt upon the great need of facts, of information upon which to act, and declared that four-fifths of the corporations in America were operating on a precarious basis because they lacked broad vision of the conditions which they must meet and were ignorant even of their own costs of production. About the same time the president of the Baldwin Locomotive Works, in addressing the National Trade Convention, exhorted his hearers to learn team work, "by which is meant correlation of the efforts of the manufacturer, merchant, banker, and investor," adding that "the creation of the Federal Trade Commission must prove to be a great benefit to our manufacturers and exporters." Less than a year later the Chairman of the Commission, in addressing the Commercial Club of Chicago, declared that business needed doctors, not lawyers; constructive governmental policies, not destructive governmental policies; and that the men administering the country's great productive enterprises must have "broad views of business and a comprehensive grasp of industry as a whole." Similar opinions had been expressed before but never so generally and authoritatively as now. In a word, consciousness that the nation was entering a new coöperative stage in industrial evolution was dawning upon the rank and file of the manufacturing public as well as upon its more farsighted leaders.

Prosecutions under the Sherman law continued, to be sure, and occupied as large a place as ever in public litigation. But the definition of illegal practices was becoming more precise; a recognized body of precedents, embodied in court decisions, was being created by which great corporations could chart their course; and a working solution of the relations between big business and the general public was gradually outlining itself in the national mind.

When, early in 1915, orders for war materials began to pour in upon American manufacturers, our moral right to supply the nations across the Atlantic with the instruments of slaughter and destruction was questioned in certain quarters. Peace societies protested against such deliveries, and in rare instances orders may have been refused on account of the abhorrence felt for their purpose or destination. In the spring of 1915 suit was brought against the Allis-Chalmers Manufacturing Company, which was making shrapnel for the Allies under a sub-contract with the Bethlehem Steel Corporation, for violating a Wisconsin law prohibiting the manufacture of munitions for foreign countries. But the Government took no steps to stop this trade, which speedily expanded to irresistible dimensions. Great Britain, followed by France, early in the war appointed John Pierpont Morgan and Company its fiscal agent and factor in the United States, through whom it made its American purchases. On May 1, 1915, Thomas W. Lamont stated in an address before the Academy of Social and Political Sciences at Philadelphia that the Allies had already borrowed $200,000,000 in the United States to finance their purchases here.

Unprecedented industrial expansion characterized the two years that followed. Not only the war market abroad but also the increased consumption of the prosperous community at home and the call for goods to meet the need of neutral countries and dependencies no longer able to supply themselves from European sources multiplied the demands upon our producers. Even before the American Government entered the war, moreover, it had begun to strengthen, on a scale hitherto unprecedented in times of peace, its naval armaments and merchant marine.

As the impressive proof of the all-importance of industrial preparedness presented by the war in Europe was borne in upon the public mind, Congress took up the project which had been before it in various forms since 1910 for creating a Council of National Defense. This resulted in the creation of a body consisting of five cabinet officers, assisted by an advisory commission of men prominent in industrial life, to develop and coordinate all forms of transportation to meet the military, industrial, and commercial demands of the nation in time of war, and to gather complete information as to the country's manufacturing and producing facilities adaptable to military needs. The Council was expected to inform American manufactures individually as to the part they would be called upon to play in a national emergency, and to form sub-committees of men actually engaged in industry, or familiar with its operations, which would be capable of mobilizing the resources of the country in an emergency. Although the power of decision rested with the Council proper, in practice the initiative lay with the advisory members, whose direct contacts with industry and with business life in general made them more competent to deal with the particular questions which the Council was designed to handle. Before war was declared this Advisory Commission had already met with the representatives of the country's leading manufacturing industries and had formed a skeleton organization for mobilizing their resources in case we became involved in hostilities.

This was the status of affairs when the United States entered the war. Under the stress of new duties and new necessities the Advisory Commission of the Council rapidly differentiated into a number of independent or quasi-independent bodies, of which the Railway Administration, the Food Administration, the Fuel Administration, and the War Industries Board stand out most prominently in the memory of Americans. It is with the last of these that we have immediately to do. This Board did not finally emerge from the medley of tentative and ephemeral organizations formed during the first few months of hostilities to deal with the industrial needs of the Government until July 8, 1917, when the National Defense Council finally brought it into existence to

. . . . "act as a clearing-house for the war-industry needs of the government, determine the most effective ways of meeting them, and the best means and methods of increasing production, including the creation or extension of industries demanded by the emergency, the sequence and relative urgency of the needs of the different government services, and to consider price factors and, in the first instance, the industrial and labor aspects of problems involved and the general questions affecting the purchase of commodities."

This Board rapidly extended its sway over the whole industrial organism of America. It was able to do this through its control of transportation and priorities, which included the allotment of both carriage and raw materials, much as the Confederate Government more than fifty years earlier had controlled its infant mills and factories by similar rationing devices, plus the powerful lever of the Conscription law. The functions of the War Industries Board, however, were far vaster and more complex than those of any predecessor. They involved maintaining an uninterrupted flow of war materials not only to the Government's own reservoirs but also to the Allies, the exchange of commodities with neutrals in return for essential materials, the provision of supplies for the civilian population, and the creation of new industries to meet the emergencies of the hour. All these things were done on a larger scale than had ever before been contemplated. In 1918 the army alone purchased "far more woolen socks than the entire normal production of the United States, twice as many blankets, three times as many part-leather gloves; it took all the wool and all the steel."[1] Modern munitions alone require scores of raw materials prepared by mani-

---

[1] All quotations in this subdivision of the chapter are from Clarkson, *Industrial America in the World War*.

fold processes; steel, brass, aluminum, and zinc wrought to the utmost accuracy; and complex and dangerous chemicals.

How these extraordinary demands were satisfied, how the highly individualistic industries of the nation, which owed their success so largely to untrammeled self-direction, were induced to march in goose step, is too long a story to be related here. That it was possible at all "was due to the transcendent spirit of the time. Business willed its own domination, forged its bonds, and policed its own subjection." When the nation's needs became paramount, we were in the midst of a runaway market for all products that could be used directly or indirectly for war purposes. Our exports to Europe had risen from $1,500,000,000 in 1914 to $4,000,300,000 in 1917. Prices had mounted to correspond. Pig iron and steel plates were costing twice as much as a few months before. It was imperative to moderate this situation, not only in the interest of the taxpayer but also in the interest of efficient production; for no man can figure ahead when market quotations are in a state of anarchy. Therefore ordinary business prudence, as well as patriotic motives, persuaded producers of basic commodities and indispensable finished goods to consent to price regulation. Steel makers and copper refiners promptly volunteered to fill the Government's requirements at one-third or more less than the market price. The Lumber Committee quoted rates considerably below those recently prevailing. Coal, coke, wool, cotton, hides and leather, zinc, lead and aluminum, all the fundamentals of industrial production, were speedily brought within the compass of reasonable costs. And this, be it remembered, was not done by official fiat but through the ordinary method of collective bargaining reinforced by the special ethical sanctions of the moment.

Prices were fixed in the simplest possible form, that is, on uniform and horizontal schedules and not on percentage ratios to the cost of production, as had been done in the Confederacy, where the Government in many instances allowed manufacturers a specified percentage of profits. This horizontal plan undoubtedly favored in many instances big business with its economy of operation, which counted for more than ever during a period of tremendous strain upon productive facilities. Smaller plants, especially those where the percentage of labor cost was high, were at a relative disadvantage; although the Government saw to it that no maker of useful goods was compelled to cease operations. Such new conditions as were established, in fact, like the substitution of the Birmingham plus rate for the Pittsburg plus rate for southern pigs, were intended to encourage smaller reproductive manufacturers. Naturally the prices set by the Government were maximum prices. They were the same for all purchasers, and they were subject to readjustment quarterly.

Not only did the Government thus curtail the profits of manufacturers and determine the articles they should produce, but also it radically restricted industries that were considered unessential or relatively less essential. The only important branch of manufacturing actually abolished however, that of intoxicating liquors, was not suspended by the War Industries Board, which limited its intervention to converting the largest whisky distilleries to producing alcohol for smokeless powder. At one time of stress, when the shortage of steel was acute and the demand for motor fuel seemed unlimited, it was proposed temporarily to suspend the production of passenger automobiles, but this project was dropped. The building trades probably suffered most from war restriction; for all new non-war construction involving an expenditure of more than $500 was prohibited, unless under special permit.

Price policies and prohibitions, however, passed away with the war. Other phases of Government control have had more enduring results. One of these was the extension of standardization, which was no new discovery in America, to be sure, but was applied with unprecedented concentration of purpose during the crisis. The result in quantity production was astonishing even to our own people, accustomed as they are to large outputs. To be sure, 51,000 army rifles a week was possibly no more than three- or fourfold the maximum output of public and private makers during the Civil War, but the rifle of today is a vastly more complicated weapon than that of 1863. But the movement spread far beyond the manufacture of specifically military supplies to their civilian accessories. For example, the principle of standardization was extended appreciably in the production of locomotives and railway rolling stock. This activity of the Government merged insensibly into another, which also has had an abiding effect—the campaign to lessen waste in industry. Waste is now recognized more clearly than before to include, in addition to the actual destruction of materials, power, and labor, losses due to their misemployment and misdirection in unnecessary models, multiplied patterns, and capricious styles.

"It was found that almost all industries were encumbered with an unbelievable amount of unexamined tradition, that resulted in duplication of effort, waste of material, and unnecessary expenditures of energy."

So patent was this condition that those who had to deal with it "ultimately became convinced that modern civilization is becoming anaemic with obesity." In farming supplies alone, manufactures reported more than 1,700 varieties of wagon gears; 326 models of plows and 784 drills and other planting machines were on the market; and even buggies, already vanishing before the automobile, rejoiced in 232 varieties of wheels and 100 kinds of axles.

A possibly permanent effect of Government war control upon the ideology of industry was its warning against extreme geographical centralization. In 1917 the nation's productive energies were threatened with paralysis by the congestion of these activities in the northeastern section of the country, which is the normal center of its metal-making and -using industries and also the region of its greatest general manufacturing development. About 60 per cent of the first orders placed for war goods were given to plants in New York, Pennsylvania, Ohio, Connecticut, and Massachusetts.

"To go elsewhere meant investigation, planning, and conversion. So the Government purchasing agents followed the path of least resistance until . . . the most extensive industrial region in America came near to nullification as a contributor to the early success of the war by being smothered under the immovable mass of its own product."

Railways and shipping terminals were overloaded until normal service became impossible, housing accommodations were overcrowded, the entire rhythm of production slowed down and threatened to come to a standstill. At one time it was proposed to shut down the steel works at Pittsburgh for several days to enable the railways to clear their yards. An order of the Fuel Administration in January, 1918, directing many manufacturing plants to close down for four consecutive days, and for every Monday thereafter until the end of March, was designed primarily to conserve fuel for necessary war industries and was rescinded within a month; but the fuel problem itself was one of transportation as well as mining. As soon as the evil of this condition was recognized, energetic steps were taken to decentralize industry. This was done by establishing regional organizations whose function was to promote the territorial concentration of the final forms of manufacture within their respective jurisdictions, thus assuring uninterrupted "production of materials, mass labor, ample power, and adequate transportation with the minimum of long hauls and the elimination of cross-hauls."

Passing over the technical problems involved in the transfer of American industry from peace production to war production, and the conversion of manufacturing plants to new and unanticipated uses—for which, by the way, countless precedents had been established both in Europe and in Canada before the problem was thrust upon America—we come to one extremely important factor in a manufacturer's success, merchandizing, which remained untouched by all these transformations. Competition was in abeyance, advertizing a superfluity. All producers were virtually members of a pool with no outsiders or revolters to worry them. Each important branch of manufacturing was administered under Government supervision by its own committee. Production was organized on what a Russian might call a bourgeois-soviet system. Naturally, manufacturers who passed through this experience could not revert completely to their prewar mentality. Therefore,

". . . . having experienced the advantages of combination for a laudable purpose, during the war, it is not unlikely that some industrial groups have sought since to continue it for their selfish benefit, and thus have effected such an intimate flow of information between themselves, intended for study from the point of view of common action for the group prosperity, that they have been able to act as units in matters of prices and regulation of production without entering technically into agreements in restriction of trade."

Whether or not this will ultimately work out to the advantage of the public is still an open question, but there is promise that under Government supervision it may do so. Other results of war-time regulation have been more unqualifiedly beneficial. In 1923 Grosvenor B. Clarkson, who shared in the activities of the War Industries Board and reviewed them after the war, wrote:

"It is probable that there will never again be such a multiplicity of styles and models in machinery and other heavy and costly articles as there was before the restrictions necessitated by the war. Undoubtedly, the discovery that traditional methods had involved the excessive use of materials for many purposes will be remembered and applied. The revelation of the possibilities of conversion and the ease with which supplies of manufactured goods can be produced to meet the most extraordinary demands will result in satisfaction with profits that will not be too attractive and in a better balance between production and consumption. It is also likely that, even if some public statistical agency does not undertake to appraise supply and demand in the whole field of industry, individual corporations and industrial groups will concern themselves much more with the gathering of data that will make possible the avoidance of periods of extreme surfeit as well as of extreme scarcity. In this manner commercial and industrial stability will be promoted. It is admitted that in many important lines producers are as deficient in their knowledge of future requirements as the army was in the beginning of the war. The efforts of the War Industries Board to ascertain all requirements —public and private—for the commodities with which it was concerned, and its complete survey of production, was a hint to thoughtful business men that some such orderly counterpoising might be possible in peace."

What is here stated partly as a prediction has, as we shall see later, been increasingly realized in practice.

IRON AND STEEL

Never in its vicissitudinous history did the American iron and steel industry experience such a sudden change of fortunes as during 1915. The previous year had closed with the subsidiaries of the United States Steel Corporation, for example, operating on the lowest scale since the organization of the Company. Nor did January promise any betterment. The year opened with mills running at from 25 to 35 per cent of their capacity; unfilled orders were below 4,000,000 tons, and dividends had been suspended. This condition was not peculiar to the big corporation, but was general throughout the industry. Although there had been some canvassing abroad for war orders shortly after the outbreak of hostilities, it was not until the armies in western Europe became immobilized in trenches after the German retreat from the Marne that Great Britain, and then France, turned seriously to the United States for iron and steel. This country, which had invented and developed barbed-wire fencing, continued to be the principal producer of that material, which it supplied to virtually the entire world. British steel makers had never entered this field extensively. But barbed wire in inexhaustible quantities was needed to protect the Allied trenches in France and Belgium, and American producers were called upon to supply it. Barbed-wire entanglements, however, and the kind of entrenchment that they connote, call for artillery preparation on a scale hitherto unknown before an enemy can successfully advance against them. Hence the Allies, who were less amply provided with the requisites of modern warfare than their opponents, found it imperative to augment immediately and on a scale never before contemplated their stores of artillery ammunition. They naturally turned to America for shell steel and shrapnel to supplement the output of their own munitions factories. Automobiles and tractors were called for in ever ascending numbers. Russia, finding her railways and railway equipment inadequate to meet their military overburden, sent urgent orders to America for locomotives, steel cars, and rails. As a result of this rush of commissions, within less than six months of the midwinter depression the United States Steel Corporation was running at 90 per cent capacity and was sending abroad one-third of the steel it produced. Notwithstanding the fact that practically all of its machinery was in motion, the Corporation's unfilled orders doubled during 1915, although they did not even then reach the high point of the boom in 1912–1913. And this was typical of the industry as a whole.

The market basis for this revival was worldwide. Our own railways suddenly discovered that they must increase their facilities to meet the heavy traffic demands that the new movement of commodities toward Europe made upon them, and South America and other sections of the world which had previously depended largely upon Great Britain and Germany for iron and steel were forced to concentrate their orders in the United States. Between January and December, 1915, the country's pig-iron output increased from the rate of 19,000,000 tons a year to about 38,000,000 tons, while the Pittsburg price for Bessemer pig rose from $14.70 to $19.65. Most of this advance occurred during the last few months of the year, for Bessemer iron rose only 30 cents a ton during the first twelve months of hostilities. Steel prices responded more quickly than those of iron to war demands, partly because these demands were concentrated upon special classes of this material. For example, plates which early in the year were selling about $1 a ton cheaper than other forms of steel, rose to $14 above them before the close of the season. Tungsten, used in making tool steel, for which every machine shop and munitions factory in the world was calling urgently, rose from 75 cents to $6 and $8 a pound. On the other hand, the domestic demand for rails fell off, since under one thousand miles of new road were built, or less than in any other year since 1864, or in any year since 1848 except during the Civil War.

The two following years witnessed a constant increase of this prosperity. In 1916 the country's pig-iron output reached 39,000,000 tons, exceeding by nearly 9,000,000 tons the previous high record. Well toward 43,000,000 tons of steel were made, of which 30,000,000 were basic open-hearth; and the production of electric steel more than doubled. Between the spring of 1915 and the end of 1916 the Pittsburgh price of Bessemer billets rose from $20 to $55 a ton, a new record equalled only by the price of wrought iron during and immediately after the Civil War. In

1917, however, the output of pig iron declined nearly 1,000,000 tons below that of the previous year, but the production of steel ingots and castings exceeded 45,000,000 tons, a point not reached again until 1925. America's entry into the war, therefore, was not accompanied by a quantitative expansion of our iron and steel industries so much as by the conversion of their product to new uses. The withdrawal of able-bodied men from productive employments, and the congestion of transportation by the movement of military trains and by the shifting of materials to new points of use or concentration, threw upon the whole industrial organism the strain that prevented the making of new records. The abnormally severe winter of 1917–1918, moreover, handicapped iron and steel makers. An acute shortage resulted, since the amount of steel required for war uses, at first estimated at less than one-fifth of the total output, was found to exceed the country's entire production.

Meanwhile prices had to be adjusted, while simultaneously old plants were converted to new uses and new plants were built at huge expense to meet abnormal, and presumably temporary, demands of the moment. Before the price of iron and steel could be determined, it was necessary to agree on prices for ore and coke. Finally the steel industry itself submitted a proposal to the War Industries Board, which was approved by the President in September, 1918, by which the price of pig iron for the remainder of the year was fixed at $33 a ton and that of steel in partly manufactured forms at from $2.90 to $3.25 a hundred. The domestic price of steel plates, now reduced to $3\frac{1}{4}$ cents a pound, had been above 12 cents a pound the previous spring, with the Japanese bidding as high as 50 cents a pound. Despite this reduction, every important steel maker in the country was pouring millions into new plants. At one time the United States Steel Corporation's expenditures under this heading alone were $14,000,000 a month, and between our declaration of war and the armistice, it invested more than $200,000,000 in war plant. When peace came, moreover, the Company had just begun to erect for the Government ordnance works at Neville Island, in the Ohio River near Pittsburgh, which were planned to cost $150,000,000.

According to an investigation of war-time costs and profits of the steel industry, made public by the Federal Trade Commission in 1925, average company earnings were somewhat over 7 per cent on their investment in 1915, 21 per cent in 1916, 29 per cent in 1917, and 20 per cent in 1918. The rate of return of the United States Steel Corporation was below this average for all years prior to 1918, when it was 21.2 per cent. As a rule, the smaller and less highly integrated companies earned the highest rate upon their investments, their profits rising to a maximum of over 55 per cent in 1917. "This was the result, apparently, of the fact that finished products advanced in price before raw materials." To be sure, the large companies produced pig iron and steel ingots at considerably lower cost than their small competitors, the margin in case of ingots amounting during the latter half of 1918 to more than $13 a ton; but this apparently did not overcome the merchandising advantage of smaller producers.

It is one of the ironies of industrial history that while the big steel companies were doing yeoman's work to help win the war, the Government was suing the United States Steel Corporation to force its dissolution as a trust, and the larger independent producers were trying to form new combinations which the Government regarded as in defiance or in evasion of the law. In 1916 the Midvale Steel and Ordnance Company acquired the Cambria Steel Company, thus securing the latter's great plant at Johnstown, Pennsylvania, a steamship line on the Great Lakes and extensive ore properties in the Lake Superior ranges. Almost simultaneously the Bethlehem Steel Corporation took over the Pennsylvania Steel Company and its subsidiary, the Maryland Steel Company, thus becoming the largest independent producer in the country.

Metallurgical progress during the war was hampered by the concentration of energy on huge outputs, especially after America entered the conflict, and for a time by a dearth of the auxiliaries for making special steels. Omitting for the moment the remarkable increase in the output of by-product coke, which was so great as to relegate beehive coke to a merely supplementary status, the most significant effect of war demands was the rapidly extending use of electricity for making steel and for heat-treating steel products. In 1915 the electric-furnace capacity of the United States for the first time surpassed that of Germany. Simultaneously the duplex process, which had been making rather slow headway, came into quickened favor because it shortened the open-hearth process by about five-sixths of its usual duration and enabled some plants, notably in the Chicago area, to increase their output with a minimum of mechanical change. The electric furnace invaded the field of the crucible furnace, so that the product of the latter rapidly declined, falling from nearly 114,000 tons in 1915 to less than 64,000 tons in 1919; while the quantity of electric steel made in the country rose between these dates from 69,000 to 290,000 tons, after reaching 511,000 tons under the stress of war demands in 1918. During the fall and winter of 1917, the Illinois Steel Company put into operation at Chicago the largest electric steel plant in the world, containing three 25-ton and two 15-ton Heroult furnaces. During the period of maximum prices some electric pigs were produced from low phosphorous steel scrap without the addition of virgin metal. About one-half of the electric ingots were of alloy steel, and before the war was over the United States led the world in ferro-alloy output, but practically all the electric castings made were of high-grade carbon steels.

When the war began only acid open-hearth steel, which required from thirteen to fifteen hours for a forty- or fifty-ton heat, was thought suitable for ordnance, but under the stress of necessity it was discovered that electric steel made on a basic bottom in a much shorter time was as good or better for this purpose. Meanwhile the domestic production of manganese, chromite, tungsten, and molybdenum, essential for the manufacture of ferro-alloys, rapidly increased; while Peruvian deposits of venadium controlled by an American company supplied our needs of this important mineral. Nevertheless steel makers still had to import a portion of their supplies of most of these ores. The shortage of ferromanganese forced a return to the use of speigeleisen, its low-grade equivalent, which had largely been abandoned by progressive steel makers. Two influences coöperated to promote the production of alloy steel at this period—the demand for ordnance and the automobile industry. Consequently, war development of this particular branch of metallurgy was more than transitory. There was some recession, to be sure, after military demands ceased, but consumers had been educated in the high qualities of electric steel and its superior adaptation to many conditions, and they continued to demand it for purposes of peace consumption.

Quantitatively, America's steel output far exceeded that of any other nation. During the four war years from 1915–1918, inclusive, it exceeded upon an average 40,000,000 long tons per annum; while that of Germany was less than one-third, and that of Great Britain less than one-fourth of this amount. In 1917, the last year reported, Russia, the next largest producer, had a total of less than 5,000,000 tons; while Austria's output was in the neighborhood of 3,000,000 tons, that of France just over 2,000,000 tons, and that of Italy about 1,250,000 tons.

NON-FERROUS METALS

Tin was the only non-ferrous metal of primary importance which was not produced within the United States in sufficient quantities for both civilian and military needs. Its war history need not detain us here. When hostilities began in Europe, more than one-half of all the aluminum produced in the world was made in the United States. During the two years that followed, the Aluminum Company of America spent $20,000,000 in extending its plants, thus doubling its capacity. In 1915 this Company acquired from French promoters large works under construction in North Carolina and began extensive hydroelectric and manufacturing developments in the Province of Quebec. The price of aluminum rose from below 20 cents in 1914 to above 60 cents two years later, but the bulk of domestic consumption was supplied by the Aluminum Company at about one-half the later figure, the high quotations applying mainly to exports. In 1918 the Government fixed the price at 32 cents a pound, raising it later to 33 cents. This metal found manifold uses during the war both in camp utensils and equipment and in the manufacture of castings of aluminum or its alloys for automobiles, airplanes, and machine-gun parts. During this period duralumin, the extremely light and strong metal used by the Germans in the framework of their Zeppelins, first came prominently to public notice. Early in the war aluminum dust was extensively employed in combination with ammonium nitrate as an explosive mixture. Altogether the demand for this metal for war purposes rose to 90 per cent of the country's production. Consequently when a severe drought during the winter of 1918 cut down by nearly one-third the output of this hydroelectric product a serious though temporary shortage occurred which stimulated the Aluminum Company still further to enlarge its capacity.

Copper, lead, and zinc were not so largely under the control of a single company. About the time the war broke out the recovery of these metals was cheapened and the sources of their supply widened by the development of the flotation process. This process consists of treating finely pulverized ores in a bath containing sulphuric acid and certain oils, so that its metal values rise to the surface in a scum and are easily separated from the residue. The amount of metal recovered from sulfide ores was greatly increased by this method, rising at certain copper works from less than 75 to 95 per cent. Moreover, metals which in nature are frequently found in combination, like silver, lead, and zinc, and which previously could be isolated only by unduly costly treatment, can be easily and inexpensively separated from each other by selective flotation, since their slimes rise in succession to the surface of the bath, where they are drawn off in turn, much as vapors of different volatility are drawn off from a retort in fractional distillation. This process made commercially workable vast quantities of Western ores which had hitherto been entirely neglected or but partially utilized.

Copper, like aluminum, was a metal of which the output of the United States from native and imported ores dominated world production. A Copper Producers' Association, organized in 1908 largely for the statistical control of the industry, was dissolved in January, 1915. Early that month a single sale of 200,000 tons of metal was made to the Allies. As a result of increased industrial activity at home and a constantly expanding military demand abroad prices had risen to 37 cents a pound by the time America entered the war. After several months of negotiation and adjustment, the price to the Government was fixed by the War Industries Board, in September, 1917, at $23\frac{1}{2}$ cents a pound. During 1916, when prices were at their peak and the United States was producing 62 per cent of the world's supply, the country's output rose to nearly 2,300,000,000 pounds of crude metal, but American refining capacity was not adequate to handle this amount. Although a great increase in plant capacity followed, production from native ores sank below 2,000,000,000 pounds in 1917 and 1918.

Lead supplies gave the country little concern during the war, although lead is a military metal of great importance. Output was fairly stable at something over half a million short tons of refined metal per annum, and prices did not rise above 7.75 cents a pound, although they were not regulated directly by the Government. Civilian consumption was never seriously curtailed. The supply of lead was not so nearly a monopoly as that of aluminum, but it was in the hands of comparatively few producers. A different situation existed in the case of zinc smelting and refining, which was not a highly centralized industry. Since the United States produced nearly one-third of the world's output, however, no acute shortage developed during the war. In fact, spelter, or slab zinc as it is now called, was relatively more abundant than most other industrial metals. It was in great request for making brass, for which the navy, the emergency fleet, and the army were calling in almost unlimited quantities. Shortly before the armistice the American Zinc Institute was formed, but it was not a war organization. Between 1914 and 1917 the spelter output of the United States rose in round numbers from 353,000 to 669,000 tons, of which a portion was reduced from foreign ores. In 1918, however, and during the years immediately thereafter, output shrank to a little over half a million tons.

ENGINEERING INDUSTRIES

Among the more notable developments of both the engineering and the metallurgical industries during the war was the increased use and more varied application of electricity. The progress of alloy steels and of heat treatment went hand in hand, for the value of the former is largely conditioned by the efficacy of the latter. Gun forgings and the rotating members of steam turbines, the employment of which on vessels extended very rapidly, must be 100 per cent reliable, or the result is disastrous. This reliability was obtained largely by eliminating ingot defects in steel and by perfecting processes for heat treating metal in larger masses and at more accurately controlled temperatures than hitherto. In fact so radical were the improvements in the annealing process that it made possible the substitution of cast-steel chains for forged chains at a time when American forges were quite unable to meet the enormously increased demand for this product to supply the emergency fleet. Autogenous welding also illustrates how electricity came to the aid of our hard-pressed metal-working industries. Its most spectacular achievement was to enable American engineers and mechanics speedily to repair the wrecked machinery of the German ships interned in our harbors when the Government declared war.

Another development, looking primarily to increased speed and volume of output, was the substitution of die castings, which are made like the slugs in a linotype from molten metal poured into dies, for forged parts of machine guns, motor trucks, bombs, and hand grenades. Their availability for such uses in turn depended upon the improvement in alloy steels and other metal combinations. Devices for centrifugal casting accompanied this development. The World War, like the Civil War, also exacted higher accuracy and precision in foundry and machine-shop practice than had previously been the rule. One reason why so many contracts for metal manufactures were concentrated in the northeastern section of the country, and particularly in the Connecticut Valley, was the greater experience its mechanics possessed in producing articles of the most refined and exacting dimensions. Indeed some contracts are said to have been shifted from other parts of the country to this center because it was the only place where the stringent requirements of ordnance officers could be satisfied. Working to 0.001-inch limits in quantity production proved to be less common than popularly supposed and to be practically unattainable except where the fine-metal-working trades had been a lifelong occupation. During the half century since the Civil War precision in shaping metals had advanced from a tolerance limit of 0.01 inch to a toleration limit of 0.001 inch or even less. At the other extreme, of shaping metal in large masses, progress was measured by the gulf that separates the planer used, in 1863, to trim armor plates 1.5 inches thick, because mills had no shears powerful enough to do this, and the 1,200-ton hydroelectric shears installed at Fairfield, Alabama, in 1919, which easily cut slabs 12 inches thick and 44 inches wide.

During 1916 and 1917 controversies arose between the Navy Department and American steel makers over the price of armor and armor-piercing projectiles. In the spring of the former year the Senate passed a bill appropriating $11,000,000 for a government armor plant. This project was vigorously opposed by the Bethelehem, Midvale, and Carnegie companies, which already had $20,000,000 invested in similar plants having a capacity of 32,000 tons of plates a year. In fact the Bethlehem people at this time offered the Government armor for $395 a ton, or $30 less than it had been paying and, it was stated, $100 or more a ton under the prices paid by the British and German admiralties. That autumn, after a summer of rising quotations, the Government contracted with the Bethelehem and Carnegie companies for over 14,000 tons of armor at prices ranging from $420 to $485 a ton; but, as we shall see later, the Navy's plant was built. A few months later the steel makers were again aroused by the bid of a British firm, at Sheffield, to supply the Navy with more than 14,000 14-inch armor-piercing shells at $356 each, as contrasted with bids ranging from $500 to $900 by leading American firms. Although the British Government for a time held up this offer, as likely to interfere with its own war needs, the bidding company contended that it had a huge surplus stock of shells on hand, that British naval vessels were fully supplied, and that the firm needed the American order "to keep its organization busy." At this date, the British Navy was simply standing guard over the North Sea and the Channel and doing very little actual fighting, while the Allied governments were already buying no small fraction of their ammunition, including ordinary shells, in the United States.

One of the heaviest quantitative demands made during the war upon our engineering industries, as well as upon our supply of steel, was for ship building. In 1915 our yards built only 225,000 gross tons or the smallest amount since 1898. The following year saw the passage of a bill creating the United States Shipping Board and appropriating $50,000,000 for the construction or purchase of ocean-going vessels. Even before this act was passed, however, the industry had experienced a marked revival, and in July, 1916, nearly 700,000 tons of shipping were under construction in American yards and over half a million tons were under contract but not yet laid down. Between that date and the end of 1917, 74 new shipyards were started in the United States, bringing the total number up to 132, and the first of the famous fabricated vessels, assembled from shapes supplied by structural plants all over the country, was launched at Chester, Pennsylvania. On February 12, 1918, the first keel was laid at the great Hog Island plant on the Delaware, and the same month the Ford Motor Company began work on a large plant on the River Rouge, just west of Detroit, to make swift submarine chasers called "eagle boats," which it was proposed to turn out by rapid production methods copied from the automobile manufacture. As a result of these encouraging conditions the burden of vessels built in the United States for American shipowners rose to over 1,000,000 tons in 1918, and to a maximum closely approaching 4,000,000 tons in 1920, when 2,067 vessels were launched; and it did not again fall below the million-ton limit until 1922. Shipbuilding requirements naturally reacted on the steel industry by creating an extraordinary demand for plates. During the period of maximum pressure the Carnegie Company erected a 110-inch plate mill to fill such orders, at West Homestead, Pennsylvania, within the remarkably short period of six months. By the date of the armistice the steel-plate capacity of the United States had been brought up to 7,000,000 tons or more per annum. This was about equal to the call for shell steel, which was the other great war demand upon our manufacturers. Meanwhile, under the combined influence of huge outputs and high labor costs the already growing tendency in rolling mills toward larger units, specialty machinery, and automatic handling was accelerated. Rapid progress in this direction was facilitated by the fact that this was a period of intensive plant construction and reorganization.

Land transportation also made heavier demands than usual upon the iron and steel industry. During the war, 170,000 railway cars were built in the United States for foreign use, and our exports of locomotives to belligerents and neutrals rose from 228, valued at about $2,000,000, in 1915 to well toward 1,500, valued at nearly $36,000,000, three years later. Orders for rails and other railway supplies rose correspondingly. The automobile manufacture, after a period of great activity during the preceding year, was restricted to one-half its normal output for the latter half of 1918; but motor trucks were classed as a military necessity, and their production, especially that of the five standardized models designed for the army, was facilitated to the utmost. Up to the armistice, omitting the demand of the Allies, our own Government had taken delivery of more than 84,000 passenger cars and trucks and 40,000 motorcycles and bicycles for military uses. Simultaneously automobile manufacturers were called upon to divert a part of their machinery and shop organization to other objects. We have already referred to the Ford plant for manufacturing eagle boats. By the end of the war, the industry's output of Liberty engines for airplanes was 150 a day. After America entered the war, the factories of the Dodge Company, as well as the Singer Sewing Machine Company, were called upon to manufacture recoil apparatus for heavy field artillery, the use of which had been granted to our Government by the French. It would require a chapter in itself to enumerate all the cases where similar plant conversions occurred.

The World War, like the Civil War, stimulated the use of farm machinery to compensate for a scarcity of labor coincident with a multiplied demand for agricultural products. This resulted in the rapid adaptation of power to small farming and a corresponding increase in the use of tractors. In fact the latter were occasionally equipped with lights, and plowing was done during the night. Just before the war the International Harvester Company, which had acquired a virtual monopoly of some branches of the farm-machinery manufacture in the United States, was divided by court order into two concerns—the International Harvester Corporation, handling principally motor trucks and tillage and planting machinery, which were relatively newer features of the business, and the International Harvester Company of New Jersey, which took over the original line of harvesting machinery together with the properties and primary industries supplying iron, coal, and timber for this virtually self-contained organization. The former company, which handled all the foreign business of both concerns, operated plants abroad, some of which were converted wholly or partially to war uses in their respective countries.

While aircraft have been built in America ever since the Wrights demonstrated the practicability of flying in 1908, the industry lagged and in 1914 employed only 16 establishments with annual product of less than $800,000. Five years later, following the stimulus of the war, there were 31 makers of airplanes and airplane parts in the country with a product exceeding $14,000,000. The first American-made planes for military use were shipped to France in February, 1918, and represented the result of the organized effort of the Government to promote quantity production. Since this was virtually a new branch of manufacture their construction was turned over largely to automobile makers, whose plants were best adapted for such work and especially for attaining the quantity output so urgently demanded. This stimulation, however, was artificial and episodic and was followed by a marked recession after the armistice.

CHEMICAL INDUSTRIES

An outstanding and enduring achievement of the war period was the expansion and refinement of certain branches of chemical manufacturing in response to the demand for explosives and for coal-tar colors. The production of both of these really begins with the by-product coke oven. As we have seen in an earlier chapter by-product coking for furnace fuel began in America about twenty years before the outbreak of the war, and it was making slow but steady progress when hostilities began. In 1914, however, by-product ovens made less than one-third of the 34,500,000 tons of coke produced, while five years later they already accounted for more than two-thirds of the total output. Moreover in 1914 the principal by-products recovered were gas, tar, and ammonia. A few plants were equipped to separate benzol and tuluol, which they were obtaining at the rate of two or more gallons of the former and one to two quarts of the latter per ton of coal. Our position relatively to Germany at this time may be inferred from the fact that while we mined twice as much coal as that country we produced considerably less than one-sixth as much benzol. But already measures were being taken to remedy this, and during 1915 eight benzol recovery plants were completed, and four others were under construction when the season ended.

The first call was for explosives, which constituted part of the earliest orders placed by the allies in America. Early in October, 1914, France contracted for 8,000,000 pounds of smokeless powder from the Du Pont Company, which was about the annual capacity of that Company's works under pre-war conditions. Two years earlier this Corporation had been unscrambled from a larger combination by an interlocutory decree of the United States Circuit Court, and when the war broke out it was operating only three smokeless powder plants with a daily capacity of some 28,000 pounds. It immediately set about enlarging these works until their output reached 1,385,000 pounds a day and employed 33,000 wage earners. In 1915 the same Company erected at Hopewell, Virginia, a plant to make nitrocellulose, of which it manufactured more than 1,000,000,000 pounds between that date and the armistice. After America entered the war the Government employed the Du Ponts to erect the Old Hickory works near Nashville, Tennessee. This establishment, which was designed to make 900,000 pounds of military powder daily and to employ 30,000 people likewise passed into the hands of the Du Ponts after the armistice. Both the Hopewell and the Old Hickory plants are now making rayon. As a result of the rapid growth of producing capacity in America, prices of explosives began to decline after November, 1915, indicating that manufacturers had not only extended facilities until they met current demands but had also paid in good part for this expansion out of profits—for the temporary character of the war market was amply discounted in such investments. This subsidence of prices continued until March, 1917, when they were considerably below the general commodity level. Another rise occurred after America entered the war, but it was comparatively moderate, and during the last months of hostilities prices were again receding.

Dyes presented a different problem; for while the production of explosives depended mainly upon plant capacity and raw materials, both of which it was easily in the power of America to augment indefinitely, the production of dyes required scientific knowledge and a skill and experience not too abundant at that moment in this country. Early in 1831, when Samuel Slater and Sons, who were then operating mills at Webster, Massachusetts, which their successors sold to the American Woolen Company in 1924, made a bargain with James Moorehouse to take over their dye house for one year, under a contract which among other things bound him to dye for them "full blues," "invisible greens," and "all wooded colors" for $2\frac{1}{4}$ cents a pound, and "all kettle colors" for 1 cent a pound, American textile manufactures were virtually on an equal footing with their transatlantic competitors in respect to raw materials, whatever their handicap may have been in regard to skilled labor and experience in the finer processes of cloth finishing.

By 1914, however, following the revolution that had accompanied the development of the chemical industries, and especially of synthetic dye manufacturing in Germany, this situation had radically changed. American consumers suddenly awakened to the fact that they were utterly dependent upon what was in war time a precarious source of foreign supply for the continuance of an important part of their operations. When the news of hostilities burst upon the world there were enough essential imported colors on hand in the United States to last about two months. Conditions remained normal until the end of December, when stocks began rapidly to dwindle. Germany, to be sure, was only too eager to replenish the color bins of her American customers, for she needed the trade and she was anxious to prevent the establishment of rival works west of the Atlantic; but for a time she would ship dyes only in return for cotton, which was an important war commodity that the British Government treated as contraband. The few dye manufacturing works outside of Germany, mostly in Switzerland, were already oversold in export markets, and in any case would have been unable to fill the needs of our manufacturers. Four or five establishments in America were, it is true, producing the simpler dyes, but they depended largely on Germany for semi-prepared materials. By 1916, therefore, the shortage of colors reached a point where a few textile mills were forced to shut down until they could procure new supplies. Germany released fixed quantities from time to time as they could be brought through the blockade. Some of these arrived by submarine.

Meanwhile American dye makers were on the alert to profit by the situation but hesitated to extend their investments on account of the possibility that an early peace would flood our market with foreign colors in the absence of a protective duty. They also had to encounter the skepticism and opposition of importers, who tried to discourage them with the prediction that "if American makers plug away at their work for the next fifteen years their product may be sufficient to supply the demands of 20 per cent of the concerns requiring dyestuffs in New York City." Nevertheless they did "plug away" and made good progress.

At the National Silk Convention in November, 1916, three months after the passage of the act levying ad valorem and specific duties upon dyes and other coal-tar products, except certain basic raw materials, the representatives of the two largest color-manufacturing concerns in America made extremely optimistic speeches. In reviewing the colors then available they asserted that manufacturers of silks and of cotton and woolen fabrics could be supplied from domestic sources with all but a relatively small number of shades, that the leather industry could obtain practically every color needed in America, and that though prices were high on account of the demand of coal-tar products to make explosives they were not above those of Europe. A year later 23 companies in the United States were producing coal tar crudes and 98 were making finished dyes. Three-fourths of the colors needed by our manufacturers were produced in America in satisfactory quantities and qualities—some of these were so abundant that they were exported to England and elsewhere. One of the principal shortages at this time was of indigo, which, however, was already manufactured synthetically in Michigan. Some criticism was provoked by the failure of American dyes in certain instances, due—the textile trade was assured—to dyers' experiments with substitutes and previously untried combinations during the previous months of extreme shortage.

That year the National Aniline and Chemical Company absorbed three of its associates, whose aggregate capital exceeded $8,000,000, and the Du Ponts began the erection of a huge plant at Wilmington, which covered 300 acres, embraced 80 buildings, and included in its army of employees more than 10 per cent of the graduate chemists of the country. In February, 1918, these works began delivering indigo, which was in great request, especially for the Navy. Meanwhile imports of vegetable dyestuffs increased fourfold. After America entered the war the Alien Property Custodian seized all dye patents owned by German subjects in this country and sold them to a fiduciary corporation, organized for the occasion, called the Chemical Foundation. This was not a profit-making enterprise, and in acquiring for a nominal sum the patents, which numbered between four and five thousand, it engaged to permit the Government to use them without compensation and to grant their use to licensed private manufacturers subject to provisions that would effectively prevent any of these from establishing a monopoly. When the war was over the legality of the transaction by which the Chemical Foundation had acquired the patents was attacked in the courts, but without success.

In short, the armistice found the United States in the possession of a thriving dye industry. This represented an achievement in the manufacturing annals of this brief period equalled only by the expansion of shipbuilding. Both were fruits of the war emergency, and both were equally artificial in a world of free competition. The difference of their respective fortunes during the years that followed illustrates both the strength and the weakness of the American economic system.

TEXTILES

Among the many industries in varying degrees essential for winning the war, textile manufacturing stands out as a group of first importance. None of its branches was notably prosperous when hostilities began. Cotton spinning was in the doldrums, particularly in New England, where average dividends had sunk far below the level of previous years. Seventeen of the thirty-seven Fall River corporations paid nothing to their stockholders during the last quarter of 1914. Makers of coarse fabrics, especially in the South, had fared better and had profited somewhat by the slump in cotton that followed the outbreak of hostilities, so that mills south of the Potomac were consuming more staple than ever before. Nevertheless the world demand for cotton fabrics, as for the raw material, was checked by the shock of the war.

During 1915, however, a gradual improvement occurred in this industry. More machinery was reported in operation with each succeeding month, and profits were on the upgrade. This betterment was due largely to the improvement of the domestic market, where buying was active, partly on account of the rapidly rising price of raw materials. The satisfactory state of business was suggested by the fact that at their various gatherings, both North and South, mill owners devoted their discussions principally to the shortage of labor and new wage demands. A series of wage increases began about this time which soon brought the weaving rate, for example, to a point double what it had been ten years before. Simultaneously dividends rose to almost record heights.

While the war thus stimulated cotton manufacturing by widening markets and increasing home demand, it had no such revolutionary effect upon the industry as it did upon the manufacture of wool, or even of silk. The only specific war fabric created was a substitute for linen to cover the wings of airplanes, developed under the auspices of the Bureau of Standards and first manufactured in 1917, at Taftville, Connecticut. Largely as a result of the wool shortage, much progress was made in the production of cotton blankets, which, thanks to the improvement of cotton napping machinery, established themselves permanently in the trade. No deterioration of standards seems to have resulted from war stress, as it did during the Civil conflict fifty years before. In fact, better staples were employed than previously; for cotton waste and linters were eagerly bought up by ammunition makers. During the cotton year ending August 1, 1918, some 490,000,000 pounds of these materials were used for explosives and other army purposes, and the Government took over the entire product.

Wool manufacturing was the textile industry most prominent in the war story. A large fraction of its raw material was imported and mainly from the British dominions or through British channels. Soon after hostilities began Great Britain assumed control of wool exports from all parts of the Empire in order to keep supplies of this essential material from reaching her enemies. Indeed at times she placed a complete embargo on the commodity. Her action forced Americans to import exclusively through licensed channels, under guaranties that the raw materials, and the goods manufactured from them, would be consumed in the United States or in countries to which they had the express permission of the British Government to export them. Machinery for handling the trade was developed around the Textile Alliance Incorporated, an organization which had been formed early in 1914 by representatives of several textile manufacturing associations to suppress what were considered objectionable practices in the purchase of dyestuffs and mill supplies.

This industry was in somewhat better shape than cotton manufacturing when the war broke out, although wool and woolens, which had been higher than the average price level up to 1914, had recently sunk below that level. After hostilities began in Europe quotations for both raw materials and finished goods continued to soar until the Government took control in 1918. Even then civilian fabrics, which were unregulated, mounted more rapidly than the price of raw materials. Until the United States entered the war, however, military demands had relatively little to do with this prosperity. Manufacturers hoped for orders for blankets and uniform cloth for foreign governments, but though some commissions of this kind were placed in America soon after the war broke out, they never bulked large in mill output. In March, 1915, more looms were idle than at the opening of the year, and only 1,106 were at that date engaged on foreign work. The following autumn something over 2,000 of the 40,000 looms reporting were manufacturing goods for the belligerents. By July, 1916, the significant feature of recent developments in the industry was reported to be "the practically complete disappearance of foreign military orders," which had been decreasing through the late winter and spring and had now been "to all intents and purposes" eliminated. But though the Allies and European neutrals—for there was at no time any possibility of supplying Germany—had adjusted their production to cover their home needs, they were not able to fill the orders of their former customers in outside markets. Consequently, American sales, especially to South America, increased to fill his void and were an important tonic to the trade. Early in 1917 the American Woolen Company organized a subsidiary corporation, The American Woolen Products Company, expressly to develop and transact its foreign business. None the less, the prosperity of the industry was based mainly on an active home demand.

America's entry into the war immediately imposed new and unprecedented tasks upon the wool manufacture. During the next year and a half the spectre of a wool famine, which had haunted mill owners at times ever since 1914, grew more intrusive and threatening. Manufacturers had inaugurated a campaign as early as 1916 to induce farmers to raise more sheep; but domestic supplies were quite inadequate, either in quantity or in variety of fiber, for the country's needs. The Government eventually took over for military purposes the entire stock of raw wool in dealers' hands or contracted for by them abroad. This forced mill owners to depend mainly upon their warehoused supplies for manufacturing civilian goods. When the war ended the authorities had either in their possession or engaged abroad some 525,000,000 pounds of wool. This temporary diversion of raw materials to military use presumably encouraged a larger employment of shoddy and other recovered wool fibers in goods for the ordinary trade; but the complaint often heard in the sixties, that our soldiers were clad in shoddy uniforms, was not repeated in 1917 and 1918. This raw-material shortage may have assisted to shift popular consumption, about this time, from worsted to woolen goods.

So far as manufacturers were working upon Government contracts, they were relieved of immediate concern as to the sources of their wool supply; and these contracts formed a very large fraction of their business. Those of the American Woolen Company, the largest corporation in this branch of manufacture, totaled more than $102,000,000, and employed over one-half of its machinery. In case of some other companies the proportion of machinery engaged upon government work was even larger; for example it exceeded three-fourths of the equipment of the great Arlington Mills.

This activity was reflected in the earnings of the principal corporations. It was during the war, but before America entered the conflict, that the American Woolen Company first began to pay dividends on its common stock. After suffering a loss of nearly $678,000 in 1913, this Company's profits rose from $2,789,000 in 1914 to a maximum of $15,665,000 in 1917, which was double the amount of the previous year. Net earnings then declined to a little more than $12,000,000 in 1918, only to rise again the following season to almost the maximum just quoted. Arlington Mills increased their earnings from somewhat over $1,000,000 in 1915 to $3,638,000 in 1917. They also experienced a shrinkage of more than $1,000,000 in profits the last year of the war but made a record income, exceeding even that of 1917, the season following the armistice.

Silk manufacturers were prosperous throughout this period, chiefly because their products were in large request to supply the place of other textiles, particularly womens dress goods, which rose excessively in price or suffered curtailed production. Beginning with 1915, a second influence directly associated with the progress of hostilities abroad stimulated the market for silk fabrics. When the German armies invaded northern France they occupied the fine wool manufacturing districts of that country. Bereft of the dress goods which that region had previously supplied, the fashion dictators of Paris turned almost exclusively to the use of silks and thus encouraged a vogue that has continued to the present day. Direct war demands for silk were limited largely to cartridge bags, which were woven from spun yarns and stimulated particularly that department of the manufacture, parachute fabric, of which a great quantity was employed in making the slow-settling flares dropped from airplanes and dirigibles, and sewing silk, which was employed exclusively to sew navy uniforms and largely used in making up other textile wares. Since raw silk reached this country freely across the Pacific and was burdened with relatively lighter freights in proportion to its value than other imported materials, the price of silks as compared with competing fabrics fell. A silk dress cost less than one of woolen, and a silk waist cost less than a cotton waist of the better grade. Last of all, the increasing employment of women at high wages in munition factories and other war work, and in civilian occupations, increased the demand for costumes suitable for a wider variety of uses, including street and office wear, than were needed at home and for household duties. To be sure, silk mills, being situated in the very heart of a region of dense general manufacturing, suffered from labor shortage. Their male workers especially were attracted by higher wages to the neighboring metal-working shops. But this was a condition also faced by other branches of textile manufacturing.

Domestic production of artificial silk more than doubled during the war, rising from about 2,500,000 pounds in 1914 to nearly 6,000,000 pounds the year of the armistice. But this did not imply an equal growth in consumption, although the latter also increased, because imports declined nearly as rapidly as domestic production rose.

No other industry of the textile group need detain us here. Flax from the Baltic countries and linen from Belgium, France, and Ireland grew scarcer as the war went on. In 1916 political disorders in Mexico plus a socialist government in Yucatan threatened to interrupt supplies of sisal urgently needed for binder twine, but eventually an arrangement was worked out by which our Government undertook to supervise the distribution of this essential commodity to American manufacturers, on behalf of the export monopoly which had been set up by the Mexicans. Had these negotiations come to an impasse the adoption of the reaper-thresher combine might have been still further hastened in the West.

One might continue almost indefinitely the enumeration of manufactures that held an important place in war production, but an excess of examples would only cloud the picture. Packers, canners, flour millers, and all other food manufacturers strained their energies to the utmost to meet the huge demands made upon them. Other groups found the call for their products diminishing and their plants partly idle. The lumber industry experienced no war boom until our Government began erecting cantonments, building wooden ships, and constructing a fleet of airplanes. But on the whole the effect of the war was to expand plant capacity beyond peace requirements, to divert machinery to emergency forms of production, to concentrate some branches of manufacturing even more than before in certain sections of the country, and to disorganize staffs of experienced workers and replace them by less skilled and less stable employees. These effects varied in different localities and in different industries. On the other hand many manufacturers profited by the lessons in coöperative control of production, plant organization, and corporate management that they learned during the era of war regulation. Some of them also got a foothold in foreign markets which they did not altogether relinquish afterward. Moreover, many accumulated large reserves of capital. Some of the steel companies made enormous profits, though these reached their maximum as a rule before America entered the war. In the food industries, Armour and Company earned nearly 16 per cent upon its investment during its best war year; the American Beet Sugar Company earned 24 per cent; and the Quaker Oats Company 20 per cent. Meanwhile the American Woolen Company earned 10 per cent, and the Central Leather Company about 14 per cent. Though these are exceptional figures, reached only in 1917, even they do not measure the augmentation in value of properties and the accumulation of surpluses which accompanied this expansion of income.

According to the census, between 1914 and 1919 the value added by manufacture to the gross product of our factories rose from under $10,000,000,000 to over $25,000,000,000. Allowing for the shrinkage of the dollar to about one-half its former value during these five years, this leaves a net increase of approximately 25 per cent. Meanwhile wages rose about 40 per cent, upon this corrected basis, and the number of wage earners some 30 per cent. These comparisons, which are but rough approximations, are between two peace years, but they are vitiated to some extent by the fact that 1914 was a season of depression and 1919 one of exceptional activity. They suggest that the volume of manufactures, so far as it can be measured by corrected monetary equivalents, grew more rapidly during the war period than during the five years immediately preceding. Progress had been slower, however, than during the interval between the census enumerations of 1904 and 1909.

CHAPTER XXI

POST-BELLUM DEVELOPMENT

Industry Becomes Socialized, 324. Tariff Laws, 328. Industrial Organization, 330. Merchandizing and Consumers' Credits, 332. Iron and Steel, 333. Engineering Industries, 336. Textiles, 339. Chemical Industries, 346. Miscellaneous Manufactures, 348.

INDUSTRY BECOMES SOCIALIZED

The war left American manufacturers with overgrown plants, an excess of raw materials, and an arsenal of new ideas. The last have probably influenced the following era more than either of the former. During many months the Government and industry had been working hand in hand—even though with clenched fists at times—and each had gained new insight into the problems of the other. This experience apparently left the authorities friendlier than before—or at least more discriminately hostile—to big industrial combinations. The statisticians of the War Industries Board inclined to the opinion that "trust-made products seem to have steadier prices than products made under conditions of free competition." Indeed the president of this Board in his final report advocated the promotion of combinations in certain lines of industry to be administered under Federal control. The first task of the moment was to stabilize prices, wages, and other conditions of production. Any form of business organization that promised to attain this object was welcome.

Production facilities of every kind were overextended. The readjustment of agriculture and coal mining to normal levels of consumption has engaged the best efforts of the entire world ever since the armistice. Excess capacity in manufacturing was more exclusively an American problem, since it was a condition not generally shared by the great industrial countries of Europe. Between 1914 and 1919 the country's fabricated-structural-steel capacity rose from 227,000 to 266,000 tons a month; and its steel-castings capacity from 86,000 to 110,000 tons. Thanks mainly to army demands for woolen cloths and blankets, the census of 1919 reported the first increase in the number of woolen mills in fifty years, from 501 to 560 establishments, and an expansion of output from $104,000,000 to $365,000,000. Progress in the worsted industry had been so much slower that the balance between these two branches of the wool manufacture was appreciably disturbed by the war interlude. Cotton machinery increased less rapidly than during the four years preceding hostilities, partly because in this industry America was approaching spindle saturation. Those engaged in exclusively war manufactures, such as making explosives, had no recourse but to scrap their excess plants with the minimum of loss, or to transfer them to entirely different lines of production.

Steel consumption had followed so closely on the heels of output during the war that stocks on hand at its close were not a serious problem. Nevertheless the trade was somewhat reassured by the statement, early in 1919, that British war supplies accumulated in the United States would be sold off gradually. Peace caught the Government with a surplus of more than 800,000,000 pounds of copper, which kept the market constantly depressed until 1922. Zinc producers had suffered from overproduction in 1917 and 1918 and therefore already had their output under good control. Aluminum was so largely in the hands of a single company that output was figured closely to market requirements. Furthermore, soon after peace was declared labor troubles in Norway and unsettled conditions in Germany widened foreign outlets for aluminum products. Of the textile fibres, wool presented the most serious disposal problem, for the Government had more than 500,000,000 pounds of this commodity on hand. An increase of some 8,000,000 pounds in the domestic clip since 1914 did not materially affect supplies, but heavy importations were foreseen as soon as the removal of war risks cheapened ocean freights. Although wool prices did not decline as precipitately as those of copper, which fell from 24.8 cents a pound in 1918 to 18.7 cents a pound the following year, their ultimate shrinkage was far greater. Producers received upon an average for unwashed fleeces 58 cents a pound in 1918, 51 cents a pound in 1919, and only 17 cents a pound in 1921.

The problem of stabilizing the conditions of which we have just indicated a few extreme examples could be solved only through coöperative action. Therefore, decided impetus was given to the movement which had already begun prior to 1914, and which would have been encouraged in any case by war experience, toward organizing producers for the purpose of pooling statistical, trade, and technical information and for collective advertising, sales promotion, and foreign marketing. In these activities they had the benevolent backing of the Government.

This resulted in the formation of some nine thousand local, interstate, and national trade organizations of which probably one-fourth represent directly manufacturing interests. The objects and the activities of these societies vary widely, as is inevitable in view of the many kinds of business that they represent and the different conditions of production and merchandizing with which they deal. Copying a name first given vogue by the iron and steel industry, several call themselves "institutes," a term suggesting the technical and research functions that they oftentimes perform. In 1921, when copper producers found themselves overstocked after the war, they organized a Copper and Brass Research Association which studied ways to promote the consumption of their product. This body, like others of similar kind, has gone after the ultimate consumer, who affords the largest as well as the most stable market, and has spent much money in the advertising pages of our magazines to convince prosperous householders that brass spouts and water pipes are desirable in their dwellings. A Copper Export Association and a National Association of Brass Manufacturers also look after the common interests of this industry. Such societies have helped to eliminate waste by standardizing and simplifying processes and products and by extending the principles of the Taylor system to industrial organization and management. This is carrying forward work begun by the War Industries Board and has been accomplished with the aid, and to no small extent upon the initiative of Government bureaus and departments. To illustrate by commonplace examples one phase of this activity, the sizes of bed blankets have been reduced from 78 to 12, and those of paper grocer's bags from 6,280 to 4,200. One of the major services of the National Automobile Chamber of Commerce is to arrange for the cross-licensing of hundreds of patents among its members, thus saving the industry large sums and great waste of energy in litigation over infringements. The American Institute of Baking has conducted researches into methods of mixing and baking bread and into the ingredients used. We have already referred in an earlier chapter to similar work done by the National Canners' Association, and in a different field by the Portland Cement Association.

In the spring of 1918, while the United States was still engaged in hostilities but when the conditions that were likely to follow peace were already evident, Congress passed an Export Trade Act to enable producers, including manufacturers and traders, to form legal combinations for promoting the sale of American goods abroad. Such combinations are exempt from the prohibitions of the anti-trust laws but are placed under the general supervision of the Federal Trade Commission. Many industries and groups of industries, ranging all the way from manufacturers of locomotives to producers of pearl buttons and clothespins, have formed associations under the law.

This trend toward industrial coöperation is not confined to separate branches of manufacture. It would take us too far afield, however, to outline what is being done by local, state, and national chambers of commerce and manufacturers' associations to bring together representatives of different trades and industries for the promotion of common objects. Such organizations are not new, but their number, influence, and functions have expanded remarkably of late.

It should not be assumed, however, that the benevolence with which the Government views such developments as these implies an abandonment of its campaign against practices constituting a restraint of trade. Shortly after the war the public, which had anticipated a return to the old price level of 1914 with the restoration of peace, conceived an idea—quite justified in some instances—that consumers were paying exhorbitant prices for the necessaries of life. As a result Congress directed the Federal Trade Commission to inquire into costs, profits, and combinations in some of the food-manufacturing industries, the shoe and leather trades, and the production of house furnishings. The principal fact brought out by these investigations seems to have been that manufacturers and merchants had based their selling prices on replacement costs during the upward movement accompanying the war but were basing them on actual costs during the subsequent market decline. The success of such a policy depended entirely upon the mood of purchasers, however, and it ended with the "buyer's strike" which introduced the sharp and short depression of 1920.

Direct government price control ceased with the war. Thereafter effort was limited to preventing price manipulation by monopolies. A long list of court decisions had established the illegality of attempts by patentees to control the prices of their products after these had left their hands. For example, owners of copyrights could not prescribe the price which dealers should place upon their books, nor could manufacturers of talking machines fix the price at which their records should be sold by retailers. Although the "trust-busting" era was over, the list of manufacturers convicted of illegal practices under the Sherman and Clayton acts was a fairly long one, but the majority of the defendants were comparatively small concerns, and the more notable cases against great corporations or corporation groups were terminated by consent decrees. The most prominent settlement of the latter kind was embodied in the decree of February 27, 1920, against Swift and Company, Armour and Company, Morris and Company, Wilson and Company, and Cudahy Packing Company, which among other things ordered the packers to cease manufacturing or trading in so-called "unrelated lines," such as canned goods, fruits, and general groceries. In 1923 the Government compelled 56 window-glass manufacturers who still employed hand blowers, in the territory between Pennsylvania and Oklahoma, to terminate an agreement to operate under the two-period plan. This plan had been originally adopted during the war to conserve fuel, but it had been continued voluntarily thereafter because it suited the interests of the trade. It provided that one-half of the works that were parties to the agreement should shut down alternately for two-week periods while the other half operated. In 1927 the Supreme Court of the United States declared illegal an association of between twenty and thirty manufacturers of sanitary pottery and fixtures on the ground that it prescribed prices and limited the sales of its members to a list of approved jobbers.

While consumers wished to return immediately to pre-war prices with the advent of peace, manufacturers, most of whom had been bound by agreements with the Government not to reduce the pay of their employees during hostilities, were equally eager to get back to the low wages of the good old days. Many of the latter thought that the returning soldiers would flood the labor market and make such reductions easy. This resulted in a period of labor unrest, accompanied by numerous strikes against wage decreases, which again called for the intervention of the Government. Some states having a large factory population, like New York and New Jersey, appointed reconstruction commissions one of whose functions was to deal with this problem. The Federal Government appointed an Industrial Commission, which occupied a prominent place on the public stage for many months to the entertainment and possibly to some small profit of the public. But the only remedies for these ills which had much effect were those discovered through the old method of trial and error by the workers and managers in each industry, and oftentimes in each industrial establishment. For many employers the war proved a liberalizing experience. The Russian Revolution, and the world-wide Bolshevist agitation which followed it, called for deft handling of industrial relationships. The spirit of coöperation so sedulously cultivated during the war had not entirely vanished. Men like Henry Ford, who stood in the public mind for conspicuous success in industry, were preaching and—what is more important—paying high wages, on the theory that this enlarged the market for their products and eventually reduced their production costs. Several great corporations, notably United States Steel, encouraged their employees to share in the ownership of the business by selling stock to them on easy terms. Labor representation in management became more common. Altogether conservative and pacifist influences increased their ascendancy in American industrial relations. Simultaneously the attitude of the public toward great industrial combinations was mollified by an increase in consumer ownership in public utilities and by a wider distribution of industrial stocks and securities among small investors.

TARIFF LAWS

On May 27, 1921, President Harding signed a bill, almost identical in its provisions with one vetoed by President Wilson a few months earlier, levying substantially increased duties upon agricultural and ranch products including grain, livestock, butter, cheese, sugar, tobacco, certain strictly industrial raw materials, like cotton and wool, and wool manufactures. This law was enacted in the midst of the greatest price decline for farm commodities that had occurred in many years. While the general price level had sunk since January, 1920, about 100 points, from 248 to 151 per cent of 1913 quotations, farm products as a group had fallen from 291 to 131, and wool from 263 to 108. This situation made ardent high tariff advocates of agriculturalists, especially in the West. Under the new law duties on wool, which had previously been admitted free, were from 15 to 45 cents a pound according to its quality and condition. The stock of this material on hand was exceptionally large, for the war hold-over had not been absorbed, great stores were in the hands of public authorities and warehousemen in the British colonies, and American woolen mills were operating on short time because of industrial depression and labor troubles. Wool imports had been heavy in anticipation of a coming duty, and the market had reached a point when the whole wool-growing industry, including the banks supporting it, faced financial ruin.

A tax of 7 cents a pound was also levied on long staple cotton, but this affected a relatively small proportion of the country's imports—not more than 200,000 bales—principally from Egypt. The duty on sugar likewise was increased to 2 cents a pound, the highest rate for many years. Beet-sugar production had increased both absolutely and relatively during the war, from an average of 1,220,000 pounds during the five years ending with 1914 to more than 2,000,000 pounds in 1921 and from 15 to 22 per cent of the total domestic consumption.

The Emergency Act was followed by the Fordney law, approved September 1, 1922, which provided for a general revision upward of nearly all import duties. During the debates upon the bill, which began while the after-war depression was still acute, new party and sectional alignments appeared. Sentiment in the West was still strongly protectionist, but the popular revolt against high prices, and a feeling that manufacturers and merchants were profiteering upon the community, made many consumers hostile to increased duties. The World War, in contrast to the Civil War, had been fought on a comparatively low tariff; for during the intervening half century sources of inland revenue, like income and excess-profits taxes, had been developed until they furnished the principal resource of the Treasury. Above all, however, America's chief industrial competitors had been practically out of the market ever since the beginning of hostilities. Consequently the public, in its preoccupation with greater issues, had been for a time comparatively indifferent to tariff questions.

When the war was over, however, the whole industrial horizon changed. The general election of 1920 returned a congress overwhelmingly Republican and, therefore, traditionally protectionist. Doctrines of national self-sufficiency and industrial preparedness were part of the patriotic propaganda of the day. New industries, like the dye manufacture, which had sprung up during the war, were considered too important to be sacrificed to transatlantic competition. As a result, the Fordney law levied higher rates than any of its immediate predecessors. It differed from them not only in the general level of the duties it applied but also in the importance it placed upon the protection of agriculture and defense against dumping. It was made popular with the farmers by retaining agricultural machinery, including vehicles, on the free list, for these were commonly regarded as trust-made articles, and in any case no foreign country was likely to intrude upon the monopoly of their American producers. Binder twine and materials for fertilizers also remained untaxed. The duty on sugar was increased to more than 2 cents, and while wool rates were nominally lowered a trifle, changes in the method of their assessment made them in practice somewhat higher than before. Duties on dyestuffs were virtually doubled both by increasing nominal rates and by providing that ad valorem rates should be assessed on the selling price in the United States instead of on foreign market values.

A new provision, embodied for the first time in this law, empowered the

President to increase up to 50 per cent of the existing rate duties upon articles manufactured in countries where production costs were so much lower than those in the United States that the schedules as they stood in the Act failed to compensate the difference. The Tariff Commission, which had been created by act of Congress in 1916, principally as a general investigating and schedule-drafting body, was required to ascertain these differences in production costs, and the power of the President to raise duties by proclamation was contingent upon the Commission's findings. In connection with these functions the duties of the Commission were considerably extended, and its authority correspondingly increased. The President was further empowered to employ the flexible provisions of the tariff to prevent discriminations by foreign governments against the commerce of the United States.

In general, therefore, the country entered upon an era of unusually high protection comparatively early in the period of after-war adjustment. American manufacturers, however, had experienced very little competition from abroad since the summer of 1914.

INDUSTRIAL ORGANIZATION

Notwithstanding the fact that the plant capacity of many industries was overextended at the end of the war, no period in American history has witnessed so large an increase of capitalization and fixed investments in manufacturing, and in power development directly subsidiary to manufacturing, as the ten years since the armistice. This growth has been accompanied by increasing concentration of control in the hands of great corporations, and of financiers rather than of captains of industry of the older type who built up great enterprises by their personal efforts. For example, the board of directors of the United States Smelting and Refining Company, which originally included a large majority of works managers and other men directly in touch with the practical operations of the business, has become preponderantly a body of bankers. The largest of several mergers, which formed part of this movement toward concentration, was the Bethlehem Steel Corporation's purchase, in 1923, of the Midvale Steel and Ordnance Company and the Cambria Steel Company, which had been combined during the war, and, a little later, of the Lackawanna Steel Company. This consolidated the only large and clearly integrated steel making corporations east of Pittsburgh. Other combinations in the Youngstown and Chicago districts also showed that the trend toward larger units in this industry had not yet ceased. It was stimulated no doubt by the after-war depression. In fact, the Bethlehem and the Lackawanna companies joined forces in the export field before the corporations were formally united. About the same time the "Big Five" in the packing industry was reduced to four when Armour and Company purchased the plants and business of Morris and Company. Efforts of the Federal Trade Commission to prevent these combinations, and still further to unscramble the International Harvester Company, which continued to dominate the domestic market for reaping machinery and enjoyed substantial advantages over its competitors through owning steel works, lumber mills, and other sources of raw material, were defeated by court decisions adverse to the Government.

Another merger, occurring in 1923, of the Winchester Repeating Arms Company, organized in 1866, and the Simmons Hardware Company, founded in 1856, was a direct outcome of the war. From 1914 until America entered the conflict the former company was actively employed on large contracts for the belligerent powers, and after that its plant was engaged to capacity on Government work. When the armistice came, therefore, this Company found itself with a huge factory at New Haven, containing 3,250,000 square feet of floor space, which it had no present prospect of utilizing in the lines for which it was originally designed. So the directors decided to enter extensively the manufacture of hardware and other metal articles and to secure an immediate market for these products by selling exclusively through retailers. This brought the Company into direct competition with the Simmons Hardware people, who were the largest jobbers in this trade in the world, and who both manufactured in their own factories and purchased from outside makers. In order to avoid ruinous competition, therefore, the two corporations merged as the Winchester-Simmons Company, thus uniting what had been primarily a sales organization with one devoted chiefly to manufacturing.

Other influences coöperated with post-bellum economic stresses to reshape the industrial landscape. Invention and scientific research—which is merely invention up to date—were the most potent of these. When prohibition condemned to idleness the great corn distilleries of Illinois, they were diverted, as we have previously seen, to the production of acetone for the manufacture of smokeless powder. One of the by-products of this process was butanol, another kind of alcohol not used in the explosives business. Large quantities of this accumulated during the war and were saved for any uses that might develop. Later when the du Ponts and others were forced to turn their war plants to new uses and perfected the manufacture of pyroxylins, of which the old and more familiar form is celluloid, butanol and its derivatives were found to be ideal solvents for certain of these new substances, converting them into the popular lacquers for which there seemed to be an almost inexhaustible market. This led to the organization, in 1919, of the Commercial Solvents Corporation, which purchased a large plant at Terre Haute, Indiana, which had been operated jointly by the United States and British governments during the war, and other works at Peoria, Illinois, and specialized in the manufacture of this product and its congeners. By January, 1927, the Company was producing more than 110 tons of solvents a day, having doubled its capacity within twelve months, and its present output is much larger than the latter figure.

That new arrival in the ranks of important manufacturing enterprises has a more imposing companion in the Radio Corporation of America, which was likewise organized the year following the armistice. This $25,000,000 company also illustrates the filiation of several of these ultra-modern undertakings. It was promoted by the General Electric Company which had become a large producer of radio apparatus, in coöperation with the Westinghouse Electric and Manufacturing Company and the United Fruit Company, which were also radio manufacturers or patent owners, and with former stockholders of the American Marconi Company, which was the original wireless communication enterprise in the United States. It is primarily a sales organization handling under contract goods produced by its parent companies and exercises market control through the ownership of several thousand patents.

MERCHANDIZING AND CONSUMERS' CREDITS

These comparatively new words in the vocabulary of business do not designate novel functions of the producer but connote methods of sales promotion that have either originated or acquired outstanding importance within recent years. Part of this change is due to new credit conditions. Soon after the Federal Reserve banks were established, the International Harvester Company urged its dealers to bring the implement business nearer to a cash business by substituting farmer's notes or acceptances for the existing system of open accounts and discounting these at the Reserve banks. In fact, the Company prepared forms of notes for dealers to use in this connection and was very active in its campaign in favor of shorter credits and a general tightening up of financial relations with the ultimate consumer. About the same time, however, the old device of instalment buying was resorted to with renewed vigor by certain manufactures in an effort to extend sales. The only features of this form of extending credit that need occupy us here are the new machinery devised to handle it and its effect upon production.

In 1915 Henry Ford notified the Wisconsin Banker's Association that he would not encourage automobile credits to farmers, because motor cars depreciated in use, thus differing radically from livestock and other farm chattels usually pledged for debt, which normally grew in value during the term of the loan. Instalment paper had begun to be used sporadically in connection with automobile sales about two years before this, by dealers who had previously accepted similar notes for buggies and other vehicles. It was not until after the war, however, that the systematic financing of automobile sales was begun by companies organized expressly for this purpose, and with the conscious object of broadening markets in order to support quantity production. The phenomenal growth of this method of sales promotion sprang out of the sudden depression that engulfed American industry in 1920 and 1921. This crisis threatened to bear with maximum severity upon the automobile manufacture, which was comparatively new, which was overextended according to all conventional measurements, and which catered to what was still considered luxury consumption. Prior to this emergency the General Motors Acceptance Corporation had been founded by the company whose name it bears and was already pointing the way for numerous imitators. By the close of 1922 that Corporation had extended financial accommodation to the amount of $337,000,000 to its customers. The following year the first Annual Automobile Financing Conference was held at Chicago, in response to the same urge toward collective action that was animating the whole business world, for the purpose of standardizing practices governing credits to purchasers, and insuring the conservative development and administration of this new aid to industry.

It exceeds the bounds of our subject to discuss the remarkable expansion of instalment selling, its alleged effect in assisting the country to recover quickly from the 1920–1921 depression, and the stimulus it is supposed to have given to our subsequent manufacturing prosperity. New credit devices, however, have promoted not only domestic consumption but also foreign commerce. Late in 1919 Congress passed the Edge bill providing for the Federal incorporation of institutions to engage in international or foreign banking. This law, among other things, gave permanent form to provisional devices through which credits had been extended to exporters during the war. The significant features of our foreign trade during the post-bellum period have been its constant average expansion, the excess of imports of raw materials and semi-manufactured products over similar exports, and a great preponderance of exports of finished manufactures over imports.

IRON AND STEEL

Shortly after the armistice an Industrial Board was organized at the instance of the Secretary of Commerce to deflate prices. This body recommended a reduction of $4.25 in the price of pig iron and an average of $7 a ton in the price of steel. The United States Steel Corporation kept close to the Board's schedule, but the independents in several instances advanced their quotations soon after official price regulation ceased. In fact, this attempt of the Government to stabilize prices broke down entirely when the Attorney General ruled that the well-intentioned plan of the Commerce Department was in contravention to the Sherman Act and was not binding even in respect to purchases by the Government, which was required by statute to buy under competitive bidding. Prior to this decision the Railroad Administration had already refused to pay the price for rails fixed by the Board. Consequently pig-iron prices ranged from $3.80 to $6 higher in December than in January, 1919, and steel naturally followed the same course. The United States Steel Corporation, however, received upon an average $6.16 a ton less on domestic orders and $12.41 less on foreign shipments in 1919 than in 1918. Simultaneously pig-iron production sank from 38,500,000 to 30,500,000 tons.

A protracted strike in the autumn of 1919, for the purpose of unionizing the steel industry, practically suspended operations at many centers, such as Buffalo, Youngstown, and Gary, but left the Pittsburgh district relatively unaffected. Subsequently strikes of coal miners, and of railway shopmen, which crippled the coal and ore roads, also acted as a temporary damper upon production. Comparatively little steel was going into construction jobs and other investment uses, but it was in active request by makers of automobiles, typewriters, and general machinery. At the end of January, 1920, the Steel Corporation's unfilled orders exceeded 9,250,000 tons, the highest point during the preceding tweve months. Market conditions continued fairly stable until late in the summer, when prices began to fall, at first gradually and then more precipitately, steel billets declining at Pittsburgh from $62.50 a ton in July, 1920, to $32.25 in the spring of the following year. By the autumn of 1920 about one-half of the machinery in the Pittsburgh-Youngstown district was idle, and the following year the proportion of shutdowns throughout the country rose to 62 per cent. Many producers, especially furnace men, who were stocked up with high-priced ore, suffered heavy losses, and some manufacturers of steel products sold their stocks on hand, confident that they could supply their needs more cheaply later. The Steel Corporation was relatively more prosperous than its competitors largely because of its previous low-price policy. The independents, whose quotations a year before had ranged above those recommended by the Industrial Board, were now cutting under them. It was at this time that the new consolidations which we have mentioned elsewhere were first mooted. In 1921 pig-iron production sank to 16,500,000 tons, and steel output to less than 20,000,000 tons. These were the lowest points since 1908. Wages of common labor in eastern Pennsylvania were back at $2 a day, or the 1915 level.

Among the first signs of recovery, late in 1921 and early in 1922, were calls for pipes for new oil fields in the Southwest and for steel from agricultural implement makers. Another stimulus from the oil region came in the form of a demand for sheets for storage tanks. During the latter year heavier sales of steel to the railways, and a record consumption by the building and automobile industries, brought the market back to normal. As a result, the season closed with 60 per cent of the country's iron furnaces in blast, as compared with 17 per cent during the depth of the depression, and with 70 per cent of the steel capacity active. This recovery was due entirely to the betterment of the domestic market, for exports of iron and steel had fallen from nearly 5,000,000 tons in 1920 to considerably less than one-half that figure two years later. In fact the foreign market has not been an appreciable factor in this trade since Europe got into civilian production after the war. Nevertheless a sagging of prices and output as these lines are written is reported to have induced United States Steel and the Bethelehem Corporation to form a new organization for the joint promotion of their sales abroad. During the upgrade movement following the depression the eight-hour shift gradually replaced the twelve-hour shift in steel works. The restoration of prosperity lasted through the years that followed. Pig-iron record outputs exceeded even the maximum of the war period in 1923, and again in 1926, while 1925 and 1926 witnessed a larger production of steel billets than any year of hostilities.

Lower prices have characterized the closing months of the period that we are describing. Pigs have reached the 1915 level, and foundry iron is quoted at $15.50 a ton at Southern furnaces. The integration as well as the concentration of the industry continues. Steel plants have become so largely self-contained that merchant furnaces, producing pigs for sale in the general market, are being forced out of business. During 1927, 22 stacks, or one-fifth of the total in the country, were dismantled, and now only 68 remain of the 131 that were active during the war. Those that survive in most instances own independent supplies of coal or ore or else are situated near big cities which afford them a varied local market for their product. One economy of integration is the fact that the big steel companies tap their smelting furnaces directly into ladles which convey the molten metal to the steel furnaces, thus saving the fuel, plant, and labor that would be used in making an extra heat. Pig-iron plants associated with steel works are also larger as a rule than merchant plants, their investment in auxiliary equipment is less per ton, and they are in more continuous operation because of the steadier outlet for their product. A Government investigation in 1924 indicated that the cost of making foundry iron was nearly $3 per ton less, or $20.34 as compared with $23.05, in integrated plants than at merchant furnaces.

Nevertheless the iron business, as a distinct branch of the larger industry, is not dead. Indeed it shows signs of rejuvenescence. Mechanical puddling is receiving new attention. Methods for refining iron in large quantities and at a cost approximating that of producing steel, without the intervention of puddling in its present form, promise shortly to reach the stage of practical application. Stainless iron, an electric-furnace product complementary to stainless steel, and heat treatment of iron castings, rendering them equal to malleable for many purposes, are other developments pointing in the same direction. Technical advances of the war period have been maintained. Electric-furnace outputs slipped back somewhat when military demands ceased, but no war year approached by 100,000 tons the product of 1925 and 1926. Recent fuel developments, such as the use of powdered coal, and of a combination of tar and coke oven gas in the open-hearth process, point the way to new economies.

In 1926 the American Iron and Steel Institute made a survey of the producing capacity of the industry, which established the fact that the nation's furnaces were able to make, as shown in actual practice, 45,000,000 gross tons of pig iron and 50,000,000 tons of steel ingots annually. Their theoretical capacity exceeded this by several million tons.

ENGINEERING INDUSTRIES

Among engineering industries in their broad definition power generation, the automobile manufacture, and the production of electrical apparatus stand out most prominently as representing the modern age. Interest in ordnance and armor and in shipbuilding, which quickly slipped back to pre-war volume, subsided with the war fever. As a result of the agitation over the price of armor plates alluded to in the preceding chapter, a huge Naval Ordnance Plant, containing some of the heaviest machinery ever set up in America, was erected at South Charleston, West Virginia. These works, which were built and operated as well as owned by the Navy Department, were not completed until the war was over. They embrace 30-ton electric furnaces for duplexing, electric cranes powerful enough to lift and carry a load of 400,000 pounds, and a 14,000-ton hydraulic press; and they are equipped to roll 18-inch armor plates 14 feet wide and weighing up to 120 tons and to forge 20-inch guns.

The automobile industry, which deserves a chapter in itself, and which with a product valued at over $3\frac{1}{3}$ billion dollars in 1927 stands at the head of American manufactures, influenced almost every other branch of engineering, as it did lines of production outside this group, both as a taker of their products and as a demonstrator of new phases of industrial technique. It affected iron and steel production by creating new demands for alloys and high-quality metal and by demonstrating the possibilities and the importance of the annealing or heat-treating process. It worked out practical applications of already familiar mechanical devices, such as the various forms of frictionless bearings, which pointed the way to their wider adoption elsewhere. Its leaders reexamined the existing scheme of industrial organization and—as we have just seen—of merchandizing, with results that have extended far beyond their own industry. In a word this manufacture has been intensely alive, and constant progress and experiment have been a fruit as well as a condition of its marvelous expansion. The plasticity of its plants and methods was never better illustrated than by the attainment at the Ford works, within a very few months during the difficult period of the war, of a production schedule of fifty Liberty motors for every eight hours of the working day without seriously crippling the other operations of that great group of establishments. In accomplishing this radically new devices were unhesitatingly adopted, such as the quantity production of pistons from steel tubing.

The armistice, therefore, found this industry, although less than a decade old as a major manufacture, fully matured in organization and technology. It had accumulated a vast capital out of its own earnings. Its engineers were concentrating intensely on new manufacturing economies in an effort to reach a constantly widening circle of consumers. Between 1915, when the system of progressive assembly or "perpetual-motion production" was first developed, and 1923, the number of man hours required to produce a car had declined from nearly 5,000 to less than 1,000 for the more expensive models, and from 1,260 to 28 for the least expensive.

This progress was accompanied by a great increase in the size of the average establishment and by the same tendency of factories to become self-contained that is observable wherever quantity production is the rule. For some years before the war makers assembled their cars in large measure from parts purchased from specialty manufacturers. This practice has by no means been abandoned, as the existence of great firms like Continental Motors and Timken-Detroit Axle testify. In 1925 the Federal Trade Commission took action to prevent the Midland Steel Products Company from acquiring two neighboring concerns—the Parish and Bingham Corporation and the Detroit Pressed Steel Company—which between them produced nearly one-half of all the automobile frames made in the United States. Simultaneously the Commission took measures to keep the Hayes Wheel Company, which made approximately 37 per cent of all the automobile wheels used in America, and the Imperial Wheel Company, a neighboring competitor, from forming a combination. Even the Ford car, though manufactured by a firm which largely controls its own sources of raw materials as well as much of its transportation by both land and sea, depends upon outside makers for some of its patented parts and fittings.

A specialty company probably can produce its particular article as cheaply as or more cheaply than the general manufacturer. An assured supply of car components, rather than lower production costs, is therefore the motive urging toward self-contained plants, and this consideration grows in importance as their size increases. In 1926 the average annual output of automobile establishments was 80,000 cars as compared with only 18,000 ten years before.

The expansion of the industry has been remarkably consistent, the only years recording positive decreases being 1917, 1921, 1924, and 1927. In 1916 the number of cars and trucks made in the United States first passed the million mark; it rose above 2,000,000 in 1920, and reached the maximum of 4,500,000 in 1926. Nearly eight passenger cars are manufactured for one motor truck, and the growth of the market that has made this increase possible is due primarily to sales inducements that appeal to personal owners. The best authority on the history of the industry cites as the chief of these the self-starter, the cord tire and demountable rim, the low-priced closed car, and the instalment system.

The salient facts relating to recent automobile history are too familiar to justify recording. The virtual elimination of steam and even of electricity, as sources of power, the growing proportion of six-cylinder cars and of closed as compared with open models, the four-wheel brake, the balloon tire, and corporate changes that are placing the control of the industry in the hands of two or three giant corporations are known to everybody. According to current statistics the largest company in the business has well over 200,000 employees upon its payrolls.

Judged by volume and historical perspective the manufacture of air craft is of minor importance in our industrial records. The combined output of airplanes, seaplanes, and amphibians increased from 789, valued at less than $7,000,000, in 1925, to 1,962, valued at well over $14,000,000, in 1927. Their production was dispersed in 61 establishments situated in 17 different states. This ratio of growth bespeaks a promising future, but the chief significance of the manufacture for the engineering industries as a whole lies in its research contributions, especially to the study of motive power and of the reliability of materials.

Power, as a commercial product, is already virtually synonymous with electricity. In that form it is shipped in great quantities for long distances, pooled, distributed to consumers everywhere, and made available for constantly multiplying forms of use. The nation's annual output of electricity will probably reach 80,000,000 kilowatt hours the present season. Hydro-electric engineering has reached a point where its progress is largely quantitative. During the last two years reported the developed horsepower of the nation's streams increased 13 per cent, and in favored sections like the Southeast 31 per cent. Already the commercially profitable limits of hydro-electric development are in sight, and conservation of waterheads will soon be enjoined upon the forester as urgently as the preservation of lumber and pulp-wood timber stands. Water turbines of 70,000 horsepower and 93 per cent efficient are now installed at Niagara Falls, as compared with 5,000 horse-power turbines, 76 per cent efficient, twenty-five years ago. In 1926 the Allis-Chalmers Company installed in southern California a 56,000 horse-power impulse wheel to operate under a head of 2,200 feet. But the present margin for technical advance, as well as for quantitative expansion, seems to be larger in case of turbogenerators propelled by steam or by metal vapors than in case of water motors. Twenty-five years ago, when the first steam turbine generator was installed at Chicago—and this was ten years after the World's Fair in that city had convinced the nation that it had reached the acme of industrial progress—its capacity of 5,000 kilowatts was regarded as a marvel. Last year the General Electric Company built for a California corporation two 94,000-kilowatt tandem turbogenerators. The great Corliss engine at the Philadelphia Centennial, in 1876, was rated at 1,400 horse-power with a steam pressure of from 15 to 20 pounds per square inch. Two years ago a Corliss engine was built at Milwaukee for the American Steel and Wire Company to carry a maximum load of 18,000 horse-power. Only yesterday steam pressures of 550 pounds were considered notable in commercial practice. More than double that pressure is now employed at a huge power station near Boston.

A novel and promising development in power generation was the installation at Hartford, Connecticut, in 1924 of a turbine to use mercury vapor. It proved so successful that the experimental unit was supplemented last year by a companion five times its size, consisting of a mercury boiler, a mercury turbine, a condenser, and necessary accessories, to generate 10,000 kilowatts per hour and, as a by-product of mercury condensation, 125,000 pounds of steam at 260 pounds pressure. By this device fuel consumption per unit of electricity is reduced by about one-half. Such apparatus would have been impossible prior to the development of autogenous welding, for no solders or gaskets could withstand the action of mercury vapor at a temperature of 850°F. Incidentally arc welding has also made it possible to eliminate costly and cumbersome castings in large electric generators and motors.

New applications of electricity in the engineering industries are recorded almost daily. Synchronous motors and anti-friction bearings have made possible satisfactory electric drives, ranging up to 7,000 horse-power, in steel mills. The rapid transformations that accompany new applications of power have kept even the oldest and best-established engineering firms on the alert lest they lag in the march of progress. Two years ago the Worthington Pump Company reported that its most perplexing recent problem had been to adapt its products to a changing market resulting from the rapid trend, particularly since the war, from vertical water works, cranks and flywheels, and direct-acting steam and power pumps, to centrifugals, and from large gas engines to turbo-electric units. At about the same time the Babcock and Wilcox Company absorbed two equipment corporations in order to be able to offer to its customers a full line of the superheaters, economizers, air heaters, chain grate stokers, oil burners, pulverized-fuel mechanism, meters, and combustion controlling devices required to equip a modern steam-generating plant.

According to recent calculations the capital investment in the electrical industry as a whole exceeds $19,000,000,000 and yields a gross revenue of $6,000,000,000 annually. There are 1,800 electrical equipment manufacturers in the United States, who do a business of nearly $2,400,000,000 yearly. And all this is virtually the creation of less than half a century!

TEXTILES

Textile manufacturing stands in strong contrast to the engineering industries in its relatively slow expansion and static stage of development. The last qualification is true, however, only in a comparative sense, for transformations are constantly occurring, though they are less dramatic than those in the automotive or the electrical manufacture. In fact the rise of rayon production is one of the most conspicuous facts in recent industrial annals.

Active cotton machinery, which increased during the war and reached a maximum the year after the armistice, has declined slightly in the country as a whole during the last eight years, though it has increased in the cotton-growing states. Since 1914 spindlage has hardly kept pace with the growth of population, which furthermore has increased twice as rapidly as the number of looms. Even allowing for the fact that each machine unit probably produces more today than it did a decade and a half ago, this indicates a considerable shrinkage of capacity. When we turn to figures of cotton consumption, to be sure, the picture changes, for mill takings in 1926 exceeded those of any previous year except 1917. This apparent paradox is explained, however, by the high spindle consumption of the South, where machinery has consistently increased, and by the more extensive employment of cotton fabrics in industry relatively to their use for apparel and in household service. During the four years ending with 1925 the quantity of "tire fabrics" woven in the United States rose from less than 96,000,000 to more than 242,000,000 square yards, to which should be added 177,000,000 square yards of "cord," which was not reported as a separate commodity the first year of this comparison. Artificial leathers, of which great quantities are used for upholstering automobiles and for automobile tops, and which are usually manufactured on a cotton base, accounted in 1925 for more than 57,000,000 square yards of cloth. Incidentally these industrial fabrics are almost a monopoly of the South. They go far toward compensating in terms of crop consumption a shrinkage of more than two-fifths during this period in New England's output of print cloth.

The South now manufactures well toward twice the quantity of woven cotton goods credited to New England, and is the principal center for the manufacture of sheetings, print cloth, denims, drills, toweling, ticking, and cotton worsteds. It surpasses New England in output of shirting, ginghams, cotton flannel, bed spreads, and table damasks, and has a monopoly of osnaburgs. New England still leads in the manufacture of twills, lawns and cambrics, and cheese cloth and bunting, and is far ahead in the production of mixed fabrics of silk and cotton. While New England makes more cotton thread than the South, the latter produces well toward four-fifths of the cotton yarns entering the general market.

Under these conditions of sectional competition it is not strange that styles and fashions should assume new importance in the eyes of northern manufacturers. Some important establishments in New England employ style directors, who make frequent trips to the centers of fashion abroad, keep in touch with the leaders of the trade in New York, and virtually dictate the designs and patterns turned out by their mills. Something of a sensation was caused in the New England textile world two years ago when it was learned that the American Print Company at Fall River, which had until recently been famous for its narrow calicoes, seldom costing more than 5 cents a yard, had discontinued their production because the market for them had vanished. This Company remodeled its plant to produce superior styled fancy prints or percales rarely sold under 25 cents a yard. It even employed designers from high-priced silk mills to bring its standards up to the best set by the competing fabric. It also turned out many styles of sheer rayon. Since the latter can be finished on the same machines as cotton, establishments like the American Print Works and the Pacific

Mill at Lawrence handle a substantial amount of the new material. These changes in production involve more than a mere shifting from one class of fabrics to another. Fashion is fickle and highly styled goods must be placed on the market quickly and sold out before their run of popularity comes to an end. This requires speeding up not only the manufacturing process but also sales procedure. These new conditions also help to explain the hand-to-mouth buying by jobbers, retailers, and garment makers, which has become the bane of all textile industries. This aversion of purchasers to making long-time commitments has been reënforced by unhappy memories of losses on stocks in hand during the price slump shortly after the war.

The turn to finer and fancier fabrics has also influenced machinery. Combed cotton yarns have acquired increased importance, and the demand for fabrics made from them has grown more rapidly than domestic production of the long staple cotton from which they are spun. It might appear paradoxical, therefore, that the number of mule spindles, which are usually employed for the finest yarns, has steadily declined. Their number fell from 3,500,000 in 1918, to less than 2,000,000 six years later. But improvements in ring spinning, of which the latest is the use of a long draft, have made it possible to turn out on frames yarns almost as soft and even as those spun on mules.

Among the new fabrics which have become popular since the armistice, one of the most notable is broadcloth shirting, which originated in England about the beginning of the war and is still largely imported from that country. As usually happens, a cheapening of quality has accompanied its wider use. The first of these cloths brought to America had a lustrous finish due to the fact that they were woven of very fine two-ply Egyptian cotton warp and filling. Domestic cloths of this character are usually woven of coarser single-strand yarns ring-spun from domestic Peeler cotton. Simultaneously American mills have taken up successfully the quantity production, in somewhat cheaper grades than the imported, of voiles, a cloth which likewise originated in England a few years before the war, and which like broadcloth shirting was at first made of ply yarns for both warp and filling. These fabrics illustrate the relation the American cotton manufacture still holds to that of England—a relation repeated in a degree between the mills of New England and of the South. The origination of new weaves, which are commonly introduced in high-quality goods, is still the function of older manufacturing countries, although many substantial fabrics have been invented and have attained their reputation in America. With the growing attention now given to style, particularly in certain New England factories and among specialty manufacturers in the Central states, we may expect to see more quality fabrics, of the class now having their origin in Great Britain and France, designed on this side of the Atlantic.

A worldwide depression in cotton manufacturing has followed the war.

It has been felt most acutely of all in England, whose mill owners have simultaneously encountered the set-backs resulting from fashion changes and the competition of new textile fibers and the loss of a substantial share of their export trade to the factories of India and the Orient. Naturally this general crisis has affected the United States. Soon after the armistice, domestic prices of cotton goods declined, in some instances 50 per cent, partly as a result of the wholesale cancellation of war contracts. Between the spring of 1918 and 1919 prints fell from 14 to $7\frac{1}{4}$ cents a yard. This drop was followed by a prompt revival, however, due to the rising price of raw cotton, for which there was an eager call from Europe. During 1920 prosperity prevailed. Print cloths rose remarkably again and were not in oversupply. An increase of $12\frac{1}{2}$ per cent in wages showed the satisfaction with which Fall River mill owners viewed a situation that had lifted their last quarterly dividends to the record height of 11.09 per cent. This was the sunshine before the storm, however, and by November, 1920, print cloths had fallen from a maximum price of 17.5 cents the previous April to 7 cents, the lowest quotation since 1917. Nevertheless dividends for the year were well maintained, out of previous earnings, approaching close to 30 per cent. They had been less than $2\frac{1}{2}$ per cent for the same period in 1898. This break in cloth prices followed a sudden decline in cotton quotations, middling uplands dropping from 43.75 cents, in July, 1920, which was the highest price since 1866, to 19.4 cents the following November. They were to sink below the 10-cent level the following year. A series of wage cuts began about this time, which were to keep the industry in a state of unrest for several seasons thereafter.

The years which have followed have not been kindly ones for cotton spinners, especially in New England, and several establishments have been dismantled or have moved to the South. To be sure, per capita consumption of cotton fabrics continues to increase, but this growth affects principally coarse goods, especially those used in the industries, which are chiefly manufactured in the South, while the finer cottons made in the North have had to meet the competition of silk and rayon.

Exports of cotton cloth, which reached their maximum in 1923, when they exceeded 219,000,000 yards, have since sunk to little more than their pre-war volume. They consist principally of such staples as duck, osnaburgs, sheetings, print cloths, ginghams, and coarser colored cloths made of carded yarns.

Although the cotton manufacture has experienced such striking ups and downs since the armistice and is undergoing a process of regional and technical readjustment, it still remains our largest textile industry. Since the beginning of the century its machinery and its volume of output have approximately doubled while the value of its products has increased six times, or to over $2,000,000,000 in prosperous years. The proportion of its spindles active ranges normally above 90 per cent. Dividends, to be sure, have declined. During the last three years their ratio to capitalization at Fall River and New Bedford has averaged but a little over 4 per cent, although it has exceeded 7 per cent in the leading textile county of the South. Nevertheless the industry preserves a good fighting spirit. One of the latest events in its history was the founding, in 1926, of the American Cotton Textile Institute, formed at the initiative of Southern mill men, but embracing members of both the American Manufacturer's Association and the National Association of Cotton Manufactures, which represent the industry in the South and in New England, respectively. This new organization promotes the production of high-quality fabrics, conducts market studies, and encourages better trade practices and merchandizing methods.

An odd coincidence of statistics indicates that between 1914 and 1925 the value added by manufacture to raw materials, by the woolen mills and by the cotton mills of the United States, increased, respectively, in the ratios of 166.8 and 166.7 per cent. It would be dangerous to assume from this, however, that the fortunes of the two industries have followed equally parallel paths. While the proportion of cotton spindles active has usually exceeded 90 per cent, the proportion of worsted and woolen spindles in operation has attained that figure but a single season out of the last six recorded and during several years has fallen below 80 per cent in one or both of the grand divisions of the industry.

The stoppage of war contracts was a greater shock to wool manufacturers than it was to those of cotton, because a larger share of their machinery—approaching two-thirds of the total—was employed on army work, and because while hostilities were in progress raw wool had been accumulated more sedulously and consumed less extravagantly than raw cotton. Cancellations, both by the Government and by buyers of civilian goods in anticipation of lower prices, were so prompt and so general that by the New Year's following the armistice two-fifths of the broad looms in the country were idle. The year 1919 was one of recovery from this acute reaction, but the extraordinarily erratic movement of wool prices during the following seasons kept the industry in a state of uncertainty, which was not alleviated by the fact that new tariff bills were under discussion at this time. By 1923, however, the period of after-war readjustment seemed to be over, and manufacturers were heartened by a new season of prosperity. Wage advances were recorded in New England and New Jersey. These were granted less because profits were high than because labor was exceptionally scarce, having been attracted to more remunerative occupations, especially in the building trades. What was called a buyer's strike by mill owners against the rise in raw wool, but was really a pause while taking stock of uncertain future prospects, slowed down operations as 1923 drew to a close and introduced a second depression which was much severer and more protracted than the crisis following the armistice. Two of the several "worst seasons on record" of which we have quoted indubitable testimony in this volume were 1925 and 1927. The intervening year was notable for a protracted strike in the Passaic worsted mills and by the withdrawal of the

Dobsons, one of the oldest and best-known firms in the industry, from the worsted business. The Pacific Mills at Lawrence passed their dividends for the first time in over forty years, after netting more than $2,000,000 the preceding season.

Many of the conditions affecting the wool manufacture were identical with those embarassing the cotton industry. Long-time contracts were giving way to hand-to-mouth buying as caprices of fashion became the determining factor in the consuming market. The vogue of woolens for men's wear, following the long ascendancy of worsteds, hung on from season to season despite the refusal of manufacturers to believe it more than a passing fancy. This preference apparently developed during the shortage of raw materials accompanying the war, when it was encouraged by manufacturers and to some extent by public opinion because a greater variety of fibers and more reworked wool and shoddy could be employed in making woolens than in making worsteds. Later it was favored during the "buyer's strike" following the armistice by the fact that carded fabrics could be sold cheaper than combed wool fabrics. Finally, woolens fitted in with the quick-delivery system of buying better than worsteds and could be produced effectively in the lighter and brighter colors that had become the vogue. This craze for "fancies" for both men's and women's attire was ascribed by some to the development of sunfast colors. Furthermore, men as well as women were wearing lighter clothing than formerly. Within fifteen or twenty years men's winter suitings declined in average weight from 20 to 13 ounces a yard. Better heating in homes and conveyances and the closed motor car accounted in part for this. Automobiles were also held responsible for a shrinkage in yardage consumption of both men's suitings and women's dress goods, because people wear old clothes more commonly when motoring then when traveling in public conveyances or walking upon the street. The popularity of cassimeres at the expense of worsted suitings was a return to the fashions of the seventies. Simultaneously women's gowns were not only abbreviated to the utmost, but when of wool were made of extremely light fabrics in order to drape like silk. The change in trading practice from buying a season in advance to buying for immediate consumption prevented mass production and shifted the financial burden of carrying stocks largely to the holder of raw materials. As a result of this revolution in the character of their output and of their system of production, many mills, both cotton and woolen, had to be remodeled.

There was but a moderate increase in worsted machinery during the period we are describing, although some expansion occurred during even the most unfavorable years. The Shawsheen mill of the American Woolen Company was the only notable establishment erected in New England. In 1924 the Southern Worsted Corporation held the first exhibition of goods of this character ever offered by an establishment in the South. A combined statement of the operations of sixteen New England woolen and worsted mills, containing more than 23,000 looms, published in the *Bulletin* of the National Association of Wool Manufacturers in October, 1927, showed a considerable shrinkage in their aggregate assets between 1923 and 1926, while a total profit of nearly $17,000,000 the former year was changed into a loss approaching $9,000,000 the latter season. Investigators of the condition of the industry agreed in finding that plant capacity was in excess of requirements and constituted a constant temptation to produce more fabrics than the market could absorb. The American Woolen Company made a vigorous effort to sell part of its product abroad through the American Wool Products Company, which it had incorporated for this purpose in 1917. Upon the whole, exports of wool manufactures, including clothing, increased consistently, reaching the neighborhood of $60,000,000 in 1926.

One must not form a too pessimistic opinion of the state of this industry, however, from gloomy descriptions of periods of depression. The steady growth of the manufacture refutes them. Early in 1928 the leaders of the two major wool manufacturing associations, after many months of consultation and negotiation, organized The Wool Institute, Inc., along much the same lines as the American Cotton-Textile Institute just mentioned, to deal with problems of production and distribution that call for united action. It may be suggestive of the ascendancy that financing and merchandizing have acquired in our complex industrial system that the headquarters of both these institutes are in New York City. Since 1902 manufacturer's associations have been fighting "truth-in-fabric" bills, somewhat along the lines of the Pure Food law, which have been almost constantly before Congress. The purpose of this proposed legislation is to require woolen goods to be branded or tagged with a description of the materials employed in their fabrication. The objection to it on the part of manufacturers has been that such descriptions as the laws propose would mislead rather than inform consumers as to the true value of the materials in the goods they buy. Several state laws of this character have been enacted, especially in the wool-growing West, but without much effect. Since 1922 the tariff has not been a live topic, and the various associations in this industry have little occasion to defend existing duties or to agitate for new ones.

Between 1914 and 1925 the value of the silk goods manufactured in America increased 218 per cent, as compared with 158 and 159 per cent, respectively, for woolens and cottons. These ratios do not measure absolute rates of expansion, because they are based upon a dollar of diminishing value, but they are accurate indications of relative progress. Since the beginning of the century imports of raw silk have increased more than sixfold, while the quantity consumed in Europe has diminished. These facts suggest a high degree of average prosperity, although the amount of idle machinery in silk mills apparently averages higher than in cotton mills. We have already, in speaking of the manufactures of the war period, alluded to some of the causes that during hostilities gave silk an advantage over other textiles. These were continuing influences so far as both fashion and economy were concerned. No period of acute depression has afflicted the industry since the armistice. At times, for example in 1919 and after the Japanese earthquake in 1923, manufacturers were temporarily embarrassed by a raw-materials shortage and attendant market uncertanties. On the other hand raw silk from Europe, especially Italy, was unusually cheap during the period of low exchange abroad. A labor shortage due to the movement of male workers to higher-paid occupations in the metal trades also followed the war.

Fashion changes, and the adaptation of fabrics to them are too ephemeral to detain us here. Novel yarn combinations of spun and thrown silk and mixtures of silk and rayon added to the variety of new products. The popularity of silk hosiery compensated in one branch of the industry for the adverse influence of short skirts upon broad-silks production. Consumers kept calling for higher grades and qualities of goods. The growing importance of style increased managerial costs, but mill outputs per operative rose 42 per cent during the ten years ending with 1923.

While the production of knit goods has not made such remarkable strides since the armistice as the manufacture of silk, the industry as a whole has prospered. Its geographical trend, instead of being southward, as in the case of cotton, has been toward the central West, where about one-fifth of the silk hosiery made in the United States is now manufactured. Full-fashion goods continued to make headway more rapidly than the cheaper tubular and cut goods, and silk underwear, now growing popular with both sexes, is to some extent taking the place of cotton. Among the developments of the war period was the establishment in the United States of the manufacture of warp-knit fabrics, which had previously been confined largely to Germany, and which are used for making gloves. Comparatively new developments in the high-grade hosiery manufacture are the extensive advertising of trade-mark goods and the practice of selling directly to consumers through traveling agents. Some large mills in the central West dispose of their entire product in this manner and manufacture no goods for stock.

It logically follows from the present emphasis on style, which is but a consumer-inspired variant of the "art-in-industry" movement, that the business of dyeing and finishing textiles should have expanded rapidy. Its product has risen in value faster than that of any branch of the primary textile manufacture, having increased nearly threefold since 1914.

CHEMICAL INDUSTRIES

Rayon forms a connecting link between the chemical industries, with which it is still grouped in census statistics, and the textile manufacture. In 1922, eleven years after production began in the United States, the output was still less than 20,000,000 pounds, virtually all of which was made by a single company. By 1927 production had risen to over 70,000,000 pounds, or more than one-quarter of the world's annual supply. The industry is in the hands of some eight or nine corporations, some of which operate more than one establishment, and at present shows a tendency to center in or near Virginia. The oldest producer, the Viscose Company, has an output of 60,000,000 pounds a year and operates the largest plant in the world at Roanoke in the latter state. The du Ponts, who entered this field in 1920, and whose first factory was at Buffalo, have plants near Richmond and in the vicinity of Nashville, Tennessee. Their establishments turn out in the neighborhood of 25,000,000 pounds per annum. The Tubize Company, making nearly 10,000,000 pounds by a different process, has its works at Hopewell, Virginia. Establishments owned by other firms, including the extensive factory of the Celanese Corporation in Maryland, are scattered from Cleveland to Connecticut.

No other textile fiber possesses the speculative possibilities of rayon, for the limits to its improvement and to the cheapening of its manufacture are not yet in sight. Already it is making serious inroads into the consumption of fabrics of other materials, although it has also given a new stimulus to certain branches of cotton, worsted, and silk weaving and to the knitting industry, because it combines well with the yarns which they employ. One source of its appeal to manufacturers is the steadiness of rayon quotations, which are not affected from season to season, by caprices of climate as are cotton and silk, or by vagaries of legislation, as is wool. This enables weavers to forecast with great certainty their costs of production. Last of all, like most products where processes of manufacture are comparatively new, it promises to grow cheaper with the passage of years, while the cost of natural fibers may increase.

The United States has the largest chemical industry in the world, with a product exceeding in value $2,250,000,000, 90 per cent of which is consumed within the country. Its qualitative, as also its quantitative, expansion dates from the World War. Details of the dye manufacture, beyond its dramatic origin described in the preceding chapter, need not detain us here. Its products have multiplied until they substantially supply the domestic market at prices that make it possible to export a surplus. Twenty-five years ago the United States paid some $2,000,000 annually for foreign indigo, three-quarters of which was the natural product imported from India. Today our dye makers regularly ship abroad synthetic indigo of their own manufacture. Colors, and even the wider range of coal-tar products as a whole, form but one group of the great array of chemicals, but they mark the most advanced stage of development that the industry has attained. Like other fields of manufacture owing their existence to organized research, this one has naturally gravitated into the hands of gigantic corporations. Two of the latter are especially prominent, E. I. du Pont de Nemours and Company, Inc., whose holdings extend far beyond this particular branch of production, and the Allied Chemical and Dye Corporation, formed in 1920 by a combination of the General Chemical Company, The Solvay Process Company, The Semet-Solvay Company, The Barrett Company, and the National Aniline and Chemical Company, all of which were already firms of the first magnitude. The General Chemical Company produced principally industrial acids, The Solvay Process Company, alkalies, and the Semet-Solvay Company, coke and its by-products, while the Barrett Company and the National Aniline and Chemical Company specialized in dyestuffs and other coal-tar derivatives. Thus the products of the five firms supplemented each other. One motive for their union, announced at the time of the merger, was to prosecute research more effectively. Several of the numerous companies controlled by the du Pont organization similarly supplement each other. Even its interest in General Motors helps to insure a steady market for its products. Lazotte, Incorporated, operating one of the first plants for the fixation of atmospheric nitrogen in the country, makes the ammonia which the other subsidiaries employ in their operations. The production of dyes and of rayon go hand in hand to some extent, as do the manufacture of pyroxylin plastics, artificial leather, and lacquers; moreover, the two latter groups of products are used extensively in the automobile manufacture. Unbreakable glass, which consists of plate glass and celluloid in laminated combination, is another connecting link between chemical and motor car production.

MISCELLANEOUS MANUFACTURES

We can do no more than sketch a few tendencies observable since the war in other industries. Concentration proceeds apace notwithstanding occasional Government efforts to check it. In the food manufacture, flour milling and baking illustrate this trend today as conspicuously as did sugar refining, packing, and tobacco in the past. Since the formation of General Mills, Incorporated, to acquire the properties of the Washburn-Crosby Company at Minneapolis and several smaller concerns in the Southwest and far West, this industry has fallen largely into the hands of six great groups. The Corporation just mentioned has a daily capacity of nearly 64,000 barrels. The five other combinations turn out from 22,000 to 40,000 barrels daily. The geography of this industry is shifting, partly in response to agricultural changes and partly on account of new transportation and marketing developments. Minneapolis continues to be the principal flour-milling center of the country; but while the value of its product increased from $85,000,000 to $113,000,000 between 1914 and 1925, that of Buffalo rose from $28,000,000 to $99,000,000. This was largely a result of the transfer of Minneapolis enterprise and capital to the latter city. Buffalo's mill expansion, so close to Rochester which occupied a prominent position in the industry two generations ago, is due to its situation in the middle of a great flour-consuming area, to the fact that lake freights for grain, which are not controlled by the Interstate Commerce Commission, are lower than flour rates by rail, and to its convenient position for grinding Canadian wheat in bond for foreign markets. Kansas City has also acquired added importance as a flour-milling center because of the great wheat area behind it. This in turn goes back to the fact that producers of the hard winter wheat raised in Kansas and the neighboring states enjoy certain economic advantages, such as more remunerative rotation crops, over producers of the hard spring wheat raised farther to the north. Hard wheats still retain their ascendancy in the milling business, because commercial bakers prefer flour made from it to the "weaker" flours made from soft wheat. Since the war, increasing costs of transportation, and perhaps the availability of electric power over larger areas than formerly, has caused some dispersion of milling to interior points strategically situated with respect to grain-raising and flour-consuming areas.

It will be recalled that makers of biscuit and other less perishable bakery products had already grouped themselves into large organizations before the war and were marketing their goods in special packages under widely advertised brands. Bread bakers began to follow the same course somewhat later, after machinery gave a definite economic advantage to larger establishments in their division of the industry also, and the automobile had greatly widened their delivery area. The first combinations were strictly local, but these gradually amalgamated and expanded until three or four large companies divided among themselves the urban markets of most of the territory east of the Rocky Mountains. An effort was made in 1926 to bring together these great producers in a single company with a fantastically high capitalization, but it was defeated by the Government. Nevertheless this business remains highly organized, and more than one-half of the bread baked for sale in the United States is now made in large establishments.

Turning to an entirely different field, a bitter controversy arose during the war over the high cost of newsprint paper. The National Newspaper Publishers Association charged manufacturers with extortion. Prices skyrocketed during 1916 from $1.65 to $3.50 per 100 pounds. These complaints led to a Government investigation, and eventually the Newsprint Manufacturers' Association accepted a court decree ordering its dissolution. Subsequently an acute shortage of paper occurred and prices remained at an unprecedentedly high level after the war was over. Among recent developments in this industry are the growth of kraft paper manufacturing in the South, an increase of self-contained mills relatively to conversion mills buying the pulp they use, and the growing part taken by the industry in forest propagation, both to secure a permanent source of raw materials and to protect its vast hydro-electric interests.

Manufacturers of leather, and of boots and shoes, have been forced since the war to adjust themselves to changing market conditions similar to those encountered by textile manufacturers, and at least our important attempt at amalgamation has occurred in the latter branch of the industry.

Fashion has incessantly demanded new shades and varieties of leather both for foot wear, which consumes four-fifths of the country's product, and for most of the varied uses that employ the remainder, with the natural concomitant of hand-to-mouth buying. Low shoes are now worn throughout the year, and lighter soles and uppers are the vogue since people took to riding in automobiles instead of walking. Machinery has been perfected until leather can be split to extreme thinness, thus multiplying its service in display if not in wear.

In the clay manufacture the organization of the General Refractories Company, in 1922, with an investment of more than $16,000,000 in plants producing some 320,000,000 firebrick per annum for furnace lining and similar employments, illustrates the size which industries entirely subsidiary to larger branches of manufacturing have attained. Potters, whose trade so long preserved its primitive lineaments, have effected great economies in their processes, notably by the invention of new slip mixtures reducing filtration costs, and of the tunnel kiln, through which the articles to be baked pass at funeral pace emerging finished at the farther end without the labor and fuel losses incident to cooling and again reheating the kilns for each batch.

Science is a destructive as well as a constructive agency in industry. It supersedes a product with a better one, sometimes of an entirely different kind, thus condemning machinery, and occasionally whole departments of manufacture, to the scrap heap. For a time the radio seemed likely to ruin the talking-machine business, until the latter likewise called science to its aid and introduced improvements that promise to restore the popularity of its products. Fewer upright pianos were made in America in 1925 than in 1919, but the number of grand pianos manufactured increased about three-fold. This was probably explained by a growth of luxury and concert consumption coincident with the displacement of household instruments by other forms of musical entertainment. In 1924, Deere and Company closed the doors of their old Reliance Buggy factory in St. Louis, thus striking their flag to the automobile.

Since we shall have occasion to refer to the changing geography of manufactures in the concluding chapter, it will be enough to remark here that in no section of the country have they suffered an actual decline. New England textile mills may move to the South, and New England capital may migrate with them, but other industries, which make the total greater than before and give the economic life of the community a better balance, rush in to fill the vacancy. Diversification of manufactures consults the public interest, alleviates depressions confined to single branches of production, and by providing a variety of employments promotes the contentment of labor. Among the latest measures of social prophylaxis adopted by municipalities and business organizations in certain of the older manufacturing sections is a conscious effort to diversify local industry.

CHAPTER XXII

CONCLUSION

Fifty-five Years' Growth, 351. Geography of Manufactures, 351. Industrial Concentration, 353. Market Policy, 355. Service Supply, 356. Manufacturing and Society, 357. Latest Developments, 358.

FIFTY-FIVE YEARS' GROWTH

In 1860 the product of our manufacturing industries was valued at less than $2,000,000,000 and our factories and work shops employed about 1,300,000 wage earners. In 1914, the last year for which we have a comparable dollar, the product had multiplied by more than twelve and exceeded $24,000,000,000, while the number of wage earners had increased over fivefold, to slightly above 7,000,000. During this interval the value added to raw materials by each industrial worker's labor more than doubled and the latter's annual earnings augmented in equal ratio.

Naturally this growth in manufactures, and in the number of persons employed in manufacturing, was much more rapid than the growth of population; and this is true even after we qualify the census figures by the fact that many more articles were made in households and in unenumerated establishments at the earlier than at the later date. Statistics of those staple industries for which figures in 1860 and 1914 are fairly comparable indicate that during this interval the number of establishments diminished, notwithstanding the vast expansion of their aggregate output; and that metal manufactures, especially those of iron and steel, increased far more rapidly than did textile manufactures. These features of our industrial history are correlated. The great expansion of manufacturing and its concentration in large establishments are due to the wider use of power and the improvement of machinery, which added to the product and the earnings of the individual worker and increased the demand for metals. Throughout the period covered by this volume, therefore, the manufacture of iron and steel was the nation's key industry, by which the progress, prosperity, and developmental tendencies of manufacturing in general were determined and illustrated.

GEOGRAPHY OF MANUFACTURES

The changing geography of American industries since the Civil War has been described in connection with their respective histories. As a whole manufacturing has moved westward, following the trend of population, although many of its branches have clung obstinately to the East, and still make that section preeminently the factory center of the country. By the end of the last century the frontier had ceased to affect the organization and regional distribution of industry. Homespun manufactures had passed away; no unsettled territories were left to provide pioneer markets; no free land remained to draw labor away from factory centers. Gristmills, sawmills, and other small manufacturing enterprises still supplied neighborhood customers, but they steadily lost ground relatively to establishments serving national markets. The local industries which survived or sprang up in minor population centers and predominantly agricultural regions were generally conducted on a large scale and sold their products over wide areas. Representative examples of such enterprises were the watch factories established in Illinois soon after the Civil War. Industries have been more nomadic in America than in Europe because of the constant discovery of new resources and the drift of population into previously unoccupied territories. Although manufacturing in general has become more widely diffused as the country grew older, many of the principal groups of industries, like the manufacture of iron and steel, agricultural machinery, automobiles, boots and shoes, and different classes of textiles, have shown a growing tendency toward regional concentration. Moreover, in what we think of as the agricultural states a movement of factories has occurred from smaller towns to larger urban centers.

It would lead us into a labyrinth of detail to trace even the more prominent migrations of specific manufactures and the reasons for their present localization. Some, like stove founding and the manufacture of agricultural machinery, have followed their market center westward; many have moved closer to fuel, as for a time to the natural-gas regions of Indiana and Kansas; still others owe their ultimate location to the neighborhood of raw materials, or abundant labor, or advantages of climate, or to a combination of all these such as encouraged cotton spinning in the South. Any such favoring condition, if sufficiently pronounced, made a district a point of crystallization, around which manufacturing establishments clustered. Thus an excess of unemployed female workers in the anthracite mining towns of Pennsylvania attracted silk mills, and the oyster beds of Chesapeake Bay made Baltimore a canning center. Before the discovery of natural gas, brick yards were rather evenly distributed throughout Kansas; a few years after that discovery nearly two-thirds of the yards in the state, and those by far the largest producers, were in the gas belt. A change of process, or of materials employed in a manufacture, often affected its location. As long as rags were the chief material used for making paper, the principal mills were in the neighborhood of cotton-manufacturing centers which supplied them with mill clippings, like Holyoke near the head of the Blackstone Valley, or accessible to large cities where rags accumulated. When pulp became the chief paper-making material, major branches of the industry moved to the forests of Maine, northern New York, and Wisconsin. On the other hand some industries owe their location almost entirely to individual initiative. That explains why most of the cameras and photographic supplies produced in this country are made at Rochester, and most of the cash registers at Dayton.

In visualizing the industrial map of the United States, we can group manufactures not only in relation to ore beds, forests, coal mines, oil and gas regions, urban centers, seaports, water powers, and transportation routes but also into two great classes, which differ markedly in their response to these attractions. A few great cities monopolize a large share of the country's printing and publishing, but nevertheless that business contributes one of the largest items to the manufacturing totals of many rural states. Omaha, while still a prairie city of medium size, had in addition to industries of national importance, like packing houses, smelters, white-lead works and linseed-oil mills, a group of strictly local service manufactures, including 52 brick yards, 8 clothing factories and a button factory, 6 furniture factories, 2 cracker factories, breweries, distilleries, and various food-preserving establishments. Despite the centralizing tendencies of the times, such dispersed industries as the latter continue to bulk large in the nation's totals.

INDUSTRIAL CONCENTRATION

The rapid mechanization of industry resulted in a temporary loss of control over the quantity of goods produced and added greatly to the normal difficulty of adjusting supply to demand. An increasingly even rhythm of production, however, is as essential a feature of economic progress as is ability to turn out an enlarged quantity and variety of articles with a given amount of human effort. Consequently the alternating crises of dearth and surplus from which our industries suffered, faced them with a problem urgently calling for solution and largely determined the change in their organization which was an outstanding feature of the period. This change was more marked and rapid in the United States than elsewhere because the country's rapid growth cooperated with the substitution of power machinery for manual skill to make more difficult an intelligent control of output. Such crises were therefore causative factors in the nation's industrial evolution. More truly than the tariff, or other facile explanations of the day, they were the mother of the trusts, and the movement toward concentration and control of which great amalgamations were the fruit appears in retrospect primarily an effort to smooth out the erratic curve of production statistics.

That does not imply that this was invariably the conscious purpose of trust promoters. Indeed such was far from being the case. Nor did this remedy apply to all manufacturing revolutionized by machinery, as the textile and the boot and shoe industries testify. A conjunction of favoring conditions was necessary to make a great combination successful. Nothing was more protean than manufacturing, which even under the reign of automatic machinery sometimes refused to crystallize into rigid forms at the behest of great financiers. The organization that seemed to solve the problem of the day often failed to fill the need of the day that followed. Trusts that were monsters when they were young became timid and ingratiating in their maturity. Finally, size proved to be largely relative and psychological, and what appeared gigantic to one generation was of commonplace dimensions to its more sophisticated successor. All these things have been taught us in a single generation, and the day has already come when America seems to be assimilating her great corporations, converting them into part of her democratic tissue by legislation and regulation and even but more largely by spontaneous and unconscious processes, such as diffusion of ownership and the pressure of a slowly educated public opinion upon their policies and administration. Thus forms of industrial organization, that were originally designed to give individuals control over production for their private emolument, in the outcome have facilitated community control to a degree that could never have been realized had manufacturing remained dispersed in the hands of a host of individual owners.

Great manufacturing combinations, in addition to regulating production and stabilizing prices, have standardized goods and services, without which price control is impossible, and created habits of consumption. In other words they have standardized not only the wares they made but also the tastes of those who use them. They have thus strengthened their hold upon their market, economized production costs, and widened their circle of consumers. On the other hand, dangers unknown in the slower days of old threaten their prosperity. A growing share of our manufacturing product now consists of unessentials—man's toys and playthings. The demand for these is determined largely by fashion and caprice. People must have shirts and shoes, but the call for mah-jong sets and talking machines is seasonal and uncertain. Furthermore, new inventions have displaced what had come to be considered staple necessities. The incandescent bulb supplanted the kerosene lamp; the furnace, the stove; the Ford car, the light buggy; the radio set, the Victrola. So new disturbances have interrupted the market rhythm just when manufacturers seemed to have discovered a way to govern its pulsations.

Yet even here the great corporation has been able to distribute its risks better than a smaller firm. The Ford works have extended to tractors and airplanes; and General Motors, to household ice machines. This tendency for a large company to engage in making several different articles, sometimes quite unrelated except in methods of manufacture, is illustrated on a broader scale by the iron and steel industry. For more than half a century after steam was employed in transportation the prosperity of American furnaces and rolling mills was determined by the demand for rails, rolling stock, and engines. This market was much larger than any that had previously existed and invited an unprecedented expansion of production, but it was undiversified and subject to simultaneous fluctuations throughout its entire area. The call for rails and equipment varied with the activity of railway building and was therefore subject to violent changes accompanied by a parallel rise and fall of prices. Gradually, however, other fields of consumption extended until they overshadowed, at least in the aggregate, that provided by transportation agencies. Consequently a slackened demand in one field did not necessarily synchronize with that in another, and prices became more stable and crises less acute. The catalogue of a great steel corporation today contains a list of major products so extensive and varied, especially when considered in connection with their ultimate uses, that the probability of a recurrence of such sudden and disastrous price collapses as afflicted the industrial world in the last century is very greatly reduced, if not entirely eliminated.

Another primary cause of the concentration of manufacturing in large units was the increasing amount of capital required to launch a new enterprise or to conduct an old one. Not only were plants more elaborate and expensive than formerly, but also the liquid funds needed to carry a payroll, to buy raw materials, and to market goods in an age of distant distribution and costly advertising necessitated a much ampler operating capital than before. To be sure credit facilities expanded *pari passu* with this need; money was easier to get; but financing machinery likewise had adjusted itself to large operations, just as factory machinery was adjusted to large outputs.

When a manufacturing enterprise attained a certain size, it was often moved to broaden its activities in order to include industries supplying its raw materials and agencies for marketing its products. Small producers, at least in former times, could trust to competition among those from whom they bought and through whom they sold for fair play in business; but this was no longer true after their purchases and sales reached a certain magnitude. Moreover it was vital for the large manufacturer to maintain a regular rhythm of production, to assure a steady flow of raw materials into finished products, and of finished products into the hands of consumers. Indeed the regularity of these functions, like the regularity of assimilation, secretion, and excretion in a physical organism, is the primary condition of industrial health. An instinctive striving to attain and preserve this equilibrium determined the development of manufacturing organization and methods throughout the period we have described.

MARKET POLICY

Since the market is the governing factor in all industrial growth, it became increasingly the first study of the intelligent manufacturer. It was no longer regarded as something of fixed or uncontrollable dimensions, to be divided among appropriators according to their aggressiveness and ability, the way unoccupied territories are divided among nations, but as a function of human well-being. This truth was particularly impressed upon manufacturers in the United States because they served predominantly a home demand, which rose and fell with the general prosperity of the country.

Gradually consuming power was recognized to be not only the barometer of good times but also their determining element. Hence the cultivation of consuming power became the direct concern of manufacturers, with results that profoundly affected wage and price adjustments. But the idea that to raise wages and reduce prices to the limits of economic possibility was the way to promote prosperity would never have occurred to the small manufacturer of the sixties, whose individual action would have had no perceptible effect upon business conditions, or at least none commensurate with his immediate sacrifice. Not until vast industrial units, like the United States Steel Corporation or the Ford Motor Company, came into existence, was it possible to inaugurate, with any hope that they would prove effective, wage and price policies designed thus to safeguard prosperity.

SERVICE SUPPLY

Since the sixties, service has acquired a new and special meaning in the manufacturing world. The multiplied use of machinery in everyday life has made its maintenance a business of large proportions. Fifty years ago the itinerant tinker and the village blacksmith supplied this need for the average community. Today the most conspicuous aid of our mechanized society is the automobile service station. But even in this technical sense, service calls for less and less manual labor and now consists chiefly in supplying machine parts, which everyone is enough of a mechanic to substitute for those that need replacement. Indeed automatic power-driven tools now shape materials so cheaply and accurately that human intervention in machine building is limited mainly to designing, testing, and assembling parts; and the last of these operations is rapidly becoming a universal art. This growing fund of mechanical knowledge accounts for the speed with which new devices like the radio have been popularized. The highly skilled tool maker is still indispensable, but the common craftsman has been displaced. His service has disappeared, and the service of the supply shop has taken its place.

When water and gas companies began to supply consumers they initiated a new kind of manufacturing service of first importance in modern civilization, which dates its great expansion from the period since the Civil War. This growth has been due chiefly to new applications of electricity, which can be divided and distributed to a wide circle of consumers and therefore is power in its most convenient form for retailing. Our mechanical age did not acquire its distinctive character until it became possible thus to parcel out and popularize power by supplying it to the general public, either from a central source or by small producing units like the internal-combustion engine. To this achievement we owe the most modern methods of locomotion, lighting, heating, refrigeration, propelling machinery, and conveying intelligence. From it spring the manifold forms of impersonal service that are so rapidly supplanting personal service and are revolutionizing the social as well as the economic structure of society.

MANUFACTURING AND SOCIETY

Modern industry affords the most arresting example of progress that the world has ever witnessed—an example that has thrust itself upon popular attention until it has influenced profoundly all forms of thought. It takes an effort for the man of today to visualize a world where changes in material environment and in the way of doing things occurred so slowly that the grandson's life was almost an exact repetition of his grandsire's. We unconsciously assume incessant change, especially as expressed in man's growing mastery over nature, to be the normal condition of the race, while it really is, in its present intensity at least, a novel aspect of human experience, dating back only two or three generations. The idea of progress, thus associated in the popular mind with mechanical inventions and improvements, has been carried over into other fields of thought and action, jogging us out of the ruts of habit and weakening the old respect for tradition and established usage. Industrial history thus throws light upon important psychological factors in modern life.

Power and machinery have quickened the pulse of the nation and accelerated the pace of the individual. The American of the eighteenth century was a less active man than his descendant of the twentieth century. European visitors remarked the deliberation, and even the indolence, of the colonists, and contemporary records abound in allusions to their slackness, sloth, and idleness. This was particularly true of rural laborers and the planting classes. De Kalb blamed Washington for his slowness. In fact the tired business man of today might sometimes be tempted to look back wistfully to the Sleepy Hollow existence of his ancestors; for the weariness that afflicts him comes chiefly from trying to keep pace with the tireless natural forces that he and his immediate predecessors have made his servant and master.

Nevertheless machinery has given to the average person more leisure than he ever enjoyed before. He has what Thoreau called a wider margin to his life. And leisure, in the curious interplay of social forces, has proved to be a powerful stimulator of markets. It creates a demand for books and periodicals, motor cars, radio sets, and musical instruments. It calls for a greater variety of clothing and a more cheerful home. This broadening margin of life is thus occupied by varied activities and interests and does not resemble the vegetative idleness of the colonist acclimatizing himself in a new country and subdued to the rhythm of the wilderness that submerged him. Moreover leisure has become a physiological necessity since the machine has set the pace and determined the form of human labor.

Thrift, which we sometimes think of as a lost virtue and imagine departed from the world with our frugal ancestors, has become socialized. We piece and patch less than our fathers did, but we utilize much more fully the resources of the country. Not only did they waste the forest and the soil, but also they spent labor and materials lavishly with a minimum result in all of their industrial processes. It is safe to say that if the cotton, wool, silk, ore, timber, coal, and other raw materials used annually in the United

States today were to be manufactured by the machinery and processes of 1860, the loss by waste alone would wipe out an appreciable fraction of our national savings and lower the general standard of living. In fact if a majority of the nation were to return to the frugal habits commended by Poor Richard, material progress would come to a halt and the country would be impoverished instead of enriched. To some extent, moreover, the larger thrift practiced by modern industry has been encouraged, and indeed made possible, by the growing size of manufacturing enterprises. Oftentimes the economy in utilizing waste does not begin until it can be handled in large quantities. A village slaughter house could not profitably convert its perishable offal into pharmaceutical products or a five-ton blast furnace manufacture slag cement.

LAST DEVELOPMENTS

Since 1914 the World War and the economic revolution that accompanied and followed that event have had a profound effect upon our industrial development—not by deflecting it from its course but by accelerating its rate of progress. There is no phase of the recent evolution that is not in logical sequence with what preceded. Statistical measurements of manufacturing expansion during this period are somewhat deceptive. Between 1914 and 1925, for example, the aggregate value of products rose in round numbers from $24,000,000,000 to $63,000,000,000, but part of this apparent increase was due to the depreciation of the currency. Between these dates, however, the primary horse-power used in manufacturing increased 70 per cent, and this item probably measures more accurately than any other in the census records our industrial growth during this eventful era.

It would be dwelling unduly upon the obvious to explain at length the immediate causes of the war expansion, which may be summarized in two words—opportunity market. More pertinent to the longer retrospects that form the theme of this history is the fact that between 1860 and 1927 domestic manufactures ready for consumption increased from 15 to 42 per cent of our total exports and simultaneously fell from 43 to 21 per cent of our total imports. This upward trend in exports of manufactures and downward trend in imports is an old phenomenon, which cannot be ascribed entirely, or mainly, to recent influences. The war demand, however, taught Americans to coördinate more efficiently agencies of production, eliminate waste, and improve already highly developed facilities for quantity output. In a word it made them push ahead more rapidly than ever in the direction which they had been advancing since the date of the first Waltham power loom, the first Springfield musket, the first Connecticut brass clock, the first sewing machine, and the first reaper.

APPENDICES

I. COLONIAL CURRENCY AND EXCHANGE

The records of prices and wages that have come down to us from colonial times are mostly in pounds, shillings, and pence. These denominations bore the same ratio to each other that they do in English money, but were of less value than the corresponding coins in sterling. The value of the American shilling fluctuated widely at different times and in different colonies, and varied at the same time in the same colony as it was expressed in coin or in paper money of different issues. Consequently, in Boston (say in the year 1740) a paper shilling of New York, of Rhode Island, of the earlier old tenor issues of Massachusetts, and of the later or new tenor issues of the same colony, all had different values; and none of them was equal in value to a shilling in the miscellaneous silver coin then in circulation, while the coin shilling itself was worth considerably less than a shilling sterling. To adjust these different values to a common denominator is a matter of some difficulty. We have three bases upon which to proceed: bullion ratios, dollar ratios, and exchange ratios.

Bullion ratios are the values, expressed in colonial shillings, of an ounce of silver. Our information as to these ratios is derived chiefly from valuations of silver plate and clipped coins or other coins exchanged by weight, either in estate inventories or in commercial transactions in which bullion in these forms was used. The precise alloy of such silver is impossible to ascertain, but as it consisted mostly of Spanish or sterling coins or of wares made from such coins it is sufficiently accurate for our purposes to use these standards. Except for some 20 years at the beginning of the eighteenth century, the official British standard was 925 fine. According to Sir Isaac Newton's assay in 1717, British coins were about 900 fine and standard Spanish coins (Seville, Mexican, pillar, and New Seville pieces of eight) were from 925 to 950 fine. In London, Spanish silver usually was quoted 3d. to 4d. an ounce higher than British silver. It is doubtful whether these niceties were much regarded in colonial exchange, and we are probably safe in assuming that the value of an ounce of coin silver, in terms of the Spanish dollar, was usually about $1.11, which was the current rate at the time of the Revolution. Where Mexican alloy is specified, the ounce is computed at $1.176.

Dollar ratios are the values of the shilling expressed in cents of the Spanish dollar. Several Spanish coins of this denomination circulated in the colonies, of different weights and standards of fineness, of which the principal and best regarded was the piece of eight. Sometimes other dollars were discriminated against by local statutes or in current accounts, but in commercial transactions the scarcity of money usually caused them to be accepted almost on a par with other coins. For the same reason clipped money passed current—as debased and mutilated coins did in England at the same period. Therefore the commercial rates at which different coins were computed into colonial currency denominations did not always correspond to their bullion value;[1] and identical coins were received

---

[1] *E. g.*, James Logan to William Penn, June 22, 1705, "Penn-Logan Correspondence," in Pennsylvania Historical Society, *Memoirs*, x, 43-44.

at different values in different colonies.[2] In 1704 the amount of pure silver in the piece of eight was estimated by the English mint as 386.8 grains, which made it worth about 4s. 6d. in sterling. This was the commercial ratio of exchange during the colonial period, the English shilling being computed at 22.22 cents or thereabouts. This dollar was debased during the following century, and at the time our present currency system was established was estimated to contain in the neighborhood of 371 grains of pure silver. Consequently the American silver dollar, which has always contained 371.25 grains of pure silver, though its total weight, on account of differences of alloy, has varied, is but a continuation of the colonial Spanish dollar. Though the piece of eight was originally worth about $1.04, as actually circulated it probably seldom exceeded in intrinsic silver content the present dollar. In the following table this coin is assumed to have been of uniform value since its first appearance in American accounts. The slight margin of error thus admitted is quite without importance in commercial quotations.

Exchange ratios are the values of colonial shillings in sterling, reduced to cents upon a basis of the actual amount of silver contained in the English pound and the piece of eight respectively. From 1600 to 1816 the pound sterling contained 1718.7 grains of fine silver, equivalent in Spanish dollars to $4.444. These ratios are of two kinds, as they indicate value in direct exchange of colonial shillings for British coins physically present in the colonies, or the ratio of colonial to British shillings in current quotations for bills on London or other British ports. Such British bills were discounted for interest according to the time and place of payment, the colonial shilling rating relatively higher for long-term than for short-term bills, and for British outport bills than for those payable in London itself. The cost of such bills was also affected by the price of silver in London, by the abundance or scarcity of money in the colonies, by the relative volume of imports and exports between the colonies and Great Britain. The par of exchange was when bills stood at the respective coin ratios of the colonial and the British shilling.

Until 1700 the value of the colonial shilling was about stationary and was equal in nearly all the colonies. Between 1640 and 1650 the New England shilling was worth 20 cents, but in 1645 the Virginia shilling was rated by law at one-sixth of a dollar, or 16.6 cents. Soon after the middle of the century Virginia temporarily raised the value of its shilling to 20 cents, while the value of the shilling in other colonies became 16.6 cents. Towards the end of the century competition for silver currency among the colonies led to a depreciation of the coin shilling in both New England and Pennsylvania. In the latter colonies, as well as West Jersey, the value of this denomination soon fell to 13.3 cents, where it remained without radical change until after the Revolution. About the same time the New York shilling gradually was reduced to 12.5 cents, which remained its common value during the eighteenth century. In New England the use of rapidly depreciating paper money caused violent changes in the value of currency units. The coin shilling remained about 16.6 cents in all these colonies, while the paper shilling gradually fell to less than one-twentieth of the value of the coin shilling. In the Carolinas paper money declined nearly as much as in New England, the shilling ultimately falling to less than 3 cents. Virginia and Maryland maintained their currency on a better basis, though the latter colony issued some paper, the value of which fluctuated, but not to the same extent as in New England and the Carolinas.

Confusion is introduced into contemporary evidence of rates of exchange by

---

[2] Lord Cornbury to the Lords of Trade, Feb. 19, 1704–1705, in O'Callaghan, *Documents Relative to the Colonial History of New York*, IV, 1131–1132; "Petition of the Merchants of the City of New York Relating to Foreign Coin," *id.*, IV, 1133–1135; Earl of Bellomont to the Lords of Trade, June 22, 1700, *id.*, IV, 669.

the fact that certain colonial officers reported their receipts in sterling at the commercial value of the shilling and their disbursements at the official value fixed in 1704 by Queen Anne's proclamation;[3] and that while officials observed proclamation standards in public accounts, rates of exchange in private dealings were determined by business custom or local statutes.[4] The latter enactments, especially laws to fix the scale at which depreciated paper money should be received in payment for old debts, do not always rate this money at the value shown in contemporary mercantile accounts.[5] Consequently official documents and legislative orders can not be accepted as guides to actual business practice. Most of the colonial prices given in the text and the following appendices have been computed at rates of coin exchange obtained from the firm ledgers and commercial letters from which the prices themselves were taken.

The price of bills on London was about the same at different colonial ports during the years for which there are enough commercial quotations to justify a generalization. Until the passage of the Stamp Act such bills usually sold above par, without considering discount for interest. Between the beginning of the Stamp Act agitation and the Revolution, except for a few months in 1767 and 1768, London bills were usually under par, falling sometimes 10 per cent below that figure. The termination of the non-importation agreements failed to raise their price on account of heavy shipments of flour to southern Europe and of flaxseed to Ireland.[6] Cheap bills on England ordinarily favored the importation of British and European manufactures.[7]

Colonial exchange on London.[8]

Date.	Place.	Per cent above or below par	Date.	Place.	Per cent above or below par.
Aug. 7, 1745	Philadelphia	6.0	Apr. 23, 1746	Philadelphia	9.0
Aug. 25, 1745	Do.	6.0	May 5, 1746	Do.	9.0
Sept. — 1745	Do.	7.0	June 5, 1746	Do.	10.5
Oct. 10, 1745	Do.	9.0	July 1, 1746	Do.	10.5
Oct. 13, 1745	Do.	9.0	Oct. 5, 1746	Do.	12.0
Oct. 31, 1745	Do.	9.0	Mar. 23, 1747	Do.	12.0
Feb. 15, 1746	Do.	15.0 to 16.5	Apr. 3, 1747	Do.	9.0 to 10.5
Apr. 16, 1746	Do.	9.0	July 9, 1747	Do.	12.0

[3] "Observations on the Mismanagement of the King's Revenue in Virginia," in Spottswood *Letters*, II, 179.

[4] Lieutenant-Governor Ingoldsby to the Lords of Trade, July 5, 1709, in O'Callaghan, *Documents Relative to the Colonial History of New York*, v, 83–84.

[5] Sometimes successive laws are contradictory; *e.g.*, Rhode Island, *Acts and Laws*, 1752, p. 105; *id.*, June, 1763, p. 31; *id.*, 1767, p. 168.

[6] *E. g.*, Smith and Son, *Manuscript Mercantile Letters*, October 29, 1770.

[7] *E. g.*, Davey and Carson, *Manuscript Mercantile Letters*, letter to William Scott, March 28, 1748.

[8] This table is computed from quotations in mercantile letters to British correspondents. The par of exchange is assumed to be 175 in New York, 165 in Philadelphia and Baltimore, and 125 in Norfolk. The exact par fluctuated, but these rates, as shown in occasional allusions in commercial correspondence, are nearly correct. *Cf.* Wright, *The American Negotiator*, lxii, which, however, is wrong as to Baltimore for the dates here quoted. The minus sign indicates below par. The percentages in the table are of 100 and not points above or below the par of exchange just mentioned.

Colonial exchange on London—Continued.

Date.	Place.	Per cent above or below par.	Date.	Place.	Per cent above or below par.
Nov. 3, 1747	Philadelphia	9.0 to 10.5	Apr. 15, 1768	Philadelphia	1.5
Nov. 9, 1747	Do	10.5 to 12.0	May 30, 1768	Do	3.0
Nov. 26, 1747	Do	12.0	July 23, 1768	Do	2.0
Dec. 5, 1747	Do	10.5 to 12.0	Aug. 20, 1768	Do	2.0
Mar. 28, 1748	Do	9.0 to 10.5	Oct. 18, 1768	New York	0.0 to − 1.5
July 27, 1748	Do	3.0 to 4.5	Oct. 25, 1768	Baltimore	− 1.5
July 29, 1748	Do	6.0	Nov. 5, 1768	Philadelphia	1.0
Sept. 4, 1748	Do	0.0	Nov. 12, 1768	Do	1.0
Oct. 20, 1748	Do	1.5	Nov. 29, 1768	Baltimore	− 3.0
Nov. 27, 1748	Do	1.5	Dec. 10, 1768	Philadelphia	− 1.5
Dec. 2, 1748	Do	0.0	Dec. 14, 1768	Do	− 3.0
Jan. 29, 1749	Do	3.0	Feb. 7, 1769	Do	− 1.5
Feb. 3, 1749	Do	3.0	Feb. 27, 1769	Baltimore	− 1.5
Mar. 21, 1749	Do	4.5	Mar. 3, 1769	New York	− 1.5
Dec. 16, 1749	Do	4.5	Mar. 25, 1769	Philadelphia	− 1.5 to − 3.0
Mar. 2, 1750	Do	4.5	Apr. 18, 1769	Do	1.5
Sept. 14, 1750	Do	1.5	June — 1769	Do	− 3.0 to − 4.5
Nov. 23, 1750	Do	0.0 to 1.5	July 12, 1769	Do	− 3.0
Dec. 6, 1750	Do	1.5	Aug. 26, 1769	Do	− 4.5 to − 6.0
June 13, 1755	Norfolk	4.0	Sept. 2, 1769	Do	− 6.0
June 13, 1755	Philadelphia	3.0	Sept. 9, 1769	Do	− 6.0
Oct. 17, 1765	Do	1.5	Sept. 17, 1769	Do	− 9.0
Oct. 30, 1765	New York	4.5	Oct. 16, 1769	Do	− 9.0
Dec. 16, 1765	Do	0.0	Oct. 20, 1769	Fairfax, Va	− 2.0
Jan. 14, 1766	Do	0.0	Oct. 31, 1769	Baltimore	− 9.0 to −10.5
Mar. 24, 1766	Do	3.0	Nov. 2, 1769	Do	−10.5
Apr. 30, 1766	Philadelphia	1.5	Nov. 10, 1769	Do	−10.0
May 3, 1766	Do	1.5	Dec. 30, 1769	Philadelphia	− 9.0
July 3, 1766	Do	3.0	Feb. 15, 1770	Do	− 7.5
July 4, 1766	New York	1.5	Apr. 17, 1770	Do	− 3.0 to − 1.5
Sept. 16, 1766	Philadelphia	1.5	July 17, 1770	Do	− 7.5
Oct. 3, 1766	New York	3.0	July 21, 1770	Do	− 8.0
Oct. 29, 1766	Philadelphia	0.0	Aug. 18, 1770	Do	− 6.0 to − 4.5
Nov. 10, 1766	Do	−3.0	Sept. 15, 1770	Do	− 4.5
Nov. 18, 1766	Do	−6.0 to − 7.5	Sept. 25, 1770	Do	− 3.0
Nov. 22, 1766	Do	−9.0 to −10.5	Oct. 9, 1770	Do	− 3.0
Dec. 11, 1766	Do	−9.0	Oct. 16, 1770	Do	− 4.5
Jan. 10, 1767	Do	−3.0	Oct. 23, 1770	Do	− 4.5
Jan. 17, 1767	New York	−3.0	Oct. 29, 1770	Do	− 4.5
Feb. 28, 1767	Philadelphia	−3.0 to − 1.5	Nov. 1, 1770	Do	− 6.0
Mar. 24, 1767	Do	0.0	Nov. 6, 1770	Do	− 6.0
Mar. 28, 1767	Norfolk	0.0	Apr. 1, 1772	Baltimore	− 1.5 to − 3.5
Apr. 2, 1767	New York	1.5	Apr. 16, 1772	Do	− 3.0 to − 4.5
May 21, 1767	Do	3.0	Nov. — 1773	Fairfax, Va	4.0
June 9, 1767	Philadelphia	3.0	Oct. 22, 1774	Baltimore	1.5
July — 1767	Norfolk	4.0	Nov. 16, 1774	Do	0.0
July 16, 1767	Philadelphia	4.5	Nov. 29, 1774	Do	0.0
Sept. 12, 1767	Do	4.5	Dec. 8, 1774	Do	0.0
Sept. 15, 1767	Do	3.0	Dec. 22, 1774	Do	− 1.5
Sept. 26, 1767	Do	3.0	Jan. 28, 1775	Do	− 3.0
Nov. 28, 1767	Norfolk	0.0	Feb. 7, 1775	Do	− 3.0
Nov. — 1767	Norfolk	0.0	Feb. 11, 1775	Do	− 3.0
Nov. 9, 1767	Philadelphia	−1.5	Feb. 16, 1775	Do	− 3.0
Nov. 19, 1767	Do	1.5	Mar. 1, 1775	Do	− 3.0 to − 4.5
Jan. 21, 1768	New York	4.0	Apr. 10, 1775	Do	− 6.0
Jan. 28, 1768	Philadelphia	3.0	May 20, 1775	Do	− 6.0
Feb. 2, 1768	Do	3.0 to 4.5	July 10, 1775	Do	− 9.0
Mar. 3, 1768	Do	1.0	Aug. 26, 1775	Do	−12.0
Mar. 11, 1768	Do	0.0			

II. COLONIAL PRICE OF LUMBER PER M FEET

[Unless otherwise stated, cash prices for inch pine boards.]

Date.	Place.	Quotation. s. d.	Price per M.	Reference.
1641..	New England...	56	$10.00	Weeden app.
1656	Massachusetts...	45	6.00	M. H. C., 2, iv, 240–250.
1664..	Maine..........	19	3.10	Williamson's Hist. Me.
1667..	New England...	45	7.50	Weeden app.
1678..	New Hampshire.	26	4.34	P. P. N. H., i, 490.
1678..	Maine..........	18	3.00	Folsom, Saco, 137.
1679..	New England...	50	8.33	Weeden app.
1682..	Connecticut.....	50	8.33	Walcott Ledger.
1682..	Maine..........	30	5.00	Me. h. c., quoted Bish., i, 99.
1682..	Do..........	20	3.33	Do.
1685..	New England...	18	3.00	Weeden app.
1686..	Boston.........	40	6.66	Merchant's Journal.
1686..	New England...	20	3.33	Weeden app.
1687..	Boston.........	23 4	3.88	Merchant's Journal.
1688..	Do..........	24	3.00	Do.
1689..	Do..........	23	2.83	Do.
1692..	New England...	36	6.00	Weeden app.
1694..	Philadelphia....	80	13.33	Phil. Merchant's Ledger.
1695..	New England...	30	5.00	Weeden app.
1697..	Do..........	25	4.16	Do.
1698..	New York......	..	10.40	Van Cortlandt ledger.
1700..	New Hampshire.	22	3.67	O'C., D. R. H. N. Y., iv, 670.
1705..	Pennsylvania....	100	13.00	Bish., Vol. I, 111.
1705..	At mill.........	80	10.40	Mem. Pa. Hist. Soc., ix, 233–234, note.
1715..	New England...	40	5.34	Lord, 72. "1¼ to 1 inch."
1719..	Do..........	55	5.34	Weeden app.
1720..	Boston.........	80	7.75	O. Brown accts.
1721..	New England...	60	5.34	Weeden app.
1728..	Philadelphia....	50	7.15	Jour. Phil. Mercht., 302.
1730..	Do..........	50	6.65	Do.
1731..	Do..........	50	6.65	Do.
1736..	Salem..........	100	4.30	T. Orne accts.
1740..	South Carolina..	276	8.56	S. C. Session Laws, 53.
1748..	Salem..........	400	8.00	T. Orne accts.
1750..	Do..........	450	10.00	Do.
1753..	Rhode Island...	400	5.70	Do.
1753..	Do..........	600	8.57	Do. "White pine."
1753..	Do..........	500	7.15	Do. "Yellow pine."
1753..	Boston.........	320	7.10	Mass. Arch., 59.
1753..	Do..........	428	9.50	Do. 59. "Clear."
1756..	Rhode Island...	700	6.35	O. Brown accts.
1756..	Salem..........	40	6.66	T. Orne accts.
1757..	Norfolk........	65	10.85	Jamieson papers.
1758..	New York......	100	12.50	Hancock accts.
1759..	New Hampshire.	225	13.33	T. Orne accts. "2 inch."
1759..	Do..........	320	18.94	Do. "Clear, 2 inch."
1761..	Salem..........	315	7.00	Do. "Merchantable."
1761..	Do..........	360	8.00	Do. "Clear."
1762..	Do..........	60	10.00	Do.
1763..	Do..........	48	8.00	Do.
1763..	Do..........	60	10.00	Do.
1765..	Norfolk........	76 8	12.77	Jamieson papers.
1765..	New York......	45	5.62	British transcripts.
1766..	Rhode Island...	60	6.30	S. Nightingale accts.

Price of lumber—Continued.

Date.	Place.	Quotation. s. d.	Price per M.	Reference.
1767..	Maryland or Virginia.........	60	$7.98	Journal M. & V. accts.
1767..	Philadelphia....	50	6.65	Merc. Letter-book.
1767..	Do........	45	6.00	Do.
1767..	New Hampshire.	30	5.00	Wm. Barrell ledger.
1767..	Do........	33	5.50	Do.
1768..	Do........	33	5.50	Do.
1768..	Do........	36	6.00	Do.
1769..	New York......	45	5.62	Smith, Tour of Four Rivers, 33.
1770..	Norfolk........	60	10.00	Jamieson papers
1771..	Virginia........	59	8.33	Va. Salt Works bill.
1772..	Do.	75	10.45	Martin Cockburn acct.
1772..	Norfolk........	67 6	11.25	Jamieson papers.
1772..	Virginia........	60	10.00	Va. Salt Works bill.
1773..	Do........	60	10.00	Do.
1773..	Connecticut.....	75	12.50	Benedict Arnold's Acct. Bk.
1775..	Rhode Island...	72	12.00	S. Nightingale accts.
1777..	Virginia........	90	15.00	Jamieson papers. "1¼ inch."
1788..	New Jersey.....	80	10.00	Potter acct. book.
1792..	Philadelphia....	90	12.00	Steph. Collins letter-book.

III. COLONIAL PRICE OF TAR PER BARREL

Date.	Place.	Quotation. s. d.	Price per Barrel.	Description.	Reference.
1670..	New England...	8	$1.33		Charters and Laws, 163.
1685..	Boston.........	7	1.17		Merchant's Journal.
1685..	Do.........	7 6	1.23		Do.
1685..	Do.........	4	.67	"small" barrel	Do.
1686..	Do.........	6 6	1.08	"great" barrel	Do.
1686..	Do.........	4 3	.71	"small" barrel	Do.
1687..	Do.........	6	1.00	"great" barrel	Do.
1687..	Do.........	4 6	.75	"small" barrel	Do.
1688..	Do.........	6	1.00	"great" barrel	Do.
1688..	Do.........	4	.67	"small" barrel	Do.
1688..	Do.........	5	.83		Do.
1689..	Do.........	5 6	.92	"great" barrel	Do.
1689..	Do.........	3 9	.63	"small" barrel	Do.
1689..	Do.........	10	1.67	"Connecticut"	Do.
1689..	Do.........	9	1.50	"Connecticut"	Do.
1693..	New York.....	12	2.00		O'C., D. R. H. N. Y., iv, 96.
1696..	Hartford.......	13	2.17		Walcott ledger.
1696..	Do.........	12 4	2.04		Do.
1698..	New York.....	13 6	2.25		Van Cortlandt ledger.
1699..	Do.........	15	2.50		Do.
1699..	Do.	10	1.67		Do.
1699..	Carolina........	8 6	1.42	tidewater	O'C., D. R. H. N. Y., iv, 558.
1706..	Salem..........	20	2.00		P. English accts.
1711..	New York.....	8	1.18		O'C., D. R. H. N. Y., v, 2, 99.
1719..	South Carolina..	7 6	1.25		McCrady, 625.
1721..	New England...	8	.72	"small" barrel	Weeden app.
1723..	Philadelphia....	9	1.20		Mercantile accts.
1723..	Do.........	12	1.70		Gibbons accts.
1728..	Do.	14	1.96		Jour. Phil. Mercht.
1730..	Do.........	14	1.86		Do.
1731..	Do.........	16	2.13		Do.
1732..	Do.........	12	1.60		Do.
1733..	Maryland......	15	2.50		Carroll Acct. Bk.
1733..	New England...	20	1.00		Weeden app.
1733..	Do.........	28	1.40		Do.
1733..	Philadelphia....	12 6	1.67		Jour. Phil. Mercht.
1733..	Do.........	12	1.60		Do.
1733..	Do.........	11	1.46		Do.
1733..	Do.........	14	1.87		Do.
1734..	Maryland.......	15	2.50		Carroll Acct. Bk.
1735..	Do.........	15	2.50		Do.
1736..	Salem..........	30	1.29		T. Orne accts.
1736..	Boston.........	26	1.12		Hancock accts.
1743..	New England...	32	1.28		Weeden app.
1751..	Salem..........	13	2.17	North Carolina	T. Orne accts.
1751..	Do.........	13 4	2.22	Do.	Do.
1757..	Do.........	6	1.00	Do.	Do.
1758..	Virginia........	11	1.83		Pagan & Co. accts.
1760..	Norfolk.........	12 6	2.08		Jamieson papers.
1761..	Maryland......	15	2.11		Md. and Va. accts.
1761..	Norfolk.........	10 6	1.75		Jamieson papers.
1762..	Do.........	9 3	1.54	wholesale	Do.
1762..	Do.........	9	1.50	Do.	Do.
1763..	Do.........	10	1.67		Do.
1763..	Do.........	11	1.83		Do.
1763..	Salem..........	12	2.00		T. Orne accts.
1763..	Maryland.......	12 6	1.87		Md. and Va. accts.
1763..	Do.........	15	2.25		Do.

Price of tar per barrel—Continued.

Date.	Place.	Quota-tion.		Price per Barrel.	Description.	Reference.
		s.	d.			
1764..	Norfolk........	12	6	$2.08		Jamieson papers.
1765..	Do........	12	6	2.08		Do.
1765..	Do........	9	6	1.58	wholesale	Do.
1766..	Do........	9		1.50	Do.	Do.
1766..	Do........	7	3	1.20	Do.	Do.
1766..	Do.	10		1.67		Do.
1767..	New Hampshire.	15		2.50		Wm. Barrell ledger.
1767..	Do........	12		2.00		Do.
1767..	Do........	16		2.67		Do.
1767..	Norfolk........	7	3	1.20	wholesale	Jamieson papers.
1767..	Do........	12		2.00		Do.
1767..	Do........	8		1.33		Do.
1768..	Do........	10		1.67		Do.
1768..	New Hampshire.	15		2.50		Wm. Barrell ledger.
1769..	Norfolk........	6	6	1.08	wholesale	Jamieson papers.
1769..	Do........	10		1.67		Do.
1770..	Do........	6	9	1.12	wholesale	Do.
1770..	Do........	8	3	1.37	Do.	Do.
1770..	Do........	7	6	1.25	Do.	Do.
1771..	Do........	11		1.83		Do.
1771..	Do........	7	6	1.25	wholesale	Do.
1772..	Do........	16		2.67		Do.
1772..	Do........	11	6	1.92		Do.
1773..	Do........	9	6	1.58	wholesale	Do.
1774..	Do........	11	6	1.92		Do.
1775..	Do........	10		1.67		

IV. COLONIAL PRICES OF SHIPBUILDING PER TON

Date.	Place.	Quotation, ton. £ s. d.	Rate, ton.	Description.	Reference.
1661	Salem........	3 5 0	$10.84	Barter.....	Essex Inst., xiii, 135.
1662	Connecticut...	4 2 0	13.67	Equipped	Caulkins, N. L., 242.
1676	New England.	4 0 0	13.33	Do.....	Hutchinson papers, ii, 252.
1697	Do.......	2 10 0	8.34	....	Mass. Arch., lxii, 70.
1700	Do.......	3 12 0	12.00	....	Mass. Arch., lxii, 328.
1701	Do.......	2 13 0	8.84	....	Mass. Arch., lxii, 397.
1712	Do.......	3 0 0	8.22	....	Essex Inst., i, 175.
1721	New England.	3 00 0	5.40	Low quality	Amory letters, 7/31.
1721	Do.......	5 00 0	9.00	High quality	Do.
1730	Philadelphia..	3 12 0	9.60	....	Jour. Phil. Mercht.
1734	Do.......	6 10 0	5.75	....	Hancock papers, 146.
1737	Do.......	12 00 0	10.32	Low quality	Faneuil Acct. Bks.
1737	Do.......	15 00 0	12.60	High quality	Do.
1755	Do.......	....	14.80	Equipped	T. Orne accts.
1761	Virginia......	2 10 0	8.33	....	Jamieson papers.
1762	Do.......	2 7 6	7.92	....	Do.
1768	New Hampshire	4 00 0	13.33	Hull only...	W. Barrell ledger.
1768	Do........	6 4 5½	21.00	Equipped...	Do.
1772	Virginia......	4 12 0	15.33	Hull only...	Jamieson papers.
1776	Maine........	....	26.50 to 33.50	Equipped...	Bishop, i, 46.
1776	Boston.......	....	40.00	Do.....	Do.
1783	Baltimore.....	4 10 0†	19.75	....	Woolsey and Salmon.
1785	Philadelphia..	8 5 0	11.37	Live oak	Ebeling, iv, 693, note.
1785	Do.......	6 10 0	9.33	White oak..	Do.
1788	Do.......	14 00 0	18.70	Green oak. equipped.	Brissot, ii, 385, note.
1788	New England.	3 00 0†	13.33	Hull.......	Brissot, iii, 395, note.
1788	Albany.......	....	27.50	Fir.........	Bishop, i, 64.
1788	South Carolina	5 05 0†	23.33	Hull.......	Bishop, i, 85.
1788	Do.......	7 7 0†	35.00	Equipped...	Do.

† Sterling.

V. COLONIAL PRICE OF IRON PER TON

1. PIG-IRON

Date.	Place.	Quotation. £ s. d.	Price.	Reference.
1653...	Lynn...........	4 10 0	$18.00	Mass. Arch., lix, 47.
1653...	Braintree.......	6 00 0	24.00	Do.
1727...	Maryland.......	10 00 0	33.33	Penn. Mag. Hist., xi, 192.
1729...	Philadelphia....	8 10 0	22.66	Jour. Phil. Mercht., 318.
1731...	Do........	8 00 0	21.33	Jour. Phil. Mercht., 426
1731...	Pennsylvania...	5 10 0*	14.66	Potts Memorial, 60.
1732...	Virginia........	4 00 0†	17.76	Byrd, Progress to Mines, 349.
1732...	Philadelphia....	8 00 0	21.33	Jour. Phil. Mercht., 488
1733...	Do........	6 00 0	16.00	Jour. Phil. Mercht., 527
1736...	Maryland.......	5 2 9†	22.84	Carroll account book.
1750...	Pennsylvania...	3 10 0*†	15.50	Acrelius, New Sweden, 169.
1750...	Philadelphia....	5 00 0†	22.22	Do.
1765...	Pennsylvania...	7 00 0*	18.70	Potts Memorial, 60.
1765...	New York......	9 10 0	23.75	W. & R. Livingstone journal.
1767...	Virginia........	7 10 0	25.00	Jamieson papers.
1767...	Pennsylvania...	8 10 0	22.67	Potts Memorial, 60
1769...	Virginia........	7 10 0	25.00	Jamieson papers.
1769...	Maryland......	7 00 0	23.33	Principio Papers (N. Y. P. L.)
1771...	Virginia........	5 10 0†	24.42	Jamieson papers.
1771...	Philadelphia....	8 10 0	22.22	Sen. Doc. 67, 21st Cong., 2d sess.
1772...	Do........	8 10 0	22.22	Do.
1773...	Do........	8 10 0	22.22	Do.
1773...	Baltimore......	8 00 0	26.66	Griffiths, Annals of Baltimore, 53.
1774...	Pennsylvania...	7 5 0	19.33	Potts Memorial, 60.
1775...	Do........	7 5 0	19.33	Do.
1776...	Do........	7 5 0	19.33	Do.
1776...	Do........	7 00 0	18.66	Potts Memorial, 61.
1776...	Philadelphia....	8 00 0	21.33	Stephen Collins accts.

2. BAR IRON

Date.	Place.	Quotation. £ s. d.	Price.	Reference.
1653...	Massachusetts...	20 00 0	80.00	Mass. Arch., lix, 47.
1686...	Boston.........	24 00 0	80.00	Merchant's Journal, "Spanish iron."
1687...	Do........	22 00 0	73.33	Do.
1688...	Do........	20 00 0	66.66	Do.
1688...	Do........	20 00 0	66.66	Merchant's Journal, "New England."
1698...	New York......	40 00 0	120.00	S. van Cortlandt ledger, 109.
1700...	Do........	28 00 0	84.00	S. van Cortlandt ledger, 191.
1708...	Salem..........	32 00 0	100.00	P. English acct. book.
1721...	Philadelphia....	37 00 0	100.00	Mercantile accts., Philadelphia.
1727...	Maryland.......	35 00 0	116.66	Penn. Mag. Hist., xi, 192.
1728...	Philadelphia....	40 00 0	106.66	Jour. Phil. Mercht., 254, 256.
1729...	Do........	40 00 0	106.66	Jour. Phil. Mercht., 281, 289.
1730...	Do........	40 00 0	106.66	Jour. Phil. Mercht., 342.
1731...	Do........	40 00 0	106.66	Jour. Phil. Mercht., 398, 450.
1731...	Maryland......	47 00 0*	156.66	Carroll acct. book.
1732...	Philadelphia....	40 00 0	106.66	Jour. Phil. Mercht., 464.

* At furnace or forge. † Sterling.

2. *Bar iron*—Continued.

Date.	Place.	Quotation. £ s. d.	Price.	Reference.
1732...	Philadelphia....	32 10 0	$86.66	Jour. Phil. Mercht., 505.
1733...	Do........	30 00 0	80.00	Jour. Phil. Mercht., 532.
1734...	Do........	30 00 0	80.00	Jour. Phil. Mercht., 581.
1734...	Do........	40 00 0	106.66	Jour. Phil. Mercht., 591.
1734...	Maryland.......	30 00 0	100.00	Carroll acct. book.
1750...	Pennsylvania...	10 00 0†	44.44	Acrelius, New Sweden, 169.
1750...	Philadelphia....	15 00 0†	66.66	Do.
1760...	Do........	32 00 0	85.33	T. Orne papers.
1762...	Pennsylvania...	34 00 0	90.66	Potts Memorial, 60.
1763...	Philadelphia....	28 00 0	74.66	T. Orne papers.
1764...	Do........	26 00 0	64.00	Do.
1764...	Norfolk........	24 00 0	80.00	Jamieson papers.
1764...	Do........	28 00 0	93.33	Do.
1765...	Do........	25 00 0	83.33	Do.
1766...	Do........	26 00 0	86.66	Do.
1766...	Do........	28 00 0	93.33	Do.
1766...	Philadelphia....	24 00 0	64.00	Mercantile letters.
1766...	Do........	25 4 6	67.73	Do.
1767...	Do........	23 10 0	62.67	Do.
1768...	Do........	23 10 0	62.67	Do.
1768...	Do........	23 00 0	61.33	Do.
1768...	Norfolk........	20 00 0	66.66	Jamieson papers.
1768...	Do........	22 10 0	75.00	Do.
1769...	Do........	25 00 0	83.33	Do.
1769...	Baltimore.......	17 17 3	59.55	Do.
1769...	Philadelphia....	24 4 2	64.55	Mercantile letters.
1769...	Maryland.......	40 00 0*	133.33	Principio papers (N. Y. P. L.)
1769...	Philadelphia....	22 10 0	60.00	Do.
1770...	Do........	23 00 0	61.33	Mercantile letters.
1770...	Do........	24 1 9	64.23	Do.
1770...	Do........	24 5 5	64.72	Do.
1770...	Maryland.......	28 00 0*	93.33	Sharf papers, v. 448.
1770...	Massachusetts...	20 00 0	66.66	Pittsfield acct. book.
1771...	Norfolk........	25 00 0	83.33	Jamieson papers.
1771...	Philadelphia....	20 00 0	53.33	Sen. Doc. 67, 21st Cong., 2d sess.
1772...	Do........	20 00 0	53.33	Do.
1772...	Norfolk........	22 10 0	75.00	Jamieson papers..
1772...	Maryland.......	28 00 0*	93.33	Sharf papers, v, 448.
1773...	Philadelphia....	20 00 0	53.33	Sen. Doc. 67, 21st Cong., 2d sess.
1773...	Baltimore.......	26 00 0	86.66	Griffith, Annals of Baltimore, 53.
1776...	Philadelphia....	24 00 0	64.00	Stephen Collins accts.
1776...	Do........	26 00 0	69.33	Do.
1776...	Baltimore.......	26 00 0	86.66	Woolsey & Salmon letter-book.
1776...	Do........	25 10 0	85.00	Do.
1776...	Maryland.......	28 00 0*	93.33	Sharf papers, v. 448.
1778...	New Jersey.....	28 00 0	74.66	Sterling collection.

* At furnace or forge.   † Sterling.

VI. COLONIAL PRICE OF FLOUR PER HUNDREDWEIGHT

Yr.	Mo.	Place.	Quotation. s. d.	Price.	Description.	Reference.
1722	Dec.	Philadelphia..	10	$1.41	....	Gibbons-Woodrop accts.
1723	Jan.	Do.......	8 9	1.23	"Country bolt"	Do.
1723	Jan.	Do.......	9 3	1.30	"Town bolted"	Do.
1723	May	Do.......	10	1.41	Do.........	Do.
1723	May	Do.......	8 6	1.20	....	Do.
1723	July	Do.......	8 6	1.20	....	Do.
1723	Aug.	Do.......	9	1.27	....	Do.
1723	Aug.	Do.......	9 3	1.31	....	Do.
1723	Nov.	Do.......	9 6	1.34	....	Do.
1723	Nov.	Do.......	9	1.27	....	Do.
1723	Dec.	Do.......	9 8	1.36	....	Do.
1723	Dec.	Do.......	8 9	1.24	....	Do.
1724	....	Do.......	9 6	1.27	....	Phil. acct. book.
1725	Aug.	Do.......	12	1.60	....	Do.
1726	July	Do.......	13	1.73	....	Do.
1726	July	Do.......	16 6	1.84	....	Do.
1728	Sept.	Do.......	10	1.41	....	Jour. Phil. Mercht., 266.
1728	Nov.	Do.......	11	1.55	....	Jour. Phil. Mercht., 273.
1729	Feb.	Do.......	10 6	1.48	....	Jour. Phil. Mercht., 280.
1730	Oct.	Do.......	11	1.47	....	Jour. Phil. Mercht., 378.
1731	Apr.	Do.......	7 9	1.03	....	Jour. Phil. Mercht., 404.
1732	Jan.	Do.......	8 3	1.10	....	Jour. Phil. Mercht., 461.
1732	June	Do.......	7 9	1.03	....	Jour. Phil. Mercht., 484.
1732	July	Do.......	10	1.33	....	Jour. Phil. Mercht., 490.
1733	Mar.	Do.......	8	1.07	....	Jour. Phil. Mercht., 524.
1733	July	Do.......	9 3	1.23	....	Jour. Phil. Mercht., 548.
1733	Aug.	Do.......	10	1.33	....	Jour. Phil. Mercht., 554.
1733	Sept.	Do.......	12 6	1.67	....	Jour. Phil. Mercht., 560.
1733	Oct.	Do.......	9	1.20	....	Jour. Phil. Mercht., 562.
1734	Mar.	Do.......	10	1.33	....	Jour. Phil. Mercht., 589.
1734	Oct.	Do.......	10 6	1.40	....	Jour. Phil. Mercht., 610.
1736	Apr.	Boston.......	40	1.65	....	Hancock accts.
1744	July	Do.......	40	1.48	....	Do.
1745	Aug.	Philadelphia..	9	1.20	....	Davey & Carson, 8/7
1745	Aug.	Do.......	10	1.33	....	Davey & Carson, 8/25.
1745	Sept.	Do.......	10 3	1.37	....	Davey & Carson, 9/13.
1745	Sept.	Do.......	9 2	1.22	....	Davey & Carson.
1745	Oct.	Do.......	8 6	1.14	....	Davey & Carson, 10/10.
1745	Oct.	Do.......	9 6	1.27	"Better quality"	Davey & Carson, 10/13.
1745	Oct.	Do.......	8 6	1.14	....	Davey & Carson, 10/31.
1745	Oct.	Do.......	7 8	1.02	....	Do.
1746	Apr.	Do.......	7 9	1.02	....	Davey & Carson, 4/16.
1746	Apr.	Do.......	8	1.07	"Rising".......	Davey & Carson, 4/23.
1746	May	Do.......	8 6	1.14	....	Davey & Carson, 5/5.
1746	June	Do.......	8	1.07	"Rising".......	Davey & Carson, 6/5.
1746	July	Do.......	10	1.33	....	Davey & Carson, 7/1.
1746	Oct.	Do.......	10 3	1.37	....	Davey & Carson, 10/5
1746	Oct.	Boston.......	100	3.00	....	Hancock accts. 10/31.
1746	Nov.	Philadelphia..	9 9	1.30	....	T. Orne papers, 11/8.
1747	Feb.	Do.......	9	1.20	....	Davey & Carson, 2/27
1747	Apr.	Do.......	8 9	1.17	....	Davey & Carson, 4/3.
1747	July	Do.......	10	1.33	....	Davey & Carson, 7/9.
1747	Nov.	Do.......	12 6	1.67	....	Davey & Carson, 11/6.
1747	Nov.	Do.......	12	1.60	....	Davey & Carson, 11/26.
1748	July	Do.......	16 6	2.20	....	Davey & Carson, 7/27.
1748	July	Do.......	15	2.00	"Falling".......	Davey & Carson, 7/29.
1748	Sept.	Do.......	18	2.40	....	Davey & Carson, 9/4.

Price of flour per hundredweight—Continued.

Yr.	Mo.	Place.	Quotation.		Price.	Description.	Reference.
			s.	d.			
1748	Oct.	Philadelphia..	21		$2.80	....	Davey & Carson, 10/20.
1748	Nov.	Do.......	21		2.80	....	Davey & Carson, 11/27
1748	Dec.	Do.......	21		2.80	....	Davey & Carson, 12/2.
1749	June	Do.......	15		2.00	....	Davey & Carson, 6/29.
1749	July	Do.......	15		2.00	....	Davey & Carson, 7/3.
1749	Nov.	Do.......	14	6	1.94	....	Davey & Carson, 11/21.
1749	Dec.	Do.......	14		1.87	....	Davey & Carson, 12/16.
1750	Mar.	Do.......	14		1.87	....	Davey & Carson, 3/2.
1750	Mar.	Do.......	13	6	1.80	....	Davey & Carson, 3/3.
1750	Sept.	Do.......	14		1.87	....	Davey & Carson, 9/14.
1750	Oct.	Do.......	13	6	1.80	....	Davey & Carson, 10/7.
1750	Nov.	Do.......	14		1.87	....	Davey & Carson, 11/23.
1750	June	Boston......	110		2.20	....	T. Orne papers.
1752	....	Rhode Island..	180		3.00	....	O. Brown accts.
1753	Sept.	New York....	15	6	1.94	"Fine".........	S. van Cortlandt ledger.
1753	Dec.	Boston.......	130		2.87	"Superfine"....	Hancock accts.
1754	Mar.	Do.......	110		2.45	....	T. Orne papers.
1754	Dec.	New York....	16		2.00	....	S. van Cortlandt ledger.
1755	Feb.	Pennsylvania..	12		1.60	....	Shippen papers, i.
1755	Oct.	New York....	17		2.12	....	S. van Cortlandt ledger.
1755	Nov.	Do.......	16		2.00	....	Do.
1755	Nov.	Do.......	19	6	2.44	....	P. Cuyler's letter-book.
1756	Mar.	South Carolina	90		3.00	....	Austin & Laurens, 3/20.
1756	June	Do.......	82		2.73	"Minnesink"...	Austin & Laurens, 6/7.
1756	Nov.	Do.......	100		3.33	....	Austin & Laurens, 11/26.
1756	Nov.	New York....	12	6	1.56	....	Austin & Laurens, 11/26.
1756	Nov.	Philadelphia..	11		1.47	....	Do.
1757	Feb.	Do.......	11		1.47	....	Austin & Laurens, 2/14.
1757	....	Do.......	12	6	1.67	....	T. Orne Papers.
1757	Apr.	Norfolk......	14		2.33	....	Jamieson papers.
1758	Dec.	Virginia......	14		2.33	....	Md. & Va. firm acct., 12/28.
1758	Dec.	Philadelphia..	16		2.13	....	T. Orne papers.
1758	Dec.	Do.......	12	8	1.69	"Common".....	Do.
1760	May	Do.......	14	3	1.90	....	Do.
1760	....	Rhode Island.	18		3.00	....	O. Brown accts.
1761	May	Philadelphia..	14	3	1.90	....	T. Orne papers.
1761	May	Do.......	15	3	2.03	....	Do.
1761	Sept.	Boston.......	20		3.33	....	Jamieson papers.
1761	Sept.	Do.......	17	4	2.90	....	Do.
1761	Nov.	Philadelphia.	15	6	2.06	....	Do.
1762	Feb.	Norfolk......	15		2.50	....	Do.
1762	May	Philadelphia..	15	3	2.03	....	T. Orne papers.
1762	June	Rhode Island.	500		3.57	"Great drouth"	S. Nightingale ledger.
1762	Sept.	Boston.......	17		2.38	....	Jamieson papers.
1763	May	Philadelphia..	19		2.53	....	T. Orne papers.
1763	June	Do.......	17		2.27	....	Do.
1763	July	Do.......	17	6	2.33	....	Do.
1763	....	Rhode Island.	600		4.28	"Fine".........	S. Nightingale ledger.
1763	July	Do.......	560		3.28	....	Do.
1763	July	New York....	18		2.25	....	J. van Cortlandt accts.
1763	Aug.	Salem........	20		3.33	....	T. Orne papers.
1763	Oct.	Norfolk......	11	6	1.92	....	Jamieson papers.
1763	Dec.	Salem........	16		2.67	....	T. Orne papers.
1764	Jan.	Philadelphia..	16	5	2.07	....	Do.
1764	Jan.	Rhode Island.	560		3.28	....	S. Nightingale ledger.
1764	Feb.	Do.......	560		3.28	....	Do.
1764	Apr.	Philadelphia..	10	8	1.42	....	T. Orne papers.
1764	May	Do.......	12	6	1.67	....	Do.
1764	June	Do.......	11	8	1.56	....	Do.
1764	June	Norfolk......	15		2.50	....	Jamieson papers.

Price of flour per hundredweight—Continued.

Yr.	Mo.	Place.	Quotation. s. d.	Price.	Description.	Reference.
1764	Aug.	Rhode Island.	18	$3.00	....	O. Brown accts.
1764	Sept.	Philadelphia..	14 6	1.93	....	T. Orne papers.
1764	Nov.	Do......	13 10	1.85	....	Do.
1765	Mar.	Norfolk......	12 6	2.08	....	Jamieson papers.
1765	Apr.	Do......	12 6	2.08	....	Do.
1765	Aug.	Philadelphia..	15	2.00	"Dry season"..	Merc. letters, 2/23.
1765	Sept.	Do......	12 6	1.67	"Falling"......	Do.
1765	Sept.	Do......	14 6	1.93	....	T. Orne papers.
1765	Sept.	Norfolk......	13 6	2.25	....	Jamieson papers.
1765	Oct.	Do......	12 6	2.08	....	Do.
1765	Oct.	Philadelphia..	14 6	1.93	....	Merc. letters, 10/26
1765	Nov.	Do......	13 10	1.84	....	T. Orne papers.
1765	Dec.	Norfolk......	14	2.33	....	Jamieson papers.
1765	Dec.	Do......	16 8	2.78	"Superfine".....	Do'
1766	Mar.	Do......	16 8	2.78	....	Do.
1766	May	Do......	14	1.87	....	Merc. letters, 5/28.
1766	June	Norfolk.......	15	2.50	"Fine".........	Jamieson papers.
1766	June	Do......	12 6	2.08	....	Do.
1766	Sept.	Do......	15	2.50	....	Do.
1766	Sept.	Philadelphia..	16 6	2.20	"Rains"........	Merc. letters, 9/30.
1766	Nov.	Do......	18	2.40	"Superfine".....	Merc. letters, 11/1.
1766	Nov.	Do......	14 6	1.94	"Common".....	Do.
1766	Nov.	Do......	16	2.13	....	Merc. letters, 11/11.
1766	Nov.	Do......	17	2.27	"Wagon flour".	Merc. letters, 11/18.
1766	Dec.	Do......	16 6	2.20	....	Merc. letters, 12/11.
1766	Dec.	Do......	17 3	2.30	"Fine".........	Merc. letters, 12/13.
1766	Dec.	Do......	16	2.13	"Common".....	Do.
1767	Mar.	Norfolk......	15	2.50	....	Jamieson papers.
1767	Mar.	Philadelphia..	16 6	2.20	....	Merc. letters, 3/24.
1767	June	Do......	18	2.40	"Wagon flour"..	Merc. letters, 6/2.
1767	June	Do......	17 6	2.33	"Shallop quick"	Do.
1767	June	Do......	17 6	2.33	....	Merc. letters, 6/9.
1767	June	Do......	17	2.27	....	Merc. letters, 6/19.
1767	July	Do......	20	2.67	"Top market" .	Merc. letters, 7/4.
1767	July	Do......	18	2.40	"Shallop".......	Do.
1767	Sept.	Do......	17 6	2.33	....	Merc. letters, 9/8.
1767	Sept.	Do......	18	2.40	....	Merc. letters, 9/26
1767	Sept.	Norfolk......	16 8	2.78	....	Jamieson papers.
1767	Oct.	New York....	21	2.62	....	J. van Cortlandt accts.
1767	Oct.	Philadelphia..	16 6	2.20	....	Merc. letters, 10/10.
1767	Oct.	Do......	16 6	2.40	....	Merc. letters, 10/19.
1767	Nov.	Do......	18	2.40	....	Merc. letters, 11/9
1767	Nov.	Do......	18	2.40	....	Smith & Co., 11/19
1767	Nov.	Do......	18 6	2.47	"Short crop"...	Smith & Co., 11/23.
1767	Dec.	Do......	21	2.80	"Superfine"....	Smith & Co., 12/12.
1767	Dec.	Do......	18 6	2.47	"Wagon flour".	Do.
1767	Dec.	New York....	20	2.50	....	J. van Cortlandt accts.
1768	Feb.	Baltimore...	16 6	2.20	....	Jamieson papers.
1768	Mar.	Do......	17 6	2.33	....	Do.
1768	Mar.	Philadelphia..	18	2.40	"Rising superfine"	Smith & Co., 3/3.
1768	Mar.	Do......	22	2.93	"Beyond reason"	Smith & Co., 3/9.
1768	Mar.	Do......	18	2.40	"Common"....	Do.
1768	Mar.	Do......	18	2.40	....	Smith & Co., 3/11.
1768	Apr.	Do......	18 6	2.47	"Needy millers accept $2.33".	Smith & Co., 4/15.
1768	Apr.	Do......	17 3	2.30	....	Jamieson papers.
1768	Apr.	Baltimore.....	17	2.27	....	Do.
1768	May	Philadelphia..	18	2.40	....	Smith & Co., 5/14.
1768	May	Baltimore....	16 6	2.20	....	Jamieson papers.
1768	June	Philadelphia..	17 6	2.33	"Shallop".....	Smith & Co., 6/-.

Price of flour per hundredweight—Continued.

Yr.	Mo.	Place.	Quota-tion.		Price.	Description.	Reference.
			s.	d.			
1768	June	Philadelphia..	18		$2.40	"Wagon"......	Smith & Co., 6/-.
1768	June	Norfolk......	12	6	2.08	....	Jamieson papers.
1768	July	Baltimore....	17		2.27	....	Do.
1768	July	Philadelphia..	18		2.40	"Wagon"......	Smith & Co., 7/23.
1768	Aug.	Do......	16	3	2.17	"Fine harvest".	Smith & Co., 8/20.
1768	Aug.	Norfolk......	15		2.50	....	Jamieson papers.
1768	Sept.	Baltimore....	14	6	1.93	....	Do.
1768	Sept.	Philadelphia..	17		2.27	"Low water"...	Smith & Co., 9/3.
1768	Sept.	Do......	17	3	2.30	Do.........	Smith & Co., 9/23.
1768	Oct.	Baltimore.....	14	6	1.93	....	Jamieson papers.
1768	Nov.	Philadelphia..	15	6	2.07	....	Smith & Co., 11/5.
1768	Nov.	Do......	16		2.13	"Rising"......	Smith & Co., 11/7.
1768	Nov.	Do......	18	6	2.47	"Fine; winter.. load."	Smith & Co., 11/12.
1768	Nov.	Do......	16		2.13	....	Do.
1768	Nov.	Baltimore....	14	6	1.93	....	Jamieson papers.
1768	Dec.	Do......	15	6	2.08	....	Do.
1768	Dec.	Philadelphia..	16	6	2.20	....	Smith & Co., 12/10.
1768	Dec.	Do......	15	6	2.07	"Open weather"	Smith & Co., 12/17; also Jamieson papers.
1768	Dec.	Do......	16		2.13	....	Smith & Co., 12/19.
1769	Jan.	New York....	20		2.50	....	J. van Cortlandt accts.
1768	Jan.	Norfolk......	15		2.50	....	Jamieson papers.
1769	Jan.	Philadelphia..	15	9	2.10	....	Smith & Co., 1/17.
1769	Feb.	Do......	15	6	2.07	....	Smith & Co., 2/7
1769	Feb.	Baltimore....	14		1.87	....	Jamieson papers.
1769	Feb.	Norfolk......	12	6	2.08	....	Do.
1769	Mar.	Philadelphia..	15	6	2.07	"Wagon flour".	Smith & Co., 3/13.
1769	Mar.	Do......	13	3	1.77	"Shallop flour"	Do.
1769	Mar.	Do......	15		2.00	....	Smith & Co., 3/29.
1769	Apr.	Do......	14	6	1.94	....	Smith & Co., 4/18.
1769	Apr.	Norfolk......	14		2.33	....	Jamieson papers.
1769	May	Do......	14		2.33	....	Do.
1769	May	Philadelphia..	15		2.00	"Wagon flour".	Smith & Co., 5/30.
1769	May	Do......	14	6	1.94	"Shallop flour".	Do.
1769	July	Do......	15	6	2.07	....	Smith & Co., 7/12.
1769	July	Do......	15	6	2.07	"Dry weather".	Smith & Co., 7/15.
1769	July	Do......	16	2	2.15	"Common flour"	Smith & Co., 7/22.
1769	Aug.	Do......	17	3	2.30	"Fine flour"...	Smith & Co., 8/26.
1769	Aug.	Do......	15	3	2.03	"Wagon flour".	Do.
1769	Sept.	Do......	15	6	2.07	....	Smith & Co., 9/2, 5, 9.
1769	Sept.	Do......	16	9	2.23	"Storm injuries".	Smith & Co., 9/16.
1769	Sept.	Do......	16		2.13	"Scarce"......	Smith & Co., 9/17.
1769	Sept.	Boston........	14	6	2.42	....	Jamieson papers.
1769	Oct.	Baltimore....	14		1.87	....	Do.
1769	Oct.	Philadelphia..	18		2.40	"Clarke's superfine".	Smith & Co., 10/16.
1769	Oct.	Do......	15	3	2.03	....	Do.
1769	Nov.	Baltimore....	14	6	1.93	....	Jamieson papers.
1770	Mar.	Philadelphia..	15		2.00	....	Smith & Co., 3/16.
1770	Apr.	Do......	15		2.00	....	Smith & Co., 4/27.
1770	Apr.	Boston.......	16		2.67	"Phila. flour."..	Jamieson papers.
1770	Apr.	Do......	14		2.33	"Norfolk flour"	Do.
1770	May	Philadelphia..	15	3	2.03	....	Smith & Co. 5/26.
1770	June	Do......	14	6	1.93	....	Jamieson papers.
1770	June	Do......	15	6	2.07	"Rising"......	Smith & Co., 6/22.
1770	July	Do......	16		2.13	....	Smith & Co., 7/3.
1770	July	Do......	16		2.13	....	Smith & Co., 7/17.
1770	July	Do......	16	3	2.17	....	Smith & Co., 7/21.
1770	Aug.	Do......	22	6	3.00	"Superfine; unconscionable"	Smith & Co., 8/10.

Appendices

Price of flour per hundredweight—Continued.

Yr.	Mo.	Place.	Quota-tion.		Price.	Description.	Reference.
			s.	d.			
1770	Aug.	Philadelphia..	17	6	$2.33	....	Smith & Co., 8/10.
1770	Aug.	Do.......	17		2.27	....	Smith & Co., 8/18.
1770	Sept.	Boston.......	16		2.67	"Phila flour"...	Jamieson papers.
1770	Sept.	Philadelphia..	17		2.27	"Common"....	Smith & Co., 9/15.
1770	Sept.	Do.......	16		2.13	....	Do.
1770	Sept.	Do.......	15	6	2.07	....	Smith & Co., 9/20.
1770	Sept.	Do.......	15		2.00	....	Smith & Co., 9/26.
1770	Oct.	Do.......	15	6	2.07	....	Smith & Co., 10/9.
1770	Oct.	Do.......	16		2.13	....	Smith & Co., 10/16.
1770	Oct.	Do.......	16	6	2.20	....	Smith & Co., 10/17.
1770	Oct.	Do.......	16		2.13	....	Smith & Co., 10/29.
1770	Oct.	Do.......	16	6	2.20	....	Smith & Co., 10/31.
1770	Oct.	Do.......	21		2.80	"Fine"........	Smith & Co., 10/29.
1770	Nov.	Do.......	16	9	2.23	....	Smith & Co., 11/6.
1770	Dec.	Boston.......	18		3.00	"Phila flour"...	Jamieson papers.
1771	Jan.	Do.......	18		3.00	....	Hancock accts.
1771	June	Baltimore....	17	3	2.30	....	Jamieson papers.
1772	Feb.	Norfolk......	12	6	2.08	....	Do.
1772	Apr.	Baltimore....	19		2.53	....	Do.
1772	Apr.	Do.......	18	6	2.46	....	Do.
1772	Oct.	Norfolk......	15		2.50	....	Do.
1772	Nov.	New York....	23		2.87	....	J. van Cortlandt accts.
1772	Dec.	Boston.......	18		3.00	"Phila. flour"..	Jamieson papers.
1773	Apr.	Norfolk......	15	6	2.58	....	Do.
1773	Aug.	Do.......	15		2.50	....	Do.
1773	Oct.	Do.......	12		2.00	....	Do.
1773	Nov.	Do.......	15		2.50	....	Do.
1774	Mar.	Do.......	15		2.50	....	Do.
1774	May	Do.......	15		2.50	....	Do.
1774	June	Do.......	16	8	2.77	"Fine flour"...	Do.
1774	Aug.	Do.......	15		2.50	....	Do.
1774	Oct.	Baltimore....	16	6	2.20	....	Woolsey & Salmon, 10/22.
1774	Oct.	Do.......	17		2.27	....	Woolsey & Salmon, 10/20.
1774	Nov.	Do.......	16		2.13	....	Woolsey & Salmon, 11/16.
1774	Nov.	Do.......	16		2.13	....	Woolsey & Salmon, 11/29.
1774	Dec.	Do.......	16	6	2.20	....	Woolsey & Salmon, 12/8.
1774	Dec.	Do.......	76	1	2.33	....	Woolsey & Salmon, 12/22.
1775	Jan.	Do.......	17		2.27	....	Woolsey & Salmon, 1/25.
1775	Jan.	Do.......	18		2.40	....	Woolsey & Salmon, 1/28
1775	Feb.	Do.......	17	6	2.33	....	Woolsey & Salmon, 2/4.
1775	Feb.	Do.......	17		2.27	"Dull"........	Woolsey & Salmon, 2/7
1775	Feb.	Do.......	16	6	2.20	"Wagon flour".	Woolsey & Salmon, 2/11.
1775	Feb.	Do.......	17	6	2.33	"Town mill flour"	Do.
1775	Feb.	Do.......	15	6	2.07	"Falling"......	Woolsey & Salmon, 2/16.
1775	Feb.	Rhode Island.	480		3.00	....	Newport store blotter
1775	Mar.	Baltimore....	15	9	2.10	"Falling from 2.13"	Woolsey & Salmon, 3/1.
1775	Mar.	Do.......	15	6	2.07	"Real price"....	Woolsey & Salmon, 3/2.
1775	Mar.	Do.......	16	6	2.20	"Expected lower"	Woolsey & Salmon, 3/-.
1775	May	Do.......	14		1.87	....	Woolsey & Salmon, 5/24.
1775	May	Philadelphia..	12	6	1.67	....	Do.
1775	May	Baltimore....	17		2.40	"Superfine"....	Woolsey & Salmon, 5/30.
1775	May	Do.......	13		1.73	....	Do.
1775	June	Rhode Island.	520		3.25	....	Newport store blotter.
1775	July	Baltimore....	16		2.13	"New crop cut"	Woolsey & Salmon, 7/11.
1775	July	Do.......	15		2.00	....	Woolsey & Salmon, 7/31.
1775	Aug.	Do.......	13		1.73	....	Woolsey & Salmon, 8/22, 26.

Price of flour per hundredweight.—Continued.

Yr.	Mo.	Place.	Quotation.		Price.	Description.	Remarks.
			s.	d.			
1775	Aug.	Baltimore....	14		$1.87	....	Woolsey & Salmon, 8/31.
1775	Sept.	Do.......	13		1.73	....	Woolsey & Salmon, 9/8.
1775	Sept.	Do.......	10	6	1.40	"Embargo, 9/10"	Woolsey & Salmon, 9/18.
1775	Dec.	Do.......	11		1.47	....	Woolsey & Salmon, 12/4
1776	Jan.	Do.......	13		1.73	....	Woolsey & Salmon, 1/3.
1776	Jan.	Philadelphia..	15		2.00	"Common"....	S. Collins ledger, 1/9.
1776	Mar.	Do.......	13	6	1.80	Do.........	S. Collins ledger, 3/2, 6, 12.
1776	Mar.	Do.......	15	9	2.10	"Superfine"....	S. Collins ledger, 3/2.
1776	Mar.	Do.......	14		1.87	"Sale flour"....	S. Collins ledger, 3/12
1776	Mar.	Do.......	14	9	1.97	....	S. Collins, ledger, 3/23, 24.
1776	Mar.	Do.......	14		1.87	"New flour" ..	S. Collins ledger, 3/24.
1776	Apr.	Do.......	14	6	1.94	....	S. Collins ledger, 4/2.
1777	Apr.	Do.......	14		1.87	....	S. Collins ledger, 4/15, 24, 25.
1776	May	Do.......	12	6	1.67	....	S. Collins ledger, 5/4.
1776	Sept.	Baltimore...	11		1.47	....	Woolsey & Salmon, 9/1–10.
1776	Sept.	Do.......	12	6	1.67	....	Woolsey & Salmon, 9/21.
1777	Jan.	Do.......	27		2.50	"Common, about"	Woolsey & Salmon, 1/16.
1777	Dec.	Virginia......	18		3.00	....	Martin Cockburn.
1778	July	Do.......	15		2.50	....	Do.

VII. GEORGE WASHINGTON'S WEAVING ACCOUNTS

Among the *Washington Papers* at the Library of Congress is a record book in George Washington's handwriting, entitled *An Account of Weaving done by Thomas Davis, etc.*, covering the years from 1767 to 1771 inclusive. An extract from this account is given on page 149 preceding. Thomas Davis was a white weaver who appears to have been continuously employed by Washington, and possibly was an indentured servant. Washington paid the passage of two members of his family from England to America, and later had various general business dealings with him. During the latter part of the period covered by this account two other weavers, who may have been negro assistants, are occasionally mentioned. The book contains dated entries of probably all the weaving done at Washington's spinning house during years when domestic industry was being actively promoted in Virginia as a measure of political retaliation against Great Britain. Cloth was woven not only for Washington himself, but also for outside customers. The entries form our best technical account of colonial textiles, because they not only describe the fabrics made, their materials, and the cost of weaving, but they give the weight of "thread" (warp) and of "shute" (weft) used, and the number of threads in width, as well as the weight and both dimensions of the finished cloth.

Data from all the complete entries for the four years ending with 1770 are summarized in the following table, and the amounts in colonial currency have been reduced to dollars and cents. It has been impossible to classify fabrics with certainty as to the materials used. The cotton goods presumably were woven with a linen warp. However, the term "thread and cotton" in a few entries would describe a cloth of this kind more accurately than "cotton" and the term "cotton filled with wool" might possibly imply that a cotton warp was sometimes used. Linens were woven in pieces about 50 yards long, but other goods were made of various dimensions. The annual earnings of the weavers appear to have varied from $148 to $180, but possibly this money was not all paid to the same person. Of the 6,557.25 yards of cloth made during these four years, 2,788.75 were linen, 1,932.25 were woolen, 973.5 were clearly mixed goods, and 862.75 were classed as cotton.

Cloth woven 1767–1770, inclusive.

Fabric.	No. of yards.	Width in yards.	Width in thr'ds.	Weight per yard, ounces.	Cost of weaving per yard.	Total cost of weaving.
COTTON.						
Bedticking	13.	0.75	800	11	$0.139	$1.81
Do	15.	.75	600	11.2	.25	3.75
Birdseye	24.	1.	1000	7.8	.333	8.00
Do	8.	.875	1000	8	.25	2.00
Do	9.	.75	900	7.5	.209	1.87
Do	38.	.875	900	8 to 8.8	.209	7.92
Do	22.	.75	900	8.4	.167	3.67
Do	21	.875	800	7.2	.167	3.50
Do	8.75	.75	700	9.9	.167	1.46
Birdseye, Double	22.75	1.	1100	7.7 to 11.4	.417	9.48
Do	9.75	.875	1000	9.8	.333	3.25

Cloth woven 1767–1770, inclusive—Continued.

Fabric.	No. of yards.	Width in yards.	Width in thr'ds.	Weight per yard, ounces.	Cost of weaving per yard.	Total cost of weaving.
COTTON.						
Birdseye diaper	13	.75	1200	5.5	$0.333	$4.33
Cotton, plaided	7.25	1.	1100	5.5	.417	3.02
Do	9.75	.875	1100	5.3	.417	4.06
Do	14.5	.75	1000	5.4	.209	3.02
Do	7.75	.75	900	5.4	.139	1.08
Do	33.75	1.	800	9.4	.139	4.69
Cotton, plain	10.25	.75	1200	4.3	.333	3.42
Do	6.5	.75	1000	5.	.167	1.08
Do	10.	.75	950	4.8	.209	2.09
Do	6.75	1.	900	5.3	.25	1.69
Do	14.	1.	900	6.	.167	2.33
Do	12.75	.75	900	5 to 6.4	.167	2.12
Do	16.75	.75	900	5.9	.139	2.30
Do	47.	.75	800	6.2	.111	5.22
Do	7.5	.75	700	7.	.111	.83
Do	16.5	.75	650	7.	.083	1.37
Do	9.	.75	600	7.5	.083	.75
Cotton, striped	8.	1.	1200	8.	.417	3.33
Do	16.5	.75	1200	5.5	.279	4.58
Do	24.25	1.	1100	8.	.25	6.06
Do	14.25	1.	1000	—	.167	2.37
Do	7.75	1.	1000	4.4	.333	2.58
Do	16.75	1.	900	5.8 to 6.1	.209	3.49
Do	13.5	.75	900	5.5	.209	2.81
Do	35.25	.75	900	5.1 to 9.2	.167	5.87
Do	9.	.875	900	6.6	.167	1.50
Do	16.75	.75	900	5.	.139	2.33
Do	20.	.75	900	5.6	.125	2.50
Do	6.5	.75	800	6.1	.278	1.80
Do	73.5	.75	800	6.1 to 7	.111	8.17
Do	13.	.75	700	8.	.111	1.44
Do	22.75	.75	700	8.	.083	1.90
Do	10.	.75	600	6.	.083	.83
Do	30.	.75	400	6.2	.069	2.08
Cotton, striped, "jumped"	7.	.875	1200	4.5	.417	2.92
Do	9.5	.75	900	8.4	.333	3.17
Do	16.	.75	900	4.2 to 5.1	.25	4.00
Cotton, striped and plaid	6.5	1.	900	5.1	.25	1.63
Counterpanes	8.75	.75	1100	8.2	.167	1.46
Do	12.	1.	600	12.3	.209	2.50
Coverlids	8.5	.75	1000	6.1	.333	2.83
Dimity	9.	.875	900	7.1	.292	2.61
Do	24.25	.875	900	7.2	.278	6.74
Dimity, "India"	13.	1.	1200	4.3	.417	5.42
Mˢ andˢ O	63.5	.75	800	6.6 to 8.6	.167	10.58
Mˢ andˢ O, plaided	23.5	.75	700	5.9	.181	4.23
LINEN.						
Huckabuck	8.5	1.	900	5.6	.209	1.77
Do	40	.75	800	4.4	.167	6.67
Linen	22.5	1.	1200	7.1	.333	7.50
Do	48.	1.	1000	8.	.167	8.00
Do	12.25	1.	800	9.8	.111	1.36
Do	50.	.75	750	8.6	.083	4.17
Do	53.	.75	700	10.	.056	2.94
Do	80.5	.75	700	7.8 to 8.8	.069	5.59
Do	66.5	.75	700	7.2	.083	5.54
Do	268.5	.75	650	7.9 ro 10.1	.056	14.85
Do	1844.25	.75	600	8.6 to 9.8	.056	102.03

Cloth woven 1767–1770 inclusive—Continued.

Fabric.	No. of yards.	Width in yards.	Width in thr'ds.	Weight per yard, ounces.	Cost of weaving per yard.	Total cost of weaving.
LINEN.						
Linen	34.	.75	600	9.8	$0.069	$2.36
Do	34.5	1.	550	14.4	.069	2.39
Do	15.75	.75	550	13.2	.056	.87
Do	108.5	.75	500	9.6 to 10.4	.056	6.03
Do	48.75	.75	400	12.6 to 12.8	.056	2.71
Linen filled with tow	53.25	.75	700	9.3	.056	2.95
MIXED.						
Cotton and silk	7.5	.75	1200	3.2	.417	3.12
Do	6.75	.875	1200	4.4	.333	2.25
Cotton and silk, plaid	7.75	1.	1000	8.2	.50	3.87
Do	6.5	1.	—	5.5	.417	2.71
Cotton striped with silk	13.5	1.	1000	4.9	.333	4.50
Cotton and wool	8.5	.75	800	9.4	.111	.94
Do	32.25	.75	800	7.9	.083	2.69
Do	25.5	.75	650	8.6	.083	2.12
Do	26.	.75	600	6.7	.111	2.89
Do	17.25	.75	600	8.3	.083	1.42
Do	7.75	.875	600	10.3	.069	.54
Do	11.75	.75	550	10.9	.069	.82
Do	27.	.75	500	7.7	.069	1.87
Cotton and wool, striped	15.75	.75	650	8.3	.083	1.32
Cotton filled with wool	22.	.75	500	14.5	.056	1.22
Fustian	14.	.75	900	6.1	.167	2.33
Do	7.	.75	800	7.1	.209	1.46
Do	8.75	.75	800	7.7	1.67	1.46
Linsey	194.	1.	300	14.3 to 18.1	.069	13.47
Do	50.5	.75	300	12.4	.056	2.80
Linsey, plaided	56.	1.	300	15.3	.083	4.67
Linsey woolsey	49.5	1	300	15.8	.083	4.12
Do	190.5	1.	300	14.9 to 15.2	.069	13.23
Roman M	7.75	1.	900	8.5	.25	1.94
Do	16.	.75	900	6.5	.167	2.66
Silk and cloth, striped	6.25	1.	1200	6.	.50	3.12
Thread and cotton	7.	1.	900	9.7	.25	1.75
Thread and cotton, birdseye	19.75	.75	600	6.8	.167	3.29
WOOLEN.						
Barracan	9.75	.75	900	9.8	.25	2.44
Do	10	.875	600	11.2	.25	2.50
Birdseye	336.75	1.	350	18.1 to 20.6	.083	28.06
Birdseye, double	99.5	1.	400	18.9	.111	11.06
Do	310.5	1.	350	19.6 to 19.8	.113	34.50
Broadcloth	17.	1.25	800	9.4	.338	5.66
Do	14.75	1.25	800	8.1	.25	3.69
Do	14.	1.25	750	10.8	.279	3.89
Do	11.	1.25	650	8.7	.25	2.75
Do	13.	1.25	650	10.7	.209	2.71
Do	15.	1.25	600	10.6	.167	2.50
Do	10.	1.25	500	13.	.209	2.08
Carpet	12.	1.	400	15.3	.333	4.00
Do	23.5	1.	250	26.5	.25	5.87
Herringbone	11.5	.875	400	16.	.083	.96
Jeans	7.85	1.	1200	6.6	.50	4.37
Do	6.5	1.	1200	10.1	.417	2.71
Do	7.5	1.	1100	7.4	.417	3.13
Do	5.75	1.	1000	8.3	.417	2.40
Do	9.	1.	1000	8.8	.333	3.00
Do	11.	1.	900	8.7	.333	3.67

Cloth woven 1767–1770, inclusive—Continued.

Fabrics.	No. of yards.	Width in yards.	Width in thr'ds.	Weight per yard, ounces.	Cost of weaving per yard.	Total cost of weaving.
WOOLEN.						
Jeans	9.75	.75	900	8.2	$0.209	$2.03
Jeans, twilled	7.	1.	1200	6.6	.50	3.50
Do	8.5	1.	1100	5.4	.417	3.54
Do	14.25	1.	1000	8.1	.333	4.75
Do	8.5	.75	1000	5.6	.25	2.13
Do	8.5	.75	900	7.	.209	1.75
Kersey	257.	1.	300	18.8 to 20.8	.069	17.85
Kersey, striped	50.	1.	350	20.1	.083	4.17
Shalloon	9.5	.875	900	7.5	.209	1.98
Woolen	15.5	1.25	700	18.5	.139	2.15
Do	8.75	1.	600	10.3	.083	.73
Do	61.	.75	400	10.1 to 11.7	.056	3.39
Do	20.	.875	400	17.6	.056	1.11
Do	54.	.75	350	14.	.056	3.00
Woolen, plaided	35.5	1.	400	16.2	.083	2.92
Do	33.5	1.	400	15.2	.111	3.72
Do	84.5	1.	350	14.1 to 14.9	.083	7.04
Woolen, striped	14.5	.75	450	9.1	.069	1.01
Do	32.75	.75	400	15.1	.083	2.72
Do	10.	.75	400	9.8	.069	.69
Do	36.5	.75	400	9.2	.056	2.03
Do	196.	1.	300	16.9	.069	13.61
Total	6557.25					$675.92

VIII. STATISTICS RELATING TO THE TARIFF

Tables 1, 2, and 3 show the net annual imports between 1821 and 1860, of dutiable commodities, of woolen manufactures, and of manufactured and unmanufactured iron and steel. Official statistics of imports and revenue during this period are sometimes contradictory and often inconsistent. Net imports of dutiable commodities and the annual rate of duties upon them are taken from the special report on customs-tariff legislation (*House Ex. Doc.*, 42 Cong., 2 sess., No. 109). Net imports of woolen manufactures are taken from the report on wool and manufactures of wool, published by the Bureau of Statistics in 1888 (*Senate Mis. Doc.*, 50 Cong., 1 sess., No. 550). The figures for net cotton manufactures have been compiled directly from the Commerce and Navigation Reports, and from the Finance Report of 1861. Statistics of manufactured iron and steel are from the same sources. In considering the first groups of figures allowance should be made for the fact that some important imports, such as tea and coffee, linen, worsted and silk, and worsted, were at times included in dutiable commodities and at times admitted free. This affects statistics of per capita consumption. Under woolen manufactures are included both dutiable and non-dutiable goods. These embrace mixtures of silk and worsted.

The averages are, as nearly as may be, true averages, based upon the computed population for years intermediate between decennial censuses. The rates of duty are given only for those years concerning which we have statistics of customs collected upon each particular group of manufactures. Duties upon woolens are based upon gross imports, and computed from figures given in the report on Wool and Manufactures of Wool already quoted. Duties upon cotton for the years 1829 and 1830 are computed from figures given in the Report on the Finances for 1832 (*Reports of the Secretary of the Treasury* III, 270, Statement M). The rates between 1844 and 1860 are taken from the Finance Report of 1861. The rate of duty on iron and steel from 1821 to 1832, inclusive, is computed from the net revenue from specific duties of iron and steel, and their manufactures, as given in the Finance Reports of those years, plus the ad valorem duties, estimated on a basis of net imports, as computed from the Commerce and Navigation reports. The duties on iron and steel from 1843 to 1846 have been computed mainly from figures given in the report of the Treasury Department, dated January 12, 1849, republished in *Senate Document*, 62 Congress, 1 sess., No. 72, part iii, 2433. Figures from 1847 to 1860 are from the Finance Report of 1861, pages 262 and following. It should be recalled that prior to January 1, 1834, cotton manufactures were appraised for customs purposes under minimum valuations higher than the true value of the goods imported. The same is true of the value of woolens between 1829 and 1832. Attention should also be called to the changing relation that per capita consumption, expressed in values, bore to per capita consumption, expressed in quantities; that is, to the fact that $1 in value represented a far larger amount of cloth or metal in 1860 than in 1821.

Tariff periods did not coincide exactly with groups of fiscal years; therefore the averages given for tariff periods possess less approximate precision than the other figures. However, the significance of the table lies rather in the relative ratios that it presents than in absolute figures.

Two groups of facts relating to the assumed influence of the tariff and foreign competition upon manufacturers are suggested by these tables. The first relates to the fluctuation of imports from year to year. This is most clearly shown by the variation of per capita imports from the mean imports of tariff periods. In the case of all dutiable imports this fluctuation was greatest under the high tariff of 1842, and greater under the tariff of 1828 than during any other 4-year period except the one just mentioned. The same is true of both cotton and woolen manufactures. In case of manufactured and unmanufactured iron and steel the maximum variation within a 4-year period was under the tariff of 1842, but the largest variation was during the last 4 years of the operation of the tariff of 1816 and 1818. These ratios are all influenced by the abnormally small importation during the 9 months that represent in official statistics the fiscal year of 1842–1843, although the tables are corrected to represent a full year in this instance. The excessive fluctuation in 1830 and 1831 occurred under the highest tariff enacted during this period. Any analysis that we may make of these figures brings us at least to the negative conclusion that rates of duty had little effect upon the fluctuation of imports from year to year, and therefore upon the evenness of foreign competition.

The average pressure of foreign competition is most satisfactorily measured by the variation from the average for the 40-year period. Yet in studying these figures it is important to bear in mind that absolute values of foreign imports through so long a period of time do not measure the competitive effect of these imports. This effect involves two other important factors—the quantitative volume of imports represented by these values and the purchasing power of the nation. The former factor has already been alluded to; the latter is illustrated by comparing per capita imports after 1850 with these for any of the earlier periods. Following the discovery of gold in California and the great increase of production due to improved machinery and communication, the purchasing power of the nation rapidly rose. Although each individual bought from $7 to $8 worth of goods abroad, where formerly he had bought less than $5 worth, it is to be presumed that the consumption of domestic manufactures had increased in even greater proportion. Therefore the rise in imports after the middle of the century does not necessarily imply an increase in competitive pressure upon American manufacturers. Comparing tables for different commodities for this period, the grouping of plus percentages within the latter years is more obvious in case of woolen than of cotton manufactures, and suggests that the latter industry was the better established of the two. The increase of metal imports during the last 8 years of this period is due, of course, in the main to railway construction. In studying the iron duties a considerable increase will be noticed after 1826, although the tariff schedules relating to these commodities were practically unchanged until the compromise law of 1833. This increase is due mostly to large importations of iron bars paying specific duties.

TABLE 1.—*Rate of duty and per cent annual variation of per capita imports from average of tariff period from 1821 to 1860, inclusive.*

Year.	All dutible imports. Rate of duty[1]	All dutible imports. Variation, per cent.	Imported woolen manufactures. Rate of duty.[1]	Imported woolen manufactures. Variation, per cent.	Imported cotton manfactures. Rate of duty.[1]	Imported cotton manfactures. Variation, per cent.	Imported manufactured and unmanufactured iron and steel. Rate of duty.[1]	Imported manufactured and unmanufactured iron and steel. Variation, per cent.
1821	32.7	−14.8	22.2	−14.5	25.0	− 6.2	28.9	−25.9
1822		27.6		39.9		29.2		18.5
1823		− 7.0		−12.1		−13.8		13.6
1824		− 5.8		−13.3		− 9.2		− 6.2
1825	38.2	19.5	30.2	28.7	(x)	30.5	31.0	− 1.5
1826		− 5.2		−10.4		−24.4		−11.8
1827		− 9.5		− 7.9		− 9.7		− 3.6
1828		− 4.8		−10.4		− 3.2		16.9
1829	39.9	−11.9	38.8	−17.3	27.7	−15.3	37.9	−13.3
1830		−23.1		−35.1	28.6	−29.4		−13.3
1831		27.2		43.2	(x)	52.2		2.5
1832		7.8		9.2	(x)	− 7.5		24.1
1833	45.2	0.0	34.0	0.0	(x)	0.0	(x)	0.0
1834	32.2	15.8	26.1	−46.8	(x)	−21.9	(x)	− 0.9
1835		−15.8		46.8		21.9		0.9
1836	22.2	18.9	20.0	43.0	(x)	29.4	(x)	3.1
1837		−18.9		−43.0		−29.4		−3.1
1838	28.3	−14.6	1.90	−22.0	(x)	−41.4	(x)	−25.6
1839		14.6		22.0		41.4		25.6
1840	27.5	−11.8	18.9	− 8.3	(x)	−31.9	(x)	−11.6
1841		11.8		8.3		31.9		11.6
1842	28.1	0.0	26.4	0.0	(x)	0.0	(x)	0.0
1843	30.5	−51.0	35.6	−61.8	(x)	−66.8	39.6	−77.4
1844		10.6		16.8	36.6	27.2		− 6.5
1845		21.0		28.2	36.7	23.5		45.2
1846		19.4		16.8	38.6	16.1		38.7
1847	25.5	−35.8	27.6	−35.7	25.3	−16.8	28.7	−44.6
1848		−22.1		−15.3		−22.7		−24.1
1849		−28.6		−24.5		−19.1		−20.5
1850		−13.7		−14.3		1.1		− 8.4
1851		3.3		− 6.1		7.0		− 6.0
1852		− 7.2		−16.3		− 9.6		0.0
1853		19.9		26.5		23.7		42.2
1854		30.0		41.8		47.4		42.2
1855		1.0		− 5.1		−31.0		7.2
1856		19.5		25.5		3.5		4.8
1857		33.7		23.5		16.5		7.2
1858	20.5	−17.5	21.3	−16.6	20.3	−27.5	22.5	− 7.3
1859		6.6		2.0		4.5		− 7.3
1860		10.9		14.6		23.0		14.6

[1] Percentage of appraised value of imports.   (x) Data not obtainable.

TABLE 2.—*Rate of duty and per cent annual variation from the average for forty years of the per capita consumption of all dutiable imports and of imported cotton and woolen manufactures and manufactured and unmanufactured iron and steel.*

Year	All dutiable imports. Rate of duty[1]	Variation, per cent.	Imported woolen manufactures. Rate of duty.[1]	Variation, per cent.	Imported cotton manfactures. Rate of duty.[1]	Variation, per cent.	Imported manufactured and unmanufactured iron and steel. Rate of duty.[1]	Variation, per cent.
1821	31.0	−25.7	22.1	−20.7	25	−12.9	26.1	−52.5
1822	27.1	11.6	21.4	30.0	25	20.0	28.8	−21.3
1823	35.1	−18.6	21.3	−19.5	25	−20.0	30.0	−24.6
1824	35.2	−17.6	24.4	−16.1	25	−15.7	29.3	−37.7
1825	31.0	2.3	28.9	16.1	....	30.0	29.3	−21.3
1826	44.0	−18.8	29.2	−18.4	....	−24.3	26.8	−29.6
1827	37.9	−22.5	31.5	−16.1	....	−10.0	34.1	−23.0
1828	41.1	−18.3	31.1	−18.4	....	2.9	32.8	− 6.6
1829	44.2	−27.8	36.0	−35.6	27.7	−22.9	36.7	−27.9
1830	47.5	−37.1	39.5	−49.4	28.6	−35.7	32.3	−27.9
1831	30.9	4.0	39.2	11.5	....	38.6	41.1	−14.8
1832	41.7	−11.8	39.8	−14.9	....	−15.7	39.7	1.6
1833	45.2	−20.7	34.0	8.0	....	−47.1	....	−13.1
1834	25.6	−22.8	36.0	−52.9	....	−27.1	....	− 6.6
1835	41.0	−43.9	22.3	46.0	....	11.4	....	− 4.9
1836	26.4	2.3	21.3	81.6	....	41.4	....	36.1
1837	17.9	−30.1	17.5	−27.6	....	−22.9	....	27.9
1838	27.7	−36.4	20.4	− 8.0	....	−51.4	....	−27.9
1839	28.7	−16.9	18.2	43.7	....	17.1	....	24.6
1840	30.6	−54.5	20.3	−29.9	....	−53.4	....	−31.1
1841	25.1	−42.4	18.4	−17.2	....	−11.4	....	−13.1
1842	28.1	−37.4	26.4	39.1	....	−31.4	....	−32.8
1843	27.4	−67.7	36.1	−77.0	....	−72.9	44.1	−88.5
1844	32.9	−27.4	35.1	−29.9	36.6	− 1.4	44.5	−52.5
1845	30.6	−20.6	34.6	−23.0	36.7	− 4.3	41.5	−26.2
1846	29.2	−21.6	34.7	−29.9	38.6	−11.4	33.5	−29.5
1847	23.6	−16.5	28.6	−27.6	26.9	0.0	29.4	−24.6
1848	25.3	1.2	27.6	− 4.6	24.2	− 7.1	28.5	3.3
1849	23.9	− 7.2	27.3	−14.9	24.2	− 2.9	28.7	8.2
1850	26.8	12.1	27.6	− 4.6	24.4	21.4	28.8	24.6
1851	26.8	34.3	27.6	5.7	24.9	28.6	28.7	27.9
1852	28.0	20.9	27.5	− 5.7	26.1	8.6	28.8	36.1
1853	26.1	55.2	27.6	42.5	25.0	48.6	28.6	92.0
1854	25.5	68.9	27.9	59.8	25.1	77.1	28.9	93.4
1855	26.3	31.3	27.3	6.9	24.3	−17.1	28.6	45.9
1856	26.0	55.3	27.3	40.2	24.4	24.3	28.5	42.6
1857	22.5	73.6	27.3	39.1	24.7	40.0	28.1	45.9
1858	22.3	10.2	21.0	13.8	22.0	−15.7	22.6	− 9.8
1859	19.8	42.4	21.2	39.1	21.8	21.4	22.6	− 9.8
1860	19.8	49.7	21.2	52.9	19.4	42.9	22.4	11.6

[1] Percentage of appraised value of imports.

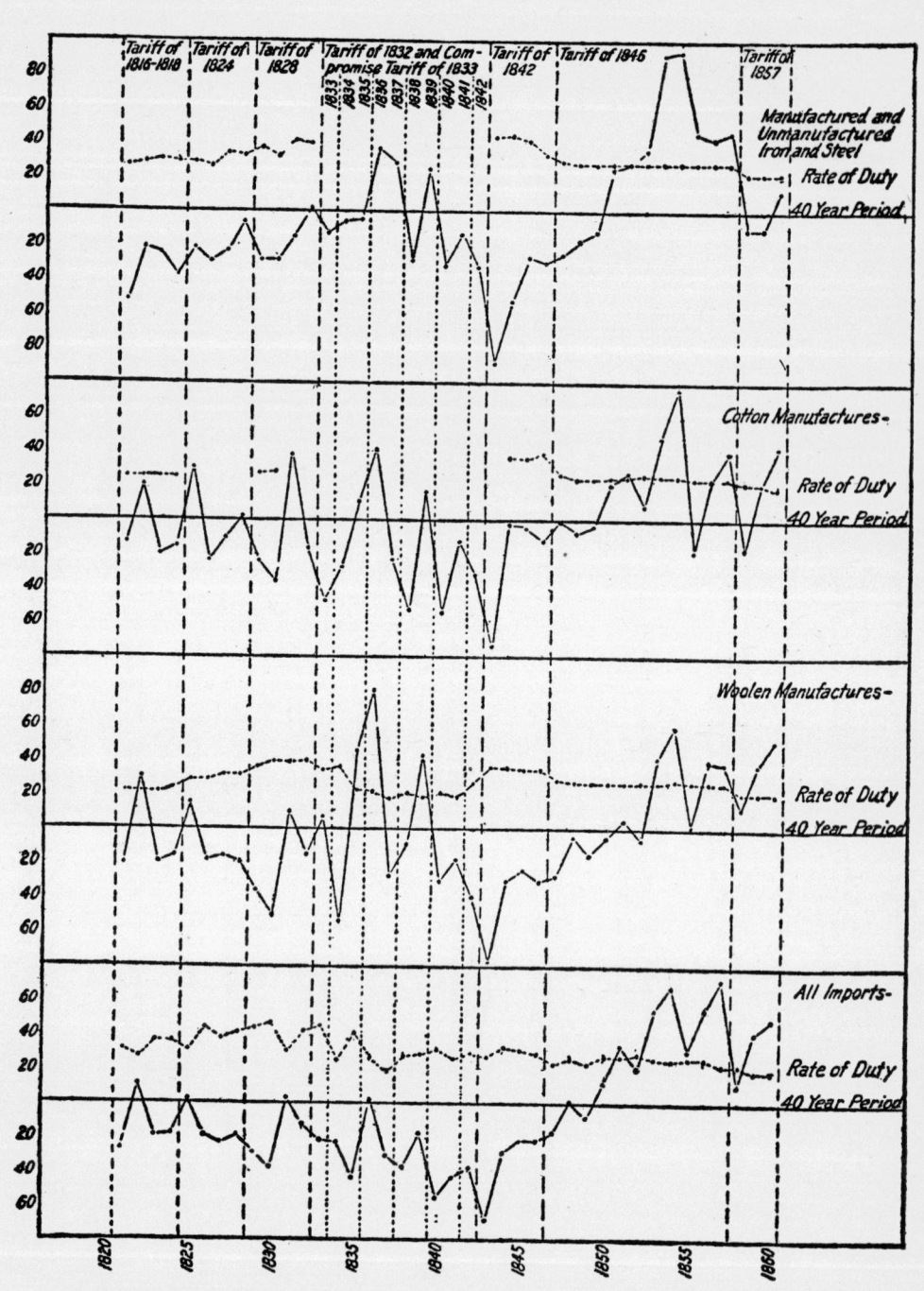

CHART I.—Rate of duty and per cent annual variation from the average for forty years of the per capita consumption of all dutiable imports and of imported cotton and woolen manufactures and manufactured and unmanufactured iron and steel.

TABLE 3.—*Net per capita imports of all dutiable commodities, of woolen and cotton manufactures, and of manufactured and unmanufactured iron and steel, from 1821 to 1860, inclusive.*

Year.	All dutiable commodities.	Woolen manufactures.	Cotton manufactures.	Manufactured and unmanufactured iron and steel.
1821	$4.23	$0.69	$0.61	$0.30
1822	6.35	1.13	.84	.48
1823	4.63	.71	.56	.46
1824	4.69	.70	.59	.38
1825	5.82	1.02	.91	.48
1826	4.62	.71	.53	.43
1827	4.41	.73	.63	.47
1828	4.64	.71	.72	.57
1829	4.10	.56	.54	.44
1830	3.58	.44	.45	.44
1831	5.92	.97	.97	.52
1832	5.02	.74	.59	.63
1833	4.58	.94	.37	.53
1834	4.39	.46	.50	.57
1835	3.19	1.27	.78	.58
1836	5.82	1.58	.99	.83
1837	3.97	.63	.54	.78
1838	3.62	.80	.34	.45
1839	4.86	1.25	.82	.76
1840	2.59	.61	.32	.42
1841	3.28	.72	.62	.53
1842	3.56	.53	.48	.41
1843	1.83	.20	.18	.07
1844	4.13	.61	.69	.29
1845	4.52	.67	.67	.45
1846	4.46	.61	.63	.43
1847	4.75	.63	.70	.46
1848	5.76	.83	.65	.63
1849	5.28	.74	.68	.66
1850	6.38	.84	.85	.76
1851	7.64	.92	.90	.78
1852	6.86	.82	.76	.83
1853	8.87	1.24	1.04	1.18
1854	9.61	1.39	1.24	1.18
1855	7.47	.93	.58	.89
1856	8.84	1.23	.87	.87
1857	9.88	1.21	.98	.89
1858	6.34	.99	.59	.55
1859	8.20	1.21	.85	.55
1860	8.52	1.36	1.00	.68

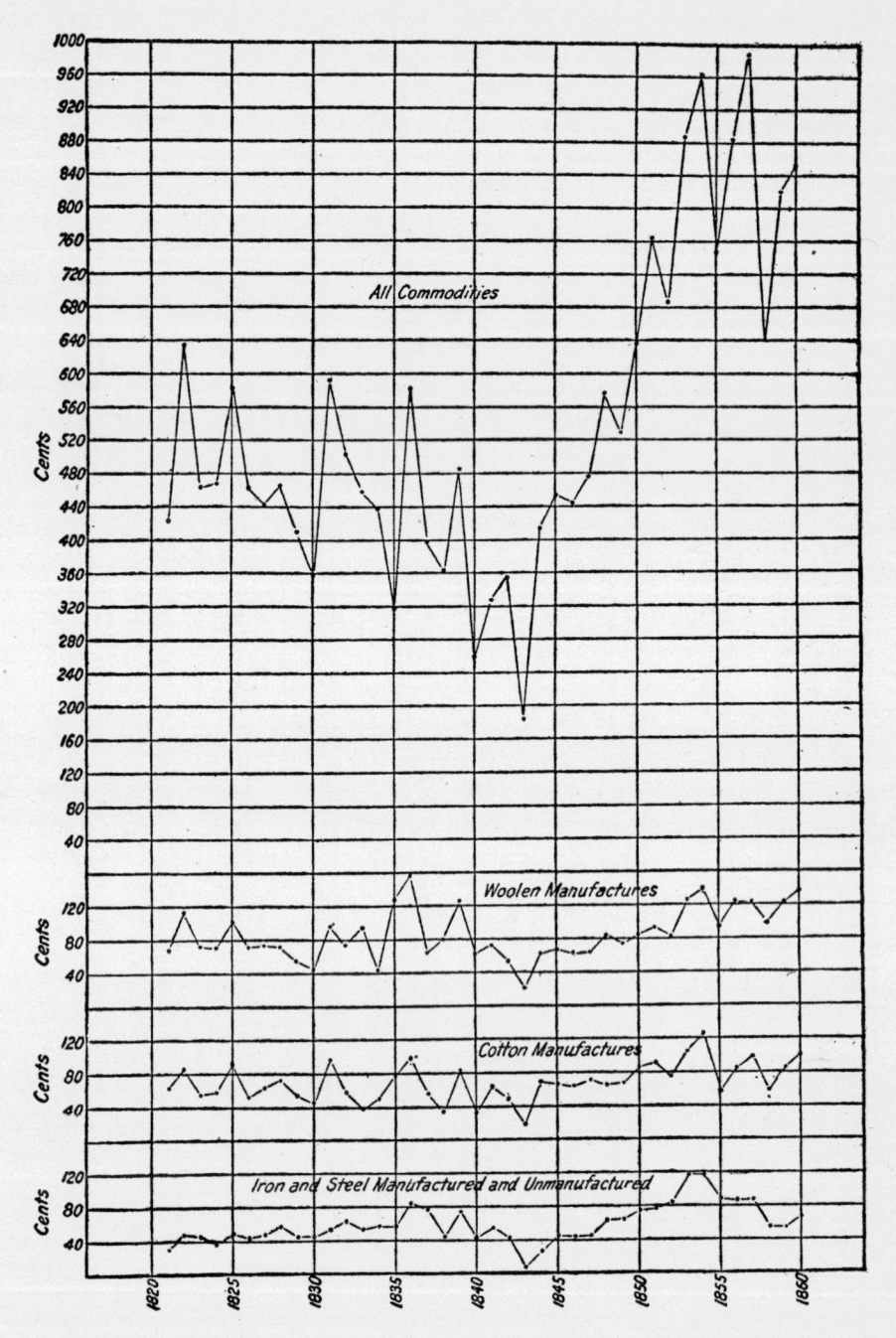

CHART II.—Net per capita imports of all dutiable commodities, of woolen and cotton manufactures, and of manufactured and unmanufactured iron and steel from 1821 to 1860, inclusive.

IX. PRICE CHANGES OF RAW MATERIALS AND MANUFACTURES

The prices given in tables 1, 2, and 3 have been taken mainly from the *New York Shipping List and Prices Current*, and the yearly averages have been computed from the first quotations of each month. However, a number of other sources have been consulted for comparison and verification. Some of these are mentioned in the notes appended to the different tables.

The first table and the accompanying chart show comparative American and English prices of cotton and pig-iron. Cotton always ranged lower in New York than in Liverpool, while iron normally was higher in this country than in Great Britain.

TABLE 1.—*Comparative average prices of cotton and iron in Liverpool and New York*

Year.	Upland cotton per pound.[1] Liverp'l	N. Y.	Pig-iron per ton.[2] Liverp'l	N. Y.	Year.	Upland cotton per pound.[1] Liverp'l	N. Y.	Pig-iron per ton.[2] Liverp'l	N. Y.
1782	....	....	$29.97	....	1822	$.182	$.14	$30.99	$35.00
1783	....	....	26.64	....	1823	.187	.147	28.02	36.25
1784	....	....	19.98	....	1824	.172	.15	35.10	40.70
1785	....	....	21.64	....	1825	.24	.167	57.45	51.50
1786	....	....	21.64	....	1826	.131	.105	45.50	42.00
1787	....	....	19.53	....	1827	.13	.105	34.53	37.00
1788	....	....	19.98	....	1828	.128	.107	30.85	37.00
1789	....	....	18.65	....	1829	.114	.095	29.57	37.50
1790	....	....	25.53	....	1830	.136	.105	24.22	35.00
1791	....	....	29.97	....	1831	.118	.092	23.24	35.00
1792	....	....	27.75	....	1832	.137	.10	23.17	35.00
1793	$0.32	....	27.75	....	1833	.175	.128	22.86	35.00
1794	.287	....	28.86	....	1834	.176	.13	22.93	35.00
1795	.378	....	28.86	....	1835	.206	.17	22.93	34.25
1796	.407	....	28.86	....	1836	.203	.167	33.48	41.75
1797	.467	....	28.86	....	1837	.142	.12	22.99	43.50
1798	.611	....	28.86	....	1838	.142	.105	23.89	37.85
1799	.607	....	28.86	....	1839	.157	.13	24.40	36.40
1800	.487	....	30.49	....	1840	.121	.085	22.16	34.25
1801	.50	....	32.19	....	1841	.135	.097	17.61	30.22
1802	.443	....	32.19	....	1842	.105	.074	16.09	27.22
1803	.228	....	33.85	....	1843	.091	.07	12.11	24.07
1804	.259	....	35.52	....	1844	.101	.075	13.28	25.66
1805	.305	....	35.52	....	1845	.083	.066	22.11	32.62
1806	.253	....	35.52	....	1846	....	.073	19.84	30.42
1807	.226	....	35.52	....	1847	.131	.11	18.91	29.46
1808	.347	....	35.52	....	1848	.091	.067	13.95	29.31
1809	.259	....	35.52	....	1849	....	.085	13.41	24.82
1810	.273	$0.155	35.52	$38.00	1850	.136	.128	18.16	22.44
1811	.203	....	35.52	....	1851	.116	.105	16.29	20.89
1812	.231	....	35.52	....	1852	.096	.09	17.67	22.23
1813	.393	....	35.52	....	1853	.101	.105	23.53	34.81
1814	.50	....	35.52	....	1854	.103	.09	28.23	38.56
1815	.321	.23	35.52	47.50	1855	.10	.092	24.53	31.18
1816	.361	.284	38.93	45.00	1856	.116	.103	27.79	32.58
1817	.395	.283	38.93	42.00	1857	.162	.14	25.91	31.12
1818	.385	.324	38.93	37.50	1858	.134	.115	21.95	24.47
1819	.294	.196	40.14	37.50	1859	.136	.115	18.54	25.27
1820	.238	.174	40.76	35.00	1860	.125	.105	18.25	23.51
1821	.19	.154	32.21	35.00					

[1] English prices from Tooke's *Thoughts and Details on Prices*, for 1793–1822; *New York Shipping List*, for 1823–1860. New York prices from *New York Shipping List*, for 1815–1845, and 1847–1850; *Finance Report of 1863*, for 1846 and 1851–1860. 1810 from *Ming's New York Price Current*.

[2] New York prices for 1810 from *Ming's New York Price Current*. New York prices from *New York Shipping List*, for 1815–1840; *Finance Report of 1856*, for 1841–1856. English Prices from Tooke's *Thoughts and Details on Prices*, for 1782–1822. See also U. S. Revenue Commission Report, 1865–1866, pp. 330–331.

Early protectionists held that foreign articles were reduced in value when they met in America the competition of similar articles of domestic manufacture, but were maintained at their former price, irrespective of foreign competition, so long as they did not meet local competition in our markets. In 1832 superfine cloths were said to be sold for the same price as 10 years previously, although flannels, which were manufactured in the United States, had fallen more than 50

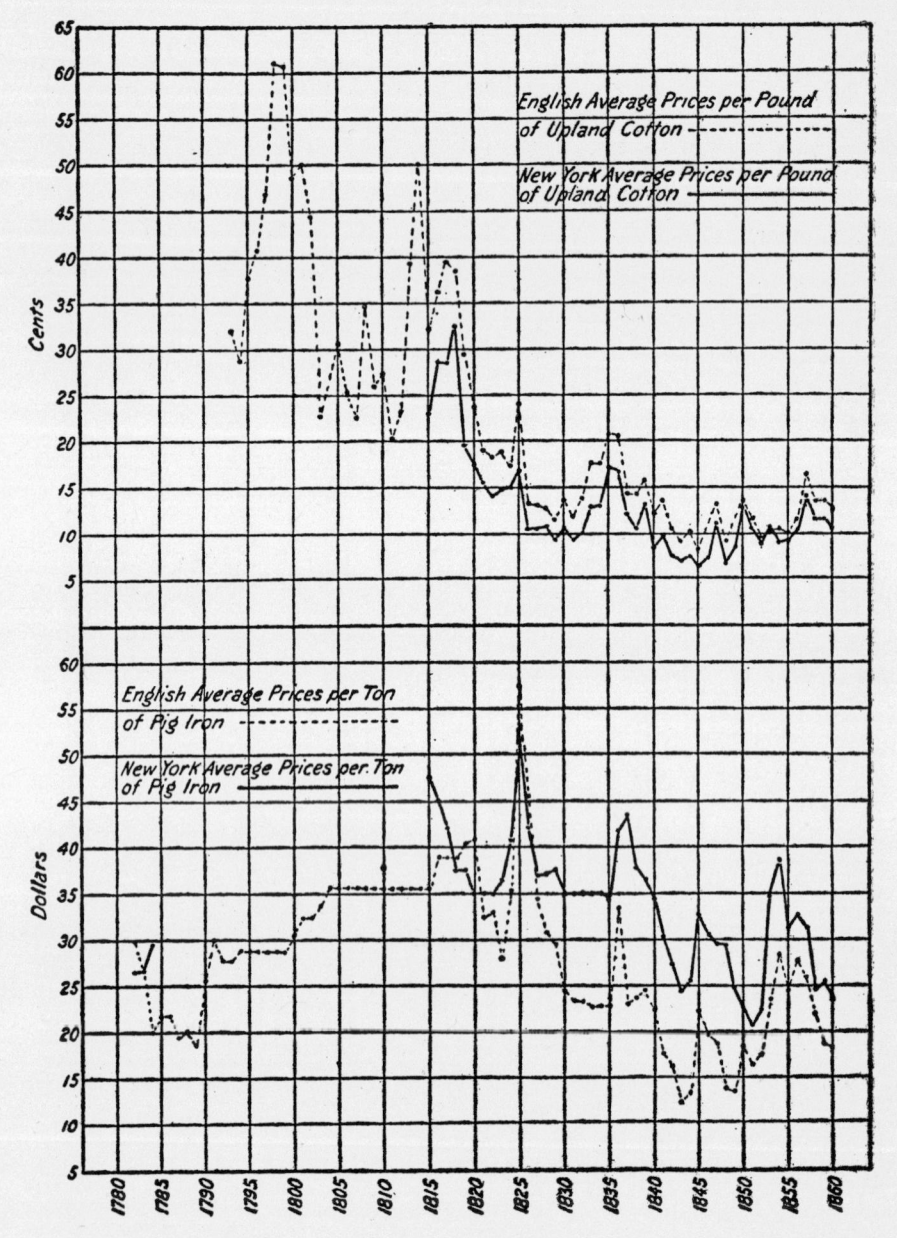

CHART III.—Comparative average prices in Liverpool and in New York, of upland cotton and of pig-iron.

TABLE 2.—*Comparative average New York prices of raw materials and manufactured articles, 1810–1860*

[Averages are computed from totals of maximum and minimum prices of each month.]

Year	Cotton. Upland per lb.[1]	Cotton. Yarn Nos. 5–13, per lb.[2]	Cotton. Brown, 3–4 shirtings, per yd.[2]	Cotton. Checks, 4–4, per yd.[2]	Wool. Merino per lb.[3]	Wool. Satinets per yd.[1]	Iron. American pig.[4]	Iron. American bar.[5]
1810	$0.155	....	....	....	....	....	$38.00	$108.00
1815	.23	....	....	....	....	....	47.50	111.00
1816	.284	....	....	....	....	....	45.00	100.00
1817	.283	....	$0.18	$0.32	....	....	42.00	92.50
1818	.324	....	.208	.327	....	....	37.50	86.00
1819	.196	....	.154	.282	....	....	37.50	92.50
1820	.174	....	.126	.244	....	....	35.00	86.00
1821	.154	....	.12	.242	....	....	35.00	82.50
1822	.14	....	.123	.237	....	$0.967	35.00	82.50
1823	.147	$0.273	.116	.185	....	.937	36.25	76.00
1824	.15	.245	.095	.167	....	.852	40.70	72.50
1825	.167	.288	.105	.194	$0.57	.85	51.50	95.00
1826	.105	.247	.087	.167	.49	.84	42.00	95.00
1827	.105	.24	.087	.166	.39	.918	37.00	95.00
1828	.107	.24	.082	.185	.37	.956	37.00	95.00
1829	.095	.208	.07	.18	.345	.975	37.50	82.50
1830	.105	.186	.075	.17	.395	.975	35.00	82.50
1831	.092	.225	.084	.17	.534	.96	35.00	82.50
1832	.10	.218	.073	.15	.473	.72	35.00	83.00
1833	.128	.222	.068	.145	.491	.84	35.00	78.00
1834	.13	.207	.067	.145	.488	1.00	35.00	74.00
1835	.17	.267	.08	.145	.543	.987	34.25	77.00
1836	.167	.302	.083	.145	.586	.95	41.75	87.00
1837	.12	.244	.073	.137	.568	.858	43.50	105.00
1838	.105	.217	.062	.115	.387	.82	37.85	100.00
1839	.13	.228	.07	.115	.512	.84	36.40	102.00
1840	.085	.17	.056	.098	.40	.825	34.25	100.00
1841	.097	.178	.055	.095	.441	.825	30.22	87.00
1842	.074	.158	.05	.092	.32	.78	27.22	76.50
1843	.07	.127	.044	.085	.304	.546	24.07	71.00
1844	.075	.16	.054	.10	.401	.574	25.66	77.50
1845	.066	.155	.057	.10	.353	.575	32.62	88.00
1846	.073	.145	.055	.085	.322	.55	30.42	91.66
1847	.11	.17	.053	.088	.353	.425	29.46	86.00
1848	.067	.15	.045	.086	.343	.425	29.31	77.00
1849	.085	.137	.04	.085	.362	.425	24.82	66.00
1850	.128	.167	.054	.085	.404	.47	22.44	60.00
1851	.105	.172	.052	.085	.425	.47	20.89	51.66
1852	.09	.155	.047	.085	.395	.47	22.23	50.00
1853	.105	.16	.052	.09	.50	.48	34.81	75.62
1854	.09	.162	.054	.11	.42	.45	38.56	87.50
1855	.092	.155	.06	.11	.37	.42	31.18	74.58
1856	.103	.15	.073	.11	.445	.40	32.58	73.55
1857	.14	.195	.08	.115	.49	.44	31.12	71.04
1858	.115	....	.074	....	.39	.45	24.47	62.29
1859	.115	....	.068	....	.492	.45	25.27	60.00
1860	.105	....	.066	....	.294	.45	23.51	58.75

[1] From *New York Shipping List*, for 1815–1845, and 1847–1850; *Finance Report of 1863*, for 1846, and 1851–1860. 1810 from *Ming's New York Price Current*.

[2] From *New York Shipping List*.

[3] From *New York Shipping List*, for 1827–1845 and 1847–1850; *Finance Report of 1863*, for 1825–1826, 1846, and 1851–1860.

[4] From *New York Shipping List*, for 1815–1840; *Ming's New York Price Current*, 1810; *Finance Report of 1856*, for 1841–1856. From Nov. 1, 1852, American pig iron ceased to be quoted. From that date, Scotch pig has been quoted as having ruled the market price of American pig. In May, 1853, American pig commanded $4.50 per ton more than Scotch pig. *Finance Report of 1856–1857*.

[5] From *New York Shipping List*, for 1810–1845 and 1847–1854; Swank's *Iron in All Ages*, for 1846 and 1855–1860. 1810 from *Ming's New York Price Current*.

per cent. Probably the growth of a national market helped to stabilize prices. In 1832, according to the correspondence of mill-owners, it was not uncommon for negro cloth of identical quality to vary more than 10 cents a yard in different cities. Doubtless the use of the telegraph, combined with cheap transportation, tended later to prevent the coëxistence of high and low prices in neighboring markets.

Table 2 and the accompanying charts give New York prices only, disregarding the local fluctuations just mentioned. Improvements in machinery and manufacturing organization were the main influences causing the curves for raw materials and for articles made from them to approach each other. Merino wool was not largely employed in satinets, but its price curve follows that of other domestic fleeces for the period for which dependable quotations of the latter can be procured.

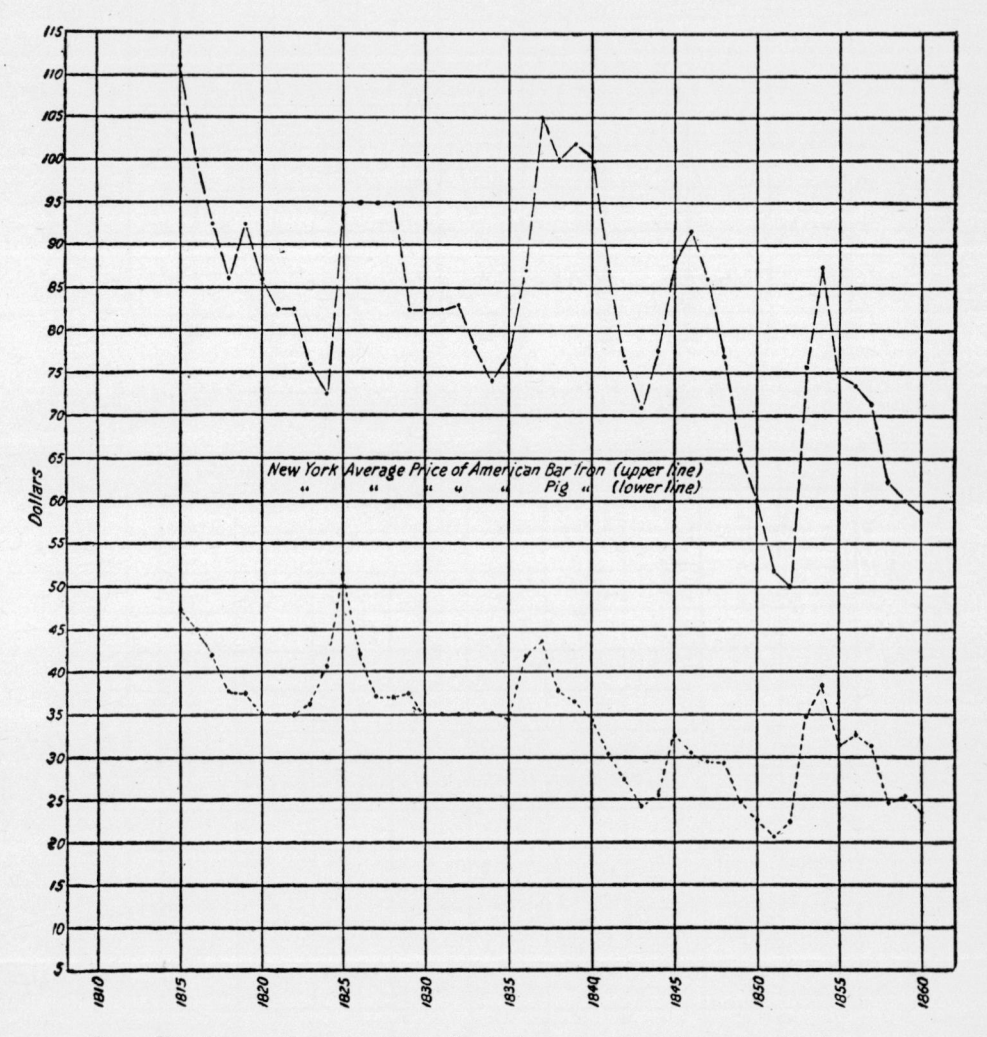

CHART IV—Comparative prices in New York of American pig and American bar iron.

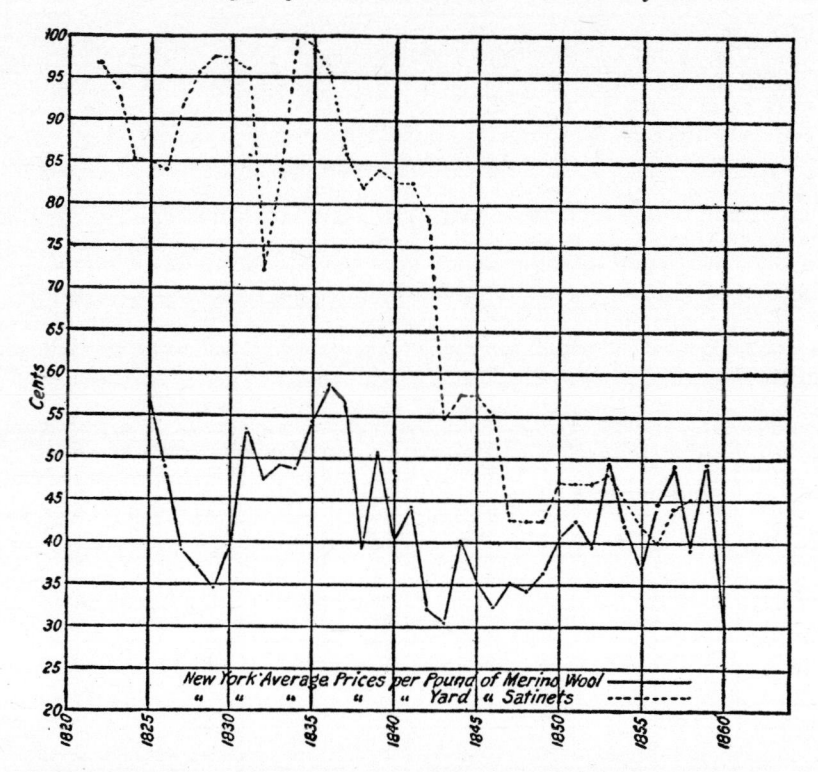

CHART V.—(A) Comparative prices in New York of merino wool and of satinets.

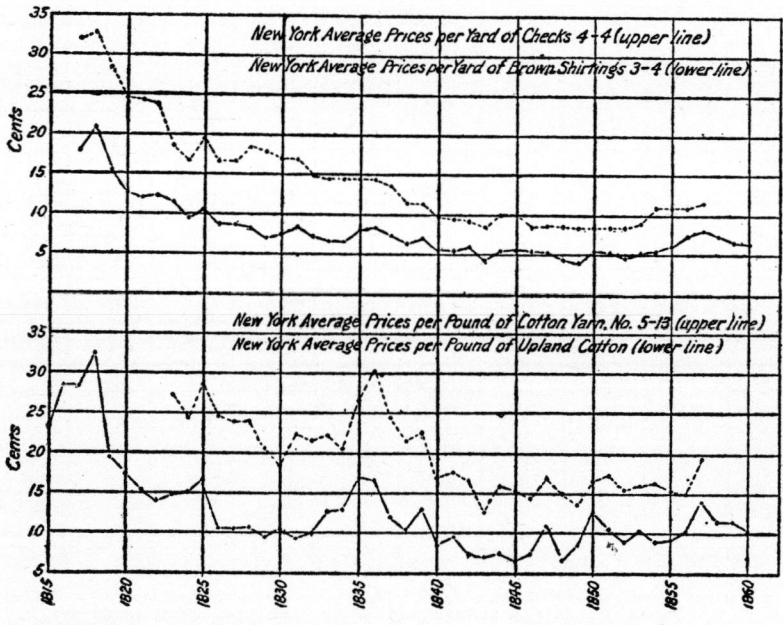

CHART V.—(B) Comparative prices in New York of upland cotton, cotton yarn, brown shirting and cotton checks.

Table 3 and the accompanying charts show the variation during each year and for a series of years in the prices of flour, sugar, and lumber. Quotations for these articles, unlike those for iron and textiles, were little affected by foreign competition, and except in case of sugar were not supposed to be governed by tariff legislation. The curves for flour and sugar follow the same general course as those for cotton, wool, iron, and their manufactures in the preceding charts. New York lumber prices rose abruptly about the time of the great fire in that city, and never again fell to their former level.

TABLE 3.—*Average prices of flour, sugar, and lumber, 1801–1860.*

[Computed from sum of maximum and minimum prices of each month.]

Year.	Flour, per bbl.[1]	New Orleans sugar per lb.[2]	North River pine boards per M feet.[3]	Year.	Flour, per bbl.[1]	New Orleans sugar, per lb.[2]	North River pine boards per M feet.[3]
1801	$10.14	....	.....	1831	$5.84	$.061	$15.00
1802	6.19	....	.....	1832	5.87	.066	15.00
1803	6.01	....	.....	1833	5.70	.072	15.50
1804	7.15	....	.....	1834	5.07	.066	16.55
1805	9.59	....	.....	1835	6.00	.076	16.50
1806	7.13	....	.....	1836	7.78	.093	17.33
1807	6.76	....	.....	1837	9.69	.069	25.83
1808	5.15	....	.....	1838	8.02	.069	37.50
1809	6.79	....	.....	1839	7.40	.071	37.50
1810	9.32	....	$16.66	1840	5.17	.061	32.50
1811	9.05	....	.....	1841	5.39	.065	34.80
1812	9.08	....	....	1842	5.67	.052	34.37
1813	7.76	....	.....	1843	5.07	.056	32.50
1814	7.76	....	.....	1844	4.61	.065	32.50
1815	8.11	....	21.00	1845	5.00	.062	34.16
1816	9.13	....	21.25	1846	5.19	.063	.....
1817	11.48	....	18.50	1847	6.80	.068	35.00
1818	9.44	....	16.66	1848	5.71	.042	34.40
1819	6.82	....	16.00	1849	5.52	.049	33.58
1820	4.86	....	16.50	1850	5.55	.054	37.68
1821	4.80	....	16.50	1851	4.52	.052	36.12
1822	6.34	....	16.50	1852	4.90	.043	38.00
1823	6.75	....	15.75	1853	5.78	.047	39.27
1824	5.67	....	14.30	1854	8.95	.047	38.75
1825	5.18	$0.082	16.25	1855	8.75	.056	38.75
1826	4.85	.081	16.80	1856	6.40	.079	41.62
1827	5.15	.08	15.40	1857	5.80	.10	43.43
1828	5.80	.08	15.90	1858	4.30	.065	39.41
1829	6.45	.07	15.33	1859	5.10	.065	34.66
1830	5.00	.072	15.00	1860	5.20	.071	36.45

[1] From *New York Shipping List*, for 1815–1830, *Report on Finances for* 1855, for 1801–1814 and 1831–1855, and *Finance Report for 1863*, for 1855–1860.

[2] From *New York Shipping List*, for 1831–1845 and 1847–1850. *Finance Report of 1863*, for 1825–1830, 1846, and 1851–1860.

[3] From *New York Shipping List*, for 1815–1860. 1810 from *Ming's New York Price Current.*

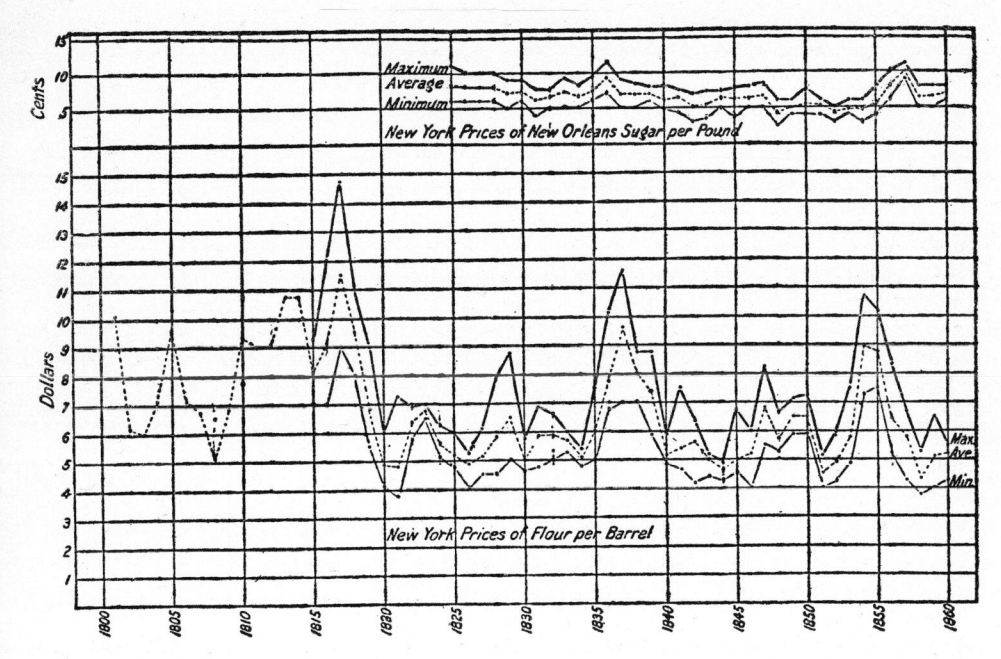

Price Changes of Raw Materials and Manufactures

CHART VI.—Annual price range of New Orleans sugar and of flour in New York.

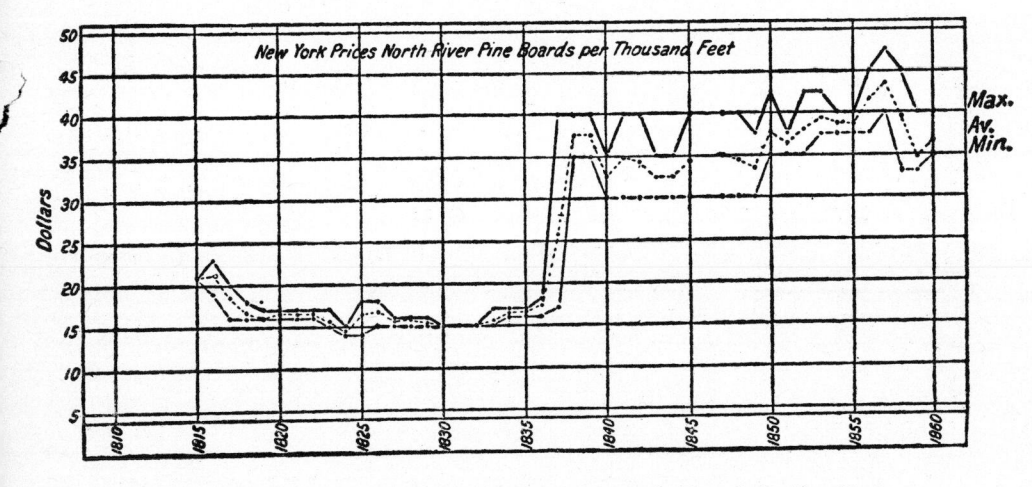

CHART VII.—Annual price range of North River pine boards in New York.

X. A BRITISH OPINION OF AMERICAN INDUSTRIAL ORGANIZATION AND LABOR IN 1854

[Extract from the *Report* of the Committee on the Machinery of the United States of America in Great Britain. *Parliamentary Papers*, 1854–1855, L, 84–85.]

"One distinguishing feature of manufacturing establishments in the United States, both public and private, is the ample provision of workshop room, in proportion to the work therein carried on, arising in some measure from the foresight and speculative character of the proprietors, who are anxious thus to secure the capabilities for future extension, and in a greater degree with a view to securing order and systematic arrangement in the manufacture.

"Another striking feature is the admirable system everywhere adopted, even in those branches of trade which are not usually considered of much importance, this applies not only to the selection and adaptation of tools and machinery, and to the progress of the material through the manufactory, but also to the discipline and sobriety of the employed.

"The observations contained in the Report upon American tools and machinery, will best explain the nature and adaptation of special tools to minute purposes, in order to obtain the article at the smallest possible cost; for this end capital is borrowed to a great extent and sunk in establishments not only adapted to a peculiar manufacture, but where a department is set apart for the express purpose of making the special tools and contrivances required in order to obtain that end in the most economical and effectual manner. This at least applies to establishments of any importance.

"The contriving and making of machinery has become so common in this country, and so many heads and hands are at work with extraordinary energy; that unless the example is followed at home, notwithstanding the difference of wages, it is to be feared that American manufacturers will before long become exporters not only to foreign countries, but even to England. . . . The advantages in a manufacturing point of view are all on the side of our countrymen, and there is nothing made in which they ought not to be able to undersell their American competitors either in England or on the continent.

"Another point, bearing on this important subject, is the dissatisfaction frequently expressed in America with regard to present attainment in the manufacture and application of labour-saving machinery, and the avidity with which any new idea is laid hold of, and improved upon, a spirit occasionally carried to excess, but upon the whole productive of more good than evil.

"The care almost universally bestowed on the comfort of the workpeople, particularly attracted the notice of the Committee; clean places for washing being provided, presses to contain their change of clothes, and an abundant supply of good drinking water, in many cases cooled with ice.

"The Committee also remarked with satisfaction, the regular attendance and cleanliness of the workmen, and the rigid exactness with which the work is continued up to the last minute of the working hours.

"A remarkable feature in the character of the native American workman is their sobriety, water is their usual beverage, and this they use inordinately in hot weather, but rarely anything stronger, clear headedness results from this and gives them a powerful advantage over those who indulge in stronger potations, which will eventually produce its effect on the national manufactures, as it now does on the intelligence and character of the individual workman.

"In the Government and private manufactories in the United States, piece-work when applicable is universally preferred to day-work, as this arrangement yields the greatest amount of work at the least cost to the employer, at the same time paying the best wages to the individual employed. . . ."

XI. EXTRACTS FROM GOVERNOR WILLIAMS'S CORRESPONDENCE RELATING TO AN EARLY COTTON FACTORY IN SOUTH CAROLINA.

(1) AN ESTIMATE OF DISPOSITION OF CAPITAL, EXPENSE AND PRODUCTION OF D. R. WILLIAMS'S COTTON FACTORY.

SOCIETY HILL, OCT. 26, 1828.

Appropriation of Capital:

Water privilege and real estate	$5000
Machinery now in the mill	2000
do new now on its passage from R. I.	859.47
2 new breakers & 1 finisher & 240 new spindles	2000
	$9859.47

Annual Expenditure:

10 little negroes too small to work out at 25 cts	$250
3 young women to reel stand winder at 75 cts	225
2 do do wool spinners at 75 cts	150
1 labourer (negro fellow)	85
1 spinner $700, 1 filer 6 months $350, 1 clerk $300	1350
5 percent wear and tear of $5000 machinery	250
Insurance estimated at 2½%	125
100 bales cotton 300 lb. each at 10 cts	3000
8000 lbs. wool at 25 cts	2000
30 gallons winter strained Sperm Oil	30
Iron and steel	30
1 cook for children $55, 1 do. for workmen $100	155
Weaving 60,000 yds. cloth at 5 cts	3000
Contingencies	500
	$11150.00

Estimate of Production:

30000 lbs. cotton will make 60,000 yds. deduct 12% waste, 3,600 = 56,400 yds.

16400 yds. osnaburghs at 11 cts	$1804
20000 do. cotton bagging at 20 cts	4000
20000 do. woolen goods at 40 cts	8000
	$13,804

"I estimate each spindle will average ¼ lb. twist per day which is for 300 days 35,000 lbs., deduct for lost time & etc. 5000 lbs. nets 30,000 lbs. Two wool spinny of 20 spindles each is 40 spindles; each spindle should turn off 1 lb. yard per day which is for 300 days 12,000 lbs. deduct ⅓ for lost time & etc. is 8000 lbs. 1 pound of wool will fill 3 yds. cloth, which gives 24,000 yds. deduct for (illegible) estimate 4,000, netto 20,000 yds. The Yankeys pay ¾ cts. for weaving by water power—one girl tends 4 looms and weaves from 100 to 120 yds. per day. 12 power looms would cost delivered here $1200, are estimated to turn out 15 yds. each per day would netto 54,000 yds. in 300 days. I estimate our weavers to cost $75 each; they will average at least six yards each per day; at which rate they will each pay a profit of 5 cts. per day on the estimated cost of 5 cts. per yard. I omitted to state one pound of cotton twist will average two yards cloth. The filling which the wool supplies, instead of cotton filling, will make out the additional width of cotton bagging, over the other widths of other cloths.

"The surplus yarns, if any, will sell in New York and Philadelphia for 22 or 23 cts. per lb."

(2) TARRIFF AND TRADE CONDITIONS IN 1830.

FEBRUARY 10, 1830.

. . . . "I have duly reflected on your information concerning prices, samples, and hoped for orders for oznaburghs—which samples and prices I hope you will still send me, for I need them. All this is only a renewed confirmation in my mind of convictions before made in relation to the patriotism of trade and the anti-tariff ebullitions of vituperation and slang-whanging as Knickerbocker calls it. If Withers of the Telescope had as good a barometer of the anti-tariff excitement as we have, in this little matter of the Factory, I verily believe he would go mad outright, or, rave less. One preference we have in the calculations of the economists and *one only*, they prefer to use *cotton* to *flax* and therefore if they can get our oznaburghs, at the same price as *foreign*, they will get it; on every other consideration 99 out of 100 go for cheapness *wholly*, and as the yankeys make theirs of *cotton* also, we may preach, till the cows come home, about *staple* and tariff imposers, etc. etc.; if we do not sell cheaper we shall have no preference; if only as cheap we stand on the same foot, with "our brethren of the north" . . .

"Any oznaburghs from N. E. not made of *coarser* numbers than ours is not good as ours; plainly for this all the *filling* from them is soft twist—all ours is hard and will last better. Ours does not look as well, for that very reason, the filling is hard twist and hence the main reason I wish for some additional machinery, mule frames to spin softer. We must consult now the whim of purchasers if we can find it out. I am satisfied the manufacturer cannot make as stout for anything *under 10 cents*. They may send a better sample but the article will come out differently, as has happened to both us."

(3) CONDITION OF THE BUSINESS IN 1835.

FACTORY MARCH 12, 1835.

. . . . "Since May twelve months there has been added to its capital upwards of $2,000 in machinery by its own means alone to January—you receive good hire for hands that would profit you but little in a cotton field even in the west—have rec. about $280 in cash or the same thing, bought your clothing for your people to that amount, and I started this week 60 additional spindles all paid for—the factory does not owe a doll. that I know of except its expences since January—this from an original investment but a few years since of $1200 I think is doing a great business. Your share is certainly worth $2500 (in this way) the $300 credited on your acct. may twelve months pays the interest in the first cost to that time buying no machinery this year but making it as my man Isack has done the 60 spindles alluded to which is the best frame in the mill—you will receive this year if the mill keeps on as she is going the usual hire for your hands which (I think is as good as they would do on a plantation) and $400 pretty certainly. If $84 is the interest on $1200 the original investment what is the principal of a sum which yields $400, answer $5714. and some odd cents, deduct ware and tare, insurance, etc. will leave you a better business I am satisfied than any planting short of Red River, even if you believe all that is said about it which is more than I do.

(*Signed*) "J. W. WILLIAMS."

(The Institution is indebted to Professor J. S. Ames, of Johns Hopkins University, for the use of Governor Williams's letters.)

(4) ACCOUNT OF A SHAREHOLDER WITH THE FACTORY IN 1830.

JUNE 19, 1830.

Col. JAMES CHESNUT

DEBTOR TO UNION FACTORY

1829.
May 9. 1525 yds. Oznaburgs at 12–1/2 cts............$190.65–3/4
      50 lbs. Twine at 32 cts.................... 16.00
                                                        $206.65–3/4

July 31.   4 pieces 114–3/4 yds. Oznaburgs at 10 cts........... 11.47–1/2
         5 lbs. No. 12 yarn at 29 cts...................... 1.45
                                                        12.92–1/2

Oct. 22.   23 pieces 611–1/2 yds. Negro cloth at 40 cts........... 244.60
        2 "   64 yds. Shirting at 13 cts................. 8.32
        5 "   142–3/4 yds. Oznaburgs at 10 cts........... 14.27–1/2
        7–1/2 lbs. Bale Rope at 25 cts..................... 1.87–1/2
                                                        269.07

Nov. 29. 4 lbs. Sewing thread at 75 cts...................... 3.00

1830.
Jan. 20. Pd. Dr. Smith for extracting William's tooth......... 1.00
Mar. 29. 1 yd. Negro cloth 45 cts........................... 0.45
         86–1/2 yds. Oznaburgs at 10 cts..................... 8.65
                                                         9.10

Apr. 7.   2005 yds. Oznaburgs at 10 cts......................... 200.50
        88 "   Shirting at 14 cts............................. 13.32
        10 lbs. Sewing thread 50 cts. Wrappers 75 cts......... 5.75
" 28.   25 "   No. 8 yarn $6.25–13/16 lb. Small twine 30.... 6.55
                                                       225.12
                                                       726.87–/4

CREDITOR.

1829.
June 2. By cash... 206.65–3/4
May 30. " 223 lb. Wool at 25 cts............................ 55.75
1830.
Feb. 17. " 1–23/30 months work of Hector & William $20....... 70.68–3/4
        " 1–1/10 months " " London at $20.............. 22.00
April 28. " 225 lb. wool at 25 cts............................ 56.25
" 30.   " Cash.. 100.00
                                                      511.34–1/2

        due the Factory............................. 215.52–3/4
        Thos. Whitaker's acct....................... 12.75
                                                 228.27–3/4

June 19. Recd. the above sum of two hundred and twenty eight dollars 27/100 for
                                      DAVID R. WILLIAMS
                                      JNO. N. WILLIAMS

XII. POPULATION, RAILWAYS, AND MANUFACTURES.

Table showing relation of population and railway mileage to value of manufactures produced in shops and factories and in households, 1840, 1850, 1860.

State.	1840 Pop. per sq. mile.	1840 Sq. miles per mile railroad.	1840 Per cap. manufactures in homes.	1850 Pop. per sq. mile	1850 Sq. miles per mile railroad.	1850 Per cap. manufactures in shops and factories	1850 Per cap. manufactures in homes.	1860 Pop. per sq. mile	1860 Sq. miles per mile railroad.	1860 Per cap. manufactures in shops and factories.	1860 Per cap. manufactures in homes.
Maine	16.8	2,717.7	$1.60	19.5	122.0	$42.29	$0.88	21.0	63.3	$60.79	$0.78
New Hampshire	31.6	169.9	1.89	35.3	19.3	72.85	1.24	36.2	13.6	115.27	0.77
Vermont	32.0		2.31	34.4	31.5	27.29	.85	34.5	16.5	46.45	.20
Massachusetts	91.8	26.7	.31	123.7	7.8	158.61	.21	153.1	6.4	207.58	.20
Rhode Island	100.3	21.1	.47	136.0	18.5	149.90	.18	160.9	9.8	233.14	.04
Connecticut	64.0	47.5	.73	76.5	12.1	127.06	.52	95.0	8.1	178.04	.11
New England	34.4	119.9	1.13	44.02	22.1	103.87	.59	50.59	16.9	149.39	.35
New York	51.0	127.3	1.91	65.0	35.0	76.71	.41	81.3	17.8	97.63	.18
New Jersey	50.1	40.5	.54	65.7	36.5	81.40	.23	90.1	13.4	113.54	.04
Pennsylvania	38.3	59.7	.76	51.4	36.3	67.07	.32	64.6	17.3	99.83	.19
Delaware	39.8	50.3	.80	46.7	50.3	50.79	.42	57.3	15.4	88.16	.16
Maryland	47.7	46.6	.37	59.1	38.3	56.68	.19	69.6	25.7	60.75	.10
Middle States	45.3	71.5	1.26	58.69	36.1	71.53	.35	73.73	17.6	96.61	.17
Ohio	37.3	1,358.7	1.22	48.6	70.9	31.66	.86	57.4	13.7	52.02	.25
Michigan	3.7	973.4	.54	6.9	167.9	28.09	.86	13.0	73.7	43.60	.19
Indiana	19.1		1.88	27.5	157.5	18.94	1.65	37.6	16.6	31.70	.73
Illinois	8.5		2.09	15.2	504.5	19.42	1.36	30.6	20.0	33.63	.54
Wisconsin	.6		.41	5.6	2,722.5	30.43	.14	14.2	60.2	35.89	.16
Minnesota						9.59		2.2		19.61	.05
Iowa	.8		.60	3.5		18.48	1.15	12.2	84.7	20.70	.47
Kansas								1.3		40.65	.23
Nebraska								.4		21.06	.55
Western States	9.9	3,371.0	1.46	12.45	475.3	25.84	1.08	14.71	53.5	38.55	.38
Virginia	19.1	440.6	1.97	21.9	134.7	20.82	1.52	24.6	37.4	31.73	.99
North Carolina	15.5	916.6	1.88	17.9	171.7	10.48	2.40	20.4	51.8	16.80	2.06
South Carolina	19.7	220.2	1.57	22.2	104.4	10.54	1.36	23.3	31.0	12.24	1.16
Georgia	11.7	318.8	2.12	15.4	91.7	7.82	2.03	17.9	32.4	16.01	1.35
Florida	1.		.37	1.6	2,582.9	7.64	.86	2.5	134.9	17.43	.45
Kentucky	19.5	1,428.6	3.36	24.6	512.8	22.10	2.50	28.9	74.9	32.82	1.81
Tennessee	19.5		3.48	24.		9.70	3.13	26.6	33.3	16.21	2.86
Alabama	11.4	1,120.4	2.80	14.9	281.6	5.87	2.51	18.7	69.4	10.98	1.89
Mississippi	8.1		1.82	13.1	617.9	4.80	1.92	17.1	53.8	8.33	1.75
Missouri	5.6		3.00	9.9		35.66	2.46	17.2	84.1	35.35	1.68
Arkansas	1.8		5.02	3.9		2.56	3.04	8.2	1,395.9	6.62	2.34
Louisiana	7.8	1,135.5	.18	11.4	567.8	13.09	.27	15.6	135.6	22.02	.71
Texas				.8		5.50	1.26	2.3	854.4	10.89	.97
South'n States	11.17	949.0	2.35	10.32	405.9	14.06	2.07	13.21	80.6	20.56	1.62

XIII. NEW ORLEANS RECEIPTS OF DOMESTIC MANUFACTURES.

New Orleans receipts of inland manufactures by river, 1822-1829.[1]

Article.	Unit.	1822.	1823.	1824.	1825.	1826.	1827.	1828.	1829.[2]
Textiles									
Kentucky bagging	Pieces	....	898	4,562	6,191	5,299	2,795	5,972	11,374
Tow linen	Yards	....	1,200	1,800	115	3,600	500	450	4,400
Do	Bales	....	21	5	.....	13	2	10	33
Bale rope	Coils	9,545	4,897	7,704	4,838	6,654	11,749	17,038	13,352
Hemp yarn	Reels[3]	414	92	269	337	99	42	256	277
Twine	Bundles	52	8	.....	.....	44	18	183	342
Do	Pounds	....	2,000	3,920	.....	500	500	129	2
Do	Boxes	....	.....	.....	19	47	41	234	85
Metals.									
Iron (bar)	Tons	....	.....	.....	.....	.....	304	525	55
Iron (pig)	Do.	....	.....	.....	.....	.....	.....	.....	293
Lead	Pigs	12,962	41,123	45,454	58,479	86,242	106,405	183,712	142,036
Do	Bars	91	63	442	306	473	1,299	471	688
Do	Pounds	1,899,520	58,908	592,853	198,244	190,292	.....	.....	409,641
Shot	Kegs	409	565	333	1,081	1,472	2,881	1,127	2,046
Do	Pounds	82,880	1,943	30,800	9,300	.....	.....	.....	.....
Do	Bags	....	221	309	15	78	551	213	146
Miscellaneous.									
Candles	Boxes	312	1,234	305	768	121	124	731	318
Glass, window	Do.	1,582	1,249	728	2,304	1,896	1,189	459	912
Gunpowder	Kegs	25	173	8	.....	10	140	100	7
Soap	Boxes	2,775	1,198	934	2,367	2,539	4,118	6,906	2.475
Grain.									
Flour	Barrels	120,159	114,735	100,929	140,546	129,094	131,096	152,593	127,490
Whiskey	Do.	21,298	9,771	18,897	32,704	10,526	35,982	44,507	20,606
Linseed oil	Do.	....	.....	191	622	708	1,723	2,637	2,004

[1] From *New Orleans Price Current.* [2] Oct. 1, 1828, to July 18, 1829. [3] About 1000 pounds.

BIBLIOGRAPHY

Colonial Period, 400. The Early Republic, 401. The Civil War and After, 405. List of Authorities, 407.

Published information concerning early manufactures in the American colonies and the United States is scanty and for the most part is scattered through books and periodicals devoted mainly to other subjects. A bibliography of works relating strictly to the manufactures of this period would therefore be too brief to cover satisfactorily our sources of knowledge, while a general survey of all the literature which casually throws light upon this topic would necessarily be either undiscriminating or very long. As a middle way out of this embarrassment an alphabetical list of the published and unpublished materials used in preparing this volume is appended to this bibliography, while the bibliography itself is confined to works that are an essential aid to all students of our industrial history.

COLONIAL PERIOD

The most ambitious and upon the whole the most valuable work of the latter class is Bishop's *History of American Manufactures*. This is a minute and accurate compilation of facts relating to the industries of the Colonies and early Republic. It is of most value for the former period, where it represents a large amount of painstaking pioneer investigation. But the arrangement of data is mechanical, and neither the grouping of material nor the elucidations of the author interpret fully the economic conditions that shaped the beginning of our industrial development.

A second and later work of a similar character, though more vitalized by interpretation, is Weeden's *Economic and Social History of New England*. The period and area covered by the author are limited to the colonial and revolutionary eras in the New England States; but within that field the book is the most important contribution to our knowledge of colonial industrial conditions since the publication of Bishop's work. On a par with Weeden's history as a product of original research, and superior to it in form and method of presentation, is Bruce's *Economic History of Virginia in the Seventeenth Century*. This is an illuminating study of both the social and economic history of our chief planting colony during the first century of settlement, and though manufactures hold a subordinate place among the topics considered, as they did among the occupations of the Virginia pioneers, they are more fully treated than in any other work. The British official reports upon manufactures in the colonies have been summarized and criticized in Chapter IX of the first volume. Much of their material is reviewed in Douglass' *British Settlements in North America* and in Chalmers' *Political Annals*. The travelers who throw most light upon the industries of the colonists are Peter Kalm and Andrew Burnaby. Information upon this same subject occurs in collections of official papers relating to the colonial period, especially in those of New York published under the supervision of O'Callaghan and in the *New Jersey Archives*, whose extracts from the colonial press contain many newspaper references to contemporary manufactures. A helpful monograph upon this and allied topics is Lord's *Industrial Experiments in the British Colonies of*

North America, which contains a chapter on general manufactures as well as a detailed study of the production and trade in naval stores. The Library of Congress has the most important single body of manuscript material relating to colonial industries. This includes the constantly increasing file of British transcripts, containing both public and private records of the commerce and manufactures of the colonists, and also a large collection of mercantile accounts, several of which are cited in the text and appendices of the present volume. Many commercial papers which incidentally contain material relating to manufactures are preserved at the Essex Institute, in Salem, and in public and historical-society libraries at Boston, Providence, Hartford, New York, Philadelphia, Baltimore, Richmond, and Charleston. The files of colonial newspapers in the American Antiquarian Library, at Worcester, also afford contemporary data regarding colonial industries.

THE EARLY REPUBLIC

Following the Revolution, when the promotion of domestic industries became a matter of avowed public concern, records of manufactures rapidly increase. Bishop covers this period, though with less thoroughness as the colonial era is left behind. The travels and descriptions of Anburey, Brissot, Crévecœur, Chastellux, and La Rochefoucault contain many allusions to industrial conditions in America during the Revolution and the period immediately following. Bagnall's *Textile Industries of the United States*, which opens with an excellent review of this branch of manufactures in colonial times, gives an accurate and detailed account of nearly every cloth manufactory and spinning mill started in this country before the War of 1812 and continues the history of those establishments, so far as they survived, down to 1880. Of contemporary writers for this early period Alexander Hamilton and Tench Coxe are the most important. Hamilton's *Report on Manufactures*, which is probably our ablest state paper upon this subject, is printed in the various editions of his works, in the finance volumes of the *American State Papers*, and in the *Reports of the Secretary of the Treasury*. Some of the original letters upon which this report is based are preserved in the *Hamilton Papers*, at the Library of Congress, and have been printed in *The Industrial and Commercial Correspondence of Alexander Hamilton*, published by the Business Historical Society. Tench Coxe was an aggressive and persistent advocate of domestic manufactures, whose writings upon the subject are influenced by propagandist bias but contain much valuable information. He was associated with Hamilton as Assistant Secretary of the Treasury and later, as purveyor of public supplies, had business relations with early American manufacturers. In the latter capacity he contracted at one time for 40,000 yards of cotton cloth from Almy and Brown, of Providence. He discussed manufactures in several pamphlets and more formal works and was the author of the *Statement of Arts and Manufactures in the United States* prefixed to our first census of manufactures in 1810. The *American Museum* is another source of contemporary information regarding post-revolutionary industries. Manuscript accounts of manufacturing establishments at this time have seldom been preserved; but two important collections, the letter-books and accounts of Almy and Brown at Providence and the accounts of the Hartford Woolen Manufactory at Hartford, have been consulted for this volume.

After 1810 materials are so abundant as to require classification. Official accounts begin with the *Gallatin Report on Manufactures* and the following *Census of Manufactures in 1810*, both of which are accessible in the second finance volume of *American State Papers*, as well as in separate editions. The statistics of manufactures gathered in connection with the census of 1820 are published in the fourth finance volume of the *State Papers*. Both of these compilations are nearly worthless from a strictly statistical point of view, but they have great descriptive interest. They are followed by the *McLane Report on Manufactures*, in 1832, which is an undigested mass of first-hand schedules, not uniform in scope or arrangement, and not summarized except in a few instances for single states. But here again, in default of more accurate information, a large collection of facts of descriptive value is presented. The censuses of manufactures in 1840 and 1850 are almost equally subject to criticism as to accuracy and completeness. Even the census of 1860, though much superior to its predecessors, reveals upon close examination many errors and inconsistencies; but the introduction to its volume on manufactures contains valuable historical and statistical information. Important historical contributions have been published also in connection with succeeding enumerations. Among these Wright's *Report on the Factory System*, Fitch's *Report on Interchangeable Mechanism*, and Part II of Swank's *Statistics of Iron and Steel Production*, all of which are in the manufactures volume of the census of 1880, have unusual interest. The national Government is likewise sponsor for the accounts of industries contained in the *Reports of the Commissioners to the International Exposition at Paris*, in 1867, and in similar reports for the Centennial Exposition at Philadelphia in 1876.

Beginning with 1837 and 1839, respectively, Massachusetts and Connecticut published, at intervals between the national census dates, tabulated accounts of their industries, based upon the assessors' returns. These are more satisfactory guides to the volume and location of manufactures in those states than the Federal enumerations. The *Reports of the Secretary of the Treasury* for 1846 and 1849 contain material worth consulting, despite its unsystematic presentation. Tariff hearings were not so elaborately conducted and reported as later, but the numerous petitions of manufacturers printed in the five finance volumes of *American State Papers*, and the hearings before the House Committee on Manufactures in 1828, in the last volume of that series, have great interest. In 1911 the Senate printed a compilation of documents relating to the tariffs of 1842, 1846, and 1857, which appear in their new form as *Senate Documents*, Sixty-second Congress, first session, Nos. 21, 71, and 72. These are the most convenient collections of official papers relating to this period.

Government accounts of manufactures are supplemented by the *Proceedings of the Harrisburg Convention*, held in 1827, and the *Journal and Reports of the New York Convention of Friends of Domestic Industry*, held four years later. The documents submitted at these public assemblies are subject to the criticism to which all partisan literature is exposed, but the information they contain is probably about as accurate as that afforded by the defective Federal returns. An earlier publication of an analogous character, the *Addresses of the Philadelphia Society for the Promotion of Domestic Industry*, gives an interesting description of the effect of the crisis of 1816–1820 upon our manufactures.

Most of the private statistical works published at this time merely summarize or restate Government figures, but Seybert's *Statistical Annals* contains data not easily accessible in official documents. Pitkin's *Statistics of the United States* has a chapter on manufactures. The works of Blowe, Bristed, and Winterbotham mentioned in the alphabetical list at the end of this bibliography are also good secondary sources for information.

The only foreign government which interested itself officially in the growth of our manufactures was Great Britain, and the *Parliamentary Papers* repay careful scrutiny. Here the most important references are to Volume VI of 1833, with its testimony upon American cotton mills; Volume VII of 1841, where the hearings of the Committee upon the Exportation of Machinery contain information regarding American patents used in England and engineering industries in the United States; the two valuable reports of the Commissioners to the New

York Exhibition of 1853 in Volume XXXVI of 1854, and the report of the Committee on the Machinery of the United States in Volume L of 1854–1855.

Foreign visitors sometimes noted with fresher interest than Americans the evidences of our industrial progress. Buckingham, Chevalier, Holmes, Kendall, Melish, Michaux, Saxe-Weimar, and the two Welds made observations upon this subject that repay perusal. Among our own travelers Mrs. Royall was perhaps the most minute recorder of industrial matters.

A complete survey of contemporary periodical literature relating to manufactures is of course impracticable. The journals containing the most important information upon this subject are *Niles' Register, De Bow's Review*, and *Hunt's Merchants' Magazine*. Early numbers of the *Scientific American*, the *Western Journal and Civilian*, and *Fisher's National Magazine*, though covering shorter periods, also devoted much space to this subject.

Cotton Manufacturing. More special literature exists upon cotton manufacturing than upon any other single branch of industry. The best guide to this is Woodbury's *Bibliography of the Cotton Manufacture*. Of works written by contemporaries the most important are Appleton's *Introduction of the Power Loom*, Baird's *American Cotton Spinner*, Batchelder's *Introduction and Early Progress of Cotton Manufactures in the United States*, Montgomery's *Cotton Manufacture of Great Britain and the United States Contrasted*, and White's *Memoir of Slater*. Secretary Woodbury's *Report upon the Cultivation, Manufacture, and Foreign Trade in Cotton* is the principal official document devoted exclusively to this topic. In the *Transactions of the Rhode Island Society for the Promotion of Domestic Industry* are reminiscences of early cotton-spinning in that State. The annual and semi-annual proceedings of the New England Cotton Manufacturers' Association, which later became the National Association of Cotton Manufacturers, and of the Southern Cotton Spinners' Association, which became the American Cotton Manufacturers' Association, contain occasional articles or addresses relating to the pioneer history of this industry. Gregg's *Essays on Domestic Industry* is the best single source of information regarding early cotton manufactures in the South. Kohn's *Cotton Mills of South Carolina* contains a good informal discussion of the same subject. The manuscript business records of the *Boston Manufacturing Company* and the voluminous *Slater Papers* are now in the keeping of the Business Historical Society at Baker Library, Harvard University. William R. Bagnall at the time of his death had in course of preparation a continuation of his *Textile Industries in the United States*. His manuscripts and notes have been purchased, edited, and indexed by the Carnegie Institution of Washington and have been used for frequent reference in the present volume. A series of historical articles in the *Wool and Cotton Reporter*, between 1899 and 1903, affords much information regarding particular textile mills in New England. Last of all Caroline F. Ware's painstaking monograph upon *The Industrial Revolution in the New England Cotton Industry, 1790–1846*, though in manuscript at present writing, is available at Widener Library, Harvard University.

Wool Manufacturing. A bibliography of historical and technical works relating to wool growing and manufacturing, both in this country and abroad, was printed in Volume XXI of the *Bulletins* of the National Association of Wool Manufacturers. These bulletins are the most important single source of information concerning the history of this industry in America. They contain Dr. S. N. D. North's *History of the New England Wool Manufacture* and other writings of the same author upon that topic and also the articles of John L. Hayes, who was the first writer to review systematically the growth of this manufacture in America. The latter's book upon *American Textile Machinery* is an excellent résumé of the improvements in both cotton and woolen machinery from Slater's and Scholfield's time until the Centennial Exposition. Kittredge's *History of the*

American Card Clothing Industry covers with more detail a special feature of this development. Another bibliography of works relating to growing and manufacturing wool is appended to Wright's *Wool Growing and the Tariff*, which contains a recent and competent review of the history of our woolen industry. Arthur H. Cole's *American Wool Manufacture*, to be mentioned later, also summarizes the history of this period. Outside of official documents statistical records of this manufacture are limited to Benton and Barry's *Statistical View of the Woolen Manufacture in 1837*, and Graham's *Statistics of the Wool Manufactures of the United States, in 1845*. Taft's *Introduction of the Woolen Manufacture into the United States* is a source book for information regarding the very early progress of this industry. Its history has also been treated briefly in a special report of the Treasury Department upon *Wool and Manufactures of Wool*, published in 1888. Valuable contemporary data in manuscript from Peace Dale Manufacturing Company, in Rhode Island are now in possession of the Business Historical Society. The early account books of Nathaniel Stevens are in the possession of the family at North Andover; and similar records of George Booth's woolen mill at Poughkeepsie, dating back to 1806, are in existence in the latter city. A good review of the progress of both wool and cotton manufactures in America forms Part II of Webber's *Manual of Power*, and Walton's *Story of Textiles* contains descriptive and historical facts relating to this group of industries in America and abroad.

Iron and Steel. Most of our information relating to the manufacture of iron in America has been collected in authoritative form in Swank's *Iron in All Ages*. The only systematic histories of domestic iron making which preceded Swank's work are French's *Iron Trade of the United States* and Pearse's *History of the Iron Manufacture of the American Colonies up to the Revolution and of Pennsylvania until the Present Time*. Lesley's *Iron Manufacturer's Guide*, published in 1859, gives a detailed view of the industry just before the Civil War. Abram S. Hewitt was the ablest contemporary writer upon this subject, and his pamphlet on the *Statistics and Geography of the Production of Iron* is still worth reading. Johnson's *Notes on the Use of Anthracite in the Manufacture of Iron* is a good sketch of the great change in methods of production that occurred soon after 1840. Two recent studies, still in manuscript, throw much more light than has hitherto been available upon the growth of iron manufacturing in particular localities. These are Kathleen Bruce's *The Rise of the Iron Industry in Virginia*, which utilizes the complete business records of the Tredegar Company; and Louis Clair Hunter's *Study of the Iron Industry at Pittsburgh before 1860*, which is available at Harvard University.

Minor Manufactures. Several books and monographs have been written upon minor manufactures. Among the best of these are Barber's books upon glass and porcelain, Lathrop's excellent study of the brass industry, and Hazard's account of boot and shoe making in Massachusetts. Abbott's *Women in Industry* also contains new material relating to early manufactures. Brockett and Wyckoff have described our pioneer silk enterprises. There is much information regarding manufactures in the *Documentary History of American Industrial Society*. Some of the articles in *One Hundred Years of American Commerce*, written by men whose personal memory or firm records go back to the ante bellum period, contain new material. Most compendia of American industrial history, like those of Bolles and of Lossing, though serving a convenient purpose, are not valuable sources of original information. Taussig's *Tariff History of the United States* and Stanwood's *Tariff Controversies* are economic or political studies rather than industrial histories, but both works, and especially the former, throw interesting side lights into the latter field. Recently several books have appeared intended primarily for classroom use, which summarize the facts of our manufacturing development in association with other phases of national economic growth. Those of Bogart, Callender, Coman, Jennings, Lippincott, Moore, Van Metre, and Wright belong to this class. Callender's *Economic History* is the only one of these that purports to be a source book; but they all contain bibliographical data of use to students, and they sometimes place in illuminating juxtaposition groups of economic facts that exhibit the relation of manufacturing to other phases of production more concisely and emphatically than is possible in a larger work devoted to a special field.

THE CIVIL WAR AND AFTER

Since the period beginning with the Civil War American manufactures have multiplied almost beyond enumeration and have expanded until each of their more important branches has a trade literature of its own. Notwithstanding this, however, only rarely has an American industry of the first importance had its history adequately recorded. Considerable monographic material has accumulated though with surprising slowness in view of America's dramatic industrial expansion during the past fifty years. For the most part, however, the facts regarding our manufacturing progress must be dug out of Government reports, court records, and, above all, the trade and financial press. Manuscript sources are only beginning to become available for the general student, and from the nature of the case, in a country as vast and varied as the United States, they will always remain the recourse of the specialist in a comparatively narrow topic.

Histories of Industries. The leading history of a major industry is Arthur H. Cole's *The American Wool Manufacture*, which covers that subject competently. It was preceded sixteen years ago by an excellent monograph entitled *Wool Growing and the Tariff*, by Chester Whitney Wright, which dealt incidentally with some aspects of this manufacture. No similar history of the cotton manufacture has as yet appeared, although M. T. Copeland's *The Cotton Manufacturing Industry of the United States*, which was printed fourteen years ago, competently analyzes the economic aspects of that industry up to that date, with the minimum of historical background necessary to illustrate its argument. Broadus Mitchell's *Rise of Cotton Mills in the South* is a competent recent work, devoted particularly to the solid establishment of the industry south of the Potomac after the Civil War. We have as yet no general record of the growth and progress of the iron and steel industry, although several histories of individual companies and corporations have appeared. Swank's *History of the Manufacture of Iron in All Ages*, is purely annalistic in treatment and was published thirty-four years ago. C. B. Kuhlmann's *Development of the Flour-Milling Industry in the United States*, which is in press as this is written, leaves little to be said upon the history of the industry of which it treats from the founding of New England until the present time. James Elliott Defebaugh's ambitious endeavor to write a comprehensive history of the lumber industry in America was unfortunately interrupted, nearly twenty years ago, by the death of the author. A comprehensive *History of the Explosives Industry in the United States*, by Arthur Pine Van Gelder and Hugo Schlatter, has adequately covered the record of that manufacture. *A History of the Silk Dyeing Industry in the United States*, edited by Albert H. Heusser, has assembled the materials in another important field. Ralph C. Epstein's *The Automobile Industry, Its Economic and Commercial Development*, published the current year, is an exceptionally able economic analysis of the history of that important manufacture; Joseph Wickham Roe's *English and American Tool Builders* contains a fund of historical and biographical as well as technical information relating to the development of this branch of engineering in America; and Grosvenor B. Clarkson's *Industrial America in the World War* will probably remain the best general first-hand account of the history of the Government's relations with industries during the World War. Popular accounts of the rise of certain manufactures prominent in the public eye, such as H. L. Barber's *The Story of the Automobile;* narrative accounts of particular industries, of which *A History of Paper Manufacturing in the United States, 1690–1916,* by Lyman Horace Weeks, is a recent and excellent example, and works like Rudolf Alexander Clemen's *American Live Stock and Meat Industry,* which set forth with some historical background the economic conditions controlling an industry, with a view to educating public opinion regarding the current conditions under which it is conducted, complete a fairly representative roll call of such books.

Government Reports. A vast amount of information regarding American manufactures is buried in Government reports. The fact that such information has been officially recorded is of course no guaranty of its accuracy. Indeed, many of these data consist of ex parte testimony submitted to congressional committees and various investigating bodies for the express purpose of influencing legislation. The great compendium of statistical facts is of course the Federal census reports which are supplemented in several instances by corresponding enumerations gathered by state authorities. From 1880 until the end of the century the Federal census volumes contain much monographic material of an historical character. Tariff hearings tend to become more voluminous as time goes on, and the nineteen volumes which contain the reports and testimony of the Industrial Commission of 1900, the reports of the former Commissioner of Corporations and the present Federal Trade Commission, and the records of evidence and briefs in suits brought by the Federal Government and by state governments under anti-trust laws contain a wealth of material for the industrial historian. This is far from exhausting such sources, however, for much data are to be found in the reports and bulletins of the Bureau of Mines, the Geological Survey, the Agricultural Department, and of state bureaus having corresponding functions. Exposition reports, both those of American and foreign commissioners, not only present a bird's-eye view of contemporary manufacturing conditions but also contain occasional historical material of interest and illuminating comparisons of industrial conditions in different countries.

Transactions and Proceedings. Within the past sixty years numerous manufacturing associations and professional societies have been organized which publish bulletins, transactions, and annual reports or volumes of proceedings of an authoritative character. The American Iron and Steel Association—now the American Iron and Steel Institute—the National Association of Cotton Manufacturers, the National Association of Wool Manufacturers, the Silk Association of America, and kindred societies have archives, or publish bulletins and proceedings, from which a fairly complete history of the industry they represent can be reconstructed. Professional bodies like the American Society of Mechanical Engineers print papers, in their transactions, which are often indispensable in tracing the technical evolution of an industry.

Trade and Financial Press. Financial journals like *The Commercial and Financial Chronicle* are the most convenient source of information for the student of industrial organization, especially of the history of the great combinations which have characterized the last forty years of manufacturing growth. Certain annuals like Moody's *Manual of Corporation Securities* supplement such data. But the most vivid picture of the state of an industry at any particular period is usually to be found in the trade journals devoted to that particular manufacture. Many of these likewise publish some historical matter, such as reminiscences of veteran manufacturers, firm histories and biographical data in obituary notices. Their advertising pages also contain source material which should not be overlooked. Unfortunately, however, the enormous growth of advertising has added to the bulk of such periodicals until many libraries have ceased to preserve them.

That fact has governed to some extent the selection of authorities cited in this book. To use a specific illustration, the *Bulletin* of the American Iron and Steel Association is much handier material, and in the experience of the author is more likely to be found bound and complete on library shelves, than the volumes of a great publication like the *Iron Age*.

Monographs. Monographs, most of which are doctorate theses stressing tariff influence, afford the best interpretative material up to the present available concerning several industries. Mussey's and Berglund's studies of the Lake Superior ore business and the United States Steel Corporation, respectively, Blakey's thesis on the beet-sugar industry and Vogt's upon sugar refining, Mason's monograph upon the silk manufacture and Jacobstein's upon the tobacco industry, and the four regional histories prepared with the assistance of the Carnegie Institution of Washington are examples cited at random of such material

Somewhat more ambitious in scope and treatment are books like Miss Hazard's *Organization of the Boot and Shoe Industry in Massachusetts* and Miss Armes' *Story of Coal and Iron in Alabama*. Similar studies of American industries of manufacturing regions have been made by foreign investigators. The most prominent group of such monographs is the series of reports to the electors of the Gartside Scholarships published by the University of Manchester, England. Besides these there are, of course, a great number of books containing incidental references to local manufacturing annals; popular accounts of great industrial enterprises, technical works in which the author occasionally indulges in a vein of reminiscence, biographies and autobiographies of manufacturers, and anniversary publications issued by old manufacturing firms, each of which contributes its mite to the nation's business annals.

LIST OF AUTHORITIES

I. PUBLISHED

ABBOTT, EDITH. Women in Industry, A Study in American Economic History (New York, London, 1910).
ABBOTT, HENRY G. The Watch Factories of America Past and Present (Chicago, 1888).
ACCOUNT OF JOURNEY OF JOSIAH QUINCY, 1801. (Massachusetts Historical Society, Proceedings, 2d series, vol. IV.)
ACRELIUS, ISRAEL. History of New Sweden, or the Settlements on the River Delaware (translated by William M. Reynolds, Philadelphia, 1874, in Pennsylvania Historical Society, Memoirs, XI).
ADAMS, GEORGE HUNTINGTON. A Hand Book of the Tariff, on Imports into the United States, the Free List, and the Bond and Warehouse System Now in Force, with Notes of Judicial Decisions and Decisions of the Secretary of the Treasury (New York, 1890).
ADAMS, JOHN. Works (ed. Charles Francis Adams, Boston, 1856).
THE ADIRONDAK IRON AND STEEL COMPANY. Report (New York, 1854; Boston Public Library).
ALDERSON, VICTOR CLIFTON. The Oil Shale Industry (New York, 1920).
ALLEN, FREDERICK J. The Shoe Industry (New York, 1921).
ALLEN, ZACHARIAH. The Science of Mechanics as Applied to the Present Improvements in the Useful Arts (Providence, 1829).
ALMON, JOHN. Tracts. A Collection of the Most Interesting Tracts lately published in England and America, on the subjects of Taxing the American Colonies and regulating their Trade (3 vols., London, 1766–1767).
ALSBERG, CARL L. Combination in the American Bread-Baking Industry with Some Observations on The Mergers of 1924–25 (Stanford University, 1926).
AMELUNG, JOHN F. Remarks on Manufactures (1878; in Boston Athenaeum Library).
AMERICAN ALMANAC AND TREASURY OF FACTS. Statistical, financial and political, for the year 1879. (ed., Ainsworth R. Spofford, New York, 1879.)
AMERICAN ANNUAL REGISTER. (ed., Joseph Blunt, 8 vols., New York, 1825–1833.)

AMERICAN CARPET MANUFACTURERS' ASSOCIATION. Protest against the Proposed Duties on Third Class Wool (addressed to the Committee on Ways and Means, Mar. 17, 1890; Boston, 1890).

AMERICAN COTTON MANUFACTURERS ASSOCIATION. Certificate of Incorporation, By-Laws and Proceedings of the Twelfth Annual Convention, Richmond, May 20-21, 1908 (Charlotte, N. C., 1908).

AMERICAN COTTON MANUFACTURERS ASSOCIATION (Southern Cotton Spinners' Association). Proceedings of Annual Convention (31 vols., Charlotte, N. C., 1897-1927. Known as Southern Cotton Manufacturers' Association prior to 1903).

AMERICAN ECONOMIC REVIEW. (Quarterly, 18 vols., 1911-date, American Economic Association Publication.)

AMERICAN FLAX AND HEMP SPINNERS' AND GROWERS' ASSOCIATION. Report for Apr. 22, 1885 (Boston, 1885).

AMERICAN HISTORICAL ASSOCIATION. Annual Reports, 1889-1904 (Washington, 1890-1906).
———— Publications. Papers (5 vols., New York and London, 1886-1891).

AMERICAN HISTORICAL REVIEW. (ed., J. Franklin Jameson, 33 vols., New York, London, 1895-date.)

AMERICAN HUSBANDRY. By an American (2 vols., London, 1775).

AMERICAN INSTITUTE OF MINING ENGINEERS. Transactions (68 vols., Philadelphia, 1871-1919).

AMERICAN IRON AND STEEL ASSOCIATION. Annual Report of the Secretary to Dec. 31, 1874 (Philadelphia meeting, Feb. 11, 1875; Philadelphia, 1875).
———— Bulletins (58 vols., Philadelphia, 1866-1914).
———— Directory of the Ironworks of the United States (Philadelphia, 1874)
———— Iron and Steel, Iron Ore, and Coal Statistics, to the end of 1901 (Philadelphia, 1902).
———— Statistics of the American and Foreign Iron Trade (41 vols., Philadelphia, 1868, 1871-1911).

AMERICAN IRON AND STEEL INSTITUTE. Annual Statistical Report, 1912, (Philadelphia, 1913).

AMERICAN IRON ASSOCIATION. Directory and Bulletins (April 1856-June 1858).

AMERICAN JOURNAL OF IMPROVEMENTS IN THE USEFUL ARTS AND MIRROR OF THE PATENT OFFICE. (ed., J. L. Skinner, Washington, 1828.)

AMERICAN JOURNAL OF SCIENCES AND ARTS. (Conducted by B. Silliman and others, 118 vols., New York and New Haven, 1819-1879.)

AMERICAN LUMBERMAN. (Weekly, 54 vols., Chicago, 1900-1927.)
———— The Curiosity Shop, or Questions and Answers Concerning the Lumber Business (Chicago, 1906).

AMERICAN MACHINIST. (Monthly, 61 vols., New York, 1877-1924.)

AMERICAN MAGAZINE. (ed. Noah Webster, New York, 1787-1788.)

AMERICAN MANUFACTURER. (Boston, 1828-1830.)

AMERICAN MANUFACTURER AND IRON WORLD. The Greater Pittsburgh and Allegany County, Past, Present, and Future (special Pittsburg ed., Oct. 7, 1898).

AMERICAN MUSEUM. (12 vols., Philadelphia, 1787-1792.)

AMERICAN QUARTERLY REGISTER AND MAGAZINE. (ed., James Stryker, 6 vols., Philadelphia, 1848-1851.)

AMERICAN REPERTORY OF ARTS, SCIENCE AND MANUFACTURES. (ed., James P. Mapes, New York, 1840-1842.)

AMERICAN SHOE MAKING. (Consolidated with Superintendent and Foreman, Weekly, 91 vols., Boston, 1901-1919.)

AMERICAN SILK JOURNAL. (Weekly, 46 vols., New York, 1882-1926.)

AMERICAN SOCIETY OF CIVIL ENGINEERS. Transactions (90 vols., New York, 1867-1927.)

AMERICAN SOCIETY OF MECHANICAL ENGINEERS. Transactions and Proceedings (49 vols., New York, 1880-1927.)

AMERICAN STATISTICAL ASSOCIATION. Collections (3 parts, Boston, 1843-1847.)

AMERICAN SUGAR REFINING COMPANY. A Century of Sugar Refining in the United States, 1816-1916 (New York, 1916).
———— Conditions in the Sugar Market, January to October, 1917 (New York, 1917).

AMERICAN TEXTILE MANUFACTURER. (Monthly, 2 vols., Philadelphia, 1880-1883.)

(AMERICAN) WOOL AND COTTON REPORTER. (Title varies slightly. Weekly, 34 vols., New York and Boston, 1891-1908.)

ANBUREY, THOMAS. Travels through the Interior Parts of America (2 vols., London, 1789).
ANDERSON, JOSEPH. The Town and City of Waterbury (3 vols., New Haven, 1896).
ANDREAS, ALFRED T. History of Chicago (3 vols., Chicago, 1884–1886).
ANDREWS, CHARLES M. Guide to the Materials for American History, to 1783, in the Public Record Office of Great Britain (Carnegie Inst. Wash. Pub. 90 A, 2 vols., 1912, 1914).
ANDREWS, ISRAEL D. On the Trade and Commerce of the British North American Colonies and upon the Trade of the Great Lakes and Rivers (House Ex. Doc. No. 136, 32d Cong., 2d sess., 1853).
ANDREWS AND DAVENPORT. Guide to the Manuscript Materials for the History of the United States, to 1783, in the British Museum, in Minor London Archives, and in Libraries of Oxford and Cambridge (Carnegie Inst. Wash. Pub. 90, 1908).
APPLETON, NATHAN. The Introduction of the Power Loom (Lowell, 1858).
ARLINGTON MILLS AT LAWRENCE, MASS. Description and Historical Sketch (Boston, 1891).
—— Tops, a New American Industry (Cambridge, Mass., 1898).
ARMES, ETHEL. The Story of Coal and Iron in Alabama (Birmingham, 1910).
ARMOUR AND COMPANY. Historical Account of Firm (Chicago, 1917).
ARNOLD, SAMUEL GREENE. History of the State of Rhode Island and Providence Plantation (2 vols., New York, 1859–1860.
ASHLEY, JOHN. Memoirs and Considerations concerning the Trade and Revenues of the British Colonies in America (London, 1740).
ASHLEY, WILLIAM JAMES. Early History of the English Woolen Industry (American Economic Association Publications, vol. II, No. 4, Baltimore, 1887).
ASHLEY, W. M. (ed.). British Industries (New York, 1903).
ASSOCIATED INDUSTRIES OF MASSACHUSETTS. Annual Reports of the General Manager, (Boston, 1926, 1927).
ATKINSON, EDWARD. Facts and Figures (Boston, 1904).
—— Report to the Boston Board of Trade on the Cotton Manufacture of 1862 (Massachusetts Historical Society).
ATLANTIC MONTHLY. (141 vols., Boston, 1857–date.)
ATWATER, EDWARD E. History of the Colony of New Haven to Its Absorption into Connecticut (New Haven, 1881).
AYER, J. C. Some Uses and Abuses in the Management of our Manufacturing Corporations (Lowell, 1863; Yale College Pamphlets No. 393).
BABSON, JOHN J. History of the Town of Gloucester, Cape Ann, Including the Town of Rockport (Gloucester, 1860).
BACHE, J. D. American Industrials (New York, 1901).
BAGNALL, WILLIAM R. The Textile Industries of the United States (Cambridge, 1893).
BAINES, EDWARD. History of the Cotton Manufacture of Great Britain (London, 1835).
BAIRD, Robert H. The American Cotton Spinner and Manager's and Carder's Guide (Philadelphia, 1851).
BALDWIN LOCOMOTIVE WORKS. Pamphlet upon the Completion of their 40,000th Locomotive (in Library of Pennsylvania Historical Society).
BALLAGH, JAMES C. Economic History of the South (vols. v and vi of The South in the Building of the Nation, Philadelphia, 1910).
BALLY, EDUARD. Industry and Manufactures of the United States (translated from the French, Boston, 1878).
BANNER OF THE CONSTITUTION. (Vols. 1–3, ed., Condy Raguet, Washington and Philadelphia, 1829–1832.)
BARBER, EDWIN ATLEE. American Glassware, Old and New (Philadelphia, 1900).
—— Pottery and Porcelain of the United States (2d ed., New York, 1901).
BARBER, H. L. The Story of the Automobile (Chicago, 1917).
BARBER, JOHN W., AND HENRY HOWE. Historical Collections of the State of New Jersey (New York, 1844).
BARNARD, J. LYNN. Factory Legislation in Pennsylvania: Its History and Administration (Publications of the University of Pennsylvania, Philadelphia, 1907).
BARRY, WILLIAM. A History of Framingham, Massachusetts, Including the Plantation, from 1640 to the Present Time (Boston, 1847).

BARTGIG'S REPUBLICAN GAZETTE. (Frederick-Town, Md., 1793–1810.)
BATCHELDER, SAMUEL. Introduction and Early Progress of the Cotton Manufactures in the United States (Boston, 1863).
—— Statistics of Cotton Manufacture, 1861 (7th annual report of the Boston Board of Trade, Boston, 1861).
BAYLES, JAMES C. Address before the Iron, Coal, and Manufacturers' Association, at Chattanooga, Tenn. Nov. 13, 1877. (Printed in full in the Chattanooga Daily Dispatch, Nov. 14, 1877.)
BEER, GEORGE L. British Colonial Policy, 1754–1765 (New York, 1907). The Commercial Policy of England toward the American Colonies (Columbia University Studies, vol. III, No. 2, 1893).
—— The Origins of the British Colonial System, 1578–1660 (New York, 1908).
BEERMANN, FRIEDRICH. Studien über die amerikanische Baumwollindustrie (Greifswald, 1913).
BELKNAP, JEREMY. History of New Hampshire (3 vols., Boston, 1791–1792).
BELL, SIR ISAAC LOWTHIAN. Iron Trade of the United Kingdom compared with that of the other Chief Iron-Making Nations (London, 1886).
—— Notes of a Visit to the Coal and Iron Mines of the United States (London, 1875).
—— Principles of the Manufacture of Iron and Steel—with some notes on the Economic Conditions of Their Production (London, 1884).
BELL TELEPHONE QUARTERLY. (6 vols., New York, 1922—date.)
BEMIS, E. W. History of Cooperation in the United States (Johns Hopkins University Studies, Baltimore, 1888).
BEMIS, SAMUEL FLAGG. Jay's Treaty (New York, 1923).
BENNETT, HUGH GARNER. The Manufacture of Leather (London, 1920).
BENTLEY, WILLIAM. Diary (4 vols., published by Essex Institute, Salem, 1906–1907).
BENTON, C., AND S. F. BARRY. Statistical View of the Woolen Manufacture (Cambridge, 1837).
BERGLUND, ABRAHAM. The United States Steel Corporation—A Study of the Growth and Influence of Combination in the Steel Industry (Columbia University Studies in History, Economics, and Public Law, New York, 1907).
BERNARD, SIR FRANCIS. Select Letters on the Trade and Government of America (London, 1774).
BEVERLEY, ROBERT. History of Virginia (reprinted from 2d rev. ed., London, 1772; Richmond, 1855).
BIGELOW, ERASTUS B. Address upon the Woolen Industry of the United States (Boston 1869; Massachusetts Historical Society Library).
—— Correspondence Relating to the Invention of the Jacquard Brussels Carpet Power Loom (Boston 1868; Massachusetts Historical Society Collections).
—— Remarks on the Depressed Condition of Manufactures in Massachusetts (Boston, 1858, in Yale College Library, Pamphlets, No. 393).
BIRKENBINE, JOHN. Changes in Manufacture of Pig Iron (in Philadelphia Engineers' Club, Proceedings XIX, 225, July, 1902).
—— The Old Charcoal Furnaces. (Contributed to the Report of Albert Williams, Jr., Chief of the Division of Mining Statistics of the U. S. Geological Survey, Washington, 1885.)
—— The Production of Iron Ores in 1891 (Washington, 1892).
BISHOP, J. LEANDER. A History of American Manufactures from 1608 to 1860 (3 vols., Philadelphia and London, 1866).
BLAKEY ROY G. The United States Beet Sugar Industry and the Tariff (Columbia University Studies in History, Economics, and Public Law, New York, 1912).
BLODGET, SAMUEL, JR. Economica: A Statistical Manual for the United States of America (Washington, 1806).
BLODGETT, LESTER. Industries of Philadelphia (Philadelphia, 1876).
BLOIS, JOHN D. Gazetteer of the State of Michigan (Detroit and New York, 1838).
BLOWE, DANIEL. A Geographical, Historical, Commercial, and Agricultural View of the United States of America (London, 1820).
BOGART, ERNEST LUDLOW. The Economic History of the United States (New York, London, 1907).
BOGART, ERNEST LUDLOW AND CHARLES MANFRED THOMPSON. The Industrial State, 1870–1893 (The Centennial History of Illinois, vol. IV, Springfield, 1920).

BOLLES, ALBERTS SYDNEY. 15th Annual Report of the Bureau of Industrial Statistics of Pennsylvania (Harrisburg, 1888).
―― The Industrial History of the United States (Norwich, Conn., 1878).
BOND, PHINEAS. Letters, in American Historical Association, Annual Report, 1896, vol. I, 552-553.
BOOT AND SHOE RECORDER. (Weekly, 91 vols., Boston, 1882-1927.)
BOSTON BOARD OF TRADE. Report on the Branch House System for the Sale of Goods Manufactured in Massachusetts, and in the Adjoining States, on Boston Capital (Boston, 1858).
BOSTON COMMERCIAL BULLETIN. (Weekly, Boston, 1859-1915).
BOSTON EVENING POST AND GENERAL ADVERTISER. (Weekly, Oct. 20, 1781-Jan. 10, 1784).
BOSTON GAZETTE. (12 vols., Boston, 1801-1815.)
BOSTON JOURNAL OF COMMERCE AND TEXTILE INDUSTRIES. (Weekly, 81 vols., Boston, 1881-1908.)
BOSTON NEWS LETTER. (ed., Jerome V. C. Smith, 2 vols., Boston, 1825-1826.)
BOSTON NEWS LETTER. (Weekly, Apr. 24, 1704-Apr. 1, 1763.)
BOSTON RECORD COMMISSIONERS. Records Relating to the Early History of Boston (39 vols., Boston, 1876-1909).
BOUCHER, JOHN NEWTON. A Century and a Half of Pittsburg and Her People (4 vols., New York 1908).
BOUCHEREAU, L. Statement of the Sugar and Rice Crops of Louisiana and Texas, 1868-1869, 1869-1870, 1870-1871, 1871-1872 (New Orleans).
BOURNE, EDWARD EMERSON. History of Wells and Kennebunk (Portland, 1875).
BOWDITCH, J. B. Industrial Development of Rhode Island (in Field, Edward, ed., State of Rhode Island and Providence Plantations, vol. III, 325-356; Boston and Syracuse, 1902).
BOWLEY, ARTHUR LYON. Wages in the United Kingdom in the Nineteenth Century (Cambridge, 1900).
BRADBURY, JOHN. Travels in the Interior of America in the Years 1809, 1810, and 1811 (London, 1817).
BRADSTREET'S. (Semi-weekly and weekly, 54 vols., New York, 1879-1928).
BRADY'S BEND IRON COMPANY. Report of October, 1858 (Boston, 1858, Boston Public Library).
―― Report upon Real Estate, Materials, Works, and Manufactures (New York, 1864, in New York Public Library Pamphlets).
BRASSEY, SIR THOMAS. Lectures on the Labour Question, (London, 1878). Works and wages (ed., J. Potter, London, 1894).
BREWSTER, SIR FRANCIS. Essays on Trade and Navigation (London, 1695).
BRIDGE, JAMES HOWARD. The inside History of the Carnegie Steel Company (New York, 1903).
BRIEF ACCOUNT OF THE RISE, PROGRESS, AND PRESENT STAGE OF THE PAPER CURRENCY OF NEW ENGLAND. (Boston, 1749, Massachusetts Historical Society Tracts.)
BRIGGS, LLOYD V. Ship Building on the North River (Boston, 1889).
BRISSOT, JEAN PIERRE (de Warville). Nouveau voyage dans les États-Unis de l'Amérique septentrionale, fait en 1788 (3 vols., Paris, 1791).
BRITISH IRON TRADE COMMISSION. American Industrial Conditions and Competition—Reports of the Commissioners appointment by the British Iron Trade Association to enquire into the iron, steel, and allied industries of the United States (Ed., J. Stephen Jean, London, 1902).
―― Annual Statistical Report of the Secretary to the members of the British Iron Trade Association on the home and foreign steel industries (London, 1880-1907).
BROCKETT, LINUS PIERPONT. The Silk Industry in America (New York, 1876).
BROOKINGS, ROBERT S. Industrial Ownership (New York, 1925).
BROUGHAM, HENRY, M. P. Speech upon the State of Agricultural Distress (Speech made in the Committee of both Houses, Apr. 9, 1816. London, 1816).
BROW, JOHN HOWARD (ed.). Lambs' Textile Industries of the United States (Boston, 1911).
BROWN, WILLIAM H. History of the First Locomotive in America (New York, 1871).
BRUCE, PHILIP ALEXANDER. Economic History of Virginia in the Seventeenth Century (2 vols., New York, London, 1895).
―― Rise of the New South (Philadelphia, 1905).

BRUCE'S MINERALOGICAL JOURNAL. (ed., Archibald Bruce, New York, 1810–1814).
BUCHANAN, JAMES (Pennsylvania). Speech in U. S. House of Representatives in Reply to Sprague of Maine on Bill levying additional duties on Hemp and Molasses (Washington, 1828).
BUCKINGHAM, JAMES SILK. America, Historical, Statistical, and Descriptive (3 vols., London, Paris, 1841).
—— The Slave States of America (2 vols., London, 1842).
BUCKLEY, E. R. Clays and Clay Industries of Wisconsin (Wisconsin Geological Survey, Madison, 1901).
BUFFALO. Annual Statement of Trade and Commerce, 1854, 1856 (compiler, John J. Henderson).
BUFFALO CHAMBER OF COMMERCE. Manufacturing Industries of Buffalo (Buffalo, 1883).
BUFFALO GAZETTE. (Buffalo, 1811–1817).
BUFFALO, MANUFACTURING INTERESTS OF. (Buffalo, 1866.)
BUREAU OF THE CENSUS. (See United States.)
BURKE, EDMUND. Works (12 vols., 7th ed., Boston, 1881).
BURKETT, C. W., AND C. H. POE. Cotton, Its Cultivation, Marketing, Manufacture, and the Problems of the Cotton World (New York, 1906).
BURNABY, ANDREW. Travels through North America (New York, 1904).
BURNLEY, JAMES. The History of Wool and Wool Combing (London, 1889).
BURRILL, JAMES, JR. AND ASSOCIATES. Petition to the Honorable Senate and House of Representatives of the United States in Congress Assembled, 1815. (Massachusetts Historical Society.)
BUSCHING, DR. PAUL. Die Entwickelung der handelspolitischen Beziehungen zwischen England und seinen Kolonien bis zum Jahre 1860 (Stuttgart und Berlin, 1902).
BUTLER, JOSEPH G., JR. Fifty Years of Iron and Steel (Cleveland, 1920).
CALHOUN, JOHN C. Correspondence (ed., J. Franklin Jameson, in American Historical Association, Annual Report, 1899, vol. 2, Washington, 1900).
CALLENDER, GUY STEVENS. Selected Readings in the Economic History of the United States (1765–1860).
CAMP, DAVID N. History of New Britain, with Sketches of Farmington and Berlin, Connecticut (New Britain, 1889).
CAMPBELL, J. P. General Commercial and Business Directory of Nashville (Nashville, 1859).
—— General Commercial and Business Directory of the South and West, 1853–1854.
CAMPBELL, LEVIN H. The Patent System of the United States (Washington, 1891).
CAREY CLIPPINGS. (Collection of newspaper clippings in several volumes, mostly without dates and names of periodicals, in the Ridgeway Branch of the Philadelphia Library.)
CAREY AND LEA. The Geography, History and Statistics of America (London, 1823).
CASSIER'S MAGAZINE. (Monthly, 44 vols., New York and London, 1891–1913.)
CATLIN, GEORGE B. The Story of Detroit (Detroit, 1923).
CAULKINS, FRANCES MANWARING. History of New London, Connecticut, from the first Survey of the Coast in 1612, to 1860 (New London, 1895).
CHALMERS, GEORGE. Introduction to the History of the Revolt of the American Colonies (2 vols., Boston, 1845).
—— Political Annals of the Present United Colonies (London, 1780).
CHAMPION, RICHARD. Considerations on the Present Situation of Great Britain and the United States of America, etc., (London, 1784).
CHAMPOMIER, P. A. Statement of the Sugar Crops made in Louisiana, 1845–6; 1859–60; 1860–1 1861–2 (13 vols., New Orleans, 1845–1862).
CHANNING, EDWARD. History of the United States (6 vols., New York, 1925).
CHAPMAN, SIDNEY J. Foreign Competition (London-New York, 1904).
—— The Lancashire Cotton Industry (Manchester University Press, 1904).
CHARLESTON DAILY COURIER. (129 vols., Jan. 10, 1803–Dec. 31, 1872).
CHASE, GEORGE WINGATE. The History of Haverhill, Massachusetts, from its first Settlement, in 1640, to the year 1860 (Haverhill, 1861).
CHASE, L. G. A Consideration of the Commercial and Manufacturing Wants and Necessities of St. Louis (St. Louis, 1869).

CHASTELLUX, FRANÇOIS JEAN, MARQUIS DE. Travels in North America (2 vols., London, 1787).
CHEMICAL AND METALLURGICAL ENGINEERING. (Monthly, semi-monthly, weekly; 29 vols., New York, 1902–1928; title varies slightly—prior to 1918 it was Metallurgical and Chemical Engineering.)
CHEVALIER, MICHEL. Lettres sur l'Amérique du Nord (3 vols., 3d ed., Bruxelles, 1838).
CHICKERING AND SONS. Commemoration of Founding, 1823–1903 (Boston, 1903).
CHILD, SIR JOSIAH. A New Discourse on Trace (London, 1694).
CHITTICK, JAMES. Silk Manufacturing and Its Problems. (New York, 1913.)
CHOATE, RUFUS (Massachusetts). Speech upon the Subject of Protecting American Labor by Duties on Imports. (Delivered in the U. S. Senate, Apr. 12 and 15, 1844. Washington, 1844.)
—— Works (ed., Samuel Gilman Brown, 2 vols., Boston, 1862).
CINCINNATI. Review of the Trade and Commerce and Manufactures, for 1850.
—— Statement of Trade and Commerce, 1855, 1858, 1859, 1860 (compiler, William Smith).
CINCINNATI BOARD OF TRADE. Semi-annual Report, Mar. 31, 1869 (Cincinnati, 1869).
CINCINNATI PRICE CURRENT. (Weekly, 1844–1889.)
CIST, CHARLES. The Cincinnati Miscellany, or Antiquities of the West (2 vols., Cincinnati, 1845–46).
CLARK, JAMES A. The Wyoming Valley (Scranton, Pa., 1875).
CLARKE, ISAAC EDWARD. Art and Industry. Education in the Industrial and Fine Arts in the United States (4 vols., Washington, 1885, 1892, 1897, 1898).
CLARKE, MAURICE D. (ed.). Manchester, A Brief Record of its Past and a Picture of its Present (Manchester, 1875).
CLARKSON, GROSVENOR B. Industrial America in the World War, (Boston and New York, 1923).
CLAY, HENRY. The Works of Henry Clay, Comprising His Life, Correspondence, and Speeches (ed., Calvin Colton, 10 vols., New York, 1904).
CLAYTON AND NELSON (compilers). History of Bergen and Passaic Counties (Philadelphia, 1882).
CLEMEN, RUDOLPH ALEXANDER. The American Livestock and Meat Industry (New York, 1923). By-Products in the Packing Industry (Chicago, 1927.)
COBB, HENRY. Preliminary Report on the Annual Value of Manufactures for the State to the Board of Trade (St. Louis, 1870).
COBBETT, WILLIAM. Selections from Political Writings (6 vols., London, 1835).
COCHRANE, CHARLES H. Modern Industrial Progress (Philadelphia and London, 1911).
COFFIN, JOSHUA. A Sketch of the History of Newbury, Newburyport, and West Newburyport, from 1635 to 1845 (Boston, 1845).
COLE, A. C. The Whig Party in the South (Washington, 1913).
COLE, ARTHUR HARRISON. The American Wool Manufacture (2 vols., Cambridge, Mass., 1926).
COLE, J. R. History of Tolland County, Connecticut (New York, 1888).
COLES, B. U. Memoir on Wheat and Flour in New York (New York, 1820).
COLLINS, J. H. The Story of Canned Foods (New York, 1924).
COLONIAL SOCIETY OF MASSACHUSETTS. Publications (14 vols., Boston, 1895–1913)
COLUMBIAN CENTINEL. (Semiweekly, 30 vols., Boston, June 16, 1790–Dec. 30, 1829).
COMAN, KATHERINE. Industrial History of the United States (New York, London, 1910).
COMMERCIAL AND FINANCIAL CHRONICLE AND HUNT'S MERCHANT MAGAZINE. (Weekly, 126 vols., New York, 1865–1928; absorbed Hunt's Merchant Magazine in 1871)
COMMERCE MONTHLY. (Issued by National Bank of Commerce, monthly, 9 vols., New York, 1919–1928.)
COMMITTEE ON ELIMINATION OF WASTE IN INDUSTRY, OF THE FEDERATED AMERICAN ENGINEERING SOCIETIES, Waste in Industry (McGraw-Hill Book Company, Inc., New York, 1921).
COMMONS, J. R. History of Labor in the United States (2 vols., New York, 1918).
CONE, ANDREW, AND WALTER R. JOHNS. Petroleum—A Brief History of the Pennsylvania Petroleum Region, from 1859 to 1869 (New York, 1870).
CONGRESSIONAL REGISTER. (Reporter, Thomas Lloyd, New York, 1789.)
CONKLING, FREDERICK A. Production and Consumption of Cotton (New York, 1870).

CONNECTICUT. Acts and Laws (New London, 1718, 1750, 1769, and sess. eds.).
—— Book of the General Laws for the People of the Province of Connecticut (Cambridge, 1673; republished, Hartford, 1865).
—— Public Records of the Colony of Connecticut, 1836–1776 (15 vols.; vols. 1–3 ed. J. H. Trumbull; vols. 4–15 ed. J. C. Hoadly, Hartford, 1850–1890).
—— Report of the Secretary of State Relative to Certain Branches of Industry (Connecticut House of Representatives Doc. No. 26, May sess. 1839; Hartford, 1839).
—— Statistics of Industry in Connecticut. (By David P. Tyler, Secretary of State, from the Assessor's returns for the year ending Oct. 1, 1845; Hartford, 1846.)
CONNECTICUT HISTORICAL SOCIETY. Collections (14 vols., Hartford, 1860–1912).
CONNECTICUT MAGAZINE. (eds., W. F. Felch, G. C. Atwell, H. P. Arms, F. T. Miller, 11 vols., 12th vol. incomplete, Hartford, 1895–1908.)
CONNELLSVILLE, PA. The Centennial History of the Borough of, 1806–1906 (Columbus, Ohio, 1906).
CONVENTION OF MANUFACTURERS, DEALERS AND OPERATIVES IN THE SHOE AND LEATHER TRADES. Proceedings (Boston, 1842, Massachusetts Historical Society).
COOK, GEORGE H. Industrial Advantages of Gloversville (Gloversville, N. Y., 1890).
COOPER, THOMAS. Some Information Respecting America, 1793 (London, 1794).
COPE, G. W. Iron and Steel Interests of Chicago (Chicago, 1890; compiled for Iron and Steel Institute).
COPELAND, MELVIN TH. The Cotton Manufacturing Industry of the United States (Harvard Economic Studies, Cambridge, Mass., 1912).
CORWIN, THOMAS. Report on the Trade and Commerce of the British North American Colonies with the United States and Other Countries (Senate Ex. Doc., 31st Cong., 2d sess., No. 23, 1851).
COTTER, ARUNDEL. The Authentic History of the United States Steel Corporation (New York, 1921).
—— The Story of Bethlehem Steel (New York, 1916).
COWLEY, CHARLES. Illustrated History of Lowell (2d rev. ed. Boston, 1868).
COXE, TENCH. Address to an Assembly of the Friends of Domestic Manufactures (Philadelphia, 1787).
—— Brief Examination of Lord Sheffield's Observations on the Commerce of the United States (Philadelphia, 1791).
—— Essay on the Manufacturing Interest of the United States (Philadelphia, 1804).
—— Memoirs of February 1817 (and of December 1818) upon the Cotton Wool Cultivation, the Cotton Trade, and the Cotton Manufactures of the United States (Philadelphia, 1817 and 1818).
—— Observations on the Agriculture, Manufactures, and Commerce of the United States (New York, 1789).
—— Reflections on the State of the Union (Philadelphia, 1792).
—— A Statement of the Arts and Manufactures of the United States of America for the Year 1810 (Philadelphia, 1814).
—— A View of the United States of America (Philadelphia, 1794, and Dublin, 1795).
CRANE, E. B. Early Paper Mills of Massachusetts (Worcester Society of Antiquity Collections, vol. VII, 1886).
CRESCENT IRON MANUFACTURING COMPANY. Report, with statistics of other manufactures at Wheeling, W. Va. (Boston, 1855, in New York Public Library Pamphlets).
CRÈVECŒUR, MICHAEL, ST. JEAN DE. Lettres d'un cultivateur Americain (3 vols., Paris, 1787).
—— Voyage dans la Haute Pensylvanie et dans l'État de New York (3 vols., Paris, 1801).
CRISSEY, THERON WILMOT. History of Norfolk (Everett, 1900).
CUNNINGHAM, WILLIAM. Growth of English Industry and Commerce in Modern Times (3d ed., 2 vols., Cambridge, 1903).
CURIOSITY SHOP, THE, OR QUESTIONS AND ANSWERS CONCERNING THE LUMBER BUSINESS, A COMPILATION OF INQUIRIES TO THE EDITOR OF THE AMERICAN LUMBERMAN AND ANSWERS THERETO (Chicago, 1906).
CURTISS, GEORGE B. The Industrial Development of Nations (Binghamton, New York, 1912).
CUSHING, THOMAS C. A Report of the Affairs of the New Hampshire Iron Company (Salem, 1810, Boston Public Library).

CUSTIS, GEORGE WASHINGTON PARKE. An address to the People of the United States on the Importance of Encouraging Agriculture and Domestic Manufactures (Alexandria, 1808).
CYCLOPEDIA OF COMMERCE AND COMMERCIAL NAVIGATION. (2 vols., eds. J. Smith Homans and J. Smith Homans, Jr., New York, 1858.)
DANA, EDMUND. Geographical Sketches on the Western Country (Cincinnati, 1819).
DANA, W. B. Cotton from Seed to Loom (New York, 1878).
DAVIDSON, J. MORRISON. Annals of Toil: being Labour-History Outlines, Roman and British (4 books, London, 1899).
DAVIS, ANDREW MCFARLAND. Corporations in the Days of the Colonies (in Colonial Society of Massachusetts, Publications, vol. I, 183–215, Boston, 1895).
—— Currency and Banking in the Province of Massachusetts Bay (Publications American Economic Association, 3d ser. vol, I, No. 4, 1900).
—— (ed.). Tracts Relating to the Currency of the Massachusetts Bay, 1682–1720 (New York, 1902).
DAVIS, CHARLES THOMAS. The Manufacture of Leather (Philadelphia and London, 1865).
DAVIS, JAMES D. History of Memphis (Memphis, 1873).
DAVIS, JOHN (Massachusetts). Speech in U. S. House of Representatives on the Tariff Bill, Mar. 12, 1828 (Washington, 1828).
DAVIS, SUSAN LAWRENCE. Authentic History of the Ku Klux Klan (New York, 1924).
DAVIS, W. T. Industrial History of New England (Boston, 1897).
—— Industrial History of Suffolk County, Massachusetts (Boston, 1894).
DAY, SAMUEL PHILLIPS. Down South; or an Englishman's Experience at the Seat of the American War (2 vols., London, 1862).
DEARBORN, NATHANIEL. Boston Notions. Being an Authentic and Concise Account of "that village" from 1630 to 1847 (Boston, 1848).
DE BOW, J. D. B. Industrial Resources of the Southern and Western States (3 vols., New Orleans, 1852–1853).
—— Statistical View of the United States (Washington 1854. See U. S. Census, 1850).
DE BOW'S COMMERCIAL REVIEW OF THE SOUTH AND WEST. (ed., J. D. B. De Bow. Old ser., 32 vols., closed 1862; revived ser., 8 vol., 1866–1870; attempted revival, 1879–1880; New Orleans).
DEFEBAUGH, JAMES ELLIOTT. History of the Lumber Industry of America. (4 vols., Chicago, 1906–1907.)
DEFOE, DANIEL. A Plan of English Commerce, Being a Complete Prospect of the Trade of this Nation (2d. ed., London, 1730).
DELAWARE. House Journal, 1807.
—— Laws for the Government of Newcastle, Kent, & Sussex, upon the Delaware (ed. Benjamin Franklin, Philadelphia, 1714–1752).
—— Laws of the General Assembly (1787).
—— Laws of the State (Washington, 1790).
DE LEON, THOMAS COOPER. Four Years in Rebel Capitals—An Inside View of Life in the Southern Confederacy from Birth to Death. From Original Notes, Collated in the Years 1861–1865 (Mobile, Ala., 1890).
DEMOCRATIC CLARION AND TENNESSEE GAZETTE. (Weekly, Nashville, 1808–1812.)
DENTON, DANIEL. A Brief Description of New York (London, 1670; reprint New York, 1845).
DEPEW, CHAUNCEY MITCHELL (ed). One Hundred Years of American Commerce, 1795–1895 (2 vols., New York, 1895).
DEWEY, DAVIS R. National Problems (New York, 1907).
DICKENSON, RUDOLPHUS. A Geographical and Statistical View of Massachusetts Proper (Greenfield, 1815).
DIX, JOHN ADAMS. Sketch of the Resources of the City of New York from the Foundation of the City to the Date of the Latest Statistical Accounts (New York, 1827).
DOCUMENTARY HISTORY OF AMERICAN INDUSTRIAL SOCIETY. (11 vols., eds. John R. Commons, Ulrich B. Phillips, Eugene A. Gilmore, Helen L. Sumner, John B. Andrews; Cleveland, 1910–1911.)
DOCUMENTS RELATING TO THE MANUFACTURE OF IRON IN PENNSYLVANIA. (Philadelphia, 1850.)
DONNELL, E. J. Chronological and Statistical History of Cotton (New York, 1872).

DORCHESTER ANTIQUARIAN AND HISTORICAL SOCIETY COMMITTEE. History of the Town of Dorchester, Massachusetts (Boston, 1859).
DOUGLASS, R. A History of Manufactures in the Kansas District (published in Kansas State Historical Collections, vol. XI, 81–215, Topeka, 1910).
DOUGLASS, WILLIAM. British Settlements in North America (2 vols., London, 1760).
—— A Discourse concerning the Currencies of the British Plantations in America (ed., Charles J. Bullock, New York, 1897).
DRAKE, BENJAMIN, AND EDWARD DEERING MANSFIELD. Cincinnati in 1826 (Cincinnati, 1827).
DRAKE, DANIEL. Natural and Statistical View, or Picture of Cincinnati and the Miami Country in 1815 (Cincinnati, 1815).
DRAKE, FRANCIS S. The Town of Roxbury (Roxbury, 1878).
DRAKE, SAMUEL GARDNER. History and Antiquities of Boston (Boston, 1856).
DRAYTON, JOHN. A View of South Carolina as Respects her Natural and Civil Concerns (Charleston, 1802).
DUNBAR, D. E. The Tin-Plate Industry (Boston and New York, 1915).
DU PONT, B. C. E. I. du Pont de Nemours, A History, 1802–1902 (Boston, 1920).
DWIGHT, TIMOTHY. Travels in New England and New York (4 vols., New Haven, 1821–1822).
DYER, WALTER ALDEN. Early American Craftsmen (New York, 1915).
EARL, HENRY HILLIARD. A Centennial History of Fall River, Mass., 1656–1876 (New York, 1877).
EATON, REV. SAMUEL J. M. Petroleum—A History of the Oil Region of Venango County, Pennsylvania (Philadelphia, 1866).
EBELINGS, CHRISTOPHER DANIEL. Erbeschreibung und Geschichte von Amerika (7 vols., Hamburg, 1793–1816).
EDMONDS, R. H. Address on Early Industrial Conditions in the South (in Southern Cotton Spinners' Association, Twentieth Century Publication, Charlotte, 1901).
EDWARDS, ALBA M. Labor Legislation of Connecticut (Publications American Economic Association, 3d ser., No. 3, New York, 1907).
EDWARDS, RICHARD (ed.) Statistical Gazetteer of the State of Virginia, for the year 1854 (Richmond, 1855).
ELECTRICAL WORLD. (91 vols., New York 1882–date.)
ELIOT, JARED. Essays upon Field Husbandry in New England (Boston, 1760).
ELLISON, THOMAS. Cotton Trade of Great Britain (London, 1886).
ELY, RICHARD T. Monopolies and Trusts (New York, 1912).
ENGINEERING. (Weekly, 116 vols., London, 1866–1923.)
ENGINEERING AND MINING JOURNAL. (124 vols., New York, 1866–1927).
ENGINEERING MAGAZINE. (51 vols., New York, 1891–1916; changed to Industrial Management.)
EPSTEIN, R. C. The Automobile Industry (Chicago, 1928)
ESSEX ANTIQUARIAN. (ed., Sidney Perley, 13 vols., Salem, 1897–1909.)
ESSEX INSTITUTE. Historical Collections (50 vols., Salem, 1859–1914).
EVANS, CHARLES H. Exports, Domestic and Foreign, from American Colonies to Great Britain, 1697–1789 (Washington, 1884).
EVANS, DAVID MORIER. The History of the Commercial Crisis of 1857–1858, and the Stock Exchange Panic of 1859 (London, 1859).
EXAMINATION OF THE COTTON FACTORY QUESTION. (London, 1819.)
EXPOSITION UNIVERSELLE INTERNATIONALE DE 1900 À PARIS. Rapports du Jury Internationale (45 vols., Paris, 1901–1903).
FARMER AND MECHANIC. (New ser., vols., I and II, New York, 1847–48.)
FAY, SAMUEL. Carpet Manufacture (Cambridge, 1866).
FEARON, HENRY BRADSHAW. Sketches of America (London, 1819).
FEDERAL REPUBLICAN AND COMMERCIAL GAZETTE (Baltimore, 1809–1814).
FELT, JOSEPH BARLOW. Annals of Salem (2d ed., Boston, 1845).
—— History of Ipswich, Essex, and Hamilton (Cambridge, 1834).
FENNER, HENRY M. History of Fall River (New York, 1906).
FERNOW, BERNHARD E. Economics of Forestry (New York, 1902).
FIELD, ARTHUR SARGENT. The Child Labor Policy of New Jersey (American Economic Association Quarterly, 3d ser. vol. XI, No. 3, Cambridge, October 1910).
FINCH, JOHN. Notes on Travel in the United States, in New Moral World (London, January to July 1844).

FINDLEY, A. I.   Review of the American Iron Trade in 1909 (Annals of the American Academy of Political and Social Science, for November 1909, Philadelphia).
FISHER, RICHARD SWAINSON.   The Progress of the United States of America from the Earliest Periods (New York, 1854).
FISHER, WILLIAM CLARK.   American Trade Regulations before 1789 (Papers, American Historical Association, vol. III, New York, 1889).
FITE, EMERSON DAVID.   Social and Industrial Conditions in the North during the Civil War (New York, 1910).
FLAX AND HEMP SPINNERS' AND GROWERS' ASSOCIATION.   Report Apr. 22, 1885 (Boston, 1885).
FLEISCHMANN, C. L.   Erwerbzweige, Fabrikwesen und Handel der Vereinigten Staaten von Nord Amerika (Stuttgart, 1852).
FLEMING, WALTER L.   Home Life in Alabama (Publications of the Southern Historical Association, 1904).
FLINT, HENRY M.   The Railroads in the United States (Philadelphia, 1868).
FLINT, JAMES.   Letters from America (Edinburgh, 1822).
FLINT, TIMOTHY.   A Condensed Geography and History of the Western States, or the Mississippi Valley (Cincinnati, 1828).
——— History and Geography of the Mississippi Valley (2 vols., Cincinnati, 2d ed., 1832).
——— Recollections of the Last Ten Years, 1815–25 (Boston, 1826).
FORCE, PETER.   Tracts and other Papers Relating Principally to the Origin, Settlement and Progress of the Colonies in North America, from the Discovery of the Country to the year 1776 (4 vols., Washington, 1836–1846).
FORD, HENRY.   My Life and Work (New York, 1923).
FOSTER, FRANK.   Engineering in the United States. (A Report to the electors to the Gartside scholarships on the results of a tour in the United States in 1904–1905. Manchester, 1906.)
FOSTER, WILLIAM E.   Stephen Hopkins, A Rhode Island Statesman (in Rhode Island Historical Tracts, 1st ser., No. 19, vol. II).
FOWLER, REV. ORIN.   History of Fall River, with Notices of Freetown and Tiverton as Published in 1841 (Fall River, 1862).
FOX, WILLIAM S.   A History of the Lumber Industry in the State of New York (U. S. Department of Agriculture, Bureau of Forestry, Bulletin 34; Washington, 1902).
FRANCIS, JAMES B.   Lowell Hydraulic Experiments (Boston, 1855).
FRANK, THEOPHIL.   Das Textilgewerbe der Stadt Freiburg im Br. bis zum Ausgang des 16 Jahrhunderts (Emmendingen, 1912).
FRANKFURTER ZEITUNG.   Das Technische Blatt (8 vols., Frankfurt-am-Main, 1919–1926).
FRANKLIN, BENJAMIN.   Works (ed., Albert Henry Smyth, 10 vols., New York, 1905–1907).
FRANKLIN INSTITUTE.   Journal (179 vols., Philadelphia, 1826–1915).
FREE TRADE AND RAW MATERIALS CONSIDERED IN ITS EFFECT UPON ALL CLASSES OF |PEOPLE. (New York, 1855.)
FREEDLEY, EDWIN T.   Philadelphia and Its Manufactures (Philadelphia, 1859).
FREEMAN, DOUGLAS SOUTHALL.   A Calendar of Confederate Papers (Richmond, Va., 1908).
FREMANTLE, LT. COL. A. T. L.   Three Months in the Southern States, April-June 1863 (Edinburgh and London, 1863).
FRENCH, B. F.   The History of the Rise and Progress of the Iron Trade of the United States, 1621–1857 (New York, 1858).
FRITZ, JOHN.   Autobiography (New York, 1912).
FULLER, GRACE PIERPONT.   An Introduction to the History of Connecticut as a Manufacturing State (Smith College Studies in History, vol. I, No. I, Northampton, 1915).
FULLER, OLIVER PAYSON.   History of the Town of Warwick (Providence, 1875).
GALLATIN, ALBERT.   Report on Internal Improvements (American State Papers, Miscellaneous, vol. I, 724).
——— Report on Manufactures (American State Papers, Finance, vol. II, 425).
GALSTER, AUGUSTA EMILE, PH.D.   The Labor Movement in the Shoe Industry (New York, 1924).
GATES, FREDERICK TAYLOR.   The Truth about Mr. Rockefeller and the Merritts (New York, 1897).
GAYARRE, CHARLES.   History of Louisiana (4 vols., New Orleans, 1903).

GEE, JOSHUA. The Trade and Navigation of Great Britain Considered (5th ed., Glasgow, 1750).
GEORGIA. Acts of Assembly, 1755–1774 (compilers, DeKenne and Jones, Wormsloe, 1881. See also Marburg and Crawford and Watkins digests).
———— Acts of the General Assembly of Georgia, 1755–1770 (printed by James Johnston, Savannah, 1763–1770).
———— Acts of the General Assembly, 1865–66 (Augusta, 1866).
———— Colonial Records of the State of Georgia, 1732–1774 (ed., Allen D. Candler, 18 vols. Atlanta, 1904–1910).
———— House Journal, Session of 1861 (Augusta, 1861).
———— House Journal, Session of 1864 (Augusta, 1864).
———— House Journal, Extra Session, 1865 (Augusta, 1865).
GEORGIA HISTORICAL SOCIETY. Collections (8 vols., Savannah, 1840–1913).
GEPHART, WILLIAM F. Transportation and Industrial Development in the Middle West (Columbia University Studies in History, Economics, and Public Law, vol. XXXIV, No. 1, New York, 1909).
GIBBINS, H. DEB. Industrial History of England (London, 1902).
———— Industry in England (New York, 1906).
GIESECKE, ALBERT ANTHONY. American Commercial Legislation before 1789 (Publications, University of Pennsylvania, Philadelphia, 1910).
GOBRIGHT, JOHN C. City Rambles, or Baltimore as it is (Baltimore, 1857).
GOODALE, STEPHEN L. (compiler) AND J. RAMSEY SPEER (ed.). Chronology of Iron and Steel (Pittsburg, 1920).
GOUGE, WILLIAM M. The Curse of Paper Money and Banking (London, 1833).
GOULDING, JOHN. Eben D. Jordan versus Agawan Woolen Company (2 vols., Boston, 1866).
GRAHAM, WILLIAM H. Statistics of the Wool Manufactures of the United States (New York, 1845).
GRANT, ULYSSES S. Personal Memoirs (2 vols., New York, 1885–1886).
GREAT BRITAIN. Acts of the Privy Council, Colonial Series (6 vols., London, 1908–1912).
———— Calendar of State Papers, Colonial Series, America and West Indies, 1574–1701 (19 vols., London, 1860–1910).
———— Committee of Lords of Privy Council. The Trade of Great Britain with the United States (January 1791; reprinted by U. S. Department of State, 1888).
———— House of Commons Journal (178 vols., London, 1742–1913).
———— House of Commons Reports from Committees, 1715–1801 (15 vols., and index, London, 1803).
———— House of Commons Reports (25 vols., London, 1801–1858).
———— Parliamentary Papers.
———— Reports on the Philadelphia International Exhibition (3 vols., London, 1877).
GREAT INDUSTRIES OF THE UNITED STATES. (Hartford, Chicago, Cincinnati, 1872.)
GREEN, JAMES. St. Louis Directory (St. Louis, 1842).
GREGG, ORMSBY. Pittsburg, Her Advantageous Position (Pittsburg, 1845).
GREGG, WILLIAM. Essays on Domestic Iudustry or an Inquiry into the Expediency of Establishing Cotton Manufactures in South Carolina (Charleston, 1845).
GREVE, C. F. Centennial History of Cincinnati (2 vols., Cincinnati, 1904).
GRIFFITH, THOMAS W. Annals of Baltimore (Baltimore, 1824).
GROSS, CHARLES. Gild Merchant (2 vols., Oxford, 1890).
HADLEY, ARTHUR T. Economic Problems of Democracy (New York, 1923).
HALL, JAMES. Letters from the West (London, 1828).
HALL, JOSEPH MARTIN. An American Industrial Center (Pittsburgh Chamber of Commerce Publications; Pittsburgh, 1891).
HAMILTON, ALEXANDER. Industrial and Commercial Correspondence (ed. Arthur Harrison Cole, Ph. D., with a preface by Prof. Edwin F. Gay; Business Historical Studies, vol. I, Chicago, 1928).
HAMILTON, DR. ALEXANDER. "Itinerarium," being a Narrative of a Journey from Annapolis, Maryland, through Delaware, Pennsylvania, New York, New Jersey, Connecticut, Rhode Island, Massachusetts, and New Hampshire from May to September 1744 (ed., Albert Bushnell Hart, St. Louis, 1907).
HAMMOND, MATTHEW BROWN. The Cotton Industry; An Essay in American Economic History (Publications American Economic Association, new ser., vol. I, New York, December 1897).

HARDIE, JAMES. Tablet of Memory, 1795 (Philadelphia, 1795).
HARGROVE, H. H., AND WILL M. STEELE. Cotton Mills and Manufactures (New Orleans, 1899).
HARKNESS, JAMES. Machine Building for Profit (Springfield, Vt., 1909).
HARPER'S WEEKLY. (62 vols., New York, 1857–1916; merged into Independent in 1916.)
HARRIS, EDWARD. Memorial of Manufactures of Woolen Goods to the Committee of Ways and Means (Washington, 1872).
HARRIS, EDWARD, AND ROWLAND HAZARD. The Tariff and how it affects the Woolen Cloth Manufacture and Wool Growers (Woonsocket, R. I., 1871).
HARRIS-GASTRELL, J. P. Report to the British Parliament on American Textile Industries (Parliamentary Papers, vol. LXVIII, 1873).
HARRISBURG CONVENTION. Proceedings of Convention, June 8, 1827 (Baltimore, 1827).
HASENCLEVER, DR. ADOLPH. Peter Hasenclever aus Remscheid-Ehringhausen (Berlin, 1922),
HASENCLEVER, PETER. The Case of Peter Hasenclever (London, 1774, in New York State Library).
HASSE, ADELAIDE R. Index of Economic Material in Documents of the States of the United States (Carnegie Inst. Wash. Pub. No. 85, 1907–1915. States thus far covered: Maine, New Hampshire, Vermont, New York, Rhode Island, Massachusetts, California, Illinois, Kentucky, Delaware, Ohio, New Jersey, Pennsylvania).
HAYES, JOHN LORD. American Textile Machinery; its Early History, Characteristics, Contributions to the Industry of the World, Relations to other Industries, and Claims for National Recognition (Cambridge, 1879).
——— The Fleece and the Loom (Boston, 1865).
——— Memorial of the Iron Manufacturers of New England, asking for a Modification of the Tariff of 1846 (Philadelphia, 1850).
——— (ed. and author). Memoirs Relating to the Wool Industry (Boston, 1872).
HAYWARD, JOHN. Prices of Forty Articles for Forty Years (Boston, 1834, in Boston Public Library).
HAZARD, BLANCHE E. Organization of the Boot and Shoe Industry in Massachusetts before 1875 (in Quarterly Journal of Economics, vol. XXVII, February 1913).
HAZARD, CAROLINE. Thomas Hazard, Son of Robert, Called College Tom (Boston, 1893).
HAZARD, SAMUEL. Register of Pennsylvania (16 vols., Philadelphia, January 1828 to December 1835).
——— United States Commercial and Statistical Register (6 vols., Philadelphia, July 1839 to June 1842).
HELD. Zur Socialen Geschichte Englands (ed., George Friedrich Knapp, Leipsig, 1881).
HENRY, J. T. The Early and Later History of Petroleum (Philadelphia, 1873).
HERKIMER COUNTY HISTORICAL ASSOCIATION. The Story of the Typewriter, 1873–1923 (Herkimer, New York, 1923).
HERR, BENJAMIN. Journal (German-American Annals, German-American Society, Publications, vol. v, January 1903).
HEUSSER, ALBERT H. (ed.). History of Silk Dyeing in America (Published by Silk Dyers' Mutual Protective Association of America, Paterson, N. J., 1927).
HEWITT, ABRAM S. Iron and Labor (in Astor Library, 1890).
——— On the Statistics and Geography of the Production of Iron (New York, 1856).
HIGGINS, SYDNEY H. Dyeing in Germany and America (Gartside Studies, Manchester University, England, 1907).
HILDRETH, SAMUEL PRESCOTT. See Ohio, First Annual Report of the Geological Survey (Columbus, 1838).
——— Original Contributions to the American Pioneer (Cincinnati, 1842).
——— Pioneer History (Cincinnati, 1848).
HILL, ISAAC [New Hampshire]. Speech in U. S. Senate on Clay's Resolution (Washington, 1832).
HILLYARD, M. B. The New South (Baltimore, 1887).
HINSDALE, BURKE AARON. The Old Northwest (New York, 1888).
HISTORICAL AND DESCRIPTIVE REVIEW OF THE INDUSTRIES OF RICHMOND. (Richmond, Va., 1884.)
HISTORY OF THE BRITISH DOMINIONS IN NORTH AMERICA, 1497–1763 (London, 1773).
HITTELL, JOHN SHERTZER. The Commerce and Industries of the Pacific Coast of North America (San Francisco, 1882).

HOFF, CURT. Die Industrieentwicklung im Bezirk Aachen. (Inaugural Dissertation, Göttingen, 1912.)
HOGAN, JOHN. Thoughts about the City of St. Louis, Her Commerce and Manufactures, Railways, etc. (St. Louis, 1854).
HOLLEY, A. L. AND LENOX SMITH. Works of the Cambria Iron Company (in Astor Library, 1878).
HOLM, THOMAS CAMPANIUS. A Short Description of the Province of New Sweden (translated by Peter S. du Ponceau, Philadelphia, 1834).
HOLMES, ABIEL. The Annals of America from the Discovery by Columbus in the year 1492 to the year 1826 (2 vols., 2d ed., Cambridge, 1829).
HOLMES, ISAAC. An Account of the United States of America, derived from Actual Observation, during a Residence of Four Years in that Republic: Including Original Communications (London, about 1823).
HOMANS, ISAAC SMITH, JR. An Historical and Statistical Account of the Foreign Commerce of the United States, 1820–1856 (New York, 1857).
HOMES, HENRY A. Notice of Peter Hasenclever, an Iron Manufacturer from 1764 to 1769 (read before the Albany Institute, Apr. 7, 1874. Albany, 1875).
HOSMER, JAMES KENDALL (ed.). Winthrop's Journal, History of New England (2 vols., New York, 1908).
HOWE, HARRISON ESTELL (ed.). Chemistry in Industry (New York, 1925).
HOWE, HENRY. Memoirs of the Most Eminent American Mechanics (New York, 1844).
HOWE, HENRY MARION. The Metallurgy of Steel (New York, 1925).
HOWELLS, WILLIAM COOPER. Recollections of Life in Ohio, from 1813 to 1840 (Cincinnati, 1895).
HULME, E. WYNDHAM. "English Glass Making in the 16th and 17th Centuries," in Antiquary, vol. xxx, 1894.
——— History of the Patent System, in Law Quarterly Review, April 1896; January 1900.
HUNGERFORD, AUSTIN N. Early Iron Furnaces and Forges in Western New Jersey. (In the American Iron and Steel Association, Bulletin xx, 257, Sept. 29, 1886.)
HUNGERFORD, EDWARD. Observations on an Outstanding American Industry (Portland Cement Association, Chicago, undated).
HUNT, GAILLARD. The Department of State of the United States (New Haven, 1914).
HUNT, JOHN WARREN. Wisconsin Gazetteer (Madison, 1853).
HUNT, THOMAS STERRY. Coal and Iron of Southern Ohio (Boston, 1881).
——— The Iron Ores of the United States (Journal Iron and Steel Institute, London, 1890).
HUNT'S MERCHANTS' MAGAZINE AND COMMERCIAL REVIEW. (eds., Freeman Hunt, 1839–1858; T. P. Kettell, 1858–1860; W. B. Dana, 1861–1870; 63 vols., New York, 1839–1870).
HUNTINGTON, REV. ELIJAH BALDWIN. History of Stamford, Connecticut, from its Settlement in 1641 to the Present Time (Stamford, 1868).
HUNZIKER, OTTO F. The Butter Industry (La Grange, 1920).
HURD, D. HAMILTON (ed.). History of Rockingham and Strafford Counties (Philadelphia, 1882).
HUSKISSON, RIGHT HONORABLE W. State of the Country (speech in the House of Commons Mar. 18, 1830. London, 1830).
HUTCHINSON, T. Papers (2 vols., in Prince Society Publications, Boston, 1865).
ILES, GEORGE. Leading American Inventors (New York, 1912).
IMPARTIAL REVIEW AND COLUMBIAN REPOSITORY. (Nashville, 1805–1808.)
INDEX, THE. (Weekly, 5 vols., London, 1862–1865.)
INDIA RUBBER WORLD. (Monthly, 68 vols., New York, 1889–1923.)
INDUSTRIAL SOUTH. (Weekly. B. F. Johnson & Co., pub., Richmond; vol. VI begins with January, 1886, at which time it was consolidated with the Virginius.)
INDUSTRY. (Organ of Associated Industries of Massachusetts, weekly, 21 vols., Boston, 1917–date.)
INGALLS, WALTER RENTON (formerly R. P. Rotherwell). The Mineral Industry, Its Statistics, Technology, and Trade (annual, 1892–date).
INQUIRY INTO THE PROPRIETY OF GRANTING CHARTERS TO THE MANUFACTURERS OF SOUTH CAROLINA. By One of the People (Charleston, 1845; Charleston College Library, Miscellaneous Pamphlets).
INSTITUTE OF AMERICAN MEAT PACKERS. The Packing Industry (Chicago, 1924).

INTEREST OF THE MERCHANTS AND MANUFACTURERS OF GREAT BRITAIN IN THE PRESENT CONTEST WITH THE COLONIES STATED AND CONSIDERED. (London, 1774.)
INTERNATIONAL CONGRESS OF APPLIED CHEMISTRY. Original Communications (26 vols., vol. XIII, Concord, N. H., 1912–1913).
IPSWICH (MASS.) MILLS. The Hosiery Industry of Ipswich, 1822–1922 (Massachusetts Historical Society).
IRON AGE. (Weekly, 120 vols., New York, 1873–1927.)
IRON AND COAL TRADE COMMITTEE, PHILADELPHIA. Letter of a Committee Appointed at a Meeting of the Iron and Coal Trade in Philadelphia to the Hon. George Evans, against the Repeal of the Duty upon Railway Iron, imposed by the Tariff Act of 1842 (Philadelphia, 1844).
IRON AND STEEL INSTITUTE OF GREAT BRITAIN. The Visit of the Iron and Steel Institute to the United States in 1890 (Journal of Iron and Steel Institute, London, 1895).
IRON TRADE REVIEW. (Weekly, 81 vols., Cleveland, 1906–date.)
IRON WORLD, THE. (Philadelphia, 1874.)
ISAACS, I. J. Industrial Advance of Rochester (Rochester, 1884).
JACOBSTEIN, MEYER. The Tobacco Industry in the United States (Columbia University Thesis, New York, 1907).
JEANS, J. S. Report on American Industrial Conditions in relation to Iron and Steel Manufactures (London, 1902).
JEFFERSON, THOMAS. Writings (ed., Andrew A. Lipscomb, 20 vols., Washington, 1904).
JENKS, JEREMIAH, AND WALTER E. CLARK. The Trust Problem (New York, 1917).
JEROME, CHAUNCEY. The History of the American Clock Business for the Past Sixty Years, and Life of Chauncey Jerome (New Haven, 1860).
JOHNSON, CAPTAIN EDWARD. Wonder-Working Providence of Sion's Savior in New England (ed., J. Franklin Jameson, New York, 1910).
JOHNSON, EMORY R., F. W. VAN METRE, G. G. HUEBNER, AND D. S. HANCHETT. History of Domestic and Foreign Commerce of the United States (Carnegie Inst. Wash. Pub. No. 215 A, 2 vols., Washington, 1915).
JOHNSON, WALTER R. Notes on the Use of Anthracite in the Manufacture of Iron (Boston, 1841, in Yale University Library).
JOHNSTON, GEORGE. History of Cecil County, Maryland (Elkton, 1881).
JOHNSTON, JAMES F. W. Notes on North America: Agricultural, Economical, and Social (2 vols., London, 1851).
JONES, CHARLES C., JR. History of Georgia (2 vols., Boston, 1883).
JONES, CHESTER LLOYD. The Economic History of the Anthracite-Tidewater Canals (Publications of the University of Pennsylvania, Philadelphia, 1908).
JONES, SAMUEL. Pittsburg in 1826 (Pittsburg, 1826).
JOURNAL OF THE FRANKLIN INSTITUTE. (179 vols., Philadelphia, 1826–1915.)
JUDD, SYLVESTER. History of Hadley, Including the Early History of Hatfield, South Hadley, Amherst, and Granby, Massachusetts (new ed., Springfield, 1905).
KALM, PETER. Travels in North America (translated by John Reinhold Forster; 2d ed., 2 vols., London, 1772).
KATAHDIN IRON WORKS. Reports (Boston, 1863; Massachusetts Historical Society).
KAYSER, I. C. & COMPANY. Commercial Directory (Philadelphia, 1823).
KEIR, MALCOLM. Manufacturing Industries in America (New York, 1923).
KELLEY, F. W. Cement is the Magic of Concrete (an address delivered at the 20th anniversary convention of the American Concrete Institute, 1924; Chicago, 1924).
KELLEY, WILLIAM D. The Old South and the New (New York and London, 1888).
KELLOGG, ROY S. Pulpwood and Wood Pulp in North America (New York, 1923).
KENDALL, EDWARD AUGUSTUS. Travels through the Northern Parts of the United States in the Years 1807 and 1808 (3 vols., New York, 1809).
KENDRICK, J. R. The Carpet Industry of Philadelphia (Pennsylvania Department of Internal Affairs, Report, 1890, Philadelphia, 1890).
KENTUCKY. Acts of the Assembly (Frankfort, 1800).
KENTUCKY BUREAU OF AGRICULTURE, HORTICULTURE AND STATISTICS. Sixth Annual Report (Louisville, 1885).
KENTUCKY GAZETTE. (Lexington, 1787–1841.)
KENTUCKY GEOLOGICAL SURVEY. Reports of Progress (2 vols., Frankfort, 1876, 1877).
KETTELL, T. P. Southern Wealth and Northern Profits (New York, 1860).

KIDDER, F. AND AUGUSTUS A. GOULD. The History of New Ipswich (Boston, 1852).
KILLEGREW, J. B. Tennessee, Its Agricultural and Mineral Wealth (Nashville, 1876).
KING, EDWARD. The Great South (Hartford, 1875).
KING, J. TRAINOR. Pittsburg, Past and Present (supplement to Pittsburg Quarterly, May 1868).
KIRK, EDWARD. The Cupola Furnace (2d ed., Philadelphia, 1903).
KITTREDGE, HENRY GOULD AND ARTHUR GOULD. History of the American Card-Clothing Industry (Worcester, Mass., 1886).
KLEIN, JOSEPH. Die Baumwollindustrie in Breuschtal (Strassburg, 1905).
KNOXVILLE GAZETTE. (Knoxville, 1791–1795.)
KOHN, AUGUST. Cotton Mills of South Carolina (News and Courier Print, Charleston, 1903).
―― The Water Powers of South Carolina (Charleston, 1907).
KRAFFT, MICHAEL. The American Distiller, or the Theory and Practice of Distilling (Philadelphia, 1804).
KUHLMANN, C. B. The Development of the Flour-Milling Industry in the United States (Boston and New York, 1928).
KURT, SORGA. Occurrences and Applications of Natural Gas at Pittsburg (translated by J. H. Stellman, 1887; original, North German Iron and Steel Association, Osnabruck, 1880).
KYRK, HAZEL, AND JOSEPH S. DAVIS. The American Baking Industry, 1849–1923. (Stanford University, 1925).
LA FOLLETTE, ROBERT MARION (ed.). The Making of America (10 vols., Philadelphia, 1905).
LAMBERT, JOHN. Travels through Canada and the United States of North America in the Years 1806, 1807, and 1808 (2 vols., London, 1813).
LAMBORN, LEEBERT LLOYD. Cottonseed Products, A Manual of the Treatment of Cottonseed for Its Products and Their Utilization in the Arts (New York, 1904).
LANCASTER COUNTY HISTORICAL SOCIETY. Publications (8 vols., Lancaster, 1897–1904).
LANDRUM, JOHN BELTON O'NEALL. History of Spartanburg County (Atlanta, 1900).
LA ROCHEFOUCAULT, LIANCOURT, FRANÇOIS ALEXANDRE FREDERIC, DUC DE. Travels through the United States of North America (2 vols., 1st ed., translated by Newman, London, 1799).
LASPEYRES, ETIENNE. Die Gruppirung der Industrie innerhalb der Nordamerikanischen Union (in Viertlejahrschrift fur Volkswirthschaft und Kulturgeschichte, vol. XXXIV, 17).
LATHROP, WILLIAM G. The Brass Industry in Connecticut. A Study of the Origin and the Development of the Brass Industry in the Naugatuck Valley (Shelton, Connecticut, 1909).
LATROBE, BENJAMIN HENRY. Journal of Benjamin Henry Latrobe (New York, 1905).
LAUER, CONRAD NEWTON. Engineering in American Industry (New York).
LAUGHLIN, G. F. Clays and Clay Industries of Connecticut (Connecticut Geological Survey, Bulletin IV, Hartford, 1902–1904).
LAWRENCE, ABBOT AND ROBERT SHAW. The Present Condition and Future Growth of Boston (Massachusetts State Library Pamphlets, 199).
LAWRENCE, W. The American Wool Interest (address before the Farmer's National Congress at Chicago, Nov. 11, 1887; Bellefontaine, Ohio, 1898).
LAWSON, W. R. American Industrial Problems (Edinburgh and London, 1903).
LE DUC, WILLIAM SALES. Genesis of the Typewriter (Minnesota Historical Society Bulletin I; St. Paul, 1916).
LEARNED, HENRY BARRETT. The President's Cabinet (New Haven, 1912).
LEE, FRANCIS BAZELY. New Jersey as Colony and State (4 vols., New York, 1902).
LEE AND SHEPARD. History of Lowell (2d rev. ed., Boston, 1868).
LEITH, CHARLES K. Economic Aspects of Geology (New York, 1921).
LEROY-BEAULIEU, PIERRE. The United States in the Twentieth Century (translated by H. Addington Bruce, New York, 1906).
LESLEY, J. P. The Iron Manufacturers' Guide (New York, 1859).
LETTER TO THE DIRECTORS OF THE NEW HAMPSHIRE IRON FACTORY. Dated London, Sept. 7, 1810 (in Boston Athenaeum Library).
LEVASSEUR, PIERRE EMILE. The American Workman (translated by T. S. Adams, Baltimore, 1900).

LEWIS, ALONZO, AND JAMES R. NEWHALL. History of Lynn, Essex County, Massachusetts, 1629–1864 (Lynn, 1890).
LEWIS, WILLIAM DRAPER. Our Sheep and the Tariff (Philadelphia, 1890).
LIBERTY HALL AND CINCINNATI GAZETTE. (Semi-weekly, 10 vols., Cincinnati, June 9, 1918, to June 22, 1827.)
LILLEY, ERNEST RAYMOND. The Oil Industry (New York, 1925).
LINGELBACH, W. E. Commercial History of the Napoleonic Era (American Historical Review, vol. XIX, January, 1914).
LIPPINCOTT, ISAAC. History of Manufactures in the Ohio Valley up to 1860 (Chicago, 1914).
LIPSON, E. The English Woolen and Worsted Industries (London, 1921).
LISBON TOWN REGISTER, 1905 (Brunswick, Me. 1905).
LLOYD, W. ALVIN. Lloyd's Southern Railway Guide (monthly, Mobile, 1863–1864).
LOGAN, GEORGE. Letter to the Citizens of Pennsylvania on the Necessity of Promoting Agriculture, Manufactures and the Useful Arts (Philadelphia, 1800).
LORD, ELEANOR LOUISA. Industrial Experiments in the British Colonies of North America (Johns Hopkins University, Studies in Historical and Political Science, extra vol. XVII, Baltimore, 1898).
LOSSING, BENSON JOHN. History of American Industries and Arts (Philadelphia, 1878).
—— The Pictorial Field Book of the Revolution (2 vols., New York, 1860).
LOUISIANA PLANTER AND SUGAR MANUFACTURER. (53 vols., New Orleans, 1888–1914.)
LYON, IRVING WHITALL. The Colonial Furniture of New England (Boston, New York, 1891).
MACBETH-EVANS GLASS COMPANY. Fifty Years of Glass Making, 1869–1919 (Pittsburgh, 1921).
MACFARLANE, JOHN J. Manufacturing in Philadelphia, 1863–1912 (published by Philadelphia Commercial Museum, 1912).
MACGREGOR, JOHN. Commercial Statistics (5 vols., London, 1844–1850).
MACPHERSON, DAVID. Annals of Commerce, Manufactures, Fisheries, and Navigation (4 vols., London and Edinburgh, 1805).
MADDOCK, THOMAS, AND SONS. Pottery, a History of the Industry and its Evolution as Applied to Sanitation (Trenton, 1910).
MAINE. Journal of the House of Representatives, 1877 (Augusta, 1877).
—— Industrial Statistics of (Kennebec, 1886).
—— Journal of the Senate, 1885 (Augusta, 1885).
—— State Board of Agriculture, 44th annual report for 1900 (Augusta, 1901).
MANCHESTER, H. H. The Story of Silk and Cheney Silks (Manchester, Conn., 1916).
MANTOUX, PAUL. La Revolution Industrielle au XVIII Siecle (Paris, 1906).
MANUFACTURERS' RECORD. (Weekly, 104 vols., Baltimore, 1882–1928.)
—— Thirty Years of Southern Upbuilding (Baltimore, 1912).
—— Blue Book of Southern Progress, 1925 (annual, Baltimore, 1925).
MARBURG, HORATIO, AND WILLIAM H. CRAWFORD. Digest of the Laws of Georgia (Savannah, 1802).
MARSHALL, LEON CARROLL. Reading in Industrial Society (Chicago, 1918).
MARTIN, JOSEPH G. History of the Boston Stock Markets, One Hundred Years (Boston, 1898).
MARYLAND. Abridgment and Collection of Acts of the Assembly of Maryland (ed., James Bisset, Philadelphia, 1759).
—— Acts of Assembly, 1692–1715 (London, 1732).
—— Acts of Assembly (July sess., 1740, Annapolis, 1740).
—— Archives (34 vols., ed., W. H. Browne, Baltimore, 1883–1914).
—— Calvert Papers (Fund Publication No. 34, selections from correspondence; Baltimore, 1894).
—— Laws, 1637–1763 (ed., Thomas Bacon, Annapolis, 1765).
—— Laws of the Province of Maryland, 1692, 1718 (publisher, Andrew Bradford, Philadelphia, 1718).
—— Laws (ed., Alexander C. Hanson, Annapolis, 1787).
—— Laws (ed., William Kilty, 2 vols., Annapolis, 1789).
MARYLAND GAZETTE. (Weekly, Jan. 17, 1745–1832.)
MARYLAND HERALD AND EAST SHORE INTELLIGENCE. (Weekly, Easton, 1790–1795.)
MARYLAND JOURNAL AND BALTIMORE ADVERTISER. (Weekly, semi-weekly, triweekly, Baltimore, Aug. 20, 1773–1797.)
MASON, FRANK R. The American Silk Industry and the Tariff (Cambridge, Mass., 1910).

MASSACHUSETTS (Massachusetts Bay). Acts and Laws (Boston, 1742).
—— Acts and Laws (and Revolves) of the Commonwealth of Masachusetts, 1780–1805 (13 vols., Boston, 1890–1898).
—— Acts and Resolves of the Province of Massachusetts Bay, 1692–1780 (18 vols., Boston, 1869–1912).
—— Annual Report of the Bank Commissioners (Boston, 1860, 1863).
—— Annual Report of the Railroad Commissioners (Boston, 1873).
—— Annual Reports of the Bureau of Statistics, Statistics of Manufactures (Boston 1886–1921).
—— Colonial Laws (ed., William H. Whitmore, reprinted from edition of 1672, with supplements through 1686; 2d ed., Boston, 1889).
—— General Laws (ed., Theron Metcalf, 2 vols., Boston, 1823).
—— Laws of the Commonwealth of Massachusetts (Boston, 1836).
—— Records of the Governor and Company of the Massachusetts Bay in New England, 1628–1686 (ed., N. B. Shurtleff, 5 vols. in 6, Boston, 1853–1854).
—— Railroad Commissioner's Report on the subject of Steel Rails (Mass. Sen. Doc. No. 47, Boston, 1870).
—— Report of the Committee on Hours of Labor (House Doc. No. 50, session of 1845).
—— Sanitary Commission Report, 1850 (Boston, 1850).
—— Special Laws (3 vols., Boston, 1805).
—— Statistical Tables of Industry, 1837 (ed., John P. Bigelow, Boston, 1838).
—— Statistics of the Condition and Products of Certain Branches of Industry in Massachusetts for the year ending April 1, 1845 (ed., John G. Palfry; in Documents Prepared and Submitted to the General Court, Boston, 1846).
MASSACHUSETTS AGRICULTURAL REPOSITORY AND JOURNAL. (3 vols., Boston, 1813–1815.)
MASSACHUSETTS BUREAU OF LABOR. Art in Industry (17th annual report, Boston, 1886).
MASSACHUSETTS CENTINEL. (Semi-weekly, 7 vols., Boston, Mar. 24, 1784, to June 12, 1790).
MASSACHUSETTS GAZETTE. (4 vols. Boston, 1785–1788.)
MASSACHUSETTS HISTORICAL SOCIETY. Collections (7th ser., 66 vols., Boston, 1794–1907).
—— Proceedings (48 vols., Boston, 1879–1915).
MASSACHUSETTS MAGAZINE OR MONTHLY MUSEUM OF KNOWLEDGE AND RATIONAL ENTERTAINMENT. (6 vols., Boston, 1789–1795.)
MATTHEWS, ALFRED, AND OTHERS. History of Butler County, Pennsylvania (Chicago, 1883).
MAXWELL, SYDNEY D. Manufacturers of Cincinnati (Cincinnati, 1866).
MCCAMANT, JOEL B. Report of the Bureau of Industrial Statistics of Pennsylvania (Harrisburg, 1884).
MCCLURE, A. K. The South—Its Industrial, Financial and Political Conditions (Philadelphia, 1886).
MCCRADY, EDWARD. History of South Carolina under the Proprietary Government, 1670–1719 (New York, 1897).
—— History of South Carolina under the Royal Government, 1719–1776 (New York, 1899).
—— History of South Carolina in the Revolution, 1775–1780 (New York, 1901).
MCCULLOCH, JOHN RAMSAY. A Dictionary, Practical, Theoretical, and Historical, of Commerce and Commercial Navigation (ed., Henry Vethake, 2 vols., Philadelphia, 1851).
MCKINNEY, J. P. Commerce and Manufactures of Cleveland (Cleveland, 1884).
MCLANE, LOUIS (Secretary of the Treasury). Report on Manufactures (2 vols., Washington, 1833; House Doc. No. 308, 22d Cong., 1st. sess.).
MCLAREN, W. S. B. Spinning Woolen and Worsted (New York, 1884).
MCMASTER, JOHN BACH. A History of the People of the United States (8 vols., New York, 1914).
MCMURTRIE, HENRY. Sketches of Louisville (Louisville, 1819).
MEASE, JAMES. The Picture of Philadelphia, an Account of its Origin, Increase and Improvements in Arts, Sciences, Manufactures, Commerce, and Revenue (Philadelphia, 1811).
MECHANICS MAGAZINE. (97 vols., London, 1823–1873.)
MEIN, JOHN. A State of Importations from Great Britain into the Port of Boston from the Beginning of January, 1770 (to June 30, 1770) (Boston, 1770).
MELISH, JOHN. Travels through the United States of America in the Years 1806, 1807, and 1809, 1810, and 1811 (2 vols., Philadelphia, 1815).

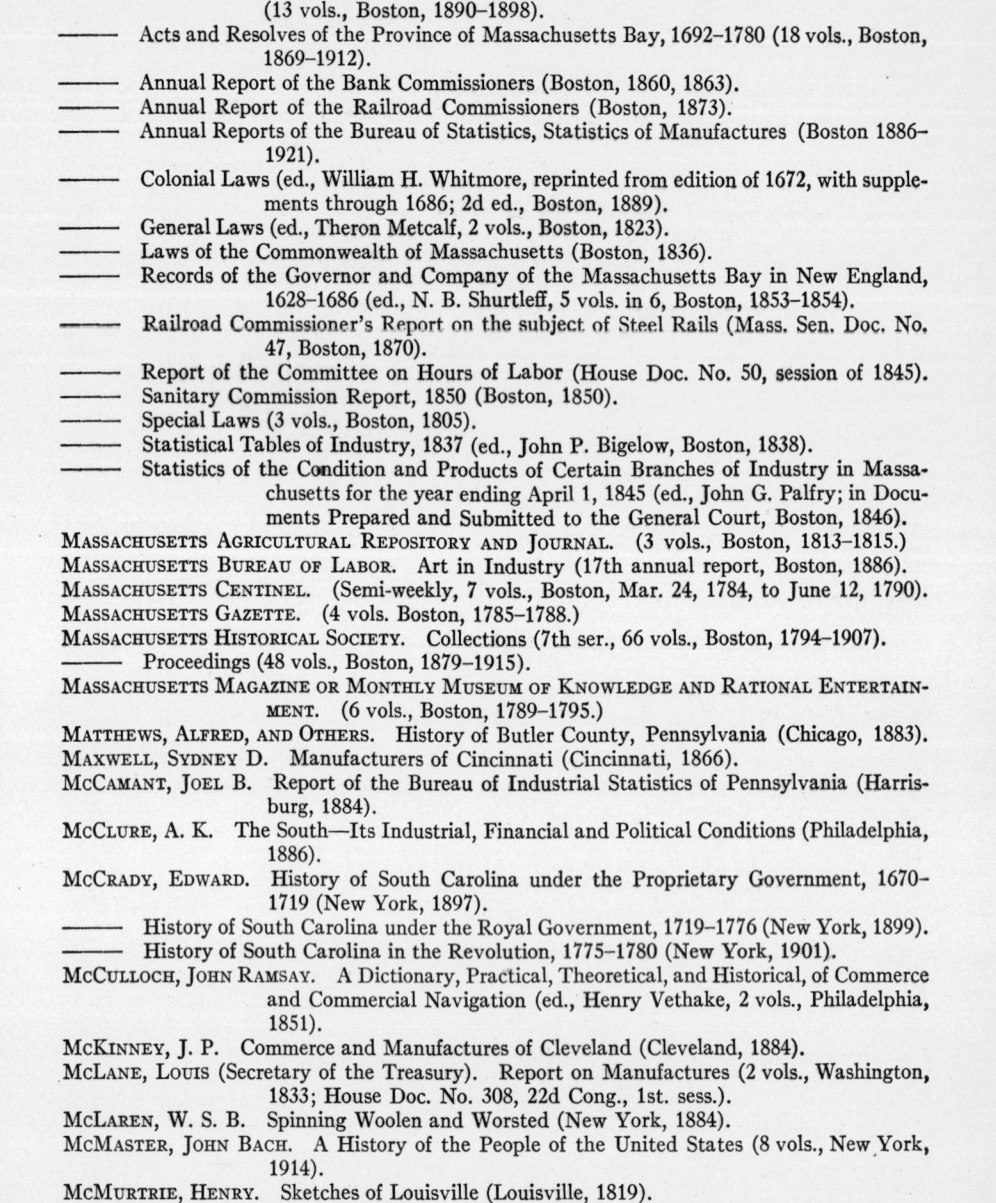

MEMPHIS MERCHANT'S EXCHANGE. Annual Statement of Trade and Commerce (Memphis, 1883–1888).
MERCHANTS' MAGAZINE AND COMMERCIAL REVIEW. (See Hunt's Merchants' Magazine.)
MESERVE, H. C. Lowell, an Industrial Dream Come True (Boston, 1923).
METALLURGICAL REVIEW. (2 vols., New York, 1877.)
METAL WORKER, PLUMBER AND STEAM FITTER. (Weekly, 94 vols., New York, 1875.)
METEYARD, ELIZA. Life of Josiah Wedgwood (2 vols., London, 1865–1866).
METROPOLITAN LIFE INSURANCE COMPANY. Research Reports (prepared for the Research Committee of the New England Council, New York—undated).
MICHAUX, F. A. Travels to the Westward of the Alleghany Mountains (translated by B. Lambert, London, 1805).
―――― Commissioner of Mineral Statistics, Mines and Mineral Statistics (Lansing, 1883–1905).
MICHIGAN. Report of the Committee on Agriculture and Manufactures (House Doc. No. 1, sess. 1844).
―――― Report of the Committee on State Affairs (Sen. Doc. No. 12, sess. 1845).
―――― State Geological Survey Report (Lansing, 1901).
―――― Commissioner of Mineral Statistics. Mines and Mineral Statistics (Lansing, 1883–1905).
―――― State Geological Survey. Report (Lansing, 1901)
MILES, HENRY ADOLPHUS. Lowell as It was and as It is (Lowell, 1845).
MILLER, ANDREW. New States and Territories on the Ohio, Indiana, Illinois, Michigan, North-. west, Missouri, Mississippi, and Alabama, in their Real Characters (1819).
MILLS, ROBERT. Statistics of South Carolina (Charleston, 1826).
MILWAUKEE SENTINEL. (Daily, 1837—.)
MINERAL INDUSTRY. (Annual, New York, 1892—).
MINNEAPOLIS CHAMBER OF COMMERCE. Historical Sketch of Milling (Minneapolis, 1903).
MISSISSIPPI VALLEY HISTORICAL REVIEW. (Quarterly, 14 vols., Cedar Rapids, Iowa, 1914—date.)
MISSOURI REPUBLICAN. Annual Reviews of the Trade and Commerce of St. Louis, 1850, 1854.
MITCHELL, BROADUS. The Rise of Cotton Mills in the South (Johns Hopkins University Studies, Baltimore, 1921).
MITCHELL, DR. JOHN. The Present State of Great Britain and North America with regard to Agriculture, Population, Trade, and Manufactures (London, 1767).
MITCHELL, JOHN L. Tennessee Gazetteer and Business Directory (Nashville, 1860).
MITCHELL, SAMUEL AUGUSTUS. Illinois in 1837 (Philadelphia, 1837).
―――― Compendium of all the Internal Improvements of the United States (Philadelphia, 1835).
MITCHELL, WESLEY CLAIR. Business Cycles (Berkeley, Calif., 1913).
―――― Gold Prices and Wages under the Greenback Standard (Berkeley, 1908).
―――― A History of the Greenbacks (Chicago, 1903).
MONTGOMERY, JAMES. A Practical Detail of the Cotton Manufacture of the United States of America and the State of the Cotton Manufacture of that Country contrasted and compared with that of Great Britain (Glasgow, 1840).
MONTGOMERY, MORTON L. History of Reading, Pennsylvania (Reading, 1898).
MOODY'S MANUAL OF INDUSTRIAL AND MISCELLANEOUS SECURITIES. (New York, 1920, 1927.)
MOONEY, THOMAS. Nine Years in America (2d ed., Dublin, 1850).
MOORE, BRENT. Study of the Hemp Industry of Kentucky (Columbia University thesis, Lexington, 1905; in Harvard University Library).
MOORE, JOSEPH ROSWELL HAWLEY. An Industrial History of the American People (New York, 1913).
MORDECAI, SAMUEL. Richmond in By-gone Days (Richmond, 1856).
MORRISON, JOHN H. History of New York Shipyards (New York, 1909).
MORSE, JEDIDIAH. The American Universal Geography: or a View of Present State of all the Kingdoms, States, and Colonies in the Known World (2 vols., Elizabethtown, 1789; Boston, 1805, 1812).
MUNSELL, JOEL. Annals of Albany (10 vols., Albany, 1850–1859).
MURRAY, HUGH. The United States of America (Edinburg, 1844).
MUSSEY, HENRY RAYMOND. Combination in the Mining Industry (Columbia University Studies in History, Economics, and Public Law; New York, 1905).

NASHVILLE UNION. (Weekly, 1836–1845.)
NATIONAL ASSOCIATION OF BAR IRON MANUFACTURERS. Statistical Report of the National Association of Iron Manufacturers for 1872 (Thomas Dunlap, secretary; Philadelphia, 1873).
NATIONAL ASSOCIATION OF COTTON MANUFACTURERS AND PLANTERS. Proceedings of First Annual Meeting, June 30, 1869 (Boston, 1869).
NATIONAL ASSOCIATION OF COTTON MANUFACTURERS (formerly New England Cotton Manufacturers' Association). Transactions (123 vols., Boston, 1868–1927).
——— Year Book. (Annual, 1918–1927.)
NATIONAL ASSOCIATION OF MANUFACTURERS. Proceedings, Cleveland Meeting, Dec. 18, 19, 1867 (Cleveland, 1867).
NATIONAL ASSOCIATION OF WOOL MANUFACTURERS. Bulletin (57 vols., Boston, 1869–1927).
——— Report of the Proceedings of the Convention of Delegates and from the Several Organizations of the Wool Growers of the United States at Syracuse, New York, December 13, 1865 (Boston, 1866).
——— Report of the Second Joint Convention of the National Association of Wool Growers and Wool Manufacturers of the United States, at Syracuse, New York, December 20, 1871 (Cambridge, 1872).
——— Statement of facts relative to Canada Wools and the Manufactures of Worsted (Boston, 1866).
——— Transactions, 1865–1866 (Boston, 1866).
——— The Woolen Tariff Defended and Explained (Cambridge, 1886).
NATIONAL ASSOCIATION OF WOOL MANUFACTURERS AND NATIONAL ASSOCIATION OF WOOL GROWERS. Joint Report of the Executive Committee (addressed to the United States Revenue Commission, Feb. 9, 1866; Boston, 1866).
NATIONAL KNIT-GOODS MANUFACTURERS ASSOCIATION. Springfield, Massachusetts, Convention, May 2, 1866 (Albany, 1866).
NATIONAL MAGAZINE AND INDUSTRIAL RECORD. (3 vols., ed., Redwood Fisher, New York, June 1845–November 1846.)
NELSON, WILLIAM. Josiah Hornblower and the First Steam Engine in America (Newark, 1883).
NEW ENGLAND COTTON MANUFACTURERS' ASSOCIATION. (See National Association of Cotton Manufacturers.)
——— Statistics of Cotton Manufacture in New England, 1866 (Boston, 1866).
NEW ENGLAND HISTORICAL AND GENEALOGICAL REGISTER. (67 vols., Boston, 1847–1913.)
NEW ENGLAND MANUFACTURES CONVENTION. Proceedings, Worcester Meeting, January 22, 1868 (Boston, 1868).
THE NEW ENGLAND STATES, THEIR CONSTITUTIONAL, JUDICIAL, EDUCATIONAL, COMMERCIAL, AND INDUSTRIAL HISTORY. (ed., William T. Davis, Boston, 1897.)
NEW HAMPSHIRE. Acts and Laws, 1696–1725 (Boston, 1726).
——— Laws (ed., Albert S. Batcheller, Manchester, 1904).
——— Perpetual Laws, 1776–1789 (Portsmouth, 1789).
——— Provincial Papers, Documents, and Records relating to the Province of New Hampshire, from 1692 to 1722 (ed., Nathaniel Bouton, Manchester, 1869).
NEW HAVEN. Records of the Colony or Jurisdiction of New Haven, from May 1653 to the Union (ed., Charles J. Hoadly, 2 vols, Hartford, 1858).
NEW JERSEY. Acts of the General Assembly of the Province (ed., Samuel Allison, Burlington, 1776).
——— Acts of the General Assembly of the Province (ed., Samuel Nevill, Philadelphia, 1752).
——— Acts of the General Assembly (ed., Peter Wilson, Trenton, 1784).
——— Archives 1st ser., 28 vols., Newark, 1881–Trenton, 1893; 2d ser., 4 vols., Trenton, 1901–1914).
——— Grants, Concessions, and Original Constitutions of the Province of New Jersey, and Acts Passed under the Proprietary Governments (eds., Aaron Leaming and Jacob Spicer, Philadelphia, 1664–1702).
——— Laws (ed., William Patterson, New Brunswick, 1800).
——— Public Laws.
NEW JERSEY GAZETTE. (Weekly, Burlington, Dec. 5, 1777; Trenton, Mar. 4, 1778–Jan. 21, 1800.)
NEW JERSEY HISTORICAL SOCIETY. Proceedings (1st ser., 10 vols., Newark, 1847–1867; 2d ser. 13 vols., Newark 1869. . . Trenton, 1899).

Bibliography

NEW JERSEY JOURNAL OR GENERAL ADVERTISER AND POLITICAL INTELLIGENCER. (1 vol., Jan. 14, 1789–Dec. 25, 1793; in Library of Congress.)
NEW ORLEANS PRICE-CURRENT AND COMMERCIAL INTELLIGENCER. (Weekly, Sept. 13, 1823; semi-weekly Jan. 2, 1858–Jan. 10, 1883).
NEW YORK (New Netherlands). (Assembly Journal, 1825, 1833).
—— Colonial Laws from the year 1664 to the Revolution (5 vols., Albany, 1896).
—— Documents Relating to the Colonial History of the State of New York. See O'Callaghan.
—— Laws and Ordinances of New Netherlands, 1638–1674. See O'Callaghan.
—— Laws of the State of New York (2 vols., Albany, 1886).
—— Laws of the State of New York in relation to the Erie and Champlain Canals, together with the Annual Reports of the Canal Commissioners (2 vols., Albany, 1825).
—— Railroad Commissioner's Annual Reports.
—— Revised Laws of the State of New York (eds., William Van Ness and John Woodworth, Albany, 1813).
—— Senate Journal, 1811, 1836.
—— State Engineer's Annual Report, 1855.
NEW YORK CONVENTION OF FRIENDS OF DOMESTIC INDUSTRY, 1831. Journal (Baltimore, 1835).
NEW YORK EVENING POST. (Daily, Nov. 16, 1801–.)
NEW YORK GAZETTE. (Weekly, Feb. 17, 1759–December 1767.)
NEW YORK GAZETTE AND WEEKLY MERCURY. (Feb. 1, 1768–November 1783.)
NEW YORK GAZETTE OR WEEKLY POST-BOY. (1746–1773.)
NEW YORK JOURNAL OR GENERAL ADVERTISER. (Weekly, New York, May 29, 1766; Kingston, 1777; Poughkeepsie, 1778–79.)
NEW YORK MERCURY. (Weekly, 1752–Jan. 25, 1768.)
NEW YORK SHIPPING AND COMMERCIAL LIST AND NEW YORK PRICE CURRENT. (Semi-weekly 73 vols., 1815–1897.)
NEW YORK TRIBUNE. (Daily, 1841—.)
NEW YORK WEEKLY POST-BOY. (1743–1746.)
NEWCOMER, MABEL. The Chemical Industry of New York and Its Environs. (Plan of New York and its environs; Economic Ser., Monograph No. I; New York, 1924.)
NILES' WEEKLY REGISTER. (eds., Hezekiah Niles, 1811–1826; Niles and Son, 1826–1830; H. Niles, 1830–1836; William Ogden Niles, 1836–1839; Jeremiah Hughes, 1839–1848; George Beatty, 1849; 75 vols., Baltimore, 1816; Philadelphia, 1849.)
NORCROSS, F. W. Wholesale Shoe Trade, 1629–1892 (Industrial History of Suffolk County, Boston, 1894.)
NORFOLK COUNTY, VIRGINIA (Lower). Records for the 17th Century (original volumes at Portsmouth, Virginia).
NORRIS LOCOMOTIVE WORKS. Circular and Testimonials (Jan. 1, 1841, in Pennsylvania Historical Society Library).
NORTH, S. N. D. Account of the History of the Woolen Industry in the United States (introduction to Eleventh Census Report on that Industry, Washington, 1897).
—— A Century of American Wool Manufacture (Boston, 1895; from National Association of Wool Manufactures, Bulletin, September 1894).
—— The New England Wool Manufacture (in Bulletin of the National Association of Wool Manufacturers, vol. XXIX, 1899–vol. XXXIII, 1903).
—— The Revision of the Wool and Woolen Schedule (statement before the Committee on Ways and Means, Jan. 7, 1897; Boston, 1897).
—— AND RALPH H. Simeon North, First Official Pistol Maker of the United States (Concord, N. H., 1913).
NORTH AMERICAN REVIEW. (Monthly, 229 vols., Boston, 1815–1877; New York, 1878–1927.)
NORTH CAROLINA. Acts of the Assembly (ed., James Davis, Newbern, 1773).
—— Acts of the Assembly (ed., James Iredell, Edenton, 1791).
—— Acts of the Assembly (ed., Samuel Swann, Newbern, 1752).
—— Report on the Subject of Cotton and Wool Manufactures and the Growing of Wool in North Carolina, by a Committee of the Legislature (Raleigh; reprinted in Philadelphia, 1828. Pamphlet in Boston Athenaeum Library).

NORTHWESTERN LUMBERMAN. (Chicago, 1887—.)
OBERHOLTZER, ELLIS PAXON. Philadelphia—A History of the City and Its People (4 vols., Philadelphia, 1912).
O'CALLAGHAN, E. B. Documentary History of the State of New York (4 vols., quarto, Albany, 1850–1851).
—— Documents Relative to the Colonial History of the State of New York (last three volumes ed. Berthold Fernow, 15 vols., quarto, Albany, 1856–1887).
—— Laws and Ordinances of New Netherlands, 1638–1674 (Albany, 1868).
ODEN, CHARLES VOLNEY. Evolution of the Typewriter (New York, 1917).
OHIO. First Annual Report of the Geological Survey (Columbus, 1838).
—— Report of the Geological Survey, Petroleum and Natural Gas (4th ser., No. 1, Columbus, 1903).
OHIO WOOL-GROWERS' ASSOCIATION. Address delivered by David Harpster, President, and The Report of the Proceedings of the Conference of a Committee of Wool-growers, etc., held at Washington, D. C., Jan. 11, 12, 13, and 14, 1888 (Columbus, Ohio, 1888).
—— 30th Annual Convention, President's Address and Proceedings, Jan. 12, 1893 (Columbus, Ohio, 1893).
OLDE ULSTER. (ed., Benjamin Myer Brink, 19 vols., Kingston, 1905–1914.)
OLMSTEAD, FREDERICK LAW. A Journey in the Back Country (New York, 1860).
—— A Journey in the Seaboard Slave States (New York, 1856).
ORTON, EDWIN. Progress of Ceramic Industry (University of Wisconsin Engineering Series, Madison, 1903).
OVERMAN, FREDERICK. The Manufacture of Iron in all Its Different Branches (2d ed., Philadelphia, 1851).
PAGE, THOMAS WALKER. Making the Tariff in the United States (New York, 1924).
PAGE, WILLIAM P. Report to the Stockholders of the New Hampshire Iron Company (Salem, 1816, Boston Public Library).
PALFREY, JOHN FORHAM. A Compendious History of New England from the Discovery by Europeans to the First General Congress of the Anglo-American Colonies (5 vols., Boston, 1858–1890).
PAPER AND PAPER MAKING. (Albany, 1876; Virginia State Library, Binder 37).
PARKER, E. W. Concentration in Pig Iron and Coal Production (American Statistical Association, Boston).
PARKER, JUDGE EDWARD E. (ed.). History of Nashua, New Hampshire (Nashua, 1897).
PARTON, JAMES. Captains of Industry (Boston, 1891).
PATTEE, WILLIAM SAMUEL. A History of Old Braintree and Quincy, Massachusetts (Quincy, 1878).
PEARSE, J. B. A Concise History of the Iron Manufacture of the American Colonies up to the Revolution, and of Pennsylvania until the Present Time (Philadelphia, 1876).
PEARSON, JOHN. Notes made during a Journey in 1821, in the United States of America, from Philadelphia to the Neighbourhood of Lake Erie; through Lancaster, Harrisburg, Carlisle, and Pittsburgh and back to Philadelphia (London, 1822).
PEASE, JOHN C., AND JOHN M. NILES. A Gazetteer of the States of Connecticut and Rhode Island (Hartford, 1819).
PECK, FREDERICK M., AND HENRY EARL. Fall River and Its Industries (Fall River, Mass., 1877).
PENNSYLVANIA. Archives. (6th ser., 96 vols., Philadelphia, 1852–1907).
PENNSYLVANIA. Session Laws.
—— Statutes at Large, 1682–1801 (eds., James T. Mitchell and Herny Flanders; 16 vols., Harrisburg, 1896).
PENNSYLVANIA DEPARTMENT OF INTERNAL AFFAIRS. The Manufacture of Coke (Annual Report, Harrisburg, 1893).
PENNSYLVANIA GAZETTE. (Philadelphia, 1735–1799.)
PENNSYLVANIA GEOLOGICAL SURVEY. Annual Reports.
PENNSYLVANIA GERMAN SOCIETY. Proceedings (21 vols., Lancaster, 1891–1910).
PENNSYLVANIA HISTORICAL SOCIETY. Memoirs (14 vols., Philadelphia, 1826–1895).

PENNSYLVANIA JOURNAL. (Philadelphia, 1775–1789.)
PENNSYLVANIA JOURNAL OF THE WEEKLY ADVERTISER. (Dec. 1742–1797.)
PENNSYLVANIA MAGAZINE OF HISTORY AND BIOGRAPHY. (27 vols., Philadelphia, 1877–1904.)
PENNSYLVANIA MAGAZINE OR AMERICAN MONTHLY MUSEUM. (Vols. 1 and 2, Philadelphia, 1775–1776.)
PENNSYLVANIA PACKET AND GENERAL ADVERTISER. (Weekly and semi-weekly, Oct. 28, 1771. Jan. 1, 1791.)
PERKINS, DAVID L. Reminiscences of Manchester (Manchester Historical Association Collections, vol. I, Part I, article 1, 1896).
PERRIGO, OSCAR F. Modern American Lathe Practice (New York, 1907).
PERU IRON WORKS. Prospectus of the Peru Magnetic Steel-Iron Works in Clinton and Essex Counties, New York (New York, 1865, in New York Public Library).
PERU MAGNETIC STEEL AND IRON WORKS. Clinton and Essex Counties (in Astor Library, New York, 1865).
PETO, SIR S. MARTIN. The Resources and Prospects of America (London and New York, 1866).
PHENIS, ALBERT. Yankee Thrift (Baltimore, 1905).
PHILADELPHIA SOCIETY FOR PROMOTION OF NATIONAL INDUSTRY. Addresses (Philadelphia, 1819).
PHILLIPS, HENRY JR. Historical Sketches of the Paper Currency of the American Colonies (2 vols., Roxbury, Mass., 1865–1866).
PHILLIPS, JOHN BURTON. Freight Rates and Manufactures in Colorado (University of Colorado Studies, Boulder, 1909).
PHILLIPS, WILLIAM B. Iron Making in Alabama (3d ed., Geological Survey of Alabama, University of Alabama, Tuscaloosa, 1912).
PITKIN, TIMOTHY. A Statistical View of the Commerce of the United States of America: including also an Account of Banks, Manufactures, and Internal Trade and Improvements (New Haven, 1835).
PITTSBURGH CHAMBER OF COMMERCE. Pittsburgh the Powerful (ed., Edward White, Pittsburgh, 1907).
PITTSBURGH GAZETTE. (Pittsburgh, 1799–1828.)
PITTSBURGH INDUSTRIAL DEVELOPMENT COMMISSION. Annual Reports (2 vols., Pittsburgh, 1911–1912, 1912–1913).
PITTSBURGH, ITS COMMERCE AND INDUSTRIES. (Pittsburgh, 1870.)
PLATT, EDMUND. Eagle History of Poughkeepsie (Poughkeepsie, 1905).
PLYMOUTH. Compact, Charter, and Laws of New Plymouth (ed., William Brigham, Boston, 1836).
PLYMOUTH CORDAGE COMPANY. 75th Anniversary, October 7, 1899 (Cambridge, 1900).
POOR, HENRY V. Manual of the Railroads of the United States, 1868–1869 (New York, 1869).
POPE, JESSE ELIPHALET. The Clothing Industry in New York (Columbia University Studies New York, 1905).
POPPLEWELL, FRANK. Some Modern Conditions and Recent Developments in the Iron and Steel Production in America (Gartside Studies, Manchester, University, Manchester, England, 1906).
POPULAR SCIENCE MONTHLY. (Monthy, 87 vols., New York, 1872–1915; continued as The Scientific Monthly, 19 vols., New York, 1915–1924.)
PORTER, CHARLES T. Engineering Reminiscences (New York, 1908).
PORTER, G. R. The Progress of the Nation (London, 1851).
POTTER, ELISHA REYNOLDS, AND SIDNEY S. RIDER. Some Account of the Bills of Credit or Paper Money of Rhode Island from the First Issue in 1710 to the Final Issue, 1786 (Rhode Island Historical Tracts, 1st ser., No. 8, Providence 1880).
POUND, ARTHUR. The Iron Man in Industry (Boston, 1922).
POWNALL, THOMAS. A Translation of the Memorial to the Sovereigns of Europe upon the Present State of Affairs between the Old and the New World (London, 1781; Massachusetts Historical Society Pamphlets).
PRINCE SOCIETY. Publications (33 vols., Boston, 1865–1911).
PRING, JOHN NORMAN. Some Electro-chemical Centers (Manchester, England, 1908).
PROVIDENCE. Census of the City of Providence, July, 1855 (eds., M. D. and Edwin M. Snow; City Document No. 6, Providence, 1856).

PROVIDENCE DAILY JOURNAL. (1829—.)
PROVIDENCE GAZETTE. (Providence, 1775–1825.)
PULLMAN, J. WESLEY. Paper on Behalf of the New Jersey Iron Ore Producer before the Tariff Commission of 1882 (Philadelphia, 1882).
QUARTERLY JOURNAL OF ECONOMICS. (Quarterly, 40 vols., Boston, 1886–1926.)
RAILROAD GAZETTE. (Titles varies slightly, being finally changed to Railway Age Gazette in 1917, weekly, 63 vols., New York, 1889–.)
RAINS, COL. GEORGE W. History of the Confederate Powder Works (address delivered before the Confederate Survivors' Association, Apr. 26, 1882; Augusta, Ga., 1882).
RAMSAY, DAVID. History of South Carolina (2 vols., Charleston, 1809).
RAMSDALL, CHARLES W. The Control of Manufacturing by the Confederate Government (in Mississippi Valley Historical Review, vol. VIII, No. 3, Cedar Rapids, Iowa, 1921).
RANDALL, HENRY STEPHENS. Sheep Husbandry (New York, 1859).
RANDOLPH, EDWARD. Documents and Letters (Prince Society Publications, vol. XXVIII; in State Papers, Board of Trade, New England, vol. v, 148).
RANKIN, CHRISTOPHER [Mississippi]. Speech on the Tariff Bill (delivered in the House of Representatives, Apr. 1 and 2, 1824; Washington, 1824).
RAUM, JOHN O. History of the City of Trenton, New Jersey (Trenton, 1875).
RAYMOND, R. W. American Iron Masters' Work (Boston, 1874).
RAYON JOURNAL. (3 vols., New York, 1927–1928.)
REBELLION RECORDS. (See United States.)
REED, NEWTON. Early History of Amenia (Amenia, 1875).
REID, WHITELAW. After the War—A Southern Tour, May 1, 1865 to May 1, 1866 (Cincinnati and New York, 1866).
REITELL, CHARLES. Machinery and Its Benefits to Labor in the Crude Iron and Steel Industries (University of Pennsylvania, thesis, Menasha, Wis., 1917).
REPORT ON THE AFFAIRS OF THE FRANKLIN COMPANY OF LEWISTON, MAINE. (1879, in Harvard University Library.)
REUSS, F. W. Calculations and Statements Relative to the Trade between Great Britain and the United States of America (London, 1833).
RHODE ISLAND. Acts and Laws (Newport, 1730, 1744, 1767; also session laws for years quoted).
——— Acts, Resolves and Reports passed by the General Assembly of the State of Rhode Island and Providence Plantations at the January Session, 1898 (Providence, 1898).
——— Public Laws (Providence, 1798).
——— Records of the Colony of Rhode Island and Providence Plantations in New England (ed., John Russell Bartlett, 10 vols, Providence, 1856–1865).
RHODE ISLAND HISTORICAL MAGAZINE. (Formerly the Newport Historical Magazine; 7 vols., Newport, 1880–1887.)
RHODE ISLAND HISTORICAL TRACTS. (1st ser., 19 vols., 2d ser., 5 vols., Providence, 1877–1896.)
RHODE ISLAND SOCIETY FOR ENCOURAGEMENT OF DOMESTIC INDUSTRY. (Transactions 21 vols., Providence, 1851–1875.)
RICE, DAVID HALL. Protection of Wool and the Protective Policy in General (speech before Commercial Club at Providence, Feb. 15, 1890; with addenda setting forth opinions of experts as to whether or not the United States can produce the wools required by our manufacturers; Boston, 1890).
RICHARDS, J. Treatise on the Construction and Operation of Woodworking Machines (London and New York, 1872).
RICHARDSON, IRVING BERDINE. Rhode Island, a Study in Separatism (Boston and New York, 1905).
RICHMOND, HER COMMERCIAL AND MANUFACTURING ADVANTAGES. (Richmond, 1884.)
RIES, HEINRICH. Clay Industries of New York (New York Museum of Natural History, Bulletin III, 12; Albany, 1895).
——— Clays of Wisconsin and Their Uses (Wisconsin Geological Survey, Bulletin XV, Madison, 1906).
———, AND HENRY LEIGHTON. History of the Clay-Working Industry in the United States (New York, 1909).
RIGHTOR, HENRY (ed.). Standard History of New Orleans (Chicago, 1900).

RILEY, ELMER A. Development of Chicago and Vicinity as a Manufacturing Center prior to 1880 (Chicago).
RINGWALT, J. L. Transportation in the United States (Philadelphia 1888).
ROE, JOHN WICKHAM. English and American Tool Builders (New Haven, 1916).
ROGERS, JAMES E. THOROLD. Six Centuries of Work and Wages, The History of English Labor (New York, 1884).
ROLPH, GEORGE M. Something about Sugar (San Francisco, 1917).
ROSS, FITZGERALD. A Visit to the Cities and Camps of the Confederate States (Edinburgh and London, 1865).
ROSSITER, W. S. A Century of Population Growth, 1790-1900 (Washington, 1909).
ROYAL GAZETTE. (Semi-weekly, Charleston, S. C., Mar. 3, 1781–Aug. 7, 1782.)
ROYALL, ANNE. Mrs. Royall's Pennsylvania or Travels Continued in the United States (2 vols., Washington, 1829).
RUPP, ISRAEL DANIEL. History and Topography of Dauphin, Cumberland, Franklin, Bedford, Adams, and Perry Counties (Lancaster, 1846).
SALMON, DR. D. E. Special Report on the History and Present Condition of the Sheep Industry of the United States (Washington, 1892).
SANFORD, NATHAN. A Report on Commerce, 1789 to 1819, made to the Senate, December 20, 1819 (in Niles Register, vol. XIX, 153–167, November 1820).
SANFORD AND KELLEY. New Bedford Manufactures, Statistics (New Bedford, 1891).
SAVANNAH DAILY GEORGIAN. (20 vols., May 10, 1823–Apr. 6, 1856.)
SAXE-WEIMAR, BERNARD, DUKE OF. Reise des Herzog's Bernhard zu Sachsen-Weimar-Eisenach durch Nord-Amerika, in 1825–1826 (Weimar, 1828).
SCHARF, JOHN THOMAS. History of St. Louis, City and County, from the Earliest Periods to the Present Day (2 vols., Philadelphia, 1883).
———, AND THOMPSON WESTCOTT. History of Philadelphia, 1609–1884 (Philadelphia, 1884).
SCHERER, JAMES AUGUSTIN BROWN. Cotton as a World Power: A Study in the Economic Interpretation of History (New York, 1916).
SCHOEPF, JOHANN DAVID. Travels in the Confederation, 1783–1784 (translator and ed., Alfred J. Morrison, 2 vols., Philadelphia, 1911).
SCHOOLCRAFT, HENRY ROWE. A View of the Lead Mines of Missouri (New York, 1819).
SCHULTZE-GAVERNITZ, G. VON. The Cotton Trade in England and on the Continent (translated by O. Hall, London, 1895).
SCHURICHT, HERMANN. History of the German Element in Virginia (Baltimore, 1898).
SCHWAB, JOHN CHRISTOPHER. The Confederate States of America, 1861–1865—A Financial and Industrial History of the South during the Civil War (New York, 1901).
SCHWEITZER, P. A Lecture on Petroleum, Its History, Commercial Importance, Uses and Dangers (Columbia, Mo., 1879).
SCIENTIFIC AMERICAN. (Vols. 1–14, Aug. 28, 1845–June 25, 1859; vols. 1–110; new ser., New York, 1845—.)
SCOBELL, HENRY. Collection of Acts and Ordinances of General Use (2 vols., London, 1657–58).
SCRIVENOR, HARRY. A Comprehensive History of the Iron Trade (London, 1841).
SELLERS, WILLIAM, & COMPANY. Report of the Judges on the Exhibit of Wm. Sellers & Company (Philadelphia, 1877).
SEYBERT, ADAM. Statistical Annals, Embracing Views of the Population, Commerce, Navigation, Fisheries, Public Lands, Post Office Establishment, Revenues, Mint, Military and Naval Establishments, Expenditures, Public Debt and Sinking Fund of the United States of America, 1789–1818 (Philadelphia, 1818).
SHEFFIELD, LORD JOHN. Observations on the Commerce of the American States (6th ed., London, 1784).
SHEPPERSON, ALFRED B. The Progress of Cotton Manufacture in the United States (New York, 1883).
SILK. (Monthly, 20 vols.; New York, 1915–1926.)
SILK ASSOCIATION OF AMERICA. Annual Reports (New York, 1873–1913).
——— The Silkworm (monthly, 8 vols., New York, 1919–1926).
SINGER, J. Die Amerikanische Stahlindustrie und der Weltkrieg (Berlin, 1917).
SINGER SEWING MACHINE COMPANY. The Story of the Sewing Machine (New York, 1901).
SLOSSON, EDWIN E. Creative Chemistry (New York, 1920).

SMART, WILLIAM. Economic Annals of the 19th Century, 1802–1820 (London, 1910).
SMITH, ADAM. An Inquiry into the Nature and Causes of the Wealth of Nations (5th ed., 3 vols., London, 1789).
SMITH, HENRY. Fifty Years of Wire Drawing (Worcester, 1884).
SMITH, J. E. S. History of Berkshire County (2 vols., New York, 1885).
SMITH, J. H. History of Duchess County (Syracuse, 1882).
SMITH, CAPTAIN JOHN. Works (ed., Edward Arber, Birmingham, England, 1884).
SMITH, RICHARD. A Tour of Four Great Rivers, in 1769 (ed. Francis W. Halsey, New York, 1910).
SMITH, W. Cincinnati, Annual Statement of Trade and Commerce of, for 1863 (Cincinnati, 1863).
SMOCK, JOHN C. Annual Report of the State Geologist of New Jersey for 1890 (Trenton, N. J., 1891).
SMYTHE, JOHN FERDINAND DALZIEL. A Tour in the United States of America (London, 1784).
SOME OBSERVATIONS RELATING TO THE PRESENT CIRCUMSTANCES OF THE PROVINCE OF MASSACHUSETTS BAY. HUMBLY OFFERED TO THE CONSIDERATION OF THE GENERAL ASSEMBLY (Boston, 1750).
SOMERS, ROBERT. The Southern States Since the War (London, 1871).
SOUTH CAROLINA. Laws of the Province of South Carolina (ed., Nicholas Trott, Charles Town, 1736).
—— The Public Laws of the State of South Carolina, from establishment of the Colony until 1790 inclusive (ed., John Foucheraud Grimké, Philadelphia, 1790).
—— Session Laws.
—— Statutes at Large of South Carolina (5 vols., ed., Thomas Cooper, Charleston, 1836–1839).
SOUTH CAROLINA AND AMERICAN GENERAL GAZETTE. (Charleston, 1768.)
SOUTH CAROLINA DEPARTMENT OF AGRICULTURE. The Cotton Mills of South Carolina (Charleston, 1880).
SOUTH CAROLINA GAZETTE. (Weekly, Charleston, Feb. 1734–May, 1775; revived as The Gazette of the State of South Carolina Apr. 1777–1800.)
SOUTH CAROLINA HISTORICAL SOCIETY. Collections (5 vols., Charleston, 1857–1897).
SOUTH CAROLINA STATE BOARD OF AGRICULTURE. South Carolina—Resources and Population—Institutions and Industries (Charleston S. C., 1883).
SOUTHERN AND WESTERN MONTHLY REVIEW AND JOURNAL OF PROGRESS. (New ser. ed., Richard Edwards; Richmond, 1854).
SOUTHERN AND WESTERN TEXTILE EXCELSIOR. (9 vols., Charlotte, 1898–1907.)
SOUTHERN COTTON MANUFACTURERS ASSOCIATION. (See American Cotton Manufacturers Association.)
—— Proceedings (Knoxville, 1905).
—— Proceedings of the Annual Convention at Charlotte, May 10, 1900 (Charlotte, N. C., 1900).
SOUTHERN COTTON SPINNERS' ASSOCIATION. Proceedings (see American Cotton Manufacturers' Association).
—— Transactions, Charlotte, 1903, May Meeting (Raleigh, 1903).
—— Twentieth Century Publication (Charlotte, 1901).
SOUTHERN HISTORY ASSOCIATION. Publications (quarterly, bi-monthly; 10 vols., Washington, 1897–1907).
SOUTHERN QUARTERLY REVIEW (16 vols., Jan. 1842–Jan. 1850, New Orleans.)
SOUTHWESTERN CONVENTION. Report of Meeting held at Memphis, Tennessee, Nov. 12, 1845 (in Cossitt Library, Memphis).
SPAFFORD, HORATION GATES. Gazetteer of New York (Albany, 1813).
SPILLANE, DANIEL. History of the American Pianoforte (New York, 1890).
SPOTTSWOOD, GOVERNOR ALEXANDER. Official Letters (2 vols. in one, Richmond, 1832, Virginia Historical Society Publications).
ST. LOUIS. Year Book of the Mercantile, Banking and Manufacturing Interests of St. Louis, 1882–1883 (St. Louis, 1883).
STANWOOD, EDWARD. American Tariff Controversies in the Nineteenth Century (2 vols., Boston and New York, 1903).
STAPLES, WILLIAM R. Annals of the Town of Providence, from its first Settlement to the Organization of the City Government in June 1832 (Providence, 1843).

STEEL DUTIES. (Pamphlet No. 2, compiled from the back numbers of the Boston Journal of Commerce, Jan. 4–Feb. 14, 1874; Boston, 1874.)
STEPHENS, THOMAS. On the Manufacture of American Potash (London, 1755).
—— Rise and Fall of Potash in America (London, 1768; New York Public Library Pamphlets).
STEVENSON, JAMES S. [Pennsylvania]. Tariff Speech in House of Representatives, March 5, 1828 (Washington, 1828).
STORY OF COAL AND IRON IN ALABAMA. (Published in behalf of the Committee named in Talladega County; in New York Public Library, Pamphlet vol. 7.)
STREET, DR. W. W. Iron and Steel Industries in the Southern States (Census Bulletin, 1890).
STUART, JAMES. Three Years in North America (2 vols., Edinburgh, 1833).
SUMMERFIELD, C. W. The Shoe Industry in Pennsylvania (Pennsylvania Department of Internal Affairs, Report, 1902; Harrisburg, 1902).
SUNDERLAND, LESTER T. Fifty Years of Portland Cement in America (Portland Cement Association; reprinted from Philadelphia Record, Jan. 8, 1923; Chicago, 1923).
SWANK, JAMES M. History of the Manufacture of Iron in All Ages, and Particularly in the United States from Colonial Times to 1891 (2d ed., Philadelphia, 1892).
—— A Record of the Remarkable Industrial Development of the Keystone State (Philadelphia, 1910).
—— Supplement to the Directory to the Iron and Steel Works of the United States (Philadelphia, 1900).
—— Twenty Years of Progress in the Manufacture of Iron and Steel in the United States (American Iron and Steel Association, Philadelphia, 1892).
SWINEFORD, A. P. Annual Review of the Iron Mining and Other Industries of the Upper Peninsula of Michigan for 1881 (Marquette, 1881).
—— Annual Review of the Iron, Copper and Other Industries of the Upper Peninsula of Michigan, for the year ending December 31, 1882 (Marquette, 1883).
—— History of the Lake Superior Iron District, its Mines and Furnaces (Marquette, 1871).
—— Mineral Resources of Lake Superior (Marquette, Mich., 1876).
—— Review of the Mines and Furnaces of Lake Superior for 1873 (Marquette, Mich., 1874).
TAFT, ROYAL C. Introduction of the Woolen Manufacture into the United States (Providence, 1882. Also published in Rhode Island Society for the Encouragement of Domestic Industry, Transactions, 1870).
TALCOTT, E. N. K. The Manufacture of Pig Iron (in Transactions of American Society of Civil Engineers, Vol. I, 193).
TANNER, HENRY SCHENCK. A Description of the Canals and Railroads of the United States (New York, 1840).
—— Memoir on the Recent Surveys, Observations and Internal Improvements in the United States (Philadelphia, 1830).
TARBELL, IDA M. The History of the Standard Oil Company (2 vols., New York, 1925).
—— The Life of Judge Gary (New York, 1924).
TAUNTON-NEW BEDFORD COPPER COMPANY. A Brief Sketch of the Business Life of Paul Revere (1928, Masachusetts Historical Society Library).
TAUSSIG, F. W. The Iron Industry in the United States, 1870–1899 (Quarterly Journal of Economics, Vol. XIV, 143–475; 2 vols., Boston, etc., 1900).
—— The Tariff History of the United States (7th ed., New York, 1923).
TAYLOR, FREDERICK WINSLOW. The Principles of Scientific Management (New York, 1911).
TEMPLE, JOSIAH HOWARD. History of Framingham, Massachusetts, early known as Danforth's Farms, 1640–1880 (Framingham, 1887).
—— History of the Town of Whately, Massachusetts (Boston, 1872).
TEXAS. Second Annual Report of the Geological Survey (E. T. Dumbel, Austin, 1891).
TEXTILE WORLD. (Published as Textile World Record, and Textile World Journal, 73 vols., New York, 1868–date.)
THOMAS, C. F. S. Manufacturing Interests of Buffalo (Buffalo, 1866).
THOMAS, DAVID. Travels through the Western Country in the Summer of 1816 (Auburn, New York, 1819).
THOMAS, GABRIEL. History of Pennsylvania (Philadelphia, 1900).
THURSTON, GEORGE HAY. Pittsburg and Allegheny in the Centennial Year (Pittsburg, 1876).
—— Pittsburg's Progress in Industry and Resources (Pittsburg, 1886).

THWAITES, REUBEN GOLD (ed.). Early Western Travels, 1748–1846 (32 vols., Cleveland, 1904–1907).
TOMPKINS, DANIEL AUGUSTUS. The Cotton Gin. The History of Its Invention (Pamphlet, Charlotte, S. C., 1901).
—— The Cotton Mill, Commercial Features (Charlotte, S. C., 1899).
—— Early Southern Cotton Mills (in New England Cotton Manufacturers' Association, Transactions, vol. LXI, 296–299).
—— History of Mecklenburg County and City of Charlotte, 1740–1903 (2 vols., Charlotte, S. C., 1903).
TOOF, JOHN. First Annual Statement of the Trade and Commerce of Memphis for the Year ending August 31, 1861 (reported to the Memphis Chamber of Commerce, Memphis, 1861).
TOWER, W. S. History of the American Whale Fishery (University of Pennsylvania Publications Philadelphia, 1907).
TOWLES, JOHN KER. Factory Legislation of Rhode Island (American Economic Association Quarterly, 3d ser., vol., IX, No. 3, October 1908).
TROYON, ROLLA MILTON. Household Manufactures in the United States, 1640–1860 (Chicago, 1917).
TRUMBULL, BENJAMIN. A Complete History of Connecticut, 1630–1764 (2 vols., New Haven, 1818).
TRUMBULL, LEVI. A History of Industrial Paterson (Paterson, N. J., 1882).
TUCKER, WILLIAM HOWARD. History of Hartford, Vermont, 1761–1889 (Burlington, Vermont, 1889).
TUNNER, PETER. Das Eisenhuttenwesen der Vereinigten Staaten (Freiberg, 1858).
TWINING, THOMAS. Travels in America One Hundred Years Ago (New York, 1894).
UNITED STATES. American State Papers:
    1. Commerce and Navigation (2 vols., Washington, 1832–1834).
    2. Finance (5 vols., Washington, 1832–1859).
    3. Miscellaneous (2 vols., Washington, 1834).
—— Bureau of Education; Education in the Industrial and Fine Arts (4 vols., Washington, 1895–1898).
—— Bureau of Mines:
    1. Coal Tar Products (Technical Paper 89, by Horace C. Porter, Washington, 1916).
    2. Alloy Steels, Manufacture and Uses (by Henry D. Hibbard, Washington, 1916).
    3. Electrical Furnance in Metallurgical Work (by Dorsey A. Lyon, Robert M. Keeney, and Joseph F. Cullen, Washington, 1916).
    4. Mineral Resources of the United States (issued by the Treasury Department up to 1875; none issued 1876–1881; 1 vol. issued annually until 1894; 2 vols. issued annually thereafter except in 1901 and 1902 when single volumes were printed, Washington, 1866–1927).
    5. Petroleum Refinery Statistics 1916–1925 (Washington, 1927).
—— Census, Bureau of the Census:
    1. Census Reports on Manufactures, 1810, 1820, 1840, 1860, 1870, 1880, 1890, 1900, 1905, 1910, 1914, 1919, 1921, 1923, 1925 (Washington).
    2. Census of War Commodities (a) Iron and Steel Products, (b) Textile Fibres (Washington, 1919).
    3. Statistical Atlas of the United States 1924, (Washington, 1925).
—— Centennial Commission Reports and Awards (8 vols., Washington, 1880).
—— Commerce and Navigation Reports (annual, Washington, 1821–1927).
—— Commissioner of Corporation's Reports:
    1. Beef Industry (Washington, 1925).
    2. Lumber Industry (3 vols., Washington, 1913–1914).
    3. Steel Industry (3 vols., Washington, 1911–1913).
—— Commissioner of Labor, Bureau of Labor Statistics:
    1. Hand and Machine Labor (2 vols., Washington, 1899).

Bibliography 435

UNITED STATES. Commissioner of Labor, Bureau of Labor Statistics:
> 2. Index Numbers of Wholesale Prices on Pre-War Base 1890–1927 (Washington, 1928).

—— Commissioners to the Paris Exposition of 1867, Reports (6 vols., Washington, 1870).
—— Commissioners to the Paris Exposition of 1878, Reports (5 vols., Washington, 1880).
—— Commissioners to the Paris Exposition of 1889, Reports (5 vols., Washington, 1891).
—— Commissioners to the Paris Exposition of 1900, Reports (6 vols., Washington, 1901).
—— Commissioners to the Vienna International Exhibition, 1873, Reports (4 vols., Washington, 1876).
—— Committee on Agriculture (House of Representatives, 51st Cong., 1st sess. Hearings on the Beveridge Amendment (Washington, 1906).
—— Committee on Ways and Means, Hearings:
> 1. Revision of the Tariff (51st Cong. 1st sess., 1889–1890, Washington, 1890).
> 2. Tariff (53rd Cong., 1st sess. Washington, 1893).
> 3. Tariff (54th Cong., 2d sess., 2 vols., Washington, 1897).
> 4. Tariff (60th Cong., 9 vols., Washington, 1909).
> 5. Tariff (62d Cong., 3d sess., 7 vols., Washington, 1913).

—— Congressional Documents, referred to under the following classification:
House Documents (15th Cong., 1st sess., to 29th Cong., 2d sess., 1817–1847, inclusive also from 54th Cong., 1st sess., 1895, to present time).
House Executive Documents (30th Cong., 1st sess., to 53d Cong., 3d sess., 1847–1895, inclusive).
House Miscellaneous Documents (30th Cong., 1st sess., to 53d Cong., 3d sess., 1847–1895, inclusive).
House Reports (15th Cong., 1st sess., 1817, to present time).
Senate Documents (15th Cong., 1st sess., to 29th Cong., 2d sess., 1817–1847, inclusive; also from 54th Cong., 1st sess., 1895, to present time).
Senate Executive Documents (30th Cong., 1st sess., to 53d Cong., 3d sess., 1847–1895, inclusive).
—— Senate Miscellaneous Documents (30th Cong., 1st sess., to 53rd Cong., 3d sess., 1847–1895, inclusive).
Senate Reports (30th Cong., 1st sess., 1847, to present time).
Customs and Tariff Legislation (ed., Edward Young, House Ex. Doc., 42d Cong., 2d sess., No. 109, Washington, 1872).

—— Department of Agriculture:
> 1. Beet Sugar Industry (Washington, 1898).
> 2. Beet Sugar Industry, Progress of (Washington, 1904).
> 3. Canning of Foods (by A. W. Bitting, Washington, 1912).
> 4. Lumber Cut in the United States, 1870–1920 (Bulletin 1119, Washington, 1923).
> 5. Sheep Industry of the United States (by Dr. D. E. Salmon, Ezra A. Carman, H. A. Heath, and John Minto, Washington, 1892).

—— Department of Commerce (and Labor):
> 1. Annual Reports of Secretary (Washington, 1915–1927).
> 2. Commercial and Industrial Organizations of the United States (Washington, 1926).
> 3. Foreign Trade of the United States (annual, Washington, 1920–1927).
> 4. Survey of Current Business (monthly, Washington, 1924–1928).
> 5. Trade Association Activities (by Irving S. Paull, J. W. Millard, and James S. Taylor, Washington, 1927).
> 6. Statistical Abstract of the United States (annual, Washington, 1878–1927).

—— Federal Reserve Board Bulletin (14 vols., 1915–1928).
—— Federal Trade Commission, Reports:
> 1. Annual (Washington, 1915–1928).
> 2. Bakery Combines and Profits (published as Sen. Doc. No. 212, 69th Cong., 2d sess., Washington, 1927).
> 3. Combed Cotton Yarn (Washington, 1921).

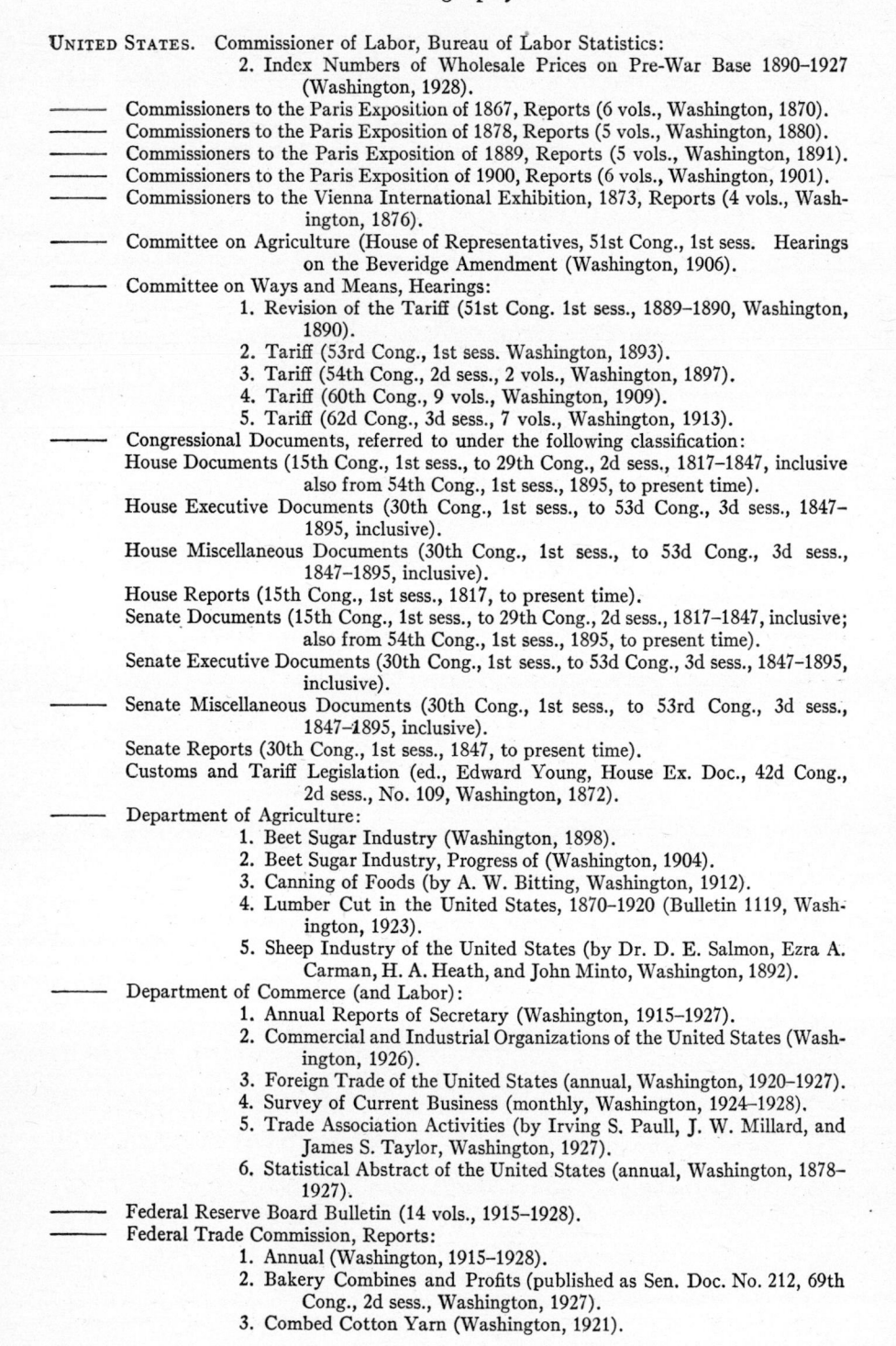

UNITED STATES. Federal Trade Commission, Reports:
    4. Electric Power Industry (published as Sen. Doc. No. 213, 69th Cong., 2d sess., and No. 46, 70th Cong., 1st sess., Washington, 1927-1928).
    5. Flour Milling (a) Commercial Wheat (Washington, 1920); (b) Wheat Flour Milling Industry (published as Senate Document No. 130, 68th Cong., 1st sess., Washington, 1924); (c) Competitive Conditions in Flour Milling (Washington, 1926).
    6. House Furnishings Industries (3 vols., and Summary, Washington, 1923).
    7. Fertilizer Industry (Washington, 1916).
    8. Leather and Shoes (a) Leather and Shoe Industries (Washington, 1919); (b) Shoe and Leather Costs and Prices (Washington, 1921).
    9. Lumber, War-Time Costs and Profits of Southern Pine Companies (Washington, 1922).
    10. Meat Packing Industry (Summary and four parts, Washington, 1919-1920).
    11. Milk and Milk Products, 1914-1918 (Washington, 1921).
    12. National Wealth and Income (Washington, 1926).
    13. News-print Paper Industry (Washington, 1917).
    14. Petroleum Industry (published as Sen. Doc. No. 61, 70th Cong., 1st sess., Washington, 1928).
    15. Radio Industry (Washington, 1924).
    16. Steel, War-Time Profits and Costs (Washington, 1925).
    17. Sugar Supply and Prices (Washington, 1920).
    18. Tobacco Products, Prices of (Washington, 1922).
—— Flax and Hemp Commission, Report (Washington, 1865).
—— Foreign and Domestic Commerce Reports (Sen. Ex. Doc. No. 55, 38th Cong., 1st sess., Washington, 1864).
—— Industrial Commission Reports (19 vols., Washington, 1900-1902).
—— Internal Revenue:
    1. Commission for a Revision of the Revenue System, Reports (Washington, 1866).
    2. Special Commissioner of the Revenue, Report for 1868 (Washington, 1868).
    3. Report for 1869 (Washington, 1869).
    4. Commissioner of the Internal Revenue, Report for 1867 (Washington, 1868).
    5. Report for 1868 (Washington, 1868).
—— National Museum. Mineral Industries of the United States (Bulletin 102, by Chester G. Gilbert and Joseph E. Pogue; Washington, 1917-1918).
—— Patent Office:
    1. Annual Reports (Washington, 1847–   ).
    2. History of, from 1790 to 1877 (Washington, 1877).
    3. List of Patents Granted by the United States, April 10, 1790, to December 31, 1836 (Washington, 1872).
—— Rebellion Records (ser. III, 5 vols., ser. IV, 3 vols., General Index, 1 vol., Washington, 1899-1901).
—— Report on the Condition of Women and Child Wage Earners in the United States (61st Cong., 2d sess., 19 vols., Washington, 1910-1913).
—— Report on Manufactures (McLane, 2 vols., House Doc. No. 30, 22d Cong., 1st sess., Washington, 1832).
—— Secretary of the Navy, Reports, 1862 (Ex. Doc. No. 1, 37th Cong., 3d sess., Washington, 1862); Report, 1863 (Washington, 1863); Report, 1864 (Washington, 1864); Report, 1865 (Washington, 1865).
—— Secretary of the Treasury:
    1. Reports (7 vols., Washington, 1828-1859).
    2. Report on the Revision of the Tariff, 1886 (Washington, 1886).
—— Secretary of War, Reports, 1861-1866 (published as House Ex. Doc. No. 1, Washington, 1861-1866).

UNITED STATES. Tariff Board. Cotton Manufacture 1909–1912 (2 vols., Washington, 1912).
—— Tariff Commission of 1882, Report (2 vols., Washington, 1882).
—— Tariff Commission:
1. (a) Cotton Cloth Industry (Washington, 1924); (b) Cotton Warp Knit Fabric (Washington, 1926).
2. Dyes, Census of (Washington, 1918, 1919, 1920, 1921, 1923, 1924, 1925, 1926).
3. Electrical Industry (Washington, 1922).
4. Emergency Tariff Act (Washington, 1922).
5. (a) Ferroalloy Industry (Washington, 1921); (b) Ferroalloy Ores (Washington, 1921).
6. Glass and Glassware (Washington, 1921).
7. Iron in Pigs (Washington, 1927).
8. Machinery (parts I and II, Washington, 1921).
9. Silk. Broad-Silk Manufacture and the Tariff (Washington, 1926).
10. Sugar. Cost of Producing Sugar Beets (Washington, 1926).
11. Wool. (a) By-Products and Wool Wastes (Washington, 1926).
(b) Tops and Yarns of Wool or Hair (Washington, 1925).
(c) Woven Fabrics (Washington, 1927).
—— Tariff Documents (documents relating to the tariffs of 1842, 1846, and 1857; Sen. Docs. Nos. 21, 71, and 72 in 3 parts, 62d Cong., 1st sess., Washington, 1911).
—— Tariff Laws (a) 1789–1897 (compiler, Robert G. Proctor, House Doc. No. 562, 55th Cong., 2d sess., Washington, 1898); (b) Tariff Act of 1922, (House Doc. No. 393, 67th Cong., 2d sess., Washington, 1922).
—— Trusts. (a) Anti-Trust Laws with Amendments 1890–1923 (Washington, 1924); (b) Decrees and Judgments in Federal Anti-Trust Cases, 1890–1918 (Washington, 1918).
—— War Industries Board. History of Prices during the War (by Wesley C. Mitchell, Washington, 1919).
—— Woodbury Report on the Cultivation, Manufacture, and Foreign Trade of Cotton (House Doc. No. 146, 24th Cong., 1st sess., Washington, 1836).
—— World's Inorganic Nitrogen Industry (by F. A. Ernst and F. S. Sherman, published as Sen. Doc. No. 211, 69th Cong., 2d sess., Washington, 1927).
—— Wool. (a) Statistics Relating to Wool and Manufactures of Wool (Special Report prepared by the Chief of the Bureau of Statistics, Washington, 1887). (b) Wool and Manufactures of Wool (House Misc. Doc. No. 550, 50th Cong.,1st sess., Washington, 1888).
UNITED STATES ASSOCIATION OF CHARCOAL IRON WORKERS. Journal, (Harrisburg, 1880–1891).
UNITED STATES INDUSTRIAL DIRECTORY (ed., John L. Hayes, Boston, 1876).
UNITED STATES NAVAL INSTITUTE. Proceedings (quarterly, Annapolis, 1874— date).
URE, ANDREW. Philosophy of Manufactures (3d ed., London, 1861).
UTTLEY, T. W. Cotton Spinning and Manufacturing in the United States (Gartside Studies, University of Manchester, Manchester, England, 1905).
VAILLATE, ACHILLE. L'Industrie Américaine (Paris, 1908).
VAN GELDER, ARTHUR P., AND HUGO SCHLATTER. History of the Explosives Industry in America (New York, 1927).
VAN HISE, CHARLES R. Concentration and Control, a Solution of the Trust Problem in the United States (rev. ed., New York, 1914).
VAN NOSTRAND'S ELECTRIC ENGINEERING MAGAZINE. (Monthly, 35 vols., New York 1869–1886.)
VAN SLYCK, J. D. New England Manufactures and Manufacturers (Boston, 1879).
VERMONT. Assembly Journal, 1823.
VILLARD, OSWALD GARRISON. John Brown, 1800–1859. A Biography Fifty Years After (Boston, New York, 1910).
VIRGINIA. Journal of the Senate, Session of December 7, 1863 (Richmond).
—— Senate Documents, Session of December 1864 (Richmond).
—— State Papers (11 vols., Richmond, 1875–1893).
—— Statutes at Large, 1619–1792 (ed., William Waller Heming; 13 vols., Philadelphia, 1823).
—— A Geographical and Political Summary. (Prepared under the supervision of the Board of Immigration; Richmond, 1876.)

VIRGINIA COMPANY OF LONDON, 1619–1624. Abstract of Proceedings (2 vols., Richmond, 1889).
VIRGINIA HISTORICAL SOCIETY. Collections (12 vols. in 11, Richmond, 1833–1892).
VIRGINIA MAGAZINE OF HISTORY AND BIOGRAPHY (eds., P. A. Bruce, 1893–1898; W. G. Stanard, 1899–1904; 11 vols., Richmond, 1893–1904.)
VISER, VICE-KONSUL KONRAD VON. Pittsburgh (Austro-Hungarian Consular Reports, 1903).
VOGT, PAUL L. The Sugar Refining Industry in the United States (University of Pennsylvania Publications, Philadelphia, 1908).
WALKER, BERNARD. The Story of Steel (New York, 1926).
WALKER, E. H. Annual Statement of the Trade and Commerce of Buffalo, 1863.
WALLIS, GEORGE. Special Report on the New York Industrial Exhibition of 1853 (in Parliamentary Papers, 1854, vol. XXXVI, No. 9).
WALTERHAUSEN, A. SARTORIUS, VON. Deutsche Wirtschaftsgeschichte, 1815–1914 (Jena, 1920).
WALTON, PERRY. The Story of Textiles (Boston, 1912).
WANSEY, HENRY. Excursion to the United States of North America in the Summer of 1794 (2d. ed., Salisbury, 1798).
WARBURG, JAMES PAUL. Cotton and Cotton Manufacturing (First National Bank of Boston Publication, Boston, 1921).
——— Hides and Skins and the Manufacture of Leather (First National Bank of Boston Publication, Boston, 1921).
——— Wool and the Wool Manufacture (First National Bank of Boston Publication, Boston, 1920).
WARD, GEORGE L., AND ASSOCIATES. Report of a Committee of the Boston Board of Trade on the Cotton Tax (Boston, 1867).
WARDEN, DAVID BAILLE. A Statistical, Political and Historical Account of the United States (3 vols., Edinburgh, 1819).
WASHBURN, CHARLES G. Industrial Worcester (Worcester, 1917).
——— Manufacturing and Mechanical Industries of Worcester (Philadelphia, 1889).
WASHINGTON, GEORGE. Diary from 1789 to 1791 (ed., J. Lossing Benson, New York, 1860).
WATERHOUSE, S. Natural Advantages of St. Louis for Iron Manufactures (St. Louis, 1869).
WATKINS, ROBERT AND GEORGE. Digest of the Laws of Georgia (Philadelphia, 1800).
WATTERSON, GEORGE, AND NICHOLAS BIDDLE VAN ZANDT. Tabular Statistical Views of the United States (Washington, 1829).
WEBBER, SAMUEL. Manual of Power, for Machines, Shafts, and Belts, with the History of Cotton Manufacture in the United States (New York 1879).
WEBER, ADNA FERRIN, PH.D. The Growth of Cities in the Nineteenth Century (Columbia University, Studies in History, Economics, and Public Law; New York, 1899).
WEEDEN, WILLIAM B. Early Rhode Island (New York, 1910).
——— Economic and Social History of New England, 1620 to 1789 (2 vols., Boston and New York, 1890).
WEEKS, LYMAN HORACE. A History of Paper Making in the United States (New York, 1916).
WELD, CHARLES R. A Vacation Tour in the United States and Canada (London, 1855).
WELD, ISAAC. Travels through the States of North America, and the Provinces of Upper and Lower Canada, during the years 1795–1797 (4th ed., London, 1800).
WELLS, DAVID A. Recent Economic Changes (New York, 1889).
WENTWORTH AND COMPANY. Iron and Metal Trades Directory (Boston, 1870).
WESTERN GAS ASSOCIATION. Gas, Coal, and Iron Sites in Western Pennsylvania (compiler, F. L. Slocum; Pittsburgh Meeting, May 1895).
WESTERN JOURNAL AND CIVILIAN (eds., M. Tarver and T. F. Risk; 13 vols., St. Louis, 1848–1855).
WESTERN RAILWAY OF MASSACHUSETTS. Report for 1844 (Boston, State House Library Pamphlets, vol. XII).
WHARTON SCHOOL OF COMMERCE AND FINANCE. Recent Development of American Industry (Philadelphia, 1891).
WHEELWRIGHT, WILLIAM B. New England's Pioneer Paper Makers (Published in Graphic Arts Section, Boston Transcript, August 29, 1922).
WHITE, GEORGE. Statistics of Georgia (Savannah, 1849).
WHITE, GEORGE S. Memoir of Samuel Slater, the Father of American Manufactures (2d ed., Philadelphia, 1836).

WHITEHEAD, WILLIAM A.   East Jersey under the Proprietory Governments (2d ed., Newark, 1875).
WHITMAN, E. A., AND J. R. LEESON.   Flax Culture in the United States (Boston, 1888).
WHITTLESEY, CHARLES.   A History of the Coal and Iron Business from Cleveland As It Is, 1872 (Yale University Library).
WHITWORTH, SIR CHARLES.   State of the Trade of Great Britain in its Imports and Exports, 1697–1773, Progressively from the year 1697, etc. (The tables in the copy in the Library of Congress, Washington, are continued, in manuscript, from 1772–1801.) (London, 1776).
WHITWORTH, JOSEPH.   Special Report on the New York Industrial Exhibition of 1853 (in Parliamentary Papers, 1854, vol. xxxvi, 103).
WILBUR, EDWARD B.   Southern Cotton Mills and Cotton Manufacturing (read before the New England Cotton Manufacturers' Association, Sept. 27, 1898).
WILBUR, W. R.   History of the Bolt and Nut Industry of America (Cleveland, 1905, in New York Public Library, Pamphlet vol. 2).
WILE, FREDERIC WILLIAM.   Emile Berliner, Maker of the Microphone, Indianapolis, 1926).
WILGUS, HORACE L.   A Study of the United States Steel Corporation in Its Industrial and Legal Aspects (Chicago, 1901).
WILKESON, JOHN.   The Manufacture of Iron in Buffalo (Buffalo, 1864, Massachusetts Historical Society Library).
WILKINSON.   The Manufacture of Iron in Buffalo (in Buffalo Historical Society Proceedings. Jan. 25, 1864; Buffalo, 1864).
WILLIAMS, JAMES M.   An American Town (New York, 1906).
WILLIAMS, JAMES S.   Old Times in West Tennessee (Memphis, 1873).
WILLIAMS, RALPH D.   The Honorable Peter White (Cleveland, 1908).
WILLIS, HENRY PARKER, AND JOHN R. B. BYERS.   Portland Cement Prices (New York, 1924).
WILSON, BECKLES.   The Great Company (Toronto, 1899).
WINSOR, JUSTIN (ed.).   Memorial History of Boston, including Suffolk County, 1630–1880 (4 vols., Boston, 1880–1882).
WINTERBOTHAM, W.   An Historical, Geographical, Commercial, and Philosophical View of the United States of America, and of the European Settlements in America and the West Indies (1st American ed., 4 vols., New York, 1796).
WINTHROP, JOHN.   History of New England from 1630 to 1649 (2 vols., ed., James Savage, Boston, 1853).
WINTHROP, JOHN.   Journal of the Transactions and Occurrences in the Settlement of Massachusetts and the other New England Colonies, from the year 1630 to 1644 (Hartford, 1790).
WOODBURY, CHARLES JEPTHA HILL.   Bibliography of the Cotton Manufacture (2 vols., Waltham, 1909–1910).
WOODWORTH, JOSEPH VINCENT.   American Tool Making and Interchangeable Manufacturing (New York, 1911).
WOOL AND COTTON REPORTER.   Our Textile Industries (vol. XIII, 146, Feb. 2, 1899, vol. XVII 474, Apr. 16, 1903).
WOOLDRIDGE, J. (ed.).   History of Nashville (Nashville, 1890).
WOOLSEY, THEODORE D.   First Century of the Republic (New York, 1876).
WORCESTER SOCIETY OF ANTIQUITY.   Proceedings for the year 1886 (Worcester, 1886).
WORCESTER SPY.   (June 1770–June 1896, Worcester, Mass.)
WRIGHT, CARROLL D.   History of Wages and Prices in Massachusetts, 1752–1883 (Boston, 1885).
——— The Industrial Evolution of the United States (Meadville, N. Y., 1897).
——— Report on the Factory System of the United States (U. S. Census, 1880, vol. 11, pp. 529–610, Washington, 1883).
WRIGHT, CHARLES E.   First Annual Report of the Commissioner of Mineral Statistics of the State of Michigan (Lansing, 1879).
WRIGHT, CHESTER WHITNEY.   Wool Growing and the Tariff. A Study in the Economic History of the United States (Harvard Economic Studies, vol. v, Cambridge and London, 1910).
WRIGHT, JOHN.   The American Negotiator (3d ed., London, 1765).
WRIGHT, WILLIAM.   The Oil Regions of Pennsylvania (New York, 1861).

WYCKOFF, WILLIAM C. American Silk Manufacture (New York, 1887).
——— The Silk Goods of America (2d ed., New York, 1880).
——— Silk Manufacture in the United States (New York, 1883).
YALE LAW SCHOOL FACULTY. Two Centuries' Growth of American Law, 1701–1901 (New York, 1901).
YEAR BOOK OF THE MERCANTILE BANKING AND MANUFACTURING INTERESTS OF ST. LOUIS, 1882–1883 (St. Louis, 1883).
YOUNG, EDWARD, PH.D. Labor in Europe and America (Washington, 1875).
——— Special Report on the Customs Tariff Legislation of the United States (Washington, 1872).
YOUNG, T. M. The American Cotton Industry (New York, 1902).

II. UNPUBLISHED

ACCOUNT BOOK No. 905. (Pennsylvania Historical Society Library.)
ALMY AND BROWN. Letter Books and Commercial Accounts (Rhode Island Historical Society Library).
ASPINWALL, WILLIAM. Notorial Records (Boston Athenaeum Library).
AUSTIN AND LAURENS. Account Books, including also the account books of Austin, Laurens, and Appleby and the letter book of B. Laurens (Charleston Historical Society Library, Charleston, S. C.).
BAGNALL, WILLIAM R. Papers relating to manufacturing establishments (4 vols., Board of Research Associates in American Economic History Manuscripts, Baker Library, Harvard University).
BOSTON GLASS HOUSE. Manuscript Receipt Book (Boston Athenaeum Library).
BOSTON MANUFACTURING CO. Manuscript Accounts, Letter Books, and Treasurer's Reports (Business Historical Society Manuscripts, Baker Library, Harvard University).
BOSTON MERCHANTS. Account of the State of Trade (Massachusetts Historical Society Manuscripts).
BOSTON AND ROXBURY MILL CORPORATION. Business Papers (Massachusetts Historical Society Manuscripts).
BRITISH MUSEUM. Additional Manuscripts: 10120 *ff*. 77–89 (letter from Mr. Taylor concerning naval stores in New England July 2, 1695).
——— *Id*., 11514. Essay on Trade in America. To the Right Honorable Earl of Halifax (signed Henry McCulloh, dated London, Dec. 10, 1756).
——— *Id*., 15485. Account of Shipping, Imports, Exports, their value and character of articles carried. 1768–1769.
——— *Id*., 28089: *f*. 6., Randolph, E., The Present State of New England.
——— *Id*., 29600. Papers relating to America, 1725–1776, chiefly about the iron industry in America (Maryland).
——— *Id*., 32901. Newcastle Papers. 33028–33030. Newcastle Papers. Papers relating to America and the West Indies.
——— *Id*., 33028. State and Condition of the British Colonies in America, 1733–1735.
——— *Id*., 34813. *f*. 88 Letter from Mathew Pope to John Jacob, York Town, Virginia, August 25, 1775.
——— *Id*., 35910. Hardwicke Papers relating to America, 1759–1764.
——— *Id*., 8133, *cf*. 234. Account of goods entered in his Majesty's custom houses in the American plantations as exported from one plantation to another. 1677–1678.
——— *Id*., 213. Journal of an Officer who travelled over a part of the West Indies and of North America in the Course of 1764 and 1765.
BRITISH MUSEUM. Edgerton Manuscripts: 2395, *ff*. 397–411. Samuel Mavericke, A Brief Description of New England.
——— Harleian Manuscripts, 1324, *ff*. 1–4. Representations of the Commissioners for Trade and Plantations to the Honorable House of Commons, Jan. 13, 1698, regarding Woolen Manufactures.
——— Kings Manuscripts: 203. Original Letters from the Rev. Dr. Cooper to Dr. Franklin, written in the years 1769–1775, on American politics. Original letters to Gov. Pownall, 1769–1774 (printed Amer. Hist. Rev., vol. VIII, 301–330).

BRITISH MUSEUM. *Id.*, 205. Reports on the State of the American Colonies, 1721 to 1768, containing copies of letters from governors and others in America.
——— Sloane Manuscripts, 2717, *ff.* 64–66 (2728-B, *ff.* 209b-212?). Petition to form a Company to supply the Colonists with Linsey-woolsey, etc.
——— Stowe Manuscripts: 318. Abstract of the Inspector General's Account of Importations and Exportations (1697–1698).
BRITISH TRANSCRIPTS. See British Museum and Public Record Office (Library of Congress).
BROWN AND IVES. Papers (office of Brown and Ives, Providence, R. I.).
BROWN, MOSES. Account Books (Rhode Island Historical Society Library).
——— Letter Books (Rhode Island Historical Society Library).
——— Papers (1st ser., 14 vols.; 2d ser., 4 vols., Rhode Island Historical Society Library).
BROWN, NICHOLAS. Papers (John Carter Brown Library, Providence, R. I.).
BROWN, OBEDIAH Account Books (Rhode Island Historical Society Library).
BRUCE, KATHLEEN. Rise of the Iron Industry in Virginia (to be published by the American Historical Association).
CALICO PRINTING MANUFACTURING SOCIETY. Minutes 1795–1798 (Massachusetts Historical Society Manuscripts).
CARROLL, CHARLES. Account Books (Library of Congress).
CHALMERS PAPERS. (New York Public Library).
COCKBURN, MARTIN. Day Book and Ledger (2 vols., 1767–1818, Library of Congress).
COLLINS, STEPHEN & CO. AND WILLIAM BARRELL. Mercantile Papers (Library of Congress).
CUSTOMS HOUSE. Papers (Pennsylvania Historical Society Library, Philadelphia).
CUYLER, PHILIP. Letter Book, 1753–1760 (New York Historical Society Library).
DAVEY AND CARSON. Manuscript Letter Book (1745–1750, Library of Congress).
EARTHENWARE DEALERS ASSOCIATION. Records 1817–1835 (Massachusetts Historical Society Manuscripts).
ERICSSON, JOHN. Papers (New York Historical Sodiety Library).
FROTHINGHAM. Papers (Middlesex Canal Records, 1795–1851; Massachusetts Historical Society Manuscripts).
GROVER AND BAKER SEWING MACHINE COMPANY. Correspondence 1860 (Massachusetts Historical Society Manuscripts).
HAMILTON, ALEXANDER. Papers: Correspondence and other papers relating to Alexander Hamilton's report on manufactures (Library of Congress).
HANCOCK, JOHN. Mercantile Account Books (Boston Public Library).
HARTFORD WOOLEN MANUFACTORY CO. Accounts and Papers (Connecticut Historical Society Library, Hartford).
HAZARD, R. Letter Books and Mercantile Accounts (Business Historical Society Manuscript, Baker Library, Harvard University.
HERZOG, JOSEPH. Letter Book (Herzog-Collins Collection, Missouri Historical Society Library, St. Louis).
HOLTON, JR., SAMUEL. Account Books (1757–1763, Library of Congress).
HUNTER, LOUIS CLAIR. A Study of the Iron Industry at Pittsburgh before 1860 (Harvard University Library).
IPSWICH COTTON MANUFACTURING COMPANY. Mill Accounts, 1829–1835 (Essex Institute Library, Salem).
JAMIESON. Papers (Library of Congress).
JOHNSON, SIR WILLIAM. Papers (New York State Library).
KLEIN, JULIUS. Manufactures on the Pacific Coast (Board of Research Associates in American Economic History Manuscript, Baker Library, Harvard University).
LAWYER'S DAY BOOK. (1769 *et seq.*, New York Historical Society Library.)
LINEN MANUFACTURING CO. Papers 1768 (Massachusetts Historical Society Manuscripts).
LIPPINCOTT, ISAAC. Manufactures in the Central Mississippi Valley (Board of Resarch Associates in American Economic History Manuscript, Baker Library, Harvard University. Published in part as History of Manufactures in the Ohio Valley up to 1860).
LYNN IRON WORKS PAPERS. (Business Historical Society Manuscript, Baker Library, Harvard University.)
MCDONALD. Papers (7 vols., Virginia State Library, Richmond.)
MASSACHUSETTS. Archives (Massachusetts State House Library, vol. LIX).

NATHAN TROTTER & COMPANY. Business Papers (Business Historical Society Manuscripts, Baker Library, Harvard University).
NEWPORT. Store Blotter (Rhode Island Historical Society Library).
NIGHTINGALE, SAMUEL. Mercantile Accounts (Rhode Island Historical Society Library).
NORTH CAROLINA HISTORICAL COMMISSION. Unlisted Papers.
ORNE, TIMOTHY. Mercantile Account Books (Essex Institute Library, Salem).
PARIS. Archives Nationales, Colonies (ser. F 3., collection Moreau de Saint Mery, 287 *tomes*).
PATTERSON, R. AND J. Ledger (Carnegie Library, Pittsburgh).
PHILADELPHIA MERCHANT. Journal, 1730 (Library of Congress).
POTTER. Mercantile Account Book (Library of Congress).
PRINCIPIO IRON CO. Letters (Maryland Historical Society Library).
——— Papers (New York Public Library).
——— Papers (see British Museum Additional Manuscripts, Nos. 29 and 600).
PUBLIC RECORD OFFICE. Colonial Office Papers (London).
SAINSBURY, E. NOEL. Abstracts of Records in British Public Record Office Relating to Virginia in the 17th Century (Virginia State Library).
SALEM INDIA RUBBER COMPANY. Cash Book, 1836–1841 (Essex Institute Library, Salem).
SALEM LEAD MANUFACTURING COMPANY. Record Book, 1824–1840 (Essex Institute Library, Salem).
SCHARF COLLECTION. (Unbound papers in Maryland Historical Society Library.)
SHENANDOAH FURNACE. Account Book (Library of Congress).
SHIPPEN PAPERS, 1747–1799. (5 vols., Pennsylvania Historical Society Library.)
SAMUEL SMITH AND CO. AND SMITH AND SONS. Mercantile Letter Books (1765–1770, Library of Congress).
SLATER, SAMUEL. Business Papers (Business Historical Society Manuscripts, Baker Library, Harvard University).
STEVENS, NATHANIEL. Letter Books and Account Books (in possession of the Stevens family North Andover, Mass.).
TILTON, DAVID. Mercantile Account Book (Essex Institute Library, Salem).
VAN CORTLANDT, JOHN & SON. Sugar House Letter Book (New York Public Library).
WALCOTT. Ledger (Connecticut Historical Society Library, Hartford).
WARE, CAROLINE F. Industrial Revolution in the New England Cotton Industry, 1790–1846 (Harvard University Library).
WASHINGTON, GEORGE. Papers (Library of Congress).
WEIR, JAMES. Letter Books (Kentucky Papers, vols. 21–22. Draper Collection, Wisconsin Historical Society, Madison).
WILLIAMS, DAVID R. Transcripts of Correspondence Relative to Cotton and Cottonseed Oil Mills in South Carolina, 1828–1835 (Board of Research Associates in American Economic History, Manuscripts, Baker Library, Harvard University).
WILTS, CHRISTIAN. Letter Book (Herzog-Collins Collection, Missouri Historical Society Library, St. Louis).
WOOLSEY AND SALMON. Mercantile Letter Book, 1774–1784 (Library of Congress).

INDEX

Abrasives, 168.
Academy of Social and Political Sciences (Philadelphia), 301.
Acetates, 243, 244.
Acids, 290; carbonic, 285; muriatic, 290; phosphoric, 290; pyrites substituted for sulpher, 285; sulphuric, 285, 286, 289, 290.
Adams (Mass.) (paper), 247.
Addyston Pipe Case, 127–128.
Adirondacks (iron ore), 37.
Advertising, beer, 278; breakfast foods, 268; growth of, 293; influence, 295; magazine, 295, 296; National Biscuit Company, 269; sugar, 275.
Advisory Commission (Council of National Defense), 301–302.
Aerial Cable Ways, 125.
Africa, 46.
Agricultural Implements, 105, 148.
Agricultural Machinery (see *Harvesters*, *Plows*), 78, 146, 147, 153, 160–161; alloys, 146; centers, 147; corporations, 146, 147; cultivators, 147; International Harvester Company, 146, 147, 315, 330–331; multiplicity of models, 304; on free list, 329; quantity production, 146; value, 147; World War, 315.
Agricultural Products (exports), 1, 10.
Aircraft (*Airplanes*), 314, 315, 354; product, 338.
Akron (Ohio) (tires), 237.
Alabama, 28, 123; cast-iron pipe, 127, 128; coal, 42; coal strike, 13; cotton, 176, 178; iron, 24–25, 31, 107, 114; iron ores, 15–18, 22, 63; New England hand cotton mills, 174; rail-making, 118; steel, 78.
Alabama and Georgia Iron Company, 27.
Alabama Consolidated Iron and Coal Company, 27, 89.
Alabama Power Company, 4.
Alabama Steel and Shipbuilding Company, 49, 61.
Alabama Steel and Wire Company, 49, 50, 51, 123.
Alaska, canning, 270; forests, 239.
Alaska Packing Company, 271.
Albany (N. Y.), 288; decline as lumber market, 241; prices, colonial, shipbuilding, Appendix IV.
Alcohol (fuel), 161.
Algeria (Algiers), 15.
Alien Property Custodian, 318
Allegheny Coke Works, 44.
Allegheny County (Pa.), iron, 23, 41.
Allegheny Iron and Steel Company, 57.
Allegheny River (navigation), 41.
Allentown (Pa.), 210; charcoal iron, 72.
Allied Chemical and Dye Corporation, 347–348.
Allis-Chalmers Manufacturing Company, 301, 338.
Alloys, 146; steel, 71, 79–80, 81, 118.

Altman and Company (electric delivery wagons), 158.
Alum, 285, 286.
Aluminum, 2, 18, 310, 325; castings, 310; Cuban ores, 17; electric process, 168; explosives, 310; price, 310.
Aluminum Company of America, 4, 310, 311.
Amalgamated Association of Iron and Steel Workers, 13; strike for closed shop, 14, 87, 101.
Amendment (eighteenth), 275.
American Agricultural Chemical Company, 290.
American Alkali Company, 287.
American Axe and Edge Tool Company, 149.
American Beet Sugar Company, 273; World War profits, 323.
American Bicycle Company, 236.
American Biscuit Manufacturing Company, 268.
American Bridge Company, 121; shipbuilding, 144.
American Can Company, 271.
American Car and Foundry Company, 138, 140.
American Cement Company, 254.
American Clay Manufacturing Company, 259.
American Cotton Manufacturers' Association, 184, 189, 343.
American Cotton Textile Institute, 343, 345.
American Cotton Oil Trust (Company), 284.
American Felt Company, 205.
American Foundrymen's Association, 89.
American Glass Company, 261.
American Glucose Sugar Refining Company, 270.
American Hawaiian Steam Navigation Company, 142, 143.
American Hide and Leather Company, 228.
American Iron and Steel Association (American iron), 68, 82, 89, 96, 102.
American Iron and Steel Institute, 89, 335.
American Iron and Steel Manufacturing Company, 88.
American Linseed Oil Company, 284.
American Locomotive Company, 89, 139, 141; electric locomotive, 166.
American Malting Company, 277.
American Marconi Company, 332.
American Net and Twine Company, 174.
American Pig Iron Storage Warrant Company, 107, 108.
American Print Company, 340.
American Radiator Company, 150.
American Railway Equipment Company, 138.
American School Furniture Company, 245
American Screw Company, 126.
American Sheet and Tin Plate Company, 133.
American Sheet Metal Company, 6.
American Sheet Steel Company, 88, 89, 132.

American Shipbuilding Company, 143, 144, 145.
American Spirits Manufacturing Company, 276.
American Steel and Wire Company, 6, 23, 54, 55, 56, 122, 123, 124, 125, 126, mammoth engine, 338.
American Steel Barge Company, 143.
American Steel Castings Company, 85.
American Steel Foundries Company, 85.
American Steel Hoop Company, 54, 59, 88, 126–127.
American Strawboard Company, 249.
American Sugar Refining Company, agreement with Claus Spreckels, 273; most unpopular "trust," 274–275.
American Switch Company, 138.
American Textile Woolen Company (southern mills), 206.
American Thread Company, 180, 181; combination of mills, 6–7.
American Tinplate Company, 54, 131, 132, 133.
American Tobacco Company, assets, 280; campaign to capture foreign markets, 279; growth, 278–279.
American Window Glass Company, 261.
American Woolen Company, 205, 206, 316; World War, 320, 321, 323; worsted mill, 344.
American Wool Products Company, 320, 345.
American Writing Paper Company, 249.
Ammonia, anhydrous, 286; by-product, 282, 286.
Anchors (use of wrought iron for), 82.
Andover Furnace, 23.
Androscoggin River (paper making), 248.
Annealing (ovens take place of kilns), 259.
Anniston (Ala.), 174.
Anthracite Coal (strike), 14.
Appalachian Forests (lumber), 238.
Argentina, 110; export meat trade, 265; wool, 191.
Arkansas, cotton, 175; furniture, 244; stave-making, 243.
Arkwright Club (Boston), 173, 184, 185.
Arlington Mills, 206; spindles and looms, 199; tops, 198; *World War*, 321.
Armor and Armor Plate (see *Iron, Steel*), 40, 68, 69, 78, 147, 148; British competition, 313; government inspection, 147; plants, 147–148, 313; prices, 313.
Armour and Company, absorb *Morris and Company*, 330; cottonseed oils, 284; Federal suits, 327; fertilizer, 290; food products monopoly, 265; World War profits, 322–323.
Arts (graphic), 293.
Ashland (Wis.) (charcoal furnaces), 24.
Asia, rugs, 203; tinplate, 133.
Asphalt Roofing, 41.
Association of American Leather Trade Chemists, 225.
Association of American Steel Manufacturers, 80.
Associations (see separate industries).
Atlanta (Ga.), 290.
Atlantic Transport Company, 144.
Atlas Company (Portland cement), 254.
Attorney-General (U. S.), 333.
Augusta (Ga.) (cotton mills), 14, 175.
Augusta (Me.) (magazine industry), 295.

Australia, 46, 112; American Tobacco Company, 279; irrigation pipes, 129; rails, 118; Railway Commissioners, 112; steamship line, 142; steel bridges, 38; wool, 191, 201, 202.
Austria-Hungary, market for southern iron, 111; speech of Premier, 10; steel, 78, 310.
Automobile Club of America, 161.
Automobiles, 151, 234; annual financing conference, 333; Benz (Carl), 157; busses, 161; clothing affected by, 344; commercial, 159, 161, 162, 163, 164; compressed air, 159, 160; credit policies, 332–333; designs, 161; Detroit, 158, 160, 164; development (pre-war), 163, 164; Duryea (Charles E.), 157, 158; effect on rubber industry, 237; electric, 157, 158, 159, 161, 162, 163, 164; engineering progress, 336; exports, 164; Flint (Mich.), 162; Ford (Henry) and Ford Works, 158, 160, 162, 163, 164, 328, 332, 336; fuel, 161; gasoline, 157, 158, 160, 164; glass consumption, 260, 348; Haynes (Elwood), 158; imports, 157, 161, 164; increased production, 81; instalment selling, 332; King (Charles B.), 158; Locomobile Company, 160, 236; machinery, 153; magnetos, 163; man hours per car, 337; manufacturing companies, 160; market, 161; merchandizing, 336; Mobile Company, 160; number of establishments, 160, 162, 164; number of vehicles, 163, 164; Olds Motor Vehicle Company, 160, 164; organization, 158–160, 164; output per establishment, 337; parts, 78; "perpetual motion" production, 336–337; pioneer, 157–158; Pope (Colonel Albert), 159; prices, 162, 163; product (value), 336, (number), 337; promoting (early), 158–160; roads, 161; Roper (S. H.), 157; Selden (George B.), 157, 163; self starter, 163; service stations, 356; shows, 160–162; specialization, 164; stage lines, 161; standardization, 161; status (1910), 162–163; steam cars, 157, 158, 160, 161, 162; steel and alloys, 80, 81; tires, 158, 229, 237; tractors, 146, 163; trucks, 159, 164, 337; value of product, 162, 163, 164; wage earners, 162, 164; Waltham buckboard, 162; World War, 304, 307, 314.
Auto-trucks, 159, 164; World War (standard models), 314.
Axes, 148, 149.

Babcock and Wilcox Company, 339.
Baking, 263; National Biscuit Company, 268, 269; New York Biscuit Company, 268; trusts, 268–269, 349.
Baking Powder, 263.
Balance of Trade, 10, 11.
Baldwin Locomotive Works, 151; agreement with Westinghouse Company, 136; electric locomotives, 166; exports, 136, 137; incorporation, 141; labor, 14; output, 137, 138, 139, 140.
Baltic Countries, flax, 322.
Baltimore (Md.), breweries, 277; canning, 352; electric locomotives, 166; exchange (colonial), Appendix I; fertilizers, 289, 290; prices (colonial, flour), Appendix VI; *id.* (iron), Appendix V; *id.* (shipbuilding), Appendix

Index

IV; shipbuilding, 144; sulphuric acid, 285; tin plate, 131, 142, 164.
Baltimore and Ohio Railroad Company, 166.
Barges (ore), 19, 63.
Baring Brothers and Company (failure), 9.
Barnum Richardson Company, 23.
Barrett Company, 348.
Bath (Maine) (shipbuilding), 144.
Bath Iron Works (shipbuilding), 144.
"*Bath-tub Trust*," 259.
Batteries, motor, 163; storage (manufacture controlled by Electric Storage Battery Company), 168.
Belfast (Ireland) (American ship plates), 112, 113, 130.
Belgium (Belgian), consumption (iron and steel), 100, 116; furnace gases for blowing engines, 153; immigrants in worsted mills, 14; iron, 92, 111; linen, 322; Solvay by-product coke ovens, 282.
Bell, Alexander Graham (inventor), 297.
Bellaire (Ohio) (glass makers' association), 261.
Berkshire County (Mass.) (wool manufactures), 196.
Berliner, Emil (gramophone inventor), 297.
Benz, Carl (automobile inventor), 157, 158.
Benzol, 282, 283, 316.
Bessemer Iron, 15, 16, 22, 24; British, 24; demanded for structural steel, 31; pool, 20; prices, 94, 95, 98, 99, 103; producers' agreement, 87–88; production, 32.
Bessemer Pig Iron Association, 88.
Bessemer Steamship Company, 142.
Bessemer Steel, 30, 34–35, 40, 42, 44, 47, 51–52, 57–58, 60, 63, 65–71, 76–82, 127; duplex process, 78; production, 44, 58, 60, 65; rails, 57, 84, 118, 119; ratio to open hearth, 63; Roberts-Bessemer, 65, 66; slag cement, 255; variants of processes, 65–66, 70–71, 77–78; wire, 124
Bethlehem (Pa.), 17.
Bethlehem Iron (and Steel), Corporation (Company, Works), 37, 39, 41, 64, 80, 86, 122, 301, 309, 313; absorbs other companies, 330; acquired by Schwab interests, 39; armor plant, 147; assets and capital, 39, 40; corporations embraced, 40; export agreement, 334; organization, 39; output, 40, 64; shipbuilding, 39–40; stock in Juragua Company, 17.
Bicarbonate of Soda, 287.
Bichromate of Potassium and Sodium, 285.
Bicycle (tricycle), ball bearings, 156; Columbia, 159; development, 155–156; skilled workers absorbed by automobile, 162; World War, 314.
Biddeford Mills, 188.
Binder Twine (see *Hemp*).
Birmingham (District) (Ala.), 36, 41, 50, 51, 88, 94, 97, 110; by-product coke ovens, 289; car plant, 139; freight, 26; iron and steel, 16, 42, 49, 62, 109; iron exports, 24, 25, 111, 112; iron shipping point, 25; "plus rate," 303.
Birmingham Cement Company, 50.
Black Sea (iron ore), 16.
Blackstone Valley (Mass.), paper, 352.
Blackwell's Island Bridge, 121.

Blaine, James G. (condemns hide duty), 229.
Bleacheries and Bleaching, 175, 285, 287.
Boilers, 128, 129, 152; plates, 68, 69; tubes, 23, 72.
Bonds (proportion of, to stocks in corporations), 7.
Boots and Shoes: agencies in Europe, 142; centers, 232; colors, 231; combination, 350; competition (western), 232; contract shops, 230; corporations, 230; exports, 231–232; finishings, 231; geography, 232–233; labor costs, 234; machinery, 232, 233–234; McKay sewed shoes surpassed by welted, 231; markets, 231, 232; mechanical improvements, 230; organization, 230; Philadelphia, 234; Rochester (N. Y.), 232; St. Louis, 232; styles and fashions, 231, 349–350; technology, 230; thread, 215, 218; value of exports, 231; welted, 231; west, 231.
Borax, 285.
Boston (Mass.), 144, 232; Arkwright Club, 173, 184, 185; automobiles, 158; Better Business Club (Bureau), 300; breweries, 278; brick, 258; cordage and hemp, 219, 220; cotton industry, 180; glass, 260; prices, colonial, flour, Appendix VI; *id.*, iron, Appendix V; *id.*, lumber, Appendix II; *id.*, shipbuilding, Appendix IV; *id.*, tar, Appendix III; publishing, 295; steam pressure, 338; steel, 34; wire market, 191.
Boston Breweries Company, 278.
Boston Duck Company (electric power), 3.
Boston Rubber Shoe Company, 235.
"*Boston System*" (tailoring), 222.
Bowling Green (N. Y.), 163.
Bowron, James, 109.
Boxer outbreak, 188.
Braddock (Pa.), 91.
Bradford System (worsted), 199.
Brady's Bend Iron Company (Works), 20.
Brandywine, 84.
Brazil, 110; Diamond Match Company, 292; imports, iron ore, 16; manganese ores, 17, 79; meat trade, 265.
Breakfast Foods (see *Cereals*): advertisements, 268; packers manufacture, 265.
Brewing, 276, 277; advertisement of brands, 278; centers, 275, 276; demand for glucose, 270; local consolidations, 277, 278; markets, 278; Milwaukee, 287; production, 278; saloons, 278; soda ash, by-product, 287.
Briar Hill Steel Company, 35.
Brick and Tiles, 50, 257, 281; centers, 258; consolidations, 258; fire, 350; Kansas, 254, 258, 352; kinds, 258, 281; paving, 258, 281; pressed, 258; production, 256, 258; sand, 258; vitrified, 258.
Bridgeport (Ohio), 89
Bridges: American Bridge Company, 121; cement, 255; exported, 38, 120, 121; standard steel specifications, 80; steel, 38, 57, 100, 119.
Bristol County (Mass.) (cotton spinning), 172.
British Columbia, 16.
British India (iron ore), 16.
British Iron and Steel Institute, 115.
British Iron Trade Association, 114.
British Iron Trade Commission, 90, 108.

British Westinghouse Electric and Manufacturing Company, Ltd., 170.
Brockton (Mass.), 232, 233.
Bromine, 285.
Brooklyn (N. Y.) bridge, 121; clothing, 223; steel imports, 114.
Brunswick (Ga.), 125.
Buckets (clam shell ore), 19.
Buckwheat, 267.
Buffalo (N. Y.), 95; charcoal furnaces, 72; flour, 348; iron, 18, 19; Niagara Falls (electricity power), 2; 166, 338; rayon, 347; shipbuilding, 141; steel, 36, 37, 89 (strike), 334.
Buggies, 350.
Buffalo and Susquehanna Iron Company, 24.
Buffalo Union Furnace Company, 24, 89.
Building trades, cement, 253, 255; Spanish War, 97; structural steel, 80, 100, 119.
Bulgaria, 129.
Bureau of Corporations established, 8.
Bureau of Navigation, 145.
Bureau of Standards, 319.
Butanol, 331.
Butter, 263, 266.
By-products, ammonia, 282, 286; coke, 49, 72–73, 282, 283, 286, 287, 289; corn, 270; cottonseed oil, 284; ovens (Semet Solvay), 49, 50; packing house, 264, 265, 266; sand paper, 265; steel, 47, 64; tar, 282.

Calcium carbide, 285, 288.
Calcutta (India), 110, 230.
California, 89, 120, 152; beet sugar, 272, 273; canning, 270, 271; electric generators, 338; electric transmission, 167; lumber, 241; tinplate market, 132; wine, 276; wool manufacture, 196.
California Fruit Canners' Association, 271.
Cambria (*Iron and Steel*) *Company*, 20, 22, 39, 41, 42, 46, 57, 64, 84, 138, 309; absorbed by Bethlehem Steel, 330; beams, 121; by-products ovens, 282; output, 64; steel cars, 139.
Camden (Me.), 82.
Camden (N. J.) (shipbuilding), 143.
Cameras, 296, 352.
Canada: American Screw Company plant, 126; American Tobacco Company factories, 279; breakfast foods, 268; canneries, 132; copper, 1; Diamond Match Company, 292; exports (leather), 230; imports, 57, 129, 133, 153, 204; locomotives, 89, 140; market, 111; paper, 246, 247, 248, 251; rails, 46; rubber tires, 237; wheat ground at Buffalo, 349.
Canaigre (tannage), 226.
Candles (shipped via New Orleans), Appendix, XIII.
Canning, Association, 270; additions of soup, etc. (1893–1914), 270; Alaska, 270; California, 270, 271; canneries, 271; cans, 271; centers, 270, 271; chemical and bacteriological control, 270, 271; fruit, 271; laboratory, 271; machinery, 271; market for tin plate, 130, 131; organization, 270; pineapple in Hawaii, 270, 271; prices, 270; specialization, 270; standardization of raw materials, 271; value of product, 270.

Canton (Mass.) (cotton), 174.
Cape Breton (Canada), 18.
Capetown (Africa) (Diamond Match Company), 292.
Capital: absorption by big corporations, 102; cotton manufactures, 186, Appendix XI; expansion of (in industrial combinations), 6–7; large operating necessary, 355; over-expansion absorbs too rapidly, 11; super-abundant, 6, 11.
Carbon dioxide, 287.
Carbon Electrodes, 169.
Carbonate of Potash, 199.
Carbonic Acid, 285.
Carborundum Company, 2.
Carey Blast Furnaces, 44.
Carnegie, Andrew, 21, 43, 44, 55, 56, 91.
Carnegie Steel Company (Works), 43–44, 46, 54, 57, 59, 67, 70, 75, 80, 91, 99, 118, 123, 129; amalgamation and lawsuits, 43–44; armor, 313; beams, 121; benzol, 282; controls iron market, 5; expansion, 43; nickel-steel rails, 80; Oliver Mining Company, 43; production of pig iron, 44, 116; property acquired, 43; purchased by United States Steel Corporation, 56; ship plates, 112, 113; steel cars, 136–137, 138; steel steamers, 143; World War, 314.
Carnegie-Oliver group, 21.
Carnegie-Rockefeller agreement, 21.
Carolina Ores, 16.
Carpets (see also *Wool Manufactures*): Axminster, 208; Berlin (price), 208; Bigelow Carpet Company (consolidation with Lowell Manufacturing Company), 209; Brussels, 208; colonial, Appendix VII; development (1893–1914), 207–209; displacement of cheap weaves, 207; exports, 204; foreign wool, 193; imports, 208; India, 208; ingrains, 207, 208, 209; linen warps, 218; looms imported, 208; markets, 208; Moquette, 208; organization, 208; Pennsylvania, 208; Philadelphia, 195; pile, 207, 208; price, 208; production, 208; rugs, 203, 207, 208; spindle increase, 208; tariff (Wilson Act), 208; territorial wool, 193; value per yard, 208; velvet, 208, 214.
Cars, railway, 136, 139; consumption of steel, 140; corporations, 138; freight, 138; gondola, 138; hopper, 138; production, 137, 139; refrigerator, 242; springs, 80; steel, 136–138, 139, 140; United States Steel Company, 59, 63; wheels, 23; World War, 314.
Carthaginia (Spain) (iron ore), 16.
Cartons, 275.
Casein, 266.
Castner Electrolytic Alkali Company, 288.
Castor-oil, 284.
Cedric (S. S.), 144.
Ceiling (metal), 89.
Celanese Corporation (rayon), 347.
Celluloid, 291.
Cellulose (substituted for carbon in electric lamps), 165.
Cement, 281; age, 253–256; bridges, 255; building and structural use, 253, 255; centers, 255; consumption per capita, 256; expansion, 254; fuel, 254, 256; imports, 253, 254; laboratory, 256; markets, 255; organization, 254, 256;

Pennsylvania, 254, 255; prices, 254, 255; processes, 253, 254, 255; Portland, 253, 254, 255–256; production, 253, 254, 255; Puzzolan, 255; raw materials, 255; slag, 254, 255; substituted for wood in buildings, 253; tariff, 253; technical advances, 255; United States Steel Company, 64.
Centennial Exhibition (see references under separate industries).
Central Foundry Company, 128.
Central Leather Company, 228; World War profits, 323.
Cereals, centers in Central West, 268; corporations, 268; intensive advertising, 268; value of products, 263.
Chapin Mines, 43.
Charcoal and Charcoal Iron (see also *Iron*), 53, 71–72; blooms, 23; furnaces, 24, 25, 72; Swedish, 72.
Charleston (S. C.), fertilizers, 290–291; knitting, 13.
Chattanooga (Tenn.) (iron freight rates), 26.
Cheese, 263; factory production, 266; packing trusts, 265.
Chemical Foundation, 318.
Chemicals (see *Dyes, Explosives*), alkalis, 287; ammonia, 286; bleaching agents, 285, 287; carbide, 288; chlorine (in cylinders), 288; increase in variety and quantity, 285; output, 7; plants, 283; pyrites (substituted for sulphur), 267–286; sulphide, 3; sulphite liquor, 285; sulphuric acid, 285, 286.
Chemistry and Chemical Industry, corn by-product experiments, 270; electrolytic process, 168, 287; food preparation, 270, 271; gases (compressed and liquefied), 288; General Chemical Company, 288; geography, 287; glass making, 259; market for clay, 256; miscellaneous, 291–293; paper making, 246, 287; production (growth), 288, 347; raw materials, 285; soda, 285, 287, 290; Solvay process, 287; sulphuric acid, 285; tariff, 288; textile schools, 180; works drift inland, 285.
Chesapeake Bay, 352.
Chester (Pa.), 36, 217; plate rolling, 84; shipbuilding, 141, 314.
Chicago (Ill.), 7, 53, 121, 122, 205; agricultural implements and machinery, 146; automobile show, 162; boots and shoes, 234; breweries, 277; brick, 258; carbide, 288; cement laboratory, 256; Commercial Club, 300; corporations, 88; electric locomotives, 166; electric vehicles, 158; Federal Steel Company, 45–47; food fats, 283; furniture, 244, 245; iron and steel, 24; packing, 229, 263; publishing, 295; steam turbine, 338; steel, 36, 45, 46, 54, 55, 57, 309, 330; tanning, 227; World's Fair, 157, 338.
Chicago Elevated Railway, 136.
Chicago Outer Belt Line Railway, 46.
Chicopee Falls (Mass.), 174.
Chile, 110; copper, 17; nitrates, 289; Tofo mines, 17, 40.
China, 188; cotton, 173, 175, 188; exports, 114; iron ore, 16, 107; locomotives, 137; raw silk, 216.
Chlorine, 287, 288.
Chrome (ore), 81, 285.

Chrome-Vanadium, 141.
Chromite, 310.
Chromium, 80, 81.
Cigarettes (see *Tobacco*), 278–279.
Cigars (see *Tobacco*), 279.
Cincinnati, boots and shoes, 232; machine tools, 150, 153, 154.
Cinema, 293.
Civil War, 37, 124, 192, 210, 216; cotton shortage, 218; Massachusetts manufactures, 298–299; iron and steel, 92, 299; printing, 293, 294; wool manufactures, 200, 299–300.
Claflin Company, H. B. (acquire cotton mills), 183.
Clapp-Griffith Steel Process, 30, 65–66.
Clarkson, Grosvenor B., 306, 405.
Clay, consumption, 256; deposits, 258; markets, 256; plants, 256–257; production, 256.
Clayton Act, 298, 327.
Clergue, Francis H. (charcoal iron), 72.
Cleveland (Ohio), breweries, 277; iron, 18, 19, 24, 87; iron offices, 19, 20; ore trade, 24; pottery, 257; rayon, 347; screw plants, 126; shipbuilding, 144; steel, 41, 87; tool making, 149.
Cleveland and Sandusky Brewing Company, 277.
Clothing, 222–224; Boston system, 222; centers, 223, 224; cloaks and coats, 223; collars and cuffs, 224; contractors, 223; electricity, 168; exports, 204; factory system, 222–223; home work, 222, 223, 224; immigrant labor, 222, 223; legislation, 222; machinery, 223; mechanization, 223; men's clothing, 197, 223; organization, 222–223; quality, improvement in, 224; sweat shops, 222; tenement house, 223; value of product, 222, 224; women's, 196, 223.
Clyde River (shipbuilding), 112, 113, 130.
Coal, 39, 123; Alabama, 42; cement fuel, 255; Connellsville, 282; consumption, 281; fields, 56; freight, 50; furnace fuel, 72; lands, 24; mining (cost), 45, 92; Pennsylvania, 24, 39; powdered, 254; roads, 80; strike, 13, 14, 28, 53; United States Steel Company, 58, 63; United States surpasses Great Britain, 281.
Coats, J. and P., Company, 180.
Coatsville (Pa.), 84.
Cobalt, 81.
Coffeyville (Kan.) (brick making), 258.
Coke (see *Coking Ores*), 41, 42, 49, 53, 72, 73, 111, 112, 123, 127; bee hive, 63, 282; "Belgian" ovens, 282; by-product, 49, 72–73; 282, 283, 286–287, 289, (World War), 315–316; Connellsville, 44, 57, 67, 95; cost, 92; fields (United States Steel Corporation), 58; freight, 50; Frick, H. C., Coke Company, 59; furnaces, 123; ovens, 27, 42, 46, 47, 53, 54, 57, 63, 282, 289; Pennsylvania, 24, 46, 57; prices, 99; production, 47, 281, 282, 283; Semet-Solvay Corporation, 49, 50; strike, 28; Tennessee Coal, Iron and R. R. Company, 48.
Colorado, beet sugar, 273; coal (strike), 53; iron and steel, 24, 78; rails, 118.
Colorado Fuel (and Iron) Company, 52–54, 57, 64, 78; adds structural department, 120; railmakers' agreement, 53.
Columbia bicycles, 159.

Columbia County (N. Y.), 53.
Columbia Electric Automobile, 159.
Columbia Mills (Columbia, S. C.), 167.
Columbia (S. C.), electric power, 3, 167; negro labor, 13; spindle center, 175.
Columbus (Ga.) cotton, 185.
Commerce, Department of (Secretary of), 333.
Commercial and Financial Chronicle, 8.
Commercial Solvents Corporation, 331.
Commissioner of Corporations, 106.
Competition, American threatens Europe, 10; trusts (devices for controlling), 5; World War, 308.
Conciliation and Arbitration Board (Great Britain), 82.
Concord (N. C.) (negro operatives), 13.
Confederate Government, Conscription Law, 302.
Conneaut (Ohio) (steel), 57, 129.
Connecticut, hardware, 148; iron, 15, 71; prices (colonial), Appendices II and IV; rayon, 347; shipbuilding, 143; silks, 211; war industries, 304; wool, 195.
Connecticut River (Valley), 4, 312.
Connellsville (Pa.), coal, 282; coke, 44, 57, 67, 95; coke ovens, 57.
Consolidated Cotton Duck Company, 182.
Consolidated Lake Superior Company, 2; failure, 102; hydroelectric power, 2–3.
Continental Match Company, 292–293.
Continental Motor Manufacturing Company (*Motors*), 164, 337.
Continental Tobacco Company, 278, 279.
Cook County (Ill.) (brick), 258.
Cook Locomotive and Machine Company, 140.
Cooperage, 242, 243.
Copenhagen (Denmark) (iron), 113.
Copper, 1, 286; electrolytic process, 3, 168; flotation process, 311; imports and exports, 1; ores (Chile), 17; prices, 311; product, 311; wires, 124; World War, 311, 325; works, 285.
Copper and Brass Research Association, 325.
Copper Export Association, 326.
Copper Producers Association, 311.
Copperas, 285.
Cordage (see *Hemp*).
Corn, products, 50, 267, 270; canned, 271; distilling, 276, 277.
Cornwall Mines, 15.
Corporations (see *Trusts*), 87–89; agricultural machinery, 146–147; conditions favoring development, 6; financial concentration in New York City, 8; financing reflects abundant money, 11; food, 263; furniture, 244–245; glass, 261; iron, 20, 21; legislation for control, 8; lumber, 241–242; number, 7; steel, 35–64; thread, 180–181; vertical, 69; woolen, 205.
"*Cosmopolitan*," 295.
Cottolene, 283–284.
Cotton, 50, 124, 218; boll weevil, 186; cargo (iron used as ballast), 50; consumption, 171–172, 185, 340; consumption per spindle, 171; crops, 171, 185; duty, 329; Egyptian, 171, 179; ginning and handling improvement, 178; gins, 284; machinery for picking, 146; planters, 147; preparation for market (improvement), 178; prices, 177, 184, 185, 186; production, 171; quality (improvement), 178; scientific testing of fibers, 178; Sea Island, 179; spinning (amount consumed), 171; transportation, 173; waste and linters, 319.
Cotton Machinery, 174; active, 343; automatic, 178, 179; carding, 178, combing, 178; Crompton loom, 178; decline after armistice, 339; Knowles loom, 178; metal drawing rolls introduced, 177; mules, 177, 181, 341; Northrop loom, 178, 189, 190; spinning (improvements), 177; tended per employe (Great Britain and United States), 190; weaving, 177, 178; World War, 324.
Cotton Manufactures (see also *South Cotton*), advantages of United States over foreign competitors, 179; airplane fabric, 319; Alabama, 176, 178; American Thread Company, 180; Arkansas, 175; artificial leather, 340; Atlantic States, 172; automatic machinery, 178, 179; Boston, 180; broadcloth, 341; bunting, 340; calicoes, 340; cambrics, 340; capital, 186; centers, 175; Central Atlantic States, 172; cheese cloth, 340; child labor, 176; China, 173, 175, 188; collective bargaining, 189; combing, 178; compared with Great Britain, 179, 187–188, 190; competition (foreign), 185, 187–188; competition (North and South), 173–175, 180, 185; concentration, 172, 180, 183; Confederacy, 218; corduroys, 189; corporations, 180, 181; cost of production, 173, 190; cottonades, 180; crises and depressions (1898), 185, 186, 221, (1914), 318–319, 341–342; damask, 340; denim, 180, 340; drills, 173, 180, 189, 340; duck, 180, 188; duties, 190; education (textile), 180; electricity (use of), 3, 167; England, 341–342; expansion, 171; exports, 173, 175, 187–188, 342; fabrics, 179–180; flannel, 340; freight, 173; fuel costs, 173; geography, 172, 174, 175; Georgia, 175; ginghams, 180, 340; growth during reconstruction, 172–177; home-work experiment, 183; hosiery, 183; hours of labor, 176; imports, 190; imports (colonial), Appendix VIII; India, 342; interownership, 183; labor, 173, 176, 177, 188–190, 190; lawns, 340; marketing, 173, 176; markets (domestic), 174, 185, 190; markets (foreign), 77, 173, 174, 175, 185, 188; Massachusetts, 172; mercerized thread and fabrics, 179; Middle Atlantic States, 173; monopoly of domestic market, 185; Mount Vernon, Appendix VII; New England, 171–173, 179–181, 185–188, 340, 341, 342; North versus South, 173–175, 340, 342; organization, 173, 180–184; Orient, 342; osnaburgs, 340; Appendix XI; output printing machine (compared with British), 179; Pennsylvania, 172; percales, 340; pool (print cloth), 181–182; power, 3, 173, 176; prices, 184, 186, 342; Appendices VII and IX; print cloths, 179, 184, 340, 342; prints, 340; production, 179, 185, 186, 342; profits, 187, 342, 342–343; Appendix XI; Providence (R. I.), 172, 174; quality, 179; rank among nations, 187; revolutionizes Southern social standards, 176; Rhode Island, 172; sheetings, 173, 180, 188, 340;

Index

shirtings, 180, 340; South, 171–180, 182–183, 185–186, 188–189, 340, Appendix XI; specialization of North in finer grades, 173, 174, 175, 178, 179, 184, 340; spindles (see *Spinning*), 171, 172, 173, 175, 177, 178, 183; spinning (see *Spindles*), 172, 177, 181; style directors, 340; technical development and progress, 177–180; thread, 215, 340; ticking, 340, Appendix VII; tire fabrics, 340; toweling, 340; trade conditions, 173, 184–187; twills, 180, 340; value of product, 188, 190; value of product compared to silk, 210; Virginia, 175; voiles, 341; wages, 14, 173, 189; West, 173; worsteds, 340; yarns, 340, (combed), 341.
Cotton Mills, 174; acquired by merchandizing houses, 183; branches of New England established in South, 174; "cooperative," 182–183; design and construction, 176; electric power, 3; elimination of small and uneconomical, 174; employes in South, 176; employment of children, 176; negro labor, 13; Southern, 175, 176.
Cotton Ties (Steel), 57, 126, 127.
Cottonseed Oil, 265; by-products, 284; corporations, 284; food manufactures, 283; meal, 174, 289; organization, 284.
Council of National Defense, 301–302.
Cramp, William and Sons (shipyards), 102, 141, 142, 143, 145, 151.
Crane (electric), 84.
Creosote, 243, 283.
Crinoline Wire, 124.
Crisco, 283.
Crisis of 1893 (see also *Panic*), 8–9, 47, 209.
Crops, 9, 10, 11.
Crown Point (N. Y.) (iron), 23.
Crucible Steel Company of America, 71, 76.
"Crushers' Association" (cottonseed), 5.
Cuba (Cuban), 40, 51; iron and coal from Alabama, 25; iron ore, 15, 16, 17, 22, 38, 39; Reciprocity Treaty, 25; sugar tariff, 273; trade, 142.
Cuban Steel Ore Company, 17.
Cudahy Packing Company, 265, 327.
Cultural Manufactures, 293–297.
Cumberland (Md.) (tinplate), 133.
Currency, colonial, Appendix I; legislation, 100.
Cutlery, centers, 149; market, 148; steel imports, 148.
Cyanamid, 290.
Cyanide (potassium), 285.
Cylinder Press (Hoe revolving), 293.

da Vinci, Leonardo, 156.
Dairy Industry, 263, 266.
Dakota (S. S.), 144, 145.
Dayton (Ohio), cash registers, 353.
De Laval Turbine, 4.
Deere and Company, 350.
Deering International Harvester Company (Works), 146; cordage, 219; motor-driven mowing machine, 160–161.
De Kalb, General, 357.
Delaware River (Valley), 40; silk mills, 211.
Delaware River Iron Shipbuilding and Engine Company, 141.
Denison (Texas) (cotton mills), 175.
Depression, general (see also *Panics*), (1894), 14, 87, (1907), 11–12, 104.
Des Moines (Iowa) (brick), 258.
Detroit (Mich.), automobiles, 158, 160, 164; chemicals, 287; shipbuilding, 145.
Detroit Pressed Steel Company, 337.
Diamond Match Company, 292.
Diamond Rubber Co. (combined with B. F. Goodrich Company), 237.
Diamond State Steel Company, 36.
Die Castings (alloy steel), 80.
Diesel Engines, 151.
Dingley Tariff, 10, 200, 201, 229, 273.
Disinfectants, 287.
Disston Saws (Works), 148.
Distillers and Cattle Feeders Trust, 276.
Distilling, Bourbon whisky, 276, 277; centers, 277; corn, 276, 277; illicit, 275; Illinois Supreme Court decision, 276; mash used to fatten cattle, 264; monopoly, 276–277; prohibition, 331; raw materials, 277; rum, 277; Peoria, 277; speculative character, 276–277; trust, 276.
Distilling and Cattle-Feeding Company, 276.
Distilling Company of America, 276, 277.
District of Columbia, 77.
Dobsons (worsted manufacturers), 344.
Docks (ore), 19, 56.
Dodge Company (automobile), 314.
Dolomite, 49.
Dominion Iron and Mill Works (Richmond, Va.), 130.
Dominion Iron and Steel Company (Sidney, Cape Breton), 18.
Douglas Axe (Company), 148.
Douglas fir, 238.
Draper, George A. (cotton loom inventor), 178.
Duluth (Minn.), 37; iron, 24; shipbuilding, 141, 144; steel, 45, 57, 61, 64.
Duluth and Iron Range Railway, 19, 47.
Dun, R. G., and Company, (Dun, Barlow and Company), 8, 95.
Dundee (Scotland), 113.
Dunkirk (N. Y.), locomotives, 139.
Dunlop Tire Company, 236.
du Pont de Nemours, E. I., Powder Company (*du Ponts*), 292, 316; dyes, 318, 347; pyroxylins, 331; rayon, 347.
Duquesne (Pa.), 43, 70.
Duquesne Steel Works, 44, 70.
Durham (N. C.), 183.
Duryea, Charles E. (automobile builder),157,158.
Dwight Manufacturing Company, 174.
Dyes (*Dyeing and Finishing*) (see *Chemicals*), 221; aniline dyes, and (coal tar) dyes, 291; duties, 329; establishments (departments in spinning and weaving factories), 221; exports, 347; importation of dyestuffs, 221, 347; labor (immigrant), 221; prices (early), 317; silk, 221; textile education, 180; World War, 316–318.
Dynamite (see *Explosives*).
Dynamos, alternating current, 165; influence in development of steam engines and turbines, 166; Niagara Falls Power Company, 86; value of, 170.

Eagle and Phoenix Mills, 185.
East Canaan (Conn.) (iron), 23.
East Douglas (Mass.) (axes), 149.
East India, 226.
East Liverpool (Ohio) (pottery), 257.
East Pittsburgh (Pa.), 166, 169, 170.
East Tennessee (Aluminum), 4.
Eastern Bar Iron Association, 87.
Eastern Shipbuilding Company, 143, 145.
Eastman Kodak Company, 296.
Easton (Pa.), 139.
Economy (Pa.), 121, 144.
Edge Law, 333.
Edinburgh (Scotland), 148.
Edinburgh "Scotsman," 236.
Edison Electric Light Company (Edison General Electric Company) (see also *General Electric Company*), 169.
Edison, Thomas, cement kilns, 255; phonograph, 296.
Education, steel (campaign for), 59; technical 12; textile, 12; 180, 207; wool classification, 192.
Egg powders, 266.
Egypt (cotton), 171, 329.
Elba (iron ore), 16.
Electric (see *Dynamos, Electricity*), apparatus (value of), 170; automobiles, 157, 158, 159, 161, 162, 163, 164; cabs, 158; capital investment, 339; conduits, 129, 134; delivery wagons, 158; dynamos, 86, 165, 166, 170; engines, 166; equipment (export of), 170; furnaces, 3, 169; generators, 155, 166–167, 170; hydroelectric development, 166; lighting, 165, 167, 169, 260, 283; locomotives, 136, 137, 139, 166; machinery (value), 170; motors (cotton mills), 167; plants, 169; power (increase, 1893–1914), 168; traction, 122, 125, 165, 166, 169, 180; transmission, 165, 167, 169, 170; value of machinery, supplies and apparatus, 170; vehicles, 158, 168.
Electric Boat Company, 169.
Electric Storage Battery Company, 158, 168.
Electrical Vehicle Company, 160.
Electricity (Electric Industries) (see also *Electric*), consumption, 152, 167–168; cotton mills, 3, 167; creates new market for clay, 256; General Electric, 168; Hartford, 338; hydro-electric power, 2–5, 166, 167, 169, 338; iron and steel, 75, 168; liberates manufacturing from geographical and physical bounds, 4–5; litigation, 169; long-distance transmission, 2, 167, 169; machine tool development (influence), 155; Niagara Falls, 166, 167, 169, 338; operation of machinery, 165; organization of industry, 168–170; paper making, 2, 168, 246; product, 338; steel mills, 339; technical progress, 165; telegraph, 165; telephone, 165; turbines (water), 338, (mercury), 338–339; turbogenerators, 338; Westinghouse, 168.
Electrolytic Process, 287.
Elevated Railroads (structural steel), 119.
Elizabeth (N. J.), electric carriages, 158; shipbuilding, 142.
Enamel Ware, 132.
Engineering Industry, depression, 136; exports (position of machinery), 153; specialities, 151; tendency toward horizontal trusts, 151; textiles, 180; works, cement, 255.
Engines, blowing, 153; compound, 5; Corliss, 338; exported, 153; gas, 151, 152–153; gasoline, 157, 158, 161, 162; horsepower, 153, 338; internal combustion, 73, 152, 153, 157, 161, 241, 283; lathes, 153, 154; reversing, 84; steam boiler, 152; steam pressure, 338; steam turbines, 5, 338.
England (English) (see also *Great Britain*), 152; bicycles, 156; capital invested in American industries, 180; cement, 254; charcoal iron, 109; coke, 48; cotton (thread), 180; iron (imports from United States), 25, 96, 111, 112; iron and steel (labor cost), 92; labor (America), 13, 14; leather (American imports), 229; paper (American office), 248; prices (iron and steel), 64, 91, 104, 105; railroads order American locomotives, 137–138; subsidy (mail steamers), 110; Tropenas process, 78; zinc and iron process, 134.
Ensley Brick Company, 50.
Erie (Pa.) (steel), 57.
Europe (European), competition, 10; copper, 1; flax-spindle statistics, 218; iron imports, 25, 107; locomotives, 137; steel, 46
Explosives, 291–292; dynamite, 291–292; nitroglycerine, 291; prices, 316; smokeless powder, 316, 331; sulphuric acid, 286.
Exchange (colonial on London), Appendix I.
Exports, 1–2, 10, 11; agricultural products, 1; automobiles, 164; boots and shoes, 231–232; bridges, 38, 120; clothing, 204; copper, 1; cotton, 1, 111, 342; dyes, 347; Edge Law, 333; engines, 153; glass, 260, 262; iron and steel, 25, 108–114; machinery, 153; manufactures, 1, 2; ore, 1; pipes, 114, 129; rails 111, 112, 113, 114, 118; saws, 148; sewing machines, 153; silk, 215; steel, 113, 114, 334; tinplate, 130–133; typewriters, 153; value, 1–2; wool manufactures, 345; World War, 303.
Export Trade Act, 326.

Fairfax (Va.), Appendix I.
Fairfield (Ala.), 313.
Fall River (Mass.), 9; cotton, 172, 180, 181, 182, 184, 185, 319, 340, 343; dividends, 342, 343; silk, 216, 340; strike, 14, 188–189; textiles, 173, 174; textile school, 12, 180.
Farrell (Pa.) (benzol works), 282.
Federal Courts (preferential jurisdiction over trusts), 8.
Federal Reserve Bank, 332.
Federal Steel Company, 45–47, 54, 55, 56, 60, 61, 98, 123; capital and charter, 46; corporations merged into, 46.
Federal Trade Commission, 300, 308, 326, 330, 337.
Felt Mills (controlled by American Felt Company), 205.
Fencing (woven wire and barbed), 57, 122, 124, 125.
Ferro-alloys (use of electricity), 168, 310.
Ferro-manganese (production of), 79.
Ferro-silicon, 76.
Fertilizer Industry, 289–291; associated with

cottonseed oil industry, 289; centers, 289, 290; corporations, 290; development in South, 289, 291; phosphate rocks, 286; plants, 284; sulphuric acid, 286.
Finns (textile mill workers), 14.
Fir, 238.
Fish (packing trust), 265.
Flax, boot and shoe thread, 218; carpet yarns, 218; corporation, 218; crash toweling, 219; decline due to cotton and woolen competition, 218; duty, 218; fiber (imported), 218; manufactures (Mount Vernon), Appendix VII; markets, 218; production (value), 219; thread, 218; twines, 218; World War, 322.
Flint (Mich.) (automobiles), 162.
Florence (Ala.) (cotton), 175.
Florida (naval stores), 243.
Flotation process, 311.
Flour, association (protective), 267; centers, 267, 348–349; consumption, 267, 269; corporations, 268, 348; exports, 267, 268; geography, 267; machinery, 267; mills, 267; Minneapolis, 268; Minnesota, 267; prices, Appendices VI and IX; production, 267; rank of States, 267; Richmond (Va.), 267; shipped via New Orleans, Appendix XIII; value of product, 263.
Food (see also *Canning, Fish, Flour, Fruit, Packing*), 263; fats (see *Cottonseed Oil*), 283.
Food Administration, 302.
Ford Automobile Works (Ford Company), (see *Automobiles*), 162, 163, 356; airplanes, 354; Liberty motors, 336; shipbuilding, 314.
Ford, Henry (automobile manufacturer), 158, 160, 162, 328, 332.
Fore River Yards (Quincy, Mass.), 40.
Forests, 238–239.
Forks, 148.
Formaldehyde, 243.
Fort Smith (Ark.) (furniture), 244.
Fort Worth (Texas), 263.
Fox Pressed Steel Equipment Company, 138.
France (French), 3, 341; American shoemaking machinery, 232; armorplate and ordnance, 147, 148; automobiles, 161, 163; band saw introduced from, 240; barrel stock from Tennessee, 243; boot and shoe industry, 232; charcoal iron, 72; employed in worsted system, 14; iron ore, 92; linen, 322; steel, 40, 310.
Franklin (Pa.), 42.
Freight and Freight Rates (see *Railroads*), cotton, 173; equipment (steel cars), 140; iron and iron ores, 19; iron and steel, 17, 19, 20, 26, 109, 110; volume moved, 139.
French Canadian (weavers), 13.
Frick, H. C., lawsuit with Andrew Carnegie, 44.
Frick (H. C.) Coke Company, 43, 44, 59.
Fuel (see *Coal, Coke, Gas, Petroleum*), alcohol, 161; consumption, 281; furnace, 72–73; industrial, 281–283; influences industrial geography, 260; oil, 281, 283–284; producing centers, 281; sawdust, 240.
Fuel Administration, 302, 305.
Fulton County (N. Y.) (gloves), 234.
Furnaces (see also *Iron, Steel*), 150; electric, 76, 309, 335; heating substituted for stoves, 150; Pittsburgh, 73; United States Steel Corporation, 60.
Furniture, association, 245; cabinet woods, 244; centers, 244; geography, 244; Grand Rapids, 244; organization, 244–245; south, 244; tables, 245.

Galesburg (Ill.) (brickmaking), 258.
Gallego Mills (Richmond, Va.), 267.
Galveston (Texas) (hemp), 219.
Gambier (tannage), 226.
Gary (Ind.), steel, 36, 62, 63, 70, 73, 140, 168; strike, 334; tinplate, 133.
Gary, Judge Elbert H., 47, 56, 122.
Gas, belt (Pittsburgh), 281; blast furnace to generate steam, 73, 168; by-product, 282; carbide, 288; cement works, 254, 256; companies, 44; compressed and liquefied, 288; consumption, 281; engines, 73, 168; fields (United States Steel Corporation), 58; fuel, 50, 72, 73, 166, 254, 256, 257, 258, 281; furnace (internal-combustion engines), 153; glass works, 260; illuminating, 260, 281, 283; iron plants, 30, 168; natural, 44, 260, 281; pipes, 129.
Gasoline, 281; car, 157, 158, 160, 164; engine, 157, 158, 161; expanding demand, 283; Standard Oil Company, 161.
Gates, John W. (steel manufacturer), 122.
Gears, bicycle, 156; wheel, 78, 80.
Gelatine, 290.
General Chemical Company, 288, 348.
General Electric Company, 168, 169, 170; giant generators, 338; radio, 332.
General Mills, Incorporated, 448.
General Motors, 348; acceptance corporation, 333; ice machines, 354.
General Refractories Company, 350.
Geography of Manufactures (see various industries), cotton, 172; iron, 15–20; leather, 226–228; silk, 210–211; steel, 34–35, 41, 69; wool, 195–196.
Georgia, charcoal iron, 71; cotton, 176; fertilizers, 289; naval stores, 243; woolen mills, 206.
Germany (German), 153, 282; alcohol fuel, 161; aluminum, 325; American shoe machinery, 232; American Tobacco Company, 279; armor, 147, 148; automobiles, 157, 161, 163; Baldwin Locomotive Works employes, 14; bricks (sand and lime), 258; cement, 253, 254; charcoal iron, 72; chemicals, 289; Diamond Match Company, 292; dyes, 317; iron and steel, 22, 32, 76, 89, 100, 105, 109, 111, 112, 114, 116, 117, 309, 310; iron ore, 16, 92; Kali Syndicate, 290; knitting industry, 220; Krupp works, 84, 129; ordnance, 147, 148; phosphate works, 289; rails, 104; steel, 66, 77; wages (woolen industry), 204.
Glasgow (Scotland), 25, 81, 110, 113.
Glass, 281; art, 260–261; associations, 261–262, 327; automobile, 260; bottle making, 259, 260; centers, 260; chimneys, 261, 262; containers, 260; cost of production, 259; exports, 260, 262; gas fuel, 260; geography, 260; hand blowing, 259; imports, 260; labor, 259–260; lamps, 260; machines, 259, 262; optical, 261; organization, 261–262; output,

260, 262; Owen's automatic glass-blowing machine, 259; plate glass, 259, 260, 261; pots, 262; pressed, 259, 260; prices, 261; processes, 259; rank of states, 260; raw materials, 260, 261, 287; selling pool, 261; shipped via New Orleans, Appendix XIII; tank system, 259; technology, 259; Tiffany, 260; trust, 261, 262; value, 260, unbreakable, 348; wages, 260; westward movement, 260, 262; wind shields, 162–163, 348; window glass, 259, 260, 327.
Glove Making, 234.
Gloversville (N. Y.), 234.
Glucose, 263, 269–270.
Glue, 266, 290.
Goat Skins (see *Hides*).
Gogebic (ores), 43.
Goluchowski, Count (speech), 10.
Goodrich, B. F., Company (combines with Diamond Rubber Company), 237.
Gorman Bill, 25.
Gould, Edwin, 292; gramophone, 297.
Grand Central Palace, 162.
Grand Rapids (Mich.) (furniture center), 244.
Graniteville (S. C.), 189.
Graphophone, 296–297.
Great Britain (British) (see also *England*), 109; American locomotives, 137; American Screw Company, 126; armor plate, 313; boots and shoes, 231, 232; bridges (American builders given preference), 120; capital invested in Southern iron furnaces, 27; cement, 253; charcoal iron, 72; coal, 281; colonial market, 82; Conciliation and Arbitration Board, 82; cotton, 171, 172, 341; dyeing, 221; furnace output, 73; hematite, 113; investments in United States, 27; imports Alabama iron and steel, 109–111; iron and steel, 32, 82, 90, 92, 100, 114, 115; knitting, 220; linen (exports), 218; machinery, 153; mackintoshes, 237; motor vehicles, 163; ordnance and armor, 147, 148; rails, 118; shoddy, 194; shoes (American machinery), 232; steel, 41, 66, 69, 77, 121, 130, 310 (war supplies in U. S.), 325; thread, 180; wool, 202, 203, 207, (war control), 319.
Great Falls (Mont.), 4.
Great Lakes, 21, 43; iron ore, 18, 143, 145; lumber, 238; ports, 57; shipbuilding, 141, 142, 143, 144, 145, 146, 153.
Great Northern Paper Company, 249.
Great Northern Railway (steel steamers), 143.
Great Northern Steamship Company, 144.
Greece (Greeks), iron ore, 15; textile mills, 14.
Greenville (S. C.) (cotton), 175.
Grey, Henry (inventor), 122.
Groceries (packers manufacture), 265.
Guayule Rubber, 237.
Gulf States (lumber), 238.
Guncotton (see *Explosives*).
Gunpowder (see *Explosives*), (shipped via New Orleans), Appendix XIII.

Hair (curled, by-product meat packers), 265.
Half-tone Process, 294, 295.
Hamilton (Ohio) (machine tools), 149.
Hammer (pneumatic), 85.
Hammond (Ind.), 45.
Hankow (China) (iron), 114.
Harding, President Warren G., 328.
Hardware, building, 148; geography and market, 148.
Harlan, Hollingsworth and Company, 40.
Harriman Railroad System, 119, 140.
Harrison (N. J.) (electricity), 169.
Hartford (Conn.), 154, Appendix III; bicycles, 156; machine tools, 154.
Harvesters (see *Agricultural Machinery*), 146; charcoal iron, 72.
Hats (fur), 221, 222; centers, 222; cloth caps, 222; soft, 222; wool, 221–222.
Haverhill (Mass.), 230, 232.
Hawaii, coastal shipping law, 142; duties, 274; pineapples, 270; sugar, 272.
Hayes Wheel Company, 337.
Haynes, Elwood (automobiles), 158.
Hazard, Rowland G. (free wool advocate), 201.
Heat-treating metals, 312.
Hemlock, paper making, 247; tannage, 225; western, 239.
Hemp (Sisal), cordage and binder twine, 124, 219, 220, 322; geography, 219–220; Manila, 219, 220; manufactures shipped via New Orleans, Appendix III; organization, 219; raw materials, 219, 220; sisal, 219, 220.
Henderson (S. C.) (knitting mills), 13.
Heroult Electric Furnace, 309.
Hides, goat skins, 226, 227, 229, 230; imports, 226; packers, 265.
High Point (N. C.) (furniture), 244.
Hill, James (iron properties), 22.
Hoe, Richard M. (revolving cylinder press), 293.
Hog Island (Delaware River), shipyard, 314.
Holland (see *Netherlands*) (market for southern iron), 111.
Holt Manufacturing Company, 163.
Holyoke (Mass.), paper 352.
Holyoke Water Power Company, 4.
Homespun Industries (in relation to railway mileage), Appendix XII.
Home Work (clothing), 183, 222–224.
Homestead Steel Works (see *Carnegie Steel Company*), 43, 44, 147; basic open-hearth steel, 70; output increased by electrically operated machinery, 75; strike, 14; structural steel, 120; Talbot process, 77.
Honolulu (T. H.), 142.
Hopedale (Mass.), 178.
Hopewell (Va.), 292, 316, 347.
Horse Shoes, 28.
Hosiery (see *Knit Goods*).
Houses (ready made), 244.
Hudson River (Valley), 160; brick, 258; paper, 248.
Hydro-electric Power, 2–3, 166, 246.

Illinois, 123; agricultural machinery, 147; brick, 258; distilling, 275, 276, 331; furniture, 244; hardware, 148; meat packing, 264; paper, 247; rails, 118; stoves and furnaces, 150; watches, 352.
Illinois Brick Company, 258.
Illinois Steel Company, 45–47, 48, 54, 57, 118; cement manufacture, 254; electric furnace, 309.

Illustrations (demand higher quality paper), 246.
Immigrants (see also *Labor*), clothing industry, 222, 223; cotton mills, 189; supplant native workers, 12.
Imperial Wheel Company, 337.
Imports, 1–2; automobiles, 157, 162, 164; carpets, 204; copper, 1; cotton, 1, 190; gold, 10; iron and steel, Appendix VIII; leather, 230; paper, 251; raw materials produced also in America, 1; silk 210, Appendix VIII; tariff and, Appendix VIII; wool, 200.
India (Indian), buffalo hides, 230; carpets, 208; cotton mills, 342; indigo, 347; iron imports, 25; locomotives, 137; manganese ores, 79; rails, 114, 118; steel bridges, 38.
Indiana, agricultural machinery, 147; cement, 255; furniture, 244; gas (natural), 260, 281; glass, 260; oil fields, 73; steel, 98; stoves, 352; strawboard, 247; timber, 239; tin plate, 131; United States Steel Company, 60; wool, 196.
Indiana Steel Company, 60.
Indianapolis (Ind.), 263.
Indigo, 347.
Industrial Board, 333.
Industrial Commission (after war), 328.
Instalment buying, 332–333.
International Automobile and Vehicle Tire Company, 158.
International Car Wheel Company, 138.
International Cotton Mills Corporation, 182.
International Cutlery Company, 149.
International Harvester Company (*Corporation*), 146, 147, 315, 330–331; credit policy, 331.
International Paper Company, 248, 249, 292.
International Power Company, 89, 151, 159.
International Rubber Company, 237.
Interstate Commerce Commission, 26, 27, 300, 348–349.
Interstate Commerce Law, 8.
Inventions, bicycle, 156; cell dryer, 221; glass blowing, 262; looms, 178; musical instruments, 296–297; photography, 296; pigments, 291; silk, 212; Tiffany glass, 260–261.
Iowa, brick, 258; coal, 45; woolen mills, 196.
Ireland (Irish), Baldwin Locomotive Works employes, 14; linen, 322; women in textile mills, 13.
Iron (see also *Nails, Pipes, Railroads, South Iron, Stoves*), Alabama 22, 24, 25, 27, 28, 31, 50, 109–110, 114; Allegheny County, 23; basic, 31, 32, 49, 63; beams, 121; Belgian, 92, 111; Bethlehem Iron Company, 37; Birmingham (Ala.), 109; bloomeries, 82; boom, 29, 100–101, 109; bridges, 32; car wheels, 23; Catalan forges, 30; centers, 23; charcoal (see also *Charcoal* and *Charcoal Iron*), 23, 32, 71, 72, 89, 94, 137; consumption, 31, 32; corporations own raw material sources, 20, 22, 28, 31; cost, 31, 92, 106, 116, 335; depressions and expansions, 49, 94–96; electric driving and smelting, 75–77; exports, 11, 24, 25, 49, 91, 96, 99, 103, 108–113; failures, 25; foreign markets, 24, 25, 111; forges, 30, 82; foundries, 27, 53, 85, 94; freight charges, 26, 50; fuel, 30, 72; furnace capacity of U. S., 335; galvanized, 134; geographical concentration, 30; imports, 29, 54, 72; Kentucky, 25; labor (conditions), 14, 28, 48, 73, 94; machinery, 71, 86, 91; markets, 5, 25, 27, 31, 49, 107–108, 111; Maryland, 23, 25; merchant iron, 53, (decline), 335; Michigan, 17, 19, 24, 42; Minnesota, 15, 19, 42, 47, 55; Missouri, 15; New England, 20, 23; New Jersey, 15, 23, 28; New York, 15, 82; North Carolina, 82; Norway, 113; organization, 30; Pennsylvania, 23, 31, 48, 55, 109; pipe (see *Tubes*), 127–129; Pittsburgh, 18, 19, 28, 49, 97, 103, 105; pools, 19, 20, 60, 87–88, 96, 108; prices, 27, 29, 31, 48, 94–114, 308, 333, 335; production, 24–25, 26, 29, 31–33, 40, 53, 60, 72, 307, 308, 333, 334, 335; profits, 31; puddled, 68; puddling, 82, (mechanical) 335; railroad building, 31; rolled (displaced by steel, 84; rolling, 84, 85, 129, 146; scrap, 33, 34, 78, 82, 84, 90; ships and shipbuilding, 32; South, 24–28; stainless, 335; statistics, 28–30; steel substituted for, 15; tariff, 107; westward movement, 23; wheels, 137; wire (see under *Steel*); Wisconsin, 17, 19; World War, 307; wrought, 72, 82, 84.
"Iron Age," 88.
Iron Furnaces (see also *Coal, Coke, Furnaces*), 23, 72, 107, 109; blast, 20, 29, 30, 38, 42, 43, 44, 45, 48, 49, 53, 54, 56, 73; capacity, 27, 28, 29, 30, 31, 38, 72; charcoal, 23, 24, 25, 27, 28, 30, 72–73, 90; construction, 71, 75; Eastern (crippled by coal strike), 14; fuel, 72; improved, 30; investments, 20; low fuel consumption, 75; merchant, 90; number, 71; output, 73–75; practice (1893–1914), 73–75; puddling, 82; smelting (electric), 75–77; Southern, 25, 28–30.
Iron Mountain (Mo.), 15.
Iron Ores, 41, 62; Adirondack, 37; Alabama, 15, 16, 18, 22, 63; analysis, 18, 19; Bessemer, 15, 42, 70; Black Sea, 16; Brazil, 16; British Columbia, 16; British India, 16; Canadian, 16; Carolina, 16; China, 16, 107; concentration, 19–22; Connecticut, 15; contracts, 20; controlled by United States Steel Company, 54, 56, 58, 59, 63; Cornwall, 15; corporations, 20, 21; cost of production, 18, 91–93; Cuban, 15, 16, 17, 22, 38, 39, 50, 75; Cuban Steel Ore Company, 17; docks, 19; duty, 16; Eastern, 15; exports, 16, 18; famine, 22; fleets, 17, 21; freights, 16, 19, 20; geography, 15–20; Gogebic, 43; Grecian, 15; handling (improved methods), 18, 19, 22; hauls, 18, 19; hematites, 16, 17, 113; imports, 16–17, 22, 113; Iron Mountain, 15; Juragua Company, 17; Lake Superior, 15, 17–19, 21, 22, 23, 36, 37, 42, 43, 46, 56, 63, 69, 71, 91, 92, 94, 95, 101, 116; Marquette range, 18, 43; Menomenee, 18; Mesabi, 15, 17, 18, 20, 21, 24, 43, 75, 91; Michigan, 17, 18, 19, 43; mining (improved methods), 18; Minnesota, 15, 19, 21, 24, 42; Mokta, 16; New Jersey, 15; New York, 15; Ohio, 23; organization of trade, 19–22; Pennsylvania, 15; Pilot Knob, 15; Pittsburgh, 18, 19, 22; pool, 19, 20, 69; Porman, 16; Port Henry, 16, 23; ports, 18; prices, 18, 20,

94–98; Saint Louis, 18; selection and sorting, 18; Seriphos, 16; sources, 17; South American, 17, 22; Southern, 16; Spanish, 15, 16, 17, 92; Spanish-American (Cuban), 17; speculation, 92; steamships, 47; Swedish, 15, 16, 17, Tafna, 16; tariff, 16; Toufo mines, 17, 40; trade, 19–22; transportation, 17, 18, 19, 57; treatment, 75; trusts (vertical), 20; unloading, 19; vessels (Rockefeller fleet), 21; Wisconsin, 17, 19.
Irondale (Wash.), 54.
Irondale Steel Company, 54.
Ironton (Ohio) (iron and steel), 45.
Isthmian Canal, 25.
Italy (Italian), armor and ordnance, 148; barrel stock from Tennessee, 243; imports, 25, 111, 112; silks, 216, 346; steel, 310; textile mills, 14.

Japan (Japanese), 3; American Tobacco Company, 279; earthquake, 346; iron imports, 24, 25, 111; matches, 292; silk exports, 222; steel bridges (imported), 38, 120; vessels (cotton carriers from Southern ports), 111.
Java, 129.
Johnson Steel Company, 35.
Johnstown (Pa.), 46, 55, 282, 309.
Joliet (Ill.), steel, 55; steel cars, 138.
Jones and Laughlin Works, 21, 57, 64, 82, 121, 123.
Juragua Iron Company, 17, 40.

Kansas, brick, 254, 258, 352; cement, 254; coal, 45; flour, 267; meat packing, 264; steel, 88; stoves, 352.
Kansas City (Mo.), flour, 349; meat packing, 263, 283.
Kentucky, distilling, 275, 277; iron, 25; whisky, 276; woolens, 206.
Kentucky Distilleries and Warehouse Company, 276.
Keokuk (Iowa) (hydro-electric power), 4.
Kidder, Peabody and Company, 144.
King, Charles B. (automobiles), 158.
Knights (of Rhode Island) (cotton manufacturers), 7.
Knit Goods (see also *Cotton, Silk, Wool*), 188, 220–221; centers, 220; cotton substituted for wool, 220; full fashioned, 220; hand operations eliminated, 220; hosiery, 214, 220, 221; labor (negro), 13; machinery, 220; materials, 220–221; mills, 181, 197, 220; Pennsylvania, 220; Philadelphia, 220; production, 220; silk, 221, 346; warp knit, 346.
Knoxville (Tenn.), 62.
Kobe (Japan), 111.
Kokomo (Ind.) (automobiles), 158.
Krupp Steel Works (Germany), 75, 81, 84, 116, 129.

Labor, child (see *Women and Children*), 176, 222; clothing industry, 222–224; convict, 48; cost, 73–74, 92; cotton, 173, 176, 177, 188–190; earnings increased by mechanical improvements, 189; education, 12; glass blowers (earnings decrease with machine introduction), 260; immigrant, 12, 14, 189, 204, 221, 222, 223, 224; iron and steel, 86–87, 94, (8-hour shift), 335, (strike) 334–335; legislation, 12, 222; locomotive works, 14; mechanical improvements reduce quantity required, 189; negro, 12, 13; Poles (Baldwin Locomotive Works), 14; Portuguese, 13; print works (Scotch), 14; Russian (locomotive works), 14; Scotch and British, 14; silk, 210, 212, 215; silk mills, 210, 215; social welfare experiments, 12; South, 13, 14; strikes, 14, 188–190; supply, 12, 103; textile, 13, 14; tinplate industry, 131; transfer (from home to factory), 224; unemployment, 94; women and children, 176, 222; wool, 195, 203–204.
Labor Unions, 87; Amalgamated Association of Iron and Steel Workers, 14.
Laboratories, canners, 271; cement, 256.
Lackawanna (Iron and) Steel Company, 23, 36–37, 60, 64, 73, 77; absorbed by Bethlehem Steel, 330.
Lake Erie, 94, 96.
Lake Erie Railroad Company, 44.
Lake Michigan, 44, 60.
Lake Ore Ports, 67.
Lake Steamers, 123.
Lake Superior (see also *Iron Ores*), mines, 43; ports, 19; steel, 45.
Lake Superior Iron Company, 43, 44.
Lake Superior Iron Ore Association, 18.
Lake Superior Power Company, 285.
Lake Superior Steel Company, 45.
Lamont, Thomas W., 301.
Lamps (see also *Glass*), 260; arc, 165; incandescent, 165.
Lancashire (England), 179, 188.
Lancaster (County) (Pa.), 196.
Lanoline Oil, 199.
Lanston Monotype, 294.
Laramie (Wyo.), 287.
Lawn Mowers, 148.
Lawrence (Kan.), 123.
Lawrence (Mass.), ranks first (woolen and worsteds), 195; textile mills, 13; woolen operators strike, 14, 202; worsteds, 199.
Lazotte, Incorporated, 348.
Lead, flotation process, 311; prices, 311; shipped via New Orleans, Appendix XIII.
Leather, artificial, 340; belting, 227; centers, 226, 227; centralization, 226, 228; chemists, 225; chrome process, 226, 227, 229; corporations, 227, 228; drawback, 229; dyes, 317, 350; exports, 229–230; fashion, 228–229; geography, 226–228; imports, 230; ladies' footwear, 227; light, 225, 229, 230; machinery (exported), 229; market, 229; organization, 226–228; packers, 228, 265; pebbled calf, 229; Pennsylvania, 226, 227; Philadelphia, 227; prices, 227; production, 7; rank of states, 226; raw materials (see *Hides*), 225, 226, 229–230; sole and heavy, 225–230; split, 350; tannages, 226, 225, 228, 230; tanners (American employed in British and German tanneries), 229; tanning, 225–227, 291; tariff, 229–230; technical progress, 225, 226, 229; trusts, 227; United States Leather Company, 227, 228; upholstery, 227, 228, 229; value, 229, 230; varieties, 228–229.

Lebanon (Pa.) (iron), 88.
Legislation, currency, 100; trust, 5–6.
Lehigh Valley, 18; cement works, 254, 255.
Leicester (England) (leather imports from America), 229.
Lewis Motor Vehicle Company, 158.
Liberty engine, 314.
Lighthouse (lenses), 261.
Lime, 18, 290.
Limestone, 41, 49, 56; cement, 255; cost, 93; quarries, 58.
Linen (see *Flax*), 218.
Lipton, Sir Thomas, 160.
Little Rock (Ark.) (furniture), 244.
Liverpool (England), 97, 109, Appendix IX.
Lobsters, 271.
Locomobile Company, 100, 230.
Locomotives (see *Baldwin Locomotive Works*), 89, 119, 136–141; American Locomotive Company, 89, 139; compound, 137, 139; depression, 136, 137, 141; electric, 136, 137, 139, 166; exports, 136, 137; machinery shipped to Russia, 110; organization, 139; Pennsylvania, 166; Pittsburgh, 139; production, 104, 136, 137, 139–141; Richmond (Va.), 139; Russia, 137; Schenectady, 139, 141; World War, 314.
London (England), 9, 113; underground railway, 165.
"*London Economist*," 94.
"*London Ironmonger*," 109.
Lorain (Ohio), ore plants, 18; steel, 35, 41, 46, 55, 57.
Lorain Steel Company, 46, 113, 165–166.
Lorimer Coke Works, 44.
Los Angeles (Calif.), 169, 244.
Louisiana, lumber, 239; naval stores, 243; sulphur, 285.
Louisville (Ky.) (freight rates), 26.
Lowell (Mass.), cotton, 186; textile schools, 12, 180; worsted machinery, 198.
Lubricants, 283.
Lucy Furnaces (Pittsburgh), 44.
Lumber, Albany, 241; areas, 227–229; articles manufactured, 243–244; associations (trade), 242; bark for tanners, 226, 227; by-products, 243; Canada prohibits log export, 239; cedar for pencils, 239; centers, 238, 239; Committee (World War), 303; corporations, 241–242; cypress, 238, 243; geography (shifting), 238–239; machinery, 240; markets, 241–242; organization, 241–242; Pennsylvania, 258; prices, 242, Appendix II, Appendix IX; production, 239; rank of states, 239; sawdust fuel, 240; sawmills, 238, 240; saws (see *Saws*); schooners, 241; South, 238; tariff, 239; technical progress, 239–241, 243; timber, 227, 238, 239, 241, 247–248; trusts, 241; wasteful methods, 239–241; West, 238; white pine, 238; Wisconsin, 239; yellow pine, 238.
Lynn (Mass.), boots and shoes, 230, 232, 233; electricity, 169; price of iron, Appendix V.
Lyon County (Nev.) (Bessemer ore), 15.
Lyons (France), 183.

Macaroni, 263.
Machine Tools, 153–155.

Machinery, agricultural (see *Agricultural Machinery*); automatic, 154, 259; automobile, 153; boots and shoes, 231–234; canning, 271; cement, 255; clothing, 223; electric, 167, 170; exports, 153; flour, 267; glass blowing, 259; knit goods, 220; lumber, 240; match, 292; metal working, 153, 154; mining, 153; paper, 246; printing, 293, 294; shoemaking, 231, 232, 233, 234; silk, 212, 213, 215; sugar, 146; tobacco, 279; Wellman charging, 69.
Madison Square Garden, 161, 162.
Magazines, 295–296.
Magnesia, 18.
Mahoning Valley, 35, 41, 95; blast furnace association, 88.
Maine, 283; canning, 271; magazine industry, 295; paper, 249, 352; prices (colonial, lumber), Appendix II; *id.* (shipbuilding), Appendix IV; wool, 195, 205.
Manchester (England), 115.
Manchester (N. H.), 139.
Manganese, 17, 18, 79, 81, 309.
Manila (Hemp), 219.
Manufactures, density of population and railway mileage, Appendix XII; exports and imports, 1–2; geography, 351–353; growth (1860–1914), 351; (1860–1927), 358; war decade comparisons, 299–300; World War expansion, 323.
Marcus Hook (Pa.), 217.
Marine engines, 39, 151, 152.
Market (*Marketing, Merchandizing*) (see various industries), automobile, 161; axes, 148; cotton, 173, 175–177, 185, 188; dumping, 1; foreign, 148, 173, 175, 177, 185, 188, 279; iron, 109, 111, 127; paper, 251; policy of modern industry, 355–356; tobacco, 278, 279; tools, 148; wool, 195, 203–206.
Marquette (Mich.), 72.
Marquette Range (ores), 18, 43.
Marshall Field and Company (acquire cotton mills), 183.
Maryland, canning, 271; fertilizers, 289; iron, 23, 25; pipes, 127; prices (colonial, iron), Appendix V; *id.* (lumber), Appendix II; *id.* (tar), Appendix III; rayon, 347; rye whisky, 277.
Maryland Brewing Company, 277.
Maryland Steel Company, 37, 57, 112, 309.
Massachusetts, 174; Bank Commissioners 298, 299; boots and shoes, 232; Bureau of Statistics, 173, 298, 299; carpets, 208; charcoal furnaces, 271; clothing, 222; cotton, 172; dyeing, 221; furniture, 244, 245; iron and steel, 23; knit goods, 220; leather (see *Boots and Shoes*), 226; legislation, 180, 222; paper, 247; prices (colonial, iron), Appendix V; *id.* (lumber), Appendix II; textile education, 180; war industries, 298, 299, 304; wool, 195, 196, 205.
Massachusetts Brewery Company, 278.
Massachusetts Bureau of Labor Statistics, 173.
Matches, 292–293.
"*McClure's*," 295.
McKay Sole-Sewing Machine, 231.
McKinley Act (see also *Tariff*), 130, 134–135.
Mechanical Rubber Company, 236.
Mediterranean (iron ore), 16.

Melbourne (Australia), 109.
Menominee Range (iron ore), 18, 59.
Merchant Fleet, 142, 145.
Mergenthaler Linotype, 294.
Merrimac (Manufacturing) Company, 176, 189.
Merrimac River (Valley), 172, 174, 180.
Merritt Family (Mesabi ore holding), 21.
Mesabi Range Mines and Ores, 15, 17–18, 19, 43, 59, 75, 123, 127.
Mexico (Mexican), American Tobacco Company, 279; cattle, 264; clothing (ready-made), 204; copper, 1; guayule rubber, 237; iron, 111; sisal, 322; steel, 57.
Michigan, 2; agricultural machinery, 147; automobiles, 161, 164; caustic soda, 287; cement, 254; charcoal, 71; engines, 152; furniture, 244; iron, 17–19, 24, 42; leather, 226; lumber, 239; ores, 17–19, 24, 42; paper, 249; stoves and furnaces, 150; sugar, 273; timber, 248; vitrified drain pipe, 258.
Michigan City (Ind.), 258.
Michigan-Peninsular-Car Company, 136.
Middlesboro (England), 25, 111.
Middlesboro (Ky.), 27.
Midland Steel Products Company, 337.
Midvale Steel (and Ordnance) Company (Works), 143, 309, 313; absorbed by Bethlehem Steel, 330.
Milk, bottles, 259; condensed, 266; used in butter substitutes, 266.
Mill(s) (see *Cotton, Iron, Silk, Wool*, etc.), construction, 4.
Millers' National Association, 267.
Milwaukee (Wis.), 229; brewing, 287; enamel and tinplate goods, 132; engines, 152, 338; steel, 55, 57; tanning, 227.
Mineral Wool, 47.
Mingo Junction (Ohio), 89.
Mining, companies (ore carriers), 142; machinery, 153.
Minneapolis (Minn.), basic open-hearth steel plant, 45; cereals, 268; flour center, 267, 268, 348; open-hearth steel, 42.
Minnesota, 24; flour, 267; iron, 15, 19, 42, 47, 55; lumber, 239; ores, 15, 19, 20, 24, 42.
Minnesota (S. S.), 144, 145.
Minnesota Iron Company, 46, 47.
Mississippi, cotton, 175; lumber, 239; wool, 195.
Mississippi River (Valley), 24; dairy products, 266; yellow pine producers, 241.
Missouri, clay, 256; iron ore, 24.
Mobile (Ala.), 110, 111, 220.
Mobile Company, 160.
Mohair (knitting), 220.
Mohawk Valley Steel and Wire Company, 125.
Mokta (iron ore), 16.
Molasses, 274.
Molybdenum, 81, 310.
Mombasa (Africa), 188.
Monell, Ambrose, 77.
Monongahela River (Valley), 41, 43.
Montour County (Pa.), 278.
Montreal (Canada), 139, 141.
Moorehouse, James (dyer), 316.
Morgan and Wright Company, 236.
Morgan, John Pierpont (and Company), 55, 56, 301.

Morgan Line, 142.
Morris and Company, 265, 327, 330.
Motor Shows, 160–162.
Motorcycles, 163, 314.
Mount Vernon (Va.), Appendix VII.
Mount Vernon-Woodberry Cotton Duck Company, 182.
Muley Saw, 240
"*Munsey's Magazine*," 295.
Muriatic Acid, 290
Musical Instruments, 293, 296–297.

Nail(s) (see also *Wire Nails*), 122, 124, 125–127; exports, 126; organization, 126; prices and production, 126; substitution of steel for iron, 125; wire (see also *Wire*), 54, 57, 69, 103, 125–127.
Nantasket Beach Railroad, 166.
Naphtha (launches), 152.
Nashville (Tenn.), 189, 316, 347.
National Alliance of Case Goods Associations, 245
National Aniline and Chemical Company, 318, 348.
National Association of Brass Manufacturers, 326.
National Association of Chair Manufacturers, 245.
National Association of Cotton Manufacturers, 179, 183, 184, 343.
National Association of Wool Manufacturers, 207.
National Automobile Chamber of Commerce, 326.
National Automobile Exhibition, 162.
National Biscuit Company, 268, 269.
National Canners' Association, 271.
National Carbon Company, 169.
National Casket Company, 245.
National Cordage Company, 219.
National Defense Council, (see *Council of National defense*).
National Enameling and Stamping Company, 54, 132.
National Glass Company, 262.
National Linseed Oil Company, 284.
National Lumber Manufacturers' Association, 242.
National Newspaper Publishers' Association, 349.
National Roofing and Corrugating Company, 89.
National Screw Company, 126.
National Shear Company, 149.
National Starch Manufacturing Company, 269.
National Steel Company, 21, 43, 55, 56, 59, 126, 132, 150.
National Straw Board Company, 250.
National Tinplate and Stamped Ware Company, 132.
National Tinplate Company, 132.
National Trade Convention, 300.
National Tube Company, 6, 54, 128–129.
National Wall Paper Company, 250.
Naval Contracts, steel, 40; stores, 243–244.
Naval Ordnance Plant, 336.
Naval Stores, 243, 244, 252.
Nebraska, 273.

Negro Labor, manufacturing company organized by, 13; South Carolina cotton mill, Appendix XI.
Netherlands, market for southern iron, 111; steel bridge, 120.
Nevada, 15.
Neville Island (Ordnance plant), 308.
New Bedford (Mass.), cotton manufactures, 174, 343; labor troubles, 14; silk, 216; textile school, 12, 180.
New Caledonia, 81.
New England, 37, 107; blast furnaces, 20; boots and shoes, 230, 232, 233; charcoal iron, 71; cotton, 10, 171, 173–177, 179–181, 183, 185, (after armistice), 340, 342, 343; flour, 267; furniture, 244, 245; hydro-electric development, 4; immigrant labor, 13; leather (see *Boots and Shoes*), 10; lumber, 238; machine tools, 153; newsprint paper, 247–248; paper, 249; pin-money clothing makers, 223; pipe prices, 127; prices (colonial lumber), Appendix II; *id.* (shipbuilding), Appendix IV; *id.* (tar), Appendix III; rum, 277; screws, 126; silk, 211, 215; spinning mills, 14; thread mills (combination), 6–7; tools, 149; wool, 10, 343.
New England Brick Company, 258.
New England Cotton Freight Claim Bureau, 184.
New England Cotton Manufacturers' Association, 3, 183, 184.
New England Cotton Yarn Company, 181.
New Hampshire, hosiery, 220; prices (colonial, lumber), Appendix II; *id.* (shipbuilding), Appendix IV; wool, 195.
New Haven (Conn.), automobiles, 159; firearms and hardware, 331; steel, 34; tool-making, 149.
New Jersey, 123, 128, 138, 180, 205, 228, 236, 276; automobiles, 158–159; cement, 254; dyeing, 221; hardware, 148; iron, 15, 23, 28; leather, 226; pottery, 257; prices (colonial, iron), Appendix V; *id.* (lumber), Appendix II; reconstruction commission, 327–328; silk, 210, 211; steel, 38, 85; tools, 149; wool manufactures, 195, 343; worsteds, 198.
New London (Conn.), 143, 145.
New Orleans (La.), 220; receipts of inland manufactures by river, Appendix XIII.
New York City, 109, 120, 340, 345; automobile show, 161–162; automobiles, 160; bakeries, 268; boots and shoes, 232; brick, 258; corporation financing, 8; electric cabs, 158; electric trucks, 159; exchange (colonial), Appendix I; flour, 268; garment makers' strike, 202, 223, 224; glass, 260; hats, 222; hemp, 220; meat packing, 263; prices (commodity), Appendix IX; prices (colonial, flour), Appendix VI; *id.* (iron), Appendix V; skyscrapers, 120; steel cars, 140; tin plate, 132; wool, 191.
New York Central Railroad, 166.
New York City Biscuit Company, 268.
"*New York Graphic*," 295.
New York Metal Exchange, 94.
New York Produce Exchange, 108.

New York Shipbuilding Company, 143, 144.
New York State, 276, 304; agricultural machinery, 147; boots and shoes, 232; brewing, 275; carpets, 208; cement, 254; cotton, 181; dyeing, 221; flour, 267; furniture, 244; hardware, 148; iron (and iron ore), 15, 82; knitting, 220; leather, 226; lumber, 238, 239; meat packing, 264; paper, 247, 248, 352; prices (colonial, iron), Appendix V; *id.* (lumber), Appendix II; pottery, 257; silk, 211; steel, 35, 85; reconstruction commission, 327–328; stoves and furnaces, 150; trusts, 6; vitrified drain pipe, 258; wool, 195.
New Zealand, 220.
Newark (N. J.), celluloid, 291; hats, 222; leather, 227.
Newport (R. I.), 291.
Newport News (Va.), 142, 143, 145.
Newport News Shipyards and Drydock Company, 142, 143, 145.
Newspapers, 292, 293, 294, 349; circulation, 295; machinery, 293, 294; Sunday and daily, 295; value in 1912, 296.
Newsprint Manufacturers' Association, 349.
Newton (Mass.), 162.
Niagara Falls (N. Y.), breakfast foods, 268; chemical industry, 287, 288; cyanamid, 290; electrical development, 2, 165–167, 169, 338.
Niagara Falls Power and Construction Company, 2–3, 86.
Nickel, 81; rails, 118; steel, 3, 80.
Nijni Novgorod (Russia), 110.
Niles-Bement-Pond Company, 149.
Nitrates (Chile), 289.
Nitrogen fixation, 348.
Nitro-Glycerine (see *Explosives*), 291.
Nixon, Lewis, 142, 144, 145.
Non-Bessemer Pig Iron Association, 88.
Norfolk (Va.), exchange (colonial, on London), Appendix I; prices (colonial, flour), Appendix VI; *id.* (iron), Appendix V; *id.* (lumber), Appendix II; *id.* (tar), Appendix III; steel tubes, 129.
North, cotton consumption, 171; cotton manufacture, 173–175; labor, 12, 13; print cloth, 175.
North Carolina, aluminum, 310; cotton (raw, imported), 176; electric power, 4; flour, 267; furniture, 244; iron, 82; naval stores, 243; pine producers trust, 241; pulp, 247.
North Chicago Rolling Mill Company (Works), 254.
Northumberland County (Pa.), 278.
Norway, aluminum, 325; bridges imported from United States, 38; ore steamers, 17; steel rails, 113; wire rods, 122.

Oak, 238, 239; bark, 225.
Ohio, automobiles, 164; blast furnaces, 42; glass making, 260; hardware, 148; iron, 23; meat packing, 264; metal-working machinery, 153; paper, 247, 249; pipes, 128; pottery, 257; steel, 35, 43, 67, 85, 88; stoves and furnaces, 150; timber, 239; tools, 149; war industries, 304.
Ohio River (Valley), 41, 95, 106, 258, 308.
Ohio Steel Company, 34.

458   Index

Oil (see *Cottonseed, Linseed, Petroleum*), linseed, 284, Appendix XIII; mills, 284; oleo, 266; refining, 287; vegetable, 283–284.
Oklahoma, brick, 258; cotton, 175; fuel, 281; glass, 327; meat packing, 264.
Old Colony Railroad, 166.
Old Hickory (Tenn.) (powder), 316.
Old Range Bessemer Iron Pool, 20.
Olds, Ransom E., 160.
Olds Motor Vehicle Company, 160, 164.
Oleomargarine, by-product, 266; meat packers, 265
Oliver Mining Company, 43, 44.
Oliver Wire Company, 126.
Omaha (Neb.) (food fats), 283; varied industries, 353.
Ontario (Canada) (prohibits log exports), 251.
Open-hearth Steel, 27, 34–35, 40–43, 45, 47–49, 51, 54, 58, 60, 63, 65–71, 76–79; advantages over Bessemer, 67–71; basic, 68, 77; duplex, 78; furnace output, 66; furnaces, 66, 70, 290; growth (1893–1914), 67–71; production, 65–68; scrap iron, 33; specified for plates and structural shapes, 68, 69.
Orange (N. J.) (hats), 222.
Ordnance, 40, 68, 147–148; World War, 308, 309, 314–315.
Oregon, 89; lumber, 241; paper, 247; timber, 238.
Organization (see *Companies, Corporations, Trusts*) (English opinion of American industrial organization), Appendix X; trade organizations extend after World War, 325.
Organs, 296.
Orient (Oriental), 46; iron, 54, 107.
Osaka (Japan), 111.
Osnaburgs (see *Flax Manufactures;* also *Cotton*), Appendix XI.
Otto, Nicholas A. (internal-combustion engine), 157.
Otto-Hoffmann (by-product coke ovens), 282.
Owens Automatic Glass-Blowing Machines, 259.
Oysters, 271.

Pacific Coast (States), 24, 114; Bessemer ores, 15; canning, 270, 271; furniture association, 245; hydro-electric power, 4; iron, 107; lumber, 238, 239; tinplate market, 130, 132.
Pacific Coast Biscuit Company, 269.
Pacific Coast Steel Company, 89.
Pacific Mail Company, 142.
Pacific Mills, (Lawrence, Mass.), 340–341, 344.
Pacific Northwest (lumber output), 238.
Packing Industry, 243, 263–266; associated with distilling, 264; beef, 264; by-products, 264–266; canning, 270; centers, 263, 266; centralization, 263, 264; chemical control, 264; Chicago, 229, 263; corporations, 264–266; Fort Worth, 263; lard and lard oil, 263, 266, 283, 284; leather, 228, 265; mutton, 264; pork, 264; rank of states, 264; refrigeration, 264, 265; Saint Louis, 263; sanitary conditions, 264; South Saint Joseph, 263; technical progress, 264; tin plate, 133; value of products, 263; veal, 264.
Pago Pago, 142.
Paint, 243, 266, 291.

Panama Canal, 17.
Panics (see *Depressions*), 104.
Panic of 1873, 12.
Panic of 1893, 1, 8–9, 12, 21, 24, 25, 28, 37, 45, 65, 87, 91, 94, 106, 284; cement, 253; cotton, 184, 186, 188; electricity, 169; iron, 31; locomotives, 136, 137; plate glass, 261; silks, 214; steel, 80; wool, 191, 199.
Paper (see *Pulp*), 294; bags, 248, 259; bleaching liquor, 285–286; Canada (drift toward), 246–248, 251; casein, 266; chemical progress, 246; chemicals, 287; competition, 249, 250; consolidations, 248–250, 349; electricity, 2, 168, 246; exports, 251–252; foreign trade, 3; geography, 246, 247, 352; hand made, 246–247; hangings, 250; imports, 251–252; kodak, 296; kraft, 349; machinery, 246; Maine, 248, 352; Manila, 248; market, 251; methods, 246; mills, 247, 248; newsprint, 246–248, 250–251; organization, 248–251; pools, 249; power, 2, 168, 246; prices, 349; production, 245, 249–250; pulp, 246–248, 251, 285; rags, 247, 248; rank of states, 247; raw materials, 247, 251, 252; reforestation, 247–248; South, 349; straw, 247, 249; strawboard, 249–251; tariff, 248, 251; technical progress, 246; value of imports, 251; wrapping, 247; writing, 249.
Paris (France) war fashions, 321.
Paris International Exposition, gas engine, 152–153; pottery (gold medal), 257; silk, 214.
Parish and Bingham Corporation, 337.
Passaic (N. J.) (strike), 202, 343.
Passaic County (N. J.) (silk mills), 210.
Passaic Steel Company, 121.
Patent Insides (newspapers), 294–295.
Patents, breakfast food, 268; electrical, 159, 168, 169; flour, 267; gasoline motor, 157–160, 162, 163; litigation, 7, 163; match machinery, 292; pressed-steel car, 138, 139; rubber tires, 158; Talbot process, 77; tanning, 226; weldless steel tubing, 128; woven and barbed wire, 57.
Paterson (N. J.), locomotives, 139; silk, 210, 211, 216; strikes, 14, 215.
Payne-Aldrich Tariff Bill, 202.
Peabody (Mass.) (leather), 227.
Pelzer (S. C.) Manufacturing Company, 167.
Pencoyd Iron Works, 77, 120.
Pendleton (Ore.) (wool), 192.
Pennsylvania, 43, 206, 304; brewing, 275; bridges,, 120; carpets, 208; cement, 254, 255; coal, 24, 39, 215; coal mines, 55; coke, 24, 46, 57; cotton, 172; dyeing, 221; engine (internal combustion), 151, 152; fuel, 281; furniture, 244; galvanized iron, 134; glass, 327; hardware, 148; hats, 222; iron, 15, 16, 30, 36, 109, 121; knit goods, 220; leather, 226, 227; lumber, 238; machine tools, 153; paper, 249; prices (colonial, iron), Appendix VI; rail making, 118; rye whisky, 277; silk mills (move to coal and iron towns), 210–212, 215, 352; steel, 35, 36, 41–43, 67, 77, 85, 88, 97; stoves and furnaces, 150; tinplate, 131; vitrified drain pipe, 258; wages, 334; wool, 195.

Index

Pennsylvania-Maryland Company, 38.
Pennsylvania Railroad, 80, 119; cars, 140; electrification, 166, 169.
Pennsylvania Steel Company, 15, 37, 38, 39, 57, 114, 121; absorbed by Bethlehem Steel Company, 40, 309; investment in Cuban mines, 17.
Pensacola (Fla.), 111, 112.
Peoria (Ill.) (distilling), 277, 331.
Peru (venadium), 310.
Petersburg (Va.) (explosives), 292.
Petroleum, brick, 258; cement, 254; containers, 133; refining, 286; Southwest development, 334; value of products (1889–1914), 283.
Philadelphia (Pa.), 9; boots and shoes, 234; carpets, 195; Centennial, 338; exchange (colonial, on London), Appendix I; iron, 16; knit goods, 220; machine tools, 154; prices (colonial, flour), Appendix VI; *id.* (iron), Appendix V; *id.* (colonial lumber), Appendix II; *id.* (shipbuilding), Appendix IV; *id.* (tar), Appendix III; publishing, 295; raw-silk market, 210; screw plants, 126; shipbuilding, 143; silk, 210; tanning, 227; textile school, 12, 180; tin plate, 133; toolmaking center, 149; worsted manufacturing, 195.
Philippines, coastal shipping law, 142; sugar, 272; tariff, 273.
Phipps, Henry, 44.
Phoenix Iron (Steel) Company, 120, 121.
Phonograph, 296, 350.
Phosphates, 285, 289, 290.
Phosphoric Acid, 290.
Phosphorus, 17, 18.
Photography, 293, 296.
Pianos (automatic), 296, 350.
Piedmont District (electric power), 4.
Pigments, 291.
Pigskin (automobile tire), 229.
Pilot Knob (Mo.) (iron ore), 15.
Pine, long leaf, 243; paper making, 247.
Pine Bluff (Ark.) (furniture), 244.
Pipes (see *Tubes*).
Pipes (tobacco), 280.
Pitch (see *Naval Stores*).
Pitt River (Reading, Calif.), 76.
Pittsburgh (Pa.), 9, 22, 49, 91, 92, 138; axes, 149; corporations, 88; furnaces (capacity), 73; galvanized iron, 134; gas fuel (belt), 281, glass, 260, 261; iron, 18, 19, 23, 28, 49, 75, 94, 95, 97, 103, 105; locomotive, 139; steel, 23, 34, 36, 41, 42, 44, 57, 62, 87, (strike), 334; wire nails, 126; wool, 191.
Pittsburgh and Lake Erie Railway, 21.
Pittsburgh Bessemer Railroad, 44.
Pittsburgh Plate Glass Company, 262.
"*Pittsburgh Plus*," 303.
Pittsburgh Reduction Company, 2.
Pittsburgh Stove and Range Company, 150.
Plainfield (N. J.) (tools), 149.
Plastics (manufacture retarded by excise on grain alcohol), 288.
Plattsburg (N. Y.) (bloomery), 82.
Plumbing Fixtures, 134.
Plymouth Cordage Company, 219.

Poles, laborers (Baldwin Locomotive Works), 14, textile mills, 13.
Pondville (Mass.), 3.
Ponemah Mills (Taftville, Conn.) (electric power), 3, 167.
Pools (see *Associations, Corporations, Trusts*), 87–89; beam, 96; cotton, 182, 185, 186; paper, 249; print cloth, 181–182, 186; rail, 87, 96, 118; steel billet, 87; trusts evolve from, 5; wire nail, 96.
Pope, Colonel Albert (bicycles), 156, 159.
Population per Square Mile, Appendix XII.
Porcelain (see *Pottery*), 257, 259; electrical supplies, 256, 257; sanitary, 256; white ware, 257.
Porman (iron ore), 16.
Port Henry (N. Y.) (iron ore), 16, 23.
Portland (Me.) (wire), 125.
Portland (Ore.) (furniture), 264.
Portland Cement, 253–256.
Portland Cement Association, 256, 326.
Porto Rico, coastal shipping law, 142; sugar, 272.
Portugal (Portuguese), barrel stock from Tennessee, 243; employment in textile mills, 13.
Potash, 199, 290.
Potassium Cyanide, 285.
Potomac River (Valley), 195; cotton mills, 175.
Pottery (see also *Porcelain*), 257; Belleek ware, 257; centers, 257; Delft, 257; East Liverpool, 257; geography, 257; organization, 258–259; product, 257; raw materials, 257; Rookwood, 257; sanitary ware, 257, 259, 327; stone ware, 256; tariff, 257; technical progress, 350; terra cotta, 256; Trenton (N. J.), 257.
Powder (see *Explosives*).
Power, hydroelectric, 2–5, 166–167, 246; water, 30, 287.
Prairie States (natural gas), 281.
Precision (metal working), 313.
Press, forging, 86; power, 155; printing, 293–295.
Pressed Steel Car Company, 99, 138, 139.
Prices, 9, 11, 12; coke, 69, 99; after war decline, 325, 328; control by monopolies illegal, 327; cotton goods, Appendix VII; flour, Appendix VI; iron in colonies, Appendix V; iron and steel, 94–115; leather, 227; lumber, 242, Appendix II; nails, 126; pipes (Addyston case), 127; pools, 87–89; print cloth, 181–182, 186; rails, 53, 91, 96, 102, 104; shipbuilding in colonies, Appendix IV; steel, 62; steel (see *Steel*); tar, Appendix III; trust influence, 5; weaving in Virginia, Appendix VII; wool, Appendix IX; World War, 303, 307, 308, 312, 313.
Prime Movers (see *Engines, Power, Turbines*), 150–153, 166.
Principio Furnace (iron), 23.
Print Cloths (see *Cotton, Silk*), 179, 180; attempted combination, 181; pool, 181–182, 186; prices, 184, 186, 342; produced mainly in North, 175; works (run by skilled English and Scotch operators), 14.
Printing, 293, 294, 295; advertising, 293, 295; centers, 295; electricity, 168; machinery,

293, 294; photolithographic, 295; product value, 293, 296; progress, 294–295.
Profits (cotton mills), Appendix XI; World War (steel), 308–309.
Providence (R. I.), cotton, 172, 174; locomotives, 139; machine tools, 154; textile education, 180; woolen, 195.
Puget Sound (iron works), 24.
Pullman (Ill.), screw plants, 126; strike, 136.
Pullman Palace Car Company (and Pullman cars), 138.
Pulp (see *Paper*), 246, 247, 248, 251; chemical, 246; duties, 199, 251; first export of dried, 3; imports, 251; mechanical, 2, 46; mills, 247; sulphite, 2, 246, 248, 251; spruce soda, 251; wood, 246, 247, 251.
Pure Food Law, 345.
Pyrites, 285; imported, 286.
Pyroxylin, 291.

Quaker Oats Company, 323.
Quebec (Canada), aluminum, 310; paper, 251; timber, 248.
Quebracho (tannage), 226.
Quincy (Mass.), 40.

Radio, 293, 350.
Radio Corporation of America, 331–332.
Rail Makers' Association (agreement), 53.
Railroads (Railways) (see *Rails* and *Transportation*), 103; cement consumers, 254; earnings, 12; electric, 165; equipment, 98, 102, 104, 136–141; Interstate Commerce Commission, 26, 27; iron and steel, 31, 97, 101; mileage and home manufactures, Appendix XII; national system, 100; New York Central, 166; Old Colony, 166; ore, 19; Pennsylvania, 80, 119, 140, 165, 169; Pittsburgh and Lake Erie Railway, 21; Pittsburgh Bessemer Railroad, 44; Pullman Company, 138; refrigerator cars, 242; Santa Fe, 81; Siberian Railway, 112; steel, 55, 59, 63; stocks, 11; street, 165, 166; Sudan, 121; surplus capital, 6; Tennessee Coal, Iron and Railway Company (see *Tennessee Coal, Iron and Railroad Company*), 50, 78; tonnage (1900–1913), 141.
Rail(s) (see *Railroads*), 21, 23, 40, 46, 53, 57, 63, 65–66, 70, 76, 80, 84, 102, 112, 118–119; alloy, 80, 81, 118; Bessemer, 40, 69, 84, 109; Colorado Iron and Coal Company, 53; cost, 91; depressions, 95; electric railway, 76, 80; exports, 111–114; geography, 118; iron, 119; mills, 38; nickel steel, 80; Pennsylvania, 118; percentage supplied by United States Steel Corporation, 57, 63; pools, 87, 118; prices, 96, 102, 104; production, 66, 79, 119; standard specifications, 80; steel, 40, 53, 63, 66, 69, 70, 76, 81, 87, 91, 118, 119; war demand, 307.
Railway (*Railroad*) *Administration*, 302, 333.
Rayon, 316, 340; popularity, 347; product, 346–347; Virginia, 347.
Reading (Calif.) (electric smelting), 76.
Reading (Pa.), iron, 88; rolling mills, 84.
Reciprocity Treaty, 25.
Refrigeration (see *Packing Industries*), 264; household, 354.

Reliance Buggy Factory, 350.
Republic Iron and Steel Company, 42, 45, 51, 55, 64, 88, 89.
Rhode Island, cotton, 172; dyeing, 221; prices (colonial, flour), Appendix VI; *id.* (lumber), Appendix II; wool, 195, 205.
Rice, 265.
Richmond (Va.), flour, 267; iron and steel, 83; locomotives, 139; rayon, 347; tin plate, 130.
Richmond Iron Company, 23.
Riker, Andrew L., 159.
Riker Electric Vehicle Company, 158.
Risdon Iron and Locomotive Works, 143.
River Rouge (Michigan) eagle boats, 314.
Roach, John, and Sons, 141.
Roanoke (Va.), 347.
Roberts, Percival, 77.
Rochester (N. Y.), 157; boots and shoes, 232; cameras, 353; flour, 348.
Rockefeller-Carnegie Agreement, 21.
Rockefeller Interests, Colorado Fuel and Iron Company, 54; holdings (sold to Carnegie interests), 5; Mesabi range, 21; ore carriers, 141, 142; U. S. Steel, 56.
Rocky Ford (Colo.) (sugar), 273.
Rocky Mountains (hydro-electric power), 4.
Rogers Locomotive Works, 140.
Rogers, W. H., 132.
Rogers Process (tin plate), 132.
Rolling Mills (see *Iron* and *Steel*).
Roofing, asphalt, 41; metal, 89.
Roosevelt (President), 298.
Roper, S. H. (steam automobile), 157.
Rosin (see *Naval Stores*).
Roswell, N. M. (auto stage), 161.
Rotterdam (Holland), 283.
Rubber, 235–237; artificial, 270; automobile tires, 237.
Rubber Goods Manufacturing Company, 236, 237.
Rubber Tire Company of America, 236.
Russia (Russians), battleships, 143, 148; Baldwin Locomotive Works, 14; locomotives, 137; manganese ores, 79; pipes for oil fields, 129; steel, 310; war with Japan (effect on wool), 202; World War, 307.

Safes (alloy steel), 80.
St. Lawrence River, 144.
St. Louis (Mo.), boots and shoes, 232; buggies, 350; enamel and tin plate, 132; food fats, 283; iron, 18; meat packing, 263; printing machine, 294; structural steel, 120.
St. Louis (S. S.), 141.
St. Paul (S. S.), 141.
Salem (Mass.), prices (colonial, flour), Appendix; *id.* (iron), Appendix V; *id.* (lumber), Appendix II; *id.* (shipbuilding), Appendix IV; *id.* (tar), Appendix III.
Salisbury (Conn.) (iron), 15, 23.
Salt, 287.
San Francisco (Calif.), 89, 125; electric transmission, 167; shipbuilding, 142, 143; steamship lines, 142; steel, 40, 54; wool-handling center, 192.
Sand, glass, 260; lime brick, 258; mixers (conveyers, blast cleaning automatic machines), 85; paper (a by-product of meat packing), 265.

Sandusky (Ohio) (breweries), 277.
Santa Fe Railroad. 81.
Santa Maria River (steel bridge), 120.
"*Saturday Evening Post*," 295.
Sault Ste. Marie, 72, 76, 102, 145, 251, 285; carbide, 288; chemicals, 287.
Savannah (Ga.) (fertilizer), 290.
Saws, American, 148; band, 240; circular, 240; gangs, 240; lumber, 240.
Schenectady (N. Y.), electric plant, 169; locomotives, 139, 141.
Schneider Works (France), 40.
Schoen Pressed Steel Company, 138.
Schools, technical, 12; textile, 12, 180.
Schuylkill Brewing Company, 278.
Schuylkill Valley, 18; silk, 210; tannery, 225.
Schwab, Charles M., address, 7, 55, 56; iron prices, 91; President Bethlehem Steel, 39; shipbuilding, 141, 145; stockholder (Carnegie Company), 44.
Scotland (Scotch), 107, 114; employed in American works, 14; iron, 92.
Scranton (Pa.), iron and steel industry transferred to Buffalo, 23, 36; locomotives, 139; silk mills, 210; steel, 37.
Screws, 126, 154.
Seattle (Wash.), 15, 16.
Seddon, Thomas, 110.
Selden, George B., 157, 160, 162, 163.
Semet-Solvay Corporation (by-product coke ovens), 49, 50, 348.
Service Supply (feature of modern industry), 356.
Sewer Pipes, 258.
Sewing Machines (exports), 153.
Shanghai (China) (cotton market), 188.
Sharon Steel Company, 59.
Shawsheen (*worsted*) *Mill* (Massachusetts), 344.
Sheep (see *Wool*), husbandry, 192; cross-bred yield better wool for worsteds, 192; number, 191; skins, 227.
Sheffield (England) (crucible steel), 71; armor plate, 313.
Shelby Steel and Tube Company, 128, 129.
Shenango Valley, 41, 95; blast furnace association, 88.
Sherman Anti-trust Law, 8, 127–128, 300, 327, 333.
Sherman (Texas) (cotton mills), 175.
Ships (see *Iron, Shipbuilding, Shipyards, Steel*), battleships, 143, 148; plates, 68, 69, 112, 113; steel, 40, 143; United States Steel Corporation, 59.
Shipbuilding (see *Iron, Steel, Ships, Shipyards*), 141–146; American Bridge Company, 144; Bethlehem Steel Corporation, 39–40; centers, 141–145; Clyde River, 112, 113; corporations, 143, 144, 145; Cramp and Sons, 102, 141, 142, 143, 145; failures, 144–145; freight, 142, 144; Government contracts, 142; markets, 142; ore carriers, 142, 145; Philadelphia, 143; price in colonies, appendix IV; ratio steel to wooden, 146; Roach, John, and Sons, 141; San Francisco, 144, 152; steel, 38, 39, 40, 112, 141, 144; tonnage, 141, 142, 145; turbines, 312; United States Shipbuilding Company, 39, 102, 145; World War, 313–314.

Shipyards (see *Shipbuilding, Ships*), Hog Island, 314; Sparrows Point, 40, 144, 145; structural steel, 129–130.
Shoe(s) (see *Boots and Shoes*).
Shrapnel, 307.
Sicily (sulphur), 285.
Sidney (N. S.), 18.
Silicon, 17, 18; removal of, 75; Talbot process, 77.
Silk Association of America, 216.
Silk, California, 216; consumption, 211; imports, 210, 211, 216, 345; markets, 210; unadulterated, 213.
Silk Machinery, automatic, 212, 213, 215; German, and Swiss replaced, 212; improved lessens dependence on skilled labor, 212; improvements, 212; labor saving, 213; ribbon looms, 212; throwing, 212; weaving, 212.
Silk Manufactures, annexes in mining towns, 210; artificial (see *Rayon*), 211, 216–217, 322; bindings, 211; braids, 211, 215; broad, 210, 211, 213, 215, 346; competition, 212, 213, 214; Connecticut, 211; cravats, 214; dress, 215; dyeing, 221; embroidery, 211; 211; exports, 215; fabrics and articles, 213–215; finishing, 211; fringes, 211; geography, 210–211, growth, 210; hosiery, 214, 346; imports, 210; influence of fashion, 213–214; international establishments, 216; knit goods, 221, 346; labels, 214; labor, 210, 211, 212, 215; laces, 190, 211; machine twist, 211, 214, 215; market, 213, 214; mills, 210; mixtures (rayon), 346; Mount Vernon, Appendix VII; movement to Pennsylvania, 210, 212; National Silk Convention (1916), 317; New England, 211, 215; New Jersey, 210, 211; New York, 210, 211; organization, 215–217; organzines, 211, 212, 213; parachute fabric, 321; Paterson (N. J.), 14, 210, 211, 215; Pennsylvania, 210, 212, 215; plushes, 211, 214, 215; prices, 213, 216; printed. 211, 214; product (increase), 345; ribbons, 210, 211, 215; sewing silks, 211, 214, 215, 321; Silk Association of America, 216; specialization, 211–212; spindle speed, 212; strikes, 14, 215; tapestries, 215; tariff, 214, 216; technical progress, 212–213; tram, 211, 212, 213; upholstery, 213; value of product, 210, 215; veils, 211; velvets, 189, 208, 211, 214, 215; warp-print, 214; weaving, 211; World War, 321–322; yarns, 211.
Silver, Appendix I; flotation process, 311; mining depression, 53; Question, 9, 97.
Simmons, Hardware, 331.
Singer Sewing Machine Company, 314.
Sisal, 219, 220.
Slater, Samuel and Sons, 316.
Sloss Iron and Steel Company, 48, 110, 112.
Sloss-Sheffield Steel and Iron Company, 28.
Soap, 243, 287; by-product packing industry, 265, 266; factories, 284; shipped via New Orleans, Appendix XIII.
Social effects of manufacturing progress, 357.
Soda, 282, 285; ash, 287; caustic, 287; Solvay process, 287.
Soda-water, 285.
Sodium Cyanide, 288.
Solvay Process (*Company*), 282, 287, 348.

South, cement, 255; cracker manufacturing companies, 269; economic recovery, 25; fertilizer, 289–291; furniture, 244; hydroelectric development, 3–4; iron and steel, 16, 24–28, 93, 105, 109, 110, 112, 113; knit goods, 220; labor, 12, 13, 14; lumber, 238, 239, 242; manufacturing growth, 25; naval stores, 243–244; paper, 349; steel, 27, 42, 47–52, 61–62; strikes, 14; whisky, 277; wire, 125; worsteds, 344.
South, Cotton, 173–177, 343; advantages, 173; capital (lack), 176; coarser fabrics, 173–175, 180; consumption, 171, (spindle), 340; cooperative mills, 182–183; education, in textile departments, 12, 180; electricity, 167; labor, 13, 14; market, 188; mills, 175; pool, 182; social standards revolutionized by, 176; trade conditions, 184–187; wages, 189.
South Africa, barbed wire, 14; irrigation. pipes, 129; rails, 118; wool, 191.
South America, 114; hides, 226, 227; iron, 16, 22, 25; locomotives, 137; rails, 118; tin plates, 133; World War market, 307.
South Atlantic States (phosphate), 289.
South Carolina, cotton-mill accounts, Appendix XI; electric power, 4; fertilizers, 289, 290, 291; prices (colonial, flour), Appendix VI; *id.* (lumber), Appendix II; *id.* (shipbuilding), Appendix IV; prices (colonial, tar), Appendix III.
South Charleston (W. Va.), 336.
South Chicago (Ill.) (steel), 37, 76.
South Chicago (Steel) Works, 45.
South Dakota (wool), 200.
South Saint Joseph (Mo.) (meat packing), 263.
Southern Car and Foundry Company, 138, 139.
Southern Cotton Oil Company, 284.
Southern Furniture Exposition, 244.
Southern Furniture Manufacturers' Association, 245.
Southern Power Company, 4.
Southern Steel Company, 51.
Southern Worsted Corporation, 344.
Southwest, oil development, 334.
Spain (Spanish), barrel stock from Tennessee, 243; iron ore, 15, 16, 17, 92; phosphate rocks, 289; shoe machinery, 232.
Spanish America, 46.
Spanish-American Iron Company, 17.
Spanish-American War, 11, 38, 97, 264, 291; increase in sugar producing area, 272; shipbuilding, 142; wool depression follows, 201.
Sparrows Point (Md.), iron, 16; rails, 38; shipyards, 40, 144, 145; steel, 38.
Spartanburg County (S. C.) (cotton), 175.
Spelter (see *Zinc*).
Spiegeleisen, 78, 79, 310.
Spirits Distributing Company, 276.
Sprekels, Claus, 273.
Springfield (Ill.) (paving brick), 258.
Spruce, 239, 247, 248, 249, 251.
Stage Lines (automobile), 161.
Standard Distilling and Distributing Company, 276.
Standard Harrow Company, 147.
Standard Manufacturing Company ("Bath Tub Trust"), 259.

Standard Oil Company, 130; articles manufactured, 3; gasoline monopoly, 161; steel tankers, 142; tin plate, 131.
Standard Rope and Twine Company, 219.
Standardization, 326; World War, 304.
Stanley Company (steam automobiles), 162.
Starch, corporations, 269; value, 263.
State Prisons (binder twine), 220.
Steam, pipes, 129; power, 4.
Steam Engines (see *Engines*), for blowing iron furnaces, 73; improvements in, 5, 338; Wisconsin, 151–152.
Steamboats and Steamships (U. S. Steel), 63.
Steel (see *Bessemer Steel, Iron, Open-Hearth Steel*), 34–35; acid, 66–70, 77, 309; Alabama, 78, 111; Allegheny County, 23, 41; Allegheny Iron and Steel Company, 57; alloys, 71, 79–80, 81, 118, 146, 310, 312; Amalgamated Association of Iron and Steel Workers, 13; American Iron and Steel Association (see *American*, etc.); American progress in, 34; American Steel Casting Company, 85; American Steel Foundries Company, 85; ammunition, 40; armor, 40 (see *Armor*); Association American Steel Manufacturers, 80, 89; automobiles and automobile parts, 81; axles, 80; basic, 45, 48, 49, 50, 66, 67, 77; beams, 119–121; Bessemer (see *Bessemer Iron and Steel, Bessemer Plants*); billets, 87, 102–103; Birmingham (Ala.), 42, 49, 61; booms, 29, 100–101, 109; Boston, 34; bridges, 38, 57 100, 119; Buffalo, 36, 37; buildings, 80, 98; capital invested, 39, 42, 47, 56, 58, 59, 64, 71; capacity U. S., 335; carbon content, 79, 80, 81; cars, 59, 63, 136, 137, 139, 140; castings, 69, 70, 76, 80, 85 (centrifugal), 312, (chains), 312, (die), 312; centers, 34, 36, 40, 41, 45–64; Chinese, 114; Clapp-Griffiths process, 30, 65–66, Colorado Fuel and Iron Company (see *Colorado Fuel and Iron Company*); combinations, 330; consumption per capita, 32; corporations, 6–7, 31, 34, 35–36, 37–44, 45–64, 107–108; cost, 42, 48, 61, 91; cotton ties, 57, 126, 127; crucible, 30, 60, 65, 71, 76, 79, 80, 81, 92, 309; depressions and prosperity, 11, 38, 49, 53, 60, 87, 94–96, 104–106, 109, 334; dividends, 46, 51; drawbacks, 113, 114, 118; duplex process, 77, 78, 309; electric furnace, 75–77, 168, 309, 335; exports, 11, 38, 50, 57, 60, 91, 102–105, 114; Federal Steel Company (see *Federal Steel Company*); financing, 51, 55; finished products, 62, 63; fleet, 43, 55, 56, 59; foreign estimates, 108; forging, 81, 82, 85–86, 170; foundries, 85, 170; France (see *France*); freight, 50, 53, 62; fuel, 69, 72–73; furnace practice, 79; furnaces (capacity), 57, 66, 79, 81; Gary, 36, 60–61, 62, 63, 70, 73, 140, 168; gas fuel, 50, 83; geography, 41, 69; Germany (see *Germany*); Great Britain (see *Great Britain*); growth, 32; hardening metals, 80, 81; hoops, 54, 57, 126, 127; hydraulic press, 120, 139; Illinois Steel Company (see *Illinois Steel Company*); imports, 71, 79, 81, 114; Krupp, 81; Lackawanna Steel Company, 36–37, 330; machine

Index

tools and shop practice, 153–154; market, 50, 51, 63, 80; marketing methods, 107–108; Maryland Steel Company, 37, 57, 112; Nails (see *Nails* and *Wire*); National Steel Company (see *National Steel Company*); Navy specifications and standards, 40; New England, 34; New Jersey, 38, 85; New York, 35, 85; nickel, 3, 80, 81; Ohio, 35, 43, 67, 85, 88; open-hearth (see *Open-Hearth Steel*); ordnance, 40, 89–90; organization, 35–36; Pennsylvania, 35, 36, 41, 42, 43, 85, 88, 97; Pennsylvania Steel Company (see *Pennsylvania Steel Company*); pipes (see *Tubes*); Pittsburgh, 23, 34, 36, 41, 42, 44, 45, 49, 57, 62, 87, 94, 95; plates, 45, 57, 68, 69, 112, 113, 114, 119; pools, 5, 55, 57, 87–89, 96, 108; prices, 58, 59, 61, 62, 69, 307, 308, 334; production, 26, 39, 42, 52, 58, 60, 61, 63, 64, 65–67, 310, 335; products, 62; profits, 38, 44, 51; puddled, 82; quality, 79; Rail Association, 57; railroads (corporations), 55, 56, 59, 63; rails (see *Rails*); Republic Iron and Steel Company, 42, 45, 51, 55; Rocky Mountain Region, 52–54; rolled, 35, 64, 65, 84–85; rolling mill trust, 42; rolling mills, 43, 56, 68, 84, 85, 146; San Francisco, 40, 54; scrap iron used in open-hearth, 69, 78; shapes, 118–135; shears, 313; shell 307, 313; sheet, 45, 57, 85, 114, 123, 129; shipbuilding, 38, 39, 40, 112, 141, 144; ships, 143; South, 27, 42, 47–52; 61–62; special, 60, 80, 81; specialization, 63; specifications (American standards), 80; speculation, 52; statistics, 63–64, 65–67; strike, 333–334; structural, 23, 31, 45, 57, 65, 68, 69, 80, 98, 113–114, 119–122, (fabricated), 324; substituted for iron, 15; tariff, 97, 107, 113; technical progress, 34, 75–76; Tennessee Coal and Iron and Railroad Company (see *Tennessee Coal, Iron and Railroad Company*); three-high mill (abandoned for improved two-high), 84; tidewater, 37–44; tin plates (see *Tin Plate*), 57, 69, 80, 129–135, 307; tools (see *Tools*), 78, 79, 80; transportation, 41, 50–51, 55, 57, 63; Troy (N. Y.), 34; tubes (see *Tubes*); Tungsten, 81; Union Works, 45; United States Government suit vs. U. S. Steel Corporation, 64; United States Steel Corporation (see *United States Steel Corporation*); wages, 48; welding, 312, 339; Wellman charging machine, 69; West, 41; westward movement, 23–24; wire (see *Wire*); wire rods, 54, 57, 103; wire rope, 122; World War, 107.
Sterlingworth Company, 139.
Stockton (Calif.), 163.
Stoves (corporations), 150; geography, of industry, 352.
Strawboard, 249, 250, 251.
Strikes, 9; after war, 327; anthracite, 14, 102; coal, 13, 14, 28, 53; coke and coal, 28, 48; cotton, 188; English, 14; Homestead, 14; iron and steel, 14, 86–87; Passaic, 202, 343; Pullman, 136; silk, 14, 215; South, 14; steel, 14, 87, 101, 333–334; textile, 14; wool, 202.
Sudan Railway, 121.

Sugar, advertisement of brands, 275; American Sugar Refining Company, 273, 274–275; beet, 272–274, 329; cane, 272; Cuba (preferential treatment), 272, 273; duties and drawbacks, 273, 274, 329; geography, 273; glucose, 263, 269, 270; legislation (State), 273; mills, 272, 274–275; molasses, 243, 273, 274; prices (New York), Appendix IX; production (value), 263, 329; refining, 272, 274, 275; syrups, 263, 274; trusts, 5, 270, 274–275; variety, 275; "wars," 274.
Sulphates, 282, 286, 289, 290.
Sulphides, 3.
Sulphite (see *Paper, Pulp*).
Sulphur, 17, 18, 285, 286.
Sulphuric Acid, 285, 286, 289, 290.
Sumatra (rubber), 237.
Superior, Lake (see *Lake Superior and Iron Ores*).
Superior (Wis.), 45, 268.
Superphosphates, 285.
Susquehanna Valley, 18; silk, 210.
Swank, James M., 96.
Sweat Shops (see *Clothing*).
Sweden (*Swedish*), charcoal iron, 72; electric smelting, 76; flax, 218; iron and ore, 15, 16, 17, 25, 71, 124; matches, 292; pulp, 251; wire rods, 122.
Swift and Company, 265, 286, 327.
Switzerland Diamond Match Company, 292; dyes, 317.
Syracuse Solvay Process Company (Detroit), 287

Tafna (ore), 16.
Taftville (Conn.), 3, 167, 319.
Tanks (cypress), 243.
Tanning (see *Leather*).
Tar (see also Naval Stores), by-products, 282; price, Appendix III; roofing, 41.
Tariff, carpets, 208; chemicals, 288; cigarettes, 279; cotton, 329; dyestuffs, 329; flaxseed and linseed oil, 284; iron and steel, 97, 107, 113; leather, 229; paper, 251; silk, 213, 214, 216; southern attitude, Appendix XI; statistical measurements of influence, Appendix VIII; sugar, 273, 329; tin plate, 130, 134–135; wool, 191, 193, 196, 199, 200, 201, 202, 205, 328.
Tariff Commission, 330.
Tariff Laws, 97, 100; of 1894, 8; Dingley, 10, 200, 201, 229; Emergency (1921), 328; Fordney (1922), 329, 330; McKinley, 130, 74–141; Payne-Aldrich, 202; Underwood, 96, 107, 202; Wilson, 130, 193, 199, 200, 201, 237, 257, 272.
Tax (see Tariff) (oleomargerine), 266.
Taylor, N. and G., Company, 133.
Taylor-White Process, 80.
Telegraph, 165; wire, 122, 124.
Telephone, 165; wire, 122.
Tennessee, 28; cedar rails for pencils, 239; iron, 25; labor (cotton mill), 189; phosphates, 285; white oak barrel stock, 243; woolen, 206.
Tennessee Coal, Iron and Railroad Company, 27, 47–52, 57, 61, 70, 78, 97, 109, 119, 123, 139; assets, 48; fertilizer, 290; foreign mar-

ket, 110, 112, 113; iron prices, 62; output, 63; steel, 48, 62.
Terre Haute (Indiana), 331.
Tesla Patents, 169.
Texas, anti-trust laws, 5; association of cotton-seed-oil mills, 5; cotton, 175; hematites, 16; iron, 24; meat packing, 264; oil (fuel), 73.
Textile Alliance Incorporated, 319.
Textiles and Textile Industry (see *Cotton, Flax, Silk, Wool*), combinations, 7–8; depression of 1896, 9; electricity, 3; employment of immigrants, 13–14; Japan, 111; output of corporations, 7; schools, 12, 180; strikes, 14.
Thames River (Conn.) (shipbuilding), 143.
Thomas Iron Company, 15, 48.
Thomasville (N. C.) (chairmaking), 244.
Thomson, Edgar, Steel Company (Works), 43, 44, 67, 75, 91.
Thomson-Houston Company, 169.
Thoreau, Henry, 357.
Thread, 180, 181; American Thread Co., 180, 218; boots, shoes, and carpets (consumers), 215; 218; mills (combination), 6, 7–8; silk, 211, 214, 215.
Tidewater Steel Company, 17, 36, 88.
Tiles (see *Brick*).
Timken-Detroit Axle, 337.
Tin-foil Factory (American Tobacco Company), 280.
Tin Plate (see *Iron, Steel*, 89, 96, 131, 132, 134; canning, 130, 131 charcoal iron, 72; competition (Welsh), 130, 131, 132, corporation, 132–133; drawbacks, 130, 131, 133; exports and re-exports, 133; geography, 131; imports, 130, 131, 133; independent plants, 133; labor, 131, 132, 133; market, 130, 131, 132, 135; mechanical improvements, 131–132; mills, 130; open-hearth steel, 69; organization, 131, 132; Pennsylvania, 131, 133; prices, 131, 132; Rogers process, 132; steel substituted for iron, 80; tariff, 130, 131, 134–135; terne plates, 134; U. S. Steel Corporation, 57; Wales, 130–133.
Tires, automobile, 158, 229, 237; bicycle, 156; pneumatic, 156, 158; rubber, 237.
Titanium, 81.
Tobacco, advertising, 278; American Tobacco Company, 278–280; cigarettes, 278, 279, 280; cigars, 279, 280; Continental Tobacco Company, 278; distribution systematized, 278, 279; machinery, 279; market, 278.
Tofo (Chile) (mines), 17, 40.
Tokyo (Japan) (iron market), 109, 127.
Toledo (Ohio) (ore), 18.
Tonawanda (N. Y.) (iron), 18, 24.
Tonawanda Iron and Steel Company, 24.
Tools, 78, 148–149; centers, 149, 150; combinations, 149; exported, 148, 149; geography, 149; high-speed cutting, 80; machine (see *Machine Tools*), 153–155; market, 148; steel (imported), 148.
Torrance (N. M.), 161.
Tractors (see *Automobiles*).
Trade (see *Exports, Imports*, etc.), associations, 245, 270; domestic, 8; foreign, 1–2, 110; river, Appendix XIII.
Trade Marks (breakfast foods), 268.

Transportation (see *Railroads, Freights*), automobiles, 161; iron and steel, 63; steel, 36, 59, 63.
Tredegar Iron Works, 83.
Trenton (N. J.), 27, 132; pottery, 257.
Tricycle, Benz (internal-combusion engine), 157.
Trolleys, 129, 165, 166.
Tropenas Bessemer Steel Process, 65, 78.
Troy (N. Y.), collars, 224; steel, 34.
Troy Furnace and Steel Works (Steel Company), 59, 77.
"*Truth in Fabric Bills*," 345.
Trusts (see *Corporations*), 59; American Steel Casting Company, 85; American Sugar Refining Company, 274–275; American Tobacco Company, 278; baking, 268–269; "Bath Tub Trust," 259; brewing, 277; brick, 258; competition (devices for controlling), 5; cordage, 219; cotton mill, 180, 181, 182–183; crises encourage formation, 353; decline, 5–8; distilling, 276; fertilizer, 290; financing, 11; food, 263; horizontal, 88; iron (see *U. S. Steel Corporation*), 107; leather, 227, 228; legislation and litigation, 5–6; lumber, 241, 242; match, 292; North Carolina pine producers, 241; multiple products, 355; packing, 265; raw materials (sources owned by), 21; Roosevelt administration, 102; Schwab, Charles (address on), 7; steel (see *U. S. Steel Co.*), 5–8, 35–64; sugar, 5, 270, 274–275; transportation, 21; United Shoe Machinery Company, 233; United States Steel Company (see *United States Steel Company*); vertical, 69, 292; War Industries Board, 324.
Tubes, 57, 127–129; Addystone Pipe Case, 127–128; cast iron, 27, 127–129; corporations, 128, 129; exports, 24; foundry, 53; markets, 129; National Tube Company, 54, 128, 129; oil and artesian well, 129; production, 129; seamless, 156; sewer, 258; steel, 57; varieties, 129; weldless steel, 128.
Tubize Company (rayon), 347.
Tuluol, 316
Tungsten, 307, 310.
Turbines, 73; 5,000–horsepower, 2; iron and steel rolling mills, 84; ships and dynamos, 151, 152; turbo-generator, 166, 338; water-wheels, 4, 152, 338.
Turpentine (see *Naval Stores*).
Two Harbors (Minn.), 56.
Type-casting and Type-setting Machines, 294, 295.
Typewriters, 153.

Underwood Coal and Iron Company, 51.
Underwood Tariff Bill, 107, 196, 202.
Union Bag and Paper Company, 249.
Union Carbide Company, 3, 288.
Union Iron and Steel Company (Chicago), 45.
Union Iron Works (San Francisco), 40, 142.
Union Mills (N. Y.) (knitting), 181.
Union Steel Company, 59.
United Breweries Company, 277.
United Cigar Stores, 279.
United Electrical Company, 3.
United Shoe Machinery Company, 230, 233.

Index

United States, battleships, 143; blast pressures, 117; chemicals, 289; divided into "pay" and "free" territory, 127; electrical equipment, 165; furnace capacity, iron and steel, 335; suits to dissolve trusts; (du Pont Powder Company), 316, (International Harvester Company), 315, (Sanitary pottery), 327, (U. S. Steel Corporation), 64, 309.
United States Baking Company, 268.
United States Biscuit Company, 268.
United States Cast Iron Pipe and Foundry Company, 88.
United States Cotton Duck Corporation, 182.
United State Envelope Company, 249.
United States Flour Milling Company, 268
United States Glass Company, 262.
United States Glucose Company, 269.
United States Leather Company, 227, 228, 292.
United States (National) Cordage Company, 249.
United States Rubber Company, 235, 236, 237.
United States Shipbuilding Company, 39, 102, 145.
United States Smelting and Refining Company, 330.
United States Steel (Company) Corporation, 30, 39, 45, 47, 52, 54–64, 69, 70, 103, 128, 146; acquires Carnegie Company, 56; acquires Rockefeller interests, 21; Amalgamated Association of Iron and Steel Workers (closed shop), 87; assets, 56, 58, 63; carriers, 56, 57, 59, 63, 145; coal, 58, 63; coke holdings and production, 57, 58, 63; companies included, 54, 56, 57, 59, 61, 123, 132, 133; depression (1907), 11, 104; dividends (reduced), 102; Duluth plant, 61, 64; electric refining, 76; expansion (1905), 60; export trade, 61, 334; federal suit, 22, 64; Gary plant, 61, 62, 63; leases Hill property, 22; limestone quarries, 58; mines, 56, 58, 63; natural gas, 58; not a monopoly, 59; ores, 56, 58, 59, 63; organization, 55–56; original investment, 58; price policy, 333, 356; production, 58, 63; rivals, 57; sale of stock to employes, 59, 328; shipping facilities, 56; stabilizes prices, 58, 59, 101; steel cars, 140; Troy works (dismantled), 34; unfilled orders, 334; World War, 306–307, 308, 309.
United States Steel Products Export Company, 60.
United States Sugar Refinery, 269.
United States Tinplate Company, 132.
United States Worsted Company, 205, 206.
Universal Cement Company, 255.
"*Unrelated lines*" decision, 327.
Uranium, 81.
Uruguay (export meat trade), 265.
Utah (sulphur mines), 285.

Vanadium, 81, 118, 121, 310.
Vancouver, 188.
Varnish, 243, 291.
Vats (cypress), 243.
Vaults (alloy steel), 80.
Vermont (cotton), 189.
Vertical Trusts, 69, 292.
Vessels (see *Ships*).
Vickers Sons, and Maxim, 143.

Victorian Railways (Australia), 112.
Virginia, chemicals, 287; fertilizer, 289; freight rates, 27; iron, 18, 25, 31; pipe prices, 127; prices (colonial, flour), Appendix VI; *id.* (iron), Appendix V; *id.* (lumber), Appendix II; *id.* (shipbuilding), Appendix IV; *id.* (tar), Appendix III; *id.* (weaving), Appendix VII; rayon, 347.
Virginia-Carolina Chemical Company, 284, 290.
Virginia Iron, Coal and Coke Company, 27.
Viscose Company (rayon), 347.
Vitriol, 285.
Vladivostock, 112.

Wages, Augusta (Ga.), 14; clothing industry, 222; cotton, 14, 189; iron and steel, 86–87, 91; Pennsylvania (1920), 334.
Wagner Palace Car Company, 138.
Wales (Welsh), 92; tin plate industry, 130–133.
Wall Street, bankers (arrangement with treasury to check exports of gold), 9; steel speculation, 52.
Walrand-Legenisel Bessemer Steel Process, 77.
Waltham (Mass.), 9.
Waltham Watch Company, 9.
War Industries Board, 302, 304, 306, 308, 311, 324, 326.
Warwick Furnace (ore), 15.
Washburn and Moen (Wire) Company, 122, 123, 124, 125.
Washburn-Crosby Company, 348.
Washington, George, 357; (weaving account), Appendix VII.
Washington (State), 89; iron, 16; lumber, 238, 239, 241; paper, 247.
Washington Mills (Lawrence, Mass.), 199.
Waste, in Industry, 194, 304, 358.
Watchmaking (see *American Watch Company, Elgin Watch Company*, etc.), 9; Illinois, 352.
Water-power, chemical industry, 287; iron furnaces, 30; wheels, 338.
Waterbury Clock Company, 9.
Watsonville Sugar Factory (Calif.), 273.
Waukegan Wire Works, 123, 125.
Weaving (see *Cotton, Flax, Hemp, Silk, Wool, and Homespun Manufactures*) (price), Appendix VII.
Webster (Mass.), 316.
Welland Canal, 18.
Wellman Charging Machine, 69.
Wellman Iron and Steel Company, 84.
West (and *Central West*), binder twine, 220; cement, 255; cotton, 173; negro labor, 13; paper, 249; steel, 40; sugar, 273.
West Duluth Car Works, 45.
West Homestead (Pa.), 314.
West Indies (boot and shoe trade), 232.
West Superior (Wis.), 45, 143.
West Virginia, 257; fuel, 281; glass, 260; iron, 24.
Western Bar Iron Manufacturers' Association, 87.
Western Nail Makers' Association, 6.
Western Steel Corporation, 15, 16.
Westinghouse Electric and Manufacturing Company, 136, 151, 168, 169, 170; radio, 332.
Wheat, 349.

Wheeling (W. Va.), 95; iron, 18; steel, 41.
Wheeling Steel and Iron Company, 129.
Wheels, American in Edinburgh, 148; car, 23; impact, 152; suspension (bicycle), 156.
Whisky (see *Distilling*) (shipped via New Orleans), Appendix XIII.
White Star Line, 144.
Whittier Cotton Mills, 174.
Whitworth Forging Press, 86.
Williams, Governor David R. (cotton mills), Appendix XI.
Wilmington (Del.), 36; dyes, 318.
Wilson and Company, 265, 327.
Wilson, President Woodrow, 328.
Wilson Tariff Law, 130, 193, 199, 200, 201, 237, 257, 272; beet sugar, 272; pottery, 257; rubber, 237.
Winchester Repeating Arms (Winchester-Simmons) Company, 331.
Window Glass Workers' Association, 261.
Wine, 276.
Wire (see *Nails*), 57, 122–125; barbed, 54, 57, 69, 123–124, 306; nails, 54, 57, 69, 103, 125–127; rods, 54, 57, 103; rope, 122; woven, 57.
Wire Nail Manufacturers Association, 87.
Wisconsin, agricultural machinery, 147; Bankers' Association, 332; butter and cheese, 266; canned peas, 271; engines, 151, 152; iron, 17, 19; knit goods, 220; law, 301; leather, 226; lumber, 239; paper, 247, 352; tan bark, 227; woolens, 196.
Wisconsin Steel Company, 45.
Women's Clothing (see *Clothing*), 196.
Wood, alcohol, 243; screws, 126.
Wood Worsted Mills, 199.
Wooden Ware, 242.
Wood Motor Vehicle Company, 158.
Woodward (Ala.) (creosoting), 283.
Wool (see also *Sheep*), 191; Argentine, 191; Australian, 201, 202; bank, 192; centers for handling, 192; classification, 192; clip, 191; concentration in two or three countries, 191; cost, 201; cotton (increase in supply of affects price), 193; cross-bred type, 192, 193; decline in East, 191; depression, 191; domestic, 193; domestic inferior packing and grading, 192; drawback, 204; duties (Wilson), 199; duties (Payne-Aldrich), 202; duties (1921–1922), 328, 329; Eastern (unscoured), 193; Exchange, 191; exports, 200; fluctuations in market, 191; foreign, 193; free (era of), 191, 193, 199, 202, 208; geography, 191; grades and kinds, 192; grading, 192; grazing areas (Asia, Southern Hemisphere), 192; imports, 192, 193, 203; market, 191; market (falling), 191; merino, 192; method of dealing in (change in), 191, 192; organization (lack of), 192; overstock after war, 325; Panic of 1893, 191; preparation for market, 192; prices, 191, 193, 201, 202, 325, Appendix IX; production, 191–193; quality changing with fashions, 191, 192, 344; San Francisco (a handling center), 192; shoddy, 194; solvent process, 199; substitutes, 194; tariff controversies, 193, 200, 202; territorial, 193; trade (domestic in chaotic condition), 192; warehouse, 192; westward shifting, 192; World War, 319, 320–321.
Wool Institute, Incorporated, 345.
Wool Manufactures (see *Clothing, Worsteds*), 190, 191; active machinery, 342; after war popularity, 344; American Woolen Company, 205, 206; army clothes, 202; blankets, 103, 196, 202; Bradford system, 199; British system, 198, 199; broadcloth, Appendix VII; by-products, 199; California, 196; cancellations after war, 343; capital losses, 345; carded fabrics, 194, 195, 197, 200, 202; carpets (see *Carpets*), Appendix VII; cassimeres, 196, 344; centers, 192; cheviots, 196, 197; Civil War, 200; combing, 198; compared with silk, 210; competition, 202–203, 204; concentration, 192, 195; Connecticut, 168; consolidations, 202, 205–207; consumption (foreign and domestic), 203, 204; corporations, 205; costs, 193, 203; depressions, 199–200, 201, 202; establishments (number), 195; export outlet (lack of), 203; exports, 204–205; fabrics, 196–197; failures, 201; flannels, 196, 197, 203; foreign, 203, 204; free wool, 191, 193, 199, 201, 202; French system, 197, 198, 199; geography, 195–196; imports, 197, 200, 202, Appendix VIII; jeans, 197, Appendix VII; kerseys, 226, Appendix VII; knit goods, 220; labor, 195, 198, 203–204; Lawrence (Mass.), 195; lighter fabrics used, 344; linsey-woolsey, Appendix VII; looms, 198; Maine, 205; market, 195, 201, 203, 204, 205; marketing methods, 206; Massachusetts, 191, 195, 196, 205; mill increase, 324; Mount Vernon, Appendix VII; New England (see *New England*); New Jersey, 195, 343; New York, 195; organization, 205–207; Pennsylvania, 195; Philadelphia, 195; plant (concentration), 207; prices, 197, 201, 202; processes, 198; product (value), 343; profits, 206; production, 195, 197, 201, 203; prosperity, 201, 202; Providence (R. I.), 195; rank of states, 195; ready-made clothing (effect on wool industry), 202, 204; Rhode Island, 195, 205; satinets and sateens, 180; serges, 197, 203; shoddy, 194; specialization, 197, 198; standard contracts, 206; strikes, 14, 202 343; style factor, 344; substitutes, 194–195; tariff, 202, 204, 205, (Dingley), 200, 201, (Payne-Aldrich), 202, (Underwood), 202, (Wilson), 193, 199, 200, 201; technical progress, 197–199; trade conditions, 199–202; tweeds, 196; value, 194, 197; wages, 203, 343; World War, 319–320; worsteds (see *Worsteds*).
Woolen Machinery, carding, 199, 205; combing (perfection of), 197; controlled by American Woolen Company, 205; domestic (more costly than foreign), 200; importation of, 198; mules, 199; worsted (imported), 198; worsted yarns on mules by French system, 197.
Worcester (Mass.), electric steel, 76; furniture, 244; machine tools, 154; steel, 51; wire, 123, 124, 125.

World War, 12, 17, 40, 52, 81, 83, 91, 105, 107, 114, 119, 133, 146, 163, 164, 184, 186, 188, 193, 196, 199, 202, 204, 210, 217, 219, 226, 228, 259, 260, 261, 265, 281, 282, 283, 285, 286, 290, 292, 298–300; 315, 329.

Worsteds (see also *Wool Manufactures*), American Woolen Company, 205; ascendancy assured, 197; British system, 198, 199; centers, 202; decline in popularity, 344; classification, 200; French and Belgian operators, 14; New Jersey, 195; French system, 198, 199; growth of (compared to carded fabrics), 194, 195, 197; imports, 196; Lawrence (Mass.), 195; machinery (imported), 198; noils, 194; New England, 344; Philadelpia (ascendancy in), 195; production, 197; Providence (R. I.), 195; Russian-Japanese War, 202; shoddy, 194; South, 344; strikes, 202; tops, 198, 199, 203, 343; value of products, 195; World War, 324.

Worthington Pump Company, 339.
Wyandotte (Mich.), alkalis, 287; chlorine, 288.

Yarn, 179; count (lowered by spindle growth in South), 175; knitting, 178, 196; labor costs, 203; New England Cotton Yarn Company, 181; United States Worsted Company, 206.
Yokohama (Japan), 111, 112, 127.
Youngstown (Ohio), 18, 34, 35, 42, 43, 67, 88, 94–95, 330, 334.
Youngstown Steel and Tube Company, 64.
Yucatan (sisal), 220, 322.

Zinc, 123, 325; annealed with iron, 134; flotation process, 311; smelters (acid as by-product), 286; spelter (slab zinc), output, 312.

Northwestern University
The Joseph Schaffner
Library of Commerce

DATE LOANED

Aug 9 '37
Mar 30 '46
MAR 2 2 '62